A Dictionary of Political Thought

Roger Scruton

A Dictionary of Political Thought

Hill and Wang · New York
A division of Farrar, Straus and Giroux

First published by The Macmillan Press, London, 1982
First American paperback edition, 1984
Printed in Great Britain
ISBN: 0–8090–1524–2

A Note on Composition

The first draft of this dictionary was written continuously, so as to achieve maximum consistency of style and minimum overlap. The articles were sent out separately to the advisors, two of whom were asked to comment on each article. The final draft was then composed, taking into account, as far as possible, all the comments received. The list of entries was gradually amended and developed in the course of writing, partly in response to suggestions received, partly in response to a developing perspective. Because of the novelty of the project, and the attempt to bring together disparate but related disciplines, it cannot be hoped that a uniform standard has been reached throughout, or that some fundamental items of political thought have not been overlooked. However, a certain synthesis has emerged, which may permit development and clarification in any future edition.

I have benefited greatly from the comments offered, and from friendly advice given by Michael Oakeshott, Amartya Sen, John Vickers and William Waldegrave. In particular, I have received inestimable benefit from the painstaking work of Sally Shreir, who read through the whole dictionary suggesting countless additions, improvements and amendments. Without her help and guidance this project would have been far more arduous and far less rewarding than it has been. It is not to be expected, however, that all errors have been eliminated, and I alone am responsible for those that remain, as well as for the tone and manner of the work, and for any expressions of opinion or manifestations of outlook.

London, April 1982 — Roger Scruton.

Note

Cross-references are indicated by an asterisk; they occur only when a major intellectual connection is in issue. Reference to authors and texts have been kept to a minimum, but are included wherever an idea seems to be specific to the thoughts of a particular school or person.

Because this is a dictionary of concepts, it has been necessary to provide not only definitions but also the sketches of arguments. These are necessarily incomplete, and may also be one-sided. The intention is to illustrate the concept, rather than to persuade the reader, and it should be borne in mind that no article can do more than suggest the arguments given for or against any particular position.

Preface

'Political thought' denotes something that all human beings engage in, whether or not knowingly. It also denotes various specialized academic disciplines which seek to explore, to support or to undermine our everyday political persuasions. Several such disciplines have contributed their terminology to this dictionary, among them political science, philosophy, sociology and economics. In addition the reader will find terms from the practical arts of law, politics and religion, together with words designed at least to draw attention to, if not to resolve, important modern controversies.

An apology may not be necessary for what follows, but some explanation of the aims and principles of such a dictionary may help the reader to gauge its utility. It is impossible to include in one small volume reference to all the concepts involved in the practice of politics, or in its related academic disciplines. The intention has been to extract, both from active debate, and from the theories and intuitions which surround it, the principal ideas through which modern political beliefs find expression. The emphasis of the dictionary is conceptual rather than factual, exploring the formulation of doctrines rather than their specific application. Political events are mentioned only when they cast light on intellectual conceptions. For this reason the few proper names contained in the dictionary are those of thinkers rather than those of political figures. Likewise nations, treaties, battles and laws are seldom mentioned, and, while it has been necessary to include discussions of the major movements and parties in contemporary politics, the detailed history of the modern world has been passed over, as outside the scope of a dictionary of concepts.

Political terms are often as obscurely understood by the person who uses them as by the person who is puzzled in hearing them used. The main purpose of this dictionary is to provide not just definitions but, where possible, clarifications of political terminology. Sometimes, as in the case of Marxism, the task is made easier by the existence of a definite and articulated theory, which the dictionary articles need only condense into appropriate form. In other cases (and this is particularly true of the main items of conservative thought) the absence of theory presents a peculiar difficulty. Here the dictionary must itself attempt a small part of a task that has not been accomplished, and perhaps not even been attempted, with the rigour that the subject demands. For this reason, while many entries will be recognized as summaries of existing doctrines, others will appear to present conceptual novelties. It is hoped that the two kinds of entry will so interlock as to give structure and coherence to the whole. It goes without saying that every attempt has been made to be impartial, and to provide equal, and equally clear, expression to the major beliefs and concepts which enjoy favour in the modern climate of political opinion. But impartiality is itself a kind of partiality, and the reader should approach the dictionary with as many inverted commas at his disposal as he might require for his peace of mind.

Some doubt may be felt as to the number of disciplines which have been called upon in the construction of this work. Why, for example, should the social sciences figure so prominently in a book designed to clarify the language of actual political discourse? It would certainly be odd to include, in a dictionary of mathematical concepts, entries dealing with the sociology of mathematical thought and practice. For what bearing could such entries have on concepts like those of number, proof, validity and integration? A sociological explanation of our mathematical habits casts no light upon their true internal logic. However, the same is not true of politics. Political thought, unlike mathematics, is permeable to its own explanation. A sociology of political belief will not leave its subject unaffected. Consider the concept of 'commodity fetishism'. While this purports to provide an explanation of certain persistent economic beliefs and practices, it contains within itself a novel way of criticizing what it explains. No sooner did the concept exist than it was used to give expression and support to political beliefs which seemed to gain in cogency through the adoption of this technical term. Similarly no exposition of modern political thought can avoid encroaching on those disciplines – economics, sociology and political science – which have political thought as part of their subject matter. Both the language and the art of politics are formed and reformed under pressure from these disciplines, borrowing their concepts, their theories, their truths and above all their confusions in the compulsive search for self-justification.

It should not be thought, however, that the subject-matter of this dictionary is either recondite or truly theoretical. On the contrary, it belongs to the mental repertoire of all active, thinking beings, and it is to be hoped that, by treating impartially conceptions which enter, however hazily, into so many current debates and disagreements. this dictionary will make some small contribution to their clarity.

A

abdication. *See* *monarchy.

abnormality. A deviation from a *norm. Abnormality is to be distinguished from eccentricity, which is the presence of noteworthy and uncommon characteristics in a *normal individual. Eccentricity is usually permitted if harmless, abnormality often regarded with suspicion whether harmless or not. Different political arrangements draw the line between the two in different ways, and the problem of defining what is normal in human nature makes dispute inevitable. Moreover the human desire to hold others responsible for the characteristics which distinguish them gives a motive to confusion. An abnormality is not part of the moral character, but part of the amoral circumstances, of the person who possesses it. To represent it as a harmful eccentricity is to justify treatment intended either to conceal the victim, or to force him to change. This thought has been extremely important in *politicized theories of *psychotherapy. The idea of the individual as essentially *responsible for his eccentricities underlies some doctrines of *authenticity.

abortion. The issue of abortion is intractable, partly because of the absence of any other case to which it can be assimilated. The relationship between a woman and her unborn child is both non-transferable and original: the child comes into existence in and through the woman, and the question of its rights and welfare cannot be considered in complete isolation from the question of the rights and welfare of its mother. Some deny that an unborn child is a *person, and on that ground deny it the *right to life. On this view the only question of *rights* is that which concerns the woman: does she have a 'right to choose' whether to give birth? If the pregnancy is unwanted, what right has another to compel her to proceed with it? It seems arbitrary, however, to say that the divide between person and non-person occurs at birth. The alternative positions are many: some see the foetus as a person, but believe that the case is one of *conflicting* rights. Others argue that the language of rights is wholly inadequate to capture the nature of the *obligation towards the unborn child. *See*, in general, *consequentialism *rights

absenteeism. *See* *industrial action.

absolutism. The theory and practice of absolute *government, i.e. government which is not *limited by any *agency internal to itself. Absolute government should be distinguished from absolute *power. Power is always contained, limited or diverted by other powers within the state; but government can be absolute even without possessing absolute power. It is so whenever there are no constitutional *checks and balances, so that no exercise of government can be criticized or opposed in the *name* of government. The principal limitation of government is the law. Defenders of absolutism, such as *Bodin and *Hobbes, have often been motivated by the thought that all government requires *sovereignty – that is, a body of decisions which cannot be questioned. Since sovereignty must be exercised through law, the sovereign himself cannot be criticized *by* the law, which is no more than his own command. On this view law is authoritative simply by virtue of the status of the person who commands it, and not by virtue of its content or of its moral or intellectual credentials.

Absolutism must be distinguished from *totalitarianism. It involves, not the total supervision by a central power of all the functions of society, but simply the possession of an unfettered power of government, which may or may not be used, and which need not be applied universally, or in every area of social existence. Sometimes, as in the European absolutism of the seventeenth and eighteenth centuries, this power may be used in order to limit the concentration of power in bodies that are not themselves sovereign, such as the nobility, the church, or the empire. Sometimes it may be used to eliminate *opposition and to establish a complete *dictatorship, as with Hitler and Stalin. Absolute rule may vest in an individual, in an *office (absolute monarchy), in a party (*democratic centralism), or in a system of administration (classical Chinese *bureaucracy).

abundance. Goods are abundant in a society whenever any member of it can obtain such of those goods as he desires by the expenditure of minimum labour. It is sometimes thought to be a criterion of *welfare that all goods which people need should also be abundant, and that the economy should have this abundance of necessaries as its aim. (*See* *need.) It is also sometimes argued that the abundance of luxuries (i.e. goods which are not needed but only desired) may be an evil: *see* *consumerism.

academic freedom. **1**. Freedom to pursue teaching, learning and research without regard for the public utility of what is taught or studied, and unconstrained by external directives (whether from the state or from elsewhere) as to the form, content or conclusions of the subject. This freedom includes the freedom to publish the results of research.

2. Specifically, the freedom of an educational body to provide its own constitution, appoint its own staff and students, and determine its own curriculum, whatever the *ideological content of what is taught. It is a disputed question whether this specific freedom does exist, or can or ought to exist. It implies that those who buy or provide the services of academics should have no power to prescribe the nature of the service rendered. Hence the provision of academic freedom requires the abolition of any contractual relation between the academy and the public.

The issue of academic freedom is to be distinguished from that of whether academic institutions ought to raise their funds, and recruit their students, without aid or direction from the state.

acceleration principle (or: accelerator principle). The hypothesis in economics, that investment in an industry varies according to the rate of change (rather than according to the level) of its output. Under standard conditions in capitalist modes of production a certain amount of capital will be required to produce a particular rate of output. If this rate of output changes then, *ceteris paribus*, the amount of capital invested must also change. It is, however, not possible to assume that the relation between them is one of direct proportionality.

This hypothesis plays an important part in theories of the *trade cycle. It implies that an increase in demand for any product brings about an increase in demand for the machines etc. used to make it. Thus a small change in the output of consumer goods tends to result in a much bigger (i.e. accelerated) change in the output of the goods used to make them. Conversely a small fall in the output of consumer goods may result in a much larger fall in the output of capital goods. It is also argued that the 'accelerator' can be brought into play by a very slight *variation* in the rate of change of output of a consumer good. Thus if output of a particular product increases by five per cent in one year and continues to increase, but only by four per cent, in the next year, this may precipitate an actual *fall* in the output of capital goods, and in the amount of capital invested.

access. The concept of political access has become increasingly important in sociological studies of political power, since, it is argued, 'power of any kind cannot be reached by a political interest group or its leaders without access to one or more key points of decision in government' (David B. Truman: *The Governmental Process: Political Interests and Public Opinion*, 1951). Access is the probability of obtaining the attention and influencing the decisions of the relevant officers of government. 'Effective access' is usually given as a function of three variables: the strategic position of the group within society, the internal characteristics of the group, and the nature of the institutions of government. A group may be without access (such as the lowest *caste in a caste system), with effective access, or with 'privileged access' (which arises when decision makers automatically take a group's interests into account). The UK aristocracy has always had privileged access, and also 'direct' access, to power through the House of Lords, whereas most other classes have had varying degrees of effective but indirect access.

Sociologists further distinguish 'loose' from 'taut' patterns of access, the first existing when there is a multiplicity of points of access to political decisions, the second when there are defined channels of *representation through which groups exert their influence. Access seems to have shifted, in the US and postwar Europe, from *party to *pressure group, perhaps as a result of modern *bureaucracy, and of the decline of trust in representation.

accommodation. **1**. In sociology, the state or process of social adjustment to conflict. To be distinguished from adaptation (structural changes brought about by biological variation and selection), assimilation (the process whereby two groups or cultures fuse), and *acculturation. Accommodation allows two groups to harmonize overtly, while leaving the real source of conflict unresolved. Thus first generation immigrants may be accommodated by adopting the food, clothes etc. of the country in which they find themselves, but they may not be acculturated, where this implies full participation in the culture of the native population.

2. In politics, accommodation is usually distinguished from *confrontation and from *conciliation. It is the process whereby hostile powers establish a *modus vivendi* which enables each to fulfil as many of its purposes as it can without overt *aggression towards the other.

accountability. Sometimes distinguished from responsibility. A is accountable to B if B may sanction and forbid his actions. It does not follow that B is responsible for A: chains of responsibility run downwards by *delegation, chains of accountability upwards; if the two chains coincide, then this is a political achievement.

acculturation. An Americanism meaning the process whereby an individual or group acquires the cultural characteristics of another through direct contact. Acculturation is a one-way process, whereby one culture absorbs another, and is to be distinguished from the two-way process of assimilation, in which homogeneity results from changes in both. The phenomenon is of increasing political significance, as war, communication and migration force the states of the world to decide whether to open or to close their frontiers to one another. Their decisions may often be affected by the extent to which acculturation of new arrivals is considered possible.

accumulation. The amassing of *capital, for purposes of either investment or expenditure. If there is to be a 'means of production' over and above what is provided by nature, then there must be accumulation, in the form of 'produced means of production'. In a *capitalist economy accumulation is in private hands; in a *socialist economy, in theory, every accumulation of any significance is *socially owned. In between those two, infinite varieties of *mixed economy can be envisaged.

Moral and political discussions of *private property often involve objections to certain levels of accumulation. Some think that all accumulation gives the person who has *control over it a further control over the lives of others. (*See* *exploitation.) Some also believe that the laws of inheritance ought not to permit constant accumulation of property across generations. Nevertheless it is difficult to envisage systems of private property rights without rights of transfer of property, and if transfer is permitted, then accumulation is always possible. Modern uses of *taxation can often be seen as attempts to permit maximum mobility of private property through exchange, while preventing accumulations beyond a certain level. (*See also* *primitive accumulation.)

activism. The German *Activismus* was used at the end of the First World War to denote the active engagement of *intellectuals in political transformation. 'Activists' are distinguished by the extent of their involvement in politics, and by the methods that they are inclined to sanction in pursuit of transformation, rather than by the nature of their views. They are not necessarily *extremists, nor are they necessarily opposed to constitutional forms of political change. *Sorel, however, defended activism in terms that also sanction extremism, arguing that activism is a necessary part of any serious political standpoint, since doing is everything, and thought only a *rationalization of what is done. On such a view it is incoherent to present a recipe for, or exhortation to, political transformation in advance of the attempt to precipitate it. Activism becomes essential to politics, and, Sorel thought, essentially violent.

act of state. **1**. Philosophical. Any act which can be attributed to no single citizen or group of citizens, and which is done for reasons connected with the interests, rights, privileges etc. of a *state, can be considered to be an act of state. Thus a declaration of war, while conveyed between statesmen and usually through diplomatic channels, is the act of one state towards another, it being impossible for any *agency less than the state to declare war. Some acts of state are directed towards other states, as in the example. Others are directed towards citizens and subject associations. It is the state that punishes the criminal, that expropriates the property owner, that nationalizes industries and enacts laws. The state can act through its officers, or through a monarch; it may also endorse or *ratify the actions of private citizens undertaken independently (as when the state annexes as a colony land captured by an adventurous citizen). In general a state has all the capacities for agency that an individual person has. Its actions may be intentional or unintentional, reasonable or unreasonable, moral or immoral. It may also *have* reasons for what it does, and respond to reasons for or against courses of action (the idea of a 'process' of government). Thus, it is often said, the state has will and responsibility, and this is one argument for thinking that, like a company in law, it is to be regarded more as an autonomous person than as an organic aggregate of subjects. This thought is given elaboration in the philosophies of *Rousseau and *Hegel.

2. Legal. Acts of state are usually defined legally so as to include only actions *between* states. Thus in English law an act of state is an act of the sovereign power performed by virtue of the *prerogative, and in the course of its relations with other powers or with the *subjects of other powers. It cannot be challenged in the courts since it lies outside their jurisdiction. Hence in English law (as also in US law), there can be no act of state against an individual subject (i.e. one who owes allegiance), and the plea of act of state can never be used by government officers in defence of an encroachment on a subject's rights. Certain provisions in other constitutions might be interpreted as allowing the same effective immunity for government actions against citizens as is granted to government actions against other states: e.g. rights to enter and search without warrant, to imprison without trial, and so on, in cases of sedition.

actually existing socialism. Soviet and East European term for the systems of government in present-day communist countries, as they really are, rather than as they ought to be. Its use is usually ironical, and is largely confined to *dissidents; it implies a distance between the actual state of communist societies and the official claims that are made for them.

adjudication. The settlement of a dispute by judicial decree, hence, in English and US law, the judgement or decision of a court.

More broadly the term is used to refer to the process of settling disputes peacefully by referring them to some body with authority to make a decision or award binding upon the parties. Thus it covers awards made by mixed commissions and arbitral tribunals as well as those made by the courts. It is a method of resolving conflicts, to be contrasted with such processes as *arbitration and *mediation, in that it issues in a statement of *rights under the law. Its nature is of great concern to students both of *jurisprudence, and of politics. It represents a particular style of government that may not exist in all places and in all times, and which may be criticized and defended for the characteristics that distinguish it. Some argue that the settling of all disputes by adjudication may confer legislative power upon judges, and thus violate the supposed requirement of a *separation of powers. Others argue that disputes should be capable of settlement by less tortuous or costly means, and that too great an emphasis on adjudication serves to limit the possibilities of settlement. Advocates of the politics of *confrontation may argue that adjudication is a way of ensuring the peaceful victory of the powers that be, through their servants, the *judiciary. Advocates of the politics of *conciliation, by contrast, value adjudication as one among many possible means of translating powers into rights while avoiding *violence. (*See* *judiciary, *law.)

admass. Term coined by J. B. Priestley in 1955 to denote the society that he thought to be emerging in postwar Europe, formed under the combined influence of *advertising and the mass *media. He considered the entire social structure to be threatened by a drive towards consumer goods, and towards all that is least serious and most expendable among the objects of human desire. (*See* *consumerism.) The term has since come to be used in many of the political criticisms made of the role of advertising in Western societies.

administered prices. *Prices which are determined by the policy of some agency which can control them, rather than by *market forces, or by whatever other less deliberative mechanism might be held to determine them. Prices can be administered by a *monopoly, by an *oligopoly, by a *cartel, or by a government.

administrative law. The branch of law which governs the activities of state administrative bodies, such as ministries, state departments, local government, commissions, and agencies. To be distinguished from *constitutional law, which is concerned not with the subordinate organs of government but with the supreme executive and legislative bodies. (There is also a large grey area between the two.) In modern government there is increasing *delegation both of government power, and, through delegated legislation, of government authority. Hence the question arises of what remedy the citizen has against a body which acts, or purports to act, with the authority of the state. In France, as a result of traditional centralization, reinforced by Napoleonic edicts, administrative bodies are now subject to strict control by special administrative courts, and by the *conseil d'état*. Hence no special remedy is provided whereby the aggrieved subject can obtain relief from an ordinary court of law. In the UK and the US there are, by contrast, established procedures of appeal to the courts, regarded as important parts of the constitutional freedom of the subject.

In the US, the supervision of the Supreme Court can prevent administrative bodies from acting **ultra vires*, it being always possible for the aggrieved citizen to seek judicial review on the grounds that he has been denied *due process of law. In the UK the courts can overturn administrative decisions by special prerogative writs. These are summonses issued to the administrative body on behalf of the aggrieved party, calling on it in the name of the Crown to account for its actions. Among such writs is the celebrated *habeas corpus, and also mandamus (ordering a public officer to perform some neglected function), and certiorari (asking for the records of a decision to be submitted). Of particular relevance in any subsequent proceedings are the principles of natural justice: has the administrative body effectively 'stood in judgement' on the plaintiff? If so, did it allow him the right of hearing? Did it review the relevant evidence? And so on. This survival of the doctrine of *natural justice in administrative law is vital if the state is to be seen as dealing at all levels on open terms with its citizens.

Adorno, Theodor (1903–69). German philosopher and social theorist. *See* *critical theory, *Frankfurt school, *progress.

adversary system. The mode of legal procedure in criminal cases whereby the prosecution (the state) acts through a counsel who is opposed in court by another counsel acting on the instructions of the accused. Each party is 'represented' before a third (the judge and jury) whose impartiality is necessary to justice, and whose existence and independence are often taken to be fundamental constituents in the *rule of law. The adversary system is to be contrasted with systems that involve 'confessional' trials, trials by ordeal, and *show trials, where the individual is pitted directly against the state as his accuser and required to exonerate himself or be condemned. Here prosecutor and judge are identical, although this identity might be masked – for example by the presence of a judge who is acting under instructions from the prosecution (the normal procedure in Soviet-style 'show trials'). Some argue that there can be no true adversary system unless the defendant who cannot afford a lawyer to represent him has an automatic right to public defence (US) or legal aid (UK).

The expression is sometimes used to describe a political system in which *opposition has a recognized function, with a place within the institutions of government, perhaps supported from public funds.

advertising. The declaration that goods or services are available for purchase, usually accompanied by attempts to persuade the public to buy them. The nature of advertising has changed radically during the course of the present century, with the development of new techniques of persuasion. Advertising has helped to form the existing character of *capitalist societies, and achieved a place in the life of the individual not unlike the place usually accorded to *propaganda in communist systems. It is the object of persistent criticism on many grounds. Some argue, for example, that advertising is an economic evil, since it creates a barrier to entry into a market, preventing firms which cannot afford expensive advertising campaigns from selling their products. Others argue that it radically alters the perceived quality of purchase and exchange, by imbuing them with acquisitive and *fetishistic impulses. Thus products become desired not because of their ability to satisfy human needs, but for reasons wholly unconnected with that, such as the desire for enhanced *status, the sense of a 'magic' power, the desire merely to have and to hold that which one is taunted for not possessing. Many go further and argue that advertising *creates* the wants that it offers to satisfy, and whose satisfaction it keeps just beyond our reach, by making sure that new wants are always created in the place of old. Thus it has an 'enslaving' effect, not unlike that described by nineteenth-century theories of *alienation. Through advertising, it is argued, the purchaser's being and activity are diverted from their natural fulfilment, in the interests of another party, so that one person is effectively *controlled by another.

From the economic point of view advertising is sometimes seen as a form of indirect *taxation, whereby the mass media are subsidized by the consumer: hence the association of the two in the term '*admass'. This is one of the few arguments that are given in its favour (namely, that it is used in support of something else). It is also sometimes said that advertising is a necessary evil, since without it the supposedly beneficial effects of competition in a market will not be obtained.

aesthetics and politics. The term 'aesthetic', introduced into modern philosophy by A. G. Baumgarten (1714–62), is now normally used to denote a kind of imaginative experience, whose object is conceived as an end in itself. It arises from the contemplation of appearances, in which questions of ultimate purpose and scientific truth are held in suspension. It was plausibly suggested by *Kant that such experience is not only essential to the life of a *rational being, but also itself inherently rational, issuing in judgements held forth as objectively binding. Moreover, despite its abstraction from particular purposes, it provides an intimation of the inherent 'purposiveness' of reality. Two questions arise: what are the political consequences, and what the political causes, of aesthetic *values so conceived?

(i) The political consequences. Some argue that, despite its non-functional character, aesthetic experience is essential both to understanding and to acting on the world. In every action appearance has a dominant part to play, since it is largely through appearances that we respond to our environment. Hence the saving of appearances may be a persistent political purpose: it is this, for example, which explains much of the concern of 'conservationists' for landscape and townscape. When people agitate on behalf of some valley that is threatened by development, they are certainly not agitating on behalf of its rights. Nor are they truly concerned with the rights of themselves or future generations. The beauty of the landscape itself seems to give sufficient reason to act. Some argue, however, that such aesthetic activism has its ultimate *raison d'être* in social life. The regard for beauty reflects a deep need for social harmony, and in agitating on behalf of aesthetic values people are really agitating on behalf of the forms of life which are consonant with them. It is certainly indisputable that appearances are of overwhelming importance in social existence, and that the sense of manners, etiquette, and 'good form' are both intimately related to the aesthetic, and also integral to our understanding of one another as persons. Hence demands for aesthetic continuity can plausibly be seen as extensions of a sense of social 'belonging'; aesthetic values seem to nourish our understanding of the ends of social existence, and therefore inevitably qualify our pursuit of the political means. Such arguments were very popular in the nineteenth century, for example among *cultural conservatives, among certain kinds of pastoral socialists, and among thinkers like Ruskin, *Morris and the critics of *industrialism. Such thinkers also extolled the aesthetic interest of the cognoscenti, as an index of the social needs of the common people. Their vision of the political significance of aesthetic value formed part of a general doctrine of the interdependence between high and common *culture.

(ii) Political causes. It is evident that aesthetic values may reflect *ideological commitments. Some argue that the 'aesthetic' way of seeing things arose, like its name, in the *bourgeois period of Western civilization. Aesthetic values arise in the mind of the person who wishes to console his economic position by a species of passive and 'functionless' contemplation that shows to be harmonious what is in reality far from being so. This is then seen as part of an ideological attempt to *naturalize reality with consoling representations; other social orders will not require, and therefore will not produce, this kind of mystery. (Thus Bertolt Brecht: *The Messingkauf Dialogues*, 1939, published 1967.) That is one example of a theory which tries to find the causes of our love of beauty in social and political circumstances. Others, unpersuaded by that, may nevertheless see individual aesthetic outlooks as reflecting both particular political arrangements, and also the position of the individual within them. The eighteenth-century aesthetic of nature, for example, may be represented as an offshoot of aristocratic control exerted over the landscape. In contemplating the beauty of nature, the aristocrat was consoled by a vision of the 'natural' quality of his power. (*See also* *architecture, *art.)

affirmative action. An Americanism,

used to denote action taken in order to advance, rather than merely to conform to, the political vision underlying a doctrine of legal rights. Thus, if it is determined that, in matters of employment, blacks and women are to be given the same rights as white men, then affirmative action on the part of an employer involves not merely conforming to the code by giving equal consideration to all candidates independently of race and sex, but also actively seeking applications from women and blacks, so 'affirming' the underlying political vision which, if merely 'conformed to', might result in the perpetuation of existing inequalities. Affirmative action is sometimes defended as a necessary part of enforcing just distribution, sometimes criticized as a form of unjust discrimination in favour of those whose position is advanced by it. It is to be distinguished from a system of 'quotas', which requires a particular outcome, rather than a particular effort.

affluence. The condition of *abundance, in which all human needs are easily satisfiable and generally catered for, and in which productive activity is directed increasingly to the production of luxuries (i.e. goods for which there is no natural *need).

In *The Affluent Society*, 1958, J. K. Galbraith argued that, when widespread poverty and want are abolished, people come to have a standard expectation of comfort. In such a society received ideas of economic theory (which tend to involve the assumption that at least *something* necessary is also scarce) cannot be applied. It is no longer rational for the *private sector to pursue increasing production or for the *public sector to refrain from interference in the means of production, distribution and exchange. In fact, however, firms continue to seek the expansion of demand, and continue to see the public sector as an obstacle to the needed diversion of resources. This unbridled private expansion can persist only by the creation of artificial or 'synthesized' demands, through *advertising and the expansion of the credit system. Because of the neglect of public works the result is a condition of private affluence accompanied by public squalor: private cars but not enough roads for them, private wealth but insufficient police to protect it, and so on.

The rise of the 'affluent worker' – i.e. the worker who receives a wage that is more than sufficient to meet the needs of himself and his family, and so more than is necessary to reproduce his *labour power – is a salient feature of modern Western *capitalism. It is held to count against the *Marxian theory of *surplus value, and to mitigate the charge of *exploitation levelled against the capitalist system. Modern advocates of state control of the economy sometimes accept this, and then go on to found new criticisms based on hostility to affluence as such. Some of these criticisms repeat age-old arguments against *luxury; others expand the objection – implicit in Galbraith's analysis – to the 'synthesized' demand, perhaps connecting this phenomenon with *alienation and *commodity fetishism. In all such discussions a distinction must be drawn between affluence that is concerned only with *consumption, and that which directs itself towards a style of life, involving, say, sumptuous ceremony and display. It is contended, e.g. by *Veblen, that the latter is simply a conspicuous version of the former. However, Veblen also argues that such conspicuous consumption provides part of the motive of accumulation and so cannot be eliminated from the productive process, which requires accumulation if it is to proceed at all. Others argue that, until naturalized by the trappings of civilization and leisure, conspicuous consumption is merely the object of envy, and so of social discontent.

agency. The faculty of action. Changes are divided into things that happen and things that are done, and philosophers and jurists dispute over the grounds and significance of the distinction. Only some forces in the world are also agencies: the wind, for example, does nothing, although it causes much to happen. Some argue that the distinctive feature of agency is that it involves intention or decision: this is disputed by others, who argue that the crucial idea is *responsibility, so that things done include many of the consequences of negligent but unintentional behaviour.

Agency belongs to many bodies and organizations besides human beings: e.g. to companies, states, committees and meetings. Perhaps this is because all such bodies are also *persons; or perhaps agency and personality are independent ideas. The distinction between actions and happenings is of immense importance: the first are justified, and criticized, by reasons; they define the responsibility and answerability of an agent; they give grounds for reciprocal actions which punish, repair, restore or reward. The political problems are typified by *revanchism, which holds a present generation responsible for things done by its ancestors, and takes revenge accordingly. But in what way is the murdered Turkish diplomat really a manifestation of the agency which killed the ancestors of his Armenian assassin?

aggregate demand. The total demand for goods and services produced within a single economy, including demands of households for consumer goods, of firms for investment, of government for goods, investment etc. and export demands. (Demands for imports are *excluded*.) Many economists hold that aggregate demand determines the level of production and hence employment. Followers of *Keynes, in particular, believe that the analysis of aggregate demand is essential to the understanding of *national income and *unemployment. Whether aggregate demand has an automatic tendency to achieve the level giving full employment of labour and of productive capacity is, however, a central point of controversy within economic theory.

aggregate supply. The total supply of goods and services to meet the *aggregate demand within an economy; i.e. domestic products + imports.

aggression. A term fundamental to international argument, which, since the First World War, has come to replace the idea of an 'offensive' act. It is argued that 'an acceptable definition of aggression and a reliable procedure for determining when an act of aggression has occurred are essential to a practicable system of collective security' (W. M. Honan: *International Conflict and Collective Security*, 1955). However, the United Nations Charter failed to define aggression, stipulating only that the Security Council and the General Assembly are authorized to call *specific* actions aggression. Two definitions were put forward in 1933, one by the Committee on Security Questions of the Disarmament Conference, the other by a 'Convention for the definition of Aggression', subscribed to by Afghanistan, Estonia, Latvia, Persia (Iran), Poland, Romania, Turkey, Yugoslavia and the USSR. While the subsequent history of those states may be held to illustrate the utility of definitions in international politics, certain distinctions were made that have been incorporated into more recent definitions. It is now normal to distinguish direct aggression between states (e.g. armed invasion, whether or not preceded or accompanied by a declaration of war) from indirect aggression (e.g. the provision of arms and relief to an existing aggressor); aggression may be military or, as in a blockade of ports or an embargo, economic – although to what extent a blockade may go without being an act of aggression is a matter of dispute (*see* *pacific blockade). Aggression may involve regular armies answerable to the sovereign power, or more or less autonomous groups of guerrillas. All attempts to arrive at a definition are motivated by the desire to outlaw aggressive war (*see* *just war), under the supposition that if there were no aggressors, but only states prepared for 'self-defence', then there would be no wars. Aggression is, therefore, the initiating act expressive of an intention to fight. The problem is to identify its instances, in particular to show how indirect aggression is manifested by such complex agencies as states.

agitprop. The acronym for the Department of Agitation and Progaganda, set up in 1920 as a section of the Central Committee Secretariat of the Soviet Communist Party, and which has gradually spread its influence into all areas of Soviet life and into many of the spheres of international politics, where it advances behind *front organizations. Now often used as a general term for left-wing agitation and propaganda, when these involve any substantial degree of organization, and also for certain kinds of cultural activity designed to establish a widespread acceptance of left-wing *ideology.

ahistorical (sometimes an-historical). A theory is described as such when it treats its subject-matter either as though it has no history, or as though its history plays no important part in the explanation of its nature. It is often said, by both conservatives and Marxists, that the *liberal theory of human nature and political institutions is ahistorical. The intention is to accuse liberalism of describing man's social and political nature without reference to the fact that these develop historically, or to the fact that historical development determines both what is politically possible and what is politically justified. Marxists often go on to add that this ahistorical vision is itself the reflection of a particular set of historical circumstances – say, those which obtained in eighteenth or nineteenth-century Europe, and perhaps even now in America. Such circumstances (it is argued) enable men to envisage a universal human type, whose essence, while in fact the product of a particular phase of capitalist development, is perceived as changeless, sempiternal, the common property of every economic and political order.

Some confusion results from the fact that any description of the essence of something (be it human nature or the nature of a plant or animal) must have universal validity: i.e. it cannot be specific with relation to time. If it is of the essence of human nature to develop through time then this is a timeless truth about human nature. A liberal theory may well rely on just such a timeless truth in constructing its fundamental doctrine of rights and duties, without incurring the charge of being 'ahistorical': yet this charge is sure to be levelled at it, simply on account of its search for universality.

aid. On the assumption that the world divides into 'developed' and 'developing' nations, and that it is better for a nation to be developed than not, the idea of international aid has come to have considerable importance in political thinking. (*See* *development.) It has been argued before the UN Conference on Trade and Development that growth in real terms in nations recognized as 'developing' can be secured only by a level of imports which exceeds their capacity to export. Hence, without foreign aid, they must inevitably decline further in real income level, as a result of the very process of trade that promises to improve their status. This idea has been used to suggest a variety of conclusions, for example: (i) that it is an inevitable effect of free trade to impoverish further the poorer nations (an argument analogous to Marx's attempt to show that private ownership of the means of production inevitably leads to the creation of a propertyless class); (ii) that there is a moral duty on richer nations to provide aid; (iii) that development is impossible without actual colonization. Others (e.g. P. T. Bauer: *Dissent on Development*, 1971) argue that the economic theories underlying the accepted wisdom concerning aid and development are in fact contentious, that it is aid which, in removing the incentive to exploit resources, leads to impoverishment, and that aid merely lines the pockets of a ruling élite, without producing a real investment.

alien. A person who, by the law of one state, is not a national or citizen of that state, though he may be resident there. The decision whether to admit aliens falls within the privilege of each sovereign state, and no state can be forced by international law to do so. The matter is however, a subject of fierce domestic disagreement. The *jus gentium* in *Roman law evolved partly in order to determine the political rights of aliens, and most states now recognize some standard of humane behaviour towards aliens on their soil.

The legal idea of an alien is bound up with those of *jurisdiction (i.e. the idea that a state has sovereign authority over a particular *territory*) and *allegiance (i.e. the idea that persons owe duties to *specific* sovereign states). In some versions of liberal internationalism, for which jurisdiction and allegiance ought to aspire to be international, the idea of an 'alien' is inherently retrograde. (*See* *Kant.)

The legal idea should be distinguished sharply from the social and political conception that certain people, classes, or races are 'alien' from the point of view of a society by which they are surrounded. In the legal sense a man is 'alien' to the state; in the socio-political sense he is 'alien' to society. That is to say, his customs, allegiances, behaviour (perhaps even the colour of his skin), mark him out as something strange, and perhaps unacceptable, in the consciousness of those with whom he must mix.

alienation. A term used to describe a state of mind or of being, and owing its modern significance to three related ideas, all of them with discernible medieval antecedents:

1. In *Hegel two terms tend to be translated as 'alienation': *Entaüsserung* (objectification), and *Entfremdung* (self-estrangement). The theory – which is not particularly associated with either term – occurs as part of a general account of the progress of spirit (**Geist*) towards knowledge of, and unity with, the 'Absolute Idea'. Spirit begins in subjectivity, and proceeds towards objective existence; spirit creates its world in the act of knowing it, and both history and individual development are to be seen as the construction and overcoming of successive 'objectifications'. At a certain 'moment' of consciousness, the spirit divides the world into good and bad, ideal and reality saved and fallen. This divorce is experienced as a divorce between the self and the objectifications which it has 'posited' as not-self. The fracture between the ideal objectification and the fallen self is experienced as a thoroughgoing imperfection in all conscious life: Hegel calls this state the 'unhappy consciousness'. Estrangement from the self is conjoined with estrangement from others. Since it is the essence of spirit to identify itself with the ideal, the world is seen as devoid of spirit, which lies beyond humanity, and not in it. Men are seen as objects, while spirit is seen as realized only in the being of a transcendent God. The practice of religion is the attempt to overcome this rift, to see man as no longer trapped in nature, and no longer aspiring hopelessly to overcome it. Alienation is overcome by the recognition of the immanence of God, and the self-transcendence of man, through the sacramental customs of religion.

2. In the early writings of *Marx, alienation (*Entfremdung*) is alienation from *species-being (*Gattungswesen*) – a term borrowed from Feuerbach (*see* *Young Hegelians) to describe the distinctive character of human social existence. Feuerbach had secularized some of the theological ideas of Hegel, and thus paved the way for Marx's view, according to which alienation is no longer inherent in man's 'being in the world', but only in his being in a *particular historical* world. Man's essence lies in his species-being, so that alienation from species-being is alienation from the human essence, and hence from self. This process occurs when men are compelled to see themselves as objects, as means to ends, with no satisfactions that they can identify as their own. They then cease to have reality for themselves; instead they project their essence and value into the objects which they pursue. Human life is seen only as a means, whereas objects are seen as ends, with an intrinsic value which in reality cannot belong to them. Since the prime activity of species-being is *labour, the primary mode of alienation is alienated labour, through which men are compelled to instil the world in their own activity of production with the forms of alienated consciousness. Marx saw this state as associated with *private property, which compels the *division of labour, and the institution of the *wage contract. By forcing men to sell themselves (i.e. in another, legal, sense, to 'alienate' their *labour power), it also compels them to engage in the production of goods which have no *use-value for them, but only *exchange-value. Such goods do not reflect back to the producer an image of himself, since they bear the imprint of no natural satisfaction. In pursuing and producing them, a man sees himself as a means to an end that is not his own. Hence he becomes an object to himself, and looks on others likewise. Only with the abolition of private property will man be restored to himself, and to the 'species-being' which constitutes his satisfaction. *See also* *master and slave.

3. In *Freud and post-Freudian psychology, alienation is seen as the condition in which man is placed by civilization, through the necessity to conform to roles and expectations, and to *repress and transform vital instincts and impulses, so that in becoming acceptable to others he becomes a stranger to himself.

Many modern thinkers (e.g. *Marcuse and Erich Fromm (b. 1900)) attempt to synthesize the Marxian and Freudian ideas. For them 'capitalist man' is a being crippled through the fatty degeneration of the will, driven to see himself always as an object and never as the originator of his acts, a person who is no longer a true person because he cannot be what he really is: he loses interest in life because it is not *he* who lives it. In this speculative social criticism alienation is often contrasted with an ideal of *authenticity or *self-realization. In none of the established usages is the notion very clear, but in all of them it expresses the search for a theory that will describe the condition of the modern consciousness, and also explain its sense of being 'separated' from some truly human way of being.

allegiance. The bond which attaches the subject to the sovereign, and also to fellow subjects. This bond can be conceived in two ways. First, as a power, consisting in emotional attachment to certain familiar conditions and expectations, of which the state is the symbol and expression. Secondly, as a duty towards the sovereign power. In the latter construction, it gives rise to the well-known problem of *political obligation: how can allegiance be *owed*, and what justifies us in asserting this? Liberals and others have attempted to find the answer in doctrines of the *social contract; Marxists and anarchists have looked forward to the creation of a state of affairs in which the problem of political obligation would not arise, believing that the highest form of society is one without sovereignty, and therefore with nothing towards which allegiance might be owed.

Conservatives, by contrast, have made the concept of allegiance, conceived as a power, fundamental to their description of the experience of society. Allegiance becomes the inescapable precondition, both of the contract which liberal thinkers suppose might justify it, and of the renunciation of sovereignty to which the anarchist aspires. Allegiance is an emotional condition, which creates the possibility of political obligation, but has no independent ground. Some – for example *Hegel in *The Philosophy of Right* – have tried to argue that the power and the obligation are one, and both examples of *piety. On this view the attempt to found political obligation in contract or consent is based on the spurious view that voluntary activity is the only thing that can put a citizen under an obligation. But it is essential to many institutions – for example the *family – that people should recognize and defer to obligations which do not arise through voluntary action. This sense of obligation towards what is safe and familiar is an ineliminable part of social consciousness and cannot be further justified. According to such views, allegiance is the true fact of the matter in political life, and any attempt to replace it with contract, consent, or some unforeseeable alternative (such as would be involved in the total abolition of sovereignty) misrepresents the fundamental bond of society, and misdescribes the subject-matter of politics. The problem for such views lies partly in determining the object of allegiance: is allegiance towards individuals, towards *society, towards the *state, or what? Moreover, how can it be brought into being if it does not already exist? Also, while 'allegiance' may describe the citizen's *sense* of obligation towards the state, it does not seem to describe, on this theory, any proven obligation.

alliance. Specifically, a nation is an ally of another if bound to it by some treaty for mutual defence. More loosely, 'allies' are those who recognize the threat of a common aggressor, and agree under certain terms to take concerted action, diplomatic, economic, or military, to counter it. 'The Allies', used to name the association of nations fighting the axis powers during the 1939 war, is a term the emotional resonance of which survives in 'The Western Alliance'. This now names the loose association of nations united to some extent by treaty (e.g. NATO), to some extent by a common apprehension of danger (e.g. from 'Russian Imperialism' – although the USSR was formerly one of 'the Allies'), most of all by similar conceptions of political *legitimacy, and by mutually dependent economies. It is disputed whether the creation of alliances is beneficial either to world peace or to the common interests of the international community, but even without the existence of alliances, the division of the world into *blocs, *spheres of influence, and spheres of *coercion and domination would presumably produce similar effects.

alternative society. A term used in the popular exposition of a certain kind of extreme liberalism (fashionable in the US and other highly developed urban-industrial societies during the 1960s), according to which the aim of individual life is to lead an 'authentic life style', achieved through independent personal choice. There is no reason to conform to the 'structures' of the 'system' into which one is born that is more compelling than the impetus to enact the authentic life style of one's own devising, and so to create, in community with one's fellows, the 'alternative society' and its associated *counter-culture. This counter-culture will be offensive to the guardians of the 'establishment', since it will threaten the easy solution by which they have chosen to live. (The terms in inverted commas are part of the rhetoric that confers on the original thought the appearance of system.)

The advocacy of the alternative society derives in part from *Sartre's existentialism, in part from the psychotherapeutic doctrines of *Reich and R. D. Laing, and in part from the radical social criticism of *Marcuse.

Althusser, Louis (b. 1918). *Neo-Marxist French philosopher, who attempts to combine 'scientific Marxism', with the *structuralism of *Lévi-Strauss. Althusser argues, in *For Marx* (1965), that there is a fundamental discontinuity ('epistemological break') between *Hegel and Feuerbach, on the one hand, and Marx on the other. He dismisses the early (pre-1845) writings of Marx as 'pre-Marxist', and finds the true, 'scientific' Marxism in the writings that follow. Althusser's major deviations from Marx's *dialectical materialism may be attributed to his conception of 'structural causation', which he argues to be implicit in the mature 'scientific' theories of Marx. Revolution and all social transformation is brought about through *contradiction, and the 'principal contradiction' is that identified by Marx, between *productive forces and *production relations. However this principal contradiction is 'inseparable from the total structure of the social body in which it is found'. The social body contains other contradictions, existing at several distinct levels within the *superstructure, and interacting systematically, as they struggle to align themselves: so contradictions pass from one level to another. Because the various contradictions develop unevenly it is possible that an economically backward country might present the sudden confluence of contradictions necessary for successful revolution (the case of Russia). Althusser calls this 'fusion of accumulated contradictions' 'over-determination', borrowing a term from *Freud. Thus while the economy may exert a powerful sway over social conditions, it alone can never be taken as the cause of social transformation (although Althusser affirms somewhat half-heartedly the thesis of *Engels, that 'economic necessity . . . in the last analysis always prevails'). Althusser has been influential, but is often criticized by other Marxists, both those who dislike his tendency to dismiss the 'immature humanism' of the early Marx, and the Marxian social criticism which has stemmed from it, and also those who think that his idea of 'contradiction' is metaphorical, and who argue that, in his reluctance to acknowledge the 'principal contradiction' as endowed with the power to explain all others, he in effect denies the thesis of *materialism. Others criticize the extreme pretentiousness and obfuscation of his approach, and his impulsive ingesting of theories which owe more to *fashion than to thought. (See, e.g., E. P. Thompson: *The Poverty of Theory*, 1978.)

altruism. The disposition to care for others, or to act knowingly in their interests. The term has been appropriated by ethologists, to describe organisms which exist partly through giving help to members of their species. *Sociobiologists have attempted to extend ethological theories of the 'altruistic organism' to the human species, in order to explain our liking for each other as a convenient evolutionary device. Whatever the value of such explanations, it is clear that altruism is a serious motive in human affairs, and one that must affect the calculations of politicians and economists. Some economists argue that *classical theorists such as *Smith did not take sufficient account of it; others try to integrate altruism into economics by ascribing to it a distinctive function, whereby it generates the *optimum economic behaviour in a group. (See, e.g. E. S. Phelps (ed.): *Altruism, Morality and Economic Theory*, 1975.)

Philosophers distinguish two distinct motives that go by the name of altruism: the emotional motives, of love, liking and *friendship, whereby another's interest is automatically mine; and the moral motive, of respect or considerateness, whereby another's interest becomes a reason for me, while not necessarily becoming mine. *See* *charity, *Kant.

amnesty. From the Greek meaning oblivion or forgetfulness. An amnesty is a general determination that whole classes of offenders shall not be prosecuted. It is juridically distinct from a pardon, which is the annulment of a penalty already prescribed. Only the criminal consequences of the absolved act are destroyed, and third parties may still have recourse to a civil action for damages.

Amnesties are offered to prisoners of war and of conscience, or to *political offenders. They may be general or particular, absolute or conditional. There is considerable dispute over who, and in what circumstances, is entitled to offer them. In the US, it seems undecided whether an amnesty is an executive rather than a legislative act. The first theory attributes the power of amnesty to the President, the second attributes it to Congress.

The term is also used, as in 'Amnesty International', to denote the general overlooking of accusations founded merely in differences of opinion between the accused and the state. Liberty of *conscience, it is thought, requires that a sincerely held belief cannot be sufficient grounds for punishment.

anarchism. The belief either that government is intrinsically evil, or that historical circumstances have conspired to make it so, together with the further belief that it is preferable and possible to abolish government, either completely, or at least in part. The anarchist believes in a *society without the institutions of a *state, and tends, also, to reject all forms of *authority that interfere with the spontaneous actions and associations of individuals. Typical anarchist beliefs are these:

(i) Men are benign by nature and corrupted by government.

(ii) The state is exploitative, and oppressive, whereas society is natural and free.

(iii) Man is a social animal, fulfilled through voluntary cooperation, but frustrated by all *coercion.

(iv) Reforms 'from above' bear the imprint of the authority that initiates them, and are therefore worthless.

(v) Social change must be brought about through revolutionary action, perhaps even *violent action.

Not all those beliefs are held by every anarchist. *Godwin, for example, believed in a society of small producers, united by cooperation, but without a state, and sought to achieve this by enlightened social reform. The Russian anarchist *Bakunin advocated 'anarchism, collectivism, atheism', in a synthesis that required immediate violent revolution. Others could be called anarchists despite rejecting all of (i) to (v): *Nietzsche, for example, who lauded the strength and egoism of the individual will, and sought to free it from all attachment to the 'herd-like' necessities whereby the multitude are governed. Much nineteenth-century anarchism was hostile towards private property, or towards some kinds of private property, as a kind of concealed slavery. *Proudhon, who attempted to make anarchism into a conscious mass movement, proposed the maxim that 'property is theft'. However he also thought that property is a necessary part of freedom, and therefore attacked *monopoly and usurpation as the principal evil forms of it. Bakunin advocated *common ownership of the means of production, but was prepared to concede private ownership in the 'means of consumption'. Godwin accepted most kinds of private ownership, on a small scale. Modern thinkers influenced by anarchism (e.g. *Nozick) are usually of a *liberal persuasion, and are therefore more tolerant towards private property, on account of the interference in freedom that its abolition seems to entail.

Another important aspect of nineteenth-century anarchism was the hostility towards organized religion: Tolstoy, for example, who believed in a society of love, argued that 'true' religion involves a complete negation of the state and all its institutions. Most anarchists have either accepted that position, or gone further, and argued that no religion is true. Violent anarchists, such as *Sorel, have been influential during the present century, and the nineteenth-century anarchists were extremely important in providing concepts to *Marx, whose '*withering away of the state' is directly inspired by their ideals.

In all its forms anarchism must assume that there is a condition of human society (or even human solitude) in which material needs and collective responsibilities will be met spontaneously, without coercion. Most anarchists are therefore disposed to reject the view of Hobbes, that the life of man outside the protection of the sovereign is 'solitary, poor, nasty, brutish and short'. The objections contained in Hobbes's remark are endorsed by many, who also see history as confirming them. Without violence, it is argued, the destruction of the state is inconceivable, and with violence, a new state must immediately replace that which is destroyed. Furthermore, the advocacy of violence seems to go against those very assumptions about human nature on which anarchism bases its vision of a new society. In the face of such difficulties certain anarchists assert (in the manner of the later Marx) that the social condition of man has first to be improved by the massive discipline of industrial production before the state can wither away and 'true human nature' reassert itself. Perhaps the view most radically opposed to anarchism is *Hegel's, that 'true human nature' requires the state, not only as means to its security, but as the highest expression of its freedom.

anarcho-syndicalism. Movement arising in the later nineteenth century from a fusion of anarchist and *trade union (syndicalist) principles, and led at first by James Guillaume, a Swiss disciple of *Bakunin, and later guided and endorsed by *Sorel. Anarcho-syndicalism advocated the use of trade union power, in order to oppose and destroy state power in all its forms. In Sorel's hands it was exhorted to *violence, and action (culminating in the final and decisive 'general strike') which would be tantamount to violence. Sorel's philosophy is often thought not to be a genuine *anarchism, since he advocated the use of organized groups in order to overthrow the established order. (*See further* *syndicalism.) The anarcho-syndicalist movement thought of trade unions as the nuclear bodies of a future society, which must prepare themselves as cohesive fighting units, in order to work for the overthrow of the capitalist state. It formed the basis of pre-Francist trade unionism in Spain, and of the US 'Industrial Workers of the World' (the 'wobblies'), but it was opposed in the UK by the existing trade union formations. Its ideals have persisted, even though the movement has collapsed, and *industrial action may still sometimes be viewed as a direct or indirect *confrontation with the state, whether or not the state is also the employer against which the action is directed.

Anglicanism. The system of religious doctrine and practice upheld by Christians in communion with the see of Canterbury, and hence by the Anglican Church of England, and its offshoots in former colonies and dependencies. The doctrine is derived from a fusion of evangelical authority and respect for local custom. The proof of doctrinal validity is to be sought in the first four centuries of Christian teaching, before the institutional structure of the Roman Catholic Church had diverted that teaching to its own peculiar usage; while in all matters of liturgy, ceremony, and the legal and social status of religious belief, local custom and tradition are respected as containing the only objective authority. Anglicanism thus comes to stand for a particular vision of the social role of the church. The 'Church of England', is not only common to Englishmen (and, by extension through the (Episcopal) 'Church of Scotland', 'Church of Ireland' etc., to Scots, Irish etc.), but also legally established within, and influenced through, a national government. It thereby attempts to incorporate into its constitution a vision of the harmony between secular and religious obligations, encapsulated in the doctrine that the head of state (the sovereign) is also the leader of the church. In the UK constitution some bishops hold seats in Parliament as of right, and all bishops are appointed by the sovereign with the advice of the Prime Minister. Equally, liturgical and doctrinal reforms require the consent of the sovereign in Parliament, a fact that has recently been resented by the Anglican Church on the grounds that it provides an impediment to reforms dictated by its evangelical mission. Clearly, the coexistence of that mission with a respect for established usage, and the incorporation of both into a legal and political superstructure of the kind currently existing in the UK, are delicate social and political artifacts. The social order that they reflect remains an object of *nostalgia on the part of some English conservatives, although others argue that it is either extinct or on the verge of extinction. (*See* *common prayer, *liturgy.)

annexation. Primarily a term in *international law, denoting the *act of state whereby territory not previously held under the sovereignty of that state is acquired. Annexation confers all powers of use, exclusion, alienation, titles to public property rights, etc., on the annexing state. Allegiance of the inhabitants of the annexed territory is automatically assumed by the new sovereign, and although existing law and *local government organization in principle remain intact, they do so only in so far as this does not conflict with the interests of the annexing state. Thus annexation is to be distinguished from the establishment of a *protectorate, or military occupation, these latter procuring for the dominant state an extension of authority, but not full *sovereignty. It is also distinct from colonization, in that actual occupation either by the authorities of the annexing state or by its citizens is not required.

Within international law annexation can only be validated when consented to by the state whose territory is annexed (in whole or in part), or (in the case of a territory not formerly held by another state) when consented to by the international community. The consent of a predecessor state may be given tacitly, under *coercion, or in the form of a *treaty. In either case, the inhabitants of the annexed territory are without rights of *self-determination. Originally annexation was intended as a mechanism whereby the discovery of new land could be both facilitated and credited to the adventuring state; it is now simply one among many means whereby major powers incorporate the territories of smaller powers.

anomie (also: anomy). Greek: without law. 'Anomy' appeared in English in the sixteenth century and was frequently used in seventeenth-century theology to mean disregard of law, particularly divine law. The French *anomie* was appropriated by *Durkheim to denote the social condition in which no established code prevails or is accepted as objectively binding, either because traditions of social conformity have broken down, or because the sense of an authority independent of the individual impulse has been dissolved. *Anomie* may be a form of personal disorganization, when the individual can recognize no social *norm as constraining him, or a form of social disorganization, when norms are in conflict or have lost authority. Durkheim argued (*Suicide*, 1897) that *anomie* is a characteristic of an immature industrial society, that has yet to develop a suitable moral climate. However, in a late essay (*The Dualism of Human Nature*, 1914) he seemed to admit the possibility that the *anomie* which he discerned in modern society, where the *division of labour isolates every man from his fellows, and where authoritative institutions exert no necessary influence, may not be overcome, and may become perpetual.

anthropology. The science of man, which has divided into several distinct but related studies, and developed an emphasis upon societies considered to be either *prehistorical or in some way isolated from too much interaction with the modern world. Anthropology has tended to concentrate on such *primitive societies, not because they are thought to require analysis in ways inapplicable elsewhere but, on the contrary, because of the assumed ease with which they might generate universal conclusions. In studying what is unfamiliar and difficult to conceptualize, the anthropologist hopes to discover hypotheses concerning *human nature and society everywhere. The following distinct branches are now recognized:

(i) physical anthropology, which merges with human biology, and deals with the physical characteristics of the species;
(ii) cultural anthropology, which studies the artifacts of separate *cultures, and looks for their general function or significance in the lives of those who make use of them;
(iii) social anthropology, which probably includes cultural anthropology, but ranges more widely, in order to explore all aspects of man's social existence, and to explain the forms which it takes;
(iv) philosophical anthropology, which is not so much a branch of anthropology as an extension of philosophy to the universal but disputed truths of human nature, in order to provide the basis for moral and political theory.

Social and cultural anthropology tend to be comparative, and this has led to the ascendancy of cultural *relativism in anthropological studies. The two principal modern schools are *structuralism, associated with the work of Lévi-Strauss, and 'functionalism', associated with Bronislav Malinowski (1884–1942). The first looks for 'meanings', the second for *functional explanations. The method of functional explanation – whereby social characteristics are explained in terms of their functional relation to the well-being of society – has impinged on *sociology and had considerable influence in all areas of political thought. Other notions important to anthropology also have wide political significance, among them *custom, *culture, *myth, *ritual, and *tradition. Anthropology has *organicist adherents, who emphasize the fragility of primitive communities and conclude that social order is organic, change in one part having unforeseeable and perhaps dangerous consequences in another. It is common for anthropologists to caution themselves against conservative conclusions, however, since what is unforeseeable to them may not be unforeseeable to the people they study, and the sense of organic complexity may be no more than an ignorance of function or a blindness to significance.

anthropomorphism. The tendency to see non-human forms and animals as endowed with human characteristics, both physical and mental, but especially with will, emotion and intelligence. It is variously held to be good, bad and indifferent that men should project their own natures into their surroundings, but it is almost universally agreed that such is inevitable (at least under 'existing social conditions'). The species of anthropomorphism known as *fetishism is offered as the explanation of things as diverse as man's tolerance of the market economy (*see* *commodity fetishism), his allegiance to the state, and his impulse to seek his salvation in a future world.

anti-. A prefix often used to denote a form of hostility supposed to express something other than a reasoned aversion to its object. Usually – as in some of the examples that follow – the explanation of the hostility is held to lie in social and economic circumstances, perhaps because these might show not only that the aversion is unreasoned, but also that it is unreasonable.

anti-clericalism. A liberal movement, which aims to reduce the political influence of the clergy and of religious institutions. Anti-clericalism is evident in much medieval literature, but its origins as a political movement lie in the eighteenth century *Enlightenment. It became an active force during the French Revolution, and in the Third Republic, was deeply intertwined with Italian, Spanish and other forms of *nationalism, inspired Bismarck's **Kulturkampf* against the Catholic church, and currently appears both outside the church (e.g. in some aspects of USSR domestic policy) and within it (in the *secularization of religious practice and doctrine).

anti-communism. The aversion towards *communism, specifically in the US, has been thought by many, whether or not themselves communists, to have a character so intense and hysterical as to be insufficiently explained by the sincere belief that communism is a bad form of government. *McCarthyism, for example, has sometimes been thought to be not merely opportunistic but also founded in self-deception. It has been accused of concentrating on obnoxious deviations from communist principles (such as *Stalinism) and ignoring the genuine and perhaps redeeming ideals which those deviations mark, in order to generate an atmosphere of hysterical fear and hatred. Explanations of this alleged hysterical character vary; some invoke the threat that communism poses to private property, others invoke its anti-individualistic message (thus explaining the prevalence of anti-communism in the US and its relative absence from Europe). The thought that communism, properly understood, could not be loathed *as such* is perhaps a curiosity of mid-twentieth century American liberalism, although it has had widespread influence.

anti-semitism. The most notorious form of *racism in politics, which has had a long history, culminating in the Nazi *holocaust, and continuing as a vital force in the modern world, e.g. in Eastern Europe (notably Poland), in the USSR, and in the Middle East, where it is partly the effect, and partly the cause, of opposition to *Zionism.

Anti-semitism has many forms. It may attribute to the Jews a debased and subject moral character, or a character of innate degeneracy (as in the Nazi ideology); it may equally accuse the Jews of cunning, success, power and conspiracy; or of a disposition to accumulate benefits through usury and injustice. Anti-semitism must be distinguished from the religious hostility to the Jews as those who had denied, and continue to deny, Christ. The two hostilities may fuel one another but, strictly speaking, the religious hostility is removed by conversion to the Christian faith, while racism remains indifferent to any change that is within its victim's power (which is one reason why it is comforting: the enemy will never deceive you by turning out to be your friend). Explanations of anti-semitism are as varied as the phenomenon. It is sometimes thought to be based on the hostility of the *petit bourgeois* towards those of his own social class who are able to obtain a livelihood through capital investment; on this view it is the hostility of the borrower towards the lender (made acute by hyper-flation) which tries to rationalize its own intensity by finding an irredeemable moral, rather than a redeemable institutional, fault. Others (e.g. *Sartre) have tried to explain the phenomenon in terms of fantasies of the Jew's sexual prowess, thus aligning anti-semitism with some kinds of hostility towards those judged to be 'primitive'. No explanation seems wholly satisfactory. Some account must be taken of habit: once a particular group which cannot defend itself is picked out as the enemy, the habit of so identifying it begins to grow. Moreover there seems to be an inveterate need for societies in a state of acute crisis to look for the 'enemy within' who causes it.

antinomianism. General name for the view – specifically advocated by *Gnostics and again at the Reformation – that Christians are set free by grace from the need to observe any moral law. Hence any view that claims absolute right of action on the grounds of absolute truth of doctrine.

anti-trust. Originally US legislation designed to control large business groupings and to prevent the formation of uncompetitive markets through *monopolies (which were often known in the nineteenth century as *trusts on account of their legal status). Anti-trust legislation is now adopted as a substantial part of much European company law, as a result of EEC legislation and policy. The Sherman Anti-Trust Act 1890 marked the first significant break with the practice of **laissez-faire* in the US, and indicated the widespread admission that law can create and control the conditions of a market, and that it may be in the public interest for the state thereby to exert substantial indirect control over the economy. *See also* *oligopoly.

apartheid. Afrikaans term meaning 'aparthood', and denoting the policy of racial segregation as practised by the National Party in South Africa since 1948. Officially it is a policy of 'separate but equal development'; it involves legislation controlling places of residence, schools, universities, and recreational facilities; as well as laws prohibiting mixed marriages, and controlling voluntary associations. The major intention is to allow political power only to the white population, and to deny to the remainder all rights that would be tantamount to political *access, including the right to vote at an election. Blacks are confined to certain autonomous 'homelands', alleged to be their 'true' historical places of residence, leaving the remaining areas to be enjoyed by whites in untroubled sovereignty. The substantial difference between the natural assets and *infrastructure of the two kinds of area is often noted; the historical justifications are for the most part considered to be either lies or *myths. Apartheid has been replaced by *neo-apartheid as the official policy of the National Party, but its pragmatic and ideological aspects remain, the second being at least partly *racist. The myths used to support the withholding of political rights from blacks have no application to the situation of the 'coloureds' who, having nothing where they are, suffer the additional grievance of having nowhere to go. (The coloureds are Afrikaans speaking, and for the most part Calvinist people, descended from Malaysians brought to the Cape Colony as slaves; the category also includes others of mixed descent, including many who are indistinguishable in every observable respect from blacks or whites.)

apolitical. A stance is called apolitical if it does not have, as part of its main purpose, intentions regarding the political order: i.e. regarding the institutions through which power is exercised. Since all social change is likely to have some *effect* on those institutions, and may even cause a necessary revision in their structure, it is always possible to give a political interpretation to a stance which is apolitical. On some views every social act or gesture also has a political meaning, in the sense of intimating some measure of criticism or acceptance of established institutions, and some idea, however sketchy, of institutions which would bring it to fulfilment. On this view there may be no important differences between those acts which have a political *intention*, and those which merely have political consequences. Typically, practices that regard *opposition as an unacceptable feature of government do not recognize the possibility of apolitical associations.

apologetics. Originally the branch of theology concerned with making religious doctrine acceptable to non-believers. All *doctrine stands in need of apology, and it is one of the characteristics of modern political thought that substantial analogues of Christian apologetics have been associated with it. It is normal for apologetics to require 'sacred texts' which are both definitive (when rightly interpreted) and also open to interpretation (and so applicable even when apparently false). It then attempts to establish the public *possibility* of beliefs associated with those texts. Thus French **gauchisme* of the 1960s and '70s managed to make Marxism acceptable to the *consumer society by rewriting it as a status-conferring intellectual *commodity. Apologetics should be distinguished from *propaganda, which seeks to make doctrine not acceptable but accepted. Propaganda always simplifies, where apologetics complicates and sophisticates, its subject.

apparat. The class of full-time servants of the Communist Party (the *apparatchiki*, those belonging to the apparatus), which evolved in the USSR as a distinctive feature of *Lenin's 'party of the new type'. Professional communists with unquestioning loyalty to the party are now sought throughout the USSR and its satellites as the core of the *civil service, and the necessary means of achieving and maintaining government by the Communist Party.

appeasement. Used in the 1920s to denote policies aiming to remove by common agreement the grievances generated by the peace settlement of 1919 – especially the grievances felt in Germany. The policy of appeasement, systematically pursued in the UK, facilitated Hitler's accumulation of power in the 1930s and the USSR's accumulation of power after the Second World War. Appeasement involves concessions in response to explicit or implied threats; it acts to the detriment of a power that does not threaten, and to the benefit of a state which makes *non-negotiable demands.

appropriation. Taking something as property. The term has various technical usages, e.g., in law, the setting aside of property or money for a particular purpose (as in bankruptcy proceedings). It also denotes a state action authorizing expenditure of public funds to be made for stated purposes. In the US appropriations are authorizations to make expenditures from the general funds of the Treasury, or from the various special funds. In the UK, by the Appropriation

Act, Parliament appropriates the supply which it grants to particular purposes. Both are in theory *legislative acts, but whereas the US Congress has a relatively free hand in determining what appropriations shall be, the UK Parliament may only decrease or delete items. Thus, so long as the *cabinet commands a majority in the House of Commons, and may make any appropriation vote a matter of confidence, it can determine the outcome. Hence appropriation in the UK has some of the character of an *executive act. The legislative nature of appropriation in the US is illustrated by the distinction between the enabling act, which establishes policy and authorizes an executive agency to do things, and the appropriation which is necessary to provide money in support of it.

approximation of laws. The policy of states, subject to treaties of commercial intent, whereby laws governing or influencing commercial transactions are aligned, thus founding common expectations and facilitating trade across frontiers. The Treaty of Rome provides extensively for approximation, involving what some regard as an effective abrogation of *sovereignty on the part of its signatories, since laws dealing with highly sensitive domestic issues – such as taxation and mobility of labour – are subject to amendment and *ratification under the terms of the treaty.

Aquinas, St Thomas (1226–74). The greatest of medieval theologians, who attempted to synthesize the newly rediscovered philosophy of *Aristotle with the articles of Christian faith, and so generated an authoritative system of theological, moral, and political doctrine which has served as the foundation for *Roman Catholic teaching. His political philosophy consists of an exposition and development of the doctrine of *natural law.

There are four kinds of law: eternal law, natural law, divine law, and human law (or *positive law). Eternal law is another name for God's conception of the ends of creation; natural law consists of the principles that rational beings will recognize and obey by nature – i.e. it is that part of the eternal law that is revealed to reason in its earthly condition. Divine law consists of God's commandments, as revealed in the scriptures, and human law (positive law) consists in the particular legal enactments that rational beings make for the good government of their institutions. Unlike the later thinkers who regarded positive law as filling in the gaps left by natural law, Aquinas often seems to argue as though natural law is sufficient in itself to generate all positive laws. If we conjoin it with the particular 'determinations' that characterize this or that social or political arrangement, then the natural law will generate the human laws which, in those circumstances, uniquely specify what is just. Thus by the natural law, all property belongs to men in common, provided that no one has been induced to labour in anticipation of a right of ownership. Once such anticipations arise, however, and once the institutions are created through which they are expressed and transmitted, the natural law generates a human law of private property, which can be violated only at the cost of injustice. A positive law that is unjust is, by this standard, felt not to be binding, indeed, not to be a genuine law, so that tyrannical law is not so much law as the perversion of law.

Aquinas favoured limited *monarchy as the ideal form of government. He also repeated arguments, to be found in Aristotle and elsewhere, for the primacy of marriage and the *family in social order, and for the primacy of *offices in forming a political *constitution. Since there is a limit set by reason to the forms of legitimate political constitution, a constitution is legitimate only when each law is a 'dictate of reason in the ruler', in which case the proper effect of law is to lead the subject to his true *virtue. In the state 'each person is related to the entire community as the part to the whole', and the state is 'the perfect community'. This Aristotelian conception of the organic perfection of political order was taken to considerable lengths. Thus Aquinas was prepared to argue that 'the individual is to the perfect community as the imperfect to the perfect', thus foreshadowing *Hegel's view of the state, as in some sense the completion and fulfilment of man's earthly existence. However 'man is not ordained to the body politic in respect of all he is and has': i.e. there are limits to what a sovereign may legitimately require of his citizens. For example all subjects have a right to resist government that has become severely oppressive. More importantly, the state cannot claim authority in matters of religion, so that, within the limits of legitimacy, it is necessary that the division between church and state be upheld, the former possessing the authority of the eternal law, the latter the authority of man's local and particularized attempts to conform to it. The church can therefore stand in judgement over princes, but cannot legislate for them except in so far as they are disposed to transgress nature's commands.

Aquinas is noteworthy for his attempt to extend the concept of natural law into the sphere of international relations, first by discussing the answerability of all princes to divine authority, secondly by laying down rules of just dealing between states. For example, he attempted to define the nature of a *just war, insisting on the distinction between war entered into in a just cause, and war prosecuted according to innate principles of just dealing between enemies (*jus ad bellum*, and *jus in bello*). This distinction and its application underlie much of the intellectual structure of the modern law of war.

Aquinas also redefined and extended the theory of the *just price, and had much to say concerning property rights, favouring local production for use over international trade, and justifying slavery, provided it were merely a form of economic domination, and did not violate principles of natural justice. (His view here was in part an apology for Aristotle, in part the expression of the theory that some men could not flourish without being guided and even controlled by others.)

arbitrage. One of the forces bringing about equality of price between markets. If goods sell in one *market at a price lower than their price in another, then 'arbitraging' may occur: that is, goods may be bought in the first market and sold in the second. The effect of this is to raise the price in the first market and lower it in the second, so that the two tend towards equality. The key element in arbitrage is that the amount of profit be determined with certainty. Because arbitrage profits involve no risk, they are hard to obtain, and such profits as do exist are normally no more than a recompense for the detailed attention and time involved in seeking out the opportunity. If that were not so goods would automatically have found their way to the market where they could most profitably be sold.

arbitrary. The exercise of *power is called 'arbitrary' when no independent reason can be given for its exercise which has weight for anyone other than the person who wields it. A power applied according to a law is not arbitrary, although someone may wish to question whether the law which validates it has any independent *authority. (*See* *autocracy.)

arbitration. The submission of a dispute, whether commercial, industrial or international, to the decision of a person or body other than a court of competent jurisdiction. Arbitration is to be distinguished from *conciliation and from *mediation on account of its quasi-judicial nature, and on account of the fact that the award rendered in arbitration is, in substance, final. Arbitration may be voluntary or (as sometimes when a government intervenes in an industrial dispute) compulsory. In either case the terms of the final settlement will normally be enforced by any subsequent judicial proceeding, unless it can be shown that they were formally defective, e.g. on account of a breach of *natural justice.

Despite this, it is an unsettled question whether arbitration is itself a kind of *adjudication: there are similarities of form, and of result; but it seems that the courts can enquire into proceedings of arbitration and adjust the result in ways that are not normally available to a court of appeal.

In international relations arbitration is a much more obviously judicial procedure. It has been significant since classical times (as exemplified in the habit of small independent cities of submitting disputes to the Senate in Rome). The precedent in modern international relations was set by the Jay Treaty between Britain and the US in 1794, allowing for arbitration by mixed commission. In 1899 The Hague conference erected at The Hague the Permanent Court of Arbitration, which has settled some twenty important issues. It is disputed whether arbitration by this court is the same as 'judicial settlement' by the International Court of Justice. Some argue that it is in effect the same, and that it is necessary to assert this if arbitration is to have the intended effect. The proposal to make arbitration obligatory was voted down at The Hague conference, but states may elect to make arbitration obligatory in dealings between them.

architecture. Described by John Ruskin (*The Seven Lamps of Architecture*, 1849) as the most political of the arts, and embroiled in political controversy throughout modern times. Being public, overt and semi-permanent, architecture exerts a certain dominion over the visual life of people; this enables it to translate political dogma into symbolic form, and to validate stylistic expression through the perceived association with political ideals. Neo-classicism – the stylistic affectation of a discipline and order intrinsic to the buildings of Greece and Rome – has been the standard architecture of the political demagogue, being associated with the French Revolution, national socialism, fascism and Stalinism, and valued for its solemn logic, and for its representation of existing public institutions as timeless and changeless. By contrast, the gothic style was propagandized in the nineteenth century as the symbol of a civil society which neither required nor tolerated the decrees of an absolute ruling power, but which arose organically out of common expectations, common beliefs and a shared experience of labour. Socialist thinkers such as Viollet-le-Duc in France and *Morris in England thus advocated the gothic as the symbolic form of natural, classless labour, working outside the tyranny of private property and enforced public order.

The Modern movement of Le Corbusier, the Russian constructivists and the Bauhaus was influenced by neo-classical ideas, and also by vaguer political aspirations based on the desire totally to remake the human environment, in order to erase the images of luxury and decadence that characterized man's former incompetence.

In all such doctrines the assumption is not just that architecture symbolizes a political expectation, but also that, by imposing itself on public perceptions, it helps to realize that expectation.

In modern times theories of a 'functionalist' kind have been influential. These may take two forms: first, that function is the primary requirement that a building must fulfil, and aesthetic standards are subordinate to it; secondly, that aesthetic standards are fulfilled simply *by* fulfilling function, perhaps in the most visually explicit way. The second view is certainly false; the first highly disputable. Some argue that such doctrines have led to a decline in respect for aesthetic values among architects, and that, in the absence of that respect, the true function of a building can never be known. Aesthetic implications are present in every human endeavour, and attention to them is necessary if its final purpose is to be understood. On this view, architecture illustrates in most vivid form the intrinsic relation between aesthetic value and social and political action. (*See* *aesthetics and politics.)

Arendt, Hannah (1906–75). German-born philosopher and social critic. *See* *essence/appearance, *people, *revolution, *work.

aristocracy. Greek: rule by the best. *Aristotle contrasted aristocracy, in which virtue is the title to power, with *oligarchy, in which the title resides in wealth. Both are forms of 'rule by the few', but only in the former case is rule by the few in the interests of the many. Aristotle's concern was with an *ideal type; nevertheless it is normal to make a corresponding distinction among actual governments, between those where power belongs to a minority *class with hereditary privileges (aristocracy), and those where power belongs to a minority group or party, without hereditary restrictions on membership (oligarchy). In this sense, there are two kinds of aristocracy: that of some Greek city-states, and related arrangements, in which the *ruling class held power without the sanction of a *monarch; and that familiar in Europe, in which aristocratic entitlements have generally been conferred or confirmed by the sovereign. The second is the more familiar, and has three aspects:

1. The legal-political aspect. The dominant features have been (a) a ruling class identified first through the possession of land and secondly through rules of succession (usually by *kinship); (b) the consequent conferring of dignities and entitlements by the sovereign which confirms a given aristocrat and his successors in the political position acquired; (c) a title bestowed on the aristocrat, signifying that, just by virtue of being successor to the powers identified in (a) and (b) (however time may have depleted and exhausted them) he may hold office in government (e.g. he may take his place in a house of *peers, or become a member of the sovereign's privy council). The net result is the existence of a hereditary *establishment and hereditary entitlements to land, goods and offices. It has usually been possible for outsiders to gain access to the aristocracy, although *social mobility in this respect has varied from place to place and time to time.

2. The economic aspect. It is almost universally accepted that the above pattern of legal relations is associated with, and perhaps also explained by, economic relations. In Marxian theory, for example, 1. is the description of a legal and political *superstructure which expresses and is explained by relations of power, in particular, by the power of the man who controls land over the man who is forced to work on it. Hence this particular kind of aristocracy is seen as an expression of *feudal relations of production, surviving as a genuine concentration of influence only to the extent that landed property confers powers distinct from those conferred by movable goods (in particular, petty sovereignty over a segment of *territory). The Marxian explanation is often criticized, mostly because it fails to explain the persistence of European (and especially British) aristocracy after the abolition of feudal tenures. (*But see* *nobility.)

3. The social aspect. This is perhaps most vivid in the popular imagination, which identifies aristocracy with all hereditary privilege and the leisure, luxury and manners generic to it. Hence aristocracy comes to stand for an idea of 'breeding', which has sometimes served as a rationalization of hereditary entitlement. There are aristocratic virtues and vices, and these have a distinct character in imaginative and moral thinking, exemplified in the mysteries of title that made it necessary for Dracula to be a count.

The old sense of aristocracy as 'rule by the best' is sometimes attached to the arrangement described, perhaps on the ground that, given the necessary imperfection of all human beings and human arrangements, the best we can hope for is that a class should be bred with the habit of power, and rewarded with the dignities and privileges necessary to make it accept the limitation of that power, and the responsibility of office. The main question is whether or not hereditary entitlement furthers rule in the interests of the many. (*See* *hereditary principle.)

Aristotle (384–322 BC) Greek philosopher and pupil of *Plato, who gave, in his *Politics* and elsewhere, a renowned and subtle account of political institutions. Aristotle held that man is a rational animal and, as such, also a political animal: it is inevitable and right that he should seek to fulfil himself through living as part of a state (Greek: *polis). Only in the perfect state can perfect human *virtue be exercised, and each kind of state will have its own peculiar virtues and vices. Aristotle classified states according to two variables: who holds power? And: in whose interest is it exercised? There are three politically possible answers to the first question (one, some and all), two politically possible answers to the second (the holder of power, and everyone). The ideal is *aristocracy: the state in which the best, who are inevitably few in number, exercise power in the interests of all. However, since that ideal is hard to achieve, and even harder to sustain, Aristotle advocated a form of mixed government, or 'polity', in which all citizens 'rule and are ruled by turn', and power is monopolized by no particular class. Aristotle was a vigorous critic both of *democracy, and of the kind of collective education advocated by *Plato. He defended the family as the nucleus of political organization, and argued for a connection between family and *household, and therefore for the necessity of *private property. He also argued that some men are naturally slaves in that they depend upon the will of others for their motivating force, so that the *division of labour required in every state is both natural and just.

Aristotle defined a citizen as anyone who can 'hold office', and his description of the ideal system of offices provides the foundation for many modern forms of *constitutionalism. The power of individuals in government is both curtailed and guided through offices, which are in turn governed by law, so that, in the Aristotelian polity, laws are supreme, and the outcome of the concentration of power in offices is a *rule of law. Moreover, government is given a character that endures from generation to generation, despite the successive changes in office holders, so that settled expectations begin to arise, and the bond between the rulers and the ruled becomes intelligible to both. In the context of his account of citizenship Aristotle raised in its modern form the question of *political obligation. He argued that political obligation is founded in distributive *justice, which is the principle that unites citizen to citizen and all to the state. Distributive justice involves 'treating equals equally'. This is possible only in the context of judicial procedure, together with the means to determine the individual rights and duties with respect to which citizens are to be compared. Aristotle favoured, as a source of such rights and duties, custom and customary law over the written statutes that can be made and remade by fiat of those in power. His defence of custom and his emphasis on the value of political stability are underpinned by a conception of the state as 'organic'. The whole, he argues, is 'prior to' its parts, which therefore depend upon it. In politics this means that the individual is incomplete until he takes part in political organization. When that organization is not merely political but also just, then the citizen may be not only complete, but also fulfilled.

armies. These take many forms. It is normal to distinguish the standing army (where an organization of armed men is kept permanently ready for war), the professional army (in which soldiers are regarded as committed to the army as to a *profession, usually with a long contract of service), the conscript army (in which citizens are 'called up', i.e. obliged to leave their occupations for some limited, or in war unlimited, period of 'military service'), and the *guerrilla army. The last fights without an overt structure of military institutions, and without subscribing to the conventions and laws of international war. It may not have a defined hierarchy of officers, it may not have uniforms, and it usually fights not openly but covertly, selecting targets so as to cause maximum damage with minimum *confrontation.

Countries with large standing armies and compulsory military service in effect subject all their citizens (or at least all their male citizens) to some years of military discipline, thus giving them a taste of the attitude to *authority and to social life that is characteristic of highly disciplined institutions with violent purposes. This was the *Spartan ideal of education, which is still adopted both as a means to an end, and also as an end in itself. The soldier acquires a distinct attitude towards offices and those holding them, towards discipline and social order, and towards actual, potential or imaginary 'enemies of the state' (or, in modern parlance, 'enemies of the people'). It is characteristic of tyranny to exploit that attitude. Conversely, the drafting into the army of men imbued with civilian values can radically change the ideology through which military institutions are guided.

Armed forces being a symbol of national or imperial power are among the most important components of the state. The existence of strong external purposes, together with a discipline which attaches the soldier to them, makes it both necessary for an army to be subject to the sovereign power, and possible for it not to be. In times of civil strife and disorder an army will always take power, not because it wants to, but because power will attach to it for a longer time than power can attach to anything else. This thought was important in motivating *Trotsky's formation of the Red Army.

armistice. The suspension of fighting pending a definite peace settlement: the term refers either to an agreement between belligerents, or to the condition existing during the term of that agreement. Armistice must be distinguished from *capitulation and *surrender, in that it is essentially bilateral, with mutual concessions and mutual restrictions, and from a treaty of peace, in that it does not end the legal state of war. It is valid only when made by the highest authorities in belligerent states, and may be repudiated if made, e.g., by military commanders.

A war that ends without armistice (e.g. those against Germany and Japan in the Second World War) ends to the disadvantage of the vanquished, though not necessarily to the advantage of the victor.

arms control. Expression introduced in the 1950s by US strategists, to denote all the ways whereby one or more states may intentionally restrain the development, testing, deployment, and danger of armaments, with the aim of reducing the likelihood and the hazards of warfare. It covers disarmament, agreements for restraint (such as the SALT agreement between the US and the USSR and the 1968 non-proliferation treaty), and unilateral acts, such as the decision by the US and others in 1969 to suspend research into biological weapons and to destroy stocks of them. Some include under 'arms control' all attempts to 'neutralize' other states, i.e. to prohibit them from joining particular military alliances.

Arnold, Matthew (1822–88). English poet, critic and social theorist, and foremost nineteenth-century advocate of *cultural conservatism. In *Culture and Anarchy*, 1869, Arnold defined *culture as 'a pursuit of our total perfection by means of getting to know, on all matters which most concern us, the best which has been thought and said in the world, and, through this knowledge, turning a stream of fresh and free thought upon our stock notions and habits'. Arnold argued that culture, and access to culture, were essential for the right direction of political power, and that, without them, there could be no true conception of the ends of human conduct, but only a mechanistic obsession with the means. He criticized many of the 'stock notions' of nineteenth-century *liberalism and *utilitarianism, both on account of their materialistic and rationalistic visions of human progress, and also on account of their *individualism. The concept of *freedom upon which so much liberal thought depends seemed to Arnold to be too abstract – 'a very good horse to ride but to ride somewhere' – and to contain no serious reasons for opposing the state in its name. The state, he argued, is 'the representative acting-power of the nation', and therefore must have power to act both in the name of freedom, and in the name of order. Without it public life must always be diverted towards the interests of one or other class (of which Arnold distinguished three, the 'barbarians' (aristocracy), the 'philistines' (middle class) and the 'populace' (working class)). When this happens, the result is anarchy; however, within each class there is a spirit opposed to anarchy, and dedicated to the common good and public order: this is the spirit which culture awakens, nourishes and refines. To achieve political order, therefore, the state must guarantee that the conditions for *humane education are as widely available as possible.

Arrow's theorem. A theorem in the theory of *social choice which demonstrates that it is impossible to design a 'constitution' that will generate complete and consistent rankings of alternative states of a society according to the preferences of its members, whilst satisfying certain further conditions. Due to the mathematical economist K. J. Arrow (b. 1925), this theorem is one of the most important theoretical results in welfare economics. The proof begins from the idea of a *social welfare function (interpreted as a set of rules for transforming the desires of individuals into concrete social choices). It then proceeds to lay down certain plausible-seeming conditions that such a function should satisfy – for example, that no member of the group should be allowed to dictate the outcome. It is shown that no such social welfare function can meet those conditions. Some economists have rejected one or more of Arrow's conditions, others have disputed their interpretation, or their applicability to politics, while others have accepted his result as showing the inherent impossibility of legislating on the basis of social choice. Others have read the result as indicating the need for a wider informational base for social choices, going beyond Arrow's use of individual preferences without any interpersonal comparison of utilities.

art. 1. There are three major views concerning the political significance of art: (i) that it is, can be, or ought to be an *expression* of political consciousness; (ii) that it is, can be, or ought to be an *agent* of political transformation; (iii) that it is, can be, or ought to be *autonomous in a way that denies the possibility of a political meaning.

Advocates of the third view defend their position from the philosophical premise that art must be appreciated not as means but as end, so that the attempt to subordinate it to political aims and ideologies is an attempt to deny its nature. Doctrines and practices such as *socialist realism and *fascist neo-classicism exhibit the inevitable degeneration, vulgarity and bad taste that ensues upon the attempt to *politicize art. According to R. G. Collingwood (*The Principles of Art*, 1938) this attempt turns art into magic, and so destroys it.

Defenders of the first view may well accept that art must be treated as end and not means, while suggesting that to appreciate an object as the expression of a state of consciousness is not necessarily to treat it as a means. It is hard to imagine art that does not gain at least some of its significance from its expressive power. And how can there be an expressive activity that is divorced entirely from social and political consciousness? (i) and (iii) may therefore be compatible.

It is characteristic of modern *totalitarianism to believe some variant of (ii). Art has an overwhelming influence on the minds and opinions of the educated. Hence it has been regarded as an important political force, perhaps even as one of the ferments that create the 'subjective conditions' of revolution (*see* *cultural revolution, *Lenin). The difficulty for that view lies in drawing the line between art and *propaganda, and in doing justice to the extreme complexity of our responses to the first in comparison with the simplicity of our responses to the second. Conservatives and revolutionaries have alike found confirmation for their views in Shakespeare, and the great artistic rumination on the tyranny of *exchange-value – Wagner's *Ring* – has never been more admired than by those who sought confirmation for the *petit bourgeois* vision of the hero.

2. Political constraint on art. Art brings about peculiar transformations of human consciousness. Attempts to diagnose the effect also lead to proposals to restrain it. *Plato would have banned all art from his Republic – save only those forms of music that seemed suitable to moral development. Plato's recommendations have sometimes been followed – notably during the 'Cultural Revolution' in China. But it is more common to pay lip-service to artistic freedom, and to argue that political interference in artistic activity is unwise or impossible, except in so far as it falls under the idea of legitimate *censorship.

3. Marxist theory of art. For classical Marxism art is part of *ideology and therefore has the unspoken but discoverable function of consolidating the political *superstructure out of which it is created. This explains why, e.g., modernist literature has so often concealed a highly conservative message (as in T. S. Eliot's *Four Quartets*, or in Joyce's covert vindication of bourgeois values in *Ulysses*). It is part of the *romantic character of contemporary *neo-Marxism that it accepts this view with reluctance, believing that art, because it must always revolutionize itself, cannot fail to be an agent of revolution. Hence the current doctrine (see, e.g., Ernst Fischer: *Art Against Ideology*, 1955; Raymond Williams: *Marxism and Literature*, 1977) that art, or true art, is essentially 'anti-ideological', concerned not to consolidate the existing political structure but rather to give expression to the 'truth' which is destined to overthrow it.

Asiatic despotism. Probably synonymous with *oriental despotism. A name sometimes given to the various forms of *despotism exemplified in Asia, from the time of the Mongol invasions onwards, in which rigid institutions combined with close surveillance of all citizens, were used to uphold unstable and therefore ruthlessly *autocratic power. The ruling class of bureaucrats was dominated by a sovereign whose powers depended mainly on the army, but also on the sanction of religious institutions, of which he was the nominal head. All insubordination was suppressed by terror, law was not respected, and decrees and institutions would be put aside as the sovereign required. This form of government was related by *Marx to *Asiatic modes of production, since the constant dissolution and refounding of the state and the unceasing changes of dynasty left the economic order untouched by the 'storm clouds in the political sky'. East European *anti-communists (e.g. Milosz) sometimes describe the government that has been imposed on the states of Eastern Europe as a form of Asiatic despotism.

Asiatic modes of production. Description often given of the self-sufficient communities of Central, Southern and Eastern Asia, in which village economy persists with minimum *division of labour, and in which production of food and other necessaries ossifies around traditional forms, remaining resistant to innovation. The existence of such modes of production (for example, in Java) tended to conflict with Marx's contention that *productive forces have an innate tendency to develop and to overthrow successive *production relations. Hence Marx often commented on 'these self-sufficing communities that constantly reproduce themselves in the same form, and when accidentally destroyed, spring up again on the same spot and with the same name'. He argued that capitalist *imperialism was necessary in order to introduce into such societies the forces necessary to true historical change.

association. The forming of a *society. A *state determines a *civil society, and within that civil society there are usually many subject associations. Lawyers, sociologists and philosophers have debated over the nature and variety of these associations, and the distinctions which they make are of the first importance in politics, in providing the models for various views of the state, and in upholding and criticizing conceptions of the role and importance of subordinate institutions. The following distinctions are particularly important:

(i) Voluntary and non-voluntary. A voluntary association (e.g. a club) is one that is constituted by the willing acceptance of its members. A non-voluntary association (e.g. a *family) exists and persists whether or not accepted. (Children may be unable to give consent, adults unable to withhold it.) In law, therefore, obligations attaching to voluntary association are contractual, whereas those of the family are not.

(ii) Purposeful and purposeless. Some associations (e.g. businesses, sports clubs) have specific purposes and expire when those purposes are fulfilled or removed. Others do not, and persist even in the absence of an identifiable aim. Among the second kind of association one must again include the family, together with certain clubs and societies of a purely conversational and friendly character. The point here is not that the family generates no purposes, or that family activities are without purpose, but rather that there is no *external* purpose, nothing that some *other* association might have fulfilled just as well. What purposes there are have to be defined by reference to the family, and not vice versa. Some sociologists theorize the distinction here in terms of **Gemeinschaft* and *Gesellschaft*. *See also* *friendship.

(iii) Incorporated and unincorporated. A legal distinction between an association that has formed itself (usually by 'articles of association') into a legal *person, with liabilities, assets, rights, obligations and *agency of its own, and associations which have not made that transition, and in which responsibility and accountability still remain with the individual members. The law chooses to regard all unincorporated associations as based in a contractual relation between members, property being vested in trustees, and legal action effected through representatives. (*See further* *incorporation.)

(iv) Constituted and unconstituted. An association may have a *constitution directing its procedures, or it may vary in accordance with the wishes and conflicts of the day. A club exemplifies the first condition, a family the second. In the former case there is an analogy of *positive law; in the latter case there is only *natural law.

All these distinctions are different and none of them is simple. The complexity partly explains the difficulty of the question, What kind of association is a state? The state might, for example, be voluntary, purposeful, and unconstituted, as some *social contract theories suggest that it is or ought to be. Or it might be non-voluntary, purposeless and constituted, as some followers of *Hegel prefer to argue. In either case it may have some of the characteristics of an autonomous legal person. If we think of the state as irreducible to its members this might be because we think that there are associations which create new entities out of old ones, as a new legal person is created by a partnership. In which case some kinds of association may be 'ontologically creative'. But which kinds, and why? These questions are considered under various headings in this dictionary. (*See* *institution, *state.)

Many theorists of *absolutism (e.g. *Hobbes) are suspicious of large associations, on account of their ability to challenge the sovereign power. For related but different reasons *totalitarianism aims to bring all associations within the orbit of the state, so that they take their nature, constitution and purposes from the central power. The 'freedom of association' is therefore an important issue in modern politics, sometimes taken to concern a basic *freedom without which elementary *human rights cannot be respected. The issue is inextricably bound up with that of the *autonomous institution. Institutions are associations which have achieved an identity independent of their members, and which can therefore become active forces which change the purposes of their members. In order to deny institutional *autonomy, it is usually necessary to restrict the freedom of association. Many who disapprove of totalitarian government may nevertheless seek this restriction, in order to abolish, e.g., private education, or monopoly.

asylum. A place of refuge. The principle that each state exercises authority over persons on its own *territory, and that other states have no authority there, implies that individuals allowed to enter a foreign *jurisdiction automatically gain asylum until it is revoked (for example, by *extradition). The migration of subjects of one state to another deemed more favourable is sometimes also described as the seeking of 'asylum', but this usage is misleading and metaphorical, unless what is sought is the *granting* of asylum by the more favourable state. Asylum then involves an informal undertaking by the state to offer protection to the refugee.

atavism. 1. The theory that ancestral types may appear as 'throwbacks' (based on a hypothesis of the geneticist Grygor Mendel, sometimes given as grounds for *racist ideology, and influential in nineteenth-century *criminology).

2. The tendency of *primitive forms of consciousness to emerge (in various disguises) in the thoughts and actions of otherwise civilized beings, as when black skin is regarded as testimony to a black character, or ownership of property is regarded as sufficient grounds for assault. The first case shows a survival of what Sir James Frazer calls 'contagious magic' (*The Golden Bough*, 1900), while the second shows a return to the ancient idea of 'hubris', according to which pride and power offend the gods and bring down judgement.

Athenian democracy. The form of government that existed periodically in Athens during the fifth and fourth centuries BC. All adult male citizens were able to vote in the assembly, where, in most cases, officials were chosen by lot, in boards of ten, one from each tribe. The chief administrative officials were the *archons* (ceremonial), the *strategoi* (military), and the *taniai* (treasurers); but there were others, and Athenian democracy is remarkable for its proliferation of offices and for the seriousness with which official duties were regarded. Three other features should be noted: the power of orators (such as Alcibiades and Demosthenes) who were able to sway opinion in the assembly, and had the kind of influence on political life that is today attributed only to the *media; the absence of any independent political and economic status for women; and the economic and political dependence of the state upon *slavery. Slaves, not being citizens, had no vote. Nevertheless the Athenians were proud of their constitutional freedoms, and of the respect for the individual which allowed them to be, in the words attributed to Pericles by Thucydides, 'free and tolerant in our private lives, in public affairs obedient to the law'.

Augustine, St (354–430). Augustine of Hippo was a doctor of the church, and the first thinker to attempt a systematic Christian philosophy of society. He exerted a profound and lasting influence on all Christian thought and practice, invented subjective literature, and was a political thinker of considerable consequence. In the *City of God* he attempted to reply to the pagans who had attributed the fall of Rome in 410 to the abolition of heathen worship. Augustine set out the fundamental contrast between the law of this world and that of the heavenly city towards which all citizens should aspire. From this description of the 'Kingdom of God' he derived an ideal system of laws and offices, adapted to the temporal world. The state mediates, or ought to mediate, between the earthly realm of sin and disharmony and the heavenly realm of absolute righteousness. All institutions of the state are forms of dominion (sovereigns over subjects, owners over property, masters over slaves) and dominion, in so far as it is a form of order, is good, although it is an order conditioned by the relative unrighteousness of its participants. The ideal order of property, for example, is that everyone should possess everything in common. Its actual order is determined by the need to subject property to the discipline of justice, in a world infected by the imperfections of avarice and greed. The state is necessary to this discipline, but not all states are equally acceptable. The ideal is rule of free men by free men through deliberation (which is the rule prescribed both by nature and by God); when that rule is displaced by masters whose authority is purely coercive, then natural order and divine law are simultaneously violated. The absolute righteousness of the City of God is an idea that corresponds to the ideal of justice given in Plato's *Republic* (by which Augustine was considerably influenced); it is also the ancestor of Christian doctrines of *natural law.

Augustine attempted to discover principles of international dispute, and presented an interesting analysis of *peace, as containing three degrees: the peace of God (*see* *pax), the peace of the just, and the peace of the unjust (i.e. of those who would make war if they were not afraid of the consequences). He also gave a theory of history which attempted to reconcile God's *providence and foreknowledge with the metaphysical *freedom of human agency.

Augustinianism is the general name for the tradition of Christian politics inspired by the *City of God*, and in particular for the attempts to extract from Augustine a coherent doctrine and policy governing relations between *church and state.

Austin, John (1790–1859), English legal philosopher. *See* *command, *jural relations, *law, *philosophical radicals, *positivism.

Austrian economics. A school of economic thought originating in the work of Carl Menger (1840–1921), who developed the still widely influential *marginal utility theory of *value. His work was further developed by Friedrich von Wieser (1851–1926), Eugen von Böhm-Bawerk (1852–1914) and Ludwig von Mises (1881–1973), and the tradition has continued into our own time, gaining renewed political influence in the thought of the philosopher-economist *von Hayek, who has tried to combine the original empirical theory of value with philosophical considerations concerning freedom, the nature of the state, and the structure of markets, so as to provide an elaborate *apologetic for modern *capitalism. (*See also* *capital.)

autarchy. Greek: self-government. Ambiguous term which may mean either absolute government (*see* *absolutism), or self-government (*see* *autonomy, political), or self-sufficiency (*see* *autarky).

autarky. Self-sufficiency; etymologically distinct from *autarchy. Now used primarily in an economic sense to denote the fact or the aim of national self-sufficiency in food, raw materials and production. The aim of autarky is part of the politics of *isolationism, and goes with resistance to *free trade, and to any form of economic or political dependence on other sovereign powers.

authenticity. The ideal, associated with the *existentialist philosophies of *Sartre and Martin Heidegger (1889-1976), according to which an individual must create himself in and through his own decisions. His freedom lies precisely in the fact that his identity is not (or need not be) determined by any arrangement external to himself. The 'inauthentic' individual is the one who abandons the responsibility to make himself what he really is and takes refuge in an external command, precept, role or moral code, wrongly imagined to be objectively binding, but in fact simply masking, without overcoming, the 'anxiety' of being (usually written 'Being'). Anxiety is confronted and overcome only in the choice that wills, not only the act, but the whole person implied in it. This ideal of authenticity freed from its metaphysical overtones, often occurs as one of the postulates of modern *liberalism.

authoritarianism. The advocacy of government based on an established system of *authority, rather than on explicit or *tacit consent. Authoritarians believe either that it is good that government should be ordered in this way, or at least that it is necessary. The sources of both beliefs are to be found in two common thoughts: first, that people need authority, and secondly that authority is not the outcome but rather the precondition of consent. More radical authoritarians may sometimes argue that there is no rational source of *political obligation, and hence there is a need to ensure stability against the advance of sceptical reflections; respect towards established institutions is thought to be at least necessary, if not sufficient, for this end.

Sometimes used to denote, not so much the above theoretical position, as a practice, in which established power is taken as having an absolute right to assert itself.

authority. That feature of a person, role, office or government which authorizes (i.e. makes legitimate, either in reality or in appearance) the acts and commands exercised in its name. Authority attaching to a person, not as the holder of an office, but as the particular person that he is, is sometimes said to arise from *charisma. This suggestion derives from *Weber (*Theory of Social and Economic Organization*, 1922), who distinguished three kinds of authority: rational-legal (in which acts are authorized by normative rules), traditional (in which immemorial tradition confers legitimacy), and charismatic. This classification is made from a sociologist's point of view, and distinguishes not so much kinds of authority, as explanations of the *belief* in it.

In all cases authority must be distinguished from *power, being a relation **de jure* and not necessarily *de facto*: authority is a right to act, rather than a power to act. It may be accompanied by power, and so upheld, or without power, and so ignored. One of the most important powers that uphold authority is the power of people's belief in it: thus, in a sense, authority can create its own power, and this gives rise to a disposition to use the two terms as though they were synonymous.

From the philosophical point of view three questions must be distinguished: (i) what causes the belief that certain individuals, institutions etc. have authority? (ii) What, if anything, shows that belief to be true? (iii) What, if anything, shows that people ought to subscribe to it?

Questions (ii) and (iii) are not identical. Many who do not think that there *is* such a thing as authority, nevertheless think that we ought to preserve our belief in it, perhaps on grounds of *utility, or public order. The following three observations relate severally to the three questions distinguished:

(i) The causes of the belief in authority are more varied than Weber's division suggests. *Habit is one cause, *custom another (both subsumed under *tradition by Weber). It may even be that the rational perception of a genuine and objectively existing *right of government is also the explanation of the belief in it. Or it may be, by contrast, that the best explanation is *functional: i.e. the belief is held because it performs a function, say in upholding an economic order, or in upholding the individual security within it. (*See* *ideology.)

(ii) The grounds of the belief in authority are explored by theories of *political obligation. Doctrines of *social contract and *consent argue that rights of action must be conferred on institutions, offices or persons by willing agreement of those subject to them, while theories of *prescriptive right argue that, in appropriate circumstances, history alone is sufficient to confer legitimacy. About this question many remain wholly sceptical.

(iii) Some find the value of the belief to stem from its being a necessary condition of government, and hence of the security brought by government. Others argue that people need to believe in an external authority if their lives are to possess inner order, the moral life being impossible without the external symbols of its objectivity. (This second view was perhaps *Hegel's.) Others, perhaps confusing authority with the power which it requires for its enactment, regard all authority as either valueless (because arbitrary) or deleterious (as an interference, or attempted interference, with *freedom).

autocracy. Literally self-rule, used to mean rule by an agent who holds all power himself, and who exercises that power in an *arbitrary manner. There may be a constitution and laws which *seem* to limit or guide his power, but in fact these can be revoked at will by the autocrat, and also disobeyed by him, there being no independent mechanism for enforcing them. Most theorists hold that true autocracy requires the concentration of power in a *single* person, and not, for example, in a *party or *caucus. Although parties may rule in a manner that admits no limitation by law, their multiple agency serves partly to restrict their power. However, there are marked similarities between party government in modern USSR and the supposedly autocratic government of the Czars which preceded it, and in the sense that the second might be called autocratic, so might the first.

The principal feature is that the ruler may affect each of his subjects at any time in any way that he pleases, and in a manner that admits of no redress. Autocracy should therefore be seen as the perversion of *absolutism, in which power is not only absolute but also arbitrary.

autonomy. Greek: living under one's own laws; hence self-government. The following are important political applications of the idea:

(i) Autonomy of the individual. This is captured by the doctrine that the *rational individual may, in the words of *Kant, 'will the maxim of his action as a law for himself'. It is held that rational beings (or *persons) do not merely respond to the promptings of appetite and desire, but also to self-imposed commands, and this is what distinguishes free action from subjection to the 'laws of nature'. Kant argued that a rational being not only may, but also must, be autonomous in this sense, and that he can be so only if his action is governed by a universal law. *Freedom thus becomes a kind of *obedience. Kant's discussion of autonomy underlies much political theory, both *liberal and anti-liberal, since it seems to generate an idea of freedom which is distinct from *licence. Moreover, it connects the freedom of the individual with a philosophy of the nature of the individual, and this philosophy, or some variant of it, has emerged in the present century as fundamental to some liberal conceptions of man. (*See also* *authenticity.)

(ii) Autonomy of the state. The autonomy of a state is partly a matter of power (of whether it has the external and internal strength to make and enforce its own laws), and partly a matter of recognized *authority (whether it is regarded by other states as the *legitimate government in a particular *territory). The first is a matter of degree: clearly, the power of a *satellite country or a *protectorate to make its own laws is limited by the surveillance of a more powerful external influence, as the power of all states to enact laws is limited by the variable tolerance of its citizens. The second is absolute in international law, since it is tantamount to the legal idea of *sovereignty. Sovereignty is both the necessary and the sufficient condition for the legal existence of a state.

(iii) Regional autonomy. The idea of autonomy has recently been extended to discuss the politics of fragmentation. By granting or recognizing a power to make laws to local bodies (e.g. councils, regional assemblies), a state confers or recognizes regional autonomy. All such grant or recognition is on sufferance, since a law-making power that cannot be overridden by the central government tends to produce a separate state (perhaps united by *federation) rather than a regional government. Hence complicated examples of regional autonomy often present an appearance of federation. Consider the states of the US, or the striking legal status of Scotland: such quasi-states are immensely difficult to describe. (*See* *devolution.)

(iv) Autonomy of *groups, and *minorities. Unlike regions, groups and minorities have no necessary claims to territory, hence they cannot be granted *jurisdiction over territory, even of a modified kind. However, it has been argued that religious organizations manifest a genuine law-making power that is independent both of territory and of the state (*see* *church and state); from the legal point of view, therefore, they are said to provide the only true examples of autonomy within a jurisdiction.

(v) Autonomy of institutions. An institution may be called autonomous for any one of three reasons: (a) when it has the capacity to make its own statutes and bye-laws; in this sense universities are usually autonomous; (b) when it is outside the direct control of some higher political body (such as a *party or government agency): in this sense universities are autonomous only to some extent and only in certain places and disciplines; (c) when it has its own peculiar or internal aims and purposes: i.e. when there is something that it does which could be done by no other institution. (All universities are autonomous in this sense, as are football teams and families.)

The maintenance of autonomous institutions of all three kinds, with their own traditions of thought, feeling and action, is often put forward as a central aim of some kinds of social *conservatism. The persistence of such institutions is regarded as guaranteeing a social and political continuity which is not enforced (but only subsumed) by the state. Thereby, it is hoped, two conservative ideals – *limited government and social continuity – which seem to be in conflict, might be reconciled. (For an important application of this view, *see* *Tocqueville.)

Specific demands for autonomy, in particular regional autonomy, will reflect the prevailing political tensions of an epoch. It is often argued that a measure of regional autonomy is always necessary when there are *separatist tendencies, since, without it, local feelings will take an overtly nationalist form.

average propensity to consume and save. The average propensity to consume (APC) is given by the total domestic expenditure on consumption goods and services within an economy, divided by the *national income of that economy. The average propensity to save (APS) is the proportion of national income which is not spent on consumption goods and services, i.e. the national income minus the APC. *Keynes suggested as a commonsense assumption that the higher the level of income, the lower the APC and therefore the higher the APS. Empirical observation suggests that this holds in the short run but not in the long run.

B

ba'ath. Arabic: resurrection. Name adopted by a pan-Arab movement and *party, which attempts to unite Marxist social analysis with a *pan-Arab idea of cultural, social and political unity, based on the common history and traditions of the Arab peoples. It thus seeks to combine socialism with the pursuit of national unity, and while resisting the appeal to *Islam as the fount of political and social ideals, celebrates it as a product of the Arab national genius. The result – which might be called national socialism – is a striking example of a political doctrine seeking to fill the vacuum left by the withering away of a religious creed, and of the political unity which the Ottoman Empire had ensured.

Babeuf, François Gracchus (1760–97). *See* *babouvism.

babouvism. Extreme *egalitarianism, along the lines proposed by François Babeuf (1760–97) in his *Conspiracy of Equals*. This was a leading document for the secret societies of the nineteenth century, which advocated absolute equality of incomes, and prepared the ground for conspiratorial and insurrectionary movements of *socialist persuasion.

Bacon, Sir Francis (1561–1626). English philosopher, essayist, jurist, and Lord Chancellor. *See* *balance of power, *equity, *humanities.

Bagehot, Walter (1826–77). English essayist and critic. *See* *bicameral government, *cabinet, *checks and balances, *peer.

Bakunin, Mikhail (1814–76). Russian revolutionary, often known as 'the father of modern *anarchism', whose conflict with Marx in 1869–71 broke up the First International. Bakunin advocated violent struggle and individual acts of *terrorism in order to bring about revolutionary change, the principal goal of which would be the immediate elimination of all political, social and religious institutions, and their replacement with a free federation of independent associations in which all would have equal rights and equal privileges, including that of secession. Bakunin is increasingly seen as a precursor of *bolshevism, in particular because of his advocacy of revolution led by a secret group of professional revolutionaries bound together by an iron discipline and subject to a single will.

balance of payments. The balance of payments accounts of a state record the economic transactions that its residents undertake with foreigners within a given period. Economists distinguish 'autonomous' and 'accomodating' items. The former include the imports and exports of goods and services, property income, and investments in long-term assets. The surplus or deficit on those items which are considered not to be within the direct control of the government of a state must be financed. Thus 'when we talk of an actual surplus or deficit in the balance of payments we shall have in mind this balance in autonomous trade and transfers. It is this sum which must be matched by what we have called accommodating finance' (J. E. Meade: *The Theory of International Economic Policy*, vol. 1, 1951). (*See also* *balance of trade, *exchange control.)

balance of power. An important concept in the description of international relations, but also of uncertain meaning. It may refer:

(i) to a policy on the part of states that deliberately aims to prevent the preponderance of any one state or *bloc, and to maintain approximate equilibrium in military potential;

(ii) to an observed principle of international politics, whereby any state which threatens to increase its power becomes at once subject to increases in countervailing power from potential belligerents;

(iii) to a political system characterized by a particular configuration of power relationships.

A distinction is usually made between *multipolar equilibrium, and simple or bipolar equilibrium. In the first a balance may be maintained either peacefully (e.g. through economic rewards and punishments), or through the use of force (as when a troublemaker is made to confront the coalition of the remaining states: e.g. the War of the Grand Alliance, 1688–97). Since the First World War critics of the European multipolar balance have often claimed that a multipolar balance eventually becomes a bipolar balance of competing alliances, thus precipitating an arms race, and war. Defenders of the multipolar balance have attributed the long periods of peace in Europe to its existence. Both sides admit that international configurations that can be called balanced are both likely to be unstable, and not certain to be peaceful. Defenders of the balance of power in Europe have included Bolingbroke, Bacon and *Hume (who wrote a famous essay on the subject). Critics have included *Rousseau and *Kant, who denounced it as an immoral sport of sovereigns (cf. *Augustine's idea of the 'peace of the unjust')

balance of terror. Term probably coined by Lester Pearson in June 1955 at the tenth anniversary of the signing of the

UN Charter: 'The balance of terror has replaced the balance of power.' Used in relation to the uneasy balance that proceeds from fear of nuclear war, and also from the ideological terrors that are fuelled by *propaganda. Balance of terror, like balance of power, may be seen either as a policy or as a system. In either case it involves, primarily, the power to deter and destroy, rather than the power to seize and defend territory. Like the balance of power, the balance of terror affords its own peculiar nature to any peace that results from it, but its novelty as a system has made it extremely difficult to describe, or predict.

balance of trade. The balance between the cost of a state's imports and the receipts for its exports, over a given period. The balance of trade is just one element of the *balance of payments.

balanced budget. The central budget of a government is in balance when current receipts are equal to current expenditure: i.e. when the sum of taxes equals the government's expenditure on goods and services. Followers of *Keynes argue that budget surpluses and deficits can be used to manage the economy, so that a balanced budget is not necessarily desirable.

balkanization. Term coined by German socialists to describe the effect of late-nineteenth-century Czarist policy on the Balkan states bordering the Russian Empire, and later used to denote the divisive effects upon those states of the treaty of Brest-Litovsk (1918). Hence: division of a region into a number of small, autonomous states, often mutually hostile, in order to remove the possibility of a serious military threat from any of them. Recent uses of the term include that by the Angolan government, in its description of the aims and effects of South African intervention in its territory.

banking. The business of safeguarding deposits and lending money at interest. The 'banking system' consists of the totality of institutions officially recognized as determining standard transactions of this kind (but does not include, for example, building societies).

The central government agencies may try to use the 'banking system' as a mechanism of monetary control (*see* *monetarism, *money supply). In offering overdrafts and loan facilities banks can augment the money supply, while by raising interest rates they may decrease it. The normal object of such a banking system is to place most of the money at its disposal to use, by lending at interest, while retaining a minimum cash balance with which to meet its obligations to depositors.

Most modern governments attempt to exert control over the creation of credit by the banking system. Thus a central bank (such as the Bank of England, or the more complex system of banks in the US known as the Federal Reserve System, whose board is appointed by the President, with the approval of the Senate) may attempt to determine rates of interest, for example, by its activities in financial markets. These 'minimum lending rates' may be enforced either directly, by legal stipulation, or indirectly, by economic pressure (exerted in the UK by dealings between the Bank of England and discount houses). An increase in the minimum lending rate causes other interest rates to rise, so making borrowing less attractive and curtailing the money supply. Economists dispute over whether this method of control is effective in the absence of additional government measures. In particular the rise of transnational banks and finance houses has led to transactions which bypass the control of any particular government.

International politics is affected, not only by the existence of such transnational corporations, but also by the perhaps more political International Bank for Reconstruction and Development (the 'World Bank'), designed to encourage investment in *developing countries. The World Bank diverts funds from contributing countries (who contribute according to their share in world trade) to those who, for lack of *capital, are unable to embark on socially necessary projects. (*See further* *world organizations.) The effect of such institutions is much debated. Some argue, for example, that they permit *primitive accumulation without *revolution, and so enable the developing countries to make a peaceful transition to *capitalist (or at any rate modern) modes of production.

bargaining theory of wages. The theory according to which wage levels are determined by a process of bargaining between the representatives of labour and management, in which each side may have recourse to powers embodied in convention, *custom, and *law, so that the outcome is not determined solely by the supply and demand of labour, or by the means of subsistence of labour. Clearly such a theory may not be universally applicable. Where it *is* applicable, the *wage contract is often considered to be entirely voluntary, and breached only at the cost of injustice to either side. It has been an important aim of Marxism and related theories to replace the bargaining theory, in order to show wages as determined by material forces which can be described without reference to ideas of justice and consent.

barter. The voluntary exchange of goods without the intermediary of *money. Systems of barter become cumbersome as soon as there are large surpluses to be disposed of or a systematic *division of labour in production; the natural tendency in those circumstances is for some standard object of human covetousness (e.g. gold) to become a standard object of exchange. (*See* *exchange-value.) Some argue that, in barter economies, production is undertaken predominantly to meet the subsistence needs of the producer himself, and that in such an economy *Say's law will be observed. (Thus, e.g., *Marx, in *Theories of Surplus Value*, II.)

base and superstructure. A distinction introduced into political thought by *Marxism, and made by *Marx in the *Preface to a Critique of Political Economy*, 1859. According to Marx it is necessary to distinguish the economic base of the social order from the legal, political and cultural superstructure which rests upon it. The base consists of the relations between men (or between classes of men) which determine their various powers of control over the means of *production, distribution and exchange: these are the *production relations, through which *productive forces operate. The superstructure consists in legal, political and social institutions which express, enforce and consolidate the relations of economic power that pertain to the base. Marxists believe that changes in the base explain corresponding changes in the superstructure, but not (or at any rate, nor normally) vice versa. Hence the most fundamental historical processes are economic ones, legal and political changes being merely changes in the social embodiment of those more basic things. If it were shown that the historical development of legal and political institutions were *autonomous, or that economic relations were normally, or at any rate not abnormally, the effects and not the causes of legal and political thought and action, then the Marxist thesis would be refuted.

A distinction between superstructure and base is a distinction between something explained and the thing which explains it. Such a distinction could therefore be upheld by someone who rejected the Marxist analysis of the two components.

It is now fairly normal among Marxists to distinguish the 'fundamentalist' from the 'dialectical' versions of the base/superstructure model. The version given above is fundamentalist, in that it tries to describe all real historical development as taking place in the base. The dialectical model, introduced by *Engels, but perhaps endorsed by the early Marx (e.g. in *The Poverty of Philosophy*, 1847), allows that developments in the superstructure can influence the base, and that there may even be a *dialectical relation between the two. Discussion of this issue is complex and scholastic. Critics of the dialectical model often argue that it attempts to save the theory by making it irrefutable, which is the same as to refute it (*see* *Popper).

behaviourism. The psychological theory that the scientific study of the mind must be confined to the study of behaviour (including language), without reference to the deliverances of introspection; alternatively, the philosophical theory that there is nothing to the mind besides behaviour, so that introspection is the observation of nothing. The psychological theory – or at least the method associated with it – has recently been extended into the socio-political sphere by B. F. Skinner, in order to give expression to a theory that is at once *utopian in its aspirations and *materialist in its assumptions. The leading idea is that behaviour is formed in response to previous behaviour, and to the 'rewards' or 'reinforcements' of the environment which *condition it, so that the self-consciousness of the subject plays no important part in the process of social development. Hence political activity should be directed towards creating the conditions which reinforce the behaviour that is desired. This raises the question, Desired by whom? Some find the pseudo-scientific optimism of *Beyond Freedom and Dignity*, 1971, to be, in the light of that question, an apology for *tyranny. Others are concerned rather to reject the theory of *human nature on which it is based.

belligerency. The legal condition or status of the parties to public war. There seem to be two requirements: an actual contest of arms, and an intention, recognition or declaration of this sufficient to attribute the contest to the parties. In international contests belligerency usually begins with a formal declaration of war, or is preceded by an ultimatum with conditional declaration.

To recognize the belligerency of two parties to a civil war is to concede that the international law of belligerency applies to them, whereas to recognize *insurgency is not to suppose that this law yet applies. The law of belligerency lays down rights and duties to be recognized by all states deeming themselves *neutral to the combat, and also rights and duties to be honoured (ideally) by the parties themselves. In international law only some states are qualified to make war – i.e. to be 'belligerents'. 'Insurgent' governments can become belligerents through the act of 'recognition' bestowed on them by other qualified states.

Benda, Julien (1867–1956). French philosopher and essayist. *See* *humanitarianism, **intégrisme*, *intellectuals, *jingoism, **trahison des clercs*.

beneficial interest. *See* *trust.

Benjamin, Walter (1892–1940). German literary and cultural critic. *See* *Frankfurt school, *politicization.

Bentham, Jeremy (1748–1832). English philosopher, economist and legal theorist, proponent of the principle of *utilitarianism, according to which the greatest total happiness of the community should be the sole aim of morality and of law. Bentham proposed a quantitative idea of happiness, as pleasure (*see* *hedonism), and a procedure for calculating the benefit of a course of action in terms of such factors as the quantity of pleasure, its probability, its proximity and duration in time. This (the 'felicific calculus') was one of the first experiments in *cost/benefit analysis. Bentham's merits as a legal and constitutional theorist stem partly from the minuteness of detail and classificatory completeness with which he approached legal and social analysis. He upheld a doctrine of legal *positivism, and opposed all ideas of *natural right, as well as the doctrine of the *social contract. He argued that *rights and obligations are created by *convention, and that the sole criterion to be applied in determining the merit of laws and maxims is the criterion of utility. He went on to deduce (*Introduction to the Principles of Morals and Legislation*, 1789) that laws should be certain, and therefore written; that they should be enforceable, and therefore adapted to the actual state of society and to the movement of social reform;

and that they should be calculated to maximize the overall prospect of pleasure. On such a basis Bentham constructed a liberal-reformist doctrine of the law and judicial procedure that has remained influential into the present century. He attempted to synthesize utilitarianism with the economic doctrines of *Smith, and put forward a plan for a *welfare state with free education, sickness benefits, minimum wages and guaranteed employment.

Bernstein, Eduard (1850–1932). German political theorist. *See* *Kautsky, *revisionism.

bicameral government. The system of government in which the *legislature, the *executive, or both, are distributed over two houses, an upper house and a lower house. The best-known examples of such arrangements – the UK *Parliament (involving House of Commons and House of Lords), and the US *Congress (involving House of Representatives and Senate) – have been taken as models for bicameral government in other countries, the second being adapted to the government of *federal states, the first having a kind of organic unity which fits it to the government of autonomous and traditionally unified societies. In theory each house acts as a check on the other, preventing hasty legislation, and enforcing deliberation. In practice, and for a variety of reasons, there is often a creeping tendency for the power of the upper house to decline, unless some countervailing force upholds its status. This force may be found in a procedure for election (as in the US *Senate), in executive control over membership, or in enhanced dignity and status, such as has been traditionally associated with the English House of Lords. Not all dignity is a form of political power, and already in 1867 Bagehot (*The English Constitution*) divided the instruments of government into the 'dignified' and the 'effective', implying that the House of Lords belongs to the first and not to the second kind. Bagehot also went on to argue for the indispensable place of that 'dignified' part in securing acceptance of the powers exercised by the effective, and this thought has often been reiterated by defenders of the *Westminster model of bicameral government.

Forms of bicameral government are many, and this means that it is extremely difficult to summarize the arguments offered for and against it. Defenders of bicameral government on the US model often refer to the *checks and balances supposedly introduced by it. Those who defend the Westminster model are often more concerned with its ability to generate a settled political establishment, which unifies the diverse allegiances within the state, offers a sop to ambition, and defuses the enthusiasm of revolutionary powers. Both forms seem to have the indirect effects of giving power to the *judiciary, and of making it comparatively easy to recognize and seek redress for official acts which are performed **ultra vires*. In the UK it has always been very important that a subject should be able to affirm his rights against an action by one house by petitioning the other.

Opponents of bicameral government are apt to be impatient with the delays that it may impose on legislation, with the difficulty with which an upper house can be persuaded to condone substantial changes in constitution or social structure, and with the complexity of *representation when the decisions of representatives stand to be ratified or amended by another body. Thus the Abbé Sieyès remarked that 'if the upper house agrees with the lower it is superfluous; if it disagrees, it ought to be abolished'. Opponents may also argue that bicameral government prevents the exercise of absolute power even in times when such power is necessary, and that no satisfactory qualification for membership of an upper house has been, or could be, devised.

Perhaps the most debated question concerning this issue is the last one: what should qualify a person for membership of an upper house? Is hereditary right acceptable (*see* *hereditary principle)? Should there be *elections? Executive privilege of appointment? The problem here is how to make the upper house into a genuine revising chamber, with some kind of sanction that enables it to represent constitutional continuity, while preventing it from becoming the principal forum of political decision-making. (*See* *peer.)

bilateralism. **1**. The advocacy of joint policies between states, e.g. in matters of aggression, defence or trade, perhaps requiring complex constitutional devices in order to secure *approximation of laws.

2. Specifically, the agreement between two states to extend to each other privileges in trade which are not extended to others (e.g. favourable tariffs). Such agreements (unlike the opposed multilateralism) act as a *de facto* restriction on international trade, and are generally opposed by those not party to them. A General Agreement on Tariffs and Trade (GATT) was therefore signed in 1947 (currently subscribed to by seventy-six states) committing the signatories to the expansion of multilateral trade and the reduction of exclusive agreements. The Soviet Union and its allies engage in extensive bilateral agreements, in order to incorporate their national plans into definite and predictable patterns of international trading.

bill. A draft or proposed piece of legislation, put before *Parliament, *Congress or some other legislative body for consideration, either by a Minister concerned with public policy, or by a 'private member' of the parliament or assembly, or by petition from a member of the public. When passed by the legislative body, a bill becomes an act.

bill of rights (also: declaration of rights). Any attempt to formulate systems of *natural rights that can be recognized by, and enforced against, particular governments. The *Constitution of Virginia*, 1776, and the French *Declaration of the Rights of Man and of the Citizen*, 1789, incorporated such declarations, and succeeded, in the first case, in enforcing them. The US Bill of Rights (or first ten amendments) is founded on eighteenth-century ideas of natural right which have their origin in *Locke. It is a constitutional device rather than a specific legal enactment, and thus has provided a genuine limit to state power, providing rights which can be fought for in open court, whatever the authority of the power which seeks to deny them. The English 'Bill of Rights' of 1689 is, by contrast, only a legal enactment, and can itself be overruled or qualified by subsequent parliamentary decisions. It is therefore not part of the constitution and provides no permanent guarantee of the rights which it designates (which include *habeas corpus). The USSR and its Eastern European dependencies have constitutions which incorporate declarations of rights (partly in order to achieve nominal conformity with the United Nations Charter of Human Rights). However, their effectiveness is disputed, since attempts by the citizen to assert them against official power lead to charges of *sedition and even *show trials. Moreover, a bill of rights is effective only if there is also *judicial independence, so that judges have power to uphold the rights specified when they are sued for. If a judge is under instruction from the state in all actions to which the state is party, then a bill of rights does not exist as a genuine constitutional device, but only as a legal fiction.

Several suggestions have been made as to the desirability of a constitutional bill of rights in the UK. It should, however, be recognized that rights have traditionally been guaranteed in the UK not by constitutional declarations, but by customary *procedures*. Thus the existence of an independent judiciary, the priority of *equity over *common law and *statute, and the entrenched disapproval of retroactive legislation, act together to provide strong barriers against parliamentary despotism, and this fact is illustrated throughout the history of English *constitutional law. The 'Bill of Rights' exists partly as a reminder of these procedures, and partly as a reassertion of the *sovereignty of Parliament against the claims of the *monarchy. It should also be recognized that a written declaration of the American variety is a guarantee of rights only when it can be upheld, and this requires just the kind of procedural detachment from executive power that is displayed by the UK judiciary.

Bismarck, Prince Otto von (1815–98). German statesman and Chancellor. *See* *anti-clericalism, *culture, *health, **Kulturkampf*, **Realpolitik*, *welfare state.

black consciousness. A movement originating among urban blacks in the US, and spreading to Africa, which urges the formation among black peoples of a consciousness of their identity and political aspirations which will be independent of the *values, aims and manoeuvres of the white nations, and independent of ways of thinking redolent of a colonial past. The idea of black consciousness is often embellished with doctrines of *oppression, which imply that blacks have accepted pictures of their own role and position which consolidate the existing domination by whites and reflect the ruling white *ideology. The elimination of this subservient consciousness is seen as a necessary preliminary to the pursuit of real political power.

Blanquism. The theory and practice of revolution by **coup d'état*, carried out by a secret *élite of armed conspirators, rather than by any mass organization. Named after the French revolutionary Louis Auguste Blanqui (1805–81), who influenced several generations of French radicals, Blanquism views a temporary élite dictatorship as a necessary means of extinguishing any remaining strains of capitalism and of imposing a revolutionary programme on the people, regardless of their support for it. The entire concentration of the doctrine is on the means of revolution; the end is taken more or less for granted.

Whilst sympathetic to Blanquism, *Marx condemned its élitism and lack of broad working-class base. Blanqui himself later came to place greater emphasis on the need for this base, and bequeathed to Marxism such fundamental concepts as *class struggle, and *dictatorship of the proletariat. Blanquism played a part in the formation of *syndicalism in France, and anticipated the actual strategy of *bolshevism.

bloc. French for block. From the habit in continental government of divergent political groups or parties gathering together to support the government in power. The term was later extended to cover groupings in an *opposition, and then transferred to international relations in order to denote political and economic concertedness of states, whether or not bound to each other by *treaty or *alliance. For example, all nations incorporated into, or overrun by, the USSR since the 'October Revolution' are, by consent or compulsion, likely to act in concert on most military, economic and political issues, and so constitute a 'bloc'.

Blocs must be distinguished from coalitions: the former are united by interest, but do not require either a truce between the parties, or a common policy.

block voting. The practice of *voting in collusion with others, and according to an agreed common policy. A block vote may involve the members of a given *faction voting against their judgement; the practice is therefore often condemned as being against the spirit of *voting. It was heavily criticized by the *Federalist*, and suggestions were made as to how a constitution might be designed to prevent it. However, the universal emergence of parties has made block voting of *some* kind a normal accompaniment of democratic procedure. Some argue that it is necessary if any kind of representation is to be effective.

blockade. The right of a belligerent to forbid access to and egress from enemy territory, usually by sea, whether on the part of the enemy or on the part of a *neutral. Under *international law such a right must be enforced impartially against all enemy and neutral nations. The Declaration of London, 1908, attempted to restrict rights of blockade, but was never *ratified. *See also* *pacific blockade.

Bodin, Jean (1530–96). French political philosopher and one of the first theorists of modern *absolutism. In his *Six livres de la république*, 1576, Bodin provided an original and highly influential examination of the concept of *sovereignty, defined as the 'most high and perpetual' power in a commonwealth and the entity which has the absolute right and duty of law-giving. Law is the expression of the sovereign's will, and binds the subject regardless of his consent. The sovereign power is, however, subject to the constraints of *natural law, and while violation of that law may absolve the subject of his duty to obey, it does not confer on him a right to rebel (political order being a benefit so great that no man has a right to overthrow it); it may, however, give to neighbouring sovereigns a right to interfere in the cause of *justice. The sovereign cannot be subject to his own laws, since they express his will, but the holding of power demands respect for the institutions of civil life, among which the family and private property are given particular emphasis.

Bodin's defence of absolute monarchy was far from a justification of *autocracy. He regarded faction and civil strife as the major causes of cruelty and injustice. To prevent them, he argued, a political arrangement must balance interests against each other, and so still their conflict. It is only when there is absolute sovereignty that there is the authoritative source of conciliation. Hence Bodin combined his absolutist doctrine with the advocacy of *minority rights in matters of religion, judicial independence, and constraints against taxation. He also gave one of the first accounts of international law, regarded as specifying the rights of a sovereign not over his subjects but against other sovereigns. The fundamental aim in all aspects of his theory was to develop a concept of sovereignty that would uphold the privileges of the French monarch, at a time of factional insurrection and religious dissent, precipitated in part by the Huguenot rebellions.

body politic. An *organicist term for *civil society. The term was popular among seventeenth-century writers, and is interesting for its implications as to how social order was conceived. Historians of ideas sometimes comment on the subsequent replacement of this and related metaphors by those of a more mechanical kind; e.g. 'the ship of state', *'checks and balances'. The influence of Newtonian mechanics is sometimes stressed, along with the emergence of the *universalist, and atomistic, vision of social order that appealed to the *Enlightenment.

Bolingbroke, Henry St John, Viscount (1678–1751). English statesman and political philosopher. *See* *balance of power, *establishment, *patriotism.

bolshevism. The revolutionary wing of the Russian Social Democratic Party became known as *bolsheviki* ('members of the majority') in 1903, at the second Party Congress in London. The *bolsheviki* were led by *Lenin in opposition to the minority *mensheviks. The name was retained in the official designation of the Soviet Communist Party from 1912 until 1952, and 'bolshevism' is now accepted as a standard term for *Leninism as practised by that party, and as theorized in the works of Lenin himself. It involves the advocacy of violent revolution as opposed to the gradual change sought by the mensheviks, together with a stringent form of *democratic centralism: all powers are to be assumed by the state in the name of the proletariat which is to dictate during the aftermath of revolution. The bolsheviks eventually seized power by **coup d'état*, and proceeded to eliminate all remaining *opposition to their rule.

Bonapartism. Attachment to and advocacy of the policies of Napoleon Bonaparte, involving belief in (a) a strong post-revolutionary concentration of power, (b) a centralized administration and '*carrières ouvertes aux talents*', (c) a system of honours and dignities issuing from the sovereign power, (d) a correspondingly ceremonial and majestic *state, (e) a foreign policy of aggression and conquest rather than defence, with a global *sphere of influence, (f) the embodiment of the power of state in the personality of a leader, who will represent *majesty in concrete form. While Bonapartism can still be seen as a characteristic of the French presidential system (albeit in diminished form), it owed its original success to the military genius of Napoleon, and to the ease with which he was able to revive and modernize the principles of *aristocratic government.

The term is sometimes used by Marxists, e.g. by *Trotsky, not in the above sense, but as an abusive description of demagogues like Hitler and Stalin. Such 'analogical' descriptions of the figures projected to eminence by history are however criticized as being inimical to the method of *historical materalism.

bourgeois/bourgeoisie. French: town-dweller, and the class thereof. The term bourgeois has two uses which have been conflated for reasons that are self-evident.

1. As appropriated by *Marx, the term denotes a particular position in *production relations, and the *class created by that position, viz. the class of property-owners under capitalist and proto-capitalist systems of production. Private property in the means of production seems to be the essential feature of this class, and the one that gives its structural description. However, Marx and *Engels also have in mind another way of identifying this class: as the 'class' of *small* property-owners, which arose during the Middle Ages and came to displace the existing *aristocracy from positions of eminence which they had formerly occupied, so that 'the bourgeoisie has at last, since the establishment of modern industry and of the world market, conquered for itself, in the modern representative state, exclusive political sway. The executive of the modern state is but a committee for managing the common affairs of the whole bourgeoisie' (*The Communist Manifesto*). The vision recurs repeatedly in Marx and subsequent writers, of a class that has *come* to hold a certain dominant position in production relations, and therefore in the state. This suggests that there is a way of identifying a class, which does not make reference to its economic position, and which also enables us to think of it as possessing power, or even *agency, of its own.

2. The term has also been used to describe the traditional division between the class of gentlemen and aristocrats, and that of their rivals, the bourgeoisie, who had newly arrived in a position of eminence through the profits of trade. This usage is exemplified in Molière's ironical title *Le Bourgeois Gentilhomme*. It is essentially the expression of a *contrast* between new, urban-based wealth, and old, land-based power. The *bourgeoisie is conceived, in this usage, as a *middle class, and its association with the life and *ethos of the town is far more important than its position in production relations. Ridicule and hostility towards the bourgeoisie has been an important part of French intellectual life since the seventeenth century, and the game of *épater les bourgeois* (Flaubert's expression) was extended in the nineteenth century to Germany, where bourgeois culture had taken over much of the impetus provided by the *romantic movement, and effectively created a style of its own in place of the bungling absence of style that had been satirized by Molière.

Emerging from 2. during the nineteenth century was the sense of the 'bourgeois' as a special kind of creature, whose thoughts, feelings and relations demanded new and so far unstudied explanations. The bourgeois is characterized by a particular kind of family relations, particular thoughts, feelings and attachments, and a characteristic *ideology. *Weber emphasized the extent to which the rising middle classes were the standard bearers of the new, 'intra-mundane' ideals of the personal and the *business ethic. Others have continued the game of ridicule, best exemplified, perhaps, by *Sartre, in *Saint*

Genet, 1952, where the bourgeois is characterized by his rejection of, and hostility to, crime, by his predilection for lasting heterosexual, as opposed to transient homosexual, relations, by his fear and suspicion of all that 'inverts' a fragile vision of 'normality'. This is a long way from the Marxian idea: to suppose that these attitudes (which are not unknown even among members of the working class) are specific to private property in the means of production is, to put it mildly, far-fetched.

Nevertheless, there are intuitive connections between the two ideas, which explain many of the current usages of the term. The major difficulty is that there are two rival ways of identifying and theorizing classes. According to one way (class = position in production relations), classes cannot rise; according to the other (class = life-style, kinship relations, and ethic), they can.

Marxists and others make a distinction between the **petit* and the *haut* bourgeois, arguing that, under the pressure of capitalist modes of production, the property-owning class has a tendency to fragment, the first being forced out of business, undergoing *proletarianization, the second acting so as to concentrate power in the hands of an ever smaller and ever more effective *ruling class.

bourgeois democracy. Term used by some Marxists to denote (and to decry) the European, and by implication American, systems of *representation, as these have emerged and evolved during the last two centuries. The label 'bourgeois' is meant to indicate that these systems are so designed that, however votes are cast and parties organized, power will always vest in the bourgeoisie or its agents, either on account of constitutional and procedural devices designed to safeguard property interests and *capitalist relations of production, or through some mechanism whereby the representative is disciplined into bourgeois principles and practice. It is usually contrasted with the true *people's democracy, in which there may not be elections to office, but in which it is a condition of the existence of an office that it be exercised only in the interests of the people as a whole, and not in the interests of any particular class – indeed, in defiance of any class that seeks dominion. Likewise, 'bourgeois civil liberties'.

bourgeois economics. Term used by Marx to denote the kind of economic theory developed by the nineteenth-century successors of Adam Smith (including *J. S. Mill, although more usually rather less self-critical figures), which treats exchange and *exchange-value as fundamental economic facts, and the laws of the *market as laws of nature. It is criticized for representing as permanent the peculiar features of developed capitalism, and thus representing the historical conditions of capitalist modes of production as essential features of human life: 'The aim is. . . to present production – see, e.g. Mill – as distinct from distribution etc., as encased in eternal natural laws independent of history, at which opportunity *bourgeois* relations are then quietly smuggled in as the inviolable natural laws on which society in the abstract is founded' (Marx, *Grundrisse*).

The label 'bourgeois economics' is still used to criticize thinkers like *Hayek and *Friedman (*see* *New Right), on the assumption that any disposition to accept the market as a fact of nature is in the end tantamount to assuming bourgeois *production relations, and hence the dominance of a property-owning *class. If the market *is* a fact of nature, then this assumption cannot be criticized; but it remains a central Marxist tenet that it is not.

boycott. Named after its original victim (Captain Boycott, an Irish landlord's agent isolated by the Irish League in 1880), a boycott implies the severance of all relations, whether economic, social or political, in order to force a recalcitrant party to change its actions or policies. Boycotting of an individual citizen or legal *person may sometimes be lawful, but it is also frequently a *conspiracy to injure. In international law it seems not to be recognized as a form of action distinct from *embargo, *sanctions etc. It is, however, fairly normal practice in international diplomacy to boycott the delegate of a state whose policies are the object of disapproval.

In *industrial action, boycotting has assumed some importance, especially in the US, although some US states have made the 'secondary boycott' (boycott of firms who patronize or supply an offending employer) illegal.

breach of the peace. In UK law, any disturbance of the public order, including particular offences such as affray and riot. If a breach is feared persons or associations may be bound over to keep the peace. This is an effective judicial power which may be used to political ends, for example in preventing potentially riotous demonstrations.

brigandage. Terrorism and violence conducted with the aim of material gain, and outside the law. Originally brigands were small groups of bandits operating in areas of China, India, Mexico, and elsewhere, where the topography and climate facilitated their exploits. There seem to be two kinds of brigandage: that arising from the dispossession, impoverishment, or persecution of some individual, group or class, which, in desperation, turns to violence; and that arising during the transition from military to civil government, when soldiers fear to lay down their arms, and also resent the loss of power that is consequent on doing so. The second kind has been important in the aftermath of wars employing mercenary soldiers, and is of some importance today. The activities of brigands have frequently come to be identified with the social aspirations of one part of a divided community; brigandage has therefore often found partisan protection, either on the part of a dominant group who use it to harass their opponents, or on the part of a foreign power with an interest in *subversion.

brinkmanship. Term coined by T. C. Schelling, based on a remark of John Foster Dulles, to denote the art of advancing to the brink of war but not engaging in it. An important feature of a certain style of foreign policy, associated with *cold war. The motivating thought seems to be that a policy of brinkmanship, coupled with the tenacious advocacy of *non-negotiable demands, must always succeed against a policy of compromise.

brotherhood of man. Slogan of the French Revolution, meant to denote a community of interests among all human beings, arising from the fact, and the perception, of equality. It has seemed impossible that this ideal should be realized if there are conflicting interests stemming from class-membership, or from the holding or not holding of *property, and it is a persistent doctrine that only the abolition of private property and the class divisions associated with it can bring about this community of human interests. The fact that at least some people are more attached to their own interests than to those of others has not (historically) been regarded as important by defenders of the ideal, although it has led some to regard the ideal as *utopian.

Buddhism. A religious system founded in India during the fifth century BC by Siddharta Gautama, who called himself the Buddha ('enlightened one'), and who preached to all willing devotees a middle path between the extremes of bodily indulgence, self-mortification and speculative philosophy. Buddhism sees the individual life as inextricably linked, both to the future incarnations of the individual (*karma*), and to the lives of all other persons and animals (*dhata*). Purity and renunciation are essential to securing a worthwhile future existence. The sense of the connectedness with other lives fosters compassion and charity, and has led to strong feelings of solidarity in Buddhistic communities. The most important type of community is the *sangha*: a social group bound together for mutual moral and spiritual enhancement. The monastic members contribute the 'gift of truth', while the lay members are responsible for the 'gift of provision'. The community is envisaged as bound together by a mutual indebtedness, religious, moral and economic, while the aim of all association is friendship and love, which transcend barriers of race, class, country and time. Hence Buddhism denies the religious ultimacy of the brahmans, and does not view the *caste system as necessary to personal salvation. It views the power of the state as based on a historically evolved contractual relationship between the sovereign and the people, which requires that the sovereign should, by executive skill and moral example, strive to earn his position.

The essence of the doctrine lies in respect for life, and absolute equality. All forms of slavery are forbidden, and the ideal community is one of complete *social justice. After the Buddha's death, however, sectarian proliferation ensued, and Buddhist communities gradually returned to hierarchical principles of organization. The religion remains as a permanent invocation to renounce the world, and to refine away the dross of *karma* so as to reach the ideal blessedness of *nirvāna*, in which the individual soul loses all that distinguishes it, and is liberated from the cycle of birth and death. Nirvana is attained by the eightfold path of morality described in the *Samyutta-nikāya*: right views, right intention, right speech, right conduct, right occupation, right effort, right mindedness, and right concentration.

budget. A plan of income and expenditure for a future period; essential in all arrangements where income and expendture are not simultaneous. The extent of government expenditure over the last few decades has meant that the government's budget has become an important instrument of policy. *Fiscal changes are often governed by the desire to modify budget surplus or deficit in the hope of achieving social and political objectives (such as a reduction in unemployment) or, alternatively, in the interests of a balanced budget.

Bukharin, N. I. (1888–1938). Russian *bolshevik, close friend and collaborator of *Lenin, social scientist and economist. Bukharin was the first editor of *Pravda*, and later became the official theorist of Soviet communism. Between 1925 and 1928 he was co-leader, with Stalin, of the Communist Party, and main architect of the more moderate economic policy which was then adopted. By 1928 he had become the main leader of the anti-Stalin faction, and continued to be seen as the symbol of the *bolshevik struggle against Stalinism until long after Stalin had had him shot. Some argue that he was the leading theoretical influence on the doctrines of Soviet communism throughout its first twenty years, although the precise nature of his thought has been effectively concealed by Soviet historiography.

bureaucracy. Rule by administrative offices. In a bureaucracy actual power is vested in those who are, from the legal point of view, administrative intermediaries between *sovereign and *subject. They (normally the civil servants, although there can also be military and religious bureaucracies) can delay or advance the causes of both sovereign and subject to an extent that gives them *de facto* control over major political transformations. *Weber (*Wirtschaft und Gesellschaft*, 1921) argued that the conflict between capitalism and socialism must be extinguished by the triumph of bureaucracy, which would prove indispensable for the *rational* attainment of the goals of any organization in industrial society. The result would be the creation of an increasingly centralized, increasingly impersonal, and increasingly 'routinized', kind of *authority.

Since administrators can master their tasks only slowly, they must perforce remain in office longer than most politicians remain in power: their activities therefore impose a continuity on successive governments which has an effect not unlike that of an unwritten *constitution. The UK *civil service – with its complex *career structure – is well known for its ability to assert continuity against every kind of radical reform, a point argued in its favour by C. H. Sisson (*The Spirit of British Administration, and some European Comparisons*, 1959). The power of the US President to appoint advisers and officers within the civil service enables him, to some extent, to break down the administrative prerogative.

In the USSR and associated states it is, by contrast, impossible to distinguish government from administration, appointment to political office and to administrative office being alike determined by the ruling party. In one sense this provides the nearest approach to complete bureaucracy that has yet been achieved. In another sense, however, it is further removed from bureaucracy than any form of government known in the West, since it prevents the existence of genuinely administrative, as opposed to political, decisions. The policies of the party are enacted at every level, from *Politbureau to factory floor. This amalgamation of politics and administration has sometimes been thought to be a feature of *oriental despotism.

Burke, Edmund (1729–97). Irish statesman, philosopher and political theorist who, despite affiliations to the *Whig faction of Lord Rockingham, became, through his writings, a founding father of modern intellectual *conservatism, his *Reflections on the Recent Revolution in France*, 1790, being often cited by adherents to that cause. Burke's thought is unsystematic but highly imaginative, attempting a synthesis of the Whig principle of freedom with the *Tory principle of order.

(i) Advocacy of social continuity. *Revolution is an evil, not only because of its violence, but also because it inevitably leads to the seizure of power by those who can neither employ it harmoniously nor renounce it peacefully. *Reform too is dangerous if taken to radical extremes, for it may then bring about a social order that can be neither understood nor accepted by its participants. Continuity is necessary if the values which motivate present action are to be understood and realized in the future, and in this sense one must 'reform in order to conserve'.

(ii) Critique of *individualism. The individual finds fulfilment only in society and only in the participation in norms, customs and institutions which reflect back to him a sense of his unity with his fellows. (Hence the family, not the individual, is the basic unit of social order.) Outside society an individual may have desires, but he cannot have long-term aims, values, achievements or rewards. The social nature of man is given as a further argument for continuity. In common with some of the *empiricist philosophers, for whom he was the greatest political spokesman, Burke regarded human nature as a permanent but uncomprehended datum, and social and political order as a delicate achievement that is more easily destroyed than created, and which we should value too much to meddle with unthinkingly.

(iii) The defence of *monarchy and *aristocracy. Inequality is inescapable in society, and guidance and leadership essential. There is also a natural sense of dependence, subordination and affection which are aroused by ability, virtue, age and social *grace. The relationship between the leader and the led may therefore be institutionalized and rendered acceptable through a hereditary aristocracy, which should leave some room for the upward mobility of new talent. Monarchy is the true central institution of political order, because it provides a 'natural' object for obedience and reverence.

(iv) Defence of *private property. Burke was influenced by liberal economic theory in the style of *Smith, and thought that it is the nature of property to be both private and unequally distributed. He argued in favour of the inheritance and *accumulation of wealth, and regarded the impediments to universal *franchise in the English constitution as justified by the need to see that property (upon which all stability depends) is adequately represented, and so achieves political responsiblity proportionate to its actual power. Parliament thus represents, not individuals, but social rank and economic influence.

Burke's political vision was diverse and diffuse; the potential conflict between liberal economics and social conservatism was never resolved, partly because his doctrines arose from intuitions about the nature of *society which were never encapsulated in a developed theory of the nature, function and legitimacy of the *state. Politics, for Burke, was a matter of 'prudence and practicability'. Conservatives value his writings for their eloquent elevation of the given, the concrete, the known and familiar, over the abstract, the unknown and the merely projected.

business cycle. Americanism for *trade cycle, gaining popularity because of the narrow implications of the word 'trade'.

business ethic. The code of conduct and *ideology which govern the transactions involved in business under conditions of open competition, private ownership, and sale and purchase in a market. It involves a respect for contract, for open dealing, for the payment of debts and the pursuit of debtors. It has also been thought to involve an assignment of monetary values to all forms of human relationship (cf. the 'goodwill' of a business, which may be bought and sold), and a respect for human fellowship as much for its expression of such monetary values, as for its independent moral lustre.

Sociologists often distinguish the business from the *professional ethic. Whereas the *professions are essentially engaged in furnishing services, business deals largely in goods; thus in business sound credit arrangements and fair profits can be emphasized to a greater degree than is compatible with professional practice.

According to some the business ethic is part of the *legitimation process of capitalist production: an ideological device that facilitates relations within a ruling class and helps to close that class to entry from outside, while representing its activities as legitimate in the eyes of those excluded. Others argue that it may in fact prevent comfortable negotiation between those who subscribe to it and those (e.g. union representatives, managers of oriental enterprises, officials of regimes not steeped in the ethos of private property) who do not.

butskellism. A British variety of *centrist politics, named after the *moderate conservative R. A. Butler, and the moderate socialist Hugh Gaitskell. It involves the search for common ground between advocates of private *property and advocates of the *welfare state, in order to find the *consensus that will facilitate constitutional government and reconcile the major interests that have emerged in the UK since 1945. (*See* *mixed economy.)

C

cabinet. The immediate entourage of ministers who confer directly with the *Prime Minister (as in the UK) or *President (as in the US). In the UK, cabinet ministers are almost always members of *Parliament, and make collective decisions in secret which are then imposed on the ruling *party in Parliament (including remaining non-cabinet ministers) through the action of the 'whips'. Hence the cabinet acts as the prime concentration of *executive power. The US constitution makes no mention of a 'cabinet', and the ministers concerned stand only in an advisory relation to the President. They have to work to establish their own links with *Congress and the President is therefore less constrained to listen to them, since they may not represent an independent political following. The cabinet is therefore much less powerful, and the President correspondingly more so. The role of the cabinet in UK politics has been frequently remarked on, as revealing both the flexibility, and the inscrutability, of the UK constitution. (See, for example, W. Bagehot: *The English Constitution*, 1867.)

cadre: French military term for the collected officers of a regiment. Appropriated *circa* 1930 by the Soviet Communist Party, to denote the groups of workers and intellectuals affiliated to the party and active in promoting its policies. Now generally used for any group of organized *activists who take concerted measures to promote common political ends.

caesaropapalism. The system whereby a *sovereign power has supreme control over the church within its dominions, and exercises this control in matters (e.g. doctrine, discipline and liturgy) normally reserved to ecclesiastical authority. Generally used to refer to the powers exercised by the Byzantine Emperors over the Eastern patriarchates, it can also be used to describe the power of the Communist Party over the same patriarchates in Russia and the Ukraine, and (to a far less extent) the power of the UK *Parliament over the *Anglican Church, which has to seek the consent of the Queen in Parliament for major doctrinal, liturgical and constitutional change. In the Byzantine case, justification was attempted through the claim that the Emperor had derived his imperial power from God, who had enjoined him to safeguard the souls as well as the bodies of his subjects.

caliphate. Arabic: *kh'alifah*, successor. The system of potentially international government by which, under the original custom of *Islam, the faithful were ruled by the 'successor' of the prophet, chosen from the tribe of the prophet, and usually establishing his claim by descent or kinship. Originally the Abassid caliphs in Baghdad exerted considerable political power, and could be thought of as the genuine rulers over the territories that had fallen to their government. Gradually however the rise of contestants for power led to a reduction in the political power of the Caliph, until, in medieval times, his role was merely to authorize the actual rule of princes (sultans) by confirming their titles – sometimes under coercion. His role was compared at the time to that of the Pope in Christendom; the comparison is misleading, however, since the office of Caliph was without specific priestly duties, nor did the Caliph have the kind of universal responsibility for the souls of the faithful that was vested in the Pope. He was a figurehead, symbol of the unity of Islam, and principal channel through which divine authority extended to the rule of princes. In due course rival caliphs emerged, and eventually princes began to dispense with the nominal separation of *power and *authority contained in the duality of sultan and caliph, and themselves assumed both titles, usually with very slender claims to legitimacy under *Islamic law. The caliphate endured under the Ottoman sultans, who ruled always as 'successors to the prophet', but it was abolished by the Turkish National Assembly in 1924. Attempts to revive it (chiefly to the benefit of the last kings of Egypt) proved abortive. It remains one of the most important examples of the manner in which, under ostensibly religious government, power and authority inevitably begin to diverge (*see* *church and state).

Calvinism. The theological system of J. Calvin (1509–64) which is accepted by most non-Lutheran reformed churches. Calvin accepted the *Lutheran doctrines of justification by faith alone, of the absence of free will since the Fall, of the absolute authority of the Bible in all matters of belief and conduct, and added the peculiar belief in the gratuitous predestination of the 'elect' to salvation, and of others to damnation. He denied the reality of divine grace, and advocated in his *Institutes*, 1536, a species of partial theocracy which he himself exercised for a while in Geneva. Calvinism, unlike Lutheranism, attempted to give a complete account of human institutions and social life, in order to replace the one that had been previously provided by the Catholic church.

Man is a creature of fellowship, who has equal need of both church and state. The concern of the church is with spiritual salvation, of the state with the regulation of external conduct and the just ordering of society (where justice includes distributive justice, so that it is the business of the state to ensure equitable distribution of benefits). Church and state must promote each other's welfare, and hence it is right that blasphemy (e.g.) should be a civil crime; however the two systems should be structurally independent, so that officials of the church do not acquire through their office a place in the state, nor officials of the state a place in the church. The ideal government is one chosen by the people from those members of the *aristocracy best suited to wielding political power. Calvin also believed in a version of the doctrine of *natural law, and thought that the magistrate held his authority ultimately from God, who is the source of the natural law.

Complex political practices have emerged from Calvinism, and from its attempts to sustain itself against the *universalist and secular thinking of the *Enlightenment. These remain influential in those parts of the world where Calvinism spread in the wake of the second 'Helvetic confession' of 1566, among them Scotland and Northern Ireland. In 1622 Calvinism became the state religion of Holland and thence passed to the Dutch colonies, notably to South Africa, where the Calvinist Dutch Reformed Church still holds considerable influence among the Afrikaans-speaking population, both white and coloured, although the once popular opinion (put about by Dr Livingstone) that the Calvinist doctrine of the elect was responsible for the harsh treatment of blacks by the Vortrekkers is now doubted.

A revival of Calvinist theology in the present century (notably in the writings of Karl Barth (1886–1968)) has led to attempts to renew the Calvinist vision of political life. Thus the Amsterdam philosopher H. Dooyeweerd, in his *New Critique of Theoretical Thought*, 1933, produced a Calvinist account of sovereignty, attempting to give a revised doctrine of the spheres of church and state, perhaps in order to reconcile the fundamentalist Christianity advocated by the one with the unchristian practice of the other. Faith is an 'ontological decision' presupposed in all Christian action; but it displays itself differently in the several autonomous spheres. Reality has 'modalities', each of which is explored by a separate science, and each of which has its own point of view and sovereignty. (A basis for this proposition is derived from *phenomenology.) Violation of the sovereignty of one sphere by the principles of another induces a confused vision of the Christian mission, which is to understand and love the world as God's creation. Each special sphere is subject to the authority of religion as recorded in the Bible. However, it proceeds according to principles of its own, and hence must be accepted in the form which those principles give to it.

This modern Calvinist *ideology opposes state intervention in the economy, since this violates the sovereignty of contrasting spheres. It is sometimes used to suggest an argument against mixed marriages, and in favour of separate development (*see* *apartheid). However, it is only under a very crude interpretation that such a conclusion can be drawn from it. For the separation of spheres is not a separation of realms (whether worldly or spiritual, economic or legal, black or white), but a separation of ways of perceiving and acting on a single reality.

Cambridge school. A school of economic thought influenced by economists at the University of Cambridge, England, following the ideas of *Keynes, and now developing the Keynesian emphasis on *macroeconomics over *microeconomics. It has opposed various *neo-classical theories, and attempted to provide an acceptable theory of the economic role of the state, and so align economics with a political vision adapted to the circumstances of modern government. It has generated various theories of economic growth and development, and has given a reasoned basis for the *mixed economy. Some of its adherents have supported certain socialist policies, in respect of ownership of the means of production and the distribution of wealth. Hence it has been a powerful influence on the thinking of recent Labour governments in the UK. It has been criticized for its comparative neglect of microeconomics. Principal members of the school include: Joan Robinson (1903–83), Nicholas Kaldor (b. 1908).

Canetti, Elias (b. 1905). Expatriate Bulgarian sociologist and writer of Spanish-Jewish descent. *See* *crowds, *leadership.

canon law. Originally, the system of law constituted by ecclesiastical legislation for the government and administration of the Christian church.

Formed from an amalgamation of *Roman law, New Testament doctrine, and doctrines of the apostolic fathers, the canon law was systematized in the twelfth century by Gratian, became increasingly refined and codified, and presented the most developed system of international *jurisdiction that the world has known, losing its direct, but none of its indirect, influence in the affairs of sovereign states at the Reformation, after which only the *Roman Catholic and *Anglican churches continued to acknowledge the authority of the canon. By the Act of Submission 1532 the English clergy agreed not to make any new canons without royal permission, so that the canon thereafter gradually lost its authority in the Anglican communion.

The canon law incorporates elaborate doctrines of evidence, inquisition and *natural justice, and laid the foundations for modern procedure in criminal trials. It also created the laws of marriage, property and succession that were to pass into European and later American legislations, and, because of its international character, contained the first attempts to specify rights of action between states, and the first legal definitions of *sovereignty.

capacity in law. The ability to bear rights and disabilities in law. Capacity is usually restricted in the case of infants, minors and people of unsound mind. It has an active and passive side, and the two may not exactly correspond: thus, in UK law, a minor has the right to enter into a contract, but not the liability to bear its enforcement. Capacity is part of the complex idea of the legal *person, and its definition reflects an intuitive understanding of *responsibility.

capital. Often defined as 'produced means of production', that is, commodities that have been produced and which are themselves employed in the production of other commodities. A distinction is sometimes drawn between fixed capital (buildings, machinery etc.) and circulating capital (e.g. semi-finished products). Alternatively it has been suggested that the essence of capital is time, in particular the way in which the passage of time can be put to productive use in capitalist production. Labour is applied, and consumption is forgone, in order to yield greater benefits in the future. On this view, capital need not involve 'produced means of production'. For example, allowing wine to mature would also be capitalistic. Thus the *Austrian school sees the capitalist method of production as a 'roundabout method' that involves 'waiting': the more waiting the more production. Yet another view is that capital is wealth: i.e. command over current output. This last view defines capital in a financial sense rather than as a feature of production.

According to Marx there is an ideological distortion in regarding capital – in the form of inanimate objects like machines and *money – as an independent *productive force. This view (sometimes stigmatized as 'capital *fetishism'), is held to neglect the fact that, without *labour, none of this accumulated stock could produce anything. If capital is to play a genuine part in production, labour must be regarded as intrinsic to it. Hence Marx distinguished 'constant' from 'variable' capital (see, e.g., *Capital*, vol. 1, Part III, ch. 8), their ratio being the 'organic composition' of capital. The first includes raw materials, machinery, and all parts of the means of production which produce no alteration in exchange-value, the second consists of labour power, which both reproduces itself, and also generates the *surplus-value necessary for capitalist accumulation. Constant capital is not a productive force, but a means of production, which, being controlled by the capitalist, enables him to extract labour hours from the worker.

Opponents of the Marxist position sometimes argue that the distinction between constant and variable capital is based on a false dichotomy, between the part played by machinery and land and the part played by labour, in the process of production. (Consider the crop which grows unattended, or the factory which is set in motion at the touch of a switch.)

Various questions have exercised political thinkers since the first attempts were made to distinguish capital from property as such. For example: how is capital possible? This is the question which concerned many nineteenth-century political economists (including Marx). What does capital do? This is a question of interest to modern economists (*see* *capital theory). Is capital necessarily private? (*See* *state capitalism.) Ought it to exist? If there can be production without capital, then this last is one of the most important questions of political philosophy. If there cannot be production without capital, then it is irrelevant.

capital theory. A branch of economics which explores the implications of the existence of *capital for the theory of prices, the theory of production, and the theory of income distribution. It is a controversial field of investigation, for many reasons. Difficult technical questions arise concerning the role of time and uncertainty. In addition there are problems concerning the factors which determine the relative distribution of income among holders of capital and suppliers of labour power, which abut directly upon the central questions of political theory. For example, the Marxian theory of income distribution and capital implies that the labourer is, but the capitalist is not, a producer. From assumptions concerning the *natural right to the product of labour (*see* *Locke) it is sometimes argued that the capitalist takes part of what belongs by right to the labourer. On that view the labourer is exploited by the capitalist (*see* *exploitation). The theories of capital advanced by the *Austrian school of economists, however, support no such implication, since capitalistic production is held essentially to be 'roundabout', involving the sacrifice of leisure and consumption for greater gain in the future.

capitalism. 1. An economic arrangement, defined by the predominant existence of capital and *wage labour, the former consisting of accumulations in the hands of private (i.e. non-government) owners, including *corporations and *joint stock companies, the latter consisting in the activities of labourers, who exchange their *labour hours (or, according to *Marxian theory, their *labour power) for wages, paid from the stock of capital. The capitalist extracts not a wage but a *profit, by realizing in a *market the value of the goods produced. Capitalism presupposes private property in the means of production, a market economy, and the *division of labour. It does not necessitate, but it may be thought to encourage, *factory production.

2. According to Marxist theory capitalism marks a transient stage of historical development, and is further characterized by the formation of capitalist and labouring *classes. The former – the *bourgeoisie – accumulates all *surplus-value, while the latter – the *proletariat – accumulates nothing, and so remains propertyless. Marx himself did not often use the term 'capitalism', but the theory is in essence his.

In both explanations 'capitalism' denotes a theoretical concept, used in the description and explanation of social arrangements that may have many aspects besides those mentioned. It is unclear whether there is or has been any society that corresponds exactly either to the Marxist or to any other conception of capitalism. It is more accurate to say that both definitions are attempts to specify an *ideal type. Moreover, some (e.g. *Weber, *Sombart), have argued that crucial elements of this type are to be found in almost all historical societies.

At least the following varieties of capitalism are recognized: commercial capitalism (in which large-scale operators control exchange), industrial capitalism (dominated by large-scale private production), finance capitalism (controlled by bankers and creditors), *state capitalism, and welfare capitalism (in which the state intervenes in the economy in the interests of social *welfare).

The term is sometimes used to denote the ideological stance which attempts to justify capitalism. Capitalism is defended either because it is seen as a necessary consequence of private property (which is in turn defended either as socially necessary (*Hegel) or as the subject of a *natural right (*Locke)), or else because it is seen as integral to the market economy. In the latter case the defence may rest on the view that a market economy has an intrinsic capacity to maximize production, and results in a rational (perhaps even *optimal) distribution of scarce resources, and so increases the material well-being of capitalist and labourer alike; or else on the more philosophical idea that the market is the economic realization of some ideal of political *freedom. Some (e.g. *Hayek) add that any attempt to destroy capitalism will lead only to a transference of power from the individual to the state, and so increase the power of the latter to the point where it is bound to be a form of *despotism. *Weber suggested that democracy in its clearest form can only occur under capitalism, while others have tried to argue that capitalism is the true cause of *limited government. Against those arguments *socialists tend to urge that capitalism, which involves the accumulation of profits in hands other than those of the producer, is inherently unjust (*see* *exploitation); that its lack of *planned economy causes imbalances and inequitable distributions; and that it creates only an illusion of democracy, since it transfers power to the small class of capitalists, who remain essentially without answerability to their employees.

capitulations. **1**. Grants of extra-territorial privileges by one state to the subjects of another; specifically, exemption from jurisdiction by *municipal courts. Much used throughout the history of empire building, capitulations existed into the present century, and represented the view that law is a personal relation between subject and sovereign, attaching to the former wherever he might be. They disappeared only with the increasing *irredentism in the nations and peoples that they were used to exploit.

2. In international law, conventions between armed forces of belligerents stipulating terms of surrender of specific towns, ships and troops.

career politics. Political process which admits of description in terms appropriate to a *profession, with recognized procedures for admission into government or party, and recognized methods of self-advancement. Career politics may permit complete change of party and political doctrine in mid career (cf. the changing allegiances of President Mitterand of France). It is becoming the standard mode of political activity in Western Europe, and is perhaps to be contrasted with prevailing eighteenth- and nineteenth-century practice, in which many assemblies were constituted by unpaid representatives, and many seats were made available by tradition or patronage and occupied by citizens who had a settled expectation of a certain level of power, but often no particular desire to increase it. It is sometimes thought that such 'amateur' politics is the real index of the *hegemony of a *ruling class which, since it already possesses power, does not need to exert itself unduly in the pursuit or exercise of office. It can then regard public office as existing 'for its own sake' (which phrase the *reductionist will interpret as 'for the sake of the ruling class').

caring society. Cant phrase introduced into modern UK politics by liberal-socialist journalism, in order to denote, not a specific form of *society, but rather a particular kind of *state, actively engaged in providing for the needy, the ill, the aged and the underprivileged, by taxing the wealthy, able, middle-aged and established.

Carlyle, Thomas (1795–1881). Scottish historian and social critic, *Calvinist by upbringing, who sought in German romantic literature (especially in Goethe) a justification for the passionate rejection of all procedures (whether religious or rationalist) for the solution of political problems. Carlyle followed *Coleridge in attempting to adapt the German vision of the organic complexity of society to the critical Anglo-Saxon spirit. He wished for a society which contains the guarantees of community and stability that others had sought in the state, and this led him to reject all materialist doctrines of the nature of man. He was also suspicious of *democracy, of **laissez-faire* economics, of liberal legal philosophy, and of all attempts to override the fact of man's social existence, in favour of some *individualistic picture of human nature. He admired Frederick the Great, longed for a German conquest of Europe, and sought in German philosophy and literature that sense of the wholeness and mystery of human fulfilment which he found lacking in prevailing *Benthamite and *utilitarian conceptions of human nature.

Carlyle's *History of the French Revolution*, 1837, attempted to portray political events dramatically, as the expression of a social condition. In this and subsequent works he elaborated his vision of society as an organism, with birth, maturity, convulsion, and death. He expressed an antagonism to the *Enlightenment, and a belief that liberal opinion is a luxury, made possible by diseased social conditions, and presaging social ruin. Carlyle's criticisms of liberalism were more influential than his favoured ideal: a society founded on the worship of heroes, involving a new aristocracy construed on the model of the Calvinist elect, and with a social and economic order of a quasi-feudal kind.

cartel. An arrangement, usually between suppliers possessing some degree of mutual independence, who agree together to set prices for their products and perhaps quotas for output and investment. Legally enforceable cartels are impossible in the UK and US, being in breach of the laws controlling *monopoly, and of *anti-trust legislation; they may also, in certain circumstances, constitute a *conspiracy at common law. Nevertheless cartels exist informally without the support of any enforceable contract. There are also international cartels which escape the controls of any particular *jurisdiction.

caste. The hereditary *class system of India consists of castes, in which each person is socially equal to every other member of his caste, having the same religious rights, and often following the same occupation or profession. There are thought to be some 3,000 castes in India, reflecting stratifications of tribe, race, occupation, territory and religion (J. H. Hutton: *Caste in India*, 1951). Until recently, social mixing between castes has been difficult or impossible, and attempts to enforce it by law have met with powerful resistance. From the outside the caste system exhibits one of the most rigid of class structures, with minimum *social mobility, and maximum hereditary determination. Because it includes a definite economic stratification, it lends itself to *functional explanation in terms of economic role. However the complexity of the system is such as to defy easy analysis in such terms.

Castroism (also *Fidelismo*). The ideology and practice introduced into the government of Cuba by Fidel Castro, since his seizure of power by **coup d'état* in 1959. Castro seems not to have been a communist when he first took power, but, in a speech in 1961, he declared himself to be a *Marxist-Leninist, and thereafter began to rationalize his own *coup d'état* in the terms suggested by that label: revolution had been achieved in Cuba not by economic development, but by popular support for a guerrilla army, acting to restore rights and privileges to a people whose economic condition was in fact primitive. (*See* *focoism.) The political system in Cuba has sustained itself through incessant military activity abroad, vigorous personal leadership (*jefatura*), and abundant aid from the USSR; it seems to have evolved in the direction of centralized government, without formal *opposition, and with effective state control over most economic activity.

casuistry. Originally a casuist was a theologian, or similar learned person, who resolves conflicts of duty and questions of *conscience. Casuistry denotes the art of so describing reality, and so prescribing action, that a given set of principles can be adhered to in actual circumstances. A casuist attempts to show how a particular principle applies in a particular case, and also to extract principles that will rationalize the moral intuitions which particular cases prompt. (*See* *double effect.)

In a wider sense 'casuistry' has come to be a slightly derogatory term, for the practice of reconciling reality with *doctrine. Thus it is part of the casuistry of capitalism to argue that the seemingly unjust distributions that result from it are not unjust at all, but the necessary consequence of just (because freely contracted) relations. It is part of the casuistry of Leninism to argue that cruelties perpetrated against opponents are justified by the 'revolutionary morality' that looks to the communist future.

casus belli. Latin: cause, or ground, of war. In international law, a situation put forward by a state as justification for war. According to the UN Charter the only recognized *casus belli*, apart from those authorized by the Security Council or General Assembly, is self-defence.

catastrophe theory. A controversial branch of applied mathematics, developed by the French mathematician René Thom, which studies the transition of systems from one dynamical configuration to another. A 'catastrophe' arises when such a transition generates points of instability within the system. On passing through such a transition (as when a wave transgresses the topological laws of surface formation at its climax) a 'catastrophe' ensues, the movement of the system being determined by a distinct law from that which had previously governed it. The theory has been applied to economics, social development and the study of political institutions. Such sciences often deal with laws of development which apply up to a certain point, but which predict only a collapse of existing structures beyond that point. The Marxist theory of revolution as precipitated by a dynamical *contradiction has been seen as a kind of catastrophe theory. The more adventurous applications of the theory remain however highly controversial.

Catholic Action. Organized action of a social and political kind on the part of *Roman Catholic laity. The term derives from a movement founded in 1922 by Pope Pius XI, to encourage flexible lay *propaganda under the direction of the clergy.

Catholicism. *see* *Roman Catholicism.

caucus. Originally US term, denoting a private meeting of members of a party prior to an election, in order to harmonize interests and policy. Since 1878 it has been used in the UK and US to denote the influencing of government by secret, semi-secret or exclusive organizations within the officially recognized party-political system, as when a group of 'hard-liners' meet in advance of official gatherings in order to decide on concerted action, while keeping other party members in ignorance of their aims and methods.

cause of action. The facts which give a citizen the right to bring an action in law. (Hence 'just cause'.)

censorship. The office of censor was a Roman magistracy, first held in 443 BC, with the function of reviewing the rolls of citizens, knights and senators, regulating morals and ritually purifying the people. From this office derives the modern use of the term 'censorship' to denote the practice of examining, restricting and prohibiting public acts, expressions of opinion, and artistic performances. It takes the following forms:

(i) Direct interference by the state prior to publication of offending material ('preventive' censorship). This is common in the USSR and its satellites, but not in the UK, US or Western Europe, and is thought to be unconstitutional in the US (*see* *prior restraint). It has been abolished in the UK with the disappearance of the office of Lord Chamberlain in 1968 – always excepting 'classified' material (*see* *official secrets) publication of which cannot be justified before a court of law.

(ii) Subsequent prosecution before a court of law ('punitive' censorship). This is the standard action of the state in the UK and US against *obscenity, blasphemy, and *sedition. Usually various defences are recognized, and the outcome depends upon judicial process.

(iii) Indirect control through responsible but autonomous bodies, such as the churches, and the Press Council, which have no legal, but some coercive, power.

(iv) Indirect control through private actions for libel (which is to be contrasted with 'seditious libel', a UK action by the state, corresponding to the 'slander of the state' familiar in the USSR and its dependencies). Private action for libel may be expensive and troublesome, and it is sometimes thought not to provide sufficient protection for the 'right of *privacy', and so to require supplementation by the creation of a criminal offence.

(v) Self-imposed censorship, as in the 'decision not to publish' based upon settled expectations as to what is socially and politically acceptable.

The justifications for state censorship will, as with all questions of state action against the citizen, lean on either utility or justice (or both), and will differ depending upon which concept is principally emphasized. Censorship may be held to contribute to political stability (and therefore to the sum of present *utility), but does it follow that the state has a right to censor? (May it not be an injustice against those who desire to publish or become acquainted with the material in question?) When liberal thinkers emphasize the limitation that censorship places on human freedom they usually (*see* *Mill) interpret the concept of freedom so that questions of freedom and questions of justice are intimately conjoined (a man being *free* to the extent that there is no interference with his rights of action). *See* *law and morality, *pornography.

census. Under Roman law, the registration of citizens and their property, for purposes of taxation and suffrage. Now used more widely, to denote any act (usually an *act of state) whereby information is collected relating to the number, situation and outlook of citizens. The importance of censuses and *opinion polls in modern politics furthers the view that the legitimacy of government depends on the opinions and situation of the governed.

centralization. The process whereby executive, administrative, economic and juridical power is concentrated in a centre, defined either geographically (e.g. as the capital city), or in terms of some single organization (such as a civil service, or a *party). Centralism, sometimes seen as an administrative necessity, is in conflict with the demand for *devolution, and for laws, institutions and economic relations which reflect more nearly the disparate local identities that may compose a state. In places where local affiliations are strong (e.g. parts of Africa) centralization can often be achieved only by force, law alone carrying no weight of authority. *Tocqueville distinguished two distinct kinds of centralization, that of administration, and that of political power, and praised the US for the extent to which it had achieved decentralization of the second kind.

centre. The supposed political position somewhere between the *left and the *right, where political views are either sufficiently indeterminate, or sufficiently imbued with the spirit of compromise, to be thought acceptable to as large a body of citizens as would be capable of accepting anything. The 'centre' is an important concept in UK politics, and the persistent aim for it – while it may involve divesting oneself of all coherent political beliefs – is nevertheless considered justifiable to the extent that politics is constituted, not by consistent doctrine, but by successful practice. The centre is seen as representing political stability, social continuity, and a recognized *consensus. It is also thought (but this is a confusion) that the centre position will be *moderate. 'Retreat from the centre' is an expression used by P. Mayer to denote the disposition among many modern politicians and intellectuals to regard the 'centre' position as unsafe, because of the abandonment of principle, and the complexity of untrustworthy *alliances that it requires, and because the confession of ignorance and uncertainty, while honest, is neither politically nor intellectually respectable.

centrism. 1. The doctrine that one should pursue the political *centre.

2. A movement within the Polish Communist Party, associated with Gomulka, which sought to liberalize Poland after Stalin's death, and which was opposed to the *extremism of the rival factions, especially that of Moczar. Centrism tried to adapt international socialism to the Polish context, by accommodating the church, working-class movements, and private property.

ceremony. The public practice whereby something is displayed, enacted or recalled, in such a way as to endow it with a symbolic value and a lasting social significance. Some follow Yeats ('A Prayer for my Daughter') in associating the decline of ceremony with a loss of innocence and grace in social relations, seeing ceremony as the force which, enacting a shared condition, makes social nature intelligible. Others regard ceremony as a form of constraint, and therefore inherently in need of justification, perhaps all the more so because of the extent to which the interests of an *establishment may be advanced by exploiting the common need for and pleasure in obligatory ceremonies.

Some liberals consider that ceremony is a feature of *civil society, and not one for which the state should take responsibility; ceremony must therefore be either spontaneous or false. But this seems to overlook the existence of ceremonies of state. These are nowhere more emphasized than by *totalitarian regimes, which attempt to create highly symbolic demonstrations of unity designed to impress on the subject the ineluctable nature of the political order which surrounds him, and also to celebrate and exhibit for the benefit of external powers both the reality of that order and the subject's all-consuming commitment to it. In this case ceremony is monopolized by the state, to form part of the enterprise of *government through symbols. But liberal democracies may also depend in mysterious ways upon ceremonies of state. The ceremonial institution of monarchy in the UK seems to inspire more affection than any other aspect of the constitution, and more respect than any political party, perhaps because it manifests itself so briefly, and to so little effect.

Ceremonies are important examples of activities which are entirely focused on themselves, having the kind of 'purposefulness without purpose' which Kant ascribed to the object of *aesthetic interest. Hence they fulfil the conservative ideal of action which inspires maximum loyalty while doing minimum damage.

chain of command. Suppose A has power and authority to command B; B to command C, C to command D, and so on. Suppose too that B is answerable to A for C's actions, C answerable to B for D's and so on. Then there exists a 'chain of command' from A downwards. Some forms of *constitutionalism insist that the true aim of government is to maintain this chain of command, by guaranteeing that when any place in it falls empty, it is at once filled by someone similarly *empowered*, and similarly *answerable*. An *office in politics may then be defined as a place in the chain of command, with recognized procedures for entry into and departure from it.

charisma. New Testament Greek: a gift of divine grace. Term used by *Weber to denote a kind of *power over others which is also perceived as *authority by those subject to it. The holder of charisma may be a human being, in which case his authority might be interpreted in terms of a myth of his divine mission, insight, or moral attributes. Alternatively, it is sometimes said, charisma can attach to an office, in which case it may be associated with an idea of that office as enshrining the history, legitimacy and mystery of a social order. Weber distinguishes charismatic from traditional and legal-rational kinds of authority. However, it is not clear how far the 'charisma of office' can be detached from the disposition to feel the power of, and attribute authority to, traditions and systems of law. (*See* *routinization.)

charity. 1. In moral contexts, 'charity' denotes the Christian virtue of love of one's neighbour. This is a distinct mode of love, being neither erotic, nor familial, nor friendly, nor reducible to any universal sense of duty (though *see* *Kant, who thought otherwise). St Paul wrote that 'though I bestow all my goods to feed the poor, and though I give my body to be burned, and have not charity, it profiteth me nothing' (I Cor. 13, 3). The famous declamation from which this comes conveys the widely accepted view that, while the end result of charity may be the betterment of the human condition, this is not its motive. What leads a person to charity is concern for *this* (irreplaceable) person, or *this* (irreplaceable) group of people, in *this* predicament. To put it another way, the end of charity is universal, but its motive is concrete. The maxim that 'charity begins at home' is a simple way of giving voice to this idea. (*See* *humanitarianism.)

2. In political discussion, charity has sometimes been held to depend upon social arrangements involving private *property. It requires that people be able to *provide* for others, which in turn requires the exercise of *gift. Universal redistribution, making the needs and powers of all people equal, might also be seen as tending to the abolition of the charitable motive, which is (to put it tendentiously) that of rejoicing in the power conferred by property through the act of giving it away. Perhaps, therefore, charity is what *Hume called an 'artificial virtue', one reflecting an actual social condition which it may not be desirable to uphold.

3. In legal contexts, the specificity of the charitable motive, together with the universality of its end, are obliquely acknowledged in its definition. A charity must benefit (according to UK and US law) some body of the public, but not necessarily a considerable body. To prove charitable status it must be shown that the motive is either sufficiently general, or specific only in the way that charity is specific. Thus the benefit conferred should not be by way of ancillary reward to a group of employees, nor a gift by way of friendship, nor any other gesture of self-interest or personal affection. The founding of a school, a hospital, a church are all allowed by this criterion, as are far more specific intentions, such as the relief of poverty in a particular parish.

Both English and US law follow judicial interpretation of a definition of charity given in the preamble to the Charitable Uses Act 1601, which defines charity by a list of examples, many of them now redundant. By a quirk of legal history, it is uncertain whether this act has now been abolished. In any case, judicial interpretation allows four kinds of charitable use: relief of poverty, advancement of learning and education, advancement of religion, and other purposes in similar spirit. Any charity, being already of public benefit, is exempt from tax. It therefore becomes a substantial political issue whether certain institutions (e.g. private schools) should be given charitable status, or even whether the law of charity, and the fiscal privilege associated with it, should survive. Moreover, as a *common law matter, the actual recognition of something as a charity is a matter for *judicial decision, and judicial decisions, say some, must inevitably reflect the interests of the property-owning class to which judges belong. Moves to undo the law of charity have been contemplated by socialist parties in the West, and no such law seems to exist in any legal system constructed on the Soviet model.

Many thinkers of a liberal persuasion also object to the existing law of charity, in that it extends fiscal benefits to institutions which may be of no true public value, and withholds them from associations based on *self-help, since the motive of these is too interested to be charitable. Thus the British Limbless Ex-Servicemen's Association is a charity, while the National League of the Blind, being organized around the principle of self-help, is not.

charter. 1. In law, a deed, granted as a rule by the sovereign power, conferring powers, rights, privileges and immunities on a subject institution or township. An important instrument in the *delegation of authority.

2. Charter of Liberties and Privileges. The first enactment of the first assembly of New York Colony, passed 1683, and later disallowed by the English Parliament.

3. UN Charter. The Charter of the United Nations Organization, drafted in 1945, consisting of a preamble and seventy articles, setting out principles of action in respect of threats to peace, instruments and procedures of international justice, and general rules for economic, social and political cooperation. Powers conferred on the Security Council (China, France, the USSR, UK and US, together with six others elected for terms of two years) exceed any that have previously been exercised by an international body, and use of these powers has changed the pattern of international politics, by giving to certain states with conflicting interests the role of supervising peace and war. The Security Council can operate only because each power has a *veto, which can effectively prevent any power from being overruled in any matter that is important to its foreign policy. The Charter thus confers as much responsibility on the major powers as is prudent, given their determination to have their own way in all things that matter.

4. Charter movements. Movements, such as the Charter 77 movement in Czechoslovakia, which present charters of rights and immunities, supposedly already recognized or implied in law, and then attempt to persuade the state to uphold them (in this case vainly).

Chartism. Working-class organization founded in England in 1838, in order to express dissatisfaction with the 1832 Reform Bill, and to seek further electoral reform. Chartism is named from the 'People's Charter' which demanded, among other things, universal male suffrage without qualification of property. It impressed on British labour the necessity for political status as a means towards economic advancement, and thus set the type for UK working-class movements, involving gestures towards trade union organization, provisions for strike action, and the recruiting of a broad base of support among the urban *proletariat.

chauvinism. Term derived from the name of Nicolas Chauvin, a French soldier fanatically devoted to Napoleon, and originally used to signify *idolatrie napoléonienne*. It was later applied to bellicose and uncritical devotion to one's country or leader, when sufficiently *xenophobic. It was further extended – as in the usage 'male chauvinism' – to denote any equally bellicose and uncritical attitude which exalts the virtues of one group (in this case men) and disparages those of another (in this case women). The general principle behind the extension is this: chauvinism is held to be a kind of self-protective hostility, which conceals the inability of the subject to enter into relations with others on equal terms. By representing the world as fraught with immovable inequalities, it appeases anxiety by making equal relations impossible.

checks and balances. A phrase which probably derives from *Jefferson, *Notes on the State of Virginia*, query XII: 'the powers of government should be so divided and balanced among several bodies of magistracy, as that none could transcend their legal limits, without being effectively checked and restrained by the others' (the direct influence on Jefferson being *Montesquieu). The phrase was similarly used by Walter Bagehot (*The English Constitution*, 1867), to denote constitutional devices whereby any power within a state can be prevented from becoming absolute by being balanced against, or checked by, another power. Such constitutional devices include the *separation of powers, *judicial review, and *bicameral government. Collectively they determine the process whereby a constitution imposes its own mould on all decisions and actions propagated through it, and reduces the prominence of particular parties, offices and individuals. Bagehot himself thought that there was a fundamental difference between the UK and the US constitution in respect of checks and balances, the first being such that the 'supreme determining power is upon all points the same', while in the second 'the supreme power is divided between many bodies and functionaries', a feature which he thought responsible for much US indecisiveness in the mid nineteenth century, since all power, even the sovereign power, as it is exercised in international relations, could be checked absolutely. Ultimately, Bagehot thought, the maintenance of checks and balances involves adherence to 'the principle of having many sovereigns, and hoping that their multitude may atone for their inferiority'. Others have objected to the mechanical model of society assumed in the phrase 'The trouble with the theory is that government is not a machine but a living thing. . . No living thing can have its organs offset against each other as checks, and live' (Woodrow Wilson). *See also* *body politic.

Christendom. 'The dominions of Christ': the collective name for nations and states the subjects of which profess Christianity. It was an important conception in international politics, when such subjects, by virtue of their faith, were bound by allegiance to the Pope. It was also of some importance subsequently, for as long as it could be assumed that the nations of Christendom would act in concert on international issues which relate to faith and doctrine, but was revealed as a moribund idea by the Holy Alliance in the nineteenth century. The concept remains interesting partly because it contains the idea of international *jurisdiction, and partly because it indicates a common source of law throughout Western countries, and a common ground for the belief in *natural law.

Christian democrats. The *moderate Roman Catholic parties in Belgium, France, the German Federal Republic (most German Protestants are in East Germany), Italy and the Netherlands. Originally *left, or left of *centre parties (e.g. as founded in Uruguay in 1910, and in Italy in 1919), they tended at first to enter into alliances with *socialist and *communist parties. Even in 1965 the Chilean Christian Democrat Party was prepared openly to condemn capitalism as 'merciless' and 'degrading of human dignity', although it also condemned communism as a form of slavery. Since 1945, especially in Europe, Christian democrats have tended to be moderate *reformist parties, professing *Christian affiliation, and representing, especially in Italy, a middle class anxious for stability, and hostile both to socialism and to communism.

Christian socialism. A nineteenth-century movement of social reform within the *Anglican Church, which owed its inspiration to *Carlyle and its opportunity to *Chartism. It saw the Anglican Church as having a vital role to play, both spiritual and social, in rectifying the social injustice and suffering caused by industrial capitalism. Its own vision of the alternative tended towards nostalgic medievalism, involving an admiration for crafts as opposed to manufactures, and a belief in cooperative production and ownership. Christian socialists sought to spread their movement to working people, in order to give enactment to their (perhaps somewhat *bourgeois) views of the dignity of labour. Neither the establishment of cooperatives nor the institution of evening classes were able to persuade the workers to adopt the prescriptions offered to them.

Christianity. The most important force in shaping the constitutions of the states of Europe, and the intermediary through which Roman law and classical morality and institutions were imposed upon our ancestors. The belief in the *church as the body of Christ in the world led to the doctrine of *ecclesiastical jurisdiction, and hence to the modern forms of *international law. It also gave rise to the problem of the relation between church and state, left largely unresolved into the present century, and thence to the medieval formulations of the problem of *political obligation. The politically significant aspects of Christian doctrine are impossible to summarize, but the following deserve mention:

(i) As in all monotheistic religions, ultimate allegiance is owed not to the *sovereign but to God, whose kingdom is not of this world. The supreme guiding principle in individual life is personal salvation, which is God's sole purpose in the creation of any individual soul, and this must therefore be put before all worldly causes.

(ii) *Charity is the fount of virtue, and pride is the fount of sin: this doctrine requires the relief of the miseries of others, and a reluctance to pursue worldly glory or power (except as a means to the exercise of charity and to the worship of God). A policy of concern for, and identification with, the underprivileged (sometimes advanced as The Imitation of Christ) has often seemed to follow from this.

(iii) The doctrine of the incarnation, i.e. that God is identical with Christ and dwells among us, as a suffering and redeeming presence, reinforces the belief that man in his compassionate aspect is nearer to God, whereas man in his pride is cast out.

The third doctrine, glossed in various ways, may provide the (mystical) thought which both reconciles the other two, and also licenses political action. For example, the traditional *Roman Catholic doctrine of the church as the body of Christ has enabled men to pursue worldly power and authority in the name of religion, and to avoid the conflict of allegiance between this world and the next. Recent Christian thinkers, more vividly impressed by the duty of charity than by the transcendence of God, have interpreted the incarnation as an invitation to political activity in the name of *social justice. The moral doctrines of the Sermon on the Mount – in which humility, meekness, poverty, and the position of the underdog are all condoned or praised – could be interpreted in an opposite sense, as inviting us to ensure that as many people as possible possess those attributes, and so come closer to salvation. Like all great religions, Christianity contains enough contradictions on these fundamental issues to enable its individual consolations to extend to people of all persuasions and in every age, so dignifying every manner of worldly activity – from the provision of guns to terrorists to the assertion of absolute monarchical power – with the character of spiritual vocation.

church. 1. Any linked configuration of religious institutions, usually with a professional priesthood.

2. In traditional and Christian teaching, the church is not just a voluntary *association of individual believers, but a *corporation, endowed with the Holy Spirit, and constituting the bodily presence of God in the world. It is characterized by unity, holiness, catholicity, and apostolicity, the last including the 'apostolic succession' under which the Pope claims authority in an unbroken chain, through St Peter, from Christ. The *Reformation introduced the modern conception of the church as an invisible body, constituted of the saved, whose membership is known only to God; together with the rival conception of the church as a visible body whose institutional form must vary from country to country, in order to preserve its spiritual essence in the contrasting conditions which surround it, and in order to avoid being subject to a potentially corrupting worldly power. (For a yet more localized conception, *see* *Anglicanism.) In both cases the church is given a partially transcendent identity, which separates it from its members and so ensures its notional survival through every diminution in its worldly influence.

3. In many nonconformist Christian practices, the term 'church' is used simply to denote a voluntary association of believers, for the purposes of religious instruction and celebration. It may not involve a professional priesthood, may have no hierarchy of authority, and no rules other than adherence to certain items of doctrine. The association is more like a club than it is like the church, as traditionally described.

church and state. The relation between church and state has been one of the most lasting issues in European politics, and continues to be a dominant political issue in parts of Eastern Europe. Either a church is so constituted as to be subject to the sovereign power, in which case it is 'established', or it is not, in which case it exists within the state not merely as an *autonomous institution but as a rival source of authority. Certain doctrines of *sovereignty (e.g., that of *Hobbes) hold the second alternative to be inherently destructive, since if the authority of some power within the state is not absolute then that power cannot be sovereign. Other doctrines attempt to explain how men can owe *political* *allegiance to one power and religious allegiance to another, even though, over many issues, the two could conflict. The church can give spiritual and moral guidance only at the risk of affecting actions in which the state has an interest. The clash between the two institutions becomes apparent when the state forbids the church some function considered necessary to its mission – e.g. education. If the state is able in fact and not just in law to do this, then the state has *de facto* sovereignty, such as was exercised through the French Law of Associations 1901, which effectively brought all the activities of religious congregations within the governance of the state. Equally, the two institutions may gain power from their harmony, and a church, in teaching obedience and humility, may act as a politically conservative force.

Full legal establishment of a church may result from its attempt to enshrine its own authority in law – as advocated by *Hooker in his defence of Anglicanism – or from the state's attempt to subjugate, and even to eliminate, the power of the church – as in the USSR, where ecclesiastical constitution and even liturgy are governed by the state, while all religious education is forbidden, and atheism propagated as part of the ideological commitment expected of the citizen. The peculiar balance found for several centuries in the Anglican Church is a reflection of a widespread political and religious consensus, the dissolution of which has led to a new crisis (however diminished) in the relations of church and state. Equally, the persistent failure of the Polish state (as governed by the Communist Party) either to *ratify or to oppose the authority of the church has led to a similar crisis of a far more cataclysmic kind.

The nature of such crises was frequently discussed by medieval thinkers, and notably by *Dante, in his *De Monarchia*, *circa* 1309: the church, as God's will in the world, calls on us freely to accept its yoke, and so to recognize that its authority binds not through tyranny but through love. The church cannot impose itself by force without negating the principle of its own authority. But the authority of the church is to be distinguished from the power of worldly princes. The latter is good only to the extent that it freely aligns itself with the former: otherwise it is a perverted power, which negates the freedom of its subjects. Hence power and authority must be separated by the two institutions, so as the better to combine; the first lies with princes, the second with the church. Hence in making *itself* into a princedom the church, Dante argued, had offended against its mission.

Cicero, Marcus Tullius (106–43 BC). Roman orator and statesman, who devoted his enforced retirement to composing works of philosophy, law and politics in which he attempted to adapt and systematize doctrines already expounded by the Greeks, in particular by *Plato and the *Stoics. His writings were extremely influential in transmitting Hellenic conceptions of the state to later thinkers, and his advocacy of the synthesis of *philosophy and *rhetoric provided the foundation for many subsequent theories of political education.

The highest human *virtue resides in the possession and employment of knowledge in practical affairs: philosophy provides the knowledge, while rhetoric makes it effective. The individual virtue generated by their union defines also an ideal of political order: a constitutional republic, in which not force but persuasion is the instrument of power and where monarchy, aristocracy and democracy are combined in a stable equilibrium. The best means to the acquisition of virtue is *liberal education, in which theoretical knowledge and practical skill are organically mingled. Cicero gave an extended account of the virtuous man (*De Officiis*), emphasizing the public responsibility which conditions his private satisfactions. In his two political works, the *Republic* (largely paraphrased from Plato and surviving only in fragmentary form) and the *De Legibus* (also surviving only in part), Cicero gave a developed account of what public responsibility amounts to. The second work introduced with admirable clarity the distinction between *power and *authority, as it has entered into much subsequent political thinking. It also provided an extended celebration of Roman law as an exemplification of constitutional authority, expounded the principles of Stoic philosophy as a basis for political life, and thereby transmitted Stoic doctrines of *natural law to Christian thinkers.

Cicero's works have been thought (partly on his own admission) to be more eloquent than original. Nevertheless, their influence – on medieval thought through the famous 'dream of Scipio' contained in the *Republic*, and on Renaissance thought through the *De Officiis* – has been as great as that of any of the Roman texts, passing ancient ideas of virtue and order into the repertoire of Christian philosophy.

citizen. **1**. The legal conception of an individual who owes *allegiance to, and receives protection from, a *state. Conditions of citizenship are determined for each state in accordance with its own legal provisions, and it is not necessary that everyone who resides within the *jurisdiction of a particular state should be a citizen of that state, even when he is a 'national' of that state and citizen of no other. Such 'statelessness' is now rare, although it was common in the ancient world. International law, however, does not recognize the distinction between citizenship and nationality and regards the first as completely determined by the second.

2. An ideological preference for the term 'citizen' over the rival 'subject' has been frequent since the American and French revolutions, it being assumed that the latter suggests a condition of subservience which the former does not. More philosophically, one can be a 'citizen' only within a certain *constitution, which defines the rights and duties of citizenship, but one can be *subject* to an unconstituted power. In political philosophy it has therefore been of great importance since ancient times to attempt to give the basis of citizenship and so justify any given legal determination. *Aristotle defines a citizen as anyone who can 'hold office', and subsequent extensions of this idea have involved the thought that citizenship (as opposed to subjecthood) is possible only where there are sufficient *offices open to all. This thought is fundamental to modern *constitutionalism, and, provided the term 'office' in not interpreted too narrowly, can be seen to capture much of the idea of mutual *responsibility invoked in the legal definition.

city state. *See *polis*.

civic. Latin: *civicus*, belonging to citizens. Now usually used in the sense 'of, or pertaining to, a town or city', as in 'civic feeling', 'civic pride', 'civic amenities', which denote specific relations between people and their place of residence. Some argue that it is only when towns inspire civic feeling that the state can command loyalty. Hence the nature and origin of civic feeling have been of concern to political thinkers. The following have been suggested as contributing to it: established and diversified employment, recognized local customs, civic ceremonies, congenial and stable architecture, and, of course, prosperity and trade. By contrast, migrancy, unemployment, large-scale demolition and neglect, the absorption of *local government into national party politics – all these things might seem to take civic feeling away. The conditions mentioned have been held to stem from the rapid flow of *capital from place to place, together with local specialisation in production, which causes towns to flourish and collapse in ways unintelligible to their occupants; though doubtless this is only one among several possible explanations. The Marxist idea of *proletarian consciousness is meant to suggest that the worker under developed capitalist conditions can acquire no civic but only a *class sentiment, since he is forced to find his identity not in local attachments, but in the governing principle of his life – his place in the relations of production.

civil disobedience. Expression given currency by Henry David Thoreau (1817–62), in an essay entitled *On the Duty of Civil Disobedience*, 1849, defending a decision not to pay taxes to a government which sanctioned slavery. The strategy of civil disobedience was made famous by the Indian statesman Mahatma Gandhi, who first employed it in 1913, and in 1920 the Indian National Congress voted overwhelmingly to adopt the strategy in order to undermine British imperial government. The phrase is now used to denote any acts of overt and deliberate lawbreaking, or acts of contested legality, which have the aim of bringing to public notice either the actual illegitimacy of certain laws, or their lack of moral or rational justification. Its success is dependent on the extent to which it can prevent or delay the judicial process. It is clear that in the most tyrannical of states civil disobedience is unthinkable as a strategy of political action, since it will be scotched as soon as it is attempted. The question whether and when civil disobedience is permissible is one part of the general question of *political obligation.

civil liberties. *See* *civil rights, *liberties.

civil rights. Those *rights which belong to the citizen by virtue of his citizenship alone, and which are protected by law. To be distinguished from *human rights, which may or may not be so protected, and which belong to all men everywhere, whether or not enshrined in law. In US political practice the two kinds of right are not always distinguished, partly because it is thought that the constitution, through its *bill of rights, and certain acts of Congress, makes all human rights into civil rights. Moreover, to deny a civil right is to deny a human right – i.e. the right to be given what has been promised. In the UK the reference to civil rights is less frequent than that to civil *liberties. Whether or not the two ideas are the same is a disputed question. On some views rights are always permissions: i.e. they consist in injunctions to others (including the state) to allow the individual to proceed about some action. On this view, to talk of civil rights and of civil liberties is to talk in different terms of the same thing. However, it is clear that not all rights which are claimed are like that: some speak, for example, of a *right to work, which imposes on others not just the obligation to leave me free to work, but also the obligation to provide work so that I may exercise this freedom. (Is this second view coherent? For this and related questions, *see* *rights.)

The civil rights movement came into existence in the US in order to enforce rights guaranteed by the constitution but, by historical and political circumstances, denied to blacks. It culminated in the Civil Rights Act 1964, containing additional provisions against discrimination. However, it is clear that the passing of a new law cannot in itself give effect to laws which already exist but have proved ineffective. Hence the concentration of the activities of the movement on seeing that the law is not only clear, but also enforced.

Civil rights movements elsewhere have sometimes had the appearance (and perhaps, as in Northern Ireland, the reality) of *front organizations for less innocent political enterprises. Thus the movements in the USSR and its satellites to uphold rights guaranteed under the written constitution, or by virtue of the Helsinki Accord, 1975, are generally treated as subversive and 'anti-socialist', and suppressed accordingly. The systematic nature of the state opposition to such movements eloquently illustrates the proposition that a piece of paper *describing* a constitution does not *create* a constitution, and without the fulfilment of further conditions (such as *judicial independence) remains a piece of paper. The relative effectiveness of the US movement is perhaps partly a consequence of the fact that the rights pursued really are *guaranteed* by the constitution, and can be fought for in open court.

civil service. The body of full-time officers (other than political or judicial officers) employed by the state in the administration of civil (as opposed to military) affairs. While containing many (and increasingly many) branches, it is fundamentally divided between the administration of home and of foreign affairs.

The genesis of the modern forms of civil service marks a radical change in the manner and content of government. In the UK the hierarchical nature of the institutions of administration – with complex rules of *answerability, careers open to talent, successive dignities and honours expected if not by right at least by convention, the whole culminating in the permanent 'under-secretaries' answerable to ministers of the crown – all this evolved from the structure of the nineteenth-century Indian civil service and its predecessor, the administrative section of the British East India Company. It is significant that an under-secretary is called 'permanent', in order to distinguish him from the merely transitory minister from whom in theory he receives instructions, but to whom in practice he may sometimes dictate. The French civil service reflects an older structure, having emerged under the absolute monarchs of the seventeenth and eighteenth centuries, while in the US the composition and structure of the civil service still expresses presidential patronage and nomination, careers being pursued at the lower rather than at the higher level of office.

The growth of the modern civil service raises large questions of *legitimacy and *right. For example, does a civil servant have a right to strike against his employer (the state)? US law says no, while UK law says yes (with certain important exceptions), perhaps because the question has never been fully considered by Parliament. Even in the UK the civil service is divided among itself as to the extent to which it should exercise this right. Does a civil servant have a right to engage in party political activity? Both US and UK law say no, on the grounds that this undermines the principle of *representation, transferring political activity from the chamber of elected representatives to the hidden corridors of administrative power. Clearly, whatever view is taken, concern over this question indicates that the civil service is not *merely* an administrative organ, and thus the prospect of a systematically disloyal civil service is one that no government, and no state, can contemplate with indifference. Some have held out this fact in support of the US system, in which the senior offices of the service are filled by political appointment, or even in support of *democratic centralism, according to which the party in power also fills every important office in the administrative machine.

civil society. 1. Term increasingly popular in the eighteenth century, and introduced into political theory largely as a result of *social contract doctrine. It denotes the state of society in which patterns of association are accepted and endorsed by the members. Most users of the term were influenced by *state of nature theory, seeing the individual as an atomic constituent of the civil society, which is composed by contract, consent or submission from these self-dependent atoms. Hence the term is often placed in inverted commas by *Marx and his followers, to denote the (to them untenable) assumption of the extra-social individual (see, for example, *Grundrisse*, 1,1).

2. In *Hegel: civil society is not *formed* by contract but is the *sphere* of contract, i.e. of free association between individuals. As such it is not a complete entity but one aspect (or 'moment') of the political order, another aspect of which is the *state. As a result of Hegel's view many political theorists now distinguish 'civil society' from 'state', using the first to denote forms of association which are spontaneous, customary, and in general not dependent upon law, and the second to denote the legal and political institutions which protect, endorse, and bring to completion the powerful but inarticulate forces of social union. Accepting such a distinction it would perhaps be right also to accept another: that between 'civil society' and 'society' *simpliciter*, the first denoting only those associations which *also* have a political aspect, the second denoting all associations generally.

civilian. 1. Traditionally, one who studied the civil law.

2. In theological usage, one who bases his values in secular considerations, especially in the virtues of *civility, as opposed to divine command.

3. (Now most frequent): a person or body not engaged in military activities. (Hence, by extension, 'non-military', as in 'civilian clothes'.)

Modern political questions about the status of civilians (sense 3.) in time of war are fraught with difficulty, just as are the associated questions concerning the existence and nature of universal *human rights, to be respected in every circumstance. This is evidently a consequence of the modern practice of 'total war' which involves acts of aggression against every citizen of a hostile state, whether or not he is himself engaged in military acts.

civility. **1**. Term often used by sixteenth-century political writers to denote civil order and government.

2. The virtue of the citizen, hence the kind of behaviour appropriate to 'good citizenship'. In particular, those parts of 'good manners' which enable people to accept one another as members of a common social order, and so treat one another with due regard for social wellbeing and quotidian moral rights.

civilization. The condition of society which is generally contrasted with its undeveloped, or 'barbarous', condition and in which, it is supposed, refined and not easily obtained advantages exist, usually in conjunction with refined and not easily obtained disasters.

The concept has played an important part in defining the aims of nineteenth- and twentieth-century politics, and various attempts have been made to define it more precisely. Thus *Coleridge (*On* *the Constitution of Church and State*, 1830) distinguishes civilization, which is the 'mixed good' consequent on general material and scientific progress, from 'cultivation', which is the unmixed good of a mind in which feeling, thought and potential have developed in harmony (*see* *culture). From the point of view of usage this distinction is an artificial one, but from the point of view of theory it is of some importance. Thus it is integral to many forms of *cultural conservatism to oppose the unqualified pursuit of material advance, and to seek to overcome political instabilities and political dissatisfactions not through economic growth, but through education. The education in question will be *humane, united to a tradition of thought and action, and expressive of a partly sceptical, partly dignifying vision of the complexity of human arrangements. Such an education, it is sometimes thought, is as likely to be impeded as propagated by material and scientific development: this is the thought behind Coleridge's distinction.

civitas. Latin term used concretely to denote the union of citizens within a state or commonwealth, and abstractly to denote the condition and rights of the citizen. In *Cicero, the term is of great importance in translating all those notions that had been associated by the Greeks with the **polis*, and which were later associated with the *state.

class. **1**. A general term subsuming all those distinctions between people which involve unequal but systematic distributions of *privileges, thus covering distinctions of rank, *caste, *estate, *status, degree, and class in sense 2., but not distinctions of *group, *role or *office.

2. Usually a theoretical term, occurring as part of an *explanation* of systematic inequalities. When so used it becomes necessary to distinguish the easily observable features which make us believe a person to be of a certain class from those features, perhaps not easily observable, which determine to what class he actually belongs. Thus in England someone may be assigned to a certain class on the basis of accent, manners, title, and membership of a social circle. In America material wealth, the nature of work, and access to leisure and luxury are likely to be given greater prominence. Theorists dispute, however, over the underlying distinctions (if there be any) of which these features are signs. Consider English upper-class characteristics: are these signs of *power or of *authority? Are they signs of economic or political position? Do they convey a particular *class consciousness which causes those who possess it to enter into privileged relation with others of their kind? Sociological theories attempt to answer such questions, some (e.g. *Weber) finding the essence of class to reside in 'life chances', some finding it in separate social or economic functions, and so on. One difficulty for such theories is that part of what makes a person upper class may be that he is taken as such by others who are upper class. So that access to a class is often achieved by representing oneself as already belonging to it. *See* *social mobility.

3. In *Marxian and similar theories, the term 'class' is used as a technical term associated with a theory of ownership and control. It denotes positions in the system of *production relations, which are held to explain all such characteristics of class-recognition as those referred to above. If an 'upper-class mentality' appears to survive in the absence of any shared economic position then this is only a lingering after-image that will vanish as economic reality makes itself perceivable. (Thus the Faubourg society described by Proust is merely the ghost of an upper class, sitting crowned upon the economic grave thereof.) For the Marxist the principal theoretical classifications are those of *master and *slave, *patrician and *plebeian, *lord and *serf (in *feudalism), and *bourgeois and *proletarian (in *capitalism).

Whether or not the Marxist theory is accepted, economic position is given increasing prominence in theories of class membership. Thus it is usual in England to speak of the lower (or working) class, the lower middle class, the middle middle class, the upper middle class, and the upper class. And since these are loosely identified in practice with labour in the first case, trade in the second, profession in the third, credit in the fourth, and landed nobility in the fifth, it is tempting to think that what is being described are fundamental distinctions of economic function. Those impressed by this idea have sometimes thought that two variables are needed in order to explain actual social inequalities: class and status (thus Weber).

In all usages it is important to distinguish theories which make it possible for classes as a whole to move from some lower to a higher position, and those which define classes in *terms* of their position, so that classes cannot move. Although Marx adopts a definition of the second kind, there is a tendency in Marxist writing to dramatize history by speaking of whole classes as though they move upwards and downwards through the social and economic hierarchy. This may be true of individual members of a class, but it can never be true of the class.

class consciousness. A term that seems to be used in two senses, to denote either:

1. the individual's sense of himself as belonging to a social *class, or

2. those features of the individual's outlook and understanding which are to be explained by his membership of a social class.

The first is sometimes distinguished from the second by referring to it as consciousness of class **identity*. This may, for example, be manifest in loyalty to one's own class, and hostility to, or suspicion towards, members of another. Depending on the theory of class adopted, either 1. or 2. or both may be taken as in part *constitutive* of class (as in E. P. Thompson: *The Making of the English Working Class*, 1968), or as ancillary to (and perhaps explained by) class (as in classical *Marxism, which distinguishes, in this respect, the class-in-itself from the class-for-itself). The second idea is more congenial to those who wish to separate matters of consciousness from the 'material conditions' which underly them (*see* *materialism). But it imposes the very real task of describing the precise nature of class consciousness, and explaining such things as social aspiration (the desire to change one's class, when this does not seem to be primarily a desire to change one's material condition), *snobbery (whether normal or inverse), and the relative absence of class consciousness in the US (as contrasted with the UK) despite very great differences of material wealth, and despite the economic relations definitive of *capitalism.

class struggle. According to much *socialist theory, the class *conflict that is the driving force of history (*see* **Communist Manifesto*), being at the root of all major changes in law, institutions, morality and religion.

*Marxists see the class struggle as intensifying under capitalism to the point of *revolution, when the whole social order is overturned in the interests of a rising class. According to this theory the class struggle is always a reality in capitalist society, but is not always apparent to its participants, since antagonistic *class consciousness may not arise, the *bourgeois devices of *legitimation sufficing to establish an uneasy acceptance of the **status quo*. Lenin went on to argue that the capitalist proletariat may achieve 'trade-union consciousness' but never true class consciousness (by which he meant consciousness of and desire for conflict), unless aided by the *intelligentsia.

By contrast with the Marxist position, *Weber saw the principal class struggle as that between creditors and debtors, with the conflict under capitalist conditions between employers and workers as merely a special case. On this view the rising class seeks always to expropriate those to whom it is indebted, while the established class seeks to sustain the law that would guarantee repayment.

No theory of the class struggle has been wholly satisfactory, partly because it is hard to accept that there always is such a thing or to accept that those conflicts which influence history can all be seen in terms of class. It is not obvious, for example, that class struggle underlies all *sectarian and religious strife, or the alleged war between the sexes; nor is it obvious that a description in such terms would be explanatory. One of the problems is that the usual theories tend to attribute to classes both *agency and the kind of collective behaviour more characteristic of associations than of economic position. Nevertheless, many struggles are *seen* in class terms; thus what some may describe as a 'struggle for control of the means of communication', others regard as a conflict between *propaganda and impartiality.

classical economics. The school of eighteenth- and nineteenth-century economists who, in opposition to the *physiocrats, emphasized the importance of manufacture and production but who, like the physiocrats, emphasized liberty and property over agriculture in the determination of prices, prosperity and distribution. Its principal exponents – among them, *Smith, *Ricardo, *Malthus, and the *Mills – shared the assumption that competition is the foundation of economic activity, and in their several ways gave grounds for the belief that market conditions, operating without interference from the state, would generate economic stability. If, at times, the market does not work for the common benefit, state interference must nevertheless be contemplated only with hesitation, since it tends to lead to inefficiency or stagnation. For Adam Smith, for example, it is not only natural but also right that economic activity should be guided by self-interest alone. (*See* *invisible hand.)

The classical doctrines were refined and perpetuated by J. S. Mill, and dominated political and economic thinking in the US and the UK in the nineteenth century. They lost credibility with the experience of *recession and the Great Depression in the 1930s, which prompted interest in the theories of *Keynes and the *Cambridge school. These attempted both to explain such facts as recession, and to justify state intervention in the economy, as a means of maintaining *aggregate demand.

clerisy. *See* *Coleridge.

closed shop. The restriction of employment in a particular place to members of a particular *trade union or unions. The practice is legally disapproved in both the UK and US, on a variety of grounds, both under statute, and under the common law of *contract. Nevertheless the practice survives, partly because it helps to concentrate the bargaining power of the work force in union representatives, a fact which has proved congenial to both sides in settling *trade disputes.

The practice is sometimes condemned as a violation of individual *liberty, thus raising the question, Is the worker more free when able to join or not to join a union which has no effective bargaining power, or when compelled to join a union which is thereby able to negotiate on his behalf? Or as some socialists (tendentiously) express it, Are you more free when coerced by your employer or when coerced by your union?

One effect of the closed shop is to oblige management to negotiate, not with all actual employees, but with the representatives of all *potential* employees. It is not always recognized that this fact makes the idea of a contractual relation between the parties into a *legal fiction (*see* *bargaining theory of wages, *industrial law). It also undermines the classical Marxist analysis of the relation between capitalist and worker (*see* *labour power).

coalition. A temporary political alliance of distinct parties or persons, who preserve their separate political identities. Coalitions may be formed for electoral purposes, for the purpose of creating a government that has sufficient power and unity to rule, or for the purpose of defeating a government (as in the 'negative coalitions' of postwar France). In the US a coalition is usually a cross-party grouping in Congress, formed in response to a particular issue, but with no long-term political objective.

A coalition government is tied by a power of *veto, since any party within it may threaten to withdraw if its policies are opposed. Hence a coalition must act in a way that is more acceptable to its members than their own withdrawal.

codification. The verbal formulation of the whole or part of the law of a state, with a view to replacing all existing *statutes, *common law, customary law, and so on: a practice introduced in Babylon in 2100 BC, and since often repeated. The tradition of codification in France began with the *ordonnances* of the seventeenth century, and culminated after the Revolution in the *Napoleonic law, which served as a model for many of the codified legal systems adopted by the nation states of Europe during the nineteenth century. Codification in Germany and Austro-Hungary proceeded on the model of codified *Roman law. It was advocated for English law by *Bentham. However, attempts to achieve codification of the UK legal system have made no progress, due to the extent and complexity of the *common law, the ascendancy of *equity, and the appreciation of the value of the present fairly flexible relations between judiciary and Parliament. US law is partly codified, but relies heavily on English common law, from which it ultimately derives.

Codification has seemed to many besides Bentham to be legally and politically desirable, since it leads to settled expectations and easy predictions; some have thought that it might even serve to make recourse to the courts unnecessary. Others have objected that it must always be too rigid to allow for proper treatment of *hard cases, and that it misrepresents the true nature of law, which is partly implicit in the procedures of adjudication, discovered by the judge in practice as much as invented by the *legislator in statutory decrees.

coercion. Any force or threat of force which reduces the freedom of an action, so that, in performing it, an agent acts less freely than he might have done, although not unintentionally. (You can be *forced* to do something which you do not do intentionally, but coercion is essentially a constraining of intentional action.) In law physical coercion makes an act legally ineffective, moral coercion does not. This reflects a distinction that we need to make, between forces which *interfere with freedom by removing it, and those which merely narrow the range of autonomous choice.

Followers of *Kant would not regard moral coercion as a form of coercion, but as a form of *influence. A person can either be influenced by reasons, in which case he retains his identity as a moral agent and the freedom which is inherent in it, or else he cannot, in which case he has lost freedom and moral integrity together. As Kant's position shows, the philosophical definition of coercion is hard to provide. The criminal law, for example, ought not to be a system of coercion, for if it were, it could never be freely obeyed; the truly autonomous agent ought then to choose to defy it. One way of looking at it is to say that the law is *two* systems, one of *authority, which influences the rational agent to obey the law, another of *power, which coerces the agent not so influenced to act in accordance with it.

cold war. Term invented by the US financier and presidential adviser Bernard Baruch in 1947, and given currency by the journalist Walter Lippmann. It denotes a state of hostility between rival *blocs (specifically the Western and the Soviet), involving economic, political and subversive action, but without overt war.

Responsibility for the condition of cold war is variously attributed to Stalin's ambitiousness, to the activities of international capitalism, to the activities of international communism (and in particular to the series of **coups d'état* organized by communists in collaboration with the USSR in Eastern Europe), to American foreign policy in the Far East, to USSR foreign policy in Europe, and so on. It is clear, however, that it could not exist without there being two immensely powerful antagonists each of whom wants to exercise a power that the other seeks to deny him.

Coleridge, Samuel Taylor (1772–1834). English poet, philosopher and social theorist. Coleridge made one of the first attempts to adapt the philosophical vision of *Kant, Schelling, and the early German *idealists to the description and evaluation of the social condition of England, thereby taking a stand against what he saw as the fragmented vision of society and the individual characteristic of *empiricism. He was particularly hostile to the *utilitarian doctrines of *Bentham, and argued that human *values cannot be understood in terms of pleasure and pain. Coleridge argued vehemently against Jacobinism and its attempt to replace the language of social *privilege with the language of *natural right, rejected the idea of human *progress as a linear movement dependent only on the growth of scientific knowledge, and felt that the enlightened *rationalism of his contemporaries ignored the instinctive, pious relations between men that form the true bond of society. He was also opposed to the influence of **laissez-faire* and *classical economics, and advocated government intervention in the economy in order to relieve poverty and hardship and to provide education.

Coleridge defended the institutions of *Anglicanism and, in *On the Constitution of Church and State*, 1830, pointed to the need to reconcile the demands of political order and constitution with the more instinctive needs that are embodied in religious institutions. Here, as elsewhere, he defended the view that *culture is an indispensable mediator between explicit law and implicit social feeling, and argued for the political importance of the 'clerisy', or learned men, in whom the culture of a nation is enshrined, and who, in taking decisions informed by that culture, act in tune with the deeper, unspoken instincts of the governed:

'The clerisy of a nation, or national church, in its primary acceptation and original intention, comprehended the learned of all denominations; – the sages and professors of the law and jurisprudence; of medicine and physiology; of music; of military and civil architecture; of the physical sciences; with the mathematical as the common *organ* of the preceding; in short, all the so-called liberal arts and sciences, the possession of which constitutes the civilization of a country, as well as the theological.'

That passage illustrates both the impulsive nature of Coleridge's thought, and also his distinctively modern faith in the role of the *intellectual, for whom he was the first true propagandist, despite his somewhat medievalist conception of the established church. His arguments for the indispensability of culture shaped many of the nineteenth-century expressions of *cultural conservatism, and also awoke *Mill to the shortcomings of the utilitarian creed. Coleridge's importance lies largely in his perception of the opposition between the empiricist and idealist visions of *human nature, and his recognition that the first typically involves a massive simplification of the facts which it claims to know by observation.

collective bargaining. The practice of settling wage claims, conditions of work, productivity and related matters through bargaining between *trade unions, representing employees, and organizations representing employers. The effect is that terms of employment are settled by *influence, *confrontation and *conciliation, after the contract of employment. The resulting terms are not (in law) terms of a contract of employment unless afterwards incorporated therein.

It could be held that the practice of collective bargaining effectively abolishes the contract of employment, and establishes (**de facto* if not **de jure*) a new kind of relation between employer and employee, which has no clear precedent in law. (*See* *industrial law.)

collective choice. An ambiguous term

used in a variety of contexts, and in connection with a variety of theories. These theories fall broadly into two kinds:

1. Theories of *social choice, which attempt to derive 'social choices' from individual choices, in accordance with principles which justify the first in terms of the second.

2. Theories of 'collective action', which attempt to describe and explain the ways in which *groups conduct their affairs, and the ways in which the actions of groups emerge from the actions of their members.

The first is a normative study, belonging to logic, political philosophy, and welfare economics. The second is a partly descriptive, partly normative, study, belonging to sociology and political science. However, it overlaps with the theory of social choice, to the extent that, in this area, description depends on the answer to normative questions: i.e. whether a choice is described as made *by* a group will depend in part on whether it can be justified in terms of the choices of the members. The second kind of theory (here considered) deals, then, with such questions as the following: how do people with an interest in a decision also influence that decision? And, when is a decision really the decision of a *group* rather than of some agent, individual or *pressure group within it? In many ways the second question is the most interesting, since, if there is no clear answer to it, then there is no clear answer to some of the most important questions of political theory. Thus advocates of *collectivization wish to see collective *control over the means of production, which involves determining when actions proceed from a genuine collective choice, and when they are imposed. In practice all of the following have been called collective choice: state decisions made by a politburo in secret; votes of activist élites at open meetings; block votes; decisions taken without consultation with, but 'on behalf of', some group and so on. Consider the procedure of voting exemplified by the UK Trades Union Congress. Each delegate casts a vote which is weighted according to the size of his union; it is therefore possible for a decision repugnant to a majority of trade unionists to be taken with the authority of their 'majority vote'. In what way can that decision be said to be a 'collective choice' made by the trade union movement as a whole?

The question illustrates the extent to which normative and descriptive questions here arise together. *Rousseau made an important distinction between the *general will, and the will of all, arguing that the first need not coincide with the second. The general will is that which is expressed in group choices; the will of all is that which is arrived at by aggregating the several individual choices. Some argue that there can only be genuine collective choices if there is also a general will, in the sense of a new kind of *agency distinct from the agencies of the members of a group. A *constitution is required to establish that agency, and the real test of the existence of collective choice lies in the nature of that constitution. (For example, is it such that the majority consented to be governed by it, or would consent if asked?)

By contrast, there seem to be things which happen as a result of individual choices which, while in some sense expressing the 'will of all', are not really the expression of a general will. This can occur when the result issues, not from a constitution, but from a mechanism. Thus, consider the *market system, as conceived by *classical economists. Here the actual behaviour of commodities is influenced by *every* choice made by sellers and purchasers, and determined by all of them. Some advocates of collectivization might argue that this could only be a real collective choice if it were mediated by a constitution: that is, by a system of rules, to which the members of society might consent. But, they might argue, if people had the choice as to whether to submit to the market mechanism or not they would refuse. Although their decisions determine the behaviour of the market, the existence of the market is not their decision.

collective consciousness. *See* *Durkheim.

collective responsibility. The principle that each member of a decision-making body should hold his membership on condition of accepting full *responsibility for all of the body's decisions. This principle, imposed on families by the primitive legislation of tribes, is also imposed on the UK cabinet by itself.

collective security. Term denoting strategies which states have adopted in order to cooperate in the prevention of *war, usually by adopting a centralized system of *security arrangements. The UN Security Council was established with collective security as its principal aim. However, since each member may *veto any decision, efforts at collective security can succeed only in so far as they are in the interests of all the parties. Hence the difficulty, some say, of dispensing with a policy of *deterrence.

collectivism. The theory and practice which advocates the 'collective' as the economic, social and political unit, as opposed to *individualism, which advocates the individual, and *state socialism, which advocates the state. A collective is an autonomous *association of individuals which is not *private in the manner of the *family, but which has a variable membership determined partly by local attachments. 'Collectivism' was originally employed to denote the kind of anarchist socialism advocated by *Bakunin, which opposed itself to both *Proudhon and *Marx. The theory and practice have shown little consistency, however, and the term now seems to have three distinct meanings:

1. (Narrow.) The theory that the means of production, distribution and exchange should be owned and controlled collectively, so that all major decisions are the result of *collective choice rather than individual preference.

2. (Broad.) Any socio-political system in which, whether or not there is collective control in sense 1., individuals act collectively in social, cultural or productive activity, perhaps under the directives of a *party, but in the name of a 'collective'. Fine semantic distinctions matter very much in describing those arrangements which might be called 'collectivist' in this sense.

3. Sometimes the term 'collectivist' is used to denote any view which allows that a collective may have rights that can override the rights of its members. For example, some think that the *state has rights; others think that lesser forms of association, such as institutions of education, religion, or recreation, also have them. A theory which holds that these rights are not always defeasible in favour of the rights of individuals may, on this usage, be called 'collectivist'.

Confusion between the senses is very common; thus many seem to think that criticisms of 3. apply also to 1. and 2. In fact the three ideas are quite independent, and the use of the term 'collectivism' would perhaps better be confined to 1. alone. In this sense the question of the possibility of collectivism is the same as the question as to the possibility of collective choice.

collectivization. The act of bringing property under collective control (*see* *collectivism 1.). Often used to denote the agricultural practice of those states governed on the Soviet model, in which private landowners have been expropriated in order to establish collective farms. In the USSR the *kolhoz* (collective farm) is, in law, if not in fact, the joint property of its members, each of whom is entitled to a share of its profits; it is to be distinguished from the *sovkhoz*, or state farm, which is the property of the state and worked by employees of the state. The legal owners of a *kolhoz* do not have the right to sell it to anyone else, other than the state, which can determine the conditions of sale unilaterally. Whether one can speak of joint ownership in such conditions is disputable. (*See* *property.)

When voluntary, collectivization is usually described as the formation of a *cooperative. This is in part to indicate the revocable nature of the act, in part to record the fact that this transaction can occur independently of any substantial political change in surrounding institutions, and in part to indicate that the members of a cooperative retain the right of transfer which the members of a *kolhoz* must forgo.

college. **1**. Educational. A particular form of educational *institution, in which members are voluntarily associated for the purposes of teaching, learning, and research, and which also has a domestic aspect – as exemplified in the colleges of older universities. Colleges developed originally out of monastic ideals of community, and the resulting institutions are peculiar in aiming to provide extensively for the social and personal needs of their members. In the UK they tend to be *corporations (usually incorporated by charter), with a highly developed social *ethos, and a capacity to influence their members in ways that are not narrowly educational. They have therefore formed the model for certain ideals of association (*see* *collegialism).

2. Electoral. *See* *electoral college.

collegialism. The theory that the church or state or both are, or ought to be, voluntary *associations, whose social and political structure is to be construed on the model of a *college, united for the pursuit of recognized ends, but generating also an ethos which is something more than devotion to those ends.

colonialism. The theory and practice of *colonization.

colonization. The establishment of a 'colony', i.e. a collection of people whose origin is in some 'mother country', and who retain the language, customs and allegiances of that country, but whose social and economic life is sustained in the place to which they have moved. Modern colonialism has usually also been imperialistic, hence the term has come to denote the particular kind of *imperialism associated with the European colonies in Africa and South-East Asia. Typically this provided for partially autonomous legal and social institutions in the colonized country, in so far as this was compatible with overriding military, political and economic objectives, combined with the retention by the mother country of supreme legislative and political powers and by the colonial community of social and political rights not normally extended to natives. It has been, in effect, a form of subjugation, in which, throughout the period of colonization, the colonized country has been deprived of true *sovereignty. Colonization also brought about highly contested boundaries between colonized countries, which reflected the limits of colonial expansion, of economic interest, or of military capacity, rather than any indigenous sense of racial, cultural and historical attachment.

It is sometimes argued that the function of colonies in recent history has been to provide raw materials for manufacturers in the mother country. If this were so, then decolonization would leave a country with developed facilities for exporting raw materials, but no facilities for employing them in production. Hence the economic (and ultimately political) dependence on the mother country (or some substitute) would survive. The argument is, however, disputed, since it is clear that the availability of cheap labour in the colonies has led to the export of capital from the mother country, and the import of *manufactured* goods. It may nevertheless be the case that *markets* formed under colonial administration are so structured as to make *autarky difficult. Moreover, cultural hegemony, through language and through a residual community of former colonists, together with the siting of educational and legal institutions in the mother country, create their own form of dependence. Thus the process of 'appeal to the Privy Council' survived until recently in many former colonies of the UK, so that the law of those countries was subject to judicial review in the former mother country.

Leninist theories of imperialism argue that it is capitalism, with its insatiable appetite for markets, that makes colonization necessary. This seems difficult to reconcile with the fact that colonization may be inspired by political motives (as in the Russian colonization of the Baltic states), social motives (as in the original colonization of North America), or even religious motives (as in the Arab conquest of North Africa).

The effect of nineteenth-century colonization on modern politics has been incalculable, and awareness of this has been responsible for several recent coinages. Thus some speak of neo-colonialism, meaning that kind of economic and cultural infiltration of *developing countries which depends neither on force nor on political alliance, but simply on the operation of skilfully managed market forces. Others refer to 'colonial ingratitude', in order to describe the resentment of colonies to the development of their resources by a colonizing power, even though this development has been to the economic advantage of the colonized country, and is recognized as such.

Comecon. Council for Mutual Economic Aid, set up by the USSR in 1949 in response to the Marshall Plan, with the intention of reducing the dependence of communist countries on trade with the West. It involves the major members of the Soviet bloc, Cuba having joined later, and Yugoslavia being represented as an 'observer'. The attempt by the USSR to impose specialization on the member states, and so increase economic interdependence, has been resisted, although implementation of the 1971 agreement in Bucharest has involved the adoption of joint five-year plans. Comecon presents a striking example of an attempt to bring economic relations into line with political ones. It contrasts with the EEC, in which a legal superstructure has developed in order to bring political relations into line with economic ones.

Cominform. Communist Information Bureau, established in 1947 in Poland, under Stalin's instructions. It stressed the division of the world into *socialist and *capitalist camps, and the irreconcilable enmity that must follow from that. Its aim of sustaining local antipathy towards the West as the seat of capitalism was never achieved, and it was dissolved in 1956.

Comintern. *See* *internationals.

comity. Friendship and good behaviour between states: international good manners. The necessary precondition for the operation of *international private law (as when the citizen of one state seeks to enforce a contract made with the citizen of another).

command. To command is to issue directives to another, and to demand that he obey them. The usual implication is that a command, to be legitimate, must be issued by someone with *authority so to do, and, to be effective, must be issued by someone with *power to enforce obedience. Hence most exercises of command are also exercises of authority and power. Actions done in response to a command are done knowingly and intentionally, although in certain circumstances a person commanded to do something (e.g. a soldier) may be less free than someone merely *influenced to do it, and less *responsible for the outcome.

Tacit command arises when a power of command has to be assumed in the explanation or justification of some human relation, even though it is never explicitly formulated in directives. Some argue that the correct way of describing, and perhaps also of justifying, the relation of *political obligation is in terms of a power of command vested in the sovereign, associated with a posture of *obedience in the subject. Such a theory may wish to add that the command is not usually explicit, but only tacit (*cf.* *tacit consent).

Command theories of political obligation have their analogue in 'command theories of law', such as that presented by the jurist John Austin: laws are to be understood as generalized commands, issuing from the sovereign power, and enforced by sanctions upon all who are subject to that power. On this theory all actual law is *positive law.

commensalism. A term of sociology, denoting a relation that involves both competition and cooperation among those who occupy similar specialized positions within a *division of labour. Some writers do not distinguish commensalism from symbiosis; however, the latter is normally taken to be a relation between those occupying dissimilar kinds of functional position within a system. Thus commensal relations underlie the *class structure, while allowing for *social mobility, whereas symbiotic relations underlie the structure of corporate groups.

commercialism. The disposition to see all social and political activity in commercial terms, and all political values as their 'cash equivalents', all political aims being identified with the commercial activities which most nearly correspond to them. For example, conservation is identified with the aims of the tourist trade. The argument as to whether or not the countryside should be protected by law is resolved by balancing the profits which would ensue upon its exploitation, from the profits that would accrue to the tourist trade should it be conserved.

commissar. A commissary, especially during and after the 1917 revolution in Russia, appointed by a soviet, a government or a party, in order to organize social, political and military activities, and to supervise indoctrination. A 'people's commissar' in the USSR is the head of a government department.

commitment. Usually used in a sense corresponding to the French *engagement*, as this term occurs in the *existentialist philosophy of *Sartre, to denote complete identification with a cause or way of life. Commitment is the expression of existential freedom, and the answer to the anxiety into which that freedom plunges me. Although I cannot be sure, for example, that the cause of revolution is just and humane, I must not hesitate for ever to espouse it, lest I should lose my nature as a political agent. There comes a point where commitment is necessary. The nature of political reality is clear only to the man who is engaged in it, since only he *exercises* his freedom, and only in the exercise of freedom can that reality be understood. Hence the value of commitment can be understood only after it has come into being.

Commitment is analogous to *faith: it involves will, but its end-point cannot be known or aimed at before it is reached. To be committed is not simply to do this or that thing in a cause, but to consign one's whole self to a cause, and so will both the act and the state of being which it expresses. Usually commitment is to one of the causes associated with the political *left, for reasons partly made clear in the definition of *praxis.

commodities. **1**. Particular kinds of raw material and 'primary product', such as grain, rubber, iron – anything, in other words, produced immediately from land.

2. More normally in economics (especially in *price theory), a commodity is an object of exchange. A commodity is associated with two *values, called by classical economists *exchange-value, and *use-value, and by many modern economists *price and *utility. Thus a £1 note has exchange-value but next to no use-value, while a glass of water can have great use-value but can be exchanged (in normal conditions) for nothing.

commodity fetishism. Defined by *Marx in *Capital*, vol. 1, as the disposition of commodities to conceal the social nature of their production. Through the seemingly autonomous laws of the *market, *exchange-value appears as an objective and intrinsic property of commodities, inducing the labour of the man who seeks to acquire them. In fact, however, this value is itself (according to the *labour theory) *produced* by human labour. The labour of men therefore appears not as a human attribute but as an illusory power in the things which men produce. Moreover this power in things appears to generate fluctuations of the market, price rises, unemployment, etc. whereas in fact the true causality of all these effects lies in the social processes of production and exchange.

common good. Political theorists sometimes distinguish conceptions of legitimacy and political obligation based in an idea of *consent, from those based in the idea of a common good. Thus T. H. Green argued that 'the state is an institution for the promotion of a common good' (*Lectures on Political Obligation*, 1924), and tried to give to the idea of a 'common good' sufficient elaboration to justify the obedience of the citizen and the extent of the law. A common good may mean at least two things: a benefit to the civil society as a whole, and a benefit to each of its members. That these need not be the same is indicated by the case of a partnership. At a certain point a partnership may thwart the purposes of its members: the good of the partnership (its active engagement in profitable business on its own account) may then run counter to the good of each partner. This possibility arises in every association of individuals that creates a new locus of *agency, so enabling us to distinguish the 'common good' from the 'good of all', rather as *Rousseau distinguishes the *general will from the will of all. (An analogous dichotomy arises in considering the idea of the *public interest.) Green seemed to interpret the common good in the second way, as involving the good of each citizen individually, and argued that the state can promote the common good only by creating the universal conditions for the growth and exercise of *virtue. Some of the paradoxes of *utilitarianism are avoided by the Kantian view that the conditions for the growth of virtue in any one individual are the conditions for the growth of virtue in all. (The common good is that which ministers to common – i.e. universal – human nature.) Any other human good might be such, however, that to extend its provision as widely as possible requires depriving at least one individual of the opportunity to acquire it. In that case, the 'common good' might begin to appear as the good of civil society as a whole, and not as the good of each and every member of it.

common law. Term used in several senses, but now principally defined by two contrasts:

1. Common law *v*. *equity. The common law is the part of the law, whether written or abstracted from cases, in which determinate legal remedies are sought and applied on the basis of definite breaches of law, the law describing the nature, scope and application of the remedy. Remedies in equity are more flexible, and are available even in the absence of breaches of law. (*See* *injunction.) They also, in UK law, take precedence over remedies in law.

2. Common law *v*. *statute. Common law is used to denote case law, i.e. the part of law that is defined through, and discoverable through, judicial decision, as opposed to the law that is laid down by parliamentary enactment.

It is part of the peculiar form of *judicial independence existing in the UK that common law in sense 2. is so important, and that common law in both senses may be overridden by equity. In French and German law the term 'common law' (*droit commun* and *Gemeinsrecht*) is used in a different sense, to denote law common to the whole state as opposed to regional law.

common market. A common market is a kind of *customs union, since its precondition is the diminution or abrogation of the powers of member states to levy duties on imports other than the common duties. However its provisions may extend beyond those normally envisaged in such a union, and involve everything which might promote exchange within a group of states, with the hope that the increase of exchange will generate an increase in economic activity and living standards.

The history of common markets is complex. Modern examples include Benelux (agreed pre-war), the Central American Common Market (1960), and the Andean Pact (1969). The most significant development in their form and nature has been the creation of the European Economic Community (EEC) by the Treaty of Rome (1957), which provides not only for the free movement of many goods, services, capital and labour throughout the member countries, but also for an elaborate administrative and judicial procedure, raising questions of *sovereignty and *international law that are perhaps without historical precedent. Thus the EEC has a parliament, with elected representatives, a court of law, and an enormous machinery of law-making and law-enforcement which, while ostensibly concerned to facilitate trade, in fact penetrates into the reaches of civil life, dictating the standard quantities and sizes of commodities, the forms and procedures of sale, and the size and nature of transportation. It indirectly affects the development of regions, investment policy, supply, demand and mobility of labour, throughout the member countries. And through the Common Agricultural Policy it controls the production of food in ways which have had major social consequences.

To some extent nations have always had to bend *municipal law in the interests of commerce, security and (more recently) international agreements. However, by the Treaty of Rome, law is not recommended to the member states by the European parliament, but *made for* those states, requiring no *ratification or domestic enactment to ensure its validity. This can be seen as an abrogation of sovereignty. Whether that is in itself a good or bad thing is another matter.

common ownership. Property rights in *x* are said to be held in common if:

1. more than one individual has a right of property in *x*, and no individual with such a right may be prevented from exercising it by any other; or alternatively if:

2. more than one individual has a right of property in *x*, and no individual may detach his right of property by consent or transfer, so as to convert it into a *private right.

UK and US law do not permit common ownership in sense 2. but insist that common ownership is a form of *trust. Each owner is then private owner of a portion of the property, and can either force sale in order to realize that portion, or detach it directly for his own exclusive use. USSR law protects common ownership in sense 2. and expressly forbids the attempt to detach private property rights from something that is owned in common. The principle of common land in feudal land law seems to be that it was held in common in sense 2. so that the rights of all owners were violated by enclosure. The notion of common ownership created by the modern law of trusts (sense 1.) is often stigmatized by *Marxists as a peculiarly bourgeois notion, whereby common ownership becomes a disguise adopted by what is in fact private property. It is sometimes retorted that 2. is common but not really a form of ownership. *See* *property.

Common Prayer. The Book of Common Prayer is the official service book of the Church of England, compiled because of Archbishop Cranmer's wish to replace the Latin service books with a vernacular text. Issued in 1549, and revised by an Act of Uniformity in 1662, it has recently been radically revised again, in an attempt to make it applicable to the experience of a modern worshipper. The battle over this revision illustrates the peculiar constitutional problem of *Anglicanism, which can revise its liturgy and practice only with the consent of the Queen in Parliament. It also illustrates a problem that has dominated conservative thinking throughout the nineteenth and twentieth centuries, that of cultural continuity.

Some argue that fundamental beliefs, such as those enshrined in a religion, are not easily detachable from the words, forms and *ceremonies in which they are embodied. Hence changes in those forms and ceremonies, and in particular the provision of a whole new *language and vocabulary of worship, cannot be assumed to leave the content of religious and moral belief significantly unaltered. Whether or not this is so is a deep philosophical problem, concerning the nature of religious and moral sentiment. The issue is of serious concern in the US, where traditional forms of religion, whether episcopalian or nonconformist, continue to provide the imagery and the vocabulary with which common predicaments are described.

commonwealth. **1**. In *Hobbes and other seventeenth-century writers, the term is used to imply that the members of some social order have a common weal, or social well-being, which it is in their collective interest to preserve. The existence of such a social well-being determines the need for politics: it is a further question what laws and institutions (if any) would minister to it. Hence the term 'commonwealth' came to be used also to mean 'state' and preserves this meaning in such titles as 'The Commonwealth of Puerto Rico'.

2. Now generally used to refer to two historical phenomena: (a) The government of the Cromwells (the Commonwealth and Protectorate) which existed between the execution of Charles I and the restoration of Charles II. This government involved the survival of the legal powers of *monarchy in the absence of legitimate succession, and also, according to some, an enhanced need for their violent exercise in those circumstances. (b) The free association of sovereign states that had been members of the British Empire. A loose, but in some ways powerful, association, united by similar legal and political institutions, but bound by no constitution or rules of membership. The UK monarch is widely recognized by the member states as head, although it is not clear what this means. The monarch cannot be head of the Commonwealth, since that is a position that bears no legal *sovereignty. Nor can she be head of each state, since that is legally impossible, and formally rejected e.g. by India, which has declared itself a republic.

The principal consequences have been legal (the persistence of appeals to the UK Privy Council, the establishment of privileges in respect of UK nationality, etc.); and economic (the establishment in 1969 of the Commonwealth Development Corporation, to channel funds to the *developing countries in the Commonwealth, and the various *bilateral agreements under the Finance Act 1957 ('Commonwealth Preference')). There is no implication of a common *foreign policy.

communalism. The theory and practice of the *commune, whether or not conjoined with *communism as the prevalent political condition.

commune. An *association whose members own everything in common (*see* *common ownership), including the product of their labour. Such associations have been advocated as a political *ideal since ancient times, but received renewed support in the works of *Owen and *Fourier. The Paris Commune of 1871 was a popular uprising which led to the brief autonomous government of the city by the *communards*. It declared that the city should be owned uniquely, entirely and in common by its people, with no citizen having a greater right to any part of it than any other. Whether through impracticality or misfortune, the objective was not realized. Communes of such a type were favoured by *Marx, and some were formed in Russia immediately after the October Revolution. However, they were soon turned into 'collective farms', and other institutions whose primary purpose is productive, with the adoption of the New Economic Policy of 1921.

It is doubtful that the modern 'commune', composed of refugees from the *bourgeois way of life, has much in common with the ideals proposed under this label, although some believe that those ideals have been, or could be, realized in the institutions of the Israeli *kibbutz, or the Chinese commune (a basic unit of agricultural collectivization, usually with about 30,000 members, subdivided into 'brigades' and 'teams'). All attempts to relinquish private property and to hold everything in common encounter problems of organization: who is to direct the process, and how?

communication. The transmission of information, ideas, emotions, values and attitudes. Since communication is essential to all social order, the theory of communication presents large political issues, including the following:

(i) The nature of *language, and its relation to *ideology. Some argue that the very act of speech, because of its social nature, is a political act, and so laden with ideological implications. This thought tends to take two forms: (a) language as such is ideological, so that political meanings are attributed to every utterance, however innocent it may seem; (b) ideological significances are to be found in the language, accent, and subjects of conversation of a particular class or classes. Class-membership is 'signalled' in speech, and this is held automatically to give an ideological meaning to its signals.

(ii) Control over the means of communication. This is often advocated by *democratic centralism as a necessary part of its political aim, and in any case is almost invariably exercised by parties who rule in the name of that idea. Here 'communication' does not mean language, but rather the *media of mass communication. The issue here turns partly on the following thought: if the party, or some other politically responsible body, does not exert control over the means of communication, then someone else will do so, less responsibly. (On this and related questions, *see* *media.)

(iii) Specific questions as to *how* means of communication are controlled (i.e. owned, licensed, censored etc.) in democratic regimes

(iv) Questions concerning the use of particular media. For example, the use of satellite communication opens whole new possibilities of propaganda, education display, trade and military manoeuvre, and it is not unreasonable to suppose that these possibilities change the character of political organization, just as they change the character of social life.

(v) More general issues concerning the media, in particular those illustrated in Marshall McLuhan's slogan that the medium is the message, and those concerning the effect of 'saturation' by communications – as when a person spends half of his life in front of a television.

(vi) The problem posed by political communication. This is held to be a two-way process, between sovereign and subject and subject and sovereign. In democracies the way is (or should be) open in both directions, whereas in some kinds of *despotism it is open only in one. How is it to be kept open? And should the way up be the same as the way down? (*See* *representation.)

communism. **1**. A social and economic arrangement defined by the fact that no participant owns significantly more than any other, either because all property is held in common, or because the institution of property does not exist, or (Marx) because ownership is confined to the means of consumption and is excluded from the means of production and exchange. To be distinguished from arrangements in which property is not owned in common but by some impersonal, but nevertheless autonomous body, such as the state. (*See* *socialism, *state capitalism, *state socialism.) Also to be distinguished from arrangements in which equality of ownership is established by isolated, or periodic, acts of redistribution, whether by common consent, by taxation, or by act of state. In all such arrangements, it has been thought, the principle of communism is not achieved, since the individual is permitted to indulge a right of ownership, and may well feel an injustice in its abolition. Moreover, periodic equalization is compatible with the institutions of barter and exchange, each of which is held to be alien to the communist ideal.

According to Marxist theory, socialism is a stage of development, and leads to communism, hence the frequent Marxist distinction between the two. True communism (or 'full communism') is incompatible with any form of exchange or *exchange-value. It is the real economic expression of *democracy and is characterized by the slogan 'from each according to his ability, to each according to his need' (Marx: *Critique of the Gotha Programme*). The emphasis on need signifies the disappearance of exchange-value, and its supersession by *use-value alone. It is this in particular which distinguishes communist society from the forms of 'redistributionism' which might otherwise be confused with it.

2. Any movement which aims to bring about the state of affairs described above, or which represents that state of affairs as a political ideal. There have been many such movements in history, but the principal one in modern times began with the European revolutions of 1848 and the publication in that year of the **Communist Manifesto* by Marx and Engels. The word 'communism' occurs frequently in their writings, but for a long time the word 'socialism' was preferred as the name of the ideal, the principal Marxist parties calling themselves *social democrats. Their political organization began with the first of the *internationals, founded in London in 1864 with the support of Marx. The Third International, or *Comintern, founded in Moscow in 1919, in the wake of the 1917 revolution, displayed the final preference for the word 'communism'. This word was adopted by *Lenin and *Trotsky in order to distinguish their ideals from the less pure intentions, as they saw them, of the European socialists and social democrats, and also in order to emphasize an affinity with the Paris Commune of 1870, which, according to Marx, involved a genuine gesture in the direction that he favoured. The Comintern gave the impetus and name to communist parties throughout the world, and since then the term 'communism' has been synonymous for many with the form of government of which Lenin was the principal inventor.

3. The system of government in which a *communist party rules, without permitting legal *opposition.

Communist Manifesto. Composed by *Marx and *Engels and published in German in 1848, at the behest of the Communist League, and in English in 1850, the *Communist Manifesto* was the principal document involved in the launching of the *Communist Party as an international organization.

In the first part an impressive summary is given of Marx's theory of history, in which the development of *productive forces under capitalism is described, together with the resulting destruction of all feudal relations and hierarchy, all true national boundaries, and all traditional modes of trade, life and consciousness. The necessary consequence is said to be the emergence of the urban *proletariat, which comes to be organized 'into a class, and consequently a party'. The manifesto, having described the condition of the proletariat, goes on to affirm the identity of interest between the Communist Party and the proletariat everywhere. The 'theoretical conclusions' of the communists are said to be founded on 'actual relations springing from an existing *class struggle'.

The remainder of the manifesto is given over to examining the proposals made by the Communist Party in support of the proletariat. These include the abolition of all 'bourgeois property', and 'in this sense, the theory of the communists may be summed up in a single sentence: Abolition of private property'. The contention is that *private property relations condemn the proletarian to be propertyless, by forcing him to accept the minimum wage. Hence he has nothing to lose by their abolition, and everything to gain from the *common ownership that will eventually displace them. Moreover, this common ownership is historically necessary, since it, and it alone, is compelled by the continuing and necessary development of the productive forces which, unleashed by capitalism, are like some uncontrollable demon now working for capitalism's crisis and destruction.

The manifesto also proposes the abolition of 'bourgeois' law and education, the abolition of the *family, a heavy progressive income *tax, and centralization of capital and *communication in the hands of the state. It concludes by analysing the various kinds of theoretical and sentimental *socialism current in its day, finds fault with all of them, and advocates the overthrow by force of all existing social conditions, since 'the proletarians have nothing to lose but their chains'.

communist parties. The word 'communism' was used in its current sense as early as 1840, and the **Communist Manifesto* spoke of 'the Communists', referring to them as a *party. Communist parties in the modern form are, however, a twentieth-century invention, emerging as a result of the split between *bolshevism and the *social democrats at the Second *International, after which *Lenin set about organizing his 'party of the new type'. The Soviet attempt to make communism into a complete system of government was inspired by Lenin's theory of the party, and has dominated the history of communist parties throughout the world. The subsequent conflict between *Stalin and *Trotsky still finds echoes in intellectual and political movements within Western parties, as does the dispute over *revisionism, the personality cult, and the role of national as opposed to international aims and aspirations.

The British Communist Party was founded in 1920, and, under Lenin's advice, unsuccessfully sought affiliation with the Labour Party, first in 1921, and then in 1922 and 1936. It has never been represented in the House of Commons by more than a few members, and its influence as a party has steadily declined. Trotskyists with communist commitments turned their attention instead to the *labour movement and have succeeded in turning trade union and Labour Party policies in directions once advocated by the Communist Party. The American party suffered much from *McCarthyism and other forms of *anti-communism, and now has little influence. The French Communist Party has existed since 1920, became highly influential after the Second World War under the *Stalinist M. Thorez (*regnavit* 1930–64), and maintained close working-class connections. The new non-Stalinist party of Georges Marchais (born 1920) has repudiated the *Marxist-Leninist doctrine of the *dictatorship of the proletariat, and its relations with the USSR have been strained. Perhaps the strongest of the Western European communist parties is the Italian, founded in 1921 by *Gramsci, and now able to receive one third of the votes cast at a general election, and to secure control of many important municipal councils.

The communist parties in Eastern Europe have suffered many calamities; first, the murder in 1919 of the founders of the German party, Rosa *Luxemburg and Kark Liebknecht; secondly, the triumph of *Nazism; thirdly, the forced imposition of Russian dominion after the war, which has turned the Communist Party into an instrument of imperial government. Its position should, however, be seen in the context of fairly effective indigenous support, and the brief ascendency of communist parties in the 1920s, when Hungary experienced communist government, and neighbouring states felt the considerable influence which that government exercised. In effect all parties in Eastern Europe must now be affiliated to and condoned by the Communist Party, which has therefore ceased to be a political *party in the Western sense of the term.

For the Chinese Communist Party, *see* *Maoism, and for the Soviet *see* *USSR, constitution and laws. *See also* *Eurocommunism.

community. A term denoting a social *group, usually identified in terms of a common habitat (such as town, village, or district), and implying both a body of common interest, a degree of social co-operation and interaction in the pursuit of them and a sense of belonging among the members. By extension, any self-identifying group of people with similar interests who attempt to advance those interests by establishing themselves in a common place, e.g. a community of artists, or of scholars.

The term has many rather vague uses and is sometimes used as a translation of **Gemeinschaft*.

community law. The directly applicable law of the EEC treaty and its instruments (on which, *see* *common market). In the event of conflict it takes precedence over *municipal law. (This is clearly necessary for the effectiveness of the treaty, but may also be an abrogation of *sovereignty on the part of its signatories.) In general, community law becomes part of the law of the UK if it is, in its nature, or under the treaty, self-executing, or is the subject of a separate parliamentary enactment, or is implemented by statutory instrument (see European Communities Act 1972, s. 2(2)). It was established in *H. P. Bulmer Ltd* v. *T. Bollinger SA*, 1974, that EEC law is to be construed by UK courts, not according to strict and literal interpretation, but in accordance with the practice of European courts, and the spirit of the treaty, so that even judicial procedure is now constrained by that treaty.

community politics. Used to describe UK Liberal Party politics in by-elections during the early 1970s, the term now has a wider application, to denote the political emphasis on matters of local concern, and the attempt to acquire support for national policies by representing them as bearing directly upon comprehensible (whether or not connected) interests of the small and localized *community.

company. Nowadays usually a form of *corporation, whose legal identity is secured by the provisions of company law, and whose essence consists in the uniting of members for a common purpose. Under the Limited Liability Act 1855, shareholders can limit their liability in law for actions of the company, thus constituting the company as an independent agent, which can contract debts and obligations which no shareholder is required to honour, and even commit crimes of which no shareholder is guilty (and be fined or dissolved in consequence).

The formation of such institutions, and the law which legitimates them, e.g. the UK Companies Acts 1862 and 1948, is one of the most important features of modern *capitalism. The principal agent in modern capitalist production is no longer the individual, and capital itself is largely detached from individual ownership, leading an autonomous (or seemingly autonomous) life of its own, so that even those who control its employment (the managers) are themselves employees, bound by a labour contract to the impersonal company which they serve. (*See* *separation of ownership from control.) This fact is important for those who wish to apply traditional (e.g. Marxian) analyses of modern capitalist production, since *profits and *control are no longer concentrated in the same agency.

All organization and accounting of incorporated companies is closely controlled by statute, in order to avoid the evident opportunities for fraud presented by limited liability.

compensation criterion (sometimes: compensation principle). A criterion for the social desirability of an economic *policy, first proposed by the economist Nicholas (now Lord) Kaldor. If those who gain from a policy could compensate in full those who lose, and yet still remain better off, then the policy is preferable to one which leaves things as they are. The principle might be compared with that offered by *Pareto optimality, which says that a policy is beneficial if no one is made worse off and someone made better off, but which, unlike the compensation principle, refers to the actual rather than to the hypothetical distribution of benefits resulting from a policy. Such principles are much used in welfare economics, which normally requires some standard of optimal satisfaction of competing claims.

The compensation principle has been much criticized, first because hypothetical benefits seem to be an incoherent object of social policy, secondly because of the paradox, noted by T. Scitovsky, that it might recommend *both* a change from A to B, *and* a change from B to A. Further inconsistencies have been noted by P. A. Samuelson, W. M. Gorman, and others.

competition. A process in which many agents rival one another, e.g. to sell their products or their labour power. The general precondition of a *market economy, competition clearly admits of degrees, and hence for the sake of economic analysis is studied in relation to an ideal of 'perfect competition', in comparison with which all actual competition is 'imperfect'. Perfect competition in a market requires (among other things) the following conditions: a large number of buyers and sellers, so that the amount bought by any buyer is negligible relative to the total transaction, homogeneous goods, perfect information possessed by all regarding selling and buying opportunities, absence of transaction costs, and freedom of entry into the market. From these and other assumptions about preferences and production conditions it can be shown that, if perfect competition pervades the economy as a whole, there will exist a set of prices at which *supply and *demand are in *equilibrium for every commodity in the economy. Yet further assumptions (e.g. concerning adjustment processes) would be needed for it to follow that the economic system will tend to equilibrium rapidly or at all.

The existence of *monopoly and *oligopoly, and the many legal, economic, and political barriers to entry into a market that have arisen in the modern world, make the theory of perfect competition more or less inapplicable, except as the study of an *ideal type, although some markets approximate to it. However, such factors have not eliminated competition altogether, but require recognition of its imperfect character; the many political and moral questions posed by the widespread dependence on competition as a controlling and motivating economic force remain. The assumption of much political theory during the eighteenth and early nineteenth centuries was that competition would also generate the *just price, since all factors contributing to the destruction of free contractual arrangements between buyers and sellers would have been removed. However, that is at best only true if the basic distribution of property rights is not unjust. It remains an open question whether normal competition generates injustice, and whether, and to what extent, it provides the conditions in which some members of society are inevitably *exploited to the benefit of the remainder.

Defenders of competition are apt to praise the 'competitive spirit', either as the source of all progress and invention, or as the necessary affirmation of the individual will (*see* *Nietzsche). It is argued that, without it, men are either less prosperous, or less dominant, over nature, and in any case in a state of imperfection or decline. This reference to the competitive spirit is an important part of the *ideology of capitalism, and also an important concept for certain religious and moral criticisms that are made of it.

Comte, Auguste (1798–1857). French philosopher and exponent of *positivism (a philosophy first enunciated in modern form by *Saint-Simon, whose secretary Comte was), and inventor of the term 'sociology', together with many parts of the study that now goes by that name.

Comte's early writings were influenced by *counter-revolutionary thought of the early nineteenth century. While he admired many of the ideals of the French Revolution, he sought to reconcile them with a respect for social order and *progress. His search for a 'middle way' between *Jacobinism and conservatism led to his development of positivism, which aimed to derive political doctrine from a science of society. He argued that social evolution proceeds through three stages, the theological or fictitious, the metaphysical or abstract, and the scientific or positive. Comte saw himself as advocating the transition from the second stage to the third, in which all phenomena subject to invariable natural laws would become the subject of scientific investigation. Man finally comes of age in this 'positive' era, and loses his dependence on religion as on all other forms of systematic illusion. However, man also requires a philosophy of life that will facilitate the transition and maintain social order. Comte therefore proposed the development of a secular system of 'common moral ideas', based on an appreciation of the normative character of all social relations, and the impossibility of social order without a publicly accepted system of values. This and similar items of sociological analysis greatly influenced *Durkheim.

In Comte's later writings, the attempt to find a system of values that would reconcile order and progress led in a new direction – that of the 'church' of positivism. 'Positive' is a term used to denote knowledge and understanding which confines itself to the actual empirical world, and refuses to transcend it in search of hidden causes and final ends. All genuine human knowledge is scientific and methodical, and no question that cannot be answered by science has an answer. The nineteenth-century man possesses an ever-growing understanding of his position, and on the basis of this can plan a total reordering of society to meet actual and scientifically determinable needs. Thus Comte summarized this aspect of his political vision (the theology of science) in the slogan: 'science whence comes prediction; prediction whence comes action'. His vision also had dogmatic and liturgical aspects, involving the worship of humanity. Comte tried to develop institutions of a quasi-ecclesiastical kind with which to transmit this faith, the result being described by T. H. Huxley as 'Catholicism minus Christianity'.

Comte was an eccentric but influential thinker, and fragments of his thought found their way into many nineteenth-century political theories, from *utilitarianism to the sociology of Marx, with whom Comte shared the ambition to strip away the veil of illusion from human things, and to reveal them, and to act on them, as they really are.

conciliation. Conciliation is the attempt by a third party to resolve a dispute. It is to be distinguished from *arbitration, on the one hand, and *mediation on the other. It is unlike arbitration in that it involves no award by the third party, and is in no sense a judicial or quasi-judicial process; it is unlike mediation in that it is not a passive intercession, but rather an active attempt to resolve a conflict. On some views conciliation provides the model for all *politics, which involves reconciling conflicting forces and opposing interests.

Methods of conciliation have been laid down in UK law since the Conciliation Act 1896; they are now largely governed by the Advisory, Conciliation and Arbitration Service, set up in 1976. In international law, conciliation is the process of settling a dispute by submitting it to a commission of enquiry, whose findings take the form of recommendations rather than legally binding judgements or awards.

concordat. A treaty between the papacy and a 'temporal' *sovereign concerning ecclesiastical affairs. Examples include that with Napoleon of 1801, accepted by most subsequent French regimes, except in periods of fervent *anti-clericalism; that of 1929 with Mussolini; that of 1933 with Hitler; and that with the Hungarian communist government in 1964, ostensibly securing freedom of worship. A concordat will tend to involve some compensatory concession by the church, e.g. articles establishing the degree of allegiance owed by the church to the particular state.

conditioning. **1**. Term from empirical psychology used to denote the establishment of a connection between stimulus and response, with the implication that this connection comes about through repetition and in a mechanical way that involves no reflection or intention on the part of the subject. (The term derives from the theory of learning advanced by the Russian psychologist I. P. Pavlov (1849–1936), for whom the 'conditioned reflex' was the paradigm of the learned response.)

Hence, any attempt to control human behaviour by repetition of mechanical and mesmerizing routines.

2. The term is also extended to refer to behaviour induced by punishment and reward (called 'operant conditioning' by B. F. Skinner) although this may be theoretically quite different from Pavlov's 'classical' or 'respondent' conditioning. It is further extended to denote all learning processes which result in the acceptance rather than in the active questioning of existing conditions – with the implication that acceptance is a kind of mechanical, 'Pavlovian' or 'Skinnerian' submission to the force of habit. 'Social conditioning' can thus come to denote any form of *education which leads to a conservative attitude to the **status quo*, whether or not that education involves serious learning as opposed to unthinking routine, or the desire for reward. (*See* *behaviourism.)

Condorcet, Marie Jean, Marquis de (1743–94). Social and political theorist. *See* *counter-revolutionary, *progress, *voting paradox.

confederacy: In *international law, an *association of *states for mutual benefit and protection.

confederation. An association of sovereign states with common means of effecting common purposes. The difference between a confederation and a *federation lies in the greater emphasis on the independence of the members in the first case, and on their unity of purpose and organization in the second. Thus the US was a confederation of states up to 1789, and thereafter a federation, until the Southern states seceded and formed a new *con*federation in 1861.

The distinction is brought out by the German distinction between a *Staatenbund* (confederation of states), and a *Bundestaat* (a federated state). In the second case there is a tendency towards the existence of only *one* *sovereign state (as in the US); in the first case there is the determined persistence of many.

conflict model of society. The sociological term for theories of history and society which see social behaviour and transformation as the outcome of conflicts between rival interests and forces, and which place less emphasis on planning, friendship, peace and creativity. The extreme example of a conflict model is *dialectical materialism.

conflict of laws. An alternative name for international private law. Suppose a citizen of the UK negligently damages property belonging to a citizen of France in the US. Which legal system provides the Frenchman with a remedy and why? The rules of conflict are not themselves international but internal to each body of national law, regulating disputes between contending factions which arise within the *jurisdiction. Hence, to answer the question, one must first determine which jurisdiction is to be recognized (in this case, the US). The principal questions determined by the rules of conflict are (a) jurisdiction, (b) which system of law applies and (c) whether any foreign judgement has to be accorded decisive authority.

confrontation. The point of conflict between two interests, when all *conciliation, *mediation, *arbitration, *adjudication and *bargaining have been put aside, and where *force is mutually recognized as the only remaining course of action. Some see *politics as the science of avoiding confrontation; others see it as the art of provoking it.

Confucianism. The philosophy and outlook of Confucius (K'ung fu-tzu, (551–479 BC)), who emphasized in his *Analects* the importance of moral *values in all social and political order. He defended the 'Way' ('Tao') of the ancients to an age that had lost religious motivation, arguing that *custom and *ceremony are the most important forces of social order and good government. Confucius represented the *hierarchical structure of traditional Chinese society as natural, while arguing that the criterion of membership of the *ruling class should be moral rather than hereditary, so that kings should 'reign not rule'. Each citizen must assume the moral obligations of his *role and station, in order to create the harmonious order in which true *virtue (*jen*, or humanity), can be practised.

Confucius's disciple Mencius (Meng-tzu, (371–289 BC)) tried further to politicize the Confucian doctrine, and to persuade the rulers of the warring Chinese states to adopt the way of virtue, arguing that obedience towards virtue is spontaneous and requires no force.

'Neo-confucianism' is the name sometimes given to the successive attempts, from the Sung revival (eleventh-century) onwards, to reintroduce the Tao into political thought and action, and *Maoism has even been seen as a late manifestation of this movement, although in the 1970s Mao was concerned to discredit Confucianism as anti-Marxist.

congress. A coming together of people, and now used to refer to certain established institutions, among which two deserve special mention:

1. The institution of the US government as formed and defined by Article 1 of the US constitution. This article vests all *legislative power in a 'Congress of the United States', consisting of the *Senate and a House of Representatives, the division into two bodies being designed to reflect certain principles of *bicameral government. Congress can legislate on all matters listed in Article 1, s. 8, such as taxation, commerce, war and peace, but not on certain matters contained in s. 9. Nor has it any power to legislate in a manner that would conflict with the *bill of rights.

Management of Congress lies to a great extent within the governance of the chairmen of 'standing committees', chosen by seniority in office. Each committee has (with certain exceptions) a majority from the party which has a majority in the House of Representatives. The importance of committees in Congress contrasts with their relative unimportance in UK parliamentary government. The congressional committees are so ordered and constituted as to be able to carry through the necessary legislation without interference from outside, each item of legislation having a standing committeee appointed to discuss it. This leads to the efficient and rapid consideration of many bills at once, but it also circumvents the general discussion of each. This circumvention is accepted partly because of widespread trust in the constitutional process, combined with a high degree of *consensus as to the form, manner and content of policy in all sections of the House. Neither this trust in constitution, nor the consensus that goes with it, exists in the UK Parliament.

2. Name of the Indian party considered to be the paramount power in obtaining independence in 1947, when led by Nehru. It arose out of the Indian National Congress, an institution founded by an Englishman (A. O. Hume) in 1885 in order to educate Indians first for the civil service and later for government, and which thus became the focus both for Indian claims to autonomy and for supporters of constitutional government after autonomy.

congressional committees. *See* *Congress 1.

congressional government. Term used to denote that type of government which separates the *executive from the *legislature and makes each independent of the other. To be contrasted with *cabinet government, which has an executive chosen by, and/or responsible to, the legislature.

conscience. If someone believes an action to be morally right or wrong, and is therefore motivated to promote or resist it, then he is moved by conscience. Some philosophers (e.g. Bishop Butler, 1692–1752) consider conscience to be a motive quite different from any other, sharply to be distinguished from passion, self-interest, or the 'cool self-love' that proceeds from a reasoned estimate of one's highest well-being. Others describe it as a desire (albeit of a peculiarly irresistible kind). Still others think of conscience not as a motive, so much as a species of appraisal or judgement, which tells us what is right without providing the spur to pursue or to avoid it.

*Kant, following Butler and other eighteenth-century moralists, argued that conscience must, of its nature, override all other considerations, not in the sense of prevailing against them, but in the sense of silencing them. Thus, while it may not have absolute *power to determine what I do, it has, of its nature, absolute *authority. The person of conscience is the person in whom the power to enact this authority is always present.

Some residue of such a doctrine is present in the thinking of those who hold that it is always an injustice to force someone to act against his conscience, since, if he has any rights, he must have the right to do as he thinks right. However, this sorts ill with the intuition that there can be error, and even corruption, of conscience, and that someone may conscientiously set about the performance of acts which it is morally and not just politically desirable to restrain. Nevertheless the phrase 'prisoner of conscience' points to a widespread view that in certain cases, where there is agreement of a special kind (perhaps of the kind referred to in doctrines of *natural justice) that an act is wrong, then it is a fundamental violation of right to imprison someone who not only thinks that it is wrong, but also refuses to do it. Hence the importance of a category of *conscientious objection, as specifying a limit to *political obligation.

conscientious objection. Objection to a *command on grounds of *conscience: specifically objection to *conscription on the ground that it is morally forbidden to be an agent of *war. Sovereigns occasionally allow conscientious objection as a sufficient reason for avoiding military service, but usually require, perhaps as proof of sincerity, but more probably in order to discourage the habit, evidence of serious *commitment to a specific, and preferably arduous, religion. Conscience that rests in moral values alone, unsupported by religious *faith, tends to be regarded with suspicion, although it is now formally accepted as a valid ground of objection by the US Supreme Court.

conscription. Compulsory enlistment for military duties was a familiar feature of war in ancient times and responsible for many of the features of the *Spartan constitution and the Jewish *theocracy. The practice was revived in modern times by the French Revolution, with its *levée en masse* of August 1793.

Most major wars are now fought by conscript armies, and conscription is often maintained in peacetime in countries which value its discipline, as one of the effective substitutes for a sentiment of *political obligation. Some argue that conscription is a good thing, war being too serious a matter to be left to professionals; others oppose it, on the grounds that it makes *total war difficult to avoid. Once used by one side, however, it is inevitable that conscription will be used by the other.

Moreover, the ethic of modern *patriotism, which legitimates such practices as conscription, has made it difficult for many to think of conscription as anything other than a natural right of the *sovereign, or to regard the *mercenary soldier (i.e. the one who kills not because commanded, but merely for financial gain) with very much sympathy.

consensus. The converging of opinion upon a common judgement. The term entered political thought through *Cicero, who wrote of the *consensus juris*, or agreement in judgement, which he thought to be a necessary condition for the existence and endurance of a republic.

A consensus will come into being automatically where there are common interests, a common understanding of those interests, and of the fact that they are shared, and a common agreement on the means to advance them. But that is not the most important example. A consensus can exist despite conflicting interests; (a) because this fact is not understood (some *Marxists argue that it is part of the function of *ideology to *conceal* conflicts of interest); (b) because differences of interest are balanced by compensating differences of opinion concerning the means necessary to secure them; (c) because of the abrogation of individual interest, in favour of some common conception of the public good – as in time of war.

An important example of the third kind of consensus is provided by *tradition, which may, at least on occasion, represent certain forms of action as legitimate, others as not, and operate as a perceived (if not always understood) background to public political speculation. Conflicts will then be resolved within a given framework perceived as defining possibilities, and there will be an immediate consensus against any act which violates it. This is the kind of consensus which has been called 'public spirit' – the *virtue of *republics, according to *Montesquieu. It is perhaps to this public spirit that appeal is made by that form of *centrism known as 'consensus politics'. This has the appearance of a search for policies designed to please as many and to offend as few as possible. It is in fact a form of political action which moves, whether towards conservation or towards change, always by emphasizing the correct *form* of what is done, and its consistency with well-tried and commonly approved procedures.

consent. 1. A mental act on the part of an *autonomous *rational agent, on the basis of understanding, whereby he agrees to participate in some action or common enterprise. Consent is to be distinguished from the decision not to resist another's act, which, if extracted by *coercion (e.g.), cannot be called consent. Consent involves taking *responsibility for an outcome, which therefore becomes 'the doing' of the consenter, even though he may not be the originator of the act which produces it. Hence, it is commonly thought, there can be no injustice to someone in compelling him to receive that to which he has already consented.

2. In law, consent is a material element in certain relations of *contract, *marriage, and sexual intercourse, which determines the nature of what is done. The legal concept of an 'age of consent' is designed to capture in a formula the two ideas of autonomy and rationality, it being assumed that both these qualities are acquired or developed through the normal process of maturation. The concept of an age of consent also serves as a *legal fiction, whereby minors may be protected from the consequences of a reckless act.

3. In political theory consent is often proposed as a criterion of *legitimacy, or as the basis of *political obligation, as in theories of the *social contract. *Locke distinguishes actual from *tacit consent, the latter being genuine consent which is, however, not overtly expressed in any gesture (unless, perhaps of a purely ceremonial kind), but which can be inferred from the conduct of the citizen. Thus a man who, knowing himself to be free to withdraw from a social arrangement, nevertheless chooses to remain within it, can be taken to have consented to it. The precise meaning of 'tacit consent' remains disputed, as does the claim that the idea provides a criterion of legitimate government.

Consent to political action is a complex matter, and it is not at all clear that there is any process – democratic or otherwise – that incontestably confers it. *See* *collective choice, *democracy, *mandate.

consequentialism. The view that the merit of an action is determined by its consequences, and not, for example, by the motive which compels it, or the character from which it springs. According to this view the fundamental concept of *morality is not obligation but *value (Greek: *axios*), hence the occasional use of the terms 'axiology' or 'axiological ethics' to denote consequentialism, in contrast to 'deontology' (Greek: *deontos*, a duty), or 'deontological ethics', in which the fundamental concept is obligation. *Utilitarianism is an example of a consequentialist system of ethics, and like other systems it generates paradoxes that are hard to overcome. For example, the good consequences of an action may be enormous, but unintended, distant, and unknown to the agent; whereas the bad may be intended, known, but temporary and slight. Does it follow that the agent acted rightly?

Consequentialism exists in various forms. One form argues that the value of an action is determined not by consequences but by intention; however, the intention is meritorious only to the extent that it is directed towards the good: in which case not actual but *intended* consequences become the criterion of merit. A still milder form of consequentialism argues only that the rational being ought to consider all the consequences of his acts, and should not regard a question of morality as closed. Hence there can be no absolute or inviolable obligations. In all versions consequentialism endorses some version of the maxim 'if the means accuse, the end excuses', and has therefore proved useful to *terrorists, *tyrants, and politicians generally (cf. *Lenin's 'revolutionary morality'). Moralists often argue that the pattern of thought involved in consequentialism is the sign of a corrupt mind, since it permits the evasion of every obligation in the interest of some further, however remote or hypothetical, good. But even if this is so, it may be difficult for a politician to take the 'deontological' view. Politics is a complicated *kind* of *agency; it seems *always* to involve balancing one outcome against another, so that, without a consequentialist ethic, it is almost impossible for the politician to avoid *dirty hands. (*See* *Machiavelli, *realism.)

conservatism. The political outlook which springs from a desire to conserve existing things, held to be either good in themselves, or better than the likely alternatives, or at least safe, familiar, and the objects of trust and affection. Conservatism has three distinct parts: an attitude to society, an ideal of government, and a political practice. All three are informed by, but not reducible to, scepticism, in particular towards proposals for radical change, towards *utopian theories and ideals, and towards liberal and socialist doctrines of human nature.

(i) The attitude to society. Typically conservatives regard society as an achievement, which, for all its imperfections, is likely to be preferable to the pre-social *state of nature. (*See* *Hobbes.) They might also hold (as against certain forms of *liberalism) that society is in some sense antecedent to the individuals which compose it, the individual being a social artifact, the product of historical conditions that ally him to customs, values and expectations without which he is seriously damaged or incomplete. (*See* *Burke, *Hegel.) These customs, values and expectations are therefore intrinsically objects of respect, and can be rejected only by casting oneself loose from the social order that makes consistent rejection possible. What then remains to a conservative when the customs and values which command his support begin to lose their authority? Modern conservatism has arisen in response to that problem, emphasizing the need for the *legitimation of values, either through the renewal of *traditions, through religious doctrine or, more commonly, through some idea of *natural justice which will provide local allegiances with their universal ground.

(ii) The idea of government. The question for a conservative is what to conserve, and how? The question is answered through an idea of 'government by institutions', and a consequent theory of the nature and function of *institutions. Power should be vested in *offices, and in individuals only as the holders of offices. These offices should be attached to institutions which fit closely to the customs and values of *civil society, arising out of them, and conserving them. Hence conservative opposition to the attempt 'to form political institutions on abstract principles or theoretical science, instead of permitting them to spring from the course of events, and to be naturally created by the necessities of nations' (Disraeli). The state is the highest institution, but can pursue the ends of conservative government only if it presides over many and diverse institutions which are both *subject, and *autonomous. Such institutions will conserve their own principles of development, and the role of government will be in part to protect them from arbitrary encroachment and erosion, and to provide the legal framework within which they might develop in answer to the needs and expectations of their members. The theory of the 'subject institution' occupies much of conservative thought, and signals the deep opposition between conservative and *totalitarian doctrine (a totalitarian state being one in which no institution is both subject and autonomous). (*See* *Machiavelli.)

The state, like other institutions, is defined by offices, and therefore by a constitution permitting redress for **ultra vires* acts. This constitution does not have to be written, but it must act so as to reconcile and harmonize existing interests and activities, while providing ceremonial and expressive form to sovereignty and authority. It is usual for a modern conservative to advocate the division of power within a state, as being the best method of reconciling unity of government with individual liberty, and with the diversity of subject institutions. The state, like society, will be seen as a complex entity more easily damaged than improved, with laws of development and self-preservation that need to be respected. It will also be seen as more closely connected with civil society than many liberal theories represent it to be.

(iii) Political practice. Conservatism is inevitably pragmatic and local in its practice, reluctant to espouse over-arching solutions and often willing to concede that there are problems and difficulties which no merely political action can solve. It is anxious to resolve conflicts within the framework of inherited institutions and the *rule of law. It believes in the exercise of power, and also in the need to conceal power through the diversity of government and the creation of a far-reaching *establishment. Its emphasis on natural social relations is often held to require the defence of *private property; even if this is so, it seems clear that conservative practice does not necessitate the defence of modern *capitalism.

Conservatism is usually criticized as the *ideology of class domination, and as the political practice which ensures that those presently holding power will continue to do so, while extracting a spurious and deceived consent from the classes that are subject to, and victims of, their rule. (*See also* *cultural conservatism.)

conservative parties. The UK, Canada, certain other *Commonwealth countries, and certain *constitutional monarchies contain influential political parties which call themselves Conservative. (In Canada the name has been changed to the oxymoronic 'Progressive Conservative' for fear that the conservative emphasis of party policies might be construed as *reactionary.) Conservative parties outside the sphere of European constitutional monarchy are rare, and, since *conservatism must necessarily take a different form from place to place, usually without much resemblance to the UK example.

The UK Conservative Party (more accurately, Conservative and Unionist Party, signifying its constitutional unity with the Liberal Unionists who had defended the Union with Scotland and Ireland) represents an alliance in defence of established institutions which, since its announcement in Peel's Tamworth Manifesto of 1834, has gradually transformed itself into an active democratic force. It is committed to slow reform, *conciliation, a *mixed economy, and the maintenance of *hierarchical and *parliamentary institutions of government. Its modern form is partly due to Disraeli, who turned the party in the direction of universal adult suffrage, and emphasized, in his 'One Nation' doctrine, the supposed unity of interest which binds the working class and the old aristocracy together and leads them to seek a common remedy against the evils of modern *capitalism, and against the socially divisive doctrine and practice of the rising middle class. The party's links with conservatism are, however, uncertain, and it has recently exhibited a sympathy for liberal, and in particular **laissez-faire*, doctrines, in both politics and economics, and so distanced itself from its nineteenth-century origins.

consolidated fund. Prior to 1787 different government funds in Great Britain were maintained for different purposes: the funds were then consolidated in a particular account of the exchequer, into which taxes are paid and from which government expenditure is drawn. Parliament passes at least two Consolidated Fund Acts in each session, in order to release money for public uses and to borrow money by the issue of treasury bills.

conspicuous consumption. *See* *Veblen.

conspiracy. In law, an agreement between two or more persons to effect some unlawful purpose. The crime is complete when the parties have agreed, and does not require further action.

The law of conspiracy raises an interesting political question, since it implies that it may be a crime to conspire to commit an act that is not in itself a crime but only a tort (civil wrong) against its victim, or even a mere 'corruption of public morals' (according to the House of Lords in *Shaw* v. *DPP*, 1962, followed in *Knuller* v. *DPP*, 1973, though the case is sometimes disapproved, e.g. in Parliament, 3 June 1964). Some object to this on the (mistaken) ground that conspiracy, like attempt, is a *lesser* crime than the overt act. The UK and US laws of conspiracy thus permit criminal action against those who plan a civil mischief, such as a vociferous protest or the occupation of an embassy (*R. v. Kamara*, 1974). Should this be permitted? Or does it licence too many judicial invasions of the civil right to do wrong?

conspiracy theory of history. The theory that effects which fall to the benefit of some *class (usually the *ruling class) are produced by *conspiracy of that class. Often attributed to *Marxists, the conspiracy theory is in fact precisely what Marx's theory of history was designed to replace, by showing that the benefit of a ruling class will be secured, in the short term, independently of the intention to secure it, and despite any (benevolent) intention to relinquish it.

constitution. **1**. The body of rules governing the structure, organization and procedure of any corporate body. A constitution sometimes has a special form, as in the charter of a university, or the articles of association of a company. Or it may have to be inferred from practice, being encapsulated in no particular document or authority.

2. (A special case of 1.) The fundamental political principles of a state, which determine such matters as the composition, powers and procedure of the *legislature, *executive and *judiciary, the appointment of officers, and the structure of *offices which authorize, express and mediate the exercise of power. Constitutions may be written or unwritten, they may depend upon explicit rules or unspoken conventions, they may be *republican or *monarchical, or *democratic (although probably not *autocratic), and so on.

Various questions arise concerning the nature of political constitutions which require careful discussion. For example: what is an unwritten constitution, and is it preferable to a written constitution? What is necessary for a constitution? What is necessary for a constitution to be enforced, and what is the status of a constitution that cannot be enforced? Can a constitution without a *bill of rights be effective in safeguarding the fundamental rights and freedoms of the citizen?

It is probably a fallacy to suppose that a constitution becomes more definite and more invulnerable through being written, since no written document makes sense without interpretation, and interpretation here means judicial interpretation, in which the written rule is interpreted in the light of actual, and dynamic, social expectations, and in which a tradition of judicial reasoning is incorporated into the current construction of every clause. The *US constitution, which is written, is now virtually unintelligible except in the light of highly complex judicial applications, and congressional amendments. The *UK constitution, which is unwritten, is neither more nor less unintelligible for that fact, and differs largely in the great role played by conventions in determining procedure. Thus it is a convention and not a law that the sovereign should invite the leader of the majority party in the House of Commons to be Prime Minister. It would probably be wrong to say that this is therefore *not* part of the constitution, since it plays precisely the same fundamental role in determining the nature and function of government as do the rules in the US constitution for the election of a President. It is sometimes put forward as an argument in favour of the unwritten constitution that it can provide a better safeguard of citizens' rights and liberties, precisely because it hesitates to formulate them, and so never exposes them to hasty or tyrannical elimination. The constitution remains procedural, and rights are guaranteed by the priority given in judicial reasoning to factors of *equity and *natural justice. However, a written constitution may protect all rights by *entrenched clauses, and even protect those clauses from amendment. Nevertheless, it should be remembered that a clause can never be so deeply entrenched that it could not die the death of judicial qualification.

A written constitution is genuine only if it can be enforced. The question then arises, enforced by whom? The obvious answer is, by the citizen, by action in open court. (Which is why judicial construction becomes all-important, whether the constitution be written or not.) If the only persons empowered to enforce the constitution are the state and its officers, then the constitution provides no genuine limitation of their actions. It may *describe* their procedure, but it cannot prescribe for it. In which case it would seem wrong to say that there *is* a genuine constitution. Such reflections naturally prompt the thought that, without *judicial independence, a constitution, even if written, remains a kind of fiction. Thus the *USSR constitution, which is a document specifying many of the rights of citizens, can be upheld in a court of law. But if the state has an interest in the outcome, then, it seems, the judge acts under instructions from the state, and there is no genuine *adjudication. In which case the constitution can provide no guarantee of the ordinary citizen's rights, even if it purports to prescribe them.

constitutional government. The mode of *limited government in which the *constitution, together with the law and offices that are prescribed by it, provide the limit and ratification of every exercise of power, and in which it is impossible for any officer to transgress the constitution without thereby ceasing to hold power legitimately, and so being removable from office. *Hobbes, *Locke, *Montesquieu and their many followers developed theories of constitutional government, versions of which are now widely accepted as giving both a true representation of political liberty, and the preferred way of exercising political power so that it expresses not the will of those who wield it, but the rights of the citizens whom it governs. Constitutional government nowadays tends to require the *separation of powers, the *rule of law, and the exercise of power through office. Fundamental to all these things is the citizen's ability to proceed against **ultra vires* acts, together with the procedural rules which make legitimate powers discernible. Constitutional government disappears once the edict of an individual or of a party becomes overriding in all matters of state, or whenever particular interests which conflict with an alleged 'constitution' cannot in fact be contained by it. Almost all modern states have written constitutions relating to every exercise of power. It seems, however, that only a minority of them are constitutional.

constitutional law. The branch of law that governs the formation, reformation and application of a *constitution. Although a written constitution may to some extent clarify the subject matter of constitutional law, the legal determination of which matters are, and which are not, constitutional (as opposed, say, to *administrative) is always to some extent open to contention. The unwritten constitution of the UK is expressed through a complex and often highly ambiguous constitutional law, which allows much latitude to the courts in determining the constitutional validity of particular acts. For example, parliamentary *privilege is frequently abused for personal, demagogic, or political ends. It is not certain that this is a breach of the constitution. Nor is it clear who, if anyone, has a cause of action, how the action would be adjudicated, and what would be the remedy.

constitutional monarchy. A *monarchy which is not absolute, but *limited by a *constitution, so that, while the *sovereignty of the state is personified in a monarch, the powers of that monarch are determined not by himself but by the law. Usually the monarch may be removed from office if he refuses to obey that law even if there is no law which expressly permits this. A constitutional monarchy is a peculiar artifact, in which most executive powers are exercised in the name of the monarch, despite the fact that the monarch himself is unable either to exercise or to forbid them. The residual power that he does possess may nevertheless be vital to the government of the state, just as his ceremonial function may be vital to the social order that is thereby governed.

constitutionalism. The advocacy of *constitutional government, i.e. of government channelled through and limited by a constitution. The major current of Western political thought in the seventeenth and eighteenth centuries was constitutionalist, and included *Hobbes, *Locke, *Montesquieu, and the *Founding Fathers of the US. There seem to be two distinct thoughts underlying constitutionalism: that a constitution is necessary in order to limit government, and that it is necessary if there is to be government by *consent. While some theorists concentrate on limiting devices (such as the *separation of powers), others concentrate on the devices necessary to obtain and elicit consent (such as *representation). Hence modern constitutionalism has tended to absorb both the traditional attacks on *absolutism, and the subsequent defences of *democracy.

consumer. **1**. In economics: whoever realizes the *use-value of a good, say, by eating food, by hanging and admiring a picture on his wall, by wearing clothes. The consumer represents the last point of the process of *production, distribution and exchange, and consumption is the aim of economic activity. The theory of consumer behaviour is a major aspect of *neo-classical economic theory. The 'means of consumption' are all those appurtenances which surround and facilitate consumption – such as a house, its furniture, and the means whereby food is prepared and clothing stored. Many socialists, who oppose private ownership in the means of production, distribution and exchange, yet favour private ownership in the means of consumption, as indispensable to human freedom and peaceful existence. (Though how far the means of consumption can be separated from the means of production is a matter of debate: for example, the car owned by a salesman may be used for his business as well as for the pleasure of his family.)

2. The term 'consumer' is *value-free in economic theory, but has a highly value-laden use in certain kinds of political discourse, notably those which recognize a distinction between the 'consumer' attitudes towards objects, and those other, less covetous, or more contemplative attitudes, in which moral and other values play a significant role. Economists make a distinction between consumer durables (objects which can be used, and still retain a use-value so as to be the subject of possible barter and exchange), and non-durables, which, like food, vanish in the act of consumption. But this does not capture the significant distinction between the value of a house and the value, say, of a friend.

'Consumerism' is a label that is beginning to be applied to those political outlooks that see acquisition and consumption as the principal ends of existence. It is therefore more or less standardly (and not just in communist rhetoric) a term of abuse. (*See* *consumer society.)

consumer organizations. Organizations, which may be either voluntary or (as in the case of the UK Consumer Protection and Advisory Committee) established under government supervision, designed to inform the *consumer and to protect him against *restrictive practices, and other factors that lead him to pay more than he need, or obtain less value than he might.

consumer society. A society in which activity is directed to an inordinate extent to the accumulation and consumption of material goods, and in which the ability to consume is held forth as a standard of social achievement to be emulated, being the reward of labour and also its aim. A loose expression used in the criticism, e.g., of *market economies, under the regime of which the motive of labour has often seemed to be little more than the fulfilment of transitory and inessential appetites. The perennial moral conviction that 'getting and spending we lay waste our powers' is thus used to criticize the structure of a certain economic arrangement, usually on the supposition that there is some alternative which escapes the criticism (cf. *commodity fetishism).

consumer surplus. The excess of the maximum amount a *consumer is prepared to pay for a certain quantity of a good (rather than to forgo that whole quantity) over the amount that he actually pays for it. Such a surplus exists because what a consumer is willing to pay for one extra unit of some good, of which he is already consuming *n* units, is less than he would have been prepared to pay for the *n*th unit when consuming *n*–1. (Example: suppose that sausages cost 10p each and that I buy three of them at a total cost of 30p. I might have been induced to part with 20p by the prospect of the first sausage (when I had none), another 15p by the prospect of the second (when I had one), and 10p by the prospect of the third (when I had two), so that the total value to me of the three is 45p and the consumer surplus is 15p. In general consumer surplus arises because of diminishing *marginal utility.)

Consumer surplus provides a monetary measure of the benefit that a consumer derives from the supply of a product, given the terms on which it is made available. It seems therefore to offer the possibility of assessing the net effect on welfare of policies that alter the terms on which different products are supplied. Economists have argued that some systems of *taxation are worse than others because they lead to a greater loss of consumer surplus.

consumption function. The relationship between total consumption expenditure in an economy and total disposable income. *Keynes introduced the consumption function into his economic theory in seeking to explain the determinants of the level of national income at a particular time, and its changes over time. *See* *multiplier.

containment, policy of. The policy pursued by the US since 1947 of containing the spread of communism within existing territorial limits, either by armed intervention (Korea, Vietnam), or by economic and technical assistance (as in Marshall Aid, and the Colombo Plan), or by military strength and a network of alliances. The first having failed in Vietnam, and the second having led to a disastrous reaction by Muslim fundamentalists in Iran, it is no longer clear that such a policy is feasible in its initial form.

contract. In law a contract is an agreement between two or more persons intended to create a legal (and legally enforceable) obligation between them. Contracts can be express, as when promises are uttered and exchanged. Or they may be implied, as when two parties act in full knowledge of each other's aims and behaviour, at least one party knowing that the other is doing what he does only on the assumption of a return which he has been led to expect. (Many quotidian sales and purchases involve such an element of implied contract.) Contracts may also be conditional, as when I agree with you the terms of a contract which is to become binding upon the fulfilment of a condition. A contract may be void (without legal effect) – as in the case of a contract to commit a crime – or voidable – as in the case of a contract made under *duress, or a contract with an infant, which is voidable at the infant's request. Contract must always be distinguished from precontractual negotiations, such as offers, invitations to treat, and tenders, which are not enforceable in law.

Behind the legal idea of contract lies an important moral idea – that of the *autonomous agent who puts himself under obligations through his own voluntary acts, and whose knowing, intentional behaviour can, when based in requisite understanding, be *sufficient* to bind him morally to the performance of some act. He is not bound when his autonomy is violated – e.g. by *coercion, *force, intimidation or fraud. Nor is he bound if he is not, or not yet, fully autonomous (the case of an infant), or when his rationality or understanding are impaired. Some Marxists have argued that the *wage contract is always coerced, and so never binding. Whether or not that particular theory is true (*see* *bargaining theory of wages, *collective bargaining), the idea of the autonomous being who *creates* his obligations is a vital one in modern political theory, since it provides the basis for many ideas of *political obligation and *legitimacy – such as those derived from the postulation of a *social contract.

*Associations can be distinguished into the contractual and the non-contractual. In the first, as in a partnership, members are bound to each other by a contract, the terms of which have been agreed, and can be released from the association by a countervailing agreement among the parties concerned. In the second, as in a *marriage, while there may be a contract to enter into the association and a contract *ancillary* to the association (providing e.g. for the nurture of children), the association itself is neither created, nor modified, by that contract, nor does it have terms that can be negotiated, renegotiated or negated. Its obligations arise in another way – one might say, from its autonomous nature, and not from the agreement of the parties. This difference between contractual and non-contractual associations is also vital to political theory, since a quite different structure of human relations pertains to the two kinds of union. Much will depend, therefore, upon whether one takes the first or the second as the model for the organization either of *civil society or of the *state.

contradiction. In logic a contradiction consists of the conjunction of a proposition with its negation – i.e. any proposition of the form '*p* and not-*p*'. Since the two conjuncts cannot both be true, the state of affairs described by a contradiction is impossible, a fact that has led some philosophers to conclude that there can be contradictions in thought but not in reality. By contrast, *Hegel's conception of the *dialectic, and various theories that have sprung from it, have fostered the belief that there *can* be contradictions in reality.

One suggestion is this: a man contradicts himself when he believes two incompatible things, and also when he *intends* each of two logically incompatible things, as when he intends to give all his money to the poor and also to buy a new car. When exposed, a contradiction becomes untenable (if the agent seems still to hold on to it, then this is proof that he does not understand it, and therefore does not really hold on to it). But a contradiction can persist just so long as it is, through ignorance, idleness, or self-deception, concealed. I may intend both to pay my debts and to enjoy myself, and persistently neglect the facts which show that I cannot do both.

By extension we can think of human

*institutions as exemplifying contradictions. This is a more interesting case, since here the persistence of the contradiction need not depend upon there being some *individual* who is in contradiction with himself. Thus if I aim at *x*, and you aim at not-*x*, we are not in contradiction, but only in *conflict*. However if an institution is such as to require that part of its membership act so as to produce *x* (whether or not knowingly) while part act so as to produce not-*x*, then it would seem reasonable to say that the institution contains a contradiction, just as an individual who aims simultaneously at *x* and not-*x* is in contradiction (and not just in conflict) with himself. An example might be an educational institution, which is so structured that all pupils learn to question the authority of their teachers, and yet which aims also to inculcate an attitude of unquestioning obedience. It is logically impossible to realize the two purposes, but it *is* possible for an institution to exist guided and convulsed by the separate pressures that tend towards the incompatible outcomes.

In some such sense it could be that complex social relations involve real (but concealed) contradictions, and not merely conflicts, among rival members or rival groups. For example, the view, held by some *Marxists, that *capitalism contains a contradiction (manifest, e.g., in the *class struggle) might be true. It would be true if it were of the *essence* of capitalism to generate incompatible aims among those bound by this form of *production relation.

Whether there can be contradictions in the material world independently of human thoughts, aims, institutions and relations, is more doubtful. Hegel's belief in such contradictions is usually considered as inseparable from his view that reality is not material. *Engels's enthusiastic affirmation of a true *dialectical *materialism* has usually been found more puzzling. However it was accepted by *Mao, who argued that contradiction is the law of all material development, under socialism and communism as much as under capitalism.

control. **1**. Of agents. One agent controls another when the first can provide the necessary and sufficient conditions for the second's actions. Actions that are controlled are intentional, but not free, although the relation of control may be the result of a free choice in both parties (as in a military commission). Control is distinct from *influence, and also from *coercion: it may lack the element of *force that is present in coercion, and is, moreover, a dispositional extended relation, governing a plurality of actions. You can be coerced only once and commanded only once, but it is doubtful that you can be controlled on only one occasion.

2. Of things. An agent controls a thing when (and to the extent that) he can do with that thing as he wishes. Thus control is a matter of degree, restraints on its exercise arising perhaps from law, perhaps from facts of nature. Only an *agent* can have control, since control is exercised in intentional acts. Sometimes 'control' is used in an absolute sense – as in 'controlling interest' – where it signifies that there is no greater control vested in any other agent.

The concept of control is important in discussing the *separation of ownership from control, collective control (which is applicable only if we can speak of *collective choice), and the distinction between the *rights and *powers of ownership.

convention. **1**. In the general acceptance of the term, convention is distinguished from both *custom and *law, although all three terms are used to describe regularities in the intentional behaviour of rational beings. Convention has the fragility and changeability of law, together with the inexplicit, natural-seeming character of custom. It may be a motive in the mind of someone who could not state or describe it, but like law, it contains an *obligation which is independent of *habit. Its arbitrariness, like the arbitrariness of *positive law, is readily understood, so that conventions change not only in the course of nature but also at will (for example, changes in dress precipitated by tailors: but *see* *fashion). At the same time there may be transactions of such complexity that they can be governed, if at all, only by convention, and not by law alone. This is fairly evidently true of the workings of an unwritten *constitution. It is a convention in the UK that the monarch must accept the advice of the ministry for the time being, but any attempt to embody this convention in a law would undermine the constitutional supremacy of the monarch and so make the convention inapplicable. The example shows the large part that conventions may play in politics: it may often be a political act of the greatest importance to uphold or defy them. The constitutional stability of the UK is perhaps partly to be explained by the manner in which rapid changes of law take place against a slowly shifting background of conventions, themselves upheld by customs sufficiently inarticulate to remain outside the forum of speculative reform.

2. The term may also denote an international meeting to discuss some matter of common interest, and is further used to describe agreements (specifically, in *international law) which may or may not also be given legal force: such as The Hague Convention and the Geneva Conventions.

cooperative movement. A political movement founded on the belief that the means of production, distribution, exchange or consumption should be owned and controlled by cooperatives, i.e. by voluntary associations owned not by investors but either by the members themselves or by patrons, and run by directors, who are also members. The aim is to secure equality by a periodic *redistribution of *profits and to eliminate *competition between the members. The cooperative is a mode of ownership of the means of production which is both compatible with (indeed, a form of) private property, and at the same time not dependent on any division between capitalist and labourer. It is, accordingly, often criticized by *Marxists as impossible, so that all actual examples are dismissed as illusions, in which the appearance of *common ownership remains only an appearance.

The movement began with the Rochdale Equitable Pioneers in 1844, who hoped to realize, within the framework of nineteenth-century capitalism, the ideals formulated by *Owen and *Fourier. The movement flourished in the UK and US (especially in the Midwest), and more recently in France, Italy and (to some extent) Germany. In the UK the emphasis has been on cooperative associations of consumers, whereas on the Continent it has been on cooperative production. From 1918 onwards cooperative movement candidates for the UK Parliament have contested elections in alliance with the *Labour Party, and the movement now has little independent political identity. However it remains an important ideal, and the modern form of cooperative known as a 'housing association' has to some extent changed the character of land tenure in UK cities.

corporate state. A state in which government represents and is answerable, not to the individual citizen, but to the various *corporations of which the individual is a functional part. The corporations are *autonomous in the manner of the medieval *estates and *guilds, and have an analogous political role, mediating between the individual and the central power, and generating independent allegiances which will be pooled and reconciled in the common submission to a single government. The idea of the corporate state has been applauded (although not usually put into practice) by *fascism, and by the governments that grew out of the fascist movement. It has been partly put into practice (although neither applauded nor acknowledged) by successive governments in the UK, which form policy in consultation with, e.g., the Trades Unions Congress, the Confederation of British Industry, and other bodies which represent corporate powers rather than individual citizens.

corporation. **1**. In law: a group of individuals, or a series of holders of an *office, that is deemed to constitute a single legal entity. A corporation is a legal *person, and is distinct, in act, liability and reward, from any individual member of it. Corporations must be distinguished from unincorporated associations, in which no independent legal entity is created or deemed to exist. (*See* *incorporation.) In UK law corporations are of two kinds: aggregate, to which more than one individual may belong (e.g. a *company), and sole, in which one individual at a time holds an office that is passed to a successor (for example, the sovereign, who is a distinct legal entity from the human being who bears that honour; or a minister).

2. More widely, any organization that acquires a corporate identity, whether or not it counts as a corporation in law. For example, a trade union, which acts and suffers very much as a single entity. In this sense 'corporation' is used in the above definition of *corporate state, to denote any entity that has some control over its members and acts on their behalf (whether or not they also have control over it), and which is also an *autonomous or at any rate partly autonomous institution. Some think that all corporations in sense 2. ought to be corporations in sense 1., so that their actions should be wholly circumscribed by law. But it is impossible in practice and difficult in theory to see how this might be done.

corporatism (or: corporativism). The theory of the *corporate state as developed in *fascist Italy. This attempted to justify the organization of the economic system into 'corporations' subordinate to the state, and argued that such an economic system would render political *representation superfluous. The economy was divided into associations (called 'syndicates') of workers, employers and the professions; only one syndicate was allowed in each branch of industry, and all officials were either fascist politicians or else loyal to the fascist cause. According to law the syndicates were autonomous, but in fact they were run by the state. The 'corporations' united the syndicates in a given industry, but made no pretence at autonomy from the state. The theory held that, because the people are not politically articulate, their interests could be consulted only through institutions related directly to their occupations. A small ruling *élite of politically competent leaders would, if placed in charge of those institutions, both guide and be guided by the people.

The term 'corporativism' was also used by *Gramsci, partly in order to criticize the fascist theory of the corporate state, and partly in order to describe what he took to be a general feature of the development of capitalist society, in which workers see their interest in terms of their place within a corporation, rather than in the universal terms required for political understanding. He defined the awakening of a class to *politics in terms of its ability to 'go beyond corporativism'.

correlation of forces. Soviet substitute for the *balance of power. The doctrine of the need for a 'correlation of forces' is founded on the premise that military power is only one of the forces which serves to advance the interests of a state, or of an international political system. In particular, capitalism, with its entrenched and concealed control over communication, international trade, and economic warfare, has an ability to threaten the communist states which far outweighs its actual military power. Hence there is need for a correlation of forces between the two political groupings, in which propaganda, infiltration, economic warfare, the erosion of morale, and the like, are all taken into consideration.

cosmopolitanism. **1**. Belief in the ancient *Stoic ideal of the 'cosmopolis', or 'world-state', to which all human beings or *rational creatures necessarily belong, and which they must attempt to realize in their actions, regardless of the local conditions which may frustrate them. The ideal underlies *Augustine's theocratic universalism, and *Dante's conception of 'world empire'. Its greatest advocate in modern times has been *Kant, whose prescription for a 'perpetual peace' involves the generation of an international government obedient to the conception, incipient in the thinking of every moral agent, of a 'kingdom of ends' in which everything is as it ought to be, and ought to be as it is.

The Stoic ideal underlies a more derogatory usage:

2. The belief in, and pursuit of, a style of life which is cosmopolitan in the sense of showing an acquaintance with, and an ability to incorporate, the manners, habits, languages and social customs of cities throughout the world. To be distinguished from *internationalism and from sense 1. (both involving the belief in and pursuit of a single way of life valid for all people everywhere) in its emphasis on the city (Greek: *polis*) and its culture, and in its desire for a kind of virtuosity, which does not so much align people as distinguish them. In this sense, the cosmopolitan is often seen as a kind of parasite, who depends upon the quotidian lives of others to create the various local flavours and identities in which he dabbles. Hence:

3. A term of abuse favoured in the USSR and its dependencies, in order to denigrate those who admire and seek to emulate the bourgeois culture of the capitalist states, and especially those who feel that the bond between European cities is deeper and more important than the distinction between the capitalist and socialist forms of government that reign in them.

cost. The cost of an action or policy consists in any harm received, or any benefit forgone, in its exercise. There are as many kinds of cost as there are varieties of human benefit and *harm.

Economists distinguish historical costs – actual costs incurred at the time of a transaction – from the current costs of that transaction. *See* *cost-benefit analysis, *opportunity cost.

cost-benefit analysis. Analysis of a social or economic policy in terms of *costs and benefits, where these are construed as widely as is thought necessary to capture the issues which the policy involves. Cost-benefit analysis does not (and should not) confine itself to immediate economic losses and gains, but endeavours to include as many as possible of the harms and benefits that will ensue upon a given policy, including long-run costs and benefits. The policy is then deemed to be reasonable only if there is a balance of benefit over cost; *optimal only if there is a greater balance of benefit over cost than might be achieved by any alternative policy.

Cost-benefit analysis is a useful tool in economics, but its wider application depends upon two assumptions: (i) that costs and benefits are all quantifiable – an assumption easy to make in the case of marketable and reproducible products, but difficult where objects held to have absolute *value (for example, human lives) are involved; (ii) that the various costs and benefits are also commensurable with one another, so that, for example, the cost of forgoing a dinner might be set against the ultimate benefit of losing weight. *Bentham invented a 'felicific calculus' which was the first systematic attempt at cost-benefit analysis, and which he sought to extend to cover the entire fields of moral, legal and political reasoning. He was able to satisfy the two assumptions above, first by estimating all costs and benefits in terms of a *single* polarity of variables – pleasure and pain – and secondly by assuming that all pleasures, whether actual or hypothetical, can be measured against each other. (Thus the pursuit of a pleasure is reasonable to the extent that it is probable, large, near at hand, and so on.) This, combined with the *utilitarian criterion of optimality, enabled Bentham to quantify every political and moral problem, and sketch solutions to such problems that have never ceased to arouse incredulity, not the least on account of the number of acts deemed rational for which it would be absurd to postulate pleasure as a motive. This has led many to say that we cannot expect the realm of human values to be so readily subjected to mathematical discipline, and that the utility of cost-benefit analysis is confined almost wholly to the economic sphere. Which is not to say that the costs and benefits of a policy should not be pondered in advance of embarking on it, but only that we should not assume that it will always be *irrational* to refuse to weigh some value in terms of benefits. But *see* *rationality.

Council for Mutual Economic Aid. *See* *Comecon.

counter-culture. Term popularized by T. Roszak (*The Making of a Counter-Culture*, 1969), and used to denote the deliberate fostering and creation of a *culture suited to an *alternative society, in overt defiance of traditional forms, customs, manners and values. It is usually assumed that a counter-culture must be expressive of the ethos of liberty, toleration, and community based on mutual respect. However, it principally expresses itself in aggressive gestures designed to offend those who are merely tolerant towards (as opposed to committed to) its values.

counter-revolutionary. Term first used in 1793, by Condorcet, who defined it as a 'revolution in the contrary direction'. However *de Maistre, who advocated counter-revolution, described it as 'not a contrary revolution, but the contrary of a revolution' (1796). The term has since been made popular by *Marxist thought and practice. It has two distinct meanings:

1. (De Maistre.) A person, act or attitude opposed to some given *revolution, or to revolution as such.

2. (Condorcet.) A person, act or attitude which seeks to produce some *new* revolution designed to overthrow the order established by the last, perhaps in the hope of restoring (in whole or in part) the original government that preceded it.

The term is also used as a term of abuse in USSR *propaganda, to denote any rebellion against USSR dominion, even on the part of those who never had a revolution, never wanted one, and assert only what they consider to be *human rights.

counterfinality. The tendency of an act or policy to thwart its own aim. Counterfinality arises frequently in cases of *social choice, and is exemplified in various problems of *game theory, such as the *prisoner's dilemma, and in social *contradictions.

countervailing power. The forces which arise, particularly in *mixed economies, which counterbalance the bargaining power of large buyers, sellers and producers: e.g. the *trade unions, organizations of distributors and consumers, government operations against *monopolies and *administered prices, and so on. The term was introduced by J. K. Galbraith (*American Capitalism: The Concept of Countervailing Power*, 1952) in order to describe the new kind of economic organization that seems to have emerged in the place of **laissez-faire* capitalism, and to have superseded classical market competition. He argued that the state should always intercede on the part of the weaker power.

country. **1**. Country, as opposed to town: those parts of a territory in which there are few and small residential areas, and in which the major part of the *land is given over to agricultural uses. The country is normally characterized by a lower *social mobility than the town, a greater attachment to traditional modes of production, to custom, and to social *hierarchy, and (normally) a greater conservatism of political outlook. The town, by contrast, exhibits social mobility, highly divided and diversified labour, *bourgeois attitudes towards trade and production, and a constant friction between social classes. Theories of the emergence of town from country emphasize these factors, and (as a rule) the distinct *production relations that they exemplify.

2. A 'country' may also be an independent *sovereign state, identified, however, not in terms of its political features, but in terms of its *territory and *jurisdiction. The frequency of this usage emphasizes the important role that territorial conceptions play in identifying and explaining political entities. It also illustrates an area of potential confusion in political thought, since the relation between state and country seems not to be determinate. Thus Russia is the same country now as in the novels of Tolstoy; but is it the same state? Could A be the same state as B but a completely different country? (Suppose a given set of political institutions is simply transported, together with language and customs, from one part of the world to another: cf. the founding of Israel, which some believe did not occur in the present century.) The problems here are not unlike those that arise in trying to describe the relation between a human *person and his body.

3. Sometimes the word 'country' is used to denote *only* the territorial aspect of a state, so that a country remains the same whatever the political institutions that govern it, and whatever people should reside within its borders. This raises the question of how countries may be counted (for normally they are counted *in terms of* the political divisions that create boundaries). Take Czechoslovakia: is it one country? Or two (since it incorporates two *nations)? Or three (Bohemia, Moravia, Slovakia)? Or arbitrarily many? Each way of counting seems to point back to some present or previous political division.

4. In UK electioneering parlance, the 'country' signifies the *electorate, and 'going to the country' is a somewhat antiquated way of describing an appeal to the electorate (usually through the declaration of a general *election) to support the existing government.

coup d'état. A change of government by *force, resulting in a change of constitution, and brought about by those who already hold some form of power, whether military or political. The instigation of a coup thereby transforms the terms on which their office is held from a public trust into a private possession. A *coup d'état* supposedly differs from *revolution in that the latter is effected by the people, or at least by those who hold no power under existing arrangements, and perhaps represent themselves as 'leaders of the people' in order to gain it.

Examples of *coups d'état* include Napoleon I's seizure of power in 1799, Napoleon III's in 1851, Mussolini's in 1925, and in all probability (although the case is disputed) the seizure of power by the *bolsheviks in October 1917.

coup de Prague. In 1948, the Czech and Slovak *communist parties, having become the largest single body within a constitutional assembly of elected *representatives, created a single party state by a combination of demonstrations, threats, and violence, while maintaining for a time the outward appearance of constitutional legitimacy. A *coup de Prague* therefore means any quasi-constitutional seizure of power, backed by subversion and force, which effectively abolishes the constitution.

courts. Originally a court was a monarch's or great lord's palace; the name was then transferred to the society surrounding him, to some of the institutions of *parliament (cf. the Spanish *cortes*), and now generally to all institutions in which men sit in judgement over each other. Certain distinctions among types of court are important in understanding the practice of *adjudication:

(i) Criminal *v*. civil. The first deals with accusations of crime brought either by the state (perhaps through a representative, such as the UK Director of Public Prosecutions) or by a private citizen; the second deals with a *dispute* between parties over some matter governed by *law.

(ii) Courts of general *v*. courts of special jurisdiction. The first can deal with more or less any kind of case, the second only with specific matters (e.g. matrimonial disputes) mentioned in their constitution.

(iii) Superior *v*. inferior courts. A superior court is one that deals with more important cases, involves more qualified and specially selected officers and judges, and so on. An inferior court may involve an unqualified (and unpaid) magistrate, sitting as judge, and often its decisions may be made subject to review by a superior court. The distinction here must not, however, be confused with that between:

(iv) Appellate *v.* trial court. Judgements of the first bind the reasoning of the second (*see* *precedent), and, in appropriate circumstances, appeal can be made from a decision of the second to the first. Appellate systems may be many-tiered, as in the UK, where appeal can be made (provided permission is granted) from the Court of Appeal to the House of Lords. The last-named court is also the upper chamber of Parliament, and embodies in institutional form the traditional right of the *subject to appeal to his *sovereign.

(v) In the US, distinction must also be made between federal and state courts. Since there are separate systems of law for each state, in addition to the federal system which governs the US as a whole, separate courts are required, with officers of distinct competence and authority.

Among courts of special jurisdiction, certain examples stand out as being of independent political interest. Courts martial, for example, have a structure that fits them for the direct imposition of a discipline that is more surveillant than the ordinary *law. Here the courts are instituted *within* the armed forces, under the special discipline there applicable, and appeal is not normally granted to any court of more general jurisdiction. Compare the recently instituted industrial tribunals (*see* *industrial law), from which appeal is normally possible. These were established in the UK in 1964, and consist of three members, of whom the chairman alone need be legally qualified; they exercise jurisdiction under statutes dealing with a wide variety of disputes between employer and employee – such as complaints of unfair dismissal – which are not covered by the contractual relation between them. In both these cases we find forms of adjudication which have developed, not so much because of the content of special laws, as because of the need to adapt the administration of justice to special institutions. There are now also international courts of special jurisdiction, including a European Court of Human Rights (est. 1954), whose power to enforce its judgements is naturally severely limited.

The French Revolution introduced a new judicial institution, the 'revolutionary court or tribunal', in which states, or even private citizens, declare themselves to be enacting in judicial form the precepts or ideals of an existing or projected *revolution. Here people are tried for offences which may be wholly unspecific, and which often do not correspond to any law knowable to the offender or interesting to his accuser. A right of defence may not exist and prosecutor and judge are almost invariably identical, if not in person at least in aim. In such arrangements, it is often argued, elementary principles of *natural justice are ignored, so that it is a misnomer to speak of the result as a form of adjudication. To call the tribunals of modern Iran or of the Italian Red Brigade 'courts' is therefore sometimes criticized as a misleading if not dangerous usage, whereby violence is turned into justice by purely semantic means. The reply, that the real difference between violence and justice *is* merely semantic, consisting in the choice of terminology best suited to the interests of a ruling or oppressing class, is seldom withheld.

covenant. In law, an 'agreement under seal' (i.e. ceremonially sealed by the signatories), or, in a deed relating to land, or implied in such a deed, a condition binding on one or the other of the parties and attached to the land. The term 'covenant' was also used more generally, to denote any particularly binding promise, such as God's covenant to Noah. It is used in this sense by *Hobbes, for example, in describing the *social contract, and has also passed into modern political usage, to denote an obligation which establishes (and therefore is not created by) *international law. Thus the 'Covenant of the League of Nations' refers to the original charter which formed the first part of the Treaty of Versailles, 1919, and which created the League of Nations as an international body.

craft. The skilful adapting of means to ends. The craftsman is normally thought of as the *complete* producer of a *commodity, who does everything necessary to its manufacture. He is therefore distinguished from the *detail labourer, who plays only a *part* in the production of any commodity, and who, while employed as a means, need have no perception of the end which he thereby furthers. Thus a craftsman (such as a shoemaker) must be the master not of one skill but of many, related skills. It may also be, as some have argued, that his work absorbs him and satisfies him more completely than the work of the detail labourer, so that he may escape from the *alienation to which the latter is habitually subject.

The last suggestion underlies much of the admiration for, and desire to restore, craft in the place of detail production among romantic socialists and cultural conservatives in the nineteenth century. Chief among these were Ruskin, *Morris and the Pre-Raphaelites, who offered penetrating psychological analyses of the phenomenon that they advocated, but few feasible projects which would tend to restore it. More recent thinkers, rejecting their ideas, have nevertheless often tried to imagine ways in which the wholeness and satisfyingness of craft can be instilled into the industrial process. In all such discussions, the important fact has been, not the mechanical nature of detail labour, so much as its unnatural isolation from the process as a whole, and the supposedly incoherent view of his own *agency that the labourer thereby obtains.

credibility. Used of a policy (especially a policy of defence) to denote its ability to persuade those who need to be persuaded that it will, in the declared circumstances, be put into effect. The term is also used of a politician, to denote his ability to persuade others that he will govern according to a professed programme or *ideology; while a 'credibility gap' (US term) exists whenever there is a perceived disparity between official utterances and the facts surrounding them.

crime. In law, any offence declared by the *state as contrary to law, whether or not it constitutes a moral wrong, and whether or not some other party has a cause of civil action in respect of it. Any conduct may be declared criminal by law, and while many moral evils are also crimes, the categories of the morally wrong and the legally criminal are almost nowhere coextensive. (*See* *law and morality.) Indeed, if *civil disobedience is ever justified, this must be because there are actions which are morally obligatory, and yet also crimes.

The most important distinguishing characteristic of crime is that it confers on the state the legal right to punish the offender (rather than the legal duty to compel him to compensate the person he has wronged, though in primitive systems of law the precise character of this distinction is often obscured). One must distinguish *common law crimes from *statutory crimes, the former including murder, theft and rape, and corresponding for the most part to antecedent moral intuitions about what must not be done. (It should be noted that theft has been lifted out of the common law of England by statutes designed to systematize judicial findings.) It is also necessary to distinguish crimes according to their seriousness. English law used to recognize treasons, felonies and misdemeanours, allowing to the third a very low degree of culpability: in other legal systems this idea of the 'petty crime' is still enshrined in law.

The most important intellectual construct involved in the understanding of crime is that of the uniting of the guilty act (*actus reus*) and the guilty mind (*mens rea*). In English and US law most important crimes require both components. For example, the *actus reus* of murder is the causing of the death of an innocent. The *mens rea* is intending death, or intending to cause 'grievous bodily harm'. Both parts of the definition of a crime may present great problems of application: what is meant by 'causing' in the definition of the *actus reus*? And what is meant by 'intending' in the definition of the *mens rea*? Such questions, ultimately philosophical, occupy much of the subject-matter of *jurisprudence, and indicate the extreme complexity of our ordinary understanding of human acts. The element of *mens rea* may cover very complex states of mind, such as negligence (a disposition that involves no specific intention), a general desire to harm, and so on. Defences of insanity, diminished responsibility and the like involve trying to disprove *mens rea*.

There exist crimes for which no element of *mens rea* is required, crimes of *strict liability. In UK and US law only statutory crimes can be such, and then only when the absence of the requirement of *mens rea* is made explicit in the statute – else, by judicial construction, the element of *mens rea* will, in the interests of *natural justice, be inferred (see the House of Lords judgement in *Sweet* v. *Parsley*, 1970). Such statutory crimes are normally (but not always) of the kind that might otherwise have been described as misdemeanours – parking offences, and the like. Some legal systems, however, seem to permit strict liability even for serious offences, and so to issue severe punishments for wholly unintended acts. (Examples: Chinese, and also, it seems, Czech law.) The existence of large areas of strict liability is an indication of the extent to which a state is prepared to control the lives of its citizens. It is sometimes suggested that the nature of a state's criminal law is one of the best indications of its true moral nature; by observing the conduct a state forbids, one can infer the desires that it awakens in its citizens. Thus there is a clear difference in moral atmosphere between a state which makes emigration without special permission into a crime, and one which does not.

criminal law. The branch of law dealing with *crime and *punishment. In England the criminal law is founded in *common law, substantially modified by statute in 1861, and further in the twentieth century. In Scotland criminal law is still, for the most part, common law, while the English common law of crime persists in the US, adapted in certain respects to the different circumstances there prevailing. In most cases the application of criminal law is governed by the following basic principles of *justice:

(i) *Nulla poena sine lege*, or no punishment without a crime. No act can be punished unless a law exists which forbids it, however immoral, anti-social or destructive it may be.

(ii) Criminal law must be clear and unambiguous, so as to give 'fair warning'.

(iii) Criminal statues are to be construed strictly and not extended by analogy.

(iv) *Retroactive legislation is impermissible, unless expressly authorized by statute.

Such provisions are widely held to capture an important element in the idea of *natural justice, and impose real constraints on judicial construction. They are tantamount to the theory that when deciding a case, the judge does not make law, but discovers it. This theory is, however, a theory about what must be thought by the participants in the judicial process, not a theory about what must be true for that process to be possible. *See further* *hard cases.

criminology. The scientific study of criminal behaviour, often thought to have been founded by Cesare Lombroso (1835–1909), who attempted to trace criminal conduct to certain physical and biological characteristics of the criminal (*see* *atavism). In fact the study had already been begun in the eighteenth century with Beccaria's *On Crimes and Punishments*, 1764, an application of *hedonist principles to the study of the causes of crime, and had been continued subsequently by *Bentham.

Modern criminology is of wide scope, and concerns itself with almost every question concerning crime and punishment, including why criminal law becomes law, why societies punish criminals in the way they do, and the nature and effects of the various kinds of punishment. Emphasis has shifted from the exclusive concentration on the criminal, towards a more general sociological analysis. An extreme version of this shift is to be found in the work of the French philosopher and social historian Michel Foucault (b. 1926), who writes as though the most important question is not what causes the criminal to behave as he does, but rather, what causes society to punish him – for neither crime nor punishment can be judged against some absolute standard as 'normal'.

crisis management. After the Cuban missile crisis of November 1962 the US Secretary of Defense (McNamara) said that 'there is no longer any such thing as strategy, only crisis management', meaning that diplomatic relations reveal their meaning and potential only in crisis, and all foreign policy is focused on surviving crises.

crisis of capitalism (or: crisis of capitalist production). An expression used by Marx, and by many Marxists, to denote the situation in which capitalism, having harnessed *productive forces and turned them to its own ends, must go on to develop those forces beyond its power to contain them, so that the *production relations of capitalism begin to fetter the productive forces. Finally, the fetters burst asunder, along with all the social and political *superstructure that rests on them. Socialists differ as to the extent of their belief in such crises, and as to the precise explanation offered for their occurrence. Some endorse the suggestion just given, that the fundamental conflict is between productive forces and production relations – a suggestion that seems to capture the original idea of Marx. Some, influenced by other aspects of Marxist theory, find the conflict to exist *in* the capitalist production relations – perhaps in the form of a *class struggle. Some speak not of conflict but of *contradiction. Some find the source of crisis in the *falling rate of profit together with the constant pursuit of *profit. In all versions of the theory the crisis is supposed to be inevitable, either because it is of the essence of capitalism to foster growth beyond the limits that can be contained by it, or because capitalism generates social oppositions that can only exacerbate over time.

crisis of socialism. Term used by defenders of *capitalism (or of a *mixed economy), in order to point to the supposed facts:

(i) that the predicted internal collapse of capitalism (*see* *crisis of capitalism) has not occurred, perhaps because *production relations have bent in conciliatory directions, perhaps because productive forces have not continued to grow at an accelerating rate;

(ii) that in those societies called socialist there seems to be no satisfactory rate of growth, but rather a constant tendency to overproduction of some essential goods, and underproduction of others.

Some add that it is only under *market conditions that *equilibrium is possible, that market conditions are not possible without private property in the means of production, and that out of private property capitalist relations must inevitably develop.

critical theory. The theoretical outlook associated with Max Horkheimer, Jürgen Habermas, Theodor Adorno and other members of the *Frankfurt school who, while professing allegiance to Marxist methods of historical analysis, have seen the principal significance of Marxism as residing not in the theory of history, nor in the explanation of economic value and the process of production, but in the conceptual tools which it provides for the critical analysis of consciousness – e.g. as *false consciousness, or as *alienated. The early Marx is valued partly because he bears the imprint of *Hegel's speculative cultural analysis, and partly because he views the conflicts involved in capitalist production through their effects in the consciousness of those who participate in it. Many other sources also enter into critical theory, including 'systems theory' or *cybernetics, and *hermeneutics. The master-thought seems to be this: that consciousness stands to be interpreted, and in its interpretation the moral nature of social arrangements is revealed, in addition to their relationship to the production relations in which they occur. Associated with this 'diagnostic' analysis of consciousness is the attempt to explain *crisis and *catastrophe in all their forms, and on all the levels of self-awareness at which they are revealed.

Croce, Benedetto (1866–1952). Italian *idealist philosopher and politician, who wrote works of aesthetics, criticism and cultural history. These were influential partly on account of their attempt to translate the idealist thought into a style accessible to all educated people. Croce developed a theory of expression, as the necessary embodiment without which the mental life of the subject is formless and uncomprehended, and in terms of this theory attempted to show the importance of individuality in our knowledge of each other and the world. He affirmed the importance of the 'spirit' in human affairs and in history, and developed a theory of history according to which all true history is contemporary history – i.e. history as now perceived. He believed that history is the 'story of liberty', in which the moral life of humanity achieves its elaboration. The true bearer of moral value and moral freedom is the individual, although he achieves his fulfilment in the 'ethical universal', which is the state as conceived by the historian, as an expression of spirit, rather than the state as conceived, e.g., by the fascist demagogues, as an instrument of control. (Croce's initial support for fascism became overt hostility in 1925, when the first fascist dictatorship was established. Thereafter he was chief intellectual spokesman for liberalism in Italy, denounced by both Mussolini and *Gramsci.)

Croce's version of *liberal individualism was expanded in such a way as to preserve the traditional Hegelian defence of social existence and shared institutions. He gave an important assessment of the value of art and culture, and was influential on both liberal and conservative thought during the first half of the twentieth century.

crowd. A mass of people gathered together, but without formal bonds of *association, which responds collectively. The emergence of the crowd as an *agent of revolution during the French Revolution transformed the contemporary perception of political events, and the important role of crowds in modern politics has stimulated the study of their social and political significance. Crowds are more powerful than individuals, in that they are larger, and also capable of generating a sense of release from all moral and social restraint; hence crowds show virtues of sacrifice and vices of cruelty which no individual can show and which most people regard with amazement or abhorrence when not themselves absorbed into a mass of people. Crowds are also less powerful than individuals, in that they are without definite will or purpose until one is provided, and are open to irrational persuasion, influence and leadership: hence crowds can be controlled in ways that an individual may resist, partly because they generate public acceptance of all common conduct. Thus crowds can be used by a leader as a means to enhance and exercise his own power, and may yet have comparatively little power of their own should the leader be removed.

Sociological studies have varied from the specific – concentrating, for example, on such phenomena as crowd hysteria – to the highly general, as exemplified by Elias Canetti in *Crowds and Power*, 1960. Canetti argues (contentiously) that the instinct to form into a crowd is founded on a spontaneous reversal of the normal fear of being touched. In this reversal individuals 'discharge' their differences and become miraculously equal, borrowing power from their sudden union. This experience is supposed to explain many political phenomena: not only war, racial persecution, ceremony, and the peculiar kinds of 'closed' crowd known as religious congregation, but also such institutional crowds as the UK *Parliament, whose behaviour is explained by the fact that parliamentary *privilege encloses its members in a crowd by extending an indefinite permission to each of them. Even the sense of justice is traced by Canetti to the feelings of equality experienced at their most vivid among crowds, while submission to the crowd identity is offered as an explanation of *leadership, of the social reality of *command, and of the strange rapt attention of the theatre audience, and the power of the conductor of an orchestra. It is arguable, however, that such a theory is too general to be explanatory.

Crown. In UK legal and constitutional usage, 'the Crown' denotes the *office of the *sovereign and all acts of the sovereign in so far as they issue from that office. Property held by the Crown may in fact not be enjoyed by the sovereign personally, and acts in the name of the Crown may be unknown to the sovereign. The concept is that of an office, and does not denote the office-holder in any other way. The rules for succession to this office are of great constitutional significance, and have, since the Act of Settlement 1700, the Union with Scotland Act 1706, and the Union with Ireland Act 1800, been settled by *statute. The sovereign of the UK has many constitutional functions which are embodied, by statute, custom and convention, in the powers, rights and obligations of the Crown. The obligations include the upholding of the Church of England, of which the monarch is head, of the Presbyterian Church of Scotland, and of the Christian religion generally; the administration of justice, the upholding of parliamentary statutes, and the acts required as commander-in-chief of the armed forces. The whole government of the UK is carried on in the name of the Crown, and this confluence of functions in a single office is designed partly to convey a sense of political unity and *sovereignty. Despite the *delegation of almost all statutory powers through ministers, it is possible that enough customary and *prerogative powers remain to render the sovereign more than a symbol of sovereignty. He may for example be able to act so as to restore political unity in a time of crisis (as did King George V in 1931, under the prerogative). However, in most respects, 'the Crown' names a collection of *legal fictions.

cult of personality. Phrase coined at the USSR Communist Party conference of 1956, primarily to denote and explain away the style of government exercised by Stalin, but of wider application. It seems to refer to the concentration of political power and authority in a person, rather than in the office which he occupies, accompanied by an enforced adulation of that person on the part of ordinary citizens, and massive propaganda designed to display his superhuman virtues.

Having found this explanation for *Stalinism, the Communist Party remained haunted by the question of whether the 'Stalinist superstructure' was the necessary outcome of the socialist economic base. If historical materialism were true, then Stalinism was inevitable; if it was not inevitable, then historical materialism could not be true. The problem was made acute for the party by *Engels' officially accepted theory of 'so-called great men': 'If a Napoleon had been lacking another would have filled the place . . the man was always found as soon as he became necessary.'

cultural conservatism. A species of *conservatism characterized by the emphasis on the continuity of a *culture (usually a high culture), both as good in itself, and as a major cause of social and political stability. England in particular has a long tradition of cultural conservatism, stretching from the beginning of the *romantic movement to the present day, and involving such thinkers as *Coleridge, *Arnold, Cardinal Newman, *Carlyle and Ruskin in the nineteenth century, followed by less broad but often equally influential twentieth-century figures, among whom F. R. and Q. D. Leavis must be given prominence. F. R. Leavis was equally the heir to a parallel American tradition, typified by Emerson and Henry James, and bequeathed to English thought by T. S. Eliot, whose *Notes Towards the Definition of Culture*,

1945, remains one of the outstanding documents of this way of thought. This American cultural conservatism is directed towards conserving the fragments of old European culture, usually with an exile's consciousness of the difficulty of the task; but, like the English version, it tries to justify itself by making large and often striking claims for the role of culture in determining the quality of life, not just of those who possess it, but also of those who do not. The monument to that doctrine is the academic subject of English as taught, at least until recently, in many English and American universities, through which the political battle between *élitist and *egalitarian values has been fought out almost entirely in terms of standards of literary taste, and, conversely, literary taste has been represented as a major vehicle of social and moral consciousness.

Perhaps the most important text of cultural conservatism is Matthew Arnold's *Culture and Anarchy*, 1869, in which high culture is represented as the repository of 'sweetness and light', the guarantee that we may still pass on to future generations that inheritance of enlightened social order, calm government, and true human values, which is celebrated in the greatest works of art. High culture is therefore the antidote to anarchy, as well as containing within itself the refutation of utilitarianism, and of every other doctrine expressive of the *philistine consciousness.

Cultural conservatism involves a belief in the power of consciousness to determine political order, and thus stands opposed to most of the materialist visions of history. Specifically it involves the belief that certain activities which some would assign to the social and political superstructure are as important as, if not more important than, activities which such thinkers assign to the *base. It can be made plausible only by overthrowing the *Marxist theory of history, perhaps by means of a doctrine of **Verstehen*. It has often been criticized for its alleged intellectual snobbery and élitism, and alternatively as a forlorn attempt to endow art and high culture with functions that can only be filled by religion, thus conserving religious feeling in secularized form. It has also been thought to provide an intellectual backing to conservatism, while remaining aloof from all explicit *doctrine.

cultural revolution. Term introduced by *Lenin, in a crucial emendation of Marxist revolutionary theory, to indicate the fact and the ideal of a revolution in consciousness which both facilitates and is facilitated by the revolutionary transformation of the social and economic basis of society. Revolution requires the fulfilment of both 'objective conditions' (material transformation), and 'subjective conditions' (the way in which social reality is perceived). Cultural revolution is a necessary part of achieving appropriate subjective conditions, and involves the breaking down of the habits and artifacts of bourgeois *culture, so as to deprive the old economic order of its cultural support.

The modern use of the term owes much to *Gramsci's theory that cultural *hegemony must be destroyed if revolution is to succeed, and also much to the cultural revolution which occurred in China in 1967–8, which began as a reaction against bureaucracy and élitism, and as an attempt to achieve the necessary subjective conditions for socialist development, and soon got out of hand, galvanizing and applauding popular manifestations of *iconoclasm. Art, music, literature and the institutions of education were purged of 'Western' and 'bourgeois' influence, while revolutionary Red Guards were licensed to demote and humiliate those who seemed most responsive to such influences. Whether this movement was really an expression of what Lenin meant by cultural revolution is not entirely clear.

culture. **1**. In *anthropology and *sociology, 'culture' denotes indifferently all manifestations of social life which are not merely concerned with the reproduction and sustenance of human beings. Thus customs, habits of association, religious observances, even specific beliefs, may be spoken of as part of a culture. The ruling idea here is that there are activities which embellish and colour the process of survival, and give to it its distinctive local forms. Culture is often argued to have a role in the creation and conservation of a social order, and might even be susceptible to *functional explanation. Alternatively, for the anthropological *structuralist, it is to be understood first as a complex of symbols, and only secondly in terms of any function that it may (perhaps as a consequence) perform.

2. Outside that wide, and perhaps over-wide, technical usage, the term 'culture' is usually reserved for habits, customs and attitudes that are specific to *leisure. In this usage it is common to distinguish 'high' from 'low' culture, the first requiring educational attainments for its exercise and understanding, the second requiring no more than membership of society. To the first belong all activities in which true *aesthetic interest is exercised, and aesthetic values pursued; to the second belong dancing, entertainment, and sport, in which relaxation and social contact are the principal aims. The distinction between the two is neither sharp nor obviously significant. Some regard the attempt to make it more precise as a form of *élitism, on the supposition that the culture called 'high' will inevitably be put forward as preferable, despite the knowledge that it is inaccessible to the majority.

The distinction between high and low culture is nevertheless important to political thinking. Many modern governments regard themselves as under an obligation to support high culture (which, because of its limited appeal, may wither away in the absence of other forms of patronage), but usually have very little coordinated policy towards low culture. (But *see* *leisure, *sport.) According to *cultural conservatism such support is necessary, since high culture, in forming the outlook of the educated class, will, through the inevitable dominance of that class, shape the expectations and customs of society. This reverses the classical Marxist doctrine, that culture is the product, and not the cause, of particular forms of society, politically significant only because of its *legitimating role.

A culture can be said to be 'common' to a nation, class or social group when there is a shared familiarity with its products and practices, so that widespread reference and allusion is made to it, causing it to be a major determinant of the form and content of communication.

Among modern political movements concerned with culture, *nationalism has been the most prominent, and cultural conservatism has often formed an integral part of it. One may also mention Bismarck's 'war of culture' (*Kulturkampf*), in which he sought to wrest the formation of the educated classes from the control of the Roman Catholic Church, and the similar wars against cultural independence on the part of *Lenin, Hitler and Stalin. *See also* *cultural revolution.

custom. A form of repeated rational action, in which past performance provides the reason for present repetition, by showing 'what is done'. Custom is distinguished from *law, in that it need not be enforced by the *state or by legal penalties; from *convention, in that it need not be exact or rule-guided; from *habit, in that it is, nevertheless, something that only rational beings engage in, and can be attributed to non-rational animals only in a metaphorical sense. To do what is customary is to act intentionally, and for a specific reason, namely, that this is what is done. The reason may be a bad one, but it has the merit of referring beyond the agent to an implied social world and its justifying context. Custom forms a background from which law may emerge, as the crystallization of settled expectations. Without custom, it is argued, law and government would be difficult if not impossible; at the same time, to attempt to impose custom by law is inherently self-defeating, since it involves removing the freedom of action which makes custom possible. Attachment to custom is an important conservative ideal; it is often held to show that an action can be wholly justifiable, even though of only local validity, and not perceivable as valid by the person who does not engage in it. Customs are therefore sometimes extolled as providing the conservative substitute for *doctrine.

customs union. An association of states for the purpose of *free trade amongst themselves, and in which the member states apply common laws and regulations to trade with non-members. The second condition distinguishes a customs union from a free-trade area, in which members may still make what provisions they choose for trade with non-member states. A free trade area may be less stable, in that these differing relations with the outside world may cause internal frictions. For example, goods may enter through member states which impose low duties, and so cause an imbalance of trade with states which charge higher duties. A *common market goes beyond a customs union in permitting free movement of all means of production, including labour, capital, and the means of distribution.

cybernetics. Greek: *kubernēs*, a steersman. The study of the control and internal governance of systems (e.g. organisms, and machines exhibiting 'artifical intelligence'), where the various operations interact reciprocally and systematically. The term was invented in 1947 by Norbert Wiener and Arturo Rosenthal, and denotes not an existing but a projected science. Sometimes the expression 'systems theory' is preferred, and sometimes the two expressions are distinguished, the one being used to denote some branch, or supposed branch, of the science denoted by the other. It is held that systems can be more or less 'closed' to influence from outside, so that many of the laws of their operation and development can be understood in terms of the reciprocal interaction among component parts. It is further held that the laws governing such systems are universal, and do not apply merely to the organic realm, as traditionally defined. The term 'feedback' has been coined to denote the return of a part of the output of a system as a new input: positive feedback increases the input, negative feedback decreases it. Negative feedback is therefore inherently stabilizing, and acts so as to reduce activity, while positive feedback may be inherently destructive. The governor of a machine will be designed to produce negative feedback, braking the machine as it races; some think that capitalist economy exhibits positive feedback (growth stimulating further growth) in a manner that would perhaps warrant the prediction of a *crisis of capitalism. As the last example indicates, social arrangements are 'systems' in the relevant sense and this has led many sociologists and political thinkers to regard cybernetics as a useful tool in explaining social and political processes, although some doubt that there is anything to be said for this approach that will serve to distinguish it from the ancient theory of *organicism.

D

Dante Alighieri (1265–1321). Florentine poet who, in his *De Monarchia*, *c.* 1309 presented a philosophical description of *monarchy, and of the state, influenced by *Aristotle and *Cicero, but containing many distinctively modern features. He argued that peace is a necessity if human powers are to be realized, and that there can be no guarantee of peace while there are national rivalries: hence the world should be governed by one prince, who is supreme over nations, and also untempted by cupidity, having no further territory to gain. Salvation for human society requires the restoration of the Empire, which will generate the true order of government and also save the papacy from corruption. Dante argued that both institutions – empire and papacy – are sanctioned by divine ordinance, and both are necessary, the one holding all legitimate temporal power, and the other all legitimate spiritual power. The papacy cannot wield temporal power without also losing spiritual authority, in particular its authority to adjudicate disputes by referring them to the law of God. Its attempt to transform itself into a princedom was therefore a lapse from its divine mission and apostolic constitution. The dualistic vision of the origins of *power and *authority was developed against the background of a philosophy of *natural law, inspired by *Aquinas. Dante's discussion was highly influential in establishing the modern conceptions of the relation between religious and political allegiance, and of *political obligation. (*See also* *church and state.)

Darwinism. The name for any *evolutionary theory conceived in the spirit of Charles Robert Darwin (1809–82), who argued in *The Origin of Species*, 1859, that evolution proceeds by natural selection, generating the 'survival of the fittest'. Darwin's theory is part of an attempt to understand *functional explanation in biology; it is therefore sometimes imitated by those who wish to extend such explanation to the social sciences. It had direct impact on politics, for example, in giving credence to certain *racist ideologies, or to philosophies which emphasized the importance of racial character in determining political conditions and social responses. It also led to 'social Darwinism', a doctrine influential in the late nineteenth century, which argued that societies, like species, are subject to the law of natural selection, and are therefore inherently progressive in character, later examples always showing greater adaptation to circumstances than earlier ones. This transfer of evolutionary theory to the social sphere, while founding a certain callow optimism, seems to be based on confusion, concerning first the kind of organization, and secondly the time-scale of development, of that to which it is applied. Nevertheless, versions of the *Marxist theory of history that incorporate an idea of functional explanation seem to bear a marked similarity to Darwin's theory

de jure/de facto. A *power exists *de jure* if its exercise is authorized by *law. To say that it exists *de facto* is to say only that it exists, with the usual implication that the question of its *legitimacy has either not arisen or been settled in the negative. *See* *rights and powers.

death. Since it is the fact about the human condition that least bears contemplation, death tends to play a subdued part in political thinking, although images of death pervade political writings, lying behind Marx's description of revolution as 'the midwife of history' (so that the old society is also killed by its monster child), and also behind the many adulations of *terror, as a purging and salutary tonic. It is possible to distinguish outlooks which encourage the acceptance of death (either as the prelude to unearthly immortality, or as the sobering premise of moral reflection) from those which abhor it, and which attempt to provide a consoling picture of social existence without reference to this fundamental fear. The first often feature as underlying philosophies of conservatism, and are typically dismissed as *reactionary by those who seek for more mortal perfections. They have a tendency to reconcile men to their condition, and to induce a stoic (some would say complacent) acceptance of the inadequacy of present arrangements. They also tend to encourage belief in *providence and *destiny, as taking history out of human hands and ensuring the constant re-enactment of an imperfect social order. Typically such views are religious, *Buddhism providing perhaps the most important example. Rival doctrines usually attempt to replace the religious conviction of man's 'fallen' condition by a belief in human powers, and in *progress, with which to deflect attention towards a future state that will be characterized by material and spiritual satisfaction. The image of perpetual youth in some *utopian writings, and in the doctrine of the *alternative society, is a striking example of this attempt to remove hesitation, by forbearing to mention the fundamental source of human anxiety. It is often argued by conservatives that it is at least as important to accept death as to provide for life, and that a doctrine (such as *Marxism-Leninism) which seeks to remove the consolations which have aided in the acceptance of death, on the grounds that they have impeded the adequate or equal provisioning for life, is founded in a mistaken vision of human self-consciousness. Thus, from *Burke to T. S. Eliot, conservative thinkers have emphasized the fundamental need for religion in social order, and have criticized their opponents for overlooking this need. Others, while not prepared to endorse religion on these grounds, have nevertheless been prepared to concede the need for social arrangements that permit and facilitate *mourning*, and the ritual and ceremony that provides its social and cathartic significance. This concession is not necessarily a small one, since it requires endorsing both a measure of freedom of association, and respect for tradition; thus funeral ceremonies became, at one point, a focus of the clash between *Maoism and *Confucianism in modern China.

To take seriously the analogy between the *body politic and the human organism inevitably leads to the view that the first, like the second, is mortal. It must therefore strive (but not officiously) to stay alive, and perhaps also to accept its death as inevitable. In opposition to that idea there is a long tradition of *constitutionalism which regards a constitution as a means of securing permanence. Thus *Cicero wrote: 'death of the state is its punishment, even though it seems to relieve all individuals of punishment; for a political body must be so constituted that it might be eternal'. This thought partly explains the reluctance among many progressivist thinkers to accept the organicist position, and the tendency to substitute for it a more mechanical, or at any rate unilinear, view of the movement of history.

decadence. The condition of society in which *values, customs and certainties are in decline, not because of economic collapse, but because of moral and spiritual exhaustion. Characteristic of decadence is the affectation of traditional values on the part of those who no longer sincerely believe in them, and also their deliberate (perhaps even orgiastic) violation by those who thereby hope to awaken in themselves some titillation of guilt, and so experience the faint after-image of conviction. Another, less sophisticated, manifestation is the wholesale pursuit of physical and sensual gratification, combined, perhaps, with an inability to understand the higher forms of human interest, or why, indeed, the word 'higher' should be chosen to denote them.

Gibbon famously attributed the decline and fall of Rome to decadence; and the decadence of human society has been a favourite theme of moralists ever since human society began. Whether things are actually worse now than they were in the time of Jeremiah is perhaps not in point; it may be fair to say, however, that the accusation is more widespread, very often with 'bourgeois society' as its principal object. Some theorists have taken an 'ontogenic' view of civilization, according to which each phase of development has a life process, with a primeval, middle, and decadent stage. Thus *Hume, Burckhardt, *Vico, and *Spengler each thought of decadence as part of an ubiquitous process of cyclical fulfilment and decay; for *Bodin, *Montesquieu, Turgot, and *Comte, however, periods of decadence are only incidental aberrations from an indomitable advance. Modern social scientists often explain decadence in terms of 'dysfunctionality': i.e. decadence arises when a social and political superstructure has ceased to fulfil the social and perhaps economic functions required of it, and can therefore no longer command the wholehearted support of the members of society.

decentralization. The process whereby *centralization is reversed, so that power is shifted from central political and administrative bodies, answerable to a single executive, to a multitude of quasi-autonomous bodies, concerned with the formulation and application of policy in particular regions and in answer to local and variable requirements.

Decentralization has often been put forward as a remedy against the concentration of power, and as a means of ensuring that the needs and expectations of the common citizen are respected. It is not clear that it need have either effect, since *sovereignty requires that the original concentration of power be conserved, even if mediated by new local institutions. Decentralization seems to occupy a midway point between mere 'deconcentration' (the *delegation of power to local officers) and *federation (the division of internal sovereignty). *See* *devolution, *federation, *local government.

decision theory. A branch of applied mathematics, designed to formalize the notion of *rational choice under conditions of risk and uncertainty. It incorporates the theory of probability, and attempts to compute the relative *costs of different courses of action on the basis of their probable outcome. (Bayesian decision theory is characterized by adherence to the theorem in probability theory put forward by Thomas Bayes (1702–61).) Decision theory is a part of *cost-benefit analysis, being largely confined to the study of the relative importance of probabilities, given an assignment of costs. It aims to provide axioms and rules of inference which convey the structure of rational choice, but is applicable only on the assumption that rational choice concerns itself with quantifiable costs and benefits which may be balanced against each other. *See also* *game theory, *preference, *utilitarianism.

deficit financing. The deliberate policy whereby a government spends more than its income. It takes the form of a budget financed by borrowing or by expanding the *money supply, usually with the object of raising the general level of purchasing power so as to stimulate economic activity and increase employment. The use of deficit financing as part of monetary policy was advocated by *Keynes.

deflation. **1**. The opposite of *inflation, signifying falling as opposed to rising prices.

2. The condition of reduced economic activity, where there is *unemployment and unused productive capacity.

*Neo-classical economists argue that if prices (including wages) are perfectly flexible, real economic activity is independent of the price level, and depends solely on relative prices. They would tend to employ the first definition. The second definition, however, is more common.

deism. A system of natural religion, classically expounded in J. Toland's *Christianity not Mysterious*, 1696, and highly influential in eighteenth-century France and Germany. Reason is the necessary and sufficient guarantee of faith, and tells us that God exists, that the world is governed by a natural moral law, and that future punishments and rewards will be based on observance of that law. God is the all-wise, all-benevolent and omnipotent creator, but it is inconsistent with his nature that he should further intervene in creation. This *demythologized belief, which sweeps the world clean of miracles and mysteries, and makes direct appeal to the deity absurd, had a profound influence on *Enlightenment thought, and notably on the moral and religious doctrines of *Kant. It accompanied the similar demythologizing of the idea of *political obligation, and furthered the *secularization of political doctrine, and the growth of religious *toleration.

delegation. The transfer of authorized power to a subordinate person or body, who acts not merely as the channel for that power, but as its agent, making decisions in its name. A delegate is authorized to act only in accordance with specific instructions, or a specific ideology. Delegation therefore differs from *representation, without being as rigidly controlled as mandation. The most important forms of delegation are military – from commanding to subordinate officer – and constitutional, from *Parliament or *Congress, for example, to bodies which are given powers to legislate in their name. (Although since Congress does not have the full *sovereignty of Parliament, it seems that its powers of delegation are limited: *Schechter Poultry Corp.* v. *US*, 1935.) Delegated legislation has become increasingly important in the UK since the Reformation, and in particular since 1832, with the growth of government influence in all spheres of administration. It is frequently criticized on account of the uncertain validity of any controversial enactment, and the uncertain competence of the legislator. The main demand in all criticism is for adequate parliamentary or congressional control. In the UK, however, challenge in the courts is often hindered by provisions which say that legislation made by the delegatee is as valid as the empowering statute, or that confirmation by a minister is to be conclusive evidence that the requirements of the statute have been complied with.

A delegate is bound by the longstanding rule of law that he cannot himself unless specifically authorized delegate the power conferred on him (*delegatus non potest delegare*), which provision is necessary if there is to be genuine delegation, as opposed to the universal diffusion, of the power of state, and genuine *answerability for the exercise of that power.

The concept is to some extent clarified by the distinction between delegation and representation. The former confers power through the directives of an original; the latter confers powers, in addition to those conferred by the original, which belong to the institutional structure through which representation is effected. In the latter case the two powers may act so as to limit each other, so that a representative cannot be bound to carry out all the directives of those whom he represents, whereas a delegate must do all that he is required to do, and sometimes nothing that he is not specifically required to do.

demagogue. Greek: a leader of the people. Now used to signify a person able to obtain political *power through *rhetoric, by stirring up the feelings of his audience and leading them to action despite the considerations which weigh against it. The demagogue is often held to require *charisma and qualities of *leadership. He at least needs to appear cogent in answer to every question, and to appear absolutely convinced of the truth of what he utters, master of himself, his audience, and his mission. In addition a demagogue is usually thought to be motivated more by the desire for power than by concern for the common good, to be prepared to appeal to irrational motives, and to be bent on policies that are disastrous for the people as a whole. He benefits by representing himself as possessing knowledge of the future, and a theory which validates that knowledge, and by urging the people to take action against powers that have conspired to delude and oppress them.

demand. The willingness and ability to pay for goods and services. A 'demand curve' is a geometric representation of the relation (the demand function) between *price per unit of product and the quantity demanded by the consumer. The demand curves of all consumers are aggregated to obtain the market demand curve which will, in general, reflect the 'law of demand': the lower the price, the greater the quantity of the product demanded (although naturally the price cannot normally become negative). Exceptions to this law include goods purchased for ostentation, where price is thought to be a sign of quality, or the ability to pay to be a sign of social distinction. An apparent exception is provided by some kinds of speculative buying, in which a rise in price evokes the hypothesis that prices might rise yet further.

demand-pull inflation. *See* *inflation.

democracy. Literally, government by the

*people as a whole (Greek: *demos*) rather than by any section, class or interest within it. The theory of democracy is immensely complicated, partly because of difficulties in understanding who the people are, and which acts of government are truly 'theirs' rather than those of some dominant group or interest. (*See* *collective choice.) The first distinction to be made is that between *direct and representative democracy: in the first all citizens participate in decision-making, say by voting and accepting a majority verdict. In the second case, the people choose (say by voting) representatives who are then answerable to them, but at the same time directly involved, and usually without further consultation, in the practice of government (*see* *representation, *and* cf. *delegation).

Apart from that distinction, however, there is little agreement as to what is important in constituting a regime as democratic. This is partly because of two conflicting criteria that might be employed in the assessment of any political decision: by whom was it taken? (which raises the problem of *collective choice) and: whose interest does it serve? (which raises the problems of social welfare, and *social choice). It is normal in the West to use the first criterion, and to call a state democratic if there is *some* way of attributing every major political decision to the people, either because they take part in making it, or because it ultimately depends upon their *consent. It is normal in the Soviet bloc to use the second criterion, and to regard decisions as democratic if they further (or perhaps only if they are intended to further) the interests of the people, even though taken by a ruling party which forbids popular membership of its ranks. (*See* *democratic centralism.) Since in practice decisions taken by a ruling party tend to be as much in the interests of that party as decisions taken by a ruling class are in the interests of that class, the first criterion is more easily recognized as embodying a principle of democracy, although many *Marxists would here speak of *bourgeois democracy, and dismiss the impression as an elaborate *ideological illusion.

As soon as societies become large, with large-scale *division of labour and complex patterns of *distribution, direct democracy seems hardly feasible. The question of principal importance then seems to be, what makes a **constitution* democratic? It is to this question that the theory of Western constitutional democracy addresses itself, burdened also by ancillary questions inherited from the long history of European constitutional government, in which what first existed as a right of appeal of every subject to the sovereign, was gradually transformed into *limited government with representational assemblies whose consent had to be sought for every legislative and executive decision. It is clear that to limit, in this way, the power of government is not of itself to transfer it to the people, and while regular *elections and universal *suffrage are now seen as essential features of a democratic constitution, they are only one part of a mode of government which may yet be undemocratic in every other particular. In particular every constitution requires a framework of *offices and *conventions which will not be subject to easy emendation by popular choice. Hence power and privilege intrinsic to that framework (e.g. that vested in a *civil service) will rarely be seen as a reflection of popular choice, however necessary it may be to making that choice effective. Moreover, a democratically elected government may proceed to enact, during its term of office, policies which are manifestly in conflict with the wishes and the interests of the people.

In representative democracies various criteria have been laid down for determining when an election really does reflect the choice of an electorate. Furthermore, attempts have been made to impose democratic organization on all subject institutions within a democracy, in order to avoid the obvious objection that the state represents only one among many concentrations of political power. The desire to extend democratic decision-making through every *autonomous body has led to much heart-searching in recent politics, partly because it has seemed that, without that extension, democracy is seriously incomplete. This thought also lies behind many justifications given for the forms of government existing in communist states. It is said that democracy can be manifest in three spheres – the political, the economic and the social – and that bourgeois democracy considers at best only the first of those. The other two are equally important, and require collective *control of the means of production (economic democracy) and the abolition of social *privilege (social democracy). 'Capitalist democracy', which exists only in the political sphere, is a device which prevents the emergence of democracy at the economic and social level; 'true democracy' can come about only when the conditions for it are prepared at those more basic levels – hence the need for a (provisional) *directed democracy in the political sphere.

democratic centralism. Term adopted by the *Communist Party in the USSR and elsewhere to designate the variety of decision-making recommended by *Lenin, and supposedly practised in Soviet government. It is held to involve free political discussion within the party, and free elections to party offices, combined with a one-party state and a strict hierarchical discipline. It has been clear since the *Comintern that the last element is the most important: 'the Communist Party will be able to fulfil its duty only if its organization is as centralized as possible, if iron discipline prevails, and if the Party centre, upheld by the confidence of the Party membership, has strength and authority and is equipped with the most comprehensive powers' (*Twenty-one Conditions of Admission to Comintern*). 'Centralism', therefore, means the concentration of all power in the central party organization, which is made responsible for the organization and development of every institution in which political influence may arise, from the school to the factory floor, and from the family to the police force, and which is therefore intolerant of every autonomous body within its sphere of influence. This centralism is 'democratic' partly because it is held to operate in the interests of the people, for example by enforcing common ownership of the means of production, and partly because of the supposed internal democracy of the party, whereby each echelon is filled by representatives voted from the one below. While some theorists (e.g. *Mao) argue that true centralism and true democracy (in the sense of answerability to popular sentiment) require each other, in practice the first seems to conflict with, and override, the second, candidates at *all* levels being subject to confirmation by the ruling élite. (*See* *influence.)

democratic despotism. Term introduced by *Tocqueville (*L'ancien régime et la Révolution*, 1856,) in order to signify the kind of *despotism which supposedly proceeds from too fervent and too uncritical an adherence to the doctrine of the *sovereignty of the *people: 'No gradations in society, no distinctions of classes, no fixed ranks – a people composed of individuals nearly alike and entirely equal – this confused mass being recognized as the only legitimate sovereign, but carefully deprived of all the faculties which could enable it either to direct or even to superintend its own government. Above this mass, a single officer, charged to do everything in its name without consulting it. To control this officer, public opinion, deprived of its organs; to arrest him, revolutions, but no laws. In principle a subordinate agent; in fact a master.'

democratic parties. Parties are normally formed in order to propose policies to an electorate and to pursue power as a means to put those policies into practice. This process may or may not occur within a framework which merits the label 'democratic'. A democratic party must nevertheless claim to uphold that framework, and this is often taken to mean upholding free and periodic elections, so that the party is committed also to guaranteeing that it may be expelled from office should it lose public support. This commitment is perhaps the only thing which all 'democratic' parties tend to share, and its existence goes no further than democratic parties in Western constitutional states. Many of the communist parties in *people's democracies declare themselves to be democratic, but, partly because of the ambiguity of the term '*democracy', they are able consistently to oppose any constitution that would make it possible for them to lose power.

The US Democratic Party deserves individual mention on account of its special relation to constitutional government as this has evolved in the present century. It was founded in 1828 and dominant until 1860, when it became identified with the South, and was unable to return a President to office until Cleveland in 1885. Since then the Democratic Party has steadily lost its conservative and agrarian image (which has instead been adopted by the rival Republican Party) and identified itself with a kind of enlightened *dirigisme, in which American ideals of liberty and self-determination are combined with active government concern for the poor and the dependent. It thus emerged after the Depression as the champion of government intervention, and embodied in the *New Deal of President Roosevelt (1933–45) the first systematic programme of social welfare for the US as a whole. The arguments before the Supreme Court that much of the programme of the New Deal was in fact unconstitutional show the extent to which a like background of policy is imposed on the two major parties in the US by the supervision of the constitution. Nevertheless the image of the Democratic Party as to the *left of the Republican has survived since that time, and determines to some extent the nature of the support that is offered to it, as well as the policies that it advances when in office. At the same time, however, it must be remembered that, in the US, 'changing one's political complexion is made easier by the fact that the conservative-liberal distinction does not coincide with party lines. The Democratic ranks are heavy with liberals, the Republican with conservatives. Each party, nevertheless, harbours an important minority of the opposite persuasion' (R. V. Denenberg: *Understanding American Politics*, 1976, 2nd edn. 1980).

democratic socialism. *Socialism pursued by *democratic means – e.g. through persuasion of the electorate in a state ruled by representative institutions. ('The parliamentary road to socialism'.) Normally contrasted with socialism and communism imposed by force, following a revolution or *coup d'état*. ('The revolutionary road to socialism'.) Not to be confused with *social democracy. Democratic socialism is professed by many Western parties, e.g. the UK Labour Party.

democratization. The introduction of features of *collective choice into institutions and associations which are not themselves parts of government: e.g. places of work, schools and universities, churches and local communities. Democratization is a major political movement in Western countries, and is often seen as an essential feature of *gradualist social reform in accordance with a respect for existing institutions.

demystification. The process of removing the mystification from things, specifically from social things, usually by attempting to reveal the true causes of social beliefs and behaviour. This may sometimes be equivalent to *demythologization, but is of wider application, arising for every item of social consciousness, however innocent of *myth. Demystification involves the critical analysis of thoughts and ideas held to conceal social realities, and its principal examples are the Marxist theories of *ideology and *false consciousness. (For example, it is normal for a Marxist to argue that the reality of wage labour is no different from that of slavery, since the labourer, owning nothing but his labour power, is compelled to sell himself to his master, the capitalist. But this reality is mystified by the contract of labour, which represents this bondage as free.) The varieties of demystification are, however, considerably wider, ranging from *critical theory and other products of academic reflection, to the *nihilism of the 'romantic twilight', and the invigorating *egoism recommended in this century by the ideologists of fascism and national socialism. In the face of this attempt to remove all mysteries from human things – which some see as founded in a deeper hostility to human *values – many conservative thinkers have emphasized the difficulty of living without mystery, some even going so far as *Plato, and advocating the 'noble lie'.

demythologization. Term introduced by the German theologian Rudolf Bultmann (1884-1976) to denote the systematic removal from the New Testament teaching of elements of *myth. Bultmann regarded belief in the bare fact of Christ crucified as sufficient for *Christian *faith, and considered that it was necessary to reinterpret as allegorical all those elements of the gospel which could not command rational assent in a modern believer. The idea of a demythologized religion has existed for at least two centuries, was given evangelical form by *deism, and found early systematic expression in *Kant's *Religion within the Limits of Reason Alone*, 1793. However, once Bultmann had made the term fashionable, its use was rapidly extended beyond theology to describe a persistent, and characteristically *modern, outlook on the world. The demythologized worldview is one in which all appearances are reviewed and amended in the light of science, and in which no supernatural beliefs are allowed to gain a foothold. Symbolic modes of thought and behaviour are perceived as such and not regarded as intimations of a world order other than that discoverable to science. The extreme form of this attitude has often been criticized under the name of *scientism, and sociologists influenced by *Weber have sometimes argued that the element of 'enchantment' in human thinking is socially indispensable. Nevertheless, even if no adequate substitutes for myth are available, it does not follow that a rational being can suspend his disbelief in it.

dependence. A state is politically dependent when its power structure and institutions are controlled from outside, economically dependent when exports and imports are necessary for survival. Both forms of dependence may be enforced by another state, either by conquest or by *Finlandization. All states are now dependent to some degree, although the ideal of political and economic *autarky is not without adherents (*see* *isolationism). The major distinction lies between those which are dependent on *one*, more powerful, state (such as the states of Eastern Europe) and those which are multilaterally dependent, in the manner of most of the states in the Western bloc. Originally, however, a dependency was not a sovereign state, but one which owed allegiance directly to a dominant sovereign power. (See, e.g., G. C. Lewis: *An Essay on the Government of Dependencies*, 1841.) In UK law this sense remains, and a 'dependency' is a state or region not annexed by the *Crown but subject to UK *jurisdiction (it is thus a wider term than 'colony').

Recent international power struggles are sometimes thought to have shown a change from old methods of securing political dependence through threat or conquest, to the newer techniques of subversion, and economic dependence, brought about, say, by the saturation of a market.

depression. The state of an economy in which labour and the means of production remain unemployed for an extended period (as opposed to *recession, where the unemployment is of shorter duration). The most significant example in recent times, which has had incalculable political consequences, was the Depression of 1929-34 – the 'world slump' – which, beginning in America, transmitted itself through international banking and uncontrolled credit transfers to central Europe and then to the UK, so that its political effects were immediate and striking throughout the capitalist world – notably in the *New Deal in the US, in the rise of *national socialism in Germany, and in the political instability of central Europe.

déracinement. French: uprootedness. Term used by French political thinkers (especially *Weil) to describe the state of man torn loose from his cultural, religious and moral origins, led to question the validity of all instinctive relations, and deprived of the forms of life through which to rehearse and renew his social nature and attachments.

Descartes, René (1596–1650). French philosopher and mathematician. *See* *false consciousness, *human nature, *natural light, *rationalism.

deschooling. A view of educational institutions advocated notably by Ivan Illich, Paul Goodman and Paolo Freire, which sees the school as an inherently political institution at the mercy of political interests (in this case, it is supposed, *international capitalism) and seeks to replace schools with 'educational networks' that will provide knowledge to the child without providing power to an institution.

desegregation. The process, begun in the US in the 1950s, of attempting to procure for blacks, not just the nominal freedom and equality guaranteed under the constitution, but actual political equality with whites, by abolishing the established separation of educational, recreational and other facilities.

despotism. From Greek, *despotēs*, meaning originally a master (for example, of a household, and so of slaves), and applied to the *absolute ruler of a people whose condition could be compared to that of *slavery. Now often applied to any form of *arbitrary or *tyrannical government, but perhaps better used to mean a form of government that is not inherently *limited by law, custom or effective *opposition, so that the power of state can encroach wherever and whenever this should please those who wield it. To be distinguished from *absolutism, which may involve real limitations on the power of government, but where those limitations are not specifically enshrined in law.

Since *Montesquieu's celebrated analysis of despotism (*De l'ésprit des lois*, 1748) it has seemed evident that a necessary condition for its existence is the concentration of powers in a single person, office or political *agent, so that there is no internal constraint on or correction of the exercise of power. (*See* *separation of powers.) The concentration of power does not have to be in an individual. The original Greek meaning suggests that the important feature of despotism is the condition of those subject to it, and it makes little material difference to that condition that all power should be concentrated in a committee, or a party, rather than an individual, except in so far as this multiplicity of *command may permit the subject to secure relief, either by exploiting disagreements, or by obtaining some covert form of *representation.

Despotism requires that power be not only concentrated but also without effective opposition within the state. It is also arbitrary, in the sense of standing above law, at least to some degree: however it is not easy for any power to be wholly arbitrary without arousing opposition stronger than itself, hence actual despotism always exists in conjunction with a system of law, however primitive, whereby to *legitimate its own exercise, and transgresses the law only when this is thought to be essential to maintaining its supremacy. Hence a fiction of legality is usually maintained.

Some writers have referred to 'enlightened despotism', to indicate, for example, the peculiar kind of absolute monarchy exercised in Prussia under Frederick the Great. In such cases it is supposed that the individual character of the despot is such as to ensure that concentrated power is used in the pursuit of ends that are worthy in themselves, and perhaps likely to recommend themselves to a liberal conscience, while needing despotic power for their realization.

destabilization. The process whereby the subject institutions of a state, and its law ful *associations (e.g. schools, businesses, armed forces) are deliberately set against the state, by agitation and *propaganda, so that the political order should become unstable, permitting conquest or *annexation by another external or internal power. Destabilization plays an important part in USSR *strategy, which often advances the thesis that *deterrence without offensive preparations is already a destabilizing act, and merits retaliatory acts of destabilization, although the argument, taken to its logical limit, clearly requires that any defence *against* the USSR merits destabilization *by* the USSR. The term has also been used of some US strategy in South America.

destiny. An impersonal force which orders the affairs of men, so as to propel them through life independently of their will, but in a manner illustrative of their character, and perhaps symbolic of their condition. The idea has existed in mystical form (which makes destiny unknowable), in religious form (which transforms destiny into *providence), and in the form of scientific or quasi-scientific doctrines about the nature of history (*see*, for example, *historical materialism, *Spengler). Most people believe that some things that happen to them are independent of their will; the singular character of a belief in destiny is the conviction that all the *important* things that happen in human affairs are independent of the will. The intermediate position is that of common sense, which holds that there is a basic 'human condition'. This is, and perhaps ought to be, independent of the will; in the context of the human condition, projects may be undertaken which can fail for the smallest reason or succeed despite the odds. Extreme forms of liberal anarchism dislike such ideas, and are reluctant to countenance the existence of unchangeable features of humanity. Matters previously assigned to destiny are, it is supposed, or ought to be, brought within the arena of *consent. Noteworthy among these matters is sexuality, previously thought to define the condition from which the individual begins, now sometimes thought to be a matter of personal choice, which may be 'tacitly consented' to, but which might easily be changed.

detail labour. *Labour that is directed entirely to some detail in the process of production, and which therefore produces a *commodity only in combination with other labour of a similar kind. A production line creates successive tasks for detail labour, and exemplifies the 'detail division of labour'. This is to be distinguished from the social *division of labour, since it is characteristic, not of *market conditions as such, but of the industrialization of production, and can, presumably, exist without a market economy.

Detail labour has been the object of much distaste, on the part of socialists and conservatives alike, both of whom have tended to see in it a dehumanization of the labourer and a source of *alienation. It is sometimes opposed to *craft, which is held to be complete and completely intelligible to the labourer, in the way that a production line cannot be. While the consequent attempt to restore craft-like modes of production (*see* *Morris) has often been criticized as short-sighted and quixotic, there seems to be general agreement that *something* is wrong with production that requires a man, for much of the day, to devote himself completely to an action that is incomplete.

*Marx attempted to offer a more 'objective' critique of detail labour – i.e. one that did not merely lean on the subjective features of the alienated consciousness which are so often in this context referred to. In *Capital* I, xiv, 4, he argued that the detail labourer produces no commodities, and that this is made possible by the control of the labour power of several labourers by a single capitalist. Detail division then constitutes a 'separation of the labourer from the means of production', which means are converted by that separation into fixed capital. (The idea being that no single labourer is now in a position to produce anything for sale, and so is necessarily dependent upon a system which denies his control over the product of his labour.) This brings about a condition of enslavement to the means of production, which Marx thought to be distinctive of capitalism, but which is presumably distinctive of any system in which detail division occurs – including modern communism as practised. (Note, however, that the term *state capitalism is here often applied precisely to denote the fact that control of the means of production remains outside the hands of the producer.)

Marx's critique was anticipated by Adam *Smith, who laments the idiocy and enslavement consequent upon detail labour, while asserting that 'in every improved and civilized society this is the state into which the labouring poor, that is, the great body of the people, must necessarily fall' (*Wealth of Nations*, v, i, ii). Whatever the truth in this lament, it seems that only a small proportion of the work force in most modern capitalist countries is employed at any moment in detail labour.

détente. French: the reduction of tension between states. The term is used largely in connection with US–USSR relations since the late 1960s, in which a policy of *peaceful coexistence has been professed by both parties, and apparently pursued, through arms limitation talks and the Helsinki Accord, 1975, on security and cooperation in Europe. Many analysts argue that the agreements reached have been regarded, by at least one of the parties, as a useful diversionary tactic, facilitating the acquisition of new armaments and even the invasion of a neighbouring state. Thus it is often pointed out that any citizen of any country within the Soviet bloc who attempts to cite the Helsinki agreement in support of a claim for *civil rights is at once savagely punished. It cannot be, therefore, that the USSR thinks that the Helsinki agreement is in any way binding. Others argue that there are necessary differences of interpretation, and that no agreement between superpowers can be expected to have quite the force of a contract.

determinism. **1**. The philosophical doctrine that everything that happens is determined by that which preceded it. More precisely: nature is governed by 'deterministic' laws, such that, given a complete description of the world at one time and a statement of those laws, a complete description of the world at any later time may be deduced. Determinism is sometimes thought to imply that all events happen by necessity, and that nothing could be other than it is. However, this obscures an important distinction, between *fatalism, and what *J. S. Mill called 'philosophical necessity', which denotes only the operation of universal natural laws.

Philosophers debate over (a) whether or not determinism is, or could be, true (for example, does the dominance of irreducibly statistical laws in microphysics refute it?); (b) if it is true, is it compatible, or incompatible, with human freedom? The thesis of 'compatibilism', variously advanced by *Spinoza, *Hobbes, *Hume, *Kant, and J. S. Mill, argues that human freedom does not require any violation of the causal order, and so is compatible with the truth of determinism.

2. In political thought 'determinism' is normally used more narrowly, to denote the view that human choice is not itself a main causal factor in the generation of social and political arrangements. Whether or not we have free will, history is determined independently of its exercise, for example, by economic processes which continue and develop however we choose to act on them. (*See* *historical materialism.)

*Vulgar Marxism, which is in part distinguished by that view, also argues that since human consciousness is a product of material conditions, those conditions cannot themselves be brought about by consciousness (i.e. by intentional action). Implausible though such a view may be, it has a certain appeal, since it seems to entail that the political action of one's opponent is based on an illusion. It also entails that political action of one's own is based on the same illusion, but this consequence is not always so clearly perceived.

deterrence. To deter is to dissuade an agent from a course of action by alerting him to consequences that he does not desire. In the theory of *punishment, deterrence is often presented as a, or the, major justification of the practice, and in that context must be carefully distinguished from retribution, vengeance, and correction. The term has achieved wider political currency from modern *strategies of defence, notably in the context of the threat of nuclear war. Strategists distinguish active or extended deterrence (which threatens retaliation to any act of aggression, whether against the state in question or against its allies), from minimum or finite deterrence, intended to protect only the state which adopts it. Graduated deterrence is the systematic strategy of demonstrating an intention to punish hostile acts in accordance with their seriousness, while mutual deterrence is the relation that exists between two hostile powers that effectively deter each other from war. *See* *balance of terror.

devaluation. An increase in the amount of domestic currency required to purchase a unit of foreign currency. Since devaluation raises the price of foreign goods and services at home, while lowering the prices of domestic goods and services to purchasers abroad, it tends to increase the volume, though not necessarily the value in money terms, of exports, and correspondingly discourages imports. Social, economic and political reasons may make governments reluctant actively to devalue. Instead a government may 'float' the currency, leaving the level of the exchange rate to be determined in the international market. *See* *exchange control.

developing country. A phrase imprecisely used, and variously defined. Generally, a developing country is one that is poor in terms of *per capita* income, and whose economic structure is backward. One theory is that developing countries have not yet reached the stage of *development sufficient to yield domestic savings which will finance further *economic growth. That definition assumes that growth has no natural limits, and that the presence of self-stimulated growth is the main thing that separates the rich from the poor among nations. Some regard the word 'developing' as evasive, since it begs the question as to the real position of the nations relative to one another. A like evasion may seem to be involved in 'underdeveloped', 'backward', and so on. The implicit assumption is that a universal process, which has occurred elsewhere, is here only in its initial stages, and that all that is necessary in order that the poorer nations should come into line with the richer is that this process should be actively stimulated. Although many of the 'developing' nations have indeed experienced economic growth, it has been at a much slower rate than that of the developed nations, thus causing the gap between the two to widen (i.e. their relative growth rate has declined). Some believe the process of trade that has this result to be for that reason unjust.

Various attempts have been made – e.g. through *aid – to alleviate the condition of the poorer nations (e.g. by the United Nations, through its Conference on Trade and Development, UNCTAD). Any solution that does not envisage substantial improvements in the *infrastructure of poorer countries is at best a temporary measure, and some argue that this improvement cannot be achieved by aid alone. (*See* * three worlds theory.)

development. Usually used to denote the process of *economic growth in *per capita* *income, and the fundamental changes in economic structure that generate that growth. Generally these include: *industrialization, the migration of *labour to industrial areas, *division of labour, etc.; the consequent revisions in *production relations, especially in the modes of tenure of *land; the steady increase in *investment.

Economic development has a precise significance. Some also speak of cultural and political development. In the first case it is not clear what is meant, since *culture, in its normal acceptation, is not something that exhibits continuous progression. On whatever scale we might measure cultural sophistication, however, cultural and economic sophistication need not go together. (Compare the fragmentary culture of modern capitalism with the sophisticated culture of the undeveloped countries of the European Middle Ages.) In the case of political development the idea of a continuous progression seems, at least in some contexts, to be more persuasive. For example, the steady limitation of the powers of European monarchs, the rise of representative institutions, and the development of constitutional constraints and democratic procedures, have all seemed at one time or another to have a kind of inevitability, and a character of steady achievement through *rationalization. For this reason some political analysts speak of constitutional, representative, and democratic institutions as more 'developed' than say *absolutism or *oriental despotism. So long as the term is not held to have any implications beyond its reference to the history of European monarchy this is not misleading. However, it is only on the assumption of what has been called the *Whig interpretation of history that such 'development' can be seen as a universal human value.

deviationism. Term of USSR political doctrine, introduced in 1921 in a resolution passed by the tenth congress of the Russian Communist Party, and used to denote the tendency within any *communist party to stray from officially sanctioned belief or policy. There are two major types of deviationism: 'dogmatism', or blind adherence to Marxist theory regardless of facts, and 'empiricism', or respect for the facts so great as to lead to a rejection of Marxist theory. In addition, deviationism can be either 'right' or 'left', depending upon whether what is advocated is tougher or milder action (the terms 'adventurism' and 'capitulationism' are also used to denote these two contrasting tendencies). Deviationism is prohibited by *Lenin's *democratic centralism, since it tends to destroy the unity of the Communist Party, and in particular prevents it from having a single policy, so reducing its otherwise enormous influence and power. Deviationism, unlike *revisionism, is not so serious a crime that it cannot be atoned for and corrected.

devolution. The transfer of legal and political powers to some subordinate institution, while retaining, in theory, complete political control over their exercise. The subordinate institution has a *territorial significance, and is designed to correspond to an existing or emergent sense of social *identity. It usually has both *executive and *legislative powers, and thus the result of devolution is to create a subordinate political identity – usually in order to cater for feelings of local allegiance which are too strong to suffer direct government, and too feeble to express themselves in concerted *irredentism.

The UK Parliament has considered devolving certain powers upon Welsh and Scottish 'assemblies', while retaining supremacy in all matters to which those powers refer. It has hesitated to proceed with the plan, partly through inertia, partly through constitutional difficulties posed by the need both to respect the decisions of the subordinate assemblies, and also to retain absolute political *sovereignty. The process of devolution is designed as a compromise; it may sometimes present an impression of contradiction. For it claims to transfer powers while affirming that they cannot be transferred without loss of *sovereignty, and therefore loss of the power to transfer them. Hence the constitutional status of the proposed subordinate assemblies seems to be uncertain: their powers would be neither *merely* delegated, nor truly autonomous. The case is quite unlike that of *federal government, where the federated states retain supremacy in at least some matters of local jurisdiction.

Dewey, John (1859–1952). American philosopher, psychologist, and theorist of education, an exponent of a modified *pragmatism, who opposed what he saw as the artificial divide between theoretical and practical knowledge fostered by *empiricist theories of the mind. Dewey argued that knowing is doing, and the objects of knowledge are the consequences of operations performed by the knower: education involves learning how to turn the world into an object of knowledge. Dewey's educational theories were extremely influential in the earlier part of the twentieth century. His social and political thought is important partly because of its attempt to reconcile *liberal individualism with a philosophy of the individual that recognizes the individual to be, as such, an abstraction. While the locus of all action is the individual agent, the thoughts and values of that agent are to be understood only by situating him in the dynamic social context of which he is a part. Dewey saw the major problem of contemporary American society as lying in the need to rework tradition (specifically, traditional customs, institutions and ways of perceiving the world) into a scientific and technological vision of reality. He believed that philosophy is the true critical instrument whereby human life, culture and institutions can be understood, and tried to advocate educational doctrines that would reconcile the pragmatist approach to science and knowledge with a respect for culture and *humane education generally. His emphasis on the active nature of experience owed much to *Kant and *idealism, although his sense of the individual as in part the active creator of the social world was more redolent of native American optimism than of the idealist philosophies of society which it distantly echoes.

dialectic. A term derived from Greek philosophy (literally: argument), and used in a variety of interconnected ways throughout the history of Western thought:

1. *Plato. The dialectic is the process of question and answer, whereby the philosopher draws his interlocutor to see for himself the truth of which the philosopher wishes to persuade him. The 'Socratic method' consists in first prompting a response, and then, by showing it to be erroneous, turning the disputant's mind in the direction of a truth that he will recognize as true without recourse to received ideas, prejudice or external authority. The 'dialectic' is supposed to show that the rational ability to perceive truth is innate, and needs only to be awakened by philosophical reflection.

2. *Kant. The dialectic is the 'logic of illusion', the process of contradictory and fallacious reasoning which follows upon the attempt to know the world absolutely, through pure reason alone, and without reference to the experience and point of view of the knowing subject. A dialectical contradiction is one in which each premise is founded on a false supposition, itself derived from the vain attempt to see the world from a 'transcendent' perspective, as a 'thing in itself'.

3. *Hegel, influenced by Kant, was concerned, however, not to bury but to praise the 'dialectical' modes of reasoning. In Hegel 'dialectic' describes both the relation between premises and conclusions in a logical argument, and also the process of historical development in reality. The essence of the dialectical movement is 'the negation of the negation', or the 'labour of the negative', whereby truth is approached by the successive generation of the negation of each concept postulated in the attempt to capture it. A concept is posited: it describes reality only partially and generates out of itself its own negation. The conflict between the two concepts is resolved (transcended) by the process of dialectical union, whereby a new, more adequate representation of the world is derived. And so on. (Later idealists sometimes used the terms 'thesis', 'antithesis', 'synthesis' to denote the three parts of the argument.) History moves in like manner, from crude formless gestures, by way of dialectical contradictions in action, to the fully realized consciousness of science, embodied in the institutions of a state. The oppositions that determine all development, whether in logical or mathematical argument, or in the human soul and society, are to be construed not as conflicts, but as *contradictions.

4. In *Marxist thought. Partly on account of Hegelian influence on both *Engels and *Marx, partly because of Russian Marxist intellectuals who refused to see any absolute divide between Hegel and Marx, the 'dialectic' has been thought to be fundamental, first to the Marxist theory of history, secondly to the hoped-for Marxist 'method' in all the human sciences. The contradictions, for Marx, however, are to be found in *material* reality, and in thought only as a consequence of that reality. (*See* *dialectical materialism.) Dialectic describes the movement of history, as generated by forces which contradict each other, but which also grow from each other. Thus capitalism generates *bourgeoisie and *proletariat, which grow in response to each other, cannot exist without each other, but remain in irreconcilable conflict until the new order emerges from their revolutionary ruin. It is supposed that this innate contradiction has an essentially *dynamic* character, as in Hegel: it is *because* of contradiction that things must change.

The dialectical 'method' is sometimes put forward as including various other theses from Hegel's logic, such as the 'transition from quantity to quality'. (Example: the addition of successive parts to a frame at a certain point produces a bicycle.) There are no abrupt transitions, only new perspectives brought about by successive change. This, and various other Hegelian ideas, are sometimes advanced as 'laws of dialectics', held to apply to subjects as disparate as formal logic and sociology.

While Marx used Hegelian rhetoric in many of his works, it is not at all clear that he relied on the 'dialectic', or that, if he did, he really needed to do so. It is, however, fundamental to much modern Marxist thought and practice, in particular to *Maoism.

dialectical materialism. Term coined by Josef Dietzgen (1828-88) and used by the Russian Marxist Plekhanov as a name for Marx's theory of history and consciousness, as expounded by Marx's friend and collaborator, *Engels. The term is now best used as a name for Engels' own version of the theory (as expounded, e.g., in the posthumous *Dialectics of Nature*, 1925). Like Marx, Engels believed that 'consciousness does not determine life, but life determines consciousness' (Marx: *The German Ideology*). *Hegel had described the movement of history as the movement of consciousness (or 'spirit') alone, arguing that this movement must proceed according to the logical order of the *dialectic. Engels agreed that the movement of history is dialectical, but denied that it is spiritual. Hence the name 'dialectical materialism'. History is the development of material forces which, while they involve human activity, consist only in that part of human activity which involves the material (or physical) transformation of nature. The movement of these forces is dialectical, in that it proceeds by generating oppositions between conflicting powers. These oppositions are described as contradictions; nevertheless, they have the power successively to resolve themselves, giving rise to new material arrangements, and the conflicts generic to them. All transformations of consciousness are to be explained as effects of these material processes. (Thus the *class consciousness of the proletariat is merely the effect of the conflict between its productive power, and the fetters placed on that power by capitalism. This consciousness does not create the conflict: it is created by it.)

Such a dialectical process could be endless. Engels thought that class conflict would be resolved in the final proletarian revolution. This would bring communism to the world, but would not remove all contradictions from the material powers that structure it, so that the laws of the dialectic would continue to govern change.

dictatorship. In the Roman Republic a dictator was a magistrate with extraordinary powers, appointed in times of civil or military crisis. He was nominated by a consul on the recommendation of the senate and confirmed by the Comitia Curiata. The office lasted for six months, but was usually laid down when the crisis was passed: other magistrates were subject to the dictators. No dictator was chosen after 202 BC, but Julius Caesar assumed dictatorial powers for ten years in 46 BC, and shortly before his assassination was given them for life.

Hence, a system of government in which one person, office, faction or party is empowered to dictate all political action and compel obedience from all other citizens. The term is not truly distinct in modern usage from 'despotism', although possibly it has the added implication that the ruling agent is active in commanding things, and not merely obstructive in resisting them. Just as there can be 'enlightened despotism', so can there be 'benign dictatorship', and indeed such was the Roman conception of the office that bore this name. Dictatorship may exist **de jure*, as in the Roman office, or merely *de facto*, as in most modern versions.

dictatorship of the proletariat. An expression used by *Marx, and adapted from *Blanqui, who had written of the need for a 'revolutionary dictatorship'. Marx never explained what he meant by 'dictatorship' (and sometimes spoke only of the 'rule' of the proletariat); nevertheless the expression has come to have a definite rhetorical significance in subsequent Marxist thinking, in order to denote the nature and the legitimacy of state power during the period of transition from revolution to true communist society. The effect of Lenin's extensive use of the term, and the constant postponing of that *withering away of the state to which Marx saw the dictatorship of the proletariat as a means, has been to provide a *social* justification (the needs of the proletariat) for a *political* dictatorship by the Communist Party, which rules in the name of the proletariat. In theory, according to *Engels, the proletariat dictates only so as to seize control of the means of production: it then 'abolishes itself as a class'. However its persistence (at least in idea) has proved necessary in order to legitimate the enormous political powers wielded in its name, hence the continuing use of the expression.

difference principle. A criterion of *social justice according to which situation *a* is to be preferred to situation *b* only if the least advantaged member of society is better off in *a* than the least advantaged individual would be in *b*. To be contrasted with *Pareto optimality, and classical *utilitarian conceptions of social welfare. The difference principle has been incorporated by *Rawls into his theory of *justice, where it is used to specify the supposed requirement of social justice, against a prior principle determining individual *rights. 'The intuitive idea is that the social order is not to establish and secure the more attractive prospects of those better off unless doing so is to the advantage of those less fortunate' (J. Rawls: *A Theory of Justice*, 1971) – an intuitive idea that is also endorsed by many of the utilitarian justifications of capitalism and private property.

differentials. A feature of the 'reward system' in employment that has become increasingly important in political thought and practice. It seems that many workers respond more vigorously to an erosion in the 'differentials' that distinguish them from the groups with which they normally compare themselves, than to many absolute changes in their living standards. The existence of a graduated system of reward, with various levels fixed relatively to one another, has therefore been held to be a functional requirement in production. If this is so, then economic stratification (whether or not accompanied by *social stratification) will be not only normal but perhaps inevitable. It seems that differentials are universal; in the USSR, for example, a general in the army earns 300 times as much as a private. Many of the sociological observations of this matter are somewhat *a priori*. However, should it be true that human beings produce more readily and more willingly in a system of differentials than in a system of equal reward, this must inevitably influence discussions of *equality.

Dilthey, Wilhelm (1833–1911). German philosopher and social theorist, influenced by *Kant, and one of the founders of the modern conception of **Verstehen*. The world is to be understood in two ways – according to scientific explanation and prediction, and according to the peculiarly human form of understanding (*Verstehen*) which is exemplified in our perception of each other, and which can be extended to all social and therefore all historical phenomena. *Verstehen* is the comprehension of a mental content – e.g. an idea, experience or intention – as this is manifest in empirically given expressions. It is not that there are two worlds, but rather two ways of understanding the world. The 'human' way of understanding is cultivated through those studies – the *Geisteswissenschaften* – which explore the concepts and relations that are integral to *Verstehen*: this is the true reason for thinking that *humane education is essential for the correct perception of the 'human world', and so of all social and political reality. The human world is a world of significances, and no human significance can be fully grasped by scientific abstractions. Every expression must be returned to its social, historical and cultural context, if its full meaning is to be revealed, and hence *Verstehen* must be educated through comparison and analysis. Without that education history and society will remain only partly intelligible. Dilthey argued against *empiricism and *individualism, and extended his theory of understanding to institutions and legal systems. He was a founder of modern *hermeneutics, and profoundly influenced the course of sociology, through his admirer *Weber.

dilution of labour. The assignment of work customarily assigned to one category of labourer to workers of another kind – specifically, the extraction from the process of production of those parts that can be performed by unskilled labourers, in order to economize on the use of skilled labour. Such economizing has been one of the major results of productivity bargaining in recent years.

diminishing returns, law of. The hypothesis that if one *factor of production is continually increased by constant amounts, while other factors remain unaltered, then – at least after some point – the resulting increases in output become steadily smaller.

This 'law' is not really a universal rule, but typically it is true. It is in fact a common-sense assumption, perhaps better captured in ordinary maxims of practical wisdom than in the technicalities of economic theory. Nevertheless, it has been given technical exposition and support by many economists.

diplomacy. The art of conducting negotiations between *states. Modern diplomacy began with the creation of permanent missions between states in the fifteenth century, but diplomatic representation is very ancient, in the form of envoys from sovereign to sovereign. The Congress of Vienna established grades of diplomatic office, and laid down rules of correct behaviour and immunity. Diplomatic privileges traditionally included *droit de chapelle* (entitlement to practise own religion), *droit de quartier* (immunity from local police), and *droit de l'hôtel*, or extra-territoriality, under which the embassy is regarded as a place exempt from local *jurisdiction and *taxation. All these are summed up under the label 'diplomatic immunity', although the extent of that immunity is now disputed. For example, does extra-territoriality give an embassy the right to construct buildings in defiance of local planning law?

Diplomacy is a mode of settling disputes without recourse to *force, or to *international law. If international *adjudication were systematic and generally enforceable, then presumably diplomacy would be less necessary. One of the most important functions of any diplomatic approach is to persuade the other party to accept a settlement under international law: thus even the application of law may require diplomacy.

direct action. Action to secure a political objective taken outside the constitutional framework, and indifferently to existing legal constraints. Direct action may be non-violent, as advocated by Gandhi and various *civil rights movements (*see* *civil disobedience, *passive resistance), or violent – in which case its extreme forms include *rebellion and *revolution.

Among familiar forms of direct action are *terrorism and strikes carried out by workers who have no legal right to strike (*see* *industrial action).

direct democracy. Any system of government in which all decisions are made by *collective choice of the citizens, and not through representatives. Direct democracy is contrasted with representative democracy (*see* *representation), and it is widely assumed that it is feasible only if the body to be governed is small, and so able to register its preferences by repeated voting. One of the most historically important systems of direct democratic government was that instituted in Athens (*see* *Athenian democracy). Some argue that only in a direct democracy is there any guarantee that the *people are *sovereign; others (including, e.g., *Paine, and *J. S. Mill) have argued for the superiority of indirect systems, which permit the emergence, at key positions in government, of experts who may be answerable to the people but who are not merely puppets of the people.

directed democracy. Term popular in leadership circles in the USSR during the 1960s and '70s, denoting the kind of government then prevailing, in which an exclusive and organized few ruled in the interest of the inclusive and disorganized many. Analogous in meaning to *Aristotle's *aristocracy, since it is assumed that the few are better fitted for government than the many would be, although it should be noted that this fitness for government is supposed to be conferred not by *virtue (as in Aristotle) but by party membership.

Directed democracy must be sharply distinguished from *direct democracy.

dirigisme. From French *diriger*, to direct. A term originally used to describe the policy of French monarchs and controllers of finance during the seventeenth century, and now used to denote the state of affairs in which the *state controls the economy by detailed intervention in economic affairs, e.g. through *nationalization, and through laws restricting private ownership, or by compelling companies to trade on certain terms, in certain areas, and with a certain work force. Its extreme form has sometimes been called *state capitalism by those socialists who have wanted to distinguish between the ideal of common ownership and the practice of state control.

Sometimes the term is used, in the context of French politics, to denote the active intervention of the state in areas of social life other than the economic – e.g. education, local planning and administration, recreation.

dirty hands. It has been argued (e.g. by *Sartre) that politics requires the politician to dirty his hands and that this is either a justification of the dirt or a reason to stay away from politics. A *consequentialist will ultimately take the first line, but his opponent, who believes in the absolute authority of a moral rule, will find it hard to avoid the second. It may be, however, that *casuistry concerning the ideas of *responsibility and *double effect may help the moral absolutist to follow the consequentialist into the breach. (*See* *morality and politics.)

disarmament. The renunciation of military means, either by agreement with a potential aggressor, or independently (*unilateral disarmament). Proposals for general (= applying to all states) and comprehensive (= applying to all weapons and forces) disarmament have been repeatedly made and discussed, for example by the League of Nations in 1927 and 1934. The United Nations set up in 1946 the Atomic Energy Commission for the elimination of the use of atomic energy for destructive purposes, and in 1947 the Commission for Conventional Armaments, 'for the general regulation and reduction of armaments and armed forces'. The commissions were separately established in order to secure maximum chance of agreement over the two issues, but were merged in the UN Disarmament Commission in 1951 when no agreement had been reached. The USSR argued that disarmament must come first and verification afterwards, and pressed for an agreement on that basis; the West argued that without provisions for verification all agreements were useless. The problem of verification continued to dominate discussion, and remained largely unresolved, despite later concessions by the USSR in the final act of the Helsinki Accord, 1975, and in 'strategic arms limitation' talks between the USSR and the US, resulting in agreements in 1972 and 1974. (*See* *arms control.) Western doubt concerning Soviet intentions was temporarily allayed by those agreements, but has recently resurged, partly because of a suspicion that they have not been honoured, and partly because the existence of suspicion, rather than certainty, shows the provisions for verification to have been inadequate.

disclericalization. Socialist and communist term, denoting the emancipation of social and individual life from the influence of organized religion. It denotes a process that is at once more active and more politically inspired than *secularization.

discrimination. The according of differential treatment to persons, bodies, or groups, usually with the implication that there is not sufficient ground for doing this in the actual differences between them. Thus 'discrimination' tends to mean irrelevant, and also invidious, distinction. Some argue that irrelevance implies invidiousness, since if the differences between *a* and *b* are irrelevant to deciding the question of what treatment should be ministered to either, then it is unjust to discriminate between them. (*See* *justice.) Intuitions about 'invidious' distinctions are frequently built into law – as in the UK Race Relations Act 1976, and Sex Discrimination Act 1975. (*See* *racism, and *sexism.)

In practice the conception that a serious difference of treatment based on an irrelevant distinction is unjust is shared by those who practise discrimination as much as by their critics. A distinction may be thought to correspond to some deep division of nature between people, and so to give grounds for differential treatment. While the search for that deep division may involve the rationalization of an irrational prejudice (e.g. in the Nazi ideology of race), it may also involve serious hypotheses concerning large and undecided questions (e.g. in the normal grounds for treating children differently from adults).

disenchantment. German: *Entzauberung*. Term given a specialized sense by *Weber, to denote the perception of the world conferred on the modern consciousness by the loss of wonder, and by the conviction that a scientific explanation can be offered for every observable fact. Disenchantment is not, normally, the outcome of any deliberate process of *demystification, or *demythologization, but consists in an irreversible shift in consciousness, with consequences that are felt throughout the realm of moral and political values, and without discernible remedy. Weber thought that it was an inevitable consequence of the acceptance, under modern conditions, of a 'legal-rational' vision of social arrangements.

The 'literature of disenchantment', thought to include such writers as Kafka, Beckett, and Rilke (whose self-conscious efforts to re-enchant his world have often been held up as an object lesson in heroic failure), is one of the most striking features of modern high culture, giving expression to, and perhaps relief from, a condition that is sometimes thought to lie at the heart of twentieth-century social consciousness.

Disraeli, Benjamin, Earl of Beaconsfield (1804–81). British statesman and novelist. *See* *conservatism, *conservative parties, *industrial law, *industrial revolution, *land, *Toryism, *trade union.

dissident. Normal translation of German *Andersdenkende*, Russian *inakomyslyashtie*, one who thinks differently, one who dissents from official doctrine. It has been defined variously in communist countries, e.g. by Jan Tesář (1979) as 'openly expressed political disagreement with the government in a totalitarian system', and although clearly there can be received ideas (and therefore dissent from them) in the absence of *totalitarianism, it is largely in order to indicate the peculiar muffled fervour of dissent in totalitarian countries that the term has been used. In this context some have distinguished 'intrastructural' from 'extrastructural' dissent, the former being dissent 'within the system' as when the ideology, codes of conduct, and political expectations of the Communist Party are quietly but deliberately flouted by someone holding office in a communist state.

Often the dissident is attempting to enforce, or encouraging the state to enforce, existing laws (usually laws concerning *civil rights). (*See* *charter.) Either the state, in adopting such laws, intended them to be obeyed, in which case there is no dissent from them, but only official lawlessness, or it did not, in which case it is in contradiction with itself, and so must be dissented from by every rational being. In this way the term 'dissident' has a misleading implication of eccentricity, for although it may be foolhardy to *express* dissent, e.g. from the edicts of the Communist Party, it may also be impossible not to feel it. Indeed, it has often been thought necessary to personal existence that the citizen in a totalitarian country should withhold his assent from much that occurs in public life, and much that he is forced overtly to condone. Thus 'the essence of dissent is the consciousness that there is no salvation except in the citizen himself, in the restoration of his feelings of self-hood (*svébytnost*) and civic responsibility' (Jan Tesář). That quotation from a Czech dissident expresses two aims of dissent: the struggle for the *autonomy of the self, as this is described by *Kantian thinkers, and the expression of that struggle through an attitude of *responsiblity towards *civil society. In external things, however, the only hope is for what T. G. Masaryk called 'small-scale work' (*drobná práce*) – the gradual bending of all public acts and institutions towards the truths that are officially denied.

distribution. **1**. Economics. The theory of distribution concerns itself with explaining how the returns to the several *factors of production (*land, *labour and *capital) are determined. Some theories focus on aggregate rent, wages and interest, while others seek to provide a far more detailed explanation; e.g. why is a professor of Greek paid more than an agricultural labourer? (Clearly the first, unlike the second, is neither essential to survival, nor in great demand.) Distribution theory has been, and remains, a controversial and unsettled area of economics.

2. More generally, political theory distinguishes distribution of goods from their production, exchange and consumption, as separate but perhaps mutually dependent parts of the process whereby nature is put to use. (*See* *production, distribution, exchange, consumption.) Considerable dispute arises over the extent to which the four parts of the process are separable, and the extent, for example, to which there could be *private property in the means of production combined with *common ownership of the means of distribution. Marxists argue that the parts of the process are in fact inseparable, and that socialist programmes of *redistribution, which attempt to reconcile an idea of equitable distribution with the existence of private property in the means of production, are misguided.

3. The question of the extent to which patterns of distribution of wealth, goods and power should be altered in the interests of justice is one that underlies much recent socialist thinking. *Aristotle's conception of distributive justice has often been taken to suggest that the concept of justice can be applied to a distribution, quite independently of its application to the acts, or supposed acts, which brought that distribution about. The question of the coherence of that conception therefore lies at the heart of much political disagreement. (*See* *justice, *social justice.)

distributive justice. *See* *justice.

divine right. The idea that a *sovereign rules by divine ordinance, or perhaps that he is himself a divinity. The theory of a divine right seems at one stage to have been widely accepted, and was consciously reintroduced by Augustus to the government of Rome as a necessary part of the *legitimation of his new-found *absolutism. In a speech before parliament in 1610, James I argued that 'Kings are not only God's lieutenants upon earth and sit upon God's throne, but even by God himself they are called gods', adding that kings 'exercise a manner or resemblance of divine power on earth'. He and his family went on to illustrate and apply what Alexander Pope was later to describe as 'the right divine of kings to govern wrong', and a defence of the doctrine – *Eikon Basilike* (Greek: *The King's Picture*) – wrongly attributed to Charles I, achieved great popularity upon the latter's execution, partly because it explained to the English public the quasi-religious horror that was then experienced. The doctrine was defended in modified form by Sir Robert Filmer (*Patriarchia*, 1680), to be attacked by *Locke, and in this version can be seen as an extended metaphysical attempt to make sense of political obligation without referring to contract or consent. Since allegiance to the sovereign defines the political condition of man, and since there is no contract or consent outside that condition, allegiance must be founded in some obligation deeper than those which have arisen through the voluntary undertakings of the subject. Whence came this obligation if it were not divinely imposed? Filmer's view was that no account of political authority could escape reference to divine *command, and that too great a separation between divine and civil ordinance was dangerous both to civil and to religious institutions.

division of labour. If each man produces all that he needs and nothing that another needs, then no-one works for another. If, however, someone acquires a skill at some particular employment such as chair-making, he may devote his time to that and exchange chairs for other goods, made by men of similarly specialized employment. Thus there arises the 'social division of labour', a phenomenon noted by *Plato in the *Republic* as fundamental to the institutions of a stable state, and one of the bonds of mutual dependence which necessitate a common system of law. The phenomenon was explored by Adam *Smith as a necessary accompaniment of market conditions, and the essence of manufacturing, and by Marx, as a distinctive feature of private property relations; it has also been a subject of considerable speculation on the part of modern sociologists, in particular *Durkheim (*De la division du travail sociale*, 1893).

It is necessary to distinguish the social division of labour just described, from the detail division of labour which occurs within a factory. Here the process of production is broken down into fine constituents, and each assigned to a different labourer. *See* *detail labour.

division of powers. *See* *separation of powers.

doctrinaire. Introduced into French usage *circa* 1815 to describe a party which attempted to mediate between extreme and warring *factions, the term is now generally used to denote any outlook or activity that is characterized by rigid adherence to *doctrine, regardless of whether circumstances show that doctrine to be impracticable, irrational or misguided.

doctrine. Literally 'teaching', the term 'doctrine' has been transferred from religious to political usage to denote any attempt to give system or coherence to political *ideals and practice. It is to be distinguished from the theory which explains doctrine (if there be such), and also from the policy which enacts it, since it aims to provide a set of reasoned beliefs and attitudes, that will recommend itself through its own intrinsic qualities, and not because it is in anybody's interest either to believe or to act as though he believed it.

Political visions differ in the extent to which they think that doctrine is desirable or possible, and the extent to which they think that doctrine can or ought to be detached from the specific historical conditions in which it is expressed. It is characteristic of certain forms of conservatism to oppose this detachment, and to argue that principles and policies must be allowed to form themselves in response to the actual conditions in which they are applied, and ought not to be formulated as abstract truths applicable to all men everywhere. (*See* *Burke, *Oakeshott.) Sometimes this opposition to doctrine is itself given a doctrinal character – an absolute truth about the human condition of universal application. Sometimes (as with *Hume) it is put forward as part of a sceptical attitude towards the human pretension to knowledge.

Liberalism and socialism are more eager in their search for doctrine, and give descriptions of human ideals and fulfilment that purport to be of universal validity. (*See* *universalism.)

dogma. In Christian theology, the term denotes a truth of religion guaranteed as such by divine revelation, and defined in detail by the *church. Dogma commands assent from the believer, since it is what has to be believed if the religion is to be adopted at all. Similarly, in politics, one may distinguish defining beliefs from peripheral beliefs in any particular standpoint, and it is part of political theory to discern which beliefs are held to dogmatically, and which can be changed without fundamental damage to the outlook. The equal right to *welfare is, for example, an item of socialist dogma, while the advocacy of religious *toleration is probably not. Likewise the right of *private property is an item of conservative dogma, while the advocacy of a **laissez-faire* economy is not. Sometimes these fundamental beliefs are called axioms, on the ground that *dogmatism is a vice, while not all such ultimate principles are invidious.

The defining characteristic of dogma is that it is ultimate, whereas the defining characteristic of *doctrine is that it is systematic.

dogmatism. The tendency to treat one's own beliefs, whatever their origin and nature, as matters of *dogma, and so to hold on to them irrationally, in the conviction that one's standpoint depends in its entirety on their preservation.

More widely, the inability to relinquish some conviction, in the face of however much evidence to the contrary. Dogmatism implies a belief in *doctrine, which gives system to all beliefs, and so shows each belief to be immovable. It is to be distinguished from bigotry: the acceptance of a dogma in the absence of any interest in doctrine.

Dogmatism is now frowned upon in most communist states, as a derogation from 'creative Marxism'; however, fear of the accusations of *opportunism and *revisionism continue to make dogmatism comparatively safe.

domestic. In politics the domestic is to be contrasted with the 'external' or *international, while in economics such expressions as 'domestic product' can be defined without reference to international trade. It should not, however, be assumed that there is any real independence of domestic from international issues or that the character of a domestic government can be determined quite independently of the *foreign policy with which it is conjoined; nor should it be assumed that the structure and volume of domestic product are independent of foreign trade.

domino theory. Expression publicized by the US National Security Council in 1950, and later much used by President Eisenhower, to denote an interdependence of neighbouring states, especially in *developing countries, of such a kind that, faced with internal crises of a similar nature (specifically, the upsurge of guerrilla warfare, armed infiltration, and communist activism), the collapse of one will lead to the progressive and consecutive collapse of its neighbours. The expression summarizes certain intuitive observations, and is not in fact the name of any formulated theory designed to explain them.

double effect. A principle of *casuistry, popularized by Roman Catholic teaching, which argues that an agent is not necessarily responsible for the unwanted side-effect of an intentional action, even though he foresees that effect and does nothing to avoid it. The important factor is not the side-effect, but the effect at which the agent aims. Suppose you are driving a trolley and the brakes fail. You see three men working on the track before you, but can switch to a side track to avoid them; unfortunately there is also a man working on the side track. You switch to the side track, thus doing something with the foreseeable result that someone will be killed. It seems hard to say that you are responsible for his death, or in any other way blameworthy, since you at no point aimed to produce it. This principle is important in discussing such problems as that of *dirty hands.

draconian laws (alternatively: draconic laws). Literally laws of the kind given to Athens by the archon Draco in 621 BC. Now used as a general designation for any legislation that is severe, inflexible, and of wide application, on the (probably false) assumption that such were the laws of Draco. (*See also* *legislator.)

due process (i.e. of law). The conduct of legal proceedings according to established principles designed to safeguard the legal *rights of the individual. The concept is rooted in English common law, and finds expression in Magna Carta, 1215, article 39, which establishes that there shall be no imprisonment without trial and that the accused shall have a right to trial by jury. It was adopted by the US constitution, Fifth Amendment (1791), and extended to state action by the Fourteenth Amendment (1867). It is now established that no federal or state government can act so as to deprive a person of 'life, liberty or property, without due process of law'.

The alleged refusal of due process has become one of the major causes of action in US *administrative law. Partly as a result of that, the complaint is now interpreted very widely, so that any legal proceeding which does not conform to intuitive requirements of *natural justice is held to violate the right to due process.

dumping. Selling in a foreign market at a price below that charged at home, or even below cost of production. An exporting state or company may tolerate the short-run losses due to dumping in order to eliminate foreign competition and so secure a monopoly, or in order to dispose of temporary surpluses. The General Agreement on Tariffs and Trade (GATT), 1948, permits defence against dumping by the levy of a duty, and dumping is expressly forbidden within the EEC by the Treaty of Rome. (*See also* *international trade.)

duress. In law: *force applied or threatened in order to *coerce, and actually coercing, someone to act in a certain way. Duress includes threats to deprive of economic benefits, and threats to spouse, parent or child. Any act performed under duress is legally altered, and a contract obtained by duress is voidable. This legal idea has its moral counterpart, and it is sometimes offered as an objection to certain *social contract theories of *political obligation that the contract which they envisage as lying at the heart of social arrangements is one that exists by duress.

(This particularly weighs against *Hobbes's view, that men are bound by contract to the warring sovereign whose peace they have accepted.)

Durkheim, Émile (1858–1917). French sociologist, a founder of modern sociology, and influential both in his attempt to synthesize theory with statistical research and in his use of the *katascopic approach. Durkheim held that the *milieu social* is as much a reality as the physical environment, but it is a 'reality *sui generis*', which cannot be reduced to physical terms. *Social facts exist independently of the individual, and exert a unique kind of constraint upon his action. Durkheim investigated such constraints, as disclosed within a system of *division of labour, where order is embodied in contractual relations. Durkheim argued that, although a contract is backed by the sanction of the law, it is the non-contractual element of a contract which both impinges most directly on the personality of the individual and also renders the contract binding. Laws can have authority only when underpinned by the 'moral authority' of internalized *norms. In industrial society, shifts in *production relations had broken down the older 'mechanical solidarity' of the 'horde', and largely replaced it with the 'organic solidarity' of the division of labour. What was previously a true 'collective consciousness', which united all members of society in a single system of values, had become a divided complex of competing norms, attached to functional groups and classes. The sole remaining common sentiment was that of humanity. But this idea was itself threatened, Durkheim thought, by pathological conditions of society, exemplified in *suicide, and characterized by **anomie*.

Durkheim introduced the idea of *functional explanation into social sciences, and argued that there are genuinely social causal relations: one social fact may cause another such fact, according to laws of social development, and these laws, together with the facts that they explain, may not be reducible to any laws or facts concerning the behaviour of individuals. Thus Durkheim rejected *individualism. He also criticized *utilitarian doctrines, and in particular the claim that increased division of labour and economic progress must necessarily bring increased happiness: on the contrary, the enforced fragmentation of industrial production gives men an individuality that they can neither want nor bear, since it detaches them from the social order in which their norms are validated.

duty. Duties may be moral, religious, legal, personal, social or political; they may be founded in nature or in convention; they may be overriding or overridable, conditional or unconditional, absolute or relative. The philosophical theory of 'deontology' regards duty and the associated idea of obligation as the fundamental concepts of morality, specifying both a reason and a motive for action. Typically such a philosophy also elevates duty over all other motives, and endows it with an absolute, unconditioned and overriding claim to obedience (*see* *Kant). To argue in such a way is, by implication, to deny the validity of *utilitarianism, as of every form of *consequentialism or *teleology, as answers to the questions of morality. Deontology will also regard legal and political perspectives as subordinate to the moral perspective, and will, typically, attempt to generate a natural law theory of political obligation. Philosophers dispute over whether *rights and duties are correlative – i.e. whether every right defines a duty and every duty a right – or whether there can be duties where no one has a right to their obedience, or rights where no one has a duty to respect them. (*See* *jural correlates.) Doctrines of natural and of human rights often neglect to settle this dispute, and therefore occasionally seem to be claiming rights while saying nothing about who has the duty to respect them or to see that they are satisfied.

Since only rational beings seem to have duties, many philosophers have tried to refer the motive of duty to reason alone, and to argue that the true objectivity of moral judgement is to be found in its appeal to duty, which is no other than an appeal to reason. (The most important example of such a philosopher is Kant, although Kant had often been anticipated, notably by *Aquinas.) Others, in the spirit of *Hume's scepticism concerning moral judgement, have argued that reason alone cannot be a motive to action, and therefore that the appeal to duty adds no independent authority to any moral law but at best merely reiterates it. In this way the concept of duty has often served as a focus for disputes both about the objectivity of morals, and about the nature of practical reason.

dyarchy. Term coined by the German historian Th. Mommsen to refer to the Roman principate, in which *sovereignty seemed to be shared between two separate *agencies, the *princeps* and the senate. Applied also to the particular form of constitutional government introduced by the UK Government of India Act 1919, which divided the provincial executive powers into two.

dynasty. Greek: *dunastēia*, lordship. A class of sovereigns or rulers, whose succession is determined by blood relationship. Dynasties often seem to have a durable political character, so that the politics of a Stuart monarch might be explained by his being a Stuart, and of a Tokugawa Sho'gun by his being a Tokugawa. How far such explanations are genuine and how far they are the residue of discredited beliefs about *heredity is a moot point: to the extent that they are genuine, it seems that there are not only rulers but also ruling families.

E

Eastern question. The many and related political problems in South-Eastern Europe and Asia Minor caused in the nineteenth century by the weakness of the Ottoman Empire and the rivalry of its powerful neighbours and successors, and by the desire of European powers to curb Russian influence, and by the desire of Russia to *destabilize the Balkan states (*see* *balkanization). To some extent these problems still exist, but have taken on a completely different complexion since the success of Kemal Atatürk in saving the nucleus of a Turkish nation state after 1918, and the success of USSR foreign policy in Eastern Europe after 1945.

ecclesiastical jurisdiction. *Courts have been founded by various religions – notably the Jewish, Muslim and Christian – with the intention of resolving spiritual disputes, whether affecting clergy or laity, by *adjudication. Since 'spiritual' disputes can be interpreted so as to cover everything from crime to the terms of a contract, the establishment of such courts has frequently amounted to a claim to jurisdiction over *territory where the church itself is not in fact *sovereign. This claim was always resisted by the state in England, but the resistance was successful partly because the *canon law and the ecclesiastical procedures and judgements that had grown from it were incorporated in part into the *common law of the land. The ecclesiastical courts were still able to reserve for themselves jurisdiction over certain matters, so that, for example, a clergyman could be punished for criminal behaviour only in an ecclesiastical court (giving rise to the much abused plea of 'benefit of clergy').

Two political consequences of ecclesiastical jurisdiction deserve mention here in that they provide precedents and examples for subsequent legislation. The first is the international character of the law applied, and the impossibility of construing its legitimacy as arising from the exercise of territorial sovereignty. (Although the doctrine of 'papal sovereignty' contains a faint echo of territorial privilege.) Hence ecclesiastical jurisdiction automatically gives rise to the idea of a *natural law, i.e. a law which is not merely *positive, since it transcends the edicts of all temporal powers. The second is the attempt of the ecclesiastical courts to impose doctrines of fair dealing between master and servant, and between parties to a contract, e.g. by the various attempts to forbid usury (still incorporated into *Islamic law), and by the doctrine of the *just price, according to which, in conditions of scarcity and unequal bargaining power, the court can be appealed to in order to settle a just price for a commodity, based on need, and on the assumption of normal conditions and open-handed dealing.

ecology. Term originally used by Ernst K. Haeckel in 1873, to denote the branch of biology which deals with the interrelationship between organism and environment (Greek, *oikos*, a home or living place). The term has been adopted by political movements which regard the conservation of the environment as an all-important, perhaps the single most important, political goal: hence the various 'ecology parties' which fight (usually with little success) for representation in European national assemblies. These are sometimes romantic in temperament, anti-industrial, with liberal or socialist leanings in matters of property and law, and favour strict legal control over every activity that can in any way alter the balance of nature, or either reduce or pollute natural resources. Often the underlying idea here is one of justice: the earth is held in trust by those who presently occupy it, and cannot be appropriated for their sole use without violating the rights of succeeding generations. In the US, however, where a majority of people seem to favour strict environmental laws, major support for ecology movements comes also from well-to-do conservative elements. The movements are sometimes opposed by those on the left as catering for the leisure and aesthetic interests of the affluent, at the expense of the productive activity which provides employment to the rest.

economic growth. The process whereby productive activity, and with it *national income, increases. The analysis of economic growth is one of the major preoccupations of political theorists and economists, partly from the questionable assumption that well-being requires growth, partly from the simpler view, upheld by some macroeconomic theories, denied by others, that full employment depends upon a steadily increasing output (*see* *unemployment). The first of these views, often criticized by moralists and philosophers, has also been abandoned by some economists. E. J. Mishan, for example, argues on various grounds that it is perfectly rational to prefer current to future consumption, and so to refrain from the investment required for growth. The reason for this may be present pleasure, or it may be more far-reaching and speculative, such as a concern for the effects of excessive growth on the environment, and on the social structure through which production is channelled (*The Cost of Economic Growth*, 1969).

Some theorists distinguish various stages of growth – for example Marx, whose theory of history is based on the idea that growth in productive forces determines successive changes in production relations, which reshape the whole social superstructure as they change. Hence there are clearly marked divisions in economies, such as that between the feudal and the capitalist, which come about quite rapidly, but also as a result of a gradual growth of the underlying productive forces. The antecendents of the Marxian theory are to be found in various eighteenth-century ideas concerning the 'four stages' of development. More recently, and perhaps less systematically, W. W. Rostow has distinguished six stages of growth (*Stages of Economic Growth*, 1960):

(i) Traditional arrangements in which custom prevents growth.

(ii) The preconditions for 'take-off', notably the preparations for modern technological development.

(iii) Take-off, in which the economy generates a surplus sufficient to provide its own investment.

(iv) The 'drive to maturity' in which there is a shift from import to export.

(v) Economic maturity.
(vi) High mass consumption.

The division here is not supposed to be arbitrary, the assumption being that there are different underlying economic structures proper to each stage. Economists have criticized Rostow's analysis, however, partly for the unclarity of the idea of 'take-off' and also for its inability to explain quite what happens between (i) and (ii). In Marx six stages are also distinguished – primitive communism, slavery, feudalism, capitalism, socialism, and mature communism – but Marx's theory seems to correspond only to a segment of the history of Europe, and then only approximately. It is normal to distinguish the stages of growth in *developing countries from those in 'mature' capitalist countries, on the assumption that the conditions of the first are to some extent dependent on conditions already reached in the second. In the light of that distinction, theories such as Marx's would seem to be of only limited application, while the classification provided by Rostow seems to have more heuristic than explanatory value. (*See also* *three worlds theory.)

economic man (*homo economicus*). The abstraction employed by much economic theory, which offers to explain the economic behaviour of actual human beings in terms of an *ideal type of rational choice. The economic man plays an important part in *classical and *neo-classical economics. He is motivated by interests or preferences, which he attempts to optimize; he therefore obeys the axioms of *decision theory, and is deflected from his purposes by no interests other than his own. Some economists argue that this creature differs from the rest of us only in his enhanced rationality; for, even when motivated by *values, we are obedient only to interests of our own. Others argue that values cannot be fitted into the usual theories of economic motivation, and that economic man is no more than a 'rational fool' (Amartya Sen).

economic warfare. Not usually a form of *war, and not in itself an act of belligerency in *international law, the mounting of trade embargoes against, the forbidding of exports to and imports from, a potentially hostile state, may nevertheless be described as economic warfare when practised sufficiently consistently and backed up by measures designed to undermine the economy of that state and compel it to sue for terms. Hence representatives have argued before the United Nations special committees for the definition of *aggression (e.g. in 1956), that certain kinds of economic pressure constitute aggression.

economics. There is no agreed definition of the subject of economics. Most suggested definitions fail to cover everything that is studied as economics. Thus L. Robbins's famous definition ('economics is the science which studies human behaviour as a relationship between ends and scarce means which have alternative uses') comprehends *microeconomics, but not *macroeconomics. Some idea of the latter is conveyed by the title of Adam Smith's famous book, *An Inquiry into the Nature and Causes of the Wealth of Nations*, which appeared in 1776.

All political thinkers are faced by the question of the extent to which their science is distinct from, incorporates, or is incorporated by, economics. Social policy always requires expenditure, and often has economic effects; all policy therefore has an economic aspect, even if it is not concerned with economic ends. Hence the permanent tendency of governments to occupy themselves with questions of economics, resulting perhaps in direct government intervention in the economy, or in a kind of dogmatic non-intervention which has just as large immediate and intended effects.

Historical materialists go further in asserting the interdependence of politics and economics, arguing that political institutions and political decisions are always the effects of economic causes, so that there are no political facts which are not, at some level of explanation, economic facts. On such a view the study of politics might seem to be entirely subsumed under economics, at least so far as concerns explanation and understanding. However, even if historical materialism were true, such a conclusion would not follow. Consider human relations. Conversation and friendship are rationally conducted only by someone who attends to the surface expression of human life, and who ignores the physiological processes which determine that expression. Likewise, there may be a rational art of politics that proceeds without reference to the underlying mechanisms that determine it. (*See also* *essence/appearance, **Verstehen*.)

Since economic ills are politically undesirable, the curing of the economy must be an essential part of politics, even if only the precondition of its successful exercise. If our view of human nature allows more to well-being than the provision of goods and services, and if we believe that politics must concern itself with well-being as a whole, then we must nevertheless admit that economics cannot constitute the whole of politics. At best there may be that kind of dynamic synthesis of the two which has sometimes been called *political economy, and which sees government of a state in terms which apply equally to the management of a *household. *But see* *positive economics.

ecumenical movement. Greek: *oikoumene*, the inhabited earth. The movement within the Christian churches towards a visible union of all believers in Christ. While a permanent feature of *Christianity (enshrined in the idea of a 'catholic' church), the movement has been a major force only since the division within the church at the Reformation, and took its principal modern impetus from the World Missionary Conference held in Edinburgh in 1910. The modern attempt to represent liturgical and doctrinal differences as peripheral, in comparison with the defining belief in Christ crucified, has seemed to some to herald the resumption of true Christian belief, to others to indicate only that Christian belief has ceased very much to matter, even to those who profess it. It has often been argued that the strongest religious sentiments emerge in hostilities between those who are united in all beliefs except one or two irrational embellishments, and that the cessation of hostilities is brought about only by the loss of the metaphysical assumptions that made them possible. On this view it is to be expected that the ecumenical movement within Christianity, unlike the continuing conflict between Sunni and Shi'ite Muslims, presages the political decline of religious doctrine.

education. The process whereby the *rational being is instructed, and through which he acquires the beliefs, emotions and *values pertaining to a *culture. How can the state stand apart from that process or regard its result with indifference? The question, explored with great vigour and skill by *Plato, has continued to occupy the thought and practice of philosophers and politicians, and is now everywhere bound up with political choices.

The definition of 'education' is no easy matter. It is now normally seen as the more formal and structured part of *socialization, and is thus defined by *Durkheim: 'Education consists of a methodological socialization of the young generation' (*Education and Sociology*, 1922). However, what distinguishes education from training, for example, or from *conditioning? One suggestion is that education essentially has a *person as its object, whereas training and conditioning may be directed towards (nonpersonal) animals. On one view this means that education must show an awareness of, and a respect for, *rights which belong to its recipient. Those philosophies which connect the ideas of person and rationality would perhaps gloss this suggestion as follows:

(i) In education, the rationality of the recipient is engaged. For example, he is given *reasons* for believing, doing and feeling things, and is not simply manipulated or bludgeoned into some finished state of unthinking acceptance of doctrine.

(ii) In education, the *autonomy of the recipient is respected. He is treated as a being with *responsibility for his own acts and judgements, and encouraged to view himself as such.

Clearly both (i) and (ii) are matters of degree, and in the early stages of education it is to be assumed that the rationality and autonomy of the recipient are only incipient. The major political question that arises out of any such definition is this: what kind of institution is best suited to educate those belonging to it? To follow the *Kantian train of thought so far entertained, it would be normal to say that the institution must be autonomous, since institutional autonomy is necessary (although not sufficient) to safeguard the autonomy of the individual subject to it. But here we must distinguish political from economic autonomy. An institution which depends upon the state for economic support may yet be autonomous in its choice of aims, methods and activities. Thus state universities in the UK are autonomous yet economically dependent, while state schools are (to some extent) dependent upon the state both for their funds and for their aims and methods. It is a defining feature of *totalitarianism that it tolerates no political autonomy and hence regards the state as possessed of an inalienable right to dictate the aims and activities of educational bodies. It does not, however, follow that the individual is thereby deprived, through his education, of his autonomy. Everything depends upon the *nature* of the control that the state exercises and on the capacity of the individual to resist it. Massive *indoctrination is usually thought to violate both the conditions offered, and this is sometimes offered in the US as an argument for *withdrawing* state support from schools which practise indoctrination (specifically religious indoctrination) on the ground that the state has an obligation to provide education, and also to foster *toleration by means of it.

*Marxist thinkers in the tradition of *Gramsci often emphasize the extent to which the autonomy of institutions may serve as an instrument of class *hegemony, so that the political freedoms enjoyed by schools in many capitalist countries are used to foster differential development, the better teachers gravitating towards the more expensive schools, and the subjects taught in those schools being such as to form an easily recognizable *élite. Thereby the children of the ruling class learn the exercise of power, the arts and graces that secure power, and the prejudices that lead them to confine that power to their own class. This is often used as an argument against schools, and against 'streaming' in 'public' schools. (NB in UK usage, a 'public school' is an independent school.) The assumption behind this argument – that the formation of a ruling class is an avoidable evil – is sometimes challenged; more usually conservatives stress that the argument, even if valid, is irrelevant, since the question concerns educational values, and what is necessary to secure them. Hence the question is inextricably bound up with that of the 'curriculum'. What are educational values, and what *should* be taught in schools? Both Plato and *Aristotle argued that *virtue is the main aim of education; later thinkers extended the idea of virtue to include *rhetoric, and this outlook was transmuted into the advocacy of *humane education and high culture by such nineteenth-century thinkers as *Arnold and *J. S. Mill. All such ideas have seemed to their critics to involve an element of élitism. Arguments as to how schools should be funded, and whether parents should have a 'right to choose' how to educate their children, often turn on this point. A 'right to choose' that extends only to one class is often seen as a mere extension of the power whereby that class controls the remainder.

The political questions of when children should attend school and for how long, and whether this attendance should be compulsory, are also bound up with the nature and value of education. In practice the 'school leaving age' has been determined in accordance with two intuitions: (a) children should stay at school until they have learned what is necessary for responsible autonomous existence; (b) they should be kept in school just so long as they would be a social nuisance elsewhere. It is often argued that both these aims would be better fulfilled in many cases by apprenticeship than by school.

egalitarianism. A somewhat vague term, best taken to denote the belief that people are or ought to be equal in at least some, possibly every, respect relevant to political decision-making. Specifically, the belief that there are no relevant differences whereby one person can be supposed to have a greater inherent *right to some benefit than another. From that it is sometimes held to follow that an unequal distribution of benefits is either unjust, since it distinguishes people on grounds which do not determine their rights, or else inherently in need of justification. (*See* *justice.)

At least the following assumptions seem to be involved in the usual forms of egalitarianism:

(i) The ultimate justification for any *distribution of benefits is to be given in terms of the rights of those receiving them.

(ii) Distribution is always within political *control, and so is always, by design or by neglect, the result of political activity.

(iii) There is some common property in all people which is the single ground of whatever rights they possess.

(iv) This common property is possessed to an equal extent by all people.

All of these assumptions may be doubted, but it is clear that (iii) and (iv) are of perennial appeal, and have been subjects of many attempted *a priori* justifications, notably by *Kant, who identifies the common property as practical reason, made manifest in the *autonomy wherefrom we act. (i) must be justified in terms of a theory of distributive justice, sufficient to eliminate all conflicting reasons (such as those stemming from *need, from *utility, or from *natural right) for distribution. In order to make (ii) seem plausible it has been common to argue that egalitarian doctrine applies, not to those benefits which are bestowed by nature, but only to those which arise from artifice. Often the principle offered here is that of *equal opportunity, meaning to refer to the opportunities available for social, political and material advancement. It is, however, true that almost any human benefit, including physical beauty and intelligence, might be conferred or withdrawn by political agency, assuming sufficient human competence. It might then seem as though the logical consequence of egalitarianism is some kind of genetic engineering, in which it is ensured that everyone has his own regulation measure of beauty, intelligence, and innate capacity for well-being. The description of this state of affairs in Aldous Huxley's *Brave New World* normally evokes revulsion, even among the most hardened egalitarians. It therefore seems that egalitarianism stands in need of a procedure for determining which benefits are to be attributed to humans as their responsibility, and which to be withheld as part of the sacred reserve of 'nature'.

Much modern egalitarianism seems to stem not from *universalist doctrines about rights so much as a *nihilistic disbelief in them. If there are no rights, no obligations, no values, but only subjective preferences, then no one has the right to anything. From which it follows that no one has the right to any more of anything than anybody else. This conclusion might then be confused with the positive doctrine (in fact incompatible with the nihilist premise) that it is *wrong* for anyone to possess more of some good than any other. Strictly speaking, given the premise, it is neither right nor wrong.

Opponents of egalitarianism might reject any of (i) to (iv). Commonly they argue that distribution can be made equal only by violating natural rights of ownership; alternatively, that utility, or human fulfilment, requires an element of struggle, competition, success and failure in the pursuit of all goods, and a background of accepted disabilities from which to embark on this struggle. (For the first, *see* *Nozick; for the second, *Nietzsche.)

egoism. The view which either describes self-interest as the true principle of *morality, or else recommends the abolition of morality in favour of a life lived for self alone. It has been advocated in modern times, to considerable political effect, partly by way of exaggerating the merits of *individualism against *collectivism, partly by way of advancing a peculiarly modern and irreligious world-view that is nevertheless held to be compatible with the reassertion of human dignity. Principal exponents of that second thought have been the *Young Hegelian Max Stirner (1806–56), and *Nietzsche. Both believed that modern socialism is nothing more than the survival of religious feeling in a bowdlerized and *sentimental form, and that its doctrines should be interpreted not in terms of what they express, but in terms of what they conceal: an envy of strength, pride and resolution; a desire to level by destroying what is superior; a small-minded resentment of the individual who is prepared to assert himself against the crowd; a wish to cripple human nature by forcing it into a single universal mould of fettered altruism. Neither Stirner nor Nietzsche could be thought of as offering a defence either of conservatism or of capitalism, their views being too resolutely self-centred to make the transition to systematic political theory. Their closest affinity is with modern *existentialism.

Various philosophies attempt to reconcile egoism and *altruism, either by arguing that it is in the long-term interest of the individual to adopt the principles and habits of an altruistic moral code (a view supported, e.g., by *Hobbes, and sometimes known as 'rational egoism'), or because the individual pursuit of self-interest acts (perhaps by an *invisible hand) in the long-term interest of society (a view associated with certain defences of the *market, notably that given by *Smith).

election. The process whereby an electorate chooses, by *voting, officers either to act on its behalf, or to *represent it in an *assembly, with a view to *government or *administration. The elements of an election are: rules of eligibility for candidates, rules for membership of the electorate, voting procedures, and officers empowered to enforce them (such as the 'returning officer' in UK law), laws relating to practice and designed, e.g., to prevent corruption, intimidation and excessive expenditure or unfair advertising. How these elements should be further specified, if the election is to result in an outcome that is in a real sense the choice of the electorate, is one of the problems of *collective choice. Many theorists try to find the distinction between *democracy and its alternatives in the nature of the procedure of an election: others seek it in the structure of the kind of *representation that results. Others look elsewhere altogether.

As an example of the issues raised by electoral procedure it is instructive to compare two electoral systems, those of the UK and the USSR. In the UK title of candidate is open, both in theory and in practice, to anyone who is able to place a deposit with the returning officer (with a few exceptions, such as *peers, and lunatics), and any candidate may announce his candidature publicly, it being an offence in law to prevent him from doing so. In the USSR there is a **de jure* right for anyone to stand as a candidate, but anyone whose name is not on the list chosen by the local committee of the Communist Party announces his candidature only at personal risk, and anyone who votes for him exposes himself to the same risk, should his vote be known. Membership of the electorate in the USSR is extended to all citizens, male or female, who have reached the age of eighteen, and all those that are entitled to vote do vote, since not to cast one's vote is to authorize the electoral officer to cast it for you, in favour of the candidate chosen by the Communist Party In the UK voting is not permitted to peers (who nevertheless are represented directly by virtue of their membership of the House of Lords), but is now open to the remainder of the population of eighteen or over, by virtue of the successive Reform Acts which have extended the *franchise. Voting procedure is open in the USSR, but the ballot is designated secret by the law (article 95 of the constitution); however, anyone who makes use of the procedure for casting his vote secretly is noted by the electoral officer, and disciplined accordingly. Finally, UK law circumscribes the amount and character of campaigning that any party may make in an election, so permitting minority parties to assert themselves as vigorously as any other, should they have the means. In the USSR all parties other than the Communist Party are illegal, and there is no legal limit to the amount of propaganda that it may issue.

It can be seen that the two practices are completely different, the one being an instrument (however crude) whereby a government subjects itself to public opinion and suffers the verdict, the other being an instrument for the ritualistic rehearsal of the rule of a single party. The important features which distinguish them seem to be the permission or lack of permission for candidates other than those officially endorsed to stand, and the adherence or non-adherence to the rule of the secret ballot. It is these two conditions which are usually referred to by the designation of 'free election'. It is a matter of dispute how far an election that is not free in that sense can actually be considered to bring about the representation of the electorate. It is still possible in theory that candidates so elected will endeavour to represent the interests of those who elected them, but the constraints that might compel them to do so will come not from the electorate but only from the ruling party, since the ruling party is the only agent that can eject them from office. The important distinction here is that between *influence and *control.

electoral college. An institution of officers (who may themselves be elected to office) responsible for electing a president, governor, prime minister, party leader, or other figure of high political power, who will obtain authority not only over them, but also over the interests which they represent. The Pope is elected by a college of cardinals, and the US President, by article II of the US constitution, by an electoral college composed of electors from each state equal in number to the total representatives of that state in the two main houses of *Congress. This procedure, which divides the election of the President from the votes cast by the *electorate, means that votes cast for a President in the college will tend to exaggerate the degree (and even to belie the absence) of popular support for the President.

An electoral college may fulfil either or both of two functions: that of making important groups with an interest in the outcome of a choice party to that choice, and that of removing key choices from direct popular control.

electorate. The class of citizens entitled to vote in an *election, by whatever procedure.

Eliot, Thomas Stearns (1888–1965). American-born poet, dramatist and critic. *See* *art, *cultural conservatism, *death, *élite, *emigration, *myth.

élite. Literally, that which has been chosen, and generally signifying the class of persons within a society who are in a position to view themselves in just that way, as chosen, either by others or by nature, to govern. Some adhere to a more specialized meaning, and distinguish government by an élite – that is, by a class that is *chosen* for the purpose, say by some ruling party – from government by a *ruling class, which obtains its powers by *prescription. (Thus T. S. Eliot, in *Notes Towards the Definition of Culture*, 1945, who distinguishes the élites of *Stalinist governments from the ruling classes that have held power elsewhere.) More generally, the term is used of any body of people who act in concert, whether or not knowingly, to maintain a shared position of social and/or political *privilege. *See also* *new class, *oligarchy.

élitism. 1. The view that *élites are desirable. The term is also used of any defence of the institutions and social relations which facilitate *oligarchy, or which pertain to a *ruling class. Élitism in this sense is usually contrasted with *egalitarianism, and is defended on a variety of grounds. Thus it may be argued that government by an élite is in the interests of the people, that the institutions which generate élites can be destroyed only by acts of injustice, or that important moral and social motives, such as pride, emulation and dignity, require the formation of élites if they are to be widely experienced. (*See* *hierarchy.)

2. The view that élites are inevitable, sometimes known as 'scientific élitism', and associated with the names of *Pareto, Mosca, and R. Michels (whose theory of the *iron law of oligarchy is discussed under that heading). Pareto distinguished the 'governing élite' from the 'non-governing élite', and both from the remainder (the non-élite). He argued that all organization, including the organization of a democracy, will generate both kinds of élite, the one dominating politics, and the other society (*Mind and Society*, 1935, vol. III). Some recent sociologists have extended Pareto's dual theory, arguing that in all developed societies there is a plurality of competing élites, which rise to eminence through the several systems of control. Politics is only one such system; others include management, trade union organizations, military organizations, and cultural and educational institutions. (*See also* *power élite.)

emancipation. The act of freeing a human being or class of human beings from the *control of another, usually when this control is enshrined in some legal privilege or right. In the case of emancipation in *Roman law various standard procedures of *manumission were developed, whereby the slave ceased to be the legal property of another. This transition from control to autonomy has been achieved in modern times largely by abolishing the existence of laws which permit human beings to be property (although note that these laws still permit some kinds of *person* to be property, such as companies). Thus emancipation of slaves in America and serfs in Russia has proceeded by government decree; however, the resurgence of laws restricting the occupation, place of residence, opinions and life-style of the Russian worker may be seen as the restoration of (partial) property rights in his body and labour, the owner now being the state rather than a nobleman. The 'emancipation' of women means, not the abolition of legal property rights in women, but the abolition of those legal, social and moral bonds which can often have the appearance of property rights; the relinquishing of women from the control of fathers, lovers, husbands and brothers is therefore a *de facto* rather than a *de jure* emancipation, and on some views not even that. (*See* *slave.)

emerging state. A *state that is in the process of securing for itself legal, constitutional, and usually economic *autonomy, by asserting itself against the vestiges of a previous colonial regime, or against the dependence on the power, protection and economic support of its neighbours.

emigration. Departure of a person from the country where he has citizenship to another, with the intention of permanent residence abroad, and usually with the intention of relinquishing the rights and duties of citizenship. The permitting of emigration is regarded by many (e.g. *Locke) as a necessary condition of legitimate power, since to forbid it is to forbid all choice to the citizen regarding the political structure to which he will be subject. It is therefore sometimes advocated as a basic *human right, and acknowledged as such even in the constitution of the USSR, which restricts it in reality.

The 'émigré' consciousness has played an important part in forming the political outlook of modern Europe. Some even argue that Western culture has become dominated by émigrés (Stravinsky, T. S. Eliot, Joyce, Nabokov, Picasso, Wittgenstein, *Popper, and many others) who have sought to find outside the country of their origin the ideal memory of a civilization that has been lost, neglected or betrayed. This is sometimes offered (e.g. by Perry Anderson: 'Components of the National Culture', *New Left Review*, 1968) as part of an explanation of the alleged *reactionary nature of the postwar intellectual establishment in Europe (the 'white émigré' syndrome). European émigrés in the last century included, however, most of the founders of modern socialism, including *Marx, *Engels and *Lenin.

eminent domain. The power of a *sovereign state to take *private property for public use, subject to making reasonable compensation, as distinct from *seizure or *expropriation. This power is recognized as a (conditional) right by certain theories of *natural law (e.g. those of *Grotius and Pufendorf); it is familiar in English law from the seventeenth century and from earlier practice, and is even permitted (subject to *due process) by the US constitution, Fifth and Fourteenth amendments. It is an important qualification to every private property right, and records the fact that no property right can easily be made absolute against the state, since the existence of a state (i.e. of a set of enforceable legal rights) is a precondition of property in any form. The power of eminent domain may be delegated, and commonly is delegated to local government bodies.

empire. Literally, rule or territory of an emperor (Latin: *imperator*), a title now of vague meaning, attached to certain kinds of *monarchy, but almost entirely in disuse. The term has been applied to states characterized:

(i) by their magnitude in area, population and power, including several *nations, peoples or subordinate states of different race or culture; and/or:

(ii) by their origin in conquest by a dominant tribe or nation which continues to form the ruling group and to monopolize *coercion; and/or:

(iii) by their political structure vesting supreme authority in a single head (emperor) from whose grant all local authority is derived; and/or:

(iv) by a theory of potentially universal jurisdiction, sanctioned by a religion, law or ideology that transcends national boundaries.

Hence *imperialism, the general name for a pursuit of power (whether economic, social or political) which acknowledges no national boundary as its natural limit. The main feature of empire is the disregard or disrespect for the *sovereignty of weaker powers, usually accompanied by a belief in the innate superiority of either the race, or the history, or the institutions of a governing people.

empiricism. The thesis that all knowledge of matters of fact is based on, or derived from, experience, so that all claims to knowledge of the world can be justified only by experience. Empiricism argues that *a priori* knowledge either does not exist, or is confined to 'analytical' truths, which have no content, deriving their validity merely from the meanings of the words used to express them; hence metaphysics, which seeks to combine the *a priori* validity of logic with the contentful character of science, is impossible. Principal empiricists have included many British philosophers (notably William of Ockham, Berkeley, *Hume, and *J. S. Mill), and also the logical *positivists. The influence of empiricism on Anglo-Saxon political thought has been very great, through what it affirms, through what it denies, and most of all through what it refuses to attend to. The following doctrines might (with varying degrees of plausibility) be attributed to empiricist influence:

(i) Experience is intelligible in isolation, or 'atomistically', without reference to the nature of its object or to the circumstances of its subject. Thus it makes sense to suggest that the object and the subject can be eliminated from all description of experience: in particular there is no need to refer to the social conditions of an experience in order to say what it is. (This seems to be implied by Hume's theory of the relation between 'idea' and 'impression', as well as by Russell's 'Logical Atomism', and other related doctrines.)

(ii) The subject of experience is the passive 'recipient' of data that are imprinted upon his intelligence irrespective of his activity, so that the subject brings nothing *to* experience and gains everything *from* it. (But *see* *pragmatism, which in some versions tries to combine empiricist ideas with the denial of (ii).)

(iii) The individual is fulfilled when the totality of his desires are fulfilled, so that there is no satisfaction of the *whole* of the human personality over and above the satisfaction of its parts. (This thesis is sometimes thought to be an essential part of *utilitarianism, at least of the kind defended by *Bentham.)

(iv) The individual is the fundamental component of, and in every important way more basic than, society: he is intelligible in isolation, and social phenomena are to be understood only by reference to him and to others of his kind. (*See* *individualism.)

(v) *Reductionism: specifically, the view that facts about society are 'reducible' to facts about the individuals that compose it. This is contrasted with the position (variously espoused by *idealists and by some *phenomenologists) that the individual is intelligible only when referred to the social arrangement which serves to constitute him (*see* (iv) above), so that any attempt to 'reduce' the society to its individual members will involve a vicious circle.

These and other doctrines all presuppose an 'atomistic' view of the world, of the relation between individual and society, and of the relation between the individual and the state. In practice not all doctrines have been espoused together, so that (iv) and (v), e.g., were rejected by Hume, who accepted (i) and (ii), while (iii) was accepted by Mill, who expressed considerable doubt about (i) and (ii). Nevertheless, there does seem to be a general tendency among philosophers who are empiricist in the strict sense given by (i) and (ii) to construe social and political institutions in an individualistic way, as agglomerates of separately intelligible parts. This has led political discussion to associate with the empiricist outlook a particular vision of the social world: composite, sceptical, individualistic, and with no patience for *social facts. In the political sphere the methodological opposite of this is *Hegel.

In the scientific sphere, empiricism generates a characteristic view of causation, which seems to be an almost inevitable consequence of its theory of knowledge. The world consists of a set of contingently connected objects and states of affairs, united by regularities rather than by necessities, and unrelated to any transcendental cause or destiny. Science investigates matters of fact, through observation and the postulation of regular connections; the aim of science is prediction, and judgements of *value have no place in it, being merely subjective preferences in the investigator, which describe no objective states of affairs.

employers' associations. Associations such as the UK Confederation of British Industry which attempt to reach agreement over strategy and tactics, in *collective bargaining, among those who are offering employment. A stone tablet recently unearthed among the ruins of Sardis testifies to the existence of such associations in the ancient world; their modern form is due partly to the ability of *trade unions to carry a dispute from one place of employment to another.

employment. The general theory of employment concerns itself with the economic conditions for full employment, and the explanation of and remedies for *unemployment, together with whatever consequences may flow from either of these conditions. The theory requires, therefore, a definition of full employment: does this mean employment of all those who *might* work, or only of some section (the 'work force')? If the latter, how is the work force to be defined? How many hours does a man have to work per week in order to be considered employed? (Official figures for the unemployed refer as a rule only to those with *no* employment, whether full-time or part-time.) Is there any requirement that his work fulfil a function, or do those also serve who only stand and wait? (The case of the matchsellers in the Strand who appeared in abundance during the Depression, or of many workers in the supposedly fully employed work forces of communist countries, who are night-watchmen where there is nothing to watch.) *Keynes defined involuntary unemployment as unemployment of those willing to work at the existing wage. Recognizing that it takes time to switch from one job to another, one might then define full employment in terms of an equality between jobs available and those who are involuntarily unemployed. However, in recent years, with growing sensitivity to the potential conflict between the goals of full employment and price stability there has been a tendency to define the employment objective as 'the lowest level to which involuntary unemployment can be reduced without bringing about an unacceptable rise in the price level'. (*See also* *over-full employment.)

Even without a definition of full employment, it is possible to study the factors which affect the *level* of employment within an economy. Keynes famously argued that one of the most important of these is the level of *aggregate demand. This hypothesis, combined with the plausible assumption that a government may act so as to increase aggregate demand, say by commissioning public works, or selectively reducing *taxation, lends economic support to the political doctrine that unemployment is the affair of government, and to be remedied by government action. It is also plausible that, the higher the level of employment, the greater the bargaining power of the work force, and the higher the consequent rate of increase in wages and so in prices; if that is so, then *inflation and employment rise together, although, beyond a certain point, inflation may produce such uncertainty as to discourage investment and therefore production, and so bring about a fall in demand, which in turn generates unemployment. Such assumptions are not everywhere accepted, even as truths about the capitalist economy of the US or the *mixed economy of the UK. Nevertheless almost all theories of employment recognize the existence of *some* connection between a high level of employment and high inflation, and propose remedies in consequence. (*See* *Phillips curve.)

A 'war economy' generates employment while imposing wage and price controls, thereby disciplining the work force not to increase its demand for wages. Even without a war economy, the production of armaments may serve to maintain the level of employment, since like the Egyptian production of pyramids discussed by Keynes, it is an activity 'the fruits of which, since they could not serve the needs of man by being consumed, did not stale with abundance' (*General Theory of Employment Interest and Money*, 1936). Another remedy, seemingly more rational, is to reduce the hours of work. It is a thesis of *Marxism that capitalism will always try to maintain the level of working hours, beyond the level required for the satisfaction of human needs, since this is a necessary consequence of the single-minded pursuit of profit. Capitalism could become stable, not through the adoption of Keynesian strategies designed to increase effective demand, but only through a 'shortening of the working day' which, in the nature of things, it cannot permit. This thesis is the residual content of the claim that capitalism must enter a *crisis from which it cannot emerge. (On the political question posed by unemployment, and the distinctions between the various types of unemployment, *see further* *unemployment.)

end state. Political philosophers sometimes distinguish those theories of justice and legitimacy that find these qualities in the nature of the act, from those which find them in the state which results from it. Only if this 'end state' (term made current by *Nozick) shows an *equitable distribution, some argue, can the transaction which leads to it be considered legitimate or just. Others regard this restriction as both too severe and also inherently disrespectful of individual rights, and attempt to develop concepts of justice and legitimacy that will eliminate reference to the final distribution in favour of reference to the constitution of the transaction that leads to it. (*See* *Rawls.) The dispute here is fundamental to the modern debate concerning *social justice, and also to *consequentialism.

Engels, Friedrich (1820–95). Lifelong friend and collaborator of *Marx, Engels was a well-to-do factory owner of Prussian origin, who spent much of his life in England, beginning his literary career with a highly influential account of the fate of the industrial *proletariat as he observed it in Manchester (*The Condition of the Working Class in England*, 1845). Thereafter he devoted himself to encouraging and supporting Marx's theoretical statement of the principles of communism, and served as co-author of many of the famous documents in which Marx's philosophy was expounded, notably *The German Ideology*, 1846, and the **Communist Manifesto*, 1848. Engels himself contributed both style and clarity to these original formulations, and influenced Marx profoundly by drawing attention to the problems of *political economy. Despite an early essay on this subject, however, he left the main enterprise of undoing the assumptions of *classical economics to Marx. Nevertheless, his thought has been extremely influential: he contributed many of the details of *historical materialism to the Marxist repertoire, and argued that both the Marxian theory of history, and the subject-matter to which it was applied, exhibit the order of the *dialectic – hence he can be considered the originator of *dialectical materialism as a distinct form of Marxism. This philosophy achieves independent (if somewhat wild) expression in Engels's late work *Anti-Dühring*, 1877–8, in which the dialectical method is extended beyond the description of human actions and institutions to the explanation of physical reality (it being part of Engels's *materialism to believe that all human facts must be shown to obey the same laws of development as govern nature as a whole). Engels's dialectical philosophy was further expounded in the posthumous *Dialectics of Nature*, and may be summarized in the three 'dialectical' laws: the transition of quantity into quality, the interpenetration of opposites, and the law of development through contradiction (or the negation of the negation); together with the idea that categories do not have fixed and immutable referents so that 'the world is not to be comprehended as a complex of ready-made *things* but as a complex of *processes*' (*Marx-Engels Selected Works*, II, 387).

In *The Origins of the Family, Private Property and the State*, 1884, Engels anticipated the modern *feminist view that monogamous marriage is the result of the subjection of one sex by another, in order to provide heirs of undisputed paternity. He adds that 'the first class-antagonism in history . . . is the antagonism between man and woman in monogamous marriage, and the first class-oppression is that of the female sex by the male'. His analysis of the interpenetration of property and family relations, and their connected developments, later proved highly influential.

As editor of Marx's posthumous work (including *Capital*), Engels probably had a great influence on the final form of the Marxian critique of political economy, but it is at present impossible to assess the extent of this influence. He was also an *activist, and an expositor of revolutionary tactics. His writings, because of their popular appeal, have been highly influential in the conduct and philosophy of modern *revolutions.

English law. Since the *UK system of law is a composite body, formed by an historical process of amalgamation, it is still necessary to distinguish English law (applicable in England and Wales) from Northern Irish law, and *Scots law. While the differences over a wide range of criminal and civil matters are now slight, there remain areas – such as the law of land – in which English and Scots law differ significantly, reflecting the greater adherence of the former to *common law, and the *Roman law influence on the latter.

Enlightenment. German: *Aufklärung*; French: *Lumières*. A name often given to the period in European history which succeeded the rise of modern science in the seventeenth century and culminated in the French Revolution, and which was characterized, so far as the educated part of society was concerned, by a scepticism towards traditional authority in matters of religion and politics, an openness of outlook, and a respect for reason as the guiding principle and defining property of the human condition. While the Enlightenment expressed itself in a variety of ways, according to national character and local conditions, its most thoroughgoing manifestations are probably French, in the works of Voltaire and Bayle, and German, in the philosophy of *Kant who, in 1784, wrote: 'Enlightenment is the liberation of man from his self-caused state of minority . . . the source [of this minority] lies not in a lack of understanding, but in a lack of determination and courage to use it without the assistance of another.' The Enlightenment was prodigious of political theory, much of it liberal, universalist, secular, and anti-authoritarian. *See*, e.g., *Kant, *Paine, *Rousseau.

In a more general sense the term 'enlightenment' is used (along with 'toleration', 'freedom of thought', 'open-mindedness') to denote the ideals of what is sometimes called the 'liberal enlightenment' view of politics. This sees a major cause of social evil in prejudice, intolerance, superstition, and attachment to custom, habit and traditional forms of association (interpreted as expressions of an outlook that forswears reason for an unthinking immersion in actual social conditions). The assumption is presumably that if all people were to think about and to question the prejudices whereby they live, then the result would be greater political understanding, and greater social harmony. Many conservatives (e.g. *Burke) argue that this assumption is itself an unargued prejudice, that it is more reasonable to suppose that matters as complicated as those involved in politics are harder to understand by reflective thought than by active engagement, that social disharmony is more often the result of critical thought than is social harmony, and that prejudice is the natural condition of every social being. But if true, then that conservative view must itself be impossible to understand through argument, so that both it and the position that it attacks must be represented as vague and vaguely articulated attitudes, rather than as *doctrines over which there might be reasoned disagreement.

entente. From French: *entendre*, to understand; and compare the etymology of **détente*. Literally, an understanding which falls short of a binding *treaty or alliance between states, especially as used in *entente cordiale*. This phrase was coined in the 1840s to denote the friendly understanding between Britain and France in matters of *foreign policy, and revived as a description of their relationship in the Anglo-French *entente* of 1904. An 'Anglo-Russian *entente*' of 1907 was, like its namesake, founded in a convention agreed between the parties, but it was far less effective in bringing the two parties together.

enterprise. **1**. Any business undertaking in which someone risks *capital in the hope of a *profit.

2. More generally, the state of mind which makes such risk-taking likely or possible.

Enterprise is 'free' when the laws of property permit the private deployment of capital in business and the private appropriation of some part of the product. The virtues of 'free enterprise' – either as an expression of a more general spirit of freedom, or as a causally efficacious factor in production and distribution – are often extolled by defenders of capitalism.

entrenched clauses. Those clauses in a written *constitution which require special legislative procedures if they are to be repealed or amended, and which are thereby protected from hasty or frequent alteration. For a fuller measure of protection the special procedure is sometimes made applicable not only to the clauses themselves but also to the clauses which provide the special procedure of protection – this is known as double entrenchment, which pushes the weak point further back. (Only an infinite regress of entrenchments could provide any protection beyond that of procedural delay, as the example shows.) The UK *Parliament is odd in that it has deeply embedded constitutional devices, which it is almost impossible to change without violence to sovereignty, and yet no possibility of entrenching legislation.

entrepreneur. French: literally, the person who undertakes an *enterprise. A name given in economic theory to the one who takes the initiative in bringing *factors of production, or buyers and sellers, together. He need own nothing to start with, but exerts some control which falls to him by virtue of his initiating role. His return is in the form of *profit or loss, rather than wages, rent or interest: i.e. it is fundamentally non-contractual, which is why he is usually seen as 'taking a risk'.

The entrepreneur corresponds to the traditional 'capitalist' of nineteenth-century theory, and like the capitalist is largely an intellectual abstraction, in that risk-taking and control of the means of production are now often separated, whether because the former lies with the state and the latter with a state functionary (as under some forms of socialism), or because risk remains with shareholders who have limited and typically only 'negative' control over production. (*See also* *separation of ownership and control.)

entryism (alternatively: entrism) The tactic of gaining clandestine admission to political organizations not directly concerned to advance one's aim in order to bend their purposes in one's favoured direction. (Usually, in the direction of *subversion or communist *revolution.) The term is now used widely, to mean any form of covert subversion (usually, but not necessarily, from the *left), effected by duplicity and through membership of some institution dedicated to purposes to which one does not adhere.

environmentalism. Concern for the environment, i.e. for natural resources, natural beauty, and for the character of cities and towns, when elevated into a political pursuit. *See* *ecology.

equal opportunity. It is often supposed that both the state and social conditions exert control, either positively or negatively, over *access to institutions which confer social or political power, and over the distribution of legal rights. The advocates of 'equal opportunity' hold that all citizens should be equally well placed to obtain such social or political benefits. In its usual form, this thesis holds that only 'relevant' considerations should be held to impede or influence the advance of any particular person. Otherwise scarce advantage may accrue to someone who does not deserve it so much as another, from whom it is withheld. What is the criterion of relevance? It is normal to argue that no one should be in a better position simply because he *already* possesses greater privilege or power. That criterion might recommend itself on grounds of *natural justice; nevertheless it is not always easy to apply. For example, is intelligence a relevant feature whereby to distinguish applicants to a university? If so, is it not a power already possessed, independently of the one sued for? Perhaps the criterion refers, however, only to man-made powers; but again, education already acquired is, common sense suggests, both a man-made power and a relevant feature. Here the advocate of equal opportunity will have to ask whether that prior education was itself acquired by equal opportunity, and so on. Often this cumulative questioning of all advantage ends by advocating *reverse discrimination, as the only feasible way of overcoming, in the long run, the unequal opportunities that are socially prevalent.

It is somewhat easier to agree that certain features are *not* relevant to the bestowal of an advantage; e.g. in the case considered, it is not relevant that the applicant's father is a party member or a governor of the university. But what about the case, much disputed, in which the applicant's father is an old member of the college to which he applies? Is it always and inevitably correct to rule that consideration out as irrelevant? To say yes is to take a *universalist view of institutions which some would rebut, on the grounds that it makes institutions unintelligible. For why, in that case, confine the applicants to citizens of one country? And consider institutions like the club and the family, both of which may have political power and privilege as a side-effect, but in which social and primary relations *must* be relevant. Much argument over equal opportunity in education seems to concern the extent to which it is legitimate to consider a school or university as bound by *private rather than *public obligations.

It is sometimes argued that supporters of equal opportunity must also support *meritocracy, as the inevitable result of opportunities being not only made available, but also seized.

equal pay. The principle, urged especially by *feminists, that people who do the same job should gain the same reward (specifically, regardless of sex, and by implication, regardless of any other feature judged irrelevant to the quality of the performance). The principle was incorporated into the first constitution of the International Labour Organization, and also in the Declaration of Philadelphia 1944, the Council of Europe's Social Charter, and the UK Equal Pay Act 1970, which also demanded equal terms and conditions of employment. Similarly for 'equal time', and so on. One of the problems with the application of such a principle lies in determining when two pieces of work are equal – i.e. in determining what is meant by 'same job'. Moreover, it seems that employers may often escape the force of the principle by redefining the jobs performed by women, so that while they are the same in fact, they are not the same in law, as those performed by men.

Some argue that there are tasks which are better done by one sex than by the other, but that nevertheless the two sexes should get the same pay for the same amount of time expended at them, since it is invidious to pay workers differently for the same job unless there is a specific agreement concerning quotas. Such questions raise intricate issues not only of *justice, but also of *utility, since it is clear that there are long-term effects on social life (particularly on the relations between the sexes, and on the nature of the family) that are brought about by all such economic equalities.

equality. Advocacy of equality as a political ideal is often thought to be a peculiarly modern attitude, although the connection between equality of treatment and *justice is enshrined in the idea of *equity, and has a philosophical ancestry that reaches back at least as far as *Aristotle. In his account of justice in Book III of the *Nicomachean Ethics*, Aristotle argues that no distinction ought to be made between men who are equal in all respects relevant to the kind of treatment in question – a conclusion that can be given an *egalitarian and an anti-egalitarian emphasis, depending upon the scope of 'relevant'. Despite the qualification, Aristotle's discussion has given inspiration to much subsequent advocacy of equality, the connection between equality and an idea of 'relevant respects' now being more or less universally acknowledged. It is clear too that equality is itself always equality in some respect; in so far as there are political ways to provide or deny equality, they can be classified according to these respects and according to the ease with which the equality in question might be secured by political activity.

1. Equality before the law. This obtains whenever an individual's *rights in law are determined simply by his being subject to the sovereign power which legislates, and to no other factor. There is never full equality in this respect, children and lunatics being treated differently from adults of a sound mind, women (as a rule) differently from men, peers (in the UK) differently from commoners, citizens differently from slaves. Hence those who fight for equality before the law usually try to determine which of these distinctions are *relevant* to legal right and privilege, which are not. **De jure* equality must then be distinguished from *de facto* equality: both rich and poor have equal *rights* in law, but it would be wrong to claim that they have equal *power* to enforce them (*see* *isonomy).

2. Political equality. Equality in respect of the ability to vote someone to office, and to stand for office oneself. This exists when the only impediment to any subject acquiring political power is his own incompetence, and the only impediment to his acquiring competence his own lack of talent. Political equality was one of the main aims of the French Revolution and was later encapsulated in the Napoleonic idea of the 'career open to talent'. It exists in varying degrees in different places but never, it would seem, absolutely. In the UK, for example, certain offices of state – notably that of *sovereign, and others whose entry requirements are hereditary – are not open to everyone.

3. Material equality. While 1. is an ancient ideal, and 2. frequently advocated, there is considerable dispute over whether a political arrangement can provide, or even ought to try to provide, material equality to those who belong to it. Does it do this by constant acts of *redistribution? Then how is this compatible with *natural justice, or with respecting the rights of people to do what they please with what is theirs? Does it do this by the abolition of *private property? Then how is this compatible with the minimal *freedom over our immediate environment that we all require? (*See* *justice, *private property.) However, it is also often argued that material equality is a prerequisite of other equalities; in which case this seeming conflict among political values cannot be easily dismissed or contained.

4. *Equal opportunity: this is usually suggested as a milder, or more politically feasible, alternative to 3., which takes the guarantee of equality as far as any merely political action can or ought to take it.

The advocacy of equality may be based on doctrines of equal rights (*see* *egalitarianism), upon a philosophy of a common *human nature (as by *Cicero, and *stoicism), or on **Realpolitik*, out of a fear that too much inequality leads to resentment and to social upheaval. The rejection of equality may be made in the spirit of 'free *enterprise', or in the name of a philosophical *egoism which rejects the idea of a 'common human nature' (cf. *Nietzsche), or in the name of a natural justice that seems threatened by too much interference in the supposedly natural inequalities that arise between men.

equilibrium. **1**. The state of balance between opposing forces. Political equilibrium must be distinguished from political stability, in which there may be no forces tending to pull asunder, although it is one plausible theory of *politics that it is the art of bringing about an equilibrium between forces within a social order, and so generating stability from potential chaos. Equilibrium is the professed aim of much international politics, involved in the pursuit of the *balance of power, *correlation of forces, etc.

'Social equilibrium' has equally been of concern to sociologists and political theorists, some, e.g. Talcott Parsons (*Towards a General Theory of Action*, 1951), arguing that all social systems have a tendency towards equilibrium, others, e.g. Marx, arguing that capitalism, for example, exhibits at best a dynamic equilibrium, as opposed to the static equilibrium of the *Asiatic mode of production. One of the most influential definitions of social equilibrium is that given by *Pareto: a social system is in equilibrium if, when 'it is artificially subjected to some modification different from the modification it undergoes normally, a reaction at once takes place tending to restore it to its real, normal state' (*The Mind and Society*, 1916).

2. In economics, the concept of equilibrium is of great importance, since it plays a crucial role in the explanation of actual movements and fluctuations, being the ideal point of rest from which the system would have no intrinsic tendency to depart. (Note that the system may or may not tend *towards* such a state, even if one exists.) The analysis of equilibrium (equilibrium analysis) and of differences between equilibria (comparative statics) is fundamental to most economic theory. Equilibrium in economies characterized by perfect *competition may be defined as that state in which, for every commodity and resource, total *supply and *demand are exactly equivalent, and the plans of all agents are fulfilled. If this equivalence exists, then, given that the only force which prompts a market to move is excess of supply over demand, or demand over supply, there will be a stasis, that lasts as long as the equivalence remains. Thus change in the system may be analysed as a movement towards or away from the equilibrium, while lack of change is explained by the fact of equilibrium. One kind of stasis that has lent itself to economic analysis is 'competitive equilibrium', in which no agent believes that prices vary with the amount that he individually buys or sells, all firms strive to maximize profit, and all individuals optimize their preferences. While actual situations may differ from that mathematical ideal, it can prove useful as a model for the behaviour of some markets.

'Equilibrium price' – the price of a commodity in equilibrium conditions – is an important concept in *price theory, since it denotes the generalizable *exchange-value of that commodity.

equilibrum model of society. The theory, to be contrasted with the *conflict model of society, that societies have a natural tendency towards *equilibrium, and that political institutions and processes develop partly in order to facilitate the return to equilibrium in times of strain or conflict. Some version of the equilibrium model underlies most modern conservative outlooks; it is also implicit in the *progressivist theories of *Comte and Spencer, and in some of the anti-revolutionary theories of socialist transformation, such as that of *Kautsky.

equity. **1**. General. Equity is another name for just dealing, and must not be confused with *equality. While it is tautologous to say that treating people equitably is just, it is certainly not tautologous, although some think it true, to say that it is just to treat them equally.

2. In legal usage, 'equity' has a distinct, highly technical sense which, while derived from 1., cannot be summarized in terms of *justice alone. Equity is a system of law, derived partly from principles of *natural justice, and partly from the peculiar historical circumstances which led to the adoption of those and related principles by the Court of Chancery in England. This court arose in the sixteenth century in order to deal with matters that had previously been the subject of appeals to the sovereign through the chancellor. Dispute between its *jurisdiction and that of the *common law was frequent, but resolved by James I on the advice of chancellors Ellesmere and Bacon, who decreed that equity should always prevail, thus ensuring that principles of natural justice may always enter into and determine the result of judicial decisions, even when common law and *statute seem to rule against them. This seems to be part of the far-reaching powers conferred by judicial independence as it exists in the UK and US (which also incorporates equitable doctrines into its law). The UK Judicature Acts 1873–5 abolished separate jurisdictions, so that the ascendancy of equitable principles is now exemplified in all the courts. Certain maxims have emerged which indicate the manner in which natural justice is envisage by the judicial mind. These 'maxims of equity' include the following: equity looks to the intent rather than to the form; he who seeks equity must do equity, and must come with clean hands; equity looks on that as done which ought to be done. In general these maxims act so as to embed and enforce judicial reasoning. Equity also provides specific remedies, such as *injunction, which are not available in the common law.

3. The law of trusts. Repeated application of equitable reasoning leads to the creation of whole new categories of legal rights, independent of those created by statute. This 'creative' aspect of equitable reasoning has been of great influence in diversifying, complicating, and adjusting claims to property. Thus equitable ownership can exist in property whose legal title vests in another: in such a case the courts grant to the equitable owner the right of use and transfer, subject to certain conditions. This is the kind of ownership known as a *trust. Doctrines of trust dominate UK and US property law, and even now enable the creative interpretation of property relations – as when a 'constructive trust' is invoked in order to give to an exploited mistress a right of property in her lover's home (*Davis* v. *Johnson*, 1978).

Erasmus, Desiderius (1466–1536) (Erasmus of Rotterdam). Early humanist and scholar, a monk by education but a critic of the monastic life who lived the life of a man of the world. Erasmus was opposed to the dogmatism of *Luther, upheld the doctrine of human free will (*see* *freedom, metaphysical), and, in a series of biting satires, endeavoured to point out both the necessary imperfection of human institutions, and also the folly of attempting to overthrow them in the name of some intellectually satisfying but untried absolute. While he criticized the formalism of the Roman Catholic Church, and upheld the aims of the *Reformation, he viewed the veneration of the individual *conscience with distaste, as the mark of a fool attempting to make his folly sovereign, and argued for continuing papal authority in matters of faith. He became one of the earliest defenders of ecclesiastical and political reform in a conservative spirit, sceptical of all recipes for perfection, and anxious to see piecemeal change within the framework of existing institutions. He was often condemned for his scepticism by those impatient of hesitation, but did much to create, by means of it, the climate of opinion that we most easily recognize as modern, in particular by presenting an image of an outlook that is serious, and committed, but without *doctrine.

Erastianism. The ascendancy of the state over the church in ecclesiastical matters, so that doctrine and ritual may be (to some extent) influenced and modified at the dictate of the state. Named after the Swiss theologian Th. Erastus (1524–83), Erastianism has been an important element in *Anglicanism, and a similar, but older, doctrine has influenced the present constitution and practice of the Russian Orthodox Church.

eschatology. The part of theology which deals with the final destiny both of the individual and of mankind. Sometimes applied by analogy to those parts of socialist doctrine (whether *utopian or scientific) which deal with the ultimate state at which we should aim, or towards which we are inexorably proceeding. Thus Norman Cohn (*The Pursuit of the Millenium*, 1957) has described medieval revolutionaries as inspired by 'eschatological fantasy', and compared Nazism to communism on the ground of their supposed like recourse to 'eschatological drama'. (*See also* *millenarianism.)

essence/appearance. A distinction of Hegelian provenance, and sometimes referred to in *Marxian economics and neo-Marxist political theory. The terms come from metaphysics, where they denote the distinction between the constitution or essence of an individual and the properties whereby we recognize it. In

Hegel they are used to conflate two separate distinctions, that between essence and accident, and that between reality and appearance, the temptation to make this conflation seeming to be deep-rooted in metaphysical thought. In Marxian economics the distinction is between the *values of commodities (as given by the labour necessary to produce them) and their *prices (which are the appearances of values). Men think of price as the essence of value partly because they fall victim to *commodity fetishism.

In the social sphere, the distinction is usually between the reality of social and historical arrangements and the beliefs, concepts and experiences through which they are perceived by their participants, and which may (perhaps) stand in a functional relation to that reality. Thus behind the 'appearance' of free contractual relations between employer and employee lies, some argue, the conflicting essence of their relation, which is one of unilateral coercion through need. To which it may sometimes be replied that 'in the realm of human affairs being and appearance are one' (Hannah Arendt: *On Revolution*, 1963), and that one no more proves the unreality of a contract by showing it to be an appearance than one proves that because redness is a secondary quality (a quality that exists by virtue of our disposition to perceive it) nothing is red. Nevertheless, the distinction is of considerable interest, and features, for example, in the *bolshevik view that society contains 'objective' enemies of the *proletariat – that is, those who, whatever their thoughts and intentions, must, by virtue of their real position in *class terms, act so as to oppress those who occupy the real position of the oppressee. This concept was extremely useful in the *show trials of the 1930s and exerts a lasting influence.

establishment. A term that is ambiguous between (i) established *power, (ii) established *right, and (iii) a third thing, lauded by certain conservatives (such as *Burke and Bolingbroke), which consists in a certain kind of synthesis of (i) and (ii) under a *rule of law. The 'right' referred to in (ii) may go beyond the narrow idea of legal right, perhaps so as to embrace conceptions of natural justice (as in Burke). Thus, one conservative writes: 'Establishment comprises both power and authority. It is a plausible assumption that power and authority mutually require each other. Power without authority is "unhappy" power. It is "at large" in the world, distributing violence without earning respect. The transformation of power into authority confers recognition, and so removes the element of arbitrary force. Power and authority seek each other. Their search is the process of politics, while establishment is the condition which their meeting creates' (Roger Scruton: *The Meaning of Conservatism*, 1980, 161–2). That conservative view is prescriptive, in that it recommends establishment, as the process of entrenching power within a system of rights, so as to provide both an internal and external corrective to, and justification for, its exercise. Others use the term descriptively, simply to describe the 'powers that be' (sense (i) above), independently of their legal or moral status, while yet others use the term largely as a term of abuse, in order to pinpoint and criticize influences that have no *other* claim to legitimacy than the fact of leaning on established power, while remaining inaccessible to the mass of people whose lives are governed by them.

However the term is used, it is clearly necessary to distinguish full legal establishment, where an institution is recognized and protected by the law, and its powers and privileges defined in law, from **de facto* establishment of the kind evinced by the Roman Catholic Church in Poland, or the Trades Union Congress in the UK, neither of which have the legal status proper to government institutions, but both of which have sufficient power to make themselves felt through government policy.

The term was originally popularized through an article in the *Spectator* by Henry Fairlie, 1955, who gave to it its slightly pejorative sense, and identified in the UK such institutions as the Monarchy, Parliament, the Church of England, the BBC and the public schools as among its components. In the US the components must be differently defined (whether for praise or abuse), while in the USSR and its satellites the establishment (in this sense) normally consists of only one institution, the Communist Party.

estates of the realm. The classes of citizens recognized by the medieval English Parliament as having distinct rights and duties and requiring (or deserving) *representation in Parliament in distinct ways. Three such classes were identified originally: the clergy, the barons and the commons, and this division persists in the modern UK Parliament, the House of Lords being composed of *peers (Lords Temporal, and Lords Spiritual, the latter being bishops), the House of Commons being forbidden to peers. The term 'estates of the realm' was used from the early fifteenth century onwards, some say by analogy with the French *états generaux*, in which the sovereign would summon to a parliament, representatives of the various estates (usually the three mentioned). Russian law traditionally recognized four 'estates': nobility, clergy, working townsmen, and peasantry, and some vestiges of legal and political distinctions between them survived until the Revolution. In the UK the press has been called (by *Carlyle) the fourth estate, the trade unions the fifth.

étatisme. Term used by French writers from the 1920s onwards to refer to the direct intervention by the state in the economic life of a capitalist society, by *nationalization, by the administering of prices and control of wages, and by social welfare legislation. In a wider sense it signifies the vesting of power in the state, as a necessary condition of political transformations.

ethics. **1**. Often used in a specific sense – as in *business ethic, *professional ethic – to mean the standards characteristic of an activity or profession, whether or not those standards reflect any accepted or acceptable morality in those who obey them.

2. More generally, any system of moral *values held forth as meriting intrinsic obedience, and not on account of some purpose which obedience might incidentally serve.

3. Now most usually used as a technical term of *philosophy, to denote the philosophical study of morality. As such, it has developed two branches: normative ethics, and meta-ethics. Normative ethics attempts, by philosophical reflection, to expound or criticize systems of moral values, e.g. by exploring consistency, conformity to human nature, ability to bring order to the experience of the moral agent. Meta-ethics engages in critical reflection on the meaning of moral judgements, and on the kinds of justification that might be given for them, and on the crucial question of whether that justification might ever be objectively binding. The two branches are related. For example a philosophy which upholds the meta-ethical doctrine of subjectivism (according to which there is no validity to any moral judgement beyond the subjective disposition to accept and act on it) is likely to find normative ethics peculiarly difficult, having deprived itself by its own arguments of the right to legislate for others. Conversely any system of normative ethics would seem to require and to stem from a view as to the justification of moral judgement.

The subject-matter of moral judgement is extremely hard to identify. It includes judgement of the ultimate value of certain courses of action, specific judgements as to what ought to be done here and now, principles of conduct, and specifications of those qualities of human mind and character that are intrinsically admirable (the *virtues). It is common to contrast ethical systems founded in the study of *human nature and virtue (such as that of *Aristotle), with those founded in the reasoned analysis of moral principles (such as that of *Kant). It is also common to distinguish those systems which argue that the value of every act is ultimately to be found in its consequences for human welfare (*see* *consequentialism), from those which argue that actions, or the motives which generate them, may sometimes possess value intrinsically, and which therefore attempt to derive a system of morality from the study of *duty. It is sometimes argued that, in the political sphere, only the consequentialist attitude is appropriate, since in this sphere the end must be allowed to justify the means, 'Deontologists' oppose such a view as intrinsically immoral, (*see* *morality and politics), and argue that if there are any moral values at all, then there will be circumstances when they simply cannot be overriden by any reason based merely in the consequences of moral obedience or disobedience.

A major source of philosophical controversy is the relations between fact and value, and that between 'is' and 'ought'. Are the distinctions here real, and do they imply that there is no inference from judgements of fact to judgements of value? *See* *value, *value-free.

ethiopianism. Term principally applied to quasi-nationalist movements among blacks in America and West India, which look to Africa (i.e. 'Ethiopia') as a symbol of a social and political condition to be recaptured through political action. A specific form ('rastafarianism') represents the former emperor of Ethiopia as a semi-divine being, the rightful protector of African *civilization, and the symbolic representative of the type of *Christianity indigenous to Africa and closest to the message of the gospels.

ethnic. Greek: *ethnos,* a tribe. Belonging to a *race or kind. Ethnic groups and ethnic minorities exist by virtue of longstanding association across generations, complex relations of *kinship, common *culture, and usually religious uniformity and common territorial attachments.

ethnicism. **1**. Originally heathen *superstition, or (used without pejorative implication) the religion of any society that does not subscribe to some variety of Judaeo-Christian belief.

2. Now more frequently, the desire (to be distinguished from that involved in *ethnocentrism) to conserve or recapture a political identity based upon race, region, or any *tradition which has its rationale in membership of an ethnic group (= a group whose members are identified not in terms of political institutions, but in terms of blood relation, *language and regional attachment).

ethnocentrism. Term used by W. G. Sumner (*Folkways,* 1906), to denote attitudes which uncritically or unjustifiably suppose the superiority of the subject's own *ethnic group. Now generally employed in a somewhat pejorative sense.

ethnographical principle. The principle that persons of the same race, language or ethnic group should be united in a common state, with its own *territory and *jurisdiction, so that political boundaries should coincide with the intuitively accepted sense of 'who belongs where'. The violation of this principle in the colonization of Africa has been widely deplored for its after-effects, as has its violent assertion by Israel in defiance of opposition from her neighbours. The principle can be seen as one of the motivating ideas behind *nationalism, and is rejected by all those who think that social and political sentiments are, and ought to be, distinct.

ethos. Greek: character. Following *Aristotle (*Rhetoric,* II, xii-xiv), used to denote the characteristic 'spirit' or 'tone' of an *association, *institution, *society, *culture or *people. An ethos is a prominent *social fact, which is often held to explain things which can be explained by no individual action or state of mind. Explanations in terms of ethos are sometimes dismissed as mere re-descriptions (as in 'the pursuit of profit is part of the ethos of capitalism'), but they may be more than that, especially for those who believe in the 'collective consciousness' discussed by such sociologists as *Durkheim.

Eurocommunism. Term probably coined by F. Barbieri in 1967 but later used to denote the attempted synthesis of *liberalism and *communism promulgated by Western European communist parties since 15 November 1975, when the French and Italian parties issued a joint declaration of policy. Their 'Eurocommunist Manifesto' recognized the right of other parties to exist, abandoned the postulate of the *dictatorship of the proletariat, advocated democratic elections, the 'parliamentary road to socialism and communism', the guarantee of civil liberties, and the right of *opposition. Denounced by the USSR as *revisionism, Eurocommunism has nevertheless gained a considerable following, especially among those who have wished to take advantage of the common political institutions and law-making capacity of the European *Common Market, in order to advance the condition of the working class throughout its member states. Eurocommunists are notable for their frequent denunciations of USSR foreign and domestic policy and their respect for political institutions denounced in the USSR as *bourgeois democracy.

Europeanism. The attitude which sees the well-being, destiny and *institutions of the major European states as so closely linked by geographical and historical circumstances that no cogent political action can be successfully pursued in one state without some reference to, and attempt to achieve integration with, the others. Ideally Europe, which created the *nation state, should also transcend it, and bear political witness to the fact of its common outlook, culture and heritage, through the creation of common legal, ecomomic and political institutions. While based in a *common market, the EEC has evolved a set of political institutions, which have the *approximation of laws as their aim, and which impinge on local customs, habits and political procedures in a manner which occasionally tends towards their abolition. This is sometimes welcomed by Europeanists, as a furtherance of true political unity.

Europeanism has been a strong undercurrent in *dissident movements in Eastern Europe, since it affirms the existence of an identity other than that insisted on by the Communist Party, and provides a real cultural and territorial claim with which to support the somewhat abstract assertion of *human rights.

euthanasia. Greek: good death. Term used since 1869 to denote the termination of human life in order to relieve the suffering of the victim, usually with his consent. Euthanasia raises in a vivid form certain questions concerning *persons, and the extent to which our duties towards them may be dissolved or overridden by their actual or supposed consent. It is normal to phrase questions concerning euthanasia in terms of the language of rights – have I the right to do this to someone, if he consents? What if he does *not* consent (supposing him to be unconscious and destined to a life as a vegetable)? Perhaps human vegetables are not persons, and have no rights? The language of rights is perhaps misleading, since the question can be phrased without it: ought I, and ought he, ever to do this, even if life holds nothing for him?

Distinction is made between the issue of euthanasia and that of *abortion, on the grounds that (i) in euthanasia consent of the victim is possible or may be inferred; (ii) abortion always requires a positive interference in the course of nature, whereas euthanasia may involve the opposite – a decision to cease medication and to let nature take its course.

evangelism. **1**. The dedicated preaching of the gospel; transferred to political contexts to denote political action which favours persuasion through *doctrine, rather than through *force, material inducement, or *conciliation. Some think that only the last is a truly *political approach to human conflict.

2. (= evangelicalism.) Term denoting various *activist tendencies within the Christian (specifically *Protestant) church, which emphasize the contents of the gospel, rather than custom or institution, as the true source of spiritual authority.

evolutionism. **1**. Belief that major social and political changes are to be understood as forms of 'evolution', whereby social structures gradually adapt themselves to material conditions, and steady improvements in institutions emerge from failed attempts. The evolutionary view of society has a long history, and versions were common in the eighteenth century, put forward, for example, by *Montesquieu and *Kant. *Saint-Simon argued that there is an evolutionary sequence through which all mankind must pass, and *Comte suggested that there are three universally observable stages of human development in the social sphere. Herbert Spencer (1820–1903) extended some of Comte's ideas in *Principles of Sociology*, 1867, arguing that social life has a natural tendency to develop from simple to complex forms, and steadily to enrich its variety. He had begun to develop his influential account of this before Darwin's *Origin of Species*, 1859, and later argued that Darwin's theory confirmed his own, thus founding the ideology of social *Darwinism, according to which adaptation of society to material conditions is to be understood in terms of the 'survival of the fittest'. *Marxism has an evolutionist side, but argues that, while society develops, it does not develop in a uniform way, and in particular undergoes periods of *revolutionary* transformation, when laws of steady development no longer apply, since the whole social organism has become dysfunctional. *Dialectical materialists describe these revolutionary periods as brought about by a 'transition from quantity to quality', which interrupts the flow of the purely quantitative development of evolution. Modern evolutionists include Teilhard de Chardin (1881–1955).

2. Any *reformist doctrine that believes in a slow and continuous process (e.g. the 'parliamentary road to socialism') as the only way to initiate beneficial change, and which therefore opposes *revolution, or the violent overthrow of existing institutions. Roughly speaking, the *social democrat parties have become evolutionists, and have been condemned as such by the *communist parties, which represent their own aims as revolutionary. Eduard Bernstein's *Evolutionary Socialism,* 1899, which advocated evolutionism from within the Marxist camp, has always been particularly distasteful to communists, and, since Lenin's attacks on it, is taken as the major text of *revisionism.

excess profits. **1**. The medieval doctrine of the *just price was an application of the view that there is a price for each commodity at which it could exchange without *exploitation of the buyer or deprivation of the seller. To sell above that price is to make a profit unjustly. This idea of a just price – to be determined by principles of justice which are independent of actual supply and demand – survives in the wartime doctrine of 'excess profits', according to which a government may determine, by criteria which do not refer to actual market forces, the level above which profit may not go without incurring a penalty. During 1939–46 excess profits were subject in the UK to an 'excess profits tax', designed to prevent the exploitation of the ordinary consumer. (*See* *usury.)

2. In economics, 'excess profit', also called 'supernormal profit', has a technical sense, for which *see* *profit.

excess supply or demand. Two kinds of economic disequilibrium (see *equilibrium). In the presence of excess demand the amount of a good or service which buyers seek to purchase at a given price exceeds the amount which sellers are prepared to sell at that price, so that (other things being equal, and failing, e.g., government constraint) prices will generally tend to rise until equilibrium is attained. In the presence of excess supply, conversely, prices tend to fall.

exchange control. The control by the *state of dealings in gold and foreign currencies, exercised through the banking system. Exchange control may affect, or even be used to fix, the rate of exchange, for example, when the price of domestic currency is artificially raised for foreign traders in order to attract *hard currency. And it may affect capital transfers, as when the transfer of domestic currency abroad is forbidden or limited. The second form of exchange control is the subject of much political controversy. It had been practised by UK governments continuously since the end of the war, until its abolition in 1979. It was then argued that the economic benefit of the measure had never been proven, and that, while it limited the citizen's ability to convert domestic assets into foreign assets, it also deterred foreign investors from converting foreign assets into domestic ones, so achieving no real improvement in the *balance of payments. The persistence of exchange control was said by some to be a form of *protectionism, which could not achieve its intended effect. It was also argued to be an unwarranted interference in individual *liberty, and became the recipient of many traditional arguments on behalf of *free trade. The issue remains, however, undecided, and the reintroduction of exchange controls is a possibility.

exchange economy. An economy in which there is specialization of activity and therefore social *division of labour, which creates the need for exchange, usually through the creation of a *market. The interdependence of division of labour and a system of exchange was pointed out by *Smith, and it persists whether or not there is private ownership of the means of production.

There is also a technical meaning of the term within economics, according to which an 'exchange economy' is a hypothetical economy in which there is exchange without production. (A possible example of this is the prisoner-of-war camp after the receipt of food parcels.)

exchange-value. A term of *classical economics. The exchange-value of a commodity consists of the quantity of some other commodity against which it will exchange in *equilibrium conditions. When the other commodity is money, exchange-value becomes *price. Exchange-value is a principal subject-matter of quantitative ecomomics, and must be distinguished from (another term of classical economics) *use-value, which requires independent theoretical treatment. According to *Marx, exchange-value is a necessary accompaniment of capitalism and also unique to it. It is also held to be the source and the object of certain damaging illusions, such as *commodity fetishism.

executive. The branch of government concerned with implementing domestic and foreign policy, and applying law. According to one version of the doctrine of the *separation of powers, the executive is contrasted with the *legislature, whose function is not to implement but to decide on policy, not to apply but to determine the law, and with the judiciary, whose function is to decide disputes as to the meaning or the applicability of the law.

In the UK the executive branch of government includes the *Crown, and the ministers of the Crown, and the *civil service (including the Foreign Office). It has two peaks of power: the *cabinet, which pursues party politics, influences as best it can the decisions taken in *Parliament, and then advises the Crown; and the civil service, which is in theory a servant of the Crown, but in practice exercises, through inertia, or habit, an executive power of its own.

Because of the influence of the doctrine of the separation of powers upon the US *constitution, the term 'executive' is used widely, to refer to all the powers of the President and his cabinet, whether or not those powers correspond precisely to any theoretical division between those which are and those which are not of an executive kind. These executive powers of the President are subject to constant scrutiny (with various sanctions, culminating in *impeachment) by both houses of Congress. The President appoints his own staff to the executive office, which may contain as many as 2,000 members, each engaged in mediating between the central apex of executive power and the various departments and agencies through which it is exercised. The constitution permits the establishment of 'executive agencies' designed to apply the legislation passed by Congress: these include the National Security Council and the CIA.

'Executive agreements' are agreements made between the US President and another head of state: they have the validity and effect of a *treaty, but do not require *ratification by the Senate. By analogy, some writers refer to 'executive war', meaning war precipitated and conducted by the President, whether in his role as commander-in-chief, or by his constitutional executive powers, which is pursued despite dissent from the people and from the two assemblies. The war in Vietnam had, at certain stages, such a character, but also resulted in legislation restricting the power to make executive war.

exile. Conceived by the Greeks and Romans as a form of punishment appropriate to grave offences, and still used as such in the USSR, where 'exile' means forced confinement in an inhospitable place, exile is now often the preferred response to *oppression. Voluntary exile – prolonged and perhaps permanent absence from one's country of origin – is therefore a common condition, with its own *ethos, and *culture, and a powerful influence in public affairs. Exile is a special case of *emigration, where what is sought is not primarily the advantages of the place to which one goes, but essentially freedom from whatever disadvantages prevailed at home. Some argue that the exile character is shaped by the thought of betrayal of those who have not been able to escape, and that this thought explains the exile's impotent refusal of existing conditions. Governments in exile are, perhaps for this reason, seldom respected either by those in exile themselves, or by those at home.

Exile with loss of citizenship is normally called expatriation, whether or not the loss was voluntary.

existentialism. Term adapted from the Danish philosopher Søren Kierkegaard (1813–55), and now denoting the philosophy of personal existence which he introduced, according to which the subjective consciousness of the individual, and his solitary 'leap into the unknown', constitute the sole legitimate premise of all metaphysical and ethical speculation. The term is also used of the philosophies of Martin Heidegger (1889–1976) and *Sartre, together with many of those who have been influenced by them, and through them, by the *phenomenology of Edmund Husserl (1859–1938). Heidegger poses the 'problem of being', and distinguishes between various kinds of being (e.g. *Sein, Dasein* and *Existenz*), with which we, as self-conscious agents, are familiar, but which need to be uncovered by philosophical reflection. It is only in the *authentic choice, whereby we take *responsibility for our own being, that our freedom is expressed and our anxiety in the face of nothingness overcome. This choice seems to precipitate a reflective posture – which Heidegger calls 'being towards death' – in which the fact of mortality becomes the premise of all practical reasoning, and the clue to acceptance of 'being in the world'. Similar doctrines, less obscurely formulated, occur in the work of Sartre, but associated there with an energetic form of political *activism, based nevertheless on the premise that an individual is answerable to himself alone, and has no responsibility greater than the responsibility to be who he (really) is. (*See* *commitment.)

If there is a political doctrine characteristic of existentialism it is to be found in that last phrase, and in the various embellishments that are offered to the idea of man as a self-created being. Sartre argues, for example, that the central fact about human beings is that they have no nature (or 'essence') but only existence. Hence there is no *natural law, and no objective morality. The individual is alone in the world, burdened by a freedom which he cannot shift since it is the precondition of all his acts, and for which he must take full and elaborate responsibility.

At the same time there is no responsibility outside the act of commitment; a political stance may provide the channel through which commitment can flow, in which case it may fulfil the obligatory existential choice of the godless agent. There is, however, a contradiction involved in this attempt to recognize absolute sovereignty only in the unmediated, untheorized, undoctrinal choice, while urging that such a choice must be, or at any rate ought to be, directed towards a political (specifically communist) end. Sartre's doctrine that contradiction is the inevitable result of the attempt to relate to anything other than oneself at least makes this course no more irrational than any other; in his followers, however, it is sometimes difficult to see the grounds for nevertheless fervent recommendations. Marxists often argue that the existentialist emphasis on subjectivity and the suffering consciousness is in fact incompatible with their vision of political agency, and incompatible with *historical (whether or not *dialectical) materialism. For Sartre, however, existentialism is, in the last analysis, only an 'enclave within Marxism'.

'Christian existentialism' is the name of the style of subjectivist *demythologizing theology that takes its inspiration from Kierkegaard, and which extols the agonizing individual who loses all for the sake of a faith that is inexpressible.

expansionism. Term coined about 1900 to refer to the advocacy of, or furtherance of, a policy of expansion, especially territorial expansion, either by inducing economic dependence in neighbouring states, or by the *subversion of their political systems in order to make them politically dependent, or by direct conquest. Economic expansionism, such as witnessed in postwar Japan, involves the constant expansion of markets, in order to capture an ever larger share of world trade.

exploitation. **1**. In common parlance, John exploits Alfred when John uses Alfred to John's advantage, and Alfred's detriment, without making just recompense (perhaps making no recompense whatsoever). Hence applications of the idea of exploitation presuppose a standard of 'just recompense'. Exploitation may involve deception (as in fraud), or *force (as in *slavery), or 'undue influence' (as when a husband exploits his wife): but its essence does not consist in any of these, which are invoked only to explain the position of the victim. Some find its essence in the idea of 'just recompense' just referred to; others in the *Kantian notion that some forms of treatment involve using others as means and not as ends – a notion itself designed to explicate the idea of injustice.

One explanation of how exploitation may arise is in terms of unequal bargaining power. This has been invoked as common ground by many of those who would criticize the institution of *wage labour, and the capitalist economic system that requires it. The crucial problem is clearly that of determining when, and how, unequal bargaining power leads to injustice. Some say that a labourer is compelled by necessity to sell his *labour power, whereas the capitalist is not compelled by any similar necessity to contract for it, and that this alone is sufficient to generate injustice. However, without further theory, that is extremely contentious: for it would have the consequence that there could never be a *just price for any commodity that is needed by the purchaser, so that the buying and selling, for example, of food, will always involve an injustice, whatever the price. Some might still be prepared to accept this consequence, but most attempt to give further theories of the wage relation. It is sometimes argued that the capitalist need only give (and therefore will only give) to the labourer sufficient to enable the reproduction of his labour power – i.e what he needs for survival. But those who argue this way (including *Marx) make the important proviso that custom and local conditions and expectancy determine what is needed to reproduce labour power: in which case this says very little about the actual amount (relative or absolute) that the capitalist must offer. Besides, it is to be supposed that unionization removes this element of absolute dependence on the capitalist's whim, as do laws governing the minimum wage and labour hours. In short, the unequal bargaining power that remains is rather like that which exists in (almost) every *contract. Is it necessary that it leads to exploitation?

2. Classical *Marxism says yes, but only by introducing a new concept of exploitation so as to imply that, whenever there is private property in the means of production, there is also exploitation. This theory is sometimes thought to be part of the *labour theory of value, but is in fact independent. It argues first that *capital is not a *productive force, but only a pattern of *production relations, with the important property that it facilitates a particularly high level of production. Nevertheless, the only producer in the capitalist enterprises is the labourer – capital (in the form of machinery etc.) being no more than the means to increase the efficiency of his labour. But the labourer does not keep the full product of his labour – part of it is kept by the capitalist, in the form of *surplus-value. This will be true whether or not the labourer receives more than the amount necessary to reproduce himself and his labour power. (In terms of the labour theory of value the point is sometimes put thus: surplus-value is the extraction of hours of unpaid labour.) Thus the labourer is deprived of some portion of the product which he, and he alone, produces. The 'rate of exploitation' is defined in terms of the ratio of the time worked to the time required for the labourer to produce the equivalent of what he receives.

While this theory speaks of exploitation, it is clear that it is stated and defended without reference to the concept of justice. If it is true, it does not follow that the labourer is exploited in sense 1. unless it is also argued, e.g., that he has a *natural right to the product of his labour. That position has been argued, e.g. by *Locke, but as part of a philosophical *defence* of private property in the means of production, and also by some of the early socialist followers of *Ricardo.

export and import. Exports are goods and services produced in one country, and sold in exchange for the goods, services, credit or currency of another: imports are what the other country thereby receives. Invisible exports are such items as financial services, shipping services, royalties, legal fees; they may constitute a considerable amount of a state's *national income (in the UK for example, invisible exports in 1975 amounted to £1,500 million). Re-export is the export of imported commodities without significant alteration, as in much of the UK trade in tea.

expropriation. Depriving some person or corporation of private property, usually by government agency, with no recompense. To be distinguished from *nationalization and 'compulsory purchase', where recompense (which may or may not relate to the *exchange-value of the property) is offered. Is there a distinction between *taxation and expropriation? If not, does that show that the former is unjust, or that the latter may sometimes be just? Some (e.g. *Nozick) regard taxation as a forced parting with property legitimately acquired; others regard all rights of private property as inherently defeasible in the interests of the state (through whose good offices they are held), so that neither taxation nor expropriation is in itself unjust, but unjust only when independent circumstances (involving, e.g., the disregard for genuine *natural rights) might make them so. (*See* *eminent domain.)

extradition. The delivery by one state to another of a person against whom the second state desires to proceed under its own criminal law. In the UK extradition is permitted only under statute, where there is an extradition treaty with the other state. In the US there can be inter-state extradition, governed by the 'Inter-state Comity' Clause (art. IV, s. 2). This clause has been held by the Supreme Court, however, to be discretionary, so that the governor of one state may refuse to return a prisoner to another whence he fled, without giving reason.

Extradition is not normally allowed, under any legal system, for *political offences, although what constitutes a political offence remains uncertain. This exception is thought necessary for a variety of reasons, but most of all in order to remove from *adjudication by the courts matters which concern diplomatic relations and foreign policy.

extremism. Vague term, which can mean:

1. Taking a political idea to its limits, regardless of 'unfortunate' repercussions, impracticalities, arguments, and feelings to the contrary, and with the intention not only to confront, but also to eliminate, *opposition.
2. Intolerance towards all views other than one's own (for which, *see* *toleration).
3. Adoption of means to political ends which disregard accepted standards of conduct, in particular which show disregard for the life, liberty and *human rights of others.

F

Fabianism. The Roman general Q. Fabius Maximus, surnamed 'Cunctator' ('the delayer'), won his campaigns by slow attrition of the enemy. Accordingly, those British socialists who wished to see their aims achieved by a policy of gradual reform within existing institutions and constitutional government, rather than by revolutionary upheaval, called their society, founded in 1884, the Fabian Society, wishing to imitate the Roman general in success as well as in name. The society has never had many members, but it has included influential intellectual figures (among them, Sidney and Beatrice Webb, H. G. Wells and G. B. Shaw), along with many Labour Party politicians. It has tirelessly pursued the task of making socialism intellectually and politically (some would also add, perhaps unfairly, socially) respectable, and, through its influence in universities (notably in Oxford) was able to win over to the Labour Party many of those best situated to obtain parliamentary seats. It has therefore been important in forming the UK Labour Party during the interwar and postwar period. It is characterized by wide-ranging, relatively undoctrinaire, and imaginative social analysis, but not by any doctrine besides the central one implied in its name.

faction. Any group organized for political ends, which defines itself at least partly by its opposition to some rival group. A faction is usually *within* a *party, *institution, or *government, and is identified by perceived common purpose rather than by rules of membership. Were a faction to achieve the level of political ascendancy necessary to announce its aims, and to invite membership, then it would tend to become a *party. Systems which do not permit *opposition parties nevertheless have still to contend with opposing factions.

Fear of, and hostility towards, faction motivated much of sixteenth- and seventeenth-century *absolutism, and subsequent *constitutionalism often had as one of its aims, the stilling of faction through permanent procedures of balance and *conciliation. The transformation of faction into legitimate opposition is often seen as one factor in political *equilibrium.

factors of production. Defined by the economist Alfred Marshall (1842–1924) as 'the things required for making a commodity', they are often grouped by economists into *land, *labour and *capital, on the assumption that these three are roughly independent factors involved in production, and that no one of them is effective alone: land provides *raw material, capital the instruments of production, and labour the necessary activity which brings these together to produce a saleable *commodity. 'Factors' are usually distinguished from 'inputs'. An input is a commodity or service, a factor of production is the recipient of some category of income (rent, wages or profit).

It is sometimes thought that this division reflects either economic error, or political prejudice, or both, in that it seems to imply (or in *certain applications* seems to imply) that the contributions of the factors are comparable, so that capital, for example, merits a return just as much as does labour. This conceals the fact, some *Marxists argue, that the owner of *capital, unlike the owner of *labour power, does not actually *do* anything – ownership exhausts his contribution, which is thereby not a contribution at all, but an indefinite tax on the product of another's labour. *Marx spoke of 'capital fetishism', as the constant illusion generated by capitalist modes of production that capital is actually a *force* active in production, rather than a position in the relations which make production possible. But, whether or not we follow Marx's argument (compare, for example, the *Austrian school theory of capital), it is clearly not absolutely necessary to have any one view about the role of capital in production just because one classifies it along with labour as a 'factor' therein. It may also be noted that much modern economics makes no use of the notion of aggregate 'factors' of production.

factory legislation. Since the beginning of the *industrial revolution in the UK there have been repeated attempts on the part of government (often acting under pressure from concerned philanthropists such as *Owen, or from increasingly organized working-class resentment) to ensure that *factory production should conform to some standard of humane conduct towards the labourer. Whether or not one accepts the (perhaps self-confirming) Marxist theory that such legislation is explained as a functional adjustment which makes capitalism more durable, it is undeniable that it has also been a major channel through which objections to unfettered capitalism – whether motivated by socialist distaste for *exploitation, or by conservative distaste for social disruption and uprootedness – have found expression. In the first acts (from that of 1802 introduced by Peel to that of 1867) the principal concern was to shorten the working day and to prevent the exploitation of children; later the emphasis shifted to provisions for health, safety and the conditions of work. In the US legislation was more tardy, and while the State of Massachusetts paved the way in a series of statutes beginning in 1836, there was no coherent body of federal legislation until the twentieth century. Even in 1916 and 1919 federal laws limiting child labour were held to be unconstitutional, and a proposed child labour amendment to the constitution was rejected in 1924. Not until the Depression did US legislation catch up with that of the UK.

factory production. That mode of production characterized by the gathering of labourers into a single place, in order to engage in *detail labour, for fixed hours, in a process which may or may not include all the operations required for the production of a *commodity. Factory production, which brings men into close relation with machines, is characteristic of a certain kind of *technological advance, itself characteristic, according to some theories, of capitalism. Its aspect of enslavement and *alienation which struck such horror into nineteenth-century observers (and presumably into nineteenth-century victims, although they had less time to be articulate about it), is one that all serious modern political doctrines attempt to confront, either by advocating the abolition of factory production (a thesis often denounced as utopian or at any rate romantic), or by suggesting modes of ownership or control that will mitigate it (although how it is mitigated by, e.g., *common ownership of the factory is a problem to which socialism returns an answer that many find unpersuasive), or (what is perhaps most reasonable) by advocating further advances that will enable men to master the machines that presently seem to master them. Whether new modes of ownership will be the necessary or desirable consequence of those advances is a fundamental matter over which socialists and their opponents dispute.

fairness. Popular term meaning *justice, perhaps with a slight leaning towards the distributive conception expressed by that term. Thus the doctrine of 'justice as fairness' advocated by *Rawls can be seen partly as advancing a claim for the primacy of distributive conceptions in settling claims over what is just, while also emphasizing that just agreements involve the discounting of all 'unfair' advantage. On the other hand, the ideas of 'fair comment' (a defence to a claim of damages in libel), 'fair trading' (concept introduced into UK law in 1973 in order to protect consumers from certain kinds of *exploitation), and 'fair wages' (introduced into UK law in 1891 in order to protect labourers from exploitation in times of over-full employment) use the term 'fair' to denote justice in transaction rather than in distribution. (On the distinction here *see* *justice.) The distributive conception is more obviously evinced by the 'fairness' doctrine in US communications law, which requires the *media of mass communication to apportion their time 'fairly' to the various candidates and parties seeking election during a political campaign. Significantly, fairness is not taken to mean that all parties should be given a share of time, or that times allotted to the various parties should be equal.

The child's cry 'It is not fair', like the more sophisticated 'It is not just that . . .', suggests a demand that the world be so arranged that justice be done. Some think that such a complaint is not only childish, but also incoherent; others see in it the basic motive of all serious political action.

faith. Regarded by the Christian churches as a supernatural rather than a natural act, faith arises from God's action on the soul, and involves an act of the will, and something surpassing an act of understanding, on the part of the subject, who voluntarily reaches out for and encounters the deity, without knowing, until he has become acquainted with God, exactly what it is that he is believing, and afterwards, in all probability, being unable or reluctant to put what he believes into words.

The underlying doctrine of faith is this: there are systems of belief so integral to the identity of the person who subscribes to them, and so far beyond intellectual definition, that they must be understood at least partly in terms of the will: an act of will is their precondition and also their result. The knowledge that results from the undertaking of faith is more like knowledge of a person ('acquaintance') than it is like knowledge of a fact, and for this reason it seems absurd to transcribe the deliverances of faith into propositions that may be doubted or believed, according to the evidence. Such an assimilation of doctrinal commitment to acts of will has its equivalent in the realm of politics, for example, in neo-conservative ideas of *tradition, and in *neo-Marxist notions of *praxis.

falangism. The *falange española* (Spanish phalanx), or falangists, were founded in 1933 by José Antonio Primo de Rivera (son of Primo de Rivera, Spanish dictator 1923–30), in order to secure working-class support for the local brand of *fascism. It continued its activities throughout the republican period, emphasizing traditional, as much as the new fascist and *collectivist, modes of social unity, and was finally successful in the civil war, under the determined leadership of General Franco. Hence 'falangism' now denotes the particular synthesis of fascism and traditionalism exemplified by Franco's subsequent dictatorship, with its emphasis on Spanish national character, on close moral and political ties between people and leadership, and on a fundamental unity between the state and all autonomous institutions, including the church.

falling rate of profit. It was several times predicted by nineteenth-century economists that, in the long run, the rate of profit of all enterprises will tend to fall, and the *accumulation of capital come to an end. *Ricardo derived this prediction from the fact that natural resources are limited: gradually more inferior land must be brought under the plough, and since the net product per labourer falls as cultivation is extended, while the exchange-value of capital against agricultural products rises, the margin of profit must inevitably dwindle. *Marx gave different reasons for the same prediction: 'organic composition' of capital tends to rise with time, i.e. the value of capital laid out on every hour of labour time is in general increasing, because of technical progress which requires the increasing use of capital. Consequently the rate of profit on capital is falling. This argument is often attacked, e.g. because output per head can rise just as fast in producing capital as in using it. Nevertheless, it founded one of the many separate predictions of a *crisis of capitalism. The prediction is no longer widely accepted, and those who accept it do not necessarily forecast the doom of capitalism. Some – for example, *Keynes, and many of his followers – look forward to a natural end to accumulation, and to the pursuit of profit that accompanies it.

false consciousness. Term of *Marxist theory, already current in 1893, when *Engels wrote, in a letter to Mehring: 'Ideology is a process accomplished by the so-called thinker consciously indeed but with a false consciousness.' It has many earlier equivalents in *Hegel, and in *Feuerbach's analysis of *fetishism, and is now popularized by writers such as *Lukács and *neo-Marxists, particularly those of the *Frankfurt school. If, as the *German Ideology* says, life determines consciousness and not consciousness life, then each mode of life will generate its own characteristic form of consciousness. Whether or not some form of *determinism is true, it is clear that this view of consciousness raises a problem concerning truth: in particular, how can one pursue truth – how can one know, that is, that the world is as one's consciousness represents it to be? The problem is made acute by the suggestion that falsehood may be generic to a particular kind of consciousness, so that even its weighing of the evidence will not guarantee the truth of its conclusions, since that very reasoning will be infected by the intrinsic falsehood that governs it.

Various responses have been made to that suggestion. One – which is at least as old as Descartes – is to argue that truths of method are ultimately self-guaranteeing, so that, with proper discipline, it is always possible for a rational being to have access to the truth, provided only that he follow the method prescribed by reason itself. (Some philosophers have also wished to derive, from this *autonomy of reason, a guarantee of human *freedom that will overthrow the deterministic implications of the Marxist thesis.) Others have accepted in part the argument given by the critics of 'false consciousness', and accepted too a rather striking conclusion of the *historical materialism with which it is conjoined: if one's vision of the world is determined by one's mode of life, specifically by one's position in a system of production relations and hence one's class, then, since thought alone cannot change that position, thought alone cannot change one's vision of reality. Hence there is no purely intellectual pursuit of truth, at least concerning matters of social and political perception. In which case not only are there modes of consciousness which are inherently false; there is also no way to change them except by action. This active move towards a mode of consciousness that is, or can be, true is sometimes called *praxis. A false consciousness is one that does not make particular errors of fact so much as general errors of reasoning and perception. Since those errors will be integral to an economic position (e.g. that of the *bourgeoisie) they can be eliminated only by changing that position. By various mixtures of rhetoric and theory many neo-Marxists try to suggest that truth belongs to the revolutionary consciousness of the proletariat and its vanguard: the reactionary consciousness of the bourgeoisie, by contrast, will always see reality in the false light of an *ideology and a *reification that serve to protect and consolidate the *status quo*.

family. From Latin *famulus*, meaning a servant, the term *familia* came to denote the *household, and then, by extension, the particular system of human relations that prevails among its occupants. The word now has two senses: (i) to refer to a system of *primary relations among people related by blood and marriage and living together (for some part of their lives) in social and economic interdependence; (ii) to refer to blood relations as such, as they extend through generations, traced according to either paternity or maternity (depending upon the prevailing social emphasis), and according to socially recognized principles of exclusion and inclusion.

In the first sense (here discussed) sociologists distinguish the nuclear from the extended family. The first is composed from immediate kin, usually monogamous parents and their children; the second involves, in principle at least, all those alive who have any degree of close kinship, through parenthood, brotherhood or sisterhood, and focuses upon the principal breadwinners, who are under an obligation to provide far-reaching support for those suitably related to themselves. In the extended family – characteristic of agricultural economy, but also determined by cultural expectations – it is normal for three or four generations to live under the same roof; in the nuclear family there are at most two. Economic explanations and radical critiques often argue for the *bourgeois nature of the nuclear family, although there is no widespread agreement about this.

In political theory the family, and the household, have played an important part, thus:

(i) *Aristotle gave a celebrated defence of marriage, the family and the household in his *Politics*, as part of his answer to *Plato's advocacy of collective nurture, education and ownership in *The Republic*. He suggested connections between the relations of domestic love and those of private property which have proved both shocking and consoling to subsequent thinkers. In the course of his discussion he adumbrated many of the arguments of later conservatives both for the family as an institution, and for private property as an immovable part of it.

(ii) *Hegel provided perhaps the most important political analysis of the family in the literature. He repeated Aristotle's arguments concerning the relation between family, household and property, and added some striking theses of his own: (a) the family is a *necessary* part of individual development, from the sphere of undifferentiated union with others to that of competitive conflict and voluntary association with them (the sphere of *civil society), and thence to the fully conscious union contained in the *state; (b) the bond of the family is not contractual but based in *piety. and this form of involuntary allegiance provides the model for political allegiance generally.

(iii) *Engels, influenced by Hegel's defence of the family, argued that the three institutions of private property, the family, and the state are connected, and that family relations develop in response to property relations. He also argued for the simultaneous abolition of the three institutions, relying on anthropological data, and upon Marxist economic analysis.

In more recent times conservatives, echoing Aristotle, have upheld the family as a social institution apparently common to all classes, and integral to social and political order, while various radical thinkers of the left follow Engels in attacking it, and in prophesying its collapse, as an institution dependent on bourgeois attitudes and bourgeois relations of production. Sometimes (as in R. D. Laing and A. Esterson: *Sanity, Madness and the Family*) the attack has been associated with neo-Freudian doctrines of suppression, and with the idea that the individual is inevitably crippled by this arrangement which surveys his personal development, and requires from him conformity to a source of authority outside himself. Such radical critiques, which have their origins in the educational theories of *Rousseau, are sometimes dismissed by conservatives as romantic and sentimental.

fascism. From Latin: *fasces*, the bundle of rods with a projecting axe-head, carried before the consuls as a sign of the state authority of Rome, and adopted as a symbol of social unity (the bundle) under political leadership (the axe). The name was given by Mussolini to the movement which he led to power in Italy in 1922, but is now used more widely, to include German *Nazism, and Spanish *falangism, on the basis more of a common *ethos than a common *doctrine. Fascism is characterized by the following features (not all of which need be present in any of its recognized instances): *nationalism; hostility to *democracy, to *egalitarianism, and to the values of the liberal *enlightenment; the cult of the *leader, and admiration for his special qualities; a respect for collective organization, and a love of the symbols associated with it, such as uniforms, parades and army discipline. In Germany the cult of *violence, together with a violent *anti-semitism, were added to these features, with notorious results. The *anti-communist and anti-liberal stance of fascist movements, together with the loathsomeness of many actual examples, have made the fight against fascism a rallying point for left and liberal causes, so that the label 'fascist' may often be applied very loosely, to denote almost any doctrine that conflicts with left-liberal ideology. In this expletive use the term conveys no very clear idea, a fact which perhaps explains its popularity.

From the intellectual point of view fascism remains an amalgam of disparate conceptions, often ill-understood, often bizarre. It is more notable as a political phenomenon on which diverse intellectual influences converge than as a distinct idea; as political phenomenon, one of its most remarkable features has been the ability to win massive popular support for ideas that are expressly anti-egalitarian (*see* *Reich). Mussolini's own doctrines were derived from a heady mixture of popular science, *Marx, *Sorel and *Nietzsche. He advocated regeneration through conquest and perpetual struggle, and spoke, in speeches seething with sexual imagery, of the need to overcome degeneracy and impotence, to make sacrifices for the nation, and to connect to the great 'dynamo' of fascism. Fascists are 'not republicans, socialists, democrats, conservatives or nationalists. They represent a synthesis of all the negations and the affirmations.' In other words, the ultimate doctrine contains little that is specific, beyond an appeal to energy, and action: it is, one might say, the form of an *ideology, but without specific content (other than can be provided by admiration towards the leader). This perhaps explains some of its appeal; it seemed to make no demand other than those which the individual himself would make had he the energy. It then provided the energy.

fashion. A fashion is a class of intentionally adopted appearances, in dress, thought or behaviour, which aims to signify membership of a dominant or influential group and to exemplify one's merit as a member of that group. A fashion therefore creates a pattern of social relations focused on display. An intellectual fashion is a theory or doctrine that is adopted not for its truth, but for its appearance, and because it signifies membership of a dominant intellectual coterie. Fashion is traditionally the property of a *ruling class, and part of its procedure of *legitimation. It is now a more widespread phenomenon, partly because of *social mobility, partly because of the influence of the *media in simultaneously standardizing and accelerating changes in socially available appearances.

fatalism. The doctrine that argues that every event is determined irrespective of human choice. The thesis is stronger than *determinism, which does not (usually) claim that human choice is without effect, but only that it, too, is determined by preceding circumstances. If fatalism is true then what will be must be. We may try to alter the future, but our trying too is predestined, and outside of our control. Action may then seem to be irrational; the least that can be said is that, believing some such thing, you have a strong motive to resign yourself, an exercise for which fatalistic philosophies usually provide recipes, often on the *Stoic model.

According to *Durkheim, fatalism is the refuge adopted by a consciousness that feels itself powerless; suicide may be explained by a fatalistic vision, in which case it is to be contrasted with the supposedly more frequent kind of suicide that results from **anomie*.

federalism. **1**. A system of *government, such as exists in the US, in which a central (or 'federal') government, both *legislature and *executive, exists side by side with state or provincial government, again with both executive and legislative powers. Both federal and state governments will derive what powers they have from the single federal *constitution, but both are supreme in their particular fields, so that (in theory at least) the state government cannot be construed as a *delegation of federal power. The *US model depends upon a written constitution, and upon highly complex political and judicial procedures for the resolution of conflicts, and for the reassertion, when necessary, of the ultimate *sovereignty of the federal government. It contrasts with the more rigid federalism of the *USSR (although whether the USSR is a genuine federation is a moot point, given that the municipalities have no real power to make decisions independently of the dictates of the Communist Party). It should be noted however, that the powers seemingly granted by the USSR constitution to its constituent republics are wider than those granted by the US constitution: thus no US state can wage war or make treaties on its own behalf, whereas these activities are permitted in theory to the USSR republics. It also contrasts with the unitary systems of government characteristic of the European *nation states, where there can be *delegation, but no genuine regional *autonomy.

2. The advocacy of 1. as a model of government, in particular as a way of abolishing nation states in favour of a mutually beneficial central government. Some forms of *Europeanism are also forms of federalism, in that they seek a transfer of sovereignty to a central government with both legislative and executive powers. In the US, federalism is a force tending in the opposite direction, i.e. to the reassertion of *states' rights, perhaps going so far as to argue that the federal government has its powers by delegation from the states, and not vice versa.

Federal Reserve System. *See* *banking.

federation. The act of forming a political unity under a federal government (*see* *federalism), and hence the unity thereby formed. Thus Syria and Egypt for a while (1958–61) formed a federation, the United Arab Republic, in order to encircle Israel and to promote pan-Arabism, with powers united under a single political authority. A federation, in which there is a single *sovereign power, must be distinguished from a *confederation. The essential difference is that the central powers of a federation have a direct power over the citizens of its component provinces or states, and can legislate for all of them at once. Switzerland, which is called a confederation, is thus really a federation, while the unity actually achieved by Syria and Egypt after a while began to seem more like that of a confederation.

feedback. The return of part of a system's output to change its input. A technical term of systems theory, or *cybernetics, widely misused to mean a response, public or private, to a question, action or policy.

fellow-traveller. From the Russian *poputchik*, used by *Trotsky (*Literature and Revolution*, 1923) to denote the intellectual supporters of the Russian Revolution whose support, however absolute-seeming, was always in fact conditional upon unstated demands of a more or less sentimental, 'bourgeois', or conciliatory kind. The term was later extended to describe sympathizers with communism (specifically with the social system of the

USSR as they take it to be), whether they confess their sympathy or do not confess it or even openly deny it. It is now used yet more widely, to cover those who sympathize with, and advance, a political cause, while not overtly belonging to it.

feminism. The advocacy of the *rights of women and of their social, political and economic equality with men. Originally a movement among the half-emancipated women of the educated classes, it has become part of a wider *women's movement, which is often activist, and which sometimes bases its stance on the belief that society, as presently known in the West, enshrines a persistent *sexism, and moreover constantly frustrates the right of a woman to be a person, and to control her own destiny. In its widest reach it argues not only that women have been accorded rights inferior to those of men, but also that in all social relations their status is implicitly taken to be, or treated as, inferior, and that this has led to their being dominated, both overtly and covertly, by men, in all their activities, thoughts and emotions.

Among the claims frequently made by modern feminists the following are of note: first, that the biological differences between men and women do not explain all the observed differences in their social status, role and behaviour; these differences must therefore be seen as a social creation, which it lies within our power to remove. Secondly, that the natural differences between the activities, physical attributes, and responses of men and women should not be taken as grounds for assigning a lower value to the 'feminine' attributes than we assign to the 'masculine'. Thirdly, that women should not be urged to think that fulfilment for them is only possible in relation with men. In particular, women should cease to think of their *identity as given by their appearance in the eyes and minds of men; hence it should be as respectable and fulfilling for a woman to associate only with her own sex as it could be for a man.

In addition, different tendencies within feminism place emphasis on various theoretical claims. 'Socialist feminism' argues that the present position of women is partly to be explained in terms of the *production relations of capitalism, which require that women be bred for a certain role in the order of private property, work, and child-rearing, and that a necessary step on the road to the elimination of invidious sexual discrimination is the elimination of the social and economic system that makes such discrimination functionally necessary.

Socialist feminists may disagree with the characteristic Marxist claim that the transition to socialist or communist production relations is *sufficient* to eliminate sexual discrimination, but they at least think that it is necessary. Others may further argue that women are to be seen as forming an oppressed *class (an idea to be found in *Engels), and that they can be redeemed from subservience only by completely overthrowing the economic arrangement that excludes them, or a vast majority of them, from *any* form of control over the means of production. Their present status is seen as that of property, rather as a slave was seen under Roman law, and rather as the proletarian is seen by the Marxist analysis of his economic condition.

'Radical feminism' is distinguished by the belief that the status of women is not dependent upon but rather far more fundamental than any system of production relations. For the radical feminist women are inevitably dominated by men when they attempt to enter into society with them, since men have an almost instinctive tendency to set up social relations and to construct institutions that are balanced in their own favour. Radical feminists often argue for complete *separatism, in which women will seek the society of their own sex to the exclusion of the other, and in which lesbian relationships will be the norm, men being perhaps used for their spermatozoa, but not for their companionship.

Anti-feminist arguments usually rely on the thought that it is no accident that the relations between men and women are as they are, and that there is a 'natural' order in which both sexes are fulfilled by mutual dependence. They may add that the appearance of male dominance is only an appearance, and perhaps that it is part of the *bourgeois nature of feminism so easily to mistake appearance for essence.

fetishism. Term current in the eighteenth century, and popularized by the anthropologist E. B. Tylor (1832–1917), who used it to denote the worship of inanimate objects, by ascribing to them a spirit, or by regarding them as endowed with magical powers. This attitude was already described by several thinkers of the *Enlightenment, and had been castigated, e.g. by *Kant, in his attack on all forms of religion that express themselves through sensory forms inadequate to the metaphysical idea of a transcendent being. (Kant's criticism had in turn been presaged by *Spinoza.) The term passed into philosophical usage through Kant's denunciation, and was extended by *Feuerbach to the whole of *Christianity (and, by implication, to the religious attitude as such). It was then borrowed by *Marx, in order to criticize, not religion, but the bourgeois economy and the attitudes and beliefs associated with it, which in Marx's view, had about them much of the force and the illusion of religious superstition. *See* *commodity fetishism. Finally, the term reappears as an important feature of *Freud's psychology of sexual behaviour, denoting the transference of sexual response to inanimate objects, or to parts of the body (such as the feet) not directly connected with the normal sexual act.

feudalism. **1**. A social and economic arrangement, characterized by a strict hierarchical organization, from *lord down to *serf, with as many intermediate steps as the penury of the dominant class, or the power of the subordinate class, could interpose. The serf (or villein) is attached to the land (or the manor), and has no right to move outside the jurisdiction of the manorial court. This court regulates his conduct and settles his disputes with his fellow serfs; since it is presided over by his lord, it will not settle disputes with *him*. The serf works the land, keeping some of the product for himself, and yielding a portion (or *corvée*) to his lord, who remains, in law, the sole owner of the land. Feudalism is characterized by production for use rather than exchange, and by the relative absence of *wage labour or freedom of movement.

2. In Marxist theory, feudalism is the system of *production relations just described, divested of any reference to law, religion, or bonds of obligation. The transition from feudalism to *capitalism is necessitated by the development of *productive forces to the point where *division of labour, and hence a *market economy, become necessary. At this point market towns are formed, and the serfs are cast out from their tenancies, to form the *industrial army necessary for *factory production. The economic relations of capitalism then come into being.

3. From the points of view both of law and of history 1. must be seen as the sketch of an *ideal type. The obligation of the serf to his lord was in fact matched by an obligation of the lord to deal justly with his serf. This second obligation could be enforced by ecclesiastical courts or by direct appeal to the sovereign. Hence relations between serf and lord were mediated by complex bodies of ecclesiastical and secular law, the serf often being able to obtain security of tenure equivalent to a property right. Moreover, in so-called feudal societies exchange was common, a merchant class existed, and the power of the clergy was usually sufficient to limit and diversify the powers of the feudal lords. Classes in feudal society came to depend upon a system of *estates in which hereditary rights and uncodified obligations played as great a part as economic potential in determining the social position of the individual. Feudal modes of land tenure were finally abolished in England by the Tenures Abolition Act 1660.

Feuerbach, L. A. (1804–72) German

philosopher. *See* *alienation, *Althusser, *false consciousness, *fetishism, *myth, *species being, *Young Hegelians.

fifth column. The Spanish nationalist general, Emilio Molo (1887–1937), when asked at a press conference which of four army columns he expected to capture Madrid, answered 'the fifth column', meaning organized sympathizers within the city. Hence: sympathizers within an opposition camp who organize its subversion.

Filmer, Sir Robert (d. 1653). English writer and royalist. *See* *divine right.

Finlandization. Following many years of dispute and war with the USSR, in which Finland had been compelled to concede large areas of territory, the postwar Prime Minister (and subsequently President) Suho Passikivi pursued a policy of *neutralism in order to escape total incorporation into the Soviet Union. Astute policies of friendly agreement, trade concessions, and yielding to pressures to buy and sell to the USSR have led to an increasing dependence of Finland on the USSR and to a conformity of Finnish foreign (and to a slight extent domestic) policy to Soviet requirements. This process of becoming covertly dependent upon, and responsive to the demands of, a powerful neighbour, for fear of being forced to concede much more, has become known as 'Finlandization'.

firm, theory of. A branch of *microeconomics concerned to explain and predict the economic behaviour of firms. The traditional theory considered firms as vehicles for the maximization of profit, and made the further assumptions that firms possess full information and complete certainty, although the theory can be extended to take account of probabilities and 'information gaps'. The firm used to be taken as a self-contained system, and the theory would not attempt to explore problems of internal organization, such as the *separation of ownership from control, or the differences of structure which arise from public as opposed to private ownership. Moreover, standard theories assumed market conditions, and did not attempt to explain the behaviour of firms in systems of ownership which reduce or eliminate *competition, such as complete *socialization or *oligopoly.

More recently, however, the theory of the firm has often dropped the all-important assumption that firms are primarily concerned to maximize profits in competitive markets. The behaviour of firms in other types of market (e.g. oligopoly) has been extensively studied. Moreover, many modern theories have suggested that firms – or their managers – maximize not profits, but growth, or sales, or 'managerial utility'. Some theories have dropped the assumption that firms maximize at all, and have proposed that the managers of firms are primarily concerned to achieve or maintain certain levels or targets (e.g. a satisfactory market share or stock market valuation). Sometimes hybrid models, which combine 'satisficing' and maximizing behaviour, are proposed – e.g. the model which assumes that the firm maximizes its rate of growth subject to the maintenance of satisfactory profits.

fiscal drag. If tax rates are progressive, then, in times of *inflation, wage increases might take people into higher tax-brackets, even though their real incomes are not rising, a situation that will not be remedied before the next budget. This tends to create a fall in demand, which acts as a drag on further growth. In order to counteract the *deflation that results from this, governments may be asked to reduce taxation, or else to increase government expenditure so as to increase the level of *aggregate demand.

fiscal policy. That part of government policy which is concerned with raising revenue for government purposes, largely through *taxation, and with deciding on its expenditure. Many modern governments adopt a fiscal policy which aims to exert some control over the level of *aggregate demand, and hence employment, the theory justifying such action being derived directly or indirectly from the work of *Keynes. Many economists oppose this, and fiscal policy continues to serve as a focus for the debate between Keynesians and *monetarists, a debate which has absorbed much intellectual energy in the UK and elsewhere.

focoism. From Spanish: *foco*, a focal point. Used to denote the kind of *guerrilla warfare strategy advocated by Ché Guevara, and by Fidel Castro, as appropriate to revolutionary activity in Latin American countries (*see* *Castroism). The aim is to establish small centres of insurrection in the countryside, to extend revolutionary activity from these bases, and only later to capture the government and administrative machinery.

force. A term that is as difficult to define as *aggression, and as important in the description of international behaviour, as well as the description and justification of every political arrangement. Force which subdues the agent against which it is used is also called *coercion; force which is opposed freely will amount to coercion only when the will of the resistant is overcome. There seem to be two ideas involved in that of force: an active and a passive. To force someone to do something involves making alternatives sufficiently undesirable to him that he will do what one desires. In other words the active idea of force is that of deliberately restricting available courses of action. The passive idea is that of being forced to do something, even though there is no *agency which is doing the forcing. Here the idea is more closely connected with that of need.

By either definition it is as much an act of force to deprive a neighbouring state of all supplies of food or water, as it is to invade that state with show of arms. But delicate issues of *responsibility arise in the application of all such definitions. I may have something which you require for your needs, but do not, simply by the fact of possessing it, *deprive* you of what you need: some relationship of mutual acquaintance and responsibility is required before I can in any way be held to be *doing* something to you by peacefully enjoying something which is necessary for your survival (else we should all in effect be murderers). Hence, when it is said, for example, that the capitalist constrains the labourer by *force into the *wage-contract, much is assumed about the relation between the contracting parties that might equally be denied.

In international law the ascendancy of ideas of agency has led to the restriction of the notion of force to 'the use of force', a notion which is held to correspond to ideas of aggression, invasion and attack. Some have asserted that 'use of force' in article 2 of the United Nations Charter includes *both* the use of arms, and any violation of international law which involves an exercise of *power within the territory of another state, even without the use of arms. Others argue that this is too broad an interpretation, and that a 'use of arms' is necessary. But this raises similar problems. Is there a use of arms when an invading army, encountering no resistance, does not fire a single shot? The International Law Commission so held when considering the German occupation of Bohemia and Moravia in 1939.

forced saving. Saving which is the result of a deficient supply of goods for consumption, rather than an actual desire to save. In a *free market forced saving exists only in a state of disequilibrium since at *equilibrium the plans of all agents are fulfilled, while in a fully *planned economy it can arise repeatedly and endure for long periods. However, in many planned economies (e.g. that of the USSR) citizens are forbidden to hold more than a certain sum in savings, and must surrender the remainder to the state.

foreign policy. Even if one thought *government to be unnecessary or undesirable in *domestic affairs, or that some form of *minimal state is the most extensive government that could be justified, the existence of other, independent states not so persuaded, and possessed of burgeoning political and economic ambitions, implies the need for sufficient government at home to permit serious policy abroad.

In practice this means a lot of government, since it is impossible to commit people to *war, to an agreement concerning *trade, or to economic sanctions, without exercising extensive domestic control. (The neglect of such issues may be responsible for the air of unreality surrounding some theories of *anarchism, and of the minimal state.)

It is sometimes argued (for example by *Machiavelli) that foreign policy is also a major instrument of domestic government, for example by creating fervent union between citizens united behind a common cause. Thus it has been suggested that USSR foreign policy is intelligible only in terms of domestic political problems and of the workings of the machinery set up to solve them. The mutual dependence of domestic and foreign policy can be seen in the constitutional and political changes that have been precipitated in the UK by the loss of empire, and in the US by the entry into and inelegant exit from the Second World War, and by the subsequent cold war in which traditional isolationism was cast aside.

Foreign policy must therefore inevitably be affected by the structure of domestic government. Monarchy, which permits and indeed encourages alliance through marriage, has a peace-making device which is not available to other forms of government; despotism, in which a single person holds power for life, or in which a single party holds power indefinitely, permits long-term foreign policy of a kind that is pursued only with great difficulty by governments whose leadership is regularly subjected to re-election. European aristocracy, under which a small number of influential families held domestic power while maintaining lasting international contact, permitted treaties and alliances which are now achieved only with the greatest difficulty (e.g. those brought about through the Congress of Vienna and subsequently). The greatest domestic effects of foreign policy stem from the need for continuity: it is this that has given to the UK Foreign Office a power which persists through changes of government, and which it is difficult, if not impossible, for any actual government to oppose.

Foreign policy provides the most vivid examples of *acts of state, and of the character of the state as an international *person, with *rights, *agency, *responsibility and *answerability as well as *power.

formalism. **1**. A doctrine in *aesthetics and art criticism which finds the merit, or the meaning, of a work of art in features of its form or structure, rather than in its representational content. Members of the school of Russian formalists which existed in Petrograd and Moscow before the Revolution in many cases welcomed the Revolution, and imagined that it would free the study of art from bourgeois preoccupations with subject-matter and morality, by exposing the literary and artistic structure as conveying the essential, and *ideological, significance of the creative act. Most members of the school were subsequently exiled or executed and all were forbidden to teach. One, however, Mikhail Bakhtine, was permitted to survive in the heartlands of Russia, and is now permitted also to publish; others – among them Tzvetan Todorov – escaped to Paris and were there influential in founding the school of *structuralist criticism.

2. As a term of abuse, used by both the *Communist and the *Nazi parties, to designate art whose perfection lies in its form, and which detaches itself from the representation of social matters and from the propagation of social values – specifically values of international, or of national socialism. Communist propaganda has contrasted 'formalism' with *socialist realism, and castigated the former for its bourgeois detachment, and for the sterile aestheticism which refuses social responsibility. The label 'formalist' has been applied to most significant twentieth-century art, in particular to abstract painting, cubism (especially Braque), constructivist sculpture and architecture, and the music of the Vienna school, which is thought to be particularly pernicious, partly because it pursues new and not easily understood musical structures, and partly because it is accompanied by theories which say that this is precisely what it *should* do.

3. A school of *sociology, associated with the name of Georg Simmel, which emphasizes the importance of the form of social relations, rather than the particular people united by them, and which attempts to explain social development in terms of *competition, cooperation, *commensalism, etc.

Foucault, Michel (b. 1926). French social philosopher. *See* *criminology, *psychotherapy.

Founding Fathers. Name generally given to the fifty-five delegates who were present at the drawing up of the US constitution by the Philadelphia Convention in May 1787. *Jefferson was not in fact there, but was represented by his luminaries, James *Madison and George Whyte, and was acquainted with more of the delegates, all of whom were committed to the notion of a stronger union.

four freedoms. Proclaimed by President Roosevelt in a speech to the US Congress on 6 January 1941, by way of summarizing certain values for which (in his own opinion, and in the opinion of many others) the US government stands. The *freedoms advocated were these: (i) freedom of speech and expression; (ii) freedom to worship God in one's own way; (iii) freedom from want (to be ensured by economic understanding between nations); (iv) freedom from fear (to be ensured by disarmament). The list is interesting in that it introduces two ideas of freedom: freedom *from* ((iii) and (iv)), and freedom *to* ((i) and (ii)). Freedom from want and from fear are, on one plausible account, the end of political activity, and require far-reaching and officious management of social and political arrangements, whereas freedom of speech and worship are to be secured by the limitation of political activity. Two of these freedoms therefore require a positive duty on the part of others (perhaps of all others), while the other two require only a refusal to meddle.

The doctrine of the 'four freedoms' seems to involve a rhetoric that ranges freely over *right and *obligation: this may be one explanation of the fact that, in subsequent international agreements, the *right to work has gained acceptance as a right on the same footing as, e.g., the rights to speak one's mind, and to practise one's religious conviction, even though the latter rights involve only a concession, and not an active undertaking, from those not concerned to exercise them.

'Four freedoms' were also advocated by Liu Shao-Ch'i (1898–73) in China, in 1953: to rent and to sell land; to hire labour; to engage in sideline economic pursuits; and to lend money at interest. Since these freedoms amount to rights of private property in land, they were attacked by *Mao, and never implemented. Liu was later denounced as a 'capitalist inroader' and expelled from the party.

Fourier, François Marie Charles (1772–1837). French social critic, and utopian socialist, active during the post-revolutionary period, who devoted his energies to the description of schemes for the salvation of mankind. Since the world had been created by a benevolent God, the actual misery of human beings could be explained only on the assumption that men had not carried out God's plans for them. These plans had been rediscovered by Fourier, but could be put into practice only by releasing man's thirteen passions, repressed by civilization, but essential to the harmony which would come in place of it. The passions are: the five senses; the four 'group' feelings of ambition, friendship, love and family feeling; the three 'series' passions of intrigue, diversification (*la passion papillone*), and combination; and the passion for harmony which synthesizes all the others.

To release the passions, humanity would have to be organized into *phalanstères* (phalanxes, or 'phalansteries') each of about 1,800 members, the different characters and inclinations being scientifically combined in a complex system of groups and series, so that each person could express his inclination in everything that he did, and avoid every activity that did not suit him. Such phalanxes would be systems of common ownership, in which a certain level of private property would also be permitted, along with inequalities necessary to the exercise of human potential.

Fourier was an influential critic of existing social conditions, and of the prevailing modes of production. His attempts to found a phalanx absorbed many of his energies. Others took up the cause, so that 'Fourierism' was for a while a popular kind of socialism, although the experimental phalanxes failed. The movement remains interesting largely because of its attempt to combine socialism with a detailed psychology of *self-realization.

France, constitution and laws. Since the Revolution France has been ruled in the name of many documents claiming to be 'constitutions' (and vividly illustrating the thesis that a mere document can be no such thing), and even the present 'fifth' Republic continues to revise itself in a manner that makes it difficult to distinguish between 'constitution' and *positive law. The French form of government is a paradigm of European *republicanism, and displays constant and far-reaching *reform within a seemingly immovable structure of republican dignities and concentrated power. The system is *bicameral, the National Assembly, or lower house, being the principal *legislative body, and the 'Council of the Republic' acting as a revising chamber with various dignifying functions. The *President is elected directly (reform introduced in 1962; previously he was appointed for a seven-year period by both chambers of parliament). The President also appoints the prime minister and *cabinet, and now holds the principal *executive power, although dependent upon the support of the National Assembly for most legislative measures. The frequent 'constitutional' changes (which may concern matters such as the reorganization of *local government, or the *decentralization of administration) are often introduced as the result of *referendums. The present appearance of the French constitution is that of a *constitutional democracy with strong presidential control over the government, outweighing the influence of any single party. The parties themselves are numerous, but only the *Gaullist, *socialist and *Communist can command a substantial vote.

For French law, *see* *Napoleonic law.

franchise. The legal right to vote at an election. Since the late eighteenth century almost all states have moved gradually in the direction of an extended, rather than a contracted, franchise, and universal adult *suffrage is now the rule rather than the exception.

Frankfurt school. The school of social thought represented by the Institute for Social Research, founded in the University of Frankfurt in 1923 and exiled to New York during the Nazi period. Principal members have been Max Horkheimer, Theodor Adorno, Walter Benjamin, *Marcuse and Jurgen Habermas, all of whom have been separately influential, and each of whom has subscribed in part to the *critical theory advocated by Horkheimer, in which social and cultural phenomena are subjected to detailed criticism, using concepts proper, so it is claimed, to a *Marxist analysis of consciousness. The Frankfurt school was instrumental in awakening interest in the early writings of *Marx, in which the influence of *Hegel's study of consciousness is still apparent, notably in the theory of *alienation. Its members opposed the *scientistic interpretation and application of *historical materialism, which, they felt, both undervalues the role of consciousness in human affairs, and also encourages a naïve and dogmatic *positivism, which is both doctrinaire in theory and highly destructive in practice. Since most members of the school have not believed in the possibility of a *value-free study of society, they have rejected the scientific claims of Marxism and attempted to adapt its concepts to the uses of cultural criticism, in order to examine institutions, practices and ways of thought that classical Marxism had referred to as *superstructure. In this way the Frankfurt school was one of the first to produce a theory of art which could claim to be Marxist in inspiration without being obviously naïve about its subject-matter. However, this very result indicates the extent to which consciousness is taken seriously as a subject for sociological analysis, and in a way that is not obviously compatible with the main tenets of Marxism. It is also possible to discern elements of *cultural conservatism in the writings of Adorno and Habermas, beside which their professions of left-wing allegiance seem more like fashion than conviction. Habermas's theory of *crisis does, however, attempt to preserve some of the structure of the Marxist theory of history, and to justify belief in the fact, if not in the value, of *revolution. (*See further* *crisis theory, *critical theory, *cybernetics.)

fraternity. The least discussed of the three aims of the French revolutionaries, although the most important, in that it attempts to specify the nature of the bond of society, without which, it is reasonable to assume, neither liberty nor equality would have value or be concrete objects of *policy. Fraternity is, literally speaking, the uniting of men in bonds of brotherly affection, though for most revolutionary purposes 'men' includes women, and 'brotherhood' sisterhood. In so far as this kind of affection extends further than immediate kin and personal friends, it is characteristic of members of a (small) tribe, and may also sometimes arise between people who act and suffer together in some dangerous enterprise, such as a battle. But whether such a feeling could actually form the bond of society within a modern democratic state is to be doubted. In contrast to the relations of *allegiance, *obedience and *political obligation, it seems to have a personal and limited character which would forbid its easy extension (except in forms that are sentimental and therefore uncommitted) to large groups of people. However, the original ideal of the advocates of fraternity was the replacement of particularized affections, such as those of the family, with sentiments thought to be more universal and less socially divisive. Some, remembering the crimes committed in the name of fraternity, prefer to drop this name from their political vocabulary; others retain it, at least for slogans and propaganda, but whether it now has a serious political application outside that use remains doubtful.

free enterprise. The situation in which people are permitted by law to begin *enterprises of production, distribution or exchange, and perhaps also to assert private rights of ownership over the result. It is often argued by defenders of capitalism that it is impossible to deny this freedom without denying some (and perhaps all) of the traditionally valued *freedoms mentioned below. Among replies given by the opponents of capitalism, two are particularly important: (a) the exercise of this particular freedom leads to the enslavement of others, since it vests in the capitalist a power to bind another, through *need, to the terms of a *wage contract that must inevitably *exploit him; (b) free enterprise acts against the third of the *four freedoms, since it prevents the organization of an economy directed to freeing the mass of people from want.

free market. A *market in which distribution and exchange lie outside the *control of the *state, and are allowed to proceed according to private agreements. The free market is an essential part of *free enterprise and, according to a thesis accepted for different reasons by both the defenders and the opponents of capitalism, is impossible without private property in the means of production. A market is rendered unfree either through government interference in its operation (e.g. through *price control), or by the transfer of property to public or common ownership. (*See* *production, distribution, exchange, consumption.)

Like all *freedoms this one is a matter of degree; nevertheless it is defended and attacked with a fervour perhaps more appropriate to an absolute condition. Some (e.g. Friedman, *Hayek and some earlier economists of the *Austrian school) argue that the free market permits economic growth, leads to stability, and respects fundamental rights that must otherwise be denied. Such arguments, expressed dogmatically, are apt to evoke a negative response. Some reply that a completely free market is unrealistic, in an age of industrialization, overpopulation and exhaustible resources; others argue more radically, against all forms of private ownership in the means of distribution. The opposition, when absolute, is no more likely to be persuasive than the defence. Are we to abolish the free market to the extent of removing every right of exchange? In which case, are we to envisage a society without sale or purchase, without *gift, and without barter? The prospect, when described in detail, is seldom found appealing. Apart from social and political considerations, some economists argue independently for the free market, on principles inherited from *classical economics, defending it as a self-regulating mechanism with a natural tendency towards *equilibrium, perhaps generating, along with that equilibrium, the conditions of social and political order.

free trade. The condition in which there is a free flow of goods and services in international trade. No trade between two nations is today absolutely free, in the sense of being shielded from all interference arising from the national interest of the states taking part in it: nevertheless, within limits, free trade still exists between trading partners with demand for each others' goods. Disputes focus upon (a) the extent to which a state ought to permit, in the interests of its citizens, free trade with others; (b) the methods which should be used, if necessary, to limit it. Classical and neo-classical economics extended the doctrine of the free market into international affairs, but some modern theories of *development question the possibility of *equilibrium conditions arising naturally between the developed and the *developing countries. Others have argued for active government intervention in order to produce surpluses on the *balance of trade (*see* *mercantilism, *neo-mercantilism), or in order to protect domestic producers (*see* *protectionism). Both those policies involve rejection of the idea that free trade is the advisable condition of international exchange, and acceptance of *tariffs, import quotas, selective *customs unions, and similar measures.

A 'free trade area' is an association of states (usually neighbouring states) under a common agreement to remove all tariffs, quotas, and similar government barriers to free trade between themselves. Each state may continue to trade with non-members on its own terms.

freedom, metaphysical. It is necessary to distinguish the metaphysical problem of 'free will' from the problem of political freedom (discussed in the next entry). Metaphysical freedom is the freedom to do one thing rather than another: it supposedly enters into every intentional act, and provides the basis on which we hold people *responsible for the consequences of what they do. Perhaps the most important question concerning metaphysical freedom is whether it is compatible with the truth of *determinism. Thus if my action and all its consequences were determined by the state of the universe before my birth, does it still make sense to say that I acted freely or am responsible for what I did? The thesis of 'soft determinism' or 'compatibilism' says yes, while 'hard determinism' says no. Clearly the problem of free will is not the same as that of political freedom: it does not concern the nature and justification of political constraints on my action, but the action's status in the light of its cause. Acts which are indisputably free from political constraint raise the problem of metaphysical freedom just as much as those which are not: when I lift this glass to my lips, do I act freely, or do the causes which determine my action also compel it, so that my sense of choice is no more than an illusion?

It is probably true to say that modern philosophical discussions of this problem have shifted the emphasis from the concept of freedom to that of responsibility, partly under the influence of 'ordinary language' methods, and partly under the influence of studies in *jurisprudence which to a great extent have provided the model for those methods. What is at stake, it is thought, is not so much whether there are acts which are 'free' in some metaphysical sense, but whether there is a true human responsibility. For it is from our descriptions of people as responsible or otherwise that the human consequences – in the form of blame, praise, *punishment and reward – follow.

freedom, political. Freedom is often advanced as one of the *values integral to a capitalist economy, and its absence is often deplored in regimes said to be *totalitarian and communist. While these common expressions of opinion are often dismissed as *ideology by those who stand accused by them, there is no doubt that they are framed in terms of a concept which is central to many traditions of political thinking, and also the subject of much philosophical reflection, which can only be hinted at in what follows.

There is a distinction to be drawn between a negative and a positive idea of freedom, the former conveyed in the expression 'freedom from', the latter in the expression 'freedom to'. A man may be free *from* constraints and threats, in a world that leaves him free *to do* very little, say because it contains no resources upon which he can exercise his powers. The distinction here is not hard and fast, and the two ideas are to some extent inter-convertible. Nevertheless there is a difference at least of emphasis between those who discern political freedom in the absence of certain constraints, and those who discern it in the presence of certain powers and possibilities. In another sense, 'positive' freedom is often described as that state of a person in which his powers are fully exercised – i.e. in which external possibilities are matched by an internal capacity to realize the self and its aims within them. (*See* *self-realization.) The interplay of the various positive and negative ideas of freedom seems to be responsible for many of the tensions and conflicts which the concept of freedom contains.

(i) The liberal position. (Expounded, for example, by *J. S. Mill in *On Liberty,* 1859.) Simply expressed, this finds freedom in the power of the individual to assert himself against the state (or even against society, Mill for various reasons omitting this distinction). The power of the state is enshrined in law, so that the measure of the freedom of the individual is not the lenience, but the scope, of the law that governs him. Are there clearly defined areas of individual life which are not governed by law, so that real choices are left open by it? A further embellishment of the liberal view construes such freedom as itself the *aim* of law; law should not merely permit these areas of untrammelled choice, but also maximize them. The thought here is an ancient one, but was given rhetoricial impetus by *Locke, in his distinction between *liberty and 'licence'. Freedom is not maximized simply by removing all law, since that is to leave the individual unprotected from the invasion of his freedom by his neighbours. The law aims to provide a system of constraints which, while limiting freedom in some respects, maximizes freedom over all. Licence is a freedom that is exercised only at risk to another's freedom: to forbid it is not to lower but to increase the sum total of individual liberty. Disputes then focus on the precise form of such a law, and whether or not it should be responsive to any requirements *other* than those of freedom. (*See* *harm, *law and morality.)

(ii) The conservative position. (Expounded, for example, by Sir James Fitzjames Stephen in *Liberty, Equality, Fraternity,* 1873, a reply to Mill.) This usually argues either that the liberal conception of freedom is mistaken, or that freedom has to be balanced against other values in a way that makes it legitimate to encroach on it. The first argument tends to emphasize that freedom is a value only for someone who can also value the activities which are permitted by it. (There is no value in a freedom which allows you to do only what you see no significance in doing.) True freedom is a more complex phenomenon than mere permission, and exists only where values exist. Men have values as a result of their perception of themselves as belonging to a social order; if freedom is to be preserved social order must be preserved as its necessary precondition. But this order requires law, and lays down a separate criterion for the validity of law. The arguments here are not exclusive to conservatives, and are often construed as attacking not liberalism as such, but only the *individualism involved in the common versions of it.

(iii) The welfare socialist view. Neither of the above positions gives sufficient attention to the conditions for positive freedom. Absence of legal constraint gives you no power to do anything, unless the world also contains food, drink, and the conditions of healthy physical (perhaps even moral) action. Such things are provided by human labour. Hence, if men are to be free, in the positive sense of possessing power to fulfil their natures, they must suffer whatever constraints are necessary to organize their labour and ensure a satisfactory distribution of its product. In response to the massive interference with human choice that tends to result from this way of thinking, liberals, and even some conservatives, have had recourse to the idea of freedom as a *natural right: i.e. as something which cannot in any circumstances, without injustice and wrongdoing, be taken away. (*See* *freedoms.)

Other specific views are mentioned elsewhere in this dictionary – e.g. under *Hegel (who argued that freedom consists, in the last analysis, not in the power to oppose the state, but in the disposition to obey it) *Mill, *Locke, *liberty, *liberalism, *individualism. In all discussions it is important to bear in mind that the freedom discussed is that of a *rational agent, who has autonomy, values, and long-term aims and projects. Hence the problem of freedom raises far-reaching problems of human nature, focusing on the tenability or otherwise of individualism.

freedoms. In political contexts, usually used to denote those choices which are, or ought to be, offered to the citizen as of *right. Doctrines of 'freedoms' are often extensions of ideas concerning *human or *natural rights; alternatively they may summarize traditions of *positive law, which have attempted to define the areas of human life from which the law withdraws or attempts to withdraw. Modern *constitutionalism, which seeks to define limits to government, often attempts to specify freedoms as one determinant of these limits. Often the choice of freedoms is dictated by a sense of the distinction between the public and the private that may be extremely hard to articulate in any other way. Common among these freedoms are freedom of speech, freedom of worship, freedom of association, freedom of assembly, freedom of contract and exchange, freedom of movement. Roosevelt's *four freedoms stepped outside the normal frame of reference of US constitutional thinking in referring not only to freedoms to *do* certain things should one choose, but also to freedoms *from* certain handicaps and disasters, specifically hunger and fear.

All the freedoms mentioned still define serious political disputes, as has been proven by the Helsinki Accord, which attempted to guarantee most of them in the states of the Western and Soviet *blocs.

freemasons. A religious brotherhood of stonemasons was established in England in the twelfth century in order to safeguard the secrets of their craft; it was abolished in 1547 but later reorganized, with educational and social aims, and without any specific connection with stonemasons. Later still it adopted the trappings of a highly symbolic, ceremonial but essentially monotheistic and even Christian religion, Mozart being among its more distinguished converts. It preserved the air of secrecy, and soon became a closed society. While the nature of freemasonry as a social and political influence is difficult to determine, there is no doubt that, because of its secrecy, and its internal ethos of *fraternity, it has often been suspected of fostering secret associations for political purposes, or in restraint of trade.

Freud, Sigmund (1856–1939). Viennese scientist and founder of psychoanalysis. Although Freud never applied his mind systematically to politics, his theories have influenced political thought in countless ways. The following (contested) ideas have all been extremely important:

(i) The theory of unconscious determination. This has given additional impetus to the thought – common to many political theories, both conservative (e.g. *Burke) and revolutionary (e.g. *Marx) – that the real motives of political action are to be found elsewhere than in the conscious reasons that might be given for it.

(ii) The theory of *repression, according to which important instincts are denied direct expression by social pressures, and consequently submerge, to re-emerge in new and surprising forms. Some political theories have been built upon this and related ideas – *see*, for example, *Reich. It should not be assumed that repression is regarded everywhere as harmful; some (including Freud) regard it as a necessary process, whereby primordial instincts are transformed into the motivating force of *civilization.

(iii) The emphasis on fundamental instincts, such as the sexual 'libido', and the 'death instinct' or 'death wish', as providing the ultimate explanation of human conduct. This emphasis has often been opposed, as being fundamentally destructive of moral values, and of the picture of man as a rational animal which sustains them. Some have welcomed it for its pessimistic implications, and as a necessary corrective to the naîveties of *progressivism. Yet others (Freud again included) have found in the Freudian account of motivation a reason to doubt the economically based theories – such as *historical materialism – which see the activity of production as the generating force of history. For Freud, both death and the sexual drive are more fundamental, and the conflicting instincts towards them, if conceived as fundamental forces in human history, must generate a historical movement that is far more complex than the linear progress imagined by the theories of nineteenth-century revolutionaries.

(iv) The doctrine of Freud's *Civilization and its Discontents,* which implies that the repression required to introduce the social forms of civilization also leads to a vast and potentially dangerous accumulation of unconscious forces, ready to erupt, and so to destroy what they have been channelled into creating. *See also* *psychotherapy.

frictional unemployment. *Unemployment resulting from the delays that people face, after leaving one employment, before entering another. Frictional unemployment can exist even where there are more jobs available than there are people seeking them.

Friedman, Milton (b. 1912). American economist. *See* *bourgeois economics, *free market, *monetarism, *New Right.

friendship. Friendship is of various kinds: intimate, casual, supportive, comradely, erotic, platonic, and so on. In all cases it exhibits the following features: (i) friendship is an end in itself and does not exist for some further purpose. To the extent that I have a ruling purpose in my relations with another (other than his well-being, and his friendship), to that extent am I not motivated by friendship towards him. The attempt to formulate this feature more precisely underlies much of the thinking behind *Kant's second categorical imperative (Act so as to treat rational beings always as ends, and never as means only); (ii) friendship is possible only between persons, who are aware of each other as persons (contrast filial dependence, and unembellished sexual desire); (iii) friendship is incapable of unjust dealings – a friendly feeling evaporates when one party discovers that the other has exploited, lied to or manipulated him; moreover the other could not have been motivated by friendship in doing so (except in very special cases).

The idea of friendship has inspired certain conservative theories of the relation between *citizens (*Aristotle) and between each citizen and the *civil society (*Oakeshott). Friendship is non-contractual (there being no common and defining purpose), and yet impregnated by obligations (which arise in the course of it); it is a source of dependence, and yet also conditional upon just dealings; it is autonomous, containing no specific purpose upon the achievement of which it will be dissolved, and yet entirely rational and pursued through intentional action. Hence friendship demonstrates that there can be relations of dependence, enacting values of justice, which are not founded in contract and not transferable from object to object. Such relations (which fall within the ancient sphere of *piety) give a model for *political obligation, which is (on some accounts) similarly structured. Political obligation (on this theory more accurately described as *allegiance) is thereby shown to be as rational as friendship.

front organizations. Organizations which profess acceptable aims, in order to conceal the unacceptable aims which really motivate them. Usually the term describes organizations which are ostensibly liberal, democratic and constitutional, with respected and respectable members, controlled by *activists owing allegiance to the Communist Party. They were much used by the *Comintern, and have been among the most successful of all instruments of USSR *foreign policy. They have also been used by *Trotskyists, and by the US Central Intelligence Agency.

Führerprinzip. Term adopted in Nazi Germany to denote the idea that a national *leader *(Führer)* is required, who would prove his merit through his personal *charisma, and so achieve and deserve absolute *authority over all citizens. In Hitler's words, this required: 'unrestricted authority downwards, unrestricted responsibility upwards'.

functional explanation. A type of explanation common in the social sciences, anthropology and biology, which attempts to incorporate into accepted models of scientific method the puzzling feature of *teleology. It can be illustrated by the theory of evolution. Birds try to escape their predators by flying, and it seems natural to say that they have wings *in order to* do this. That is the germ of a *teleological explanation, or explanation in terms of an end. We can rewrite this explanation and at the same time eliminate the reference to purpose, by using the idea of a function: wings have a function, in relation to the bird's need to survive. *That* wings have this function may then be invoked in order to explain the fact that birds possess them. Such an explanation no longer refers to an end (a succeeding state of affairs) but to a cause (a preceding state of affairs). It is because wings have this function in relation to the condition of birds at time t that birds have wings at time $t + \delta$. *How* the explanation works (i.e. what theory might be invoked to entail it) may vary from case to case. The further details of the theory of evolution, as given by *Darwin, are supposed to make the functional explanation more plausible. Thus, in the light of the theoretical hypothesis of natural selection, one can show *how* the function of wings determines their existence. But the functional explanation might have been correct, even though the theory of natural selection (which entails it) was not.

In a similar way, an anthropologist may explain ceremonies, and other social practices, in terms of a function that relates them to the well-being of a tribe. Such an explanation may eliminate all reference to purpose, in particular to the avowed purpose with which their practices are engaged in by the members of the tribe. The social cohesion, for example, that results from and explains a ceremony of propitiation will not typically be the purpose of those who engage in it, who seek not to unite with their fellows, but to propitiate a deity.

Some advocates of the materialist theory of history phrase the theory in terms of functional explanation. Social and political *superstructures have the function of consolidating some pattern of economic relations: this is what causes them to exist. Of course one may look for further explanations which show *how* that is possible. One may not find those further explanations, and yet still be persuaded that the functional explanation is true.

Many think that without some account of mechanism (such as is provided by the theory of evolution) functional explanations are not really explanations; on this view the use of functional explanation in the social sciences is illegitimate, involving an inference from the (uncontentious) idea that dysfunctionality causes the disappearance of something, to the (unwarranted) idea that functionality *causes* its appearance.

functionalism. *See* *anthropology, *architecture, *functional explanation.

fundamentalism. A movement within any religion towards the fundamental doctrine out of which the religion has grown, and a refusal to depart from it in order to accomodate extraneous social or moral requirements. The term may also be applied to political doctrine, in order to distinguish the central from the deviant cases.

G

Galbraith, John Kenneth (b. 1908). American economist. *See* *affluence, *countervailing power, *use-value.

game theory. A branch of mathematics (developed by O. Morgenstern and J. von Neumann) that offers a way of formalizing many social and political problems and activities. A game includes a number of *players*, each having a choice between certain *strategies*, and receiving a *pay-off*, defined for each combination of strategies by the rules of the game. In the general case the pay-off to each is determined by the choices of all, and it is this feature that has led people to think that the theory of games might provide a suitable model for social interaction. It is an assumption of the theory, however, that each player chooses *rationally*, in the sense that he has a consistent *preference ordering among possible outcomes and attempts to secure the best pay-off to himself. Choices made without prior communication are *independent*. The game has a *solution*, if each player has a uniquely best (or 'dominant') strategy or if, after repeated play, an outcome emerges which no player has reason to avoid. Games are of varying degrees of complexity, and the theory can be extended to take account of those situations in which there are many players, and in which information is uncertain.

Distinctions are made between types of game. In **zero-sum* games, the pay-offs to the players add up to zero or, more generally, to some constant amount. Such games are games of *conflict*: one player's gain is another's loss. In non-zero-sum games that is not the case, and there is a potential for mutual gain. At the extreme are games in which the players have identical preferences. Nevertheless there may be difficulties of *coordination* in such games if there is no possibility of communication. Such difficulties may be resolved by the emergence or establishment of some convention or habit, such as the English habit of keeping to the left in a subway. Alternatively there may be some obvious or *salient* feature which is conducive to coordinated choice, even in the absence of any formal communication. Games are described as *cooperative* or *non-cooperative* according to whether players have the ability to engage in preplay communication and to make joint binding agreements.

It is no part of game theory, as a branch of applied mathematics, to suggest that human nature conforms or ought to conform to the paradigm of *rationality from which it begins. But it is a significant addition to political thought only if there are political problems or strategies which possess the form of a game, and for which the theory can determine at least an ideal, if not an actual, outcome. Some writers urge that human nature and political institutions are too complex to permit such an easy mathematical reduction. Others have gone so far as to suggest that almost all political choice could be seen on the model of the particular problem in game theory known as the *prisoner's dilemma.

Gandhi, Mahatma (1869–1948). Indian statesman. *See* *civil disobedience, *direct action, *non-violent resistance, *passive resistance.

gauchisme. French: leftism. A term in use since the nineteenth-century, but now mostly used to denote the *anarchist movement within the intellectual and student *left in France, particularly as this was manifested in and around 1968. The essential elements seem to be exuberant contempt for *bourgeois values, *Marxizing theory, and strongly *romantic prescriptions in answer to the question, What is to be done?

Gaullism. French political movement centred on the policies, principles and character of General (later President) Charles de Gaulle (1890–1970), beginning with the Rassemblement du Peuple Français (1947), and supplying a majority in the National Assembly as the Union de la Nouvelle République (1958). It has survived the death of de Gaulle to become a major political coalition capable of commanding considerable support among the French electorate. It tends to change its name with almost every election, and became the Rassemblement pour la République when Jacques Chirac reformed the Gaullists in 1976. According to one observer such 'terminological problems' express 'both the party's essential continuity . . . and the uncertainty of its role and impermanence of its organizational structure' (Michael Steed: *Political Parties in the European Community*, 1979).

The distinctive philosophy of Gaullism emphasizes nationalism, leadership, and an independent foreign policy, conducted for the most part outside the structure of the Western alliance. The advocacy of capitalist economy, traditional French *centralism, and Roman Catholic morality is combined with a strongly republican outlook which often appears conservative in its evident emphasis on military security, political stability and economic growth, but which also has some of the volatility of its Napoleonic archetype.

Geist. German: spirit or soul. Term used by *Hegel and his followers to refer to the basic substance the inner nature of which is the object of all self-consciousness and which strives to realize itself both 'subjectively' through our own *self-realizations, and also 'objectively' through the dialectical transformations which constitute history. (Hence the Hegelian division of phenomena into those of subjective and those of objective spirit.) *See* **Volksgeist*, **Zeitgeist*.

During the nineteenth-century the term *Geisteswissenschaften* was coined, to denote those branches of study which have the human soul and human institutions as their subject-matter, it being assumed by followers of *Dilthey (himself a disciple of *Kant and Hegel) that these studies exemplify methods different from those employed in the physical sciences. *See* *humane education, **Verstehen*.

Gemeinschaft* and *Gesellschaft. German: community and society. Terms employed by the sociologist Ferdinand Tönnies (*Gemeinschaft und Gesellschaft*, 1887, tr. *Community and Association*, 1955) in order to distinguish two kinds of association, one based in bonds of affection, kinship etc., the other in *division of labour, self-interest and *contract. The theory of the distinction concerns two *ideal types, and it is important in providing two contrasting models of political association and political obligation, the one (that of non-contractual allegiance) popular among traditional conservatives, the other (that of quasi-contractual obligation) popular among liberal individualists.

general strike. *See* *anarcho-syndicalism, *industrial action, *myth, *Sorel, *syndicalism.

general will (*volonté générale*). Term introduced by *Rousseau, who distinguished the 'general will', which is the will of a society in its political aspect, from the 'will of all', which is the majority preference on this or that occasion. The two may conflict (for example, a majority may seek to disobey a law enacted by a constitution to which all agreed under the terms of a *social contract). The general will is expressed in law and is thought to be a 'real force, superior to the action of any particular will'. In being forced to conform to the general will, Rousseau argued, a citizen is being 'forced to be free'.

The idea has been important in shaping modern political thought, particularly since it seems to capture a *paradox of democracy, namely, that citizens may consent to arrangements that thereafter constrain and restrict their choices. Subsequent applications range from *Hegel's theory of the personal *state, to modern theories of *social choice, which sometimes argue that results such as *Arrow's theorem show that there can be no consistent democratic constitution based on the 'will of all', but only on some impersonal (but dictatorial) general will.

genocide. Term coined by Raphael Lamkin, to denote the deliberate destruction of a *race, usually motivated by a theory as to the nature of races, whereby to distinguish the 'higher' from the 'lower' (eliminable) varieties. Classified as a crime under *international law by the UN General Assembly in 1948. *See* *holocaust, *racism.

gentleman. **1**. A man of 'gentle' birth. This originally signified a definite position in the social *hierarchy. A gentleman required inherited material wealth, usually in the form of land, and an education (when he had one) derived from recognized institutions of learning closed to those who did not belong or aspire to the upper *class. It is questionable whether the 'gentry' now form a class in any precise or theoretical sense since (a) their economic position is fairly indeterminate; (b) it is easy to become or cease to be a gentleman; (c) the classification seems from its beginning to have been subordinate to an ideal of civilized conduct. Hence:

2. A man who displays certain distinctive social characteristics, being courteous, liberal, honest, and well-spoken. These virtues have been thought to be more easily achieved by someone who is both attached to the land and relieved of the necessity of working it. Such a man, who has neither the vulgarity of the merchant, nor the avarice of the farmer, may exhibit, even in those conditions of poverty and ill-fortune that are the test of virtue, the social graces of a gentleman.

The vagueness of 1. combined with the broad application of 2. have led to the sense that a man can become a gentleman simply by representing himself to be one. No man can become an aristocrat in that way. Hence the term has come to express an idea of *social mobility. By representing oneself as a gentleman in sense 2. one is better placed to become a gentleman in sense 1. But even if that is true, the social mobility of women is unlikely to be improved by it.

Those who subscribe to a *power theory of politics will not regard sense 2. as denoting a politically significant category. Thus Bertrand Russell (an aristocrat, but no gentleman) wrote: 'whatever the prevalent conception of manners may be, it is only where power is (or lately was) hereditary that men will be judged by their manners . . . What survives in the way of admiration of the "gentleman" depends upon inherited wealth, and must rapidly disappear if economic as well as political power ceases to pass from father to son' (*Power*, 1938).

gentry. The class of *gentlemen. Used specifically to denote the class of small entrepreneurial landlords which existed in England from the early Renaissance onwards, and which provided much of the base for the political power struggles which shaped and reshaped modern English parliamentary institutions. Hence the 'gentry controversy', a parochial dispute, initiated by R. H. Tawney and H. R. Trevor-Roper, concerning the role of this class in the phenomenon in mid-seventeenth-century England which is by some called a *rebellion, and by others a *revolution.

geopolitics. A science, or pseudo-science, associated principally with the name of R. J. Kjellen (1864–1922) and Karl Haushofer, which conceives geographical location as an important and perhaps major determinant of political identity, political thought and political action, and which sees *nations as organisms struggling with each other for the occupancy of space. Haushofer coined the term *Lebensraum* (space for living), which played an important role in the *Nazi rhetoric of conquest.

gerontocracy. Greek: *geron*, an old man. Rule by the elderly, a frequent practice among primitive tribes and in those societies where it is considered that only age can provide the knowledge, wisdom or influence necessary for government. For different reasons gerontocracy has become the characteristic form of government in China, the USSR, and many of the satellites of the USSR.

ghetto. Probably from Italian: *borghetto*, small (part of a) city. Originally used to denote the quarter of a town (principally in Italy) to which the Jews were by law confined, and now denoting any urban area in which people of one race or ethnic group congregate, either by consent, or by coercion, or by economic constraint. The usual implication is that the living conditions in a ghetto are less desirable than those in surrounding areas, and that the occupants of the ghetto form part of an underprivileged *minority.

Giffen goods. Goods which do not obey the law that less is bought as price rises (the 'law of demand'). Named after Sir Robert Giffen (1837–1910), who observed that when the price of bread rose the labouring classes bought more of it, and when the price fell, less. Such goods are not now regarded as exceptions to the 'law of demand', which has been supplemented by the theories of *income effect and *substitution effect, whereby the behaviour of Giffen goods may be explained.

gift. The voluntary transfer of property to another, or into *common ownership, without receipt of any property in exchange. Gift between private persons requires private property, and its importance in expressing and cementing indispensable human relationships has provided one of the frequently used arguments for private property: the right of property being extolled as a necessary condition for its own renunciation, much as chastity has been extolled as the necessary condition for those relations which are founded on its demise. This sentiment received expression, for example, in *Hegel and *Burke. Conversely many who have been opposed to private property have for that reason been opposed to gifts, and in many socialist communities gifts are severely curtailed by law; even capitalist economies may subject gifts to punitive *taxation in the interest of *social justice and *redistribution.

A specific form of gift – that from the dead to the living – has frequently evoked this hostility in an acute form, since it seems to be the principal means whereby the power of individual families and even classes germinates. (*See* *hereditary principle.) Some think that it is unjust that one person should begin life with inherited wealth, others argue that it is in any case politically unacceptable that such constant accumulation across generations should be possible, and therefore advocate total or partial confiscation of wealth on death. Inheritance may, however, be both upheld and abolished in the name of a more feudal conception of private property. According to this conception property is held not absolutely, but subject to the will of the sovereign to whom allegiance is owed. Thus property is at best a right for life, with ownership reverting to the sovereign (i.e. the state) on death, to be redistributed in accordance with the will of the sovereign (i.e. in accordance with the law). The law may designate, for example, the eldest male son as heir, thus upholding inheritance. This does not alter the fact that transfer across generations has now ceased to be a gift, and has become, instead, the reassumption of ownership by the sovereign, followed by its re-allocation according to the law. This is probably the correct way to understand the medieval concept of 'entail', which makes the holder of an estate into a kind of trustee for those entitled in succession. This way of seeing inheritance also shows how it is possible for private property to be subject to state supervision, so that no interference in the right of property as commonly understood need be involved in any measures designed to prevent accumulation beyond a certain level (specifically beyond the level at which the subject begins to appear comparable in power to the sovereign).

No such intellectual construction can be used to rationalize the forbidding (or permitting) by law of gifts *inter vivos*, and the question of their admissibility continues, therefore, to raise important questions concerning the nature and justification of private property.

Gleichschaltung. German: levelling or regularizing of government. The general idea of political coordination or bringing into line, so that policy decisions harmonize. The term was given a more sinister use by Hitler, to signify (what some consider to be a necessary part of political coordination) the systematic elimination of *opposition and of those who instigate it.

glory. Glory can name either the splendour generosity and ostentation of a style of life, or the esteem due to *virtue, especially to courage and effort expended in a public cause. To some extent both those ideas have been subsumed under the traditional French political value of *gloire*, which at first referred to the reputation and dignity of the true public figure and later (after the trappings of monarchy had been borrowed by Napoleon) to that kind of public recognition and display which is the reward of heroic action. (The direct influence here was the Roman idea of *gloria* as the reward of *virtue.)

In a lesser sphere the pursuit of glory has often been thought (e.g. by *Aristotle) to be an ineliminable part of the political motive, since it is nothing more than an attempt to represent objectively the subjective pride which is essential to virtue. In so far as all political order requires courage it also requires the motive of honour, and that in turn requires the satisfaction of honour, which is the public recognition that is symbolized in acts of display. Some have argued that the modern world has not escaped the need for that display. For example, some defend a system of *honours, on the ground that public service should find a reward in the form of recognition and social status, rather than in financial advantage or naked power. Glory, as an end in itself, thereby removes the motive from a certain kind of corruption.

gnosticism. A religious movement of pagan origins which influenced Christianity in the second century, and which held that no redemption is possible without 'gnosis' – the revealed knowledge of God and man's destiny – and (sometimes) that possession of gnosis is a sufficient guarantee of redemption. The term has been borrowed by Eric Voegelin to describe political doctrines which claim to reveal a truth about man and history which is sufficient to show the way to a secular redemption. Voegelin argues that the gnostic idea of salvation through knowledge, while quickly condemned as a heresy by the church, represents a permanent temptation of the human intelligence, and is a source of fantasy in religion, morality, and politics.

Gobineau, Arthur (self-styled Comte de) (1816–82). French political theorist, diplomat and polemicist, widely known as the father of modern *racism, who wrote powerfully and trenchantly of the condition of European civilization in the nineteenth century, and who also sought to develop a theory of *race that would explain the simultaneous technological advance and spiritual insecurity of the European powers, and the relative backwardness and innocence of the Africans. Gobineau was fascinated by Arab and Middle-Eastern civilization, which presented a striking challenge to many of his theories, and was a tireless collector of anthropological evidence in his attempt to show that physical environment has no influence on culture, and that all flourishing and all degeneracy can be traced to the influence of race. He recognized three races – the white, the yellow and the black, in descending order of superiority – and argued that the luxury and *decadence of his countrymen was but one small consequence of the fact that the white race had all but disappeared in a mess of hybridization. All races achieve their characteristic greatness when unmixed, and hybridization is the downfall of all.

Godwin, William (1756–1836). British political theorist and novelist who, in his *Enquiry Concerning Political Justice*, 1793, gave what was perhaps the first extended modern defence of *anarchism, based on principles of *natural justice, utility, and the *rights of man. He argued for 'primeval equality' – i.e. for the view that man outside society can recognize no distinctions among his kind that might justify unequal treatment. All inequality is created by the condition of society, which generates class distinctions, sentiments of nationality and territory, and all the aggressive activities that we have learned to associate with them. Only the total removal of political *institutions can restore man to his natural rights, and permit him to engage in genuine as opposed to constrained *social contract with his fellows. Godwin's anarchism was liberal in inspiration; however, since there is a right, in Godwin's view, only to what maximizes utility, his preferred list of natural rights does not resemble that normally offered by liberal theory. Despite his influence on the intellectuals of the romantic period (notably on the poets Shelley and Wordsworth), Godwin was never associated with any definite political movement.

good offices. In *international law 'good offices and mediation' signifies the intervention in a dispute by a *state not party to it, in order to procure a settlement. 'Good offices' are in theory distinct from 'mediation', the first denoting the preparatory moves towards securing negotiation between the parties, the second involving the actual initiation of the negotiations.

government. The exercise of *influence and *control, through *law and *coercion, over a particular group of people, formed into a *state. Government has many kinds, and the following distinctions should be noted:

(i) Constitutional and non-constitutional: in the first, power is limited by a *constitution, in the second it is not. Many governments pretend to be constitutional: a common sign of this is a written constitution, which carefully specifies the rights of the citizen while neglecting to mention how he might enforce them (See e.g. many of the post-colonial African constitutions.)

(ii) Absolute and limited (*see* *absolutism and *limited government). This distinction concerns the extent to which a government's power is limited by other agencies within the state (law being principal among them), as opposed to other states.

(iii) Political and non-political, for which *see* *politics. Certain institutions, concerned with the *representation, *arbitration, *adjudication and *conciliation of interests within the state, are deemed to have a 'political' character, the most important of them being courts of law. Government can, however, exist without such institutions, and even without law – in which case it may be *despotic, or merely *primitive (as in the government of a tribe by a single chieftain in accordance with *custom).

(iv) In addition to those basic distinctions, various classifications of government have evolved, for example according to who holds power and in whose interest (the influence here being *Aristotle). The principal ones now recognized are *monarchy, *democracy, *aristocracy, *oligarchy, and *tyranny.

Theories of government are legion, but it is always important to distinguish between those which see government as a means to an end, and those which see it as an end in itself. *Hegel's theory is an example of the latter; standard *liberal and *socialist theories are examples of the former. If there are human ends for which government is necessary, then probably government must always be considered (at least to some extent) as a means to them. Thus if government is necessary for *peace, *friendship, *production and social life, then government must be conceived as a means to these basic and indispensable goods. But if *anarchism is right, and those goods are obtainable without government, then government may yet be defensible as an end in itself – i.e. as defining a form of life (that of political *allegiance or *obligation) which is desirable in itself (say, because it is the full expression of man's *freedom – roughly Hegel's view). In reality most political practice recognizes that government is both a means to order, and an end of social existence, and has a dual value founded in compromise between these two.

Since the subject-matter of this dictionary is government, it would be impertinent to extend this entry.

government through symbols. The kind of government in which the state, its power, and its authority, are given periodic demonstration of a symbolic kind. The purpose may be to increase the *authority of the state, as in the ceremonies and pageants that occur in monarchies, and which involve not the display of power but only the rehearsal of traditional allegiances, or in the flags, national anthems, parades and tournaments upon which virtually every government relies for the image of legitimacy. In this sense all government needs symbols, since it is through symbols that values, including those of political obligation, are understood. Alternatively, the purpose may be to increase the *power of the state, as in the show trials organized periodically by communist states, or in the *auto da fé* of the church, which exist to inspire awe and terror in the citizen, and to remind him in a vivid form of his subjection to an overriding power.

grace. **1**. The supernatural assistance of God, bestowed with a view to the salvation of a human soul.

2. The ability to appear in society so as to attract the interest, sympathy and obedience of others, without offending their pride.

The second indicates a style of politics that has often appealed to Europeans; the first indicates a belief that has sometimes enabled them to achieve it.

gradualism. The view, sometimes associated with *social democracy, that the transformation of social and political life cannot be achieved by sudden *revolution, but can be achieved by steady and systematic 'permeation' of existing political institutions. (*See also* *evolutionism, *Fabianism.)

Also, more loosely, any political doctrine which advocates slow and steady rather than sudden and disruptive advances towards its aims. Gradualism has been a major cause of Fabians, and was passionately advocated by Sidney and Beatrice Webb, and by G. B. Shaw.

Gramsci, Antonio (1891–1937). Founder of the Italian *Communist Party, and imprisoned by Mussolini, Gramsci wrote works (some while in prison) which were subsequently to be highly influential. He attempted to reformulate certain of the theses of *Marxism – in particular *historical materialism – in a way that would reflect native Italian conceptions of the role of institutions, consciousness and culture. A *humanist and hater of tyranny, Gramsci has achieved renown as a symbol of an intellectual communism of Italian manufacture which (partly because it was snuffed out by Mussolini) can be thought of as the true source of doctrine to which the Italian intellectual should turn in his search for the reasoned grounds of revolutionary activity. His term *hegemony has entered political rhetoric, although not always with a meaning of which he would approve. For Gramsci a hegemony consists of complex and concealed modes of *class domination, whereby positions of influence throughout society are always, by a hidden mechanism, filled by the members of an already ruling class. Classical Marxism asserts that when *productive forces have developed to the level at which existing *production relations can no longer contain them or serve their further growth, revolution is precipitated and in the ensuing crisis all institutions crumble and disappear. The theory of hegemony tries to explain why that does not happen: a powerful mechanism of consolidation exists within social and political *superstructure, which helps to stabilize the ascendancy of a class at the limiting point of production compatible with its continuity. Hence an important task of the revolutionary is to infiltrate the *autonomous institutions (schools, councils, universities, the church) through which hegemony is covertly exercised, so as to remove their internal staying power and let loose the flood of revolution that is surging from below.

Revolution should involve the construction of a new hegemony, which will gradually expand, spreading the influence of the Communist Party into all areas of civil society. Gramsci wished for a revolution but not for a coercive state, and thought that through this new hegemony, which would involve the gradual *democratization of all institutions and the involvement of the whole people in all aspects of their life, the area of state coercion could be gradually eliminated. The ideal was not a state but a 'regulated society', in which *consensus would replace the rule of force. (*See also* *corporatism.)

grass roots. US political slang, originating *circa* 1912, and used to designate support for a policy or party within the ranks of citizens who do not possess any more power than is contained in the ability to vote. 'Grass roots politics' denotes a political practice that seeks to instigate and fulfil policy by influencing the opinion and involving the sentiments of those outside political office, and which usually represents itself as being at one with some popular *consensus. (*See also* *populism.)

Great Leap Forward. Term used to denote the policy of forced industrialization and political mobilization initiated in China in 1958, and which aimed at an annual rate of *economic growth of twenty-five per cent. The attempt failed, in 1961 more moderate policies were introduced, and the continuing crisis of Chinese socialism took the form of a *cultural rather than an industrial revolution.

Great Officers. In English parlance, Great Officers of the Realm (elsewhere Officers of State (Scotland) or Great Officers of State) are the holders of those political offices through which executive powers are exercised in the name of the sovereign. The usage is antiquated, and does not now correspond to the true centre of executive power (the *Prime Minister and *cabinet), but only to a traditional sense of the manner in which monarchical privilege is represented. In the UK the Great Officers include the Lord Chancellor (who is responsible for the execution of law and judicial process), the Lord President of the Council, the Lord Privy Seal, and twelve othere. Only the first of these is of necessity a peer, and all are bound by an order of precedence. Absolutism in

France was accompanied by the virtual disappearance of Great Officers of State (with the exception of the Chancellor), while in most other states the importance of these officers steadily diminished through the nineteenth century.

Greek constitutions. Since much of our political philosophy has it origin in discussions prevalent in ancient Greece, the constitutions of the Greek city states (*see* ***polis*) are often taken as models with which to guide discussion of the *nation states which have long since succeeded them. The two principal Greek constitutions now discussed are those of Athens (*see* *Athenian democracy) and *Sparta: in the former a kind of partial *democracy prevailed, while in the latter intense political organization of all aspects of social life coexisted with extraordinary social divisions. Sparta was esteemed for its inner discipline by *Plato, who expressed, in the *Republic*, and the *Laws*, his admiration for a constitution that could so easily provide political answers to every social question. In the *Laws* Plato compares many Greek constitutions, and enables us to see how the familiar problems of political theory – the role of law, the problem of securing limited government, the nature and status of labour, and the problem of social class – are generic to government, and not peculiar to our time.

Extant are a constitution of Athens, attributed to Xenophon but in fact written by an Athenian oligarch about 425 BC, which disguises bitter criticism of democracy behind a 'descriptive' façade; an incomplete history and analysis of the Athenian constitution by *Aristotle, and a 'constitution of the Lacedaimonians' (i.e. of Sparta) by Xenophon, which says, however, very little about its subject-matter. Plato's *Laws* remain therefore an indispensable source.

Green, Thomas Hill (1836–82). English philosopher. *See* *common good.

Gresham's law. 'Bad money drives out good', named after Sir Thomas Gresham (1519–79), a businessman and economic adviser to King Edward VI and Queen Elizabeth I of England. The idea is this: if the face value of two coins differs from the bullion value, then the one with the higher bullion value can be melted down and so will exchange against the other at an advantageous rate; eventually it will disappear from circulation. Sometimes, when the *exchange-value of a coin as bullion is less than its exchange-value as money, a law may be passed to *take* it out of circulation.

gross domestic product. A measure of the total flow of goods and services produced by the economy – i.e. the aggregate value added – over a specified period (normally a year). Intermediate products (i.e. those which re-enter the production process) are not included. 'Gross' product does not allow for depreciation. The GDP is 'domestic' in that it is a measure of the actual level of production *within* the economy: contrast *gross national product.

gross national product. *Gross domestic product plus *income accruing from overseas investments and minus income earned in the domestic market by those residing abroad.

Grotius, Hugo (Huig de Groot) (1583–1645). Dutch jurist, philosopher and man of letters, a *humanist and disciple of *Erasmus, Grotius wrote a famous pamphlet in defence of the freedom of the seas (*Mare Liberum*, 1609) and, after escape from life imprisonment on political charges, wrote the first, and the greatest, exposition of modern *international law (*De Jure Belli ac Pacis*, *On the Law of War and Peace*, 1620–25). The purpose was to devise a system of international law suitable to the new *nation states of Europe, which would not rely upon *ecclesiastical jurisdiction, but harmonize with, and gain support from, normal principles of adjudication. He argued that such a system of law must be founded in *natural law, which is instinct in human nature, and independent of the command of God: 'Natural law is so immutable that it cannot be changed by God himself.' This law has authority in all rational beings, and therefore can command assent at all times and places, irrespective of whether there is some power, secular or ecclesiastical, able to give support to its manifest moral authority. Natural law is distinct from *positive law, and provides the criterion whereby positive law might be tested, and to which appeal may be made when the positive laws of separate nations conflict. One principle of natural law is of particular importance in international jurisdiction, as the foundation of all legal dealings between states: *pacta sunt servanda*, i.e. promises and treaties are to be adhered to. Other postulates offered by Grotius in the name of natural law are perhaps more parochial than this one, which he clearly regarded as the most important, in founding what he called the *jus voluntarium* (the 'voluntary legislation') characteristic of dealings between states. On the basis of his exploration of this concept, Grotius offered a famous analysis of the *just war, arguing that no war could be just if purely aggressive (*see* *aggression) and hence that only acts of defence and retaliation could be countenanced. Grotius's ideas on this subject have since been taken seriously, and to a great measure applied, through the legal determinations of the United Nations.

Grotius defended a *social contract doctrine, although unlike later theorists (such as *Hobbes, *Locke and *Rousseau) he believed that this contract actually occurred, preceding the state of society in every community governed by law (hence the natural law principle of *pacta sunt servanda* also provides the ultimate basis of *political obligation).

Grotius's writings were voluminous; he is notable for his attempt to give a full account of man as rational agent, and for the extent to which he presaged, in that account, many doctrines that were to acquire their full modern dress in the moral philosophy of *Kant.

group. Usually defined by political scientists as a number of individuals with a common interest, whether or not associated for the pursuit of interest. Groups vary according to size, organization and interest, and many contain sub-groups and *factions. Studies of *collective choice make increasing reference to groups, and 'group theory' (exemplified, e.g., in Arthur Bentley: *The Process of Government*, 1949; and Sidney Verba: *Small Groups and Political Behaviour*, 1961) is now an important part of the sociology of politics. *See also* *interest group, *pressure group.

growth. Growth usually means *economic growth, although naturally many other factors of social life exhibit principles of growth – e.g. population, knowledge, understanding, sympathy. *Progressivism, the view which sees all forms of growth as related and as occurring together, is to be contrasted with the view that economic growth is an independent social feature, that might occur whether or not there is any corresponding movement in political and social institutions, and without determining growth in anything else.

guerrilla warfare. *Guerrilla* is the Spanish term for a kind of irregular and usually undeclared warfare carried out by autonomous units without a coordinated high command but, it is assumed, with a concerted (and usually *revolutionary or *nationalist) purpose. The potential of guerrilla warfare for undermining an established government has led to considerable theoretical work by those revolutionaries (e.g. *Mao, Ché Guevara) committed to its success. In his theory of the 'people's war' Mao argued that guerrillas have an essential part to play in arming the people, and in directing their efforts towards the seizure of power. Others (e.g. the French communist Régis Debray) argue that the support of the people is not necessary, and that guerrilla activity may alone be sufficient to create the conditions of revolution, through an 'insurrectional focus' (*see* *focoism). Such theories require the guerrilla army to perform both a military and a political function, capable of commencing and consolidating the policies of the party for which it fights.

The 'urban guerrilla' is a familiar exponent of modern *terrorism, although no comparable dignifying role has yet been written for him.

Guevara, Ernesto, 'Ché' (1928–67) Argentinian-born revolutionary. *See* *focoism, *guerrilla warfare.

guilds. Permanent voluntary associations serving a common interest of their members: this interest was usually occupational, but not always so (thus universities began in England as guilds). Deriving from the Roman *collegia* (*see* *college), guilds emerged in Europe at about the beginning of the eleventh century as organizations of skilled labourers and craftsmen concerned to promote the social, professional and religious interests of their members, to help those in need, and to promote their education and welfare. They could effectively forbid someone from practising a vocation by closing their doors to him, and anticipated in their dealings with their members some of the social and political organization of modern *trade unions, differing largely in the nature of the employments supervised by them, and in the greater emphasis on social, recreational and ceremonial embellishments to the life of labour and craft. They had their own bodies of customary law, and were later always governed, in England, by statute (e.g. the Statute of Artificers 1562). Guild organization broke down under the impact of *industrialization, *detail labour, and **laissez-faire*.

guild socialism. A movement within the British *labour movement, guild socialism existed as an active force from 1906 to 1923 (becoming the National Guilds League), and as a dwindling idea thereafter. The central aim was to incorporate into the modern labour organizations the social concern and sense of wholeness characteristic of the *guilds, and to develop, out of small autonomous associations, modes of common ownership and control that would be organically linked to the leisure and social life of their members. These guilds were to be the true locus of economic activity, and also to provide the basis for all social and political existence, with the state reduced to the status of arbitrator and adjudicator of disputes and conflicts. Ideally, even parliamentary government could be abolished if power was properly vested in these self-sufficient social units. The principal exposition of the idea is A. J. Plenty: *Restoration of the Guild System*, 1906.

H

habeas corpus. In English law, a *prerogative writ (i.e. a summons by a legal officer issued on behalf of the sovereign), calling for the liberty of a subject. Originally habeas corpus was a command to bring the person before a court; now it is simply a general order to release from imprisonment. The existence of this writ (named after its opening words in Latin: 'In that you have the body of . . .') is seen as one of the fundamental guarantees of traditional English liberty. It is older than Magna Carta, 1215, and was established in the seventeenth century as the appropriate process for securing release from illegal detention. The writ may now be validly used against the *Crown, its officers and ministers, and therefore vests absolute power in a judge to enquire into the validity of any restraint, except where ordered by a court of competent jurisdiction (when the enquiry would be tantamount to retrial), and in certain rather peculiar cases (as when a member of the House of Commons is committed to the Tower for breach of *privilege).

The writ also exists in the US, transplanted from English law, and now issued as an original proceeding by the Supreme Court. Abraham Lincoln worried about the suspension of the writ during the civil war emergency, and it then became a public issue of the first importance: to what extent does the US constitution guarantee the rights and liberties of the citizen in the absence of this writ? Habeas corpus has also become an issue recently, because of its increasing use to take issues out of state courts and into federal courts, a practice that is frequently deplored by *federalists. No equivalent of habeas corpus exists in USSR law.

Habermas, Jurgen (b. 1929). German philosopher and social critic. *See* *critical theory, *Frankfurt school, *legitimation.

harassment. A form of *coercion, much practised, easily recognized, but difficult to define. A legal definition is offered by, and for the purposes of, the UK Protection from Eviction Act 1977, s. 1(3), which extends an intuitive idea from the Administration of Justice Act (s. 40, forbidding harassment of debtors) to the harassment of occupiers, and makes it an offence to do acts calculated to interfere with the peace or comfort of an occupier and his family, with the intention of getting him to renounce his rights of occupancy.

hard cases. From the maxim 'hard cases make bad law'; a phenomenon singled out by the American jurist and philosopher Ronald Dworkin (*Taking Rights Seriously*, 1977), as posing fundamental questions concerning the nature of *law and legal reasoning. A hard case is a case in law whose outcome seems not to be determined by an antecedent rule, and where, while the judge may follow a *precedent, the disparity between the present case and the one with which it is compared is too great to permit any simple assimilation of the one to the other. Attention to such cases brings into focus the all-important question: does the judge make, or discover, the law? On the one hand, there is no antecedent rule determining his decision (which makes it seem as though he makes the law to fit this case); on the other hand, he cannot *think* of himself as making the law, for that would suggest that the law came into existence after the action that is being tried, in which case injustice (in the form of *retroactive legislation) will be the inevitable consequence of his decision. The problem is rendered more, not less, acute, as *statute comes to replace *common law, since this seems to emphasize the conventional, man-made character of the law, and to cast doubt on the interpretation of judicial reasoning as a process of discovery.

hard currency. A currency, traded in a foreign exchange market, for which the demand is persistently high, on account of its purchasing power or stability. Governments with 'soft' currencies often control exchange in order to acquire hard currency at favourable rates (*see* *exchange control). The softness of a currency is often taken as a sign of the economic fragility of the state which issues it, so that the constant search on the part of *communist states for hard currency has often been taken as an index of the economic instability of communist modes of production. The retort is sometimes made that this is a distortion, due to the fact that the institutions of international exchange are all in the hands of capitalists.

harm. A concept important in articulating *liberal conceptions of the nature and function of *law, and in formulating plausible limits to the scope of law. One popular idea (which finds expression in some of the writings of *J. S. Mill) is that the prime function of law is to prevent the individual from doing harm to others and to himself. Intuitively appealing though that conception is, it has presented immense problems in its application, for what constitutes harm? What harms a plant may not harm a dog, what harms a dog may not harm a person; and conversely. Roughly, *x* harms *y* whenever *x* prevents *y* from existing or flourishing according to *y*'s nature; disputes about harm are therefore usually disputes about *human nature. Since the flourishing of a *person may not be identical with, and may be quite independent of, the flourishing of the human animal in which he is, as it were, incarnate, enormous philosophical controversies arise. For example, am I harmed by something just *because* I do not consent to it? What then is the criterion of my consent to a law? That I voted for the party whose majority secured its enactment? Clearly this criterion, when combined with the original liberal idea of the function of law, leads to enormous scepticism about laws which are both deeply entrenched in all legal systems, and perhaps even essential to good government. (And, in another, more plausible sense, people often consent to things which harm them.)

Some accounts of harm attempt to do justice to the complexity of the idea of the person, by defining his harm as an invasion of his interests, where his interests include, or are exhausted by, his *rights (sometimes his *natural rights). Then the true function of law may be construed as the protection of natural rights. This provides a more objective criterion than 'consent', and one that has often seemed plausible; but how are natural rights to be determined? This problem is perhaps as difficult as the one which 'harm' was invoked to solve.

Harrington, James (1611–77). English political philosopher and scholar, who set forth, in his *The Commonwealth of Oceana*, 1656, a *utopian picture of the ideal *republican state. The work has a philosophical basis in *empiricism, and defines the types of rule (monarchy, oligarchy, etc.) in terms of the distribution of property among members of the state (thus presaging later theories of *class), while attempting to discover the general conditions for stability. Harrington was an admirer of *Machiavelli and also a philosophical *hedonist, who attempted to vindicate private property and to show that republican government in an essentially bourgeois society – a 'commonwealth for increase' – would be the most stable political system. In the course of this he argued for a written constitution, *bicameral government, a *separation of powers, rotation of *office, secret ballot, indirect election of a *president, and many other extremely interesting features of the ideal constitution, which was to be, in his famous words, 'an empire of laws, not of men'. His work was to exert a powerful influence upon many of the Founding Fathers of the US constitution, and to influence the content of that constitution itself. Harrington was imprisoned on a trumped-up charge of treason in 1661, became insane while in prison, and never recovered his wits after his eventual release.

Hayek, F. A. von (b. 1899). Political philosopher and economist of the *Austrian school, whose denunciation (especially in *The Road to Serfdom*, 1945) of the *totalitarian systems of government imposed upon Europe first by Hitler and then by Stalin did much to create the postwar consciousness of liberty at bay. Hayek has attempted to reformulate the doctrine of the *free market, as a self-regulating mechanism whose social benefits outweigh its harms, and to adapt it for modern consumption by giving it *constitutionalist form. A liberal by inclination, Hayek sees the economic structure of capitalism, however modified by historical contingencies, as an essential part not only of economic prosperity, but also of the freedom of action to which all social beings aspire. Nevertheless, freedom is only possible when guaranteed by a constitution, and it is no easy matter to develop a constitution which permits liberty, while forbidding licence and anarchy. His later work, therefore – notably *The Constitution of Liberty*, 1961 – attempts to give an account of the ideal constitution of a modern capitalist state. The result is a mitigated traditionalism, in which many of the constitutional devices of the Anglo-American political tradition are upheld, as guarantees of stability which also permit the possibility of reform. Hayek supports democracy in principle, but argues that the mechanisms whereby power is exercised in democracies prevent the emergence of genuine *collective choice, and that no political system provides as real an instance of collective choice as is provided by the operation of a market. Moreover, whereas in an economic market each individual acts under a budget constraint, under most majority-rule democracies politicians are under no similar constraint, or at least, not immediately: hence the self-regulating conditions of the market cannot easily be achieved in the political sphere.

head of state. The individual who *represents the state according to law and in international relations. He need not in fact wield political power, and his function may be more or less ceremonial. Thus he may be a hereditary *monarch, whose only political act is to *ratify the decisions of others. Alternatively he may be a *president, elected for a certain period, and with enormous *prerogative powers (as in the US), yet subject to review and limitation by a Supreme Court and Congress, in the light of a constitution that is designed precisely for that purpose. He may also be a *dictator or *tyrant, who cannot be removed from office by constitutional means, and who exercises power without fear of legal sanction.

Often supreme executive power may be vested in an individual who is not the head of state, but who submits his decisions to some president or monarch for ratification, even though the head of state has no choice but to ratify (on pain of removal from office, exile or death). In such a case the head of state may serve as a symbol of *authority, acting so as to give sanction to naked *power: but without *some* residual legal powers, it is difficult to see how he might do even this. Such is the attraction of power that popular sentiment is always apt to identify the head of state with the actual holder of power. Thus there arises in the UK what is – from the constitutional point of view – an illusion, namely, that the *Prime Minister is *leader of the nation.

The distinction between head of state and prime minister (or some equivalent distinction, involving the separation of the dignities and ceremonies of state from the actual exercise of power) is sometimes urged as a necessary constitutional device, providing a focus for national loyalties which stands apart from direct involvement in domestic politics, and therefore retains some power to unite warring factions. It also gives symbolic expression to the distinction between power and authority, and emphasizes that political offices are more durable and more important than their passing occupants. On this view it is *important*, and not just eccentric, that the UK head of state has a ceremonial role, is the titular head of the *Anglican Church, has a vestigial royal prerogative, accedes to office by hereditary entitlement rather than by the struggle for power – and so on. All those are essentially 'dignifying' attributes, which confer authority, and power only in so far as the constitution makes use of that authority.

health. One of the most important issues in modern politics has been that of *welfare provision, in particular provision for the health of citizens who cannot otherwise afford to obtain treatment for their illnesses. While measures to control the outbreak of disease have always been recognized as a public responsibility, the detailed provision of proper medical services to the poor emerged as a political objective only in the nineteenth century. It was introduced for the first time by Bismarck in Prussia, and then gradually imitated by Austro-Hungary, by Tsarist Russia, by England and – most recently – by France. The US has yet to renounce the doctrine that properly supervised private insurance is equally effective, although it is clear that moves in the European direction are constantly being made, e.g. through 'Medicare' and 'Medicaid'.

Modern arguments tend to focus on the question whether a private medical service – one that is sustained through *contractual relations between doctor and patient, perhaps supported by schemes of private insurance – should survive at all. Arguments of justice, utility and freedom are offered on both sides. They may be summarized thus:

(i) For private medical care. (a) Justice. If someone is prepared to pay for a good, and another prepared to offer it, and if they freely contract between them, is there not an injustice to both parties in making that contract impossible? In particular, is it not unjust to the doctor, whose training (for which he sacrificed time and effort) gives him something that others both need and demand? Moreover, if doctors are supposed to provide their services to all comers for fixed reward, do they not have a right to refuse them? Or is the state entitled to compel them, just because of their qualifications, to work, and perhaps for a reward that lies outside the scope of their asking? (Various embellishments to this theme can be imagined, by taking particular cases, in the manner of *Nozick, and attempting to force the opponent to admit that the doctor's rights are being infringed.)

(b) Utility. If properly rewarded, and according to agreement, resources will be allocated more efficiently than they could be allocated by the state, and facilities would have a constant tendency to improve, through *competition. The poor too must benefit from this and those hours which a doctor may be required to work for the state will be more useful than in arrangements of fully socialized medicine.

(c) Freedom. Patients are less free when, whatever sacrifices they are prepared to make, nothing can be achieved in the way of superior treatment; doctors are less free when their labour hours are commandeered by the state.

(ii) Against private medical care. (a) Justice. Any kind of differential treatment makes it inevitable that better treatment will be available to the rich than to the poor. This means, in effect, that people will be offered differential medical treatment on grounds *other* than their state of health. But the only *relevant* ground for medical treatment is the state of health. All discrimination between people based in grounds irrelevant to the allocation of a good is an injustice. (*See* *social justice.) Hence the rights of the poor are infringed by private medicine.

(b) Utility. The complete socialization of medicine brings into the 'public sector' all the talent that might otherwise gravitate to the exclusive hospital. In comparison to the good done to private patients, the good done to everyone under socialized medicine must surely be greater. (The precise form of the argument here will depend upon which criterion of *optimality is to be chosen.)

(c) Freedom. The freedom of the rich is indeed enhanced by private medicine: but only at the expense of the freedom of the poor, whose possibilities are seriously diminished by all differentials of this kind.

The dispute captures, in miniature, two classical and recurring positions in the philosophy of social *welfare.

hedonism. **1**. Psychological: the view that people never pursue anything except pleasure, or the avoidance of pain. They may pretend to be pursuing nobler things, but this is an illusion; moreover, all the particular objects of desire are desired only because of the pleasure that they bring.

2. Philosophical: the view that pleasure and pain are the only criteria in terms of which the *value of any action may be estimated, and hence must figure as the grounds of all practical reasoning.

Bishop Butler (1692–1752) rebutted psychological hedonism by pointing to the absurdity of the view that if I want a plate of fish, then what I want is really the pleasure produced by it. For then it would be irrational of me to respond with amazement to the offer of a book, a lover or a cocked hat in place of it. Philosophical hedonism has perhaps had more of a following, partly on account of the efforts of *Bentham, partly because it seems to promise a mathematical structure to practical reasoning. But it is probably no more plausible (*see* *value).

Hegel, G. W. F. (1770–1831). German philosopher, founder of modern *idealism, and perhaps the greatest influence on modern political thought after *Marx, whose outlook he did much to make possible. Hegel's philosophy contains many parts, but of particular concern to politics are the following:

(i) The theory of the *dialectic. In Hegel this has two sides: (a) all reasoning is dialectical, proceeding from the positing of a concept, via the extraction of its negation and the consequent 'labour of the negative', to a new concept which transcends and makes 'determinate' the content of the first. Through the dialectical process a definite reality is gradually 'determined', the universality of the concept finds the 'particularity' of its object, and so generates knowledge. (b) Reality itself has the structure of thought (the fundamental thesis of idealism). Hence all processes in the world, whether the world of nature or the world of history, exhibit the order and development of the dialectic, passing from 'undifferentiated' beginnings to ever more determinate ends. An example of this is the progress of man himself, from the primitive undifferentiated consciousness of the member of the tribe, to the final self-realized and self-conscious individual, who postulates his ideal aim and satisfaction as his own, and so challenges the world to match his individuality. (In the folds of this progression all human history lies concealed, although only its end result, the German *romantic *individualism exemplified at its highest in Hegel, is immediately knowable.)

(ii) The theory of *self-realization. The dialectical process in the individual is one of steady advance towards the determinate 'self', which is 'for itself'. The individual knows himself through his efforts to create a determinate reality: thus man realizes himself in labour, in art, in political life, and in each case the increasing self-knowledge and increasing power represent a gain in *freedom. In this way Hegel came to view true (realized) human nature as an acquisition, rather than a gift, a fact which coloured his whole political philosophy. In particular he argued that social interaction *precedes* the creation of the individual, and so cannot be explained as a matter of individual choice. His complex account of self-realization includes the celebrated theories of *alienation, and of the relation between *master and slave.

(iii) The theory of history. History is the human spirit writ large – the 'march of reason in the world' – and its movement must inevitably exemplify the dialectical movement that is contained in every manifestation of the spirit. (*See* **Geist*.) Hence it proceeds from undifferentiated union (the equivalent of the pure concept of 'Being' from which the dialectic begins), through struggle and opposition (*see* *master and slave), to the highest forms of self-consciousness. Self-consciousness thereby emerges from the conflicts of religion (alienation), into the pure air of science, which sees everything as it is, since for science appearance has become transparent to essence. (*See* *essence/appearance.) At every period the spirit manifests itself as a specific **Zeitgeist*, determining the forms of social life, political order, knowledge, religion and art. The *progressivist tendency in Hegel is mitigated by his sense that reflective knowledge arrives always too late ('the owl of Minerva spreads its wings only at the gathering of the dusk'), so that the understanding of the human condition vouchsafed to him was also the guarantee that he could not remedy it.

(iv) The theory of the state. In *The Philosophy of Right*, 1821, Hegel produced an extremely succinct exposition of law, politics, and morality, in which he proposed the state as the highest expression of man's freedom, resulting from the transcendence of the (philosophically antecedent) conditions of *family and (in dialectical opposition to it) *civil society. The elements of the theory are these:

(a) The bond of the family is not contractual but one of *piety. The family is an indispensable 'moment' (a term not to be understood in a temporal sense) of political existence, without which the free being cannot emerge; (b) civil society is the sphere of justice, in which men freely secure and contract away their rights. Here the doctrine of the *social contract may seem to give a picture of social union, but only because those 'contracting' already possess the *autonomy which the family provides and which the state protects; (c) the unstable opposition between particularized loyalty to the family and universal loyalty to all free (contracting) beings is transcended and resolved in a new, self-conscious piety that orders all conflicting claims – that to the state, as the body of institutions which express, uphold and endorse the laws through which conflict is resolved. The state becomes the highest expression of man's freedom, and allegiance to it a necessary condition of full self-realized individuality; (d) *private property is justified as a necessary part of the dialectical process displayed in (a) to (c), as are *marriage, retributive punishment and adherence to a written code of law.

hegemony. Greek: *hegemon,* a chief or ruler. Term used since the last century to denote the influence of one state over others; hence 'hegemonism', which describes the politics of those powers that cow their neighbours and dependants into submission.

In political thought the term is now as often used in the sense given to it by *Gramsci, in which it denotes the ascendancy of a *class, not only in the economic sphere, but through all social, political and ideological spheres, and its ability thereby to persuade other classes to see the world in terms favourable to its own ascendancy. Gramsci advocated the construction of a rival hegemony, through the infiltration and transformation of those small-scale institutions by which class ascendancy, once achieved, is sustained. This struggle for hegemony is seen as a transforming factor as important as any development of *productive forces, and corresponds to *Lenin's 'subjective conditions' for revolution.

Heidegger, Martin (1889–1976). German philosopher. *See* *authenticity, *existentialism, *hermeneutics.

hellenism. Admiration for, and imitation of, ancient Greek *virtues: in the political sphere this involves admiring and attempting to sustain the vision of public life celebrated by Thucydides in words attributed to Pericles: 'Our constitution is called a democracy because power is in the hands not of a minority but of the whole people. When it is a question of settling private disputes, everyone is equal before the law; when it is a question of putting one person before another in positions of public responsibility, what counts is not membership of a particular class, but the actual ability which the man possesses . . . and just as our political life is free, so is our day-to-day dealing between ourselves . . . free and tolerant in our private lives, in public matters obedient to the law,' (*Peloponnesian War,* 2, 37). Associated with that idealized vision of *Athenian democracy is the respect for the ancient virtues of courage, honour and endurance. In the writings of *Arnold, Hellenism, as a social and political ideal, is contrasted with 'Hebraism', the detailed dependence on the dictatorial will of God.

helot. *See* *Sparta.

Herder, Johann Gottfried von (1744–1803). German philosopher and critic, a powerful intellectual opponent of the *Enlightenment, and a force behind the *romantic movement in Germany and central Europe. Herder emphasized the active nature of the human mind, and argued against *empiricist views of knowledge and experience, on account of their attempt to construe all knowledge as a passive reception, and also on account of their inability to explain the true complexity of *language, *culture and social life. He expounded an influential philosophy of history, and a view of language as expression, according to which the language of a people encapsulates not only its common experiences, but also its historical identity and an underlying consciousness of unity. This unity is expressed through cultural artifacts, but it is also in part constituted by them. Language is therefore seen as the repository of all that is distinctive of and precious to the group who speak it. In due course, as a result of Herder's influence, language was to become the object of solicitious political feelings. Thus he inspired many of the romantic *nationalist movements of central Europe, which sought to use language and culture to provide the 'natural' political boundaries which the various imperial alignments had obliterated. (*See also* **Volksgeist*, **Volksstaat*.)

hereditary principle. The principle either that there are hereditary *natural rights (e.g. the right of a child to enjoy some part of its deceased parents' *property), or that there ought to be (for whatever reason) hereditary legal rights. (For the distinction here, *see further* *positive law.) The two important hereditary rights generally considered are: title to property, and title to *nobility (construed as conveying social and political *privilege). The second is sometimes thought to be a late arrival in European legal systems; according to *Maitland, for example, titles such as 'earl' originally denoted offices, and only later, under Norman influence, were these offices thought of as hereditary – a feature which Maitland significantly describes as the 'tendency of every office to become hereditary, to become property' (*Constitutional History of England*, 1908), as though the inheritance of property is so natural a thing as to *explain* the inheritance of political rights and privileges. However, this extension of the hereditary principle to offices is probably only a rationalization of widespread feelings about family and kinship which manifest themselves even in the expressly anti-aristocratic governments of the US and the USSR.

Many who do not object to the inheritance of property rights as such, nevertheless object to the inheritance of political status (as under the *apartheid system) and especially the inheritance of *office, as under the peerage system, even though the acquisition of property may confer political advantages that far outweigh the very slight political privilege conferred by membership of a house of *peers. In the last case, this is partly because *titles* of nobility have an independent significance, as part of a system of *honours – and it seems absurd that anyone should bear an honour that he has not earned. It is sometimes replied that this preference for inherited property over inherited *status is nothing more than *bourgeois ideology, and that whatever arguments may be given against the one will weigh equally against the other. Presumably the same goes for arguments *for* the hereditary principle. Thus conservatives such as *Burke have thought that inherited status is useful for the generation of a permanent and competent *ruling class, united by bonds of family across generations, and so committed to the maintenance of social continuity (and its own rule as part of that continuity); this argument, if it justifies titles, also justifies inherited property.

The arguments over the hereditary principle continue to exercise political thinkers in the UK, largely on account of the persistence of a house of peers in *Parliament. It is clear that inheritance, whether of title or property, may lead to extraordinary powers being conferred on idiots, degenerates and fools. However, it is also clear that democratic election is equally likely to lead to great power being placed in the hands of idiots, degenerates and fools, so that arguments conducted at this level remain inconclusive, not to say ridiculous. It seems that the main conservative arguments *for* the principle concentrate rather on the ideas of continuity and *tradition, and the effect of hereditary office in defusing the urgency of the scramble for power, and tempering ambition and preferment with safe expectation and leisure – attributes which may be necessary in government, but not easily acquired through professional politics. The main liberal and socialist arguments against the principle seem to dwell first on ideas of *social justice, secondly upon the supposed obnoxiousness of class distinctions and class rule.

heredity and environment. Of vital consequence and almost impenetrable intricacy, the dispute as to the roles of heredity and environment in forming the moral and social attributes of people underlies many of the current conflicts of political opinion. *Racism emphasizes what it takes to be the overwhelming importance of heredity in determining not only intelligence and temperament, but also customs, character, morals – indeed, in its extreme form, everything from table manners to political doctrine. Likewise those accused of *sexism often complain that they seek only to affirm that the inherited characteristic of sex (or 'gender') is sufficient to determine, independently of social environment, different patterns of thought, feeling and social response among men and women.

Often the arguments simply dwell upon the totally unproven nature of the opponent's view. The obvious moral and scientific difficulties posed by the testing of any particular theory, combined with the somewhat obscure and perhaps irrelevant evidence provided by the breeding of 'character' in animals, must lead to caution. It must also encourage the development of a doctrine of rights that does not depend upon the truth of any particular hypothesis. If, for example, you have to believe that there is no inherited difference in intelligence, aggressivity, etc. between blacks and whites in order to accord equal rights to both, that surely shows that your doctrine of rights – in pre-empting the answer to an unsettled scientific question – is confused, or at least ill-considered. (A sophisticated, perhaps sophistical, rejoinder has it that to treat such questions as though they are 'scientific' is *already* racist: *see* *scientism.)

hermeneutics. The science of interpretation, traditionally applied to the discovery of the real but hidden meanings of sacred texts (specifically the gospels), but given a more universal interpretation by F. D. E. Schleiermacher (1768–1834) and then, much later, by Martin Heidegger (1889–1976). As currently understood, the term denotes the activity of understanding the world not as a physical system, but as an object of human thought and action (as *Lebenswelt* or 'human world'). The premises of modern hermeneutics (derived in part from the work of *Dilthey) are: (i) that scientific explanation is not the only form of understanding (*see* **Verstehen*); (ii) that we understand the human world only through asking questions of it, and every question is determined in form and content by an interest that underlies it; (iii) that a question already embodies a partial interpretation of the thing questioned. From these premises arises the 'hermeneutical circle': no interpretation is possible until interpretation has begun. This is supposed not to be a vicious circle, but simply to reflect the fact that our world exists as an object of consciousness only in and through language, which is the continuous expression of our being.

The more specialized applications of hermeneutics in literary criticism have remained recondite and obscure. However the underlying vision has had considerable influence on continental (especially German) social and political thought. Thus Hans-Georg Gadamer (b. 1900) has propagated hermeneutics as a supposed 'method' appropriate to the social sciences that will avoid the fallacies of *scientism. He has also attempted to give a philosophical account of the nature of *tradition. Since there is no *first* question asked of the human world but only a continuous flow of never-ending questions and answers, it is only through immersion in that continuity that social reality can be understood. The continuity involves language, culture and social interaction (both the last two themselves offshoots of language), and immersion in that continuity is what is meant by 'tradition'.

hierarchy. Greek: sacred rule. Term adopted to denote the power given by Christ to his apostles and their successors to form and govern the *church. It is now used more widely to denote any system in which the distributions of *power, *privilege and *authority are both systematic and unequal. The result is a society arranged according to 'degree', with power, privilege and authority varying together. Such an arrangement was defended by Shakespeare's Ulysses in *Troilus and Cressida,* Act I, scene iii: 'Take but degree away, untune that string, and Hark what discord follows!' – a speech which asserts an indissoluble connection between the existence of degree and the perception of the world in terms of *right and authority, rather than in terms of power. Thus for many of Shakespeare's day the structure of hierarchy seemed necessary in order for power to be perceived as legitimate rather than arbitrary, and hence for justice to be a live social value.

Hindu law. A system of law whose *jurisdiction is not determined by the boundaries of a state but by adherence to a religion. Its sources are in ancient Sanskrit texts (e.g. the Upanishads), and its aim, as in *Jewish law, is to provide practical guidance for those who seek to be righteous in the eyes of God. It upholds the *caste system, and determines family law and rights of inheritance. However, since British rule in India, and the subsequent efforts to evolve a genuine national law, Hindu law has fallen into disrepute. It is to some extent protected from extinction by its obscurity, and by its organic closeness to the *customs around which it is built.

historical jurisprudence. The study that tries to find the nature and meaning of *law through understanding its historical development, rather than through the reasoning given for the enactments of *legislators. It is associated with *Vico and *Montesquieu, and has been exemplified by thinkers as diverse as *Burke, who saw law as the final conscious reflection of a spirit that has its true significance in unconscious custom, and F. C. von Savigny (1779–1861), perhaps its most important exponent. Savigny argued against the Napoleonic codification of German law on the ground that law is discovered not made: in the course of this argument he produced a classic statement of the benefits of *common law and the harm of *statute. *Marx also expounded a kind of historical jurisprudence, through his argument that law is to be understood as the encapsulation in a system of rights of historically developing relations of power.

historical materialism. The fundamental tenet of *Marxism in all its 'classical' varieties. History is the product not of conscious decisions and ideas (*see* *voluntarism), but of 'material' processes and conditions which can be identified and described without reference to the mental states of those who participate in them. (*See* *materialism.) It is the changes in these material conditions which make necessary and bring about those changes in social, political and institutional *superstructures which in aggregate form the substance of history. The process of change has been variously described as *dialectical (*see* *dialectical materialism), as one of unceasing development of *productive forces, and as a *class struggle in which the participants are driven by their economic condition to act as they do. Although it is likely that these ideas are not compatible, Marxists often tend to assume that they are.

historicism. A term with many meanings, of which the three principal ones are:

1. The view that no society or period of history can be understood exclusively in terms of ideas current at the time of understanding, but that each period must be seen in terms of ideas contemporary to it. (This may be advanced as part of the general doctrine of **Verstehen,* and clearly leads to paradoxical consequences if taken to extremes: for how can I understand the conceptions of a former time except by translating them into conceptions of my own?)

2. (In the writings of *Popper.) Any belief in over-arching laws of historical development, such as those expounded by *Hegel, *Marx and *Spengler, which claim to reveal the necessity in historical processes and which have the effect of subduing or undermining the belief in human *agency and ingenuity. Popper criticizes historicism as such, arguing that it is a mask for uncritical attachment to a *totalitarian ideology, using the 'inevitability' of history as the justification for acts of tyranny and arbitrary violence. He also criticizes individual historicist theories by attempting to show that they are so phrased as to be compatible with any seemingly recalcitrant experience, and so, being irrefutable, are empty of empirical content.

3. (Especially in architectural theory, e.g. that of the early Pevsner.) The love of and *nostalgia for the culture of a previous age, and the attempt to recapture it by stylistic imitation in the absence of the social conditions which made it possible, or which gave to it the character of a sincere expression. (Thus the Gothic revival has been criticized as historicist, although it is often replied that every architectural style has begun as 'historicist' in this sense: *see* *architecture.)

historicity. Term coined by continental Marxists to refer to the fact that human institutions and human consciousness gain part of their significance from their nature as historical phenomena, developing in accordance with processes which are larger than themselves. Thus law, for example, possesses 'historicity', and any attempt to deprive it of this historicity (for instance, by describing it as an autonomous system of reasoning answerable to no external constraints) will inevitably falsify its social and political nature. (Ditto for *art, *culture, *religion.)

Hitler, Adolf (1889–1945). German statesman and Nazi leader. *See* *absolutism, *appeasement, *concordat, *culture, **Führerprinzip,* **Gleichschaltung,* *Hayek, *ideology, *myth, *national socialism, *persuasive definition, *Spengler, *sport.

Hobbes, Thomas (1588–1679). English political theorist and philosopher. A royalist, whose perception of the chaos and brutality of the Civil War, and consequent attempt to understand the conditions of peace and good government, was combined with a sceptical, largely *empiricist outlook on human knowledge and society. Hobbes wrote several political works, and his *Leviathan,* 1651, is one of the few universally recognized masterpieces of political theory (and also one of the great stylistic achievements in English). He attempted in that work to give a systematic account of *human nature, *sovereignty, *political obligation and *law, free from limitation to any particular social or political predicament. To understand sovereignty, he thought, we should first try to understand the condition of man without it. He believed in natural law, as a system of principles the validity of which all rational beings will recognize, but thought that natural law could not be enforced or obeyed in a *state of nature, which is a state of the 'war of every man against every man', since natural law has *authority, but no intrinsic *power. Security lies in a kind of *social contract, first, between men, to set up the sovereign who will command and protect them, and, perhaps derivatively, between each man severally and the sovereign power under which he places himself, and on whom he confers the power to enforce the contract with his fellows. (Although it should be noted that the sovereign is in some sense 'outside' the original contract and cannot therefore forfeit his right to obedience.) Sovereignty may be embodied in one man or in an assembly of men, but once established, it has absolute authority in making law, and can be rejected by the *subject only by an act of *rebellion which, in breaking the contract which confers supreme entitlement on the sovereign, must always amount to injustice.

The state of nature must be thought of, not as a state which precedes the institution of sovereignty, but as a state which will certainly succeed upon its dissolution. It is also a state in which sovereigns exist in relation to each other, since here too there is no overriding sovereign whose command has the force of law. The complete absence of any power that will enforce rights in a state of nature confers an absolute obligation on the subject to obey the sovereign in return for whatever rights the sovereign may guarantee. It seems then, that there can be no justification for *civil disobedience, although Hobbes somewhat inconsistently goes on to argue that there are real limits imposed on the legitimacy of state action by that natural law which, without the state, could never be upheld.

Hobbes's thought shows considerable similarity to that of *Bodin, and together they have been thought of as the supreme theorists of *absolutism, although what emerges from Hobbes – on one reading at least – is an argument which justifies government absolutely, and *limited goverment as the preferred variety. He attempted to lay bare the components of the institution of sovereignty in a manner that is certainly original, and which has often been thought to be exemplary. His principle that there can be 'no obligation on any man which ariseth not from some act of his own' introduces a great strain into his theory, however, in that it seems to suggest that all legitimacy and political obligation must eventually be traced to contract or consent. His attempt to find the basis of natural law in the inherent injustice of requiring a man to destroy his own life was influential on later thinkers – notably *Locke – but leads to obscure reasoning about all subsidiary 'natural rights'.

holism. **1**. The theory that the whole is more than the sum of its parts, exhibiting what *Hegel called the 'transition from quantity to quality'. Thus it might be argued that a society is something greater than the aggregate of individuals which composes it, since it has features, and performs actions, which cannot be attributed to any aggregate. (For example, a society has laws and institutions which outlast the individuals subject to them.)

One part of that metaphysical doctrine is the view (variously espoused by *Burke, *Hegel and certain *Marxists) that the individual acquires part of his nature from the historical totality of which he is part. Thus Robinson Crusoe, according to *Marx (*Grundrisse,* ch. 1), is not really an 'atomic' individual, but rather a personification of all the social attributes of *bourgeois economy, arbitrarily transported to an empty place. To think that his nature, aims, intentions and values, and the conception of freedom so integral to his dramatic function, could belong to him independently of the historical condition that defines him, is like thinking that the hand of a human being might have performed all its functions even though severed from the body with which it is organically united.

2. The view that, in some cases – e.g. that of organic life, perhaps that of social life – only 'holistic explanation' is possible. That is, the behaviour of each part must be explained in terms of a theory which makes essential reference to laws governing the whole.

3. A term of abuse sometimes used (e.g. by *Popper) for anti-individualistic philosophies of history, with no more precise meaning than that which can be assigned to *collectivism in its more popular sense. (*See* *individualism.)

4. The philosophical system of Jan Smuts (1870–1950), South African statesman, who emphasized the 'holistic factor' in history, in opposition to the supposed effect of individual decisions.

Clearly all of the above theories exhibit different departures from the same basic idea.

holocaust. Greek: the burning of everything. Term used by Jewish historians for the *genocide of the Jews practised by the *Nazis and named by them more euphemistically 'the final solution' (*Endlosung*).

home. *See* *household.

homosexuality. *See* *sexual conduct.

honours. The 'honours system', whereby public service is recognized through conferring an intangible benefit such as a title, membership of an order of knighthood, a medal, or some similar right to sport ribbons on one's chest and letters about one's name, is widely accepted as a necessary feature of government. In the US, however, it exists only in an attenuated form – this being regarded by some as the effect of democratic informality, by others as one of those far-reaching consequences of a *constitution which set out to remake the social world. In the UK and the USSR, by contrast, it provides one of the essential motives both for civil servants, and for all others who may attract the attention of the public.

Against the honours system it is sometimes argued that it helps to form and perpetuate distinctions of *class (which is an argument only if such distinctions are bad); that it distributes privilege inequitably; that it forms and consolidates a ruling or dominant *establishment within the state (again only an argument if that can be shown to be bad). In its favour the argument is brought that it rewards loyalty to the state with a purely symbolic entitlement, and that the desire for this symbolic recognition is both purer than the pursuit of naked power or wealth, and more immediately consonant with the continuing loyalty of the subject who has acquired it: a title, for example, being a dignity to live up to, rather than an asset to dispense.

In the UK it should be noted that honours include peerages, and hence may involve the direct gift of political *office, even as a reward for writing operas.

Hooker, Richard (1553–1600). English divine and political theorist whose *Laws of Ecclesiastical Polity*, 1593 *et seq*., contains an examination of the theoretical principles behind the idea of an established church. Hooker reinterpreted the doctrines of *natural law, and other features of the political philosophy of *Aquinas, in order to fit them for the new constitutional position of the Anglican Church. He also anticipated many arguments that were to reappear in *Locke (whom he greatly influenced), and tried to demonstrate how the secular and religious authority could be combined into a single sovereign power, while still permitting a real distinction in practice between the legitimate and illegitimate exercise of power. While the body of his work is ostensibly concerned with the organization of a church under the principles of revealed religion, it contains many important disquisitions upon political problems generally, and on the concepts of *law, *justice, and *jurisdiction.

Horkheimer, Max (1895–1973). German philosopher and social scientist. *See* *critical theory, *Frankfurt school.

hospitality. Hospitality is in many societies a sacred duty, and almost always among *nomads. It requires that food, shelter and gifts be offered to someone who is not part of the *family, or *community, simply because he finds himself temporarily in the same *household. Hospitality requires the relinquishing, passing or extending of a right of property, and anyone who argues that there should be no private property argues by implication that there should be no private hospitality. Hospitality is a form of *gift, but most gifts are not obligations. The difference presumably lies in the fact that, within the household, property is already embodied in a common right of use – 'mine', as *Hegel puts it, overreaches itself into 'ours'. Hence, to invite someone into the household is to invite him to share in a common right, and the obligation arises ceremonially to confer that right upon him.

hours of work. Ever since the radical reformers and socialists of the nineteenth century advocated the 'shortening of the working day' as the first objective of *welfare legislation, a move towards limited hours of work has become the norm in developed economies. Although some argue that it is inherent in capitalism that it will force to the limit the extraction of 'unpaid hours of labour' (*see* *surplus-value), it seems that the normal working week has settled at about forty hours in both capitalist and socialist economies (in so far as either are exemplified in the actual world) since the last war. Among the professional classes the average is higher, indicating either increased incentive, or increased sense of obligation, to work, or perhaps a function that requires hours of work beyond those contracted for.

household. With a few exceptions, recent

political theory has neglected to discuss the institutions for which 'household' is the collective name, and which exemplify a peculiar synthesis of *private and *common ownership: private in that there is a *right to exclude; common, in that this right is shared indivisibly among members whose number may be indeterminate. Along with their defences of the *family as the first locus of social existence, *Aristotle and *Hegel each argued for this specific mode of ownership, Hegel finding in it new reason for the defence of private property. The household is the forum of consumption, and its stability is integral to social and political stability. However it is formed (whether out of one family or many, as a *commune or as a nuclear family, contractually or non-contractually), its behaviour and nature will be of equal interest to both economists and political theorists. One general political characteristic of the household has been the frequent absence of any legal determination of property rights within it, the presumption of common ownership being paramount (unless expressly disavowed, e.g. by a contract ancillary to marriage). Another traditional characteristic of some significance is the *division of labour within the household (often according to sex and age), which seems to be independent of the existence of a *market. A market can exist between members of a household only by dividing the household into several.

Houses of Parliament. *See* *Parliament.

human nature. All political *doctrine must be founded in a theory of human nature, and disputes commonly reflect differences (whether or not argued) over what this nature is. Thus it seems that communism must assume that the aggressive, acquisitive, competitive and dominion-seeking feelings of men (which lead them to pursue and secure private property, status, and hegemony) are not natural, but the product of changeable social conditions. Likewise liberalism must assume that the desire for freedom is natural and fulfillable, and that its fulfilment will contribute to human happiness. Many conservatives argue as though human nature were entirely inscrutable, revealed by the actual facts of human history, but not easily describable except in terms which are either too platitudinous to found a distinctive doctrine, or too much the product of doctrine to have any universal value. It may certainly be true that the *monism of much socialist and liberal thought – the first emphasizing almost exclusively questions of ownership and control, the second those of liberty – must indicate a simplified view of the nature of the political being. But the scepticism of much conservative doctrine exemplifies a similar simplification, often emphasizing the ineffability of human things only in order to dignify its own reluctance to remedy them.

Philosophers have found a recurrent problem in the seeming duality of human nature. Human beings are organisms, obeying laws of growth and decline. They are also *rational beings, as are gods and angels. It seems difficult to resist the view that each of those attributes determines a nature or essence of the thing that possesses it. Thus there are well-known philosophical problems concerning the possibility that the organism might continue without the attributes of the rational being, or that the rational being might continue without the attributes of the organism. Is this vegetable really identical with John, the victim of the accident? And is this new body, which has all John's character, memories, intentions and thoughts, not perhaps really John, translated into a new existence? Those intuitive problems — which seem to suggest a separation between person and body – also give support to philosophical theories which define the rational agent wholly without reference to his body, either in the manner of Descartes (the 'Cartesian ego') or in the manner of *Kant (the transcendental self, which has a perspective *on* the empirical world, but no identity within it). Kant's idea of the rational being as entirely *autonomous, standing apart from the laws of empirical nature, provides the philosophical basis for the concept of autonomous choice, or choice in which the whole self is implicated. This concept is necessary in formulating the underlying values of liberalism. Hence the Kantian theory of human nature often recurs, in however transmuted a form, in modern political thinking. Followers of *Hegel object that the autonomous being of Kant is a social artifact; he should therefore be seen as the product of a political order and not as the atom from which that order is constructed. This reversal of metaphysical priorities brings about a profound shift in political focus. From this rival view of human nature the liberal standpoint is often found far less plausible. *Idealists have further criticized the political outlook of *empiricists and *utilitarians largely on account of a supposed naïvety in the vision of human nature underlying it. The deep questions aroused by that conflict remain the overt or covert subject-matter of much modern debate.

human rights. A label which is designed (a) to denote the idea of *natural rights, (b) to propagate and win sympathy for that idea in the peculiar political atmosphere of the modern world. Since the doctrine of natural rights is rehearsed and endorsed in the US constitution (following the *Virginia Declaration of Rights* of 1776), and since fairly specific rights are therein associated with it and declared to be binding, the idea of human rights has also come to be seen as an *ideological conception, behind the veil of which the interests of *international capitalism take their devious way. Human rights of a fairly standard kind (including freedom of speech, worship, and peaceful assembly) are endorsed in the UN Charter (exercised through a UN commission that can at least report on their absence, if not assure their presence), and more recently in the Helsinki Accord of 1975, which tries to use international sanctions in order to compel the respect for human rights in states not given to upholding them. Those in the USSR and its *satellites who have cited this accord in their battle for *civil liberties have found themselves savagely persecuted for doing so. While the 1977 constitution of the USSR purports to guarantee certain human rights, it adds crucially, that 'the citizens' exercise of their human rights must not harm the interests of society, the state or other individuals'.

The Helsinki agreement is interesting in that it poses a fundamental problem for the philosophy of *rights: are all rights really *freedoms, in the sense of being limitations on the acts of others? Or are some rights also duties, requiring the active provision of something not available without human effort? The first list of rights, proposed by nations of the Western alliance, followed the pattern of freedom – i.e. it consisted in a set of limitations on what the state might *do* to the citizen (e.g. arrest him arbitrarily, imprison him without trial, punish him for receiving 'forbidden' literature, and so on). The states of the Soviet bloc insisted that certain other rights should be added – notably the *right to work, which requires the state (or, if not the state, some other *agency) actively to provide opportunities, and not merely to permit things to happen. It may be doubted that such a 'positive' conception of rights is coherent; nevertheless it has proved useful in the subsequent international rhetoric.

The problems facing the defender of human rights are threefold: (a) Is the doctrine that there are natural rights defensible? (b) Which rights are natural, and which merely local? (c) Can a natural right always override a conventional (or legal) right which conflicts with or denies it? Most doctrines neglect to answer those questions and end up with lists of rights that are either too wide (e.g. the *four freedoms), or too narrow, to be universally applicable. (Consider the attempt to impose the idea of 'human rights' upon the Islamic state of Iran.) There is one human right which seems, however, to command universal assent when understood, and to precipitate the transition from *tyranny to constitutional government when upheld – the right to *due process and to the *judicial independence which that requires.

humane education. Term used since the early Renaissance to denote those subjects which were traditionally (in Roman schools of *rhetoric and their tributaries) thought to be integral to *liberal education; in its original form *studia humaniora*, 'the more human studies'. This last expression is Petrarch's, used by him to denote classical literature and scholarship, as opposed to the 'more divine' studies of theology and cosmology. Nowadays the term tends to denote those subjects which involve academic discipline, and perhaps an associated tradition of scholarship, but which do not exemplify scientific method. The scientific revolution (presaged in Bacon's *Advancement of Learning*, 1605) brought with it the view that certain subjects have a peculiar claim to objectivity, and are characterized, first, by the attempt to understand the world as an entity independent of our ways of perceiving it, secondly, by a potential for progress (since discovery is cumulative – hence the title of Bacon's work). In the absence of these two features it is very unclear how we may speak of 'method' and 'objectivity', so that the 'humanities' stand in need of defence as educational subjects. The debate surrounding them has often assumed a political dimension, partly on account of a surviving sense (associated by some with a *hegemony which dominates the traditional institutions of *education) that political and administrative advancement has often been made easier for those versed in the humanities than for those with a knowledge of science. It is often argued that this reverses the natural priorities; scientific education fits people for public life, not by giving them meretricious gifts of rhetoric, but by conferring a real understanding of the material world, and of *technology. The reply often involves a general defence of the *Geisteswissenschaften*, perhaps by attempting to represent them as more appropriate to the understanding of the human world than any natural science (*see* **Verstehen*), or by arguing, in more traditional manner, for their role in inculcating *virtue, and transmitting *culture.

humanism. **1**. The outlook, prevalent particularly in Renaissance Europe, and often summed up in the ancient apophthegm 'man as the measure of all things'. which emphasizes the human, as opposed to or at least in addition to the divine, as a centre of significance, a repository of virtue, a source of strength, purpose and discovery, and a principle of artistic, moral and political expression.

2. The modern outlook, perhaps first given rhetorical expression by Baron d'Holbach and other eighteenth-century encyclopaedists, but more characteristic of the twentieth century than of any earlier period, which emphasizes the human as the *sole* but *sufficient* source of all our *values. For humanism, the moral atheist is the type of the enlightened man, and it is by looking to the human capacities for knowledge and virtue that hope will be regenerated and the misery of the human condition overcome. Such an attitude does not usually involve militant atheism, since that would indicate too stark an intolerance towards a common human weakness, and a departure from the principle urged by Terence in the words 'Homo sum, et nihil humanum mihi alienum puto' – 'I am a man and hold nothing human alien to myself.' Nevertheless the principal opponent, for the humanist, is the man of *faith, who regards our 'fallen' condition as a self-evident fact, and human effort as worthless without the assistance of *grace.

humanitarianism. A term of vague meaning, defined by Julien Benda (*see* **trahison des clercs*) thus: 'I should like to draw a distinction between humanitarianism as I mean it here – a sensitiveness to the abstract quality of what is human, to Montaigne's "whole form of the human condition" – and the feeling which is usually called humanitarianism, by which is meant the love for human beings existing in the concrete.' Both senses, Benda affirms, are to be distinguished from *cosmopolitanism. The 'love for human beings existing in the concrete' is a vague idea, but presumably corresponds to the warm-hearted and essentially particularized love that is also known as *charity. The contrast between this concrete love and the abstract virtue of duty to one's neighbour is a familiar theme of moral thought, some (e.g. *Kant) thinking that only the abstract duty can be meritorious, others (e.g. Dostoevsky) arguing that the abstract duty is worthless and that the only thing that matters is love for the individual, here and now, no other love being true to our mortal nature. Both the abstract and the concrete love are to be distinguished from another thing known as 'humanitarian sentiment', namely, compassion towards humanity as a whole, which *Rousseau called 'le zèle compatissant' ('compassionating zeal'), and which *Nietzsche dismissed as 'slave morality'. Benda's idea perhaps corresponds to none of the familiar usages, but rather to a modern sceptical, and perhaps somewhat anguished, version of *humanism, sense 1.

Hume, David (1711–76). Scottish philosopher, historian and essayist, whose radical *empiricism has had a far-reaching influence on modern thought. His political and economic writings do not represent a substantial part of his output: nevertheless their distinctive tone and vision has often been identified, both by conservatives and by liberals, as expressing thoughts fundamental to their outlook. Hume was a Tory, and thought that this particular, historically determined political vision was both consonant with his scepticism and also commendable to common sense. His influence was not, however, confined to British conservatism: several of the *Founding Fathers of the US found inspiration in Hume's defence of *mixed government, and many nineteenth-century *utilitarians saw Hume as their intellectual ancestor. Had Rousseau taken time off from sentimental compassion for friendship, he too might have been influenced; but despite Hume's exemplary kindness, Rousseau did not find cause to extend his compassionate zeal towards this particular benefactor.

Hume attacked the doctrine of the *social contract, arguing that the criterion of *tacit consent is inapplicable, most people being inevitably constrained by cultural, linguistic and habitual ties to stay where they are, whatever the government that should exert jurisdiction over them. He also argued that the only true basis for any conception of *legitimacy or *political obligation must be *utility, thus laying foundations for the utilitarian views of political order espoused by *Bentham and *Mill. (Although it is doubtful that Hume would have been in sympathy with nineteenth-century *utilitarianism, or that he would have condoned the particular idea of utility that it employed.) Hume believed that politics, as a 'moral' science, could be deduced from the study of human nature, and that controversies would dissolve if the true structure of the human sentiments could be discerned. The principal sentiments involved in political order he identified as sympathy and benevolence, and he regarded the sentiment and idea of justice as ultimately derived from them. Justice, he thought, required the establishment and defence of private rights, principal among which was the right of private property, for which he gave a classic utilitarian defence. He defended staunchly the liberties that he associated with the British constitution as this had emerged from the 'Glorious Revolution' and its aftermath, although he was extremely doubtful that those liberties could be easily guaranteed or that a formula could be found wherein to summarize them. His own preference was for a form of mixed *republican and *monarchical government, such as he argued was exhibited in Great Britain, where the two kinds of power oppose and limit each other.

The unsystematic nature of Hume's political reflections stems from his scepticism. Used against orthodoxies, that scepticism was devastating. His writings on economics include the first serious analysis of the *balance of payments mechanism, and were highly influential on *classical theorists.

Husserl, Edmund Gustav Albert (1859–1938). German philosopher. *See* *existentialism, *phenomenology.

Huxley, Aldous (1894–1963). English novelist and critic. *See* *egalitarianism.

hyperflation. *Inflation that is so rapid as to move uncontrollably towards a radical breakdown in the monetary system, and the complete collapse of all long-term expectations concerning price, so that in a very short time money is no longer effective as a medium of exchange.

I

iconoclasm. Greek: the breaking of images, applied originally to the destruction of religious symbols and images, usually in obedience to the sentiment that to use an image in worship is to worship the image, and so be guilty of idolatry. (A sentiment which, while founded in a *non sequitur*, remains an immovable part of the nonconformist *Protestant outlook.)

The term is now used in two related senses: (i) to denote any destructive activity directed against the substance of a belief through ridiculing the symbols upon which it is nourished, and in which it finds expression; political iconoclasm is a significant modern pastime, usually severely punished in any state which relies on *government through symbols (e.g. most of the states of Eastern Europe); (ii) since icons are, by extension, ideas, to denote the assailing and ridiculing of cherished beliefs.

ideal. Any state of affairs which exists as idea and aspiration, rather than as reality, usually as an example of moral or political perfection. To possess ideals is to possess *values that are incommensurate with the actual, hence the opposite of the 'idealist' is the 'realist'. The realist tends to believe that small improvements and practical manoeuvres within the existing state of affairs may constitute true moral virtue, whereas the idealist thinks of virtue in terms of a sacrifice demanded from the agent, who must act so as to defy reality.

To have values is not necessarily to have ideals: values may be informed by a sense of the actual, and of the difficulty of moving from it. Nevertheless at least one philosopher – *Kant – has argued that all values are in effect ideals, since all values postulate not what is, but what ought to be. Through them the agent is inevitably constrained to aim at that 'kingdom of ends' in which only reason is sovereign.

ideal types. A term introduced by *Weber, roughly in order to denote social arrangements peopled by ideally rational beings. It is now used to describe theoretical models of institutions, social relations, and political systems which are 'ideal' in the sense of being construed entirely according to theoretical laws that explain them, and not according to observation of the actual world. At the same time the models are chosen so as to correspond as nearly as possible to the actual world. If there were an instance of such an ideal type in reality, then we should be able to explain *all* its features; even if there is not, however, it is hoped that the proximity of real arrangements to an ideal type will explain their *principal* features. (Examples of ideal types include, e.g., *feudalism, *capitalism, and *communism as described by *Marx; the *family as described by Hegel; the US *state as described by its *constitution.) There is a problem in the philosophy of science as to whether, and if so how, the postulation of an ideal type can really explain something that only imperfectly copies it. Is the case like that of axiomatic geometry, which, while it corresponds only roughly to the disordered lines of the perceivable world, nevertheless describes the laws which govern them? Unfortunately geometry is a descriptive science, and does not really explain why something that exemplifies its laws is as it is; the 'ideal type', however, is supposed to show *why* the actual events that mimic it develop as they do.

idealism. **1**. Metaphysical. The only things that exist (or which 'ultimately' exist) are ideas or mental entities, so that the whole structure of reality is to be understood in terms of consciousness. Thus, in Berkeley's philosophy, the world is held to consist of the infinite mind of God, the finite minds of his creatures, and the mental states ('ideas') of all of them. Berkeley is often cited as a paradigm metaphysical idealist although, from the political point of view, it is fair to say that he is without significance. The major forms of metaphysical idealism that have had political influence are those given by *Plato, *Kant, and *Hegel. Kant's 'transcendental idealism' argues that the world as known bears the imprint of the knower, so that all attempts to know the world 'as it is in itself' are empty. The one guarantee that we have of the existence of the 'thing-in-itself' comes through practical reason; hence the 'moral law' which guides practical reason is also the foundation of metaphysics. The resulting vision of the sovereignty of the moral law had profound political influence, in giving a reasoned foundation for *universalism and *natural law.

Hegel's 'objective' idealism begins from the doctrine that reason and the concepts of reason contain within themselves the seeds of knowledge: reason does not so much discover as 'posit' reality, which is a perpetually developing object of consciousness, deriving its nature from the concepts through which it is known. The development of reality is, like the development of an argument, *dialectical, and proceeds towards that absolute idea which is both the object and the subject of ultimate knowledge. The world, although it is none other than the absolute idea which knows it, is always known as *object*: so that objective reality is understood as distinct from, even though ultimately identical with, the knowing subject. The result of this thoroughgoing idealism is that, in Hegel's words, 'the real is rational and the rational real'. So that despite all appearances to the contrary, the world as object exhibits the 'cunning of reason'. This doctrine has far-reaching implications, among them:

(a) the structure of reason and its concepts is prior to that of history, so that the former explains the latter;

(b) the essence of historical processes may be concealed by their appearance, even (and especially) to the participants, who exist at a stage of rational development that does not enable them to perceive the underlying reality (it being part of reason's 'cunning' to hide itself from its progeny). (*See* *essence/appearance.)

*Historical materialism is a theory which, in its usual forms, accepts (b) (or something like it) while denying (a), the force of the word 'materialism' lying in the belief that ideas are powerless to produce events, and are at best the product of them. (a) and (b) are characteristic only of Hegel's idealism, and not, for example, of Plato's or Kant's. The underlying metaphysic is remarkable for its attempt to reconcile the two ideas contained in (a) and (b) – i.e. that the fundamental stuff of the world is consciousness, and that consciousness itself remains only imperfectly conscious of the world.

Sometimes, when *Marxists use the term 'idealist', they mean to refer to any theory which rejects the thesis that 'life determines consciousness, not consciousness life', whether or not that theory involves the metaphysical commitment here identified as the defining feature of idealism. (Thus *Gramsci is sometimes called an idealist, since the Gramscian theory of hegemony attributes to the consciousness of a ruling class a large role in securing its ascendancy.) This usage is not really respectable, since what is meant can be said in another way, and the controversy referred to is saturated with dead philosophical arguments. (*See also* *materialism.)

2. Moral and political idealism. The pursuit of, and unwillingness to renounce *ideals of conduct, even when present reality conflicts with them, and even when their future realization seems unlikely or impossible, perhaps with a reluctance to believe in that impossibility. In international affairs idealists are often contrasted with *realists, the former seeing international relations at least partly in terms of moral precepts, justice, trust and obligation, the latter seeing them only in terms of power.

identity. Normally used, in political contexts, to denote not the relation which everything bears to itself, but rather self-identification. Only conscious beings or things which contain conscious beings as members, such as societies, states, clubs and institutions, have identity. An institution has an identity, when the members are able not only to distinguish it from other institutions, but also to convey its distinctive character in words, gestures and practice, so as to reassure themselves that it *should* exist and that they have reason to belong to it. Thus the emergence of a 'national identity' involves a growing sense among people that they belong naturally together, that they share common interests, a common history, and a common destiny. The search for an 'identity' in this sense is a major political motive.

ideology. Term coined by the French philosopher Destutt de Tracy in 1795, to denote the general science of ideas, which was to clarify and improve the public mind. Given currency by the rhetoricians of the French Revolution (*les idéologues*), by Napoleon, and by *Marx, the term developed in many directions and now has two principal and partly conflicting significances:

1. Any systematic and all-embracing political *doctrine, which claims to give a complete and universally applicable theory of man and society, and to derive therefrom a programme of political action. An ideology in this sense seeks to embrace everything that is relevant to man's political condition, and to issue doctrine whenever doctrine would be influential in forming or changing that condition. Most things taught in the name of *Marxism are ideology, and it is sometimes said that *totalitarian government – as opposed to 'liberal democracy' – stands in need of ideology to justify its endless intrusion into personal existence. Ideology is the principal object of much conservative criticism (e.g. that given by *Oakeshott), largely on the grounds that political doctrine, if possible at all, is not detachable from the particular circumstances in which it is conceived, and can never be given the universal, all-embracing character to which ideology aspires.

2. In Marxist and *Marxian theories 'ideology' denotes any set of ideas and values which has the social function of consolidating a particular economic order, and which is explained by that fact alone, and not by its inherent truth or reasonableness. (*See* *functional explanation.) The function of ideology is to *naturalize the **status quo*, and to represent as immutable features of human nature the particular social conditions which currently persist. Ideology wins support for class rule, by persuading oppressed classes to accept the descriptions of reality which render their subordination 'natural'. It therefore has three principal functions: to legitimate, to mystify, and to console.

It is a part of classical Marxism to argue that ideology is necessary only under certain social conditions (specifically those of feudalism and capitalism) and that, with the coming of communism, the veil of ideology will be torn aside: society and human nature will at last be perceived as they really are. One of the problems faced by such a theory is this: how do we, who do not exist in that ideal or future state, distinguish the ideological from the non-ideological among our beliefs? If we cannot make the distinction, how do we know that we are not, in all our social beliefs (including, say, the belief in communism), victims of a *false consciousness? One answer to those questions is contained in the doctrine of *praxis.

As examples of ideology Marxists have offered the beliefs of *bourgeois economics, together with religion (which partly explains the connection with sense

1.), moral systems which enshrine the sanctity of contract and promise (and which thereby consolidate the market economy of capitalism), art which dignifies the dominance of a ruling class (such as neo-classical architecture, most fervently propagated in our time by Hitler and Stalin).

immigration. The entrance into an alien country of people who intend permanently to reside there. The introduction of immigration controls into the law of most modern states has accompanied an increased possibility of movement between states. The traditional idea (given philosophical importance by *Locke in his theory of political obligation) that the freedom to emigrate is a necessary condition of legitimate government is still upheld in the law of most Western countries; but the freedom to immigrate, having no such doctrinal basis, is equally often denied there. Henry Sidgwick upheld it in the name of a liberal sentiment that was avowedly *universalist and *cosmopolitan: 'the business [of government] is to maintain order over the particular territory which historical causes have appropriated to it, but not in any way to determine who is to inhabit the territory, in order to restrict the enjoyment of its natural advantages to any particular portion of the human race' (*Elements of Politics*, 1891). To which the reply may be made that it is unlikely that 'historical causes' should mark out a territory for government without also marking out a people to be governed. *Nationalist philosophies of the state go further, arguing that some measure of ethnic and social unity is the precondition of government. On this view a state is possible only where there is customary conformity over a large area of social life.

To some extent this nationalist sentiment is falsified by the experience of America, which, being a society entirely constructed by immigrants, developed laws and institutions which made immigration acceptable. (A comparable example is provided by Brazil.) These led to the creation of a highly supple *federal structure. Ever new waves of immigrants have been able to settle and to recognize the binding character of the *jurisdiction. It is no doubt unwise, however, to generalize from this system of government. Perhaps the situation in the US should be compared with that in the USSR where, in order to force acceptance of a unitary state on what was nominally (but only nominally) a federation of autonomous regions, forced migration was resorted to, so as to remove the motive for *secession.

In the nation states of Europe immigration, in particular from other continents, has become an acknowledged political problem. Some argue that the aversion to it is largely a species of *xenophobia or even *racism, and that the European states (especially the UK) are obligated by their colonial past to overcome those feelings. Others argue, either in the spirit of nationalism, or more pragmatically, in terms of limitation of resources, that unrestricted immigration is a social ill. The West German and French laws, which in effect permit the temporary importation followed by the forced expulsion of cheap labour, are often held up as typifying the kind of exploitation that underlies immigration controls, although how one could persuade the present population of a state to accept immigration on terms that are not to its own advantage is a problem which such objections do little to overcome.

impeachment. Broadly, a criminal accusation brought in a *legislative body. It is not the same as removal from office, but is more like a criminal indictment. In the UK, US, France and almost all South American states the function of accusation is vested in the lower house of the legislature and the function of trial and sentence in the upper house.

The ancient Greek *eisangelia*, whereby a citizen could be brought before the public assembly and accused of misconduct in public office, closely resembled impeachment. Its use in the UK was discredited by the impeachment of Warren Hastings, 1788, and has been rendered largely obsolete by the doctrine of ministerial responsibility and by *administrative law. It remains an important power of the US Congress, although the constitution provides that 'judgement shall not extend further than removal from office, and disqualification to hold and enjoy office of honour, trust or profit under the US'. Impeachment can be directed against the President, the Vice-President, the federal judiciary and federal officials, and provides a major constitutional limitation to *executive power, as was abundantly illustrated in the case of President Nixon. It has been used in all only thirteen times since Congress was established, but persists as the symbolic and effective expression of the sovereignty of Congress in a state which vests supreme executive power not in Congress but in a President.

The power to impeach has been frequently defended by advocates of *limited government. Perhaps the first important exposition of the reasoning behind this view occurs in *Machiavelli (*Discourses on the First Decade of Titus Livy*, I, VIII).

imperfect competition (or: monopolistic competition). A technical term of economic theory, denoting a *market in which there are many firms whose outputs are close but not perfect substitutes, either because there is 'product differentiation' (differences of brand name, social appearance, etc.) or geographical fragmentation of the market. Since the products are not homogeneous one firm may raise its prices relative to its competitors without losing all its sales, so that its 'demand curve' (which relates price per unit to quantity sold) is downward sloping, rather than horizontal as in *perfect competition. The theory of imperfect competition, developed in the 1930s by E. H. Chamberlin and Joan Robinson, is an important part of the modern analysis of markets.

imperial preference. An economic doctrine, canvassed by Joseph Chamberlain in 1897, according to which British dominions and colonies were to be given economic preference through *protection, largely by imposing high tariffs on imports from outside the colonial network. Running counter to the *free trade dogma of the time, this doctrine received no support until the Depression. Analogous policies have been instigated by a variety of imperial powers, most recently by the USSR through the institutions of *Comecon.

imperialism. The extension of power through conquest, or the pursuit of 'empire', i.e. of a global influence so dominant as to amount to virtual *sovereignty wherever it is successful. Empire was advocated in the UK in the 1880s by Joseph Chamberlain, in opposition to the 'Little Englanders' who favoured a policy of *isolationism. Chamberlain argued that the expanding influence of France and Germany must be counterbalanced by the expanding influence of the UK. This defence facilitated the once fashionable economic analysis of imperialism as a search for captive markets, offered in 1902 by J. A. Hobson, who criticized imperialism as a form of *exploitation. The criticism was taken up by *Lenin, who in *Imperialism as the Highest State of Capitalism*, 1917, argued that imperialism is an economic necessity for the capitalist economy, in order to overcome the otherwise inevitable *falling rate of profit that spells its doom. (Lenin was thus able to explain why Marx's prediction of a falling rate of profit had not been fulfilled.) Imperialism is the last state since it leads to international competition in order to secure markets and exploit resources, and hence to 'imperialist war'. This, as Lenin later thought was demonstrated by the emergence of the Russian Revolution from the chaos of the First World War, creates the conditions for the seizure of power by the international proletariat.

Lenin's theory has provided support for the claim that innocent-seeming gestures on the part of capitalist powers are nevertheless expressions of imperialism (or at any rate 'neo-imperialism'). This complaint was given theoretical elaboration by K. Nkrumah (1909–72) in *Neo-Colonialism, The Last Stage of Imperialism*, 1965. However, armed invasion by communist powers is also part of the international role of the Communist Party, in offering assistance to the proletariat everywhere. Hence the term 'imperialist' has, in communist rhetoric, acquired a very distinctive and misleading flavour. Thus social and economic *influence from capitalist countries may be called imperialism, while military *coercion from communist countries is usually called liberation. *See also* *colonialism, *Lenin.

implied powers. Powers of the US President and Congress implied but not specified by the constitution, specifically by virtue of the clause (Art. 1, s. 8) giving power to make 'all laws which shall be necessary and proper for carrying into execution the foregoing powers, and all other powers vested by this constitution in the Government of the United States, or in any Department or Office thereof'. Initially controversial, this clause has since been widely used to extend the powers of government.

impossibility theorems. *See* *Arrow's theorem, *Paretian liberal.

incentive. The expected benefit which induces someone to incur a *cost, especially a labour cost. The theory of incentives is an important part of the controversy between defenders of capitalist and socialist modes of production, it being argued in favour of capitalism that it alone is compatible with a realistic view of human inducements. The socialist reply often argues that, under new socialist conditions, a new human nature will emerge (*see* *new man), and that 'moral' and 'collective' incentives will then be stronger than their 'material' and 'individual' counterparts.

income. The flow of money, goods and services accruing to a particular economic unit (individual, household, group or shareholder) over a period of time, or the flow of money with which the economic unit acquires the flow of goods and services. (Hence the distinction between *real and money income). Income is an important concept in modern economics, and it is often argued that much economic behaviour is to be explained in part by the attempt to maximize income, and that limits on income constrain consumption. The theory of what determines the aggregate flow of income within the economy forms an important part of *macroeconomics, largely pioneered by *Keynes, and now one of the major areas in which economic thinking influences political policy. According to the Keynesian theory the rate of production of goods and services, and hence the level of *national income, is determined – to put it simply – by the level of *aggregate demand, which is in turn dependent partly on the level of income (a mutual dependence known as the 'circular flow of income') and partly on the prevailing rate of *interest. Hence the factors determining the rate of interest become important in the theory of income determination. Among these factors the *money supply is often considered to be particularly important. Keynesians, however, tend to emphasize the role of government expenditure in raising aggregate demand by more direct and efficacious means.

income and capital. Much discussion of the politics of *distribution focuses upon the relative merits of redistributing *capital and *income, usually in the name of some egalitarian ideal. In the USSR, where enormous inequalities of income are normal – some say despite, others say because of, the fact that the state is, in the end, the single important employer – private capital *accumulation is nevertheless severely limited, so that all capital greater than a certain amount (specified by the requisites of a comfortable household) must be surrendered to the state. In practice corruption has made this legal provision ineffective; however, its intention is clear: the only major holder of capital must be the state, otherwise *private property in the means of production might arise. The level of income, meanwhile, can be allowed to rise as high as is necessary to provide incentives, provided that all income is spent in *consumption, and none is saved. By contrast, many *capitalist countries permit vast accumulations of capital, but tend to limit inequalities of income, usually by progressive *taxation. It has been argued that the process of *collective bargaining has tended to close the gap between the income of the work force and that of the owners of capital.

income effect. The effect which a change in the price of a good has on a consumer's demand for it, by way of the change induced in his *real income. Thus, if the price of *x* drops by 10p a unit, someone who is used to buying ten units of *x* a week finds his real income increased by £1 per week because he could continue to spend his income as before and still have £1 left over. The quantity of *x* purchased may rise, e.g. because *x* is something which the consumer wants more of than he could previously afford. Alternatively, it may fall, e.g. because *x* was an 'inferior good', destined to be replaced as soon as more real income becomes available to spend on better things. Thus the income effect might be positive, zero, or (less commonly) negative. The *substitution effect, via the change induced in relative prices, is, however, always negative. The combined effect is usually that price and quantity demanded are inversely related. (But *see* *Giffen goods.)

income tax. *See* *taxation.

incomes policy (or: prices and incomes policy). A policy for controlling (and in practice usually restraining) *prices and *incomes in money terms, usually in order to achieve stability in the former and so to control *inflation. Such a policy seeks to control prices directly, and not by regulating the *money supply, or *aggregate demand. The hope is to preserve the balance of the economy intact as far as possible, and so to control inflation without precipitating *unemployment.

The wisdom of such a policy is disputed. However, the relative concreteness of the practice, together with its intelligibility, has led to the temporary imposition of an incomes policy by several postwar governments in the UK and the US. Many economists continue to argue that the objectives of stable prices, full employment and economic growth are, in the end, incompatible. It is debated whether temporary incomes policies can have more than temporary effects, and whether an incomes policy can be made permanent. (*See* *Keynes, *monetarism.)

incorporation. **1**. The creation of a *corporation – i.e. an *association which is a distinct legal entity, with *rights, *duties, and *agency of its own.

2. The doctrine of 'incorporation' in law holds that *international law is part of the law of a state only if made so by domestic enactment.

incrementalism. Term used to denote policy-making that settles always on small circumscribed objectives, while remaining as sensitive as possible to influences from existing policies and decisions. Thus C. E. Lindblom writes (*The Policy-Making Process*, 1968): 'usually – though not always – what is feasible politically is policy only incrementally, or marginally, different from existing policies'. Nevertheless this approach may be not only necessary, but also beneficial, since it concentrates the mind on what is knowable, not only theoretically, but also practically, and thus enables the policy-maker to estimate the effects of any particular decision. Lindblom cites, as an example, the practice of the Anti-trust Division of the Department of Justice, in extending laws controlling mergers and prices.

independence. **1**. The ability of a *state to exercise *rights of *government in its own *territory without encroaching on the rights of other states: an essential condition for the recognition of a state as a distinct legal *person in *international law. Independence implies that no other state has the legal right to interfere in the internal affairs of the state which possesses it, whether directly or indirectly.

2. Freedom from dependence – economic, military or political – on any other power. In this sense (*de facto* independence rather than *de jure*), no state has total independence, and independence is always a matter of degree.

index (or: index number). A number which gives a synthetic 'average' level or value of a set of related items, used particularly to show changes over time, e.g. of the prices of different commodities, or the outputs of different industries. If the various items whose behaviour is thus aggregated show distinct tendencies over time, then the economist is faced with a statistical problem in determining how to encapsulate their economic behaviour in a single figure. This is the 'index number problem', which arises whenever different factors have to be weighed against each other, and a choice of mean has to be made.

indexation. The linking of a monetary obligation to the price level, so that the former changes in proportion to the latter. Thus the indexation of pensions to the level of prices means that their real value will not be affected by the level of inflation at the time of their receipt. Some economists consider that the indexation of all monetary obligations helps to reduce expectations of inflation, and so contributes to the control of inflation. By the operation of English *common law the indexation of damages in civil action seems to be automatic; in Brazil (e.g.) indexation of *all* monetary obligations is obligatory. Indexation can be partial, as in the Italian *scala mobile* for the indexation of wages.

indifference curve. A theoretical construct much used in economics. An individual is indifferent between two bundles of goods if he regards each as being at least as good as the other. On a graph of commodities demanded, a curve can then be drawn connecting the graphical representation of these points of 'indifference'. For example, if five apples and eight oranges were regarded as neither better nor worse than six apples and six oranges, then these figures determine two points on an indifference curve. The properties ascribed to these curves will reflect assumptions about the psychology of consumers. For example, an assumption that the curves are continuous implies that the consumer is always willing to receive a quantity of one of the goods as an exact compensation for some reduction in the quantity of the other. (*See also* *preference.)

The device of the indifference curve can be extended beyond economics in order to give theoretical representations of problems in morality and politics, where commitments to distinct values are in issue. In morality it is often objected that values cannot be seriously weighed against each other by the moral agent, who, when asked to choose between respect for life and respect for liberty, say, may find himself in a dilemma, but not in a resoluble dilemma, since the two goods may not be commensurate. In politics, however, where it might be argued that responsibilities fall less directly, the economist's indifference curve may be a useful device. Thus a government may be indifferent between 90% employment and 10% inflation on the one hand, and 95% employment and 20% inflation on the other. The construction of an indifference curve will then be significant, on the assumption that employment and inflation vary together.

indirect rule. A system of *colonial government by *delegation of power to indigenous institutions, modified so as to conform to the legal and constitutional requirements of the metropolitan government. Introduced into Nigeria by Lord Lugard in 1898, and thereafter widely imitated, notably by the USSR.

individualism. **1**. The attitude which sees the individual human person, his rights, and his needs, as taking precedence over all collectives (whether family, corporation, civil society or state), in moral and political decision-making. Usually justified by the basic theory that only individuals have rights (or, at any rate, only individuals have natural rights): the attribution of rights to a collective being simply a way of summarizing the rights held by individuals by virtue of their membership of it. Important modern defenders of this kind of individualism include *Nozick and (probably) *Rawls.

2. The more metaphysical position that the individual human person may exist apart from any social arrangement, and is therefore intelligible, in principle, independently of society. On this view all *social facts are complex facts about individuals, societies themselves being nothing more than constructs out of the individual people who compose them. (*See* *reductionism.) Even *institutions – such as the law, and the state – are thought to have no reality independently of the individuals who compose them, and so play no constitutive part in the nature of those individuals.

A characteristic individualistic doctrine is that of liberal individualism, which argues that the state must be seen as a system of constraints on the activities of the individual, justifiable only in so far as it protects his freedoms and rights, society being a voluntary association of individuals, which may be renounced by any of them by a simple change of mind. Only in this way, the liberal individualist argues, will we see the true basis of political obligation.

Anti-individualists tend to argue that the individual human being may indeed exist outside society, but the same is not true of the individual human *person,* since the essence of the person is social. This doctrine of 'social essence' has not always been put quite as clearly as that (*see,* for a particularly confused, but influential version, *species-being). It claims that the person – the bearer of rights – is (i) a product of social and institutional arrangements, and (ii) able to flourish only in the appropriate social conditions. It is therefore wrong to think that individuals can be understood without reference to the social relations in which they participate. Moreover, in an important sense, institutions might have to be considered as prior to individuals, and so no more to be thought of as aggregates of individuals than organisms are to be thought of as aggregates of cells.

Individualism is central to many liberal and *Enlightenment doctrines, while anti-individualism is an important component, both of idealist doctrines of the state (notably *Hegel's), and of certain forms of *Marxism, the latter often objecting to the attempt to divorce, in thought, the individual from the *production relations which determine his social nature. (*See* *bourgeois economics, *holism.)

3. 'Methodological individualism'. The attempt to study society and social facts while making as little reference as possible to institutions and 'social wholes', and exploring instead the actions, intentions etc., of individual men.

indoctrination. 'Indoctrination' does not mean the transmission of *doctrine, nor even *education that has the transmission of doctrine as its ultimate purpose, but rather the inducement of specific beliefs and attitudes (which may lack system, cogency, or any other ingredient thought to be necessary to doctrine) by methods that are not genuinely educational, and which involve the abrogation of reason and intellectual autonomy on the part of the recipient. All education leads to the acquisition of at least some irrational beliefs; hence we cannot distinguish genuine education from its false substitute in terms of the end result but only in terms of the method used. Not respecting the autonomy of the recipient, indoctrination prevents the exercise of those rational faculties that it purports to develop; either the recipient remains sceptical of what he is told, or he believes it simply as *dogma. Indoctrination is designed to induce beliefs, whether or not they are true; to the extent that someone knows he is being indoctrinated, to that extent will he cease to believe what he is told without independent evidence.

industrial action. Term orginally used by the French *syndicalists in order to denote action located in the centre of production (the factory) designed to force the transfer of ownership from management to the *trade union. The term is now used more widely, to signify any form of strike, go-slow, or unilateral constraint on the part of the work force, designed to compel the other side (management, capitalist or the state) to comply with certain demands. These demands will include anything from a change in terms and conditions of work, to a change in government policy (increasingly, whether or not the state is in fact party to the wage contract, it being assumed that the state can be compelled to join any dispute in which the national interest is at stake). The object may also be more personal, such as the exclusion of a particular worker from the work force, for whatever reason (but *see* *industrial law). Action is 'official' if instigated or recognized by the appropriate trade union, otherwise 'unofficial'.

The following now form standard parts of the repertoire of industrial action: strike, in which the work force joins together to withdraw labour; secondary strike, in which other work forces do likewise in order to prevent alternative modes of production or distribution; general strike, in which some large section of the entire work force of a state withdraws its labour, either to enforce a demand on the part of some section of it, or else to enforce a demand on the part of the whole; picketing, whereby workers attempt both to announce their action, and to persuade others neither to enter the place of work, nor in any other way to behave so as to make the action nugatory; secondary picketing, in which workers from one place of work picket another place whose productive activities thwart or hamper the aims of their action.

All the above are permitted, with qualifications, by UK statute, even though they all amount to *conspiracy in *common law. However, it is established that no industrial action must be such as to constitute a 'breach of the peace', a rule which makes much picketing ineffective. US labour law, which has provided the model for much legislation (including that in the UK), has evolved during the present century, from a situation in which industrial action was almost invariably frustrated by the courts, through the granting of *injunctions, to one in which most common varieties of industrial action are permitted, circumscribed and controlled by statute. The famous Taft-Hartley Act 1947, enacted after Congress had overridden a presidential *veto, was much criticized by the trade unions, in that it attempted to define and make illegal certain types of 'unfair labour practice' and so to assert the rights of an individual against his union. It has been subject to amendments, but its provisions remain, so that the US law is now thought to be more biased in favour of management than is the UK law. Needless to say this is an area of great legal and constitutional intricacy, for which it is impossible to envisage a universal solution that might be applied regardless of the nature and constitution of the state as a whole.

industrial army. Term sometimes used to refer to the work force as a whole. Also 'industrial reserve army', a term used by *Marx to refer to the mass of dispossessed peasantry which, according to the theory of *primitive accumulation, was created in the early period of *capitalism and lay always ready to fill any place of work in exchange for the means of subsistence, and also (by parity of reasoning), to the mass of the *unemployed whose need would constantly force down the price of labour to the minimum required for the reproduction of *labour power.

Industrial Christian Fellowship. An *Anglican mission founded in 1918 to present Christian faith to industrial workers, and also to relate its theory and practice to the conditions of *factory production.

industrial democracy. Industrial production in which workers, whether or not they have ownership of the means of production, at any rate exert *control over it, by participating in the decisions governing its management. (*See further* *collective choice, *democracy, *democratization.) Workers may participate directly, through voting at the crucial decisions, or indirectly, through representatives (who may in turn be officers of a *trade union). The usual form of participation contemplated is one in which workers sit in a representative capacity on the board of directors of the firm, so taking part in all executive decisions. But a variety of other practices could be devised, each of which might equally be called 'industrial democracy'.

In favour of industrial democracy (with or without private property in the means of production) the following arguments are often urged: it serves to identify the interests of the work force more closely with those of the company, and so increases the motive of labour; it removes the antagonism between labour and management, who can perceive more clearly their common interest; it awakens an interest in the end of production in the worker who had otherwise seen himself only as a means; it promises some relief from *alienation, perhaps by virtue of that last feature. Arguments offered against the arrangement are similarly various: it is said to violate the right of property, by vesting too much control in people who have neither ownership nor an interest in ownership (*see* *separation of ownership and control); it paralyses the firm by electing on to its board of directors workers who have no expertise in management; it *politicizes the wage contract, and puts the directors of the firm at the mercy of a trade union which may have no interest in the firm's survival; it exaggerates the antagonism between labour and management by acquainting the first with the superior position of the second; it perpetuates the subjection of the worker through creating a new illusion of interest in the machine that exploits him. And so on.

industrial law. Not a distinct branch of law, but a name for all those aspects of law which deal with industrial relations and disputes, with the formation and conduct of *trade unions, and with the dealings between employer and employee concerning hours of work, wages, and conditions of employment. Some 'industrial legislation' is in fact *factory legislation, which concerns not the specific contracts of employment, or the apparatus involved in forming, disputing or amending them, but those general conditions of work regarded as legally and politically acceptable.

Attempts to introduce law governing disputes between labour and management have been characteristic of modern *constitutionalist tendencies in government. These have abhorred disputes which, while ostensibly arising under contracts, are in fact irresoluble by the law of contract, and so resolve themselves through *confrontation rather than *adjudication. Some have seen practices such as the *closed shop, and certain forms of *industrial action such as secondary picketing and sympathetic strikes, as already containing elements of lawlessness, independently of any violent or anarchic use to which they might be put. At the same time it seems that trade unions cannot possibly carry out their appointed task – which, on one interpretation at least, is that of giving to their members sufficient collective power to redress the balance of the wage contract against a class that must otherwise necessarily exploit the labourer – without acting in ways that the law of contract could not countenance. Thus already in the UK Trade Disputes Act 1906 unions were granted large privileges and immunities from legal liability in respect of actions done 'in the course of or in contemplation of' an industrial dispute. The principle of such immunity remains fundamental to UK industrial law. Two justifications might be offered for this. One is the radical *left argument, that law is a *bourgeois artifact designed to conceal the *class struggle and to uphold the **status quo*, so it is better to take that struggle out of the realm of law altogether by a declaration of immunity: this argument might also be used by someone of the *right, in order to argue for immunities granted by law rather than those seized by power, so that the artifact of a *rule of law may endure, even in this area of near open conflict. The other justification refers to the particular nature of the wage contract, pointing out the extent to which it determines the life and livelihood of the labourer who sells his entire productive powers to another, and the inevitable element of *coercion introduced by this, the idea of a free contract becoming very like a legal fiction.

Industrial tribunals were established in the UK in 1964, to deal with complaints in the first instance arising under matters covered by industrial legislation – e.g. unfair dismissal. These have given additional credence to the view that industrial law is only nominally a branch of the law of contract, and is really a new and developing branch of the law, analogous to family law, which has grown up in response to a new and only partly contractual relation between people. The call to make the relation between employer and employee no more easily severable than that between husband and wife may be seen as a desire to inject into the relations of production what Disraeli called the 'feudal principle'. At least it shows an awareness that the capitalist relations of production involve just the same element of 'unfree obligation' that attached to the feudal relations. In this way it could be seen as an objective of modern radical conservatism to define a new status for industrial law, so as to endorse the popular sentiment that the relation governed by it is not, or ought not to be, contractual.

industrial revolution. The introduction into many branches of manufacturing industry of innovations in technique (originally machinery, steam power, railways, etc.), which occurred in Britain during 1760–1860, and which is called a *revolution because of the radical social transformation that it precipitated. (The phrase originated in France, and was used in order to compare the industrial revolution with the French Revolution.) The phenomenon fascinated subsequent political theorists, largely because it seems to demonstrate the demonic force of economic transformation, which precipitates changes in every aspect of social and political life. The industrial revolution involved demographic restructuring, changes in communications, in style of life, in obligations and relationships, in religion and morality, and in the nature of political institutions. It also created, or seemed to create, a new alignment of classes, and a new class antagonism. It was probably this, as much as the history of the French Revolution, that led to the Marxist analysis of society in terms of *base and superstructure, and to the theory of revolution that found the true determinants of revolutionary transformation in the economic base, rather than in the institutions that rest upon it. Modern historians tend to dispute the Marxist claim that the industrial revolution led to a fall in the standard of living for industrial workers, although all agree that the experience of the industrial revolution is one of the most important factors in the emergence of the working class as a political force.

English conservatives of the nineteenth century tended to argue that political adjustments could in fact ensure legal and social continuity even through this transformation, and Disraeli, in his famous 'One Nation' doctrine, perhaps gave the most politically effective expression to that idea. The adjustments in franchise, property law, and parliamentary institutions that were thereby made have often been thought to be instrumental in preventing true social revolution in the UK, a fact which is sometimes regarded as providing a challenge to the doctrine of base and superstructure, or alternatively as illustrating the supple quality of class hegemony.

Later industrial revolutions include that in Germany beginning in the 1860s and 1870s, and that which, on some accounts, is being experienced throughout the modern world as a result of 'microchip technology'. *See* *technology.

industrialism. The advocacy and pursuit of *industrialization. It is a strong element in those socialist theories which claim to have a scientific foundation that industrialization, even though it involves the evils of *detail labour and the separation of the labourer from the product of his labour, is a necessary condition of the material advance without which all such evils will not be overcome. (Complete industrialization not being an evil, since it will involve mastery of the mechanical process that presently seems to master us.) Some romantic conservatives – notably *Carlyle and *Coleridge – condemned industrialism, not only because of its blindness to the dehumanizing effects of *factory production, but more particularly because of its erosion of natural bonds of attachment between man and man and between man and place. It was always a challenge for such thinkers to build their criticism into creative politics, and to offer a vision of the future that would not be merely pastoral.

industrialization. The process whereby production becomes, not necessarily industrious, but industrialized – e.g. centres of *factory production arise, in which every kind of machine is involved in the production process, and new conditions of work created, together with the population demanded by those conditions. Many early critics of capitalism took as their starting point the miseries of the labourer under industrialization, although, since industrialization is not only compatible with social ownership, but also actively pursued by regimes which profess social ownership as their aim, such criticisms are no longer fashionable. The social effects of rapid industrialization have often been studied – in particular the growth of large centres of production such as the English Victorian cities, the depopulation of the countryside, and the rapid erosion of all traditional bonds based on a sense of place and natural *piety, under the impulse of the new *mobility of labour.

Industrialization does not necessarily mean factory production: there can be industrialization in agriculture also, where the principal features are the growth of the farm, the use of ever larger and more efficient machinery, the breaking down of small fields and hedgerows, and the rationalization of crops.

infiltration. Used either of the clandestine movement of an army into territory occupied by an opponent, or else of the clandestine entry into a party, institution or faction, by agents of some opposing force. A specifically modern form of infiltration, interesting both for its theory and for its results, is *entryism.

inflation. The state of an economy in which prices are steadily rising, resulting in a steady fall in the value of money. Theories of its cause are often (at least since *Keynes) divided into 'cost-push' and 'demand-pull' theories. The first attributes inflation to increased costs of production independently of the state of demand. Thus if there were a general difficulty in obtaining some essential commodity, or if trade unions acted in concert to push up the level of wages without guaranteeing any corresponding increase in productivity, this would automatically increase costs of production. Critics of the theory argue that the wage demands of trade unions are not so much a cause as an effect of inflation; such critics may espouse the 'demand-pull' theory, which holds that inflation is created by an excess of demand over the total of goods and services, at constant prices, independently of supply conditions. *Monetarism is such a theory, arguing that inflation results to a great extent from governments increasing the supply of money, perhaps with the aim of increasing the level of demand.

Emphasis on demand-pull inflation partly explains the fashionable call to governments to cut public spending, while emphasis on cost-push partly explains the call for incomes policies. (Although, in both cases, views about the relation between government spending and *unemployment are highly influential.) On all these subjects *see* *Keynes, *monetarism, *price control.

The bad effects of inflation are variously identified: the possibility of *hyperflation, and the consequent collapse of the monetary system; the arbitrary and unplanned redistribution of income, e.g. away from those, such as pensioners, with incomes that are not indexed; the possible discouraging of saving and *investment, and the consequent exacerbation of the disparity between demand and supply; the deleterious effects on the *balance of payments, the exchange rate, and international trade; and so on. Virtually no political thinker welcomes inflation (unless he also welcomes political instability, say because it prepares the way for *revolution), and modern governments seem to be united in the determination to reduce it. However, because of its redistributive effect it may be favoured by those (notably borrowers and mortgagees) who seek to gain from it, and these may constitute a group sufficiently large and powerful effectively to resist policies designed to counter inflation.

It should be noted that, perhaps because the two rival explanations given are (rightly or wrongly) often associated respectively with defences of private property and social ownership, the discussion of the issue reaches further than questions of economics. Even there, it will tend to take into account the phenomenon of unemployment, since many theories seem to accept that employment and inflation rise together, so that the ideal of full employment and stable prices may be impossible to achieve. (*See* *Phillips curve.)

inflationary gap. The gap between *aggregate demand and aggregate supply which precipitates demand-pull *inflation.

influence. One of the basic concepts of political science but, like many such concepts, extremely difficult to define. It is left undefined in international law, and although municipal law makes use of such concepts as 'undue influence' it is usually assumed that an intuitive understanding of the idea will suffice. The major problems concern the relations and distinctions between influence and *control, *force, *coercion, *interference, and *power. As defined in this dictionary, influence is a *form* of power, distinct, however, from control, coercion, force and (probably) interference. It involves affecting the conduct of another through giving reasons for action short of threats; such reasons may refer to his advantage, or to moral or benevolent considerations, but they must have weight for him, so as to affect his decision. The influenced agent, unlike the agent who is coerced, acts freely. He may choose to ignore those considerations which influence him, and he may himself exert control over the influencing power.

As illustrations of the vital distinction between influence and control, consider the following two cases: the USSR claims that Eastern Europe is a *sphere of influence. However, it *seems* to be a 'sphere of control', in that the USSR can dictate a vast number of key political decisions within that sphere. Again *democratic centralism is said to be democratic because the people can influence all decisions; the Western theory of constitutional democracy tends to assume that influence is not enough: the people must exert some control over political decisions, for example by being able to eject a representative from office. The theory of *representation and *election is therefore a theory not of popular influence but of popular control.

infrastructure. Literally an underpinning, or substructure; now used in three separate contexts in diverging ways:

1. Economics. The infrastructure of a state denotes underlying capital *accumulations, embodied in such things as roads, communications systems, and other capital items, including, on some accounts, such intangibles as *education and *law.

2. Military theory. The infrastructure of an army or military zone consists in bases, installations and so on, which support and supply the military activities of the soldiers that make use of them.

3. In politics. Sometimes the word 'infrastructure' is used to denote the *base of social institutions, in the context of a *Marxian or analogous theory of their economic determination. Some also refer to 'ideological infrastructure', meaning to imply that, even in the realm of *ideology, there are more fundamental beliefs, values and perceptions, which connect together to support transient and fragile superstructures of thought and feeling.

injunction. A remedy, granted by courts on application from a plaintiff who stands to be injured by some action or inaction, whereby the courts order someone to refrain from doing (restrictive injunction) or to do (mandatory injunction) the thing in question. The remedy was not available in *common law, which is applied only *after* misdemeanour and never before it; however it is a long-standing principle of *equity that, in cases where injury would be irreparable, continuous and inadequately remedied by damages, the courts have power to grant an injunction. They may also grant such ancillary relief (including damages) as is appropriate and just, but, because the remedy is equitable, they will also look to the conduct of the parties in deciding whether an injunction should be granted (i.e. the 'maxims of equity' apply).

Breach of injunction amounts to contempt of court and is therefore a criminal act, for which the usual penalty is imprisonment. Hence many have objected to the wide powers of injunction in the UK and US courts, on the ground that they can be used to import criminal sanctions into civil disputes. Injunction has been extensively used in the US, not only to ensure protection of rights guaranteed by the constitution, but also in highly controversial areas, such as labour disputes. (*See also* *prior restraint/subsequent punishment.)

injustice. *See* *justice.

institution. Widely defined by the *OED* as 'an established law, custom, usage, practice, organization, or other element in the political or social life of a people; a regulative principle or convention subservient to the needs of an organized community or the general ends of civilization'. Some sociologists attempt to bring order into the discussion of institutions by distinguishing four types: the political (concerned with regulating the pursuit and exercise of *power), the economic (concerned with establishing and maintaining production and *production relations), the cultural (involving *education, *culture, and *leisure), and institutions of *kinship (including the *family). This division is helpful only to the extent that these four spheres of social life do not completely interpenetrate; moreover it is associated with no accepted theory of the general nature and function of institutions. Nevertheless the concept of an institution is indispensable to political thought, and it is important to clarify it. It is for example a frequent complaint made by conservatives that neither the liberal nor the socialist gives a satisfactory account of institutions, or attempts to show how his respective ideals might be *embodied* in institutions. Whether or not the accusation is fair, the failure of *democratic centralism to generate any institution that commands the respect of those governed by it has frequently been noted, and has often been thought to be connected with the *Marxist attempt to eliminate reference to institutions from the description of the underlying forces of history. Among important features of institutions the following deserve mention:

(i) Institutions contain 'members', but are not identical with any member, even when there is only a single member, as in the institution of *monarchy.

(ii) Institutions have independent *agency, and sometimes even personality. There are things done and suffered by institutions which are not done or suffered by any of their members; and institutions may have rights and obligations that do not belong to any member. (Some *individualists doubt both these propositions.) The conferring of a degree is an act of a university, but not necessarily of any individual member of it, just as the condemning of a criminal is the act of a court, but not of any individual officer of the court. These two features seem to belong to institutions whether or not they are voluntary associations, whether or not they are recognized as persons in law, and whether or not they are *incorporated. (Thus a football club may be *blamed* for damage caused by its members, even though it is a voluntary association without legal personality.)

(iii) Institutions may endure beyond the life of any particular member, and have a history which is not simply the history of their members.

(iv) Institutions manifest their existence through the intentional acts of their members; they also form and govern the intentions of their members, partly by influencing the conceptions from which the members act. A complex example of this is a parade: soldiers on parade are doing something which is unintelligible without the existence of military institutions; they are also doing it with an intention that can be expressed only in military terms.

Institutions may or may not have a *constitution; they may or may not have rules, laws and *conventions; they may or may not be *autonomous. The defence of autonomous institutions (and the required *freedom of association) is an important conservative and liberal cause. Autonomy can mean either or both of two things: (a) the autonomous institution is self-governing, answerable to no external constraints other than those contained in the criminal and civil law; (b) the autonomous institution has its own internal purposes which could not be fulfilled in some other way, but which require just *this* institutional arrangement (*see*, e.g., *education, *sport). The proliferation of both kinds of autonomy might be thought to be necessary for the accommodation of the diversity of social life, as well as for the protection of the realms of *leisure and the *private from the encroachments of the state. A state may also be defined as totalitarian on the grounds that it does not permit autonomous institutions in any sphere in which the state has an interest – e.g. in education, trade union organization, and so on

The continuity of society is something which many conservatives extol, and which they seek to embody in the continuity of autonomous institutions (rather than in the state). Such thinkers are also apt to refer to the necessary fragility of institutions, which, like life, are always easier to destroy than to create, while being so deeply implicated in the moral development of the individual that he may well be unable to know what he loses in destroying them, or to envisage, except in negative terms, the value of a world that is not conditioned by their presence. (These conservative theories are to be found, for example, in *Burke, and through him have been extremely influential.) However it should not be thought that conservative thought has a monopoly over this concept, which is fundamental also to that 'constitution of liberty' which liberalism has, in its reflective moments, attempted to prescribe.

institutional economics. School of economic thought (also known as institutionalism), which flourished in the US in the 1920s and which held, partly under the influence of *Veblen, that economists err in attempting to understand economic behaviour without taking account of the non-economic, specifically institutional, contexts in which it occurs.

insurgency. A term used in *international law and generally in order to denote an uprising ('insurrection') against constituted government which falls short of *revolution, *rebellion or *civil war. Hence 'insurgent', a belligerent in such an insurrection. To call the Afghan tribesmen who fight the present Soviet-backed government 'insurgents' is to avoid the question of the legal status of their war. At the same time it is to suppose that the government against which they fight is not that of a foreign power, nor one established by *usurpation. Nevertheless in certain circumstances (e.g. for the purposes of negotiation, settlement, trade and cooperation) it may be necessary to deal directly and legally with 'insurgent governments', which may therefore be accorded *international personality.

integration. Different groups within a jurisdiction may have the same *rights in law, but nevertheless enjoy unequal *privileges, and disparate social, educational and recreational institutions. Integration is the process whereby all such institutions are made available to all members of the state, regardless of creed, race, and origin, with the intention of forming a unified *civil society within the jurisdiction of a unified *state. The aim of integration may, however, partially conflict with that of *toleration, which requires some measure of respect towards those groups (whether ethnic, religious, or however formed) which determine among themselves to remain socially distinct from other groups within the state, and who, while perhaps anxious for equal legal rights, are equally anxious for separate social institutions. This problem is of considerable importance in the US, on account of the federal structure designed to allow for just such a separation between state and civil society, and on account of the constitution, which, through the bill of rights, acts so as to impose uniform legal expectations.

intégrisme. Term coined by the French *right-wing intellectual Charles Maurras, to denote the aim of bringing all distinct characteristics of a *nation within the purview of its political organization, so that, e.g., the *Roman Catholic Church in France would be regarded as an integral part of the political structure of the country, along with the language, customs and traditions of the people. A form of late *nationalism, it has also been denounced as *fascist by some of its opponents, on account of the attempt to incorporate the functions of *civil society into those of the *state. It may be that this accusation overlooks the distinction between asserting the political relevance of an institution or *social fact, and advocating state participation in it. Maurras and his followers evoked the famous charge of the **trahison des clercs*, from the pen of Julien Benda, a liberal intellectual who believed that no intellectual should lend his support to the politics of prejudice. *See also* *royalism.

intellectuals. Byron (who rhymed 'intellectual' with 'how hen-peck'd you're all') was one of the first writers to use this term in its modern sense, so as to denote someone for whom ideas, science, art and culture are so important as to determine not only the aims of everyday life, but also the roots of political thought and action. The *clerisy of *Coleridge was described in terms that celebrate the role of the intellectual as guardian of cultural and social values, and throughout the nineteenth century intellectuals produced similar apologies for their own condition. In *Leninism the *intelligentsia are given a crucial role in the preparation and instigation of revolution, and are even regarded as suitable members of a subsequent (and, according to the theory, provisional) government. By contrast, conservative thinkers have often tended to dismiss intellectuals as either politically ineffective, or not to be trusted, since it is easier to go wrong when attempting to articulate a *doctrine than when following a *prejudice. The effect of the intellectual, on this view, is to draw a veil of abstraction around the immediacies of practical life, and to sever politics from the instincts of the people. That *populist idea can be found in *Burke, as part of his denunciation of the French Revolution and of the role of intellectuals in bringing about its worst excesses.

The view of Coleridge and *Arnold, which attributes to intellectuals the irreplaceable task of preserving the gift of culture, so as to secure it from the assaults of barbarism and from the blight of indifference, is equally, however, a conservative view, just as Julien Benda's attack on the intellectual presumption of a right to rule (*see* **trahison des clercs*) is an anti-conservative defence of liberal values. Since it is only intellectuals who are anxious to articulate, rather than to enact, political ideas, it is only they that will be bothered by this dispute over their own status. However, there is evidence that they are worried by it. Many left intellectuals, disturbed by the classical *Marxist position which assigns much intellectual activity to the *superstructure and to *ideology, have tried to develop theories of intellectual production, with which to secure the intellectual more firmly to the base and so to the labouring activity with which he expresses solidarity. (*See* *technological determinism.) Thus *Gramsci, for example, argued that intellectuals occupy key positions in the organization of society, and have a functional significance which confers on them vast *de facto* power, both economic and political.

intelligence. The gathering of 'intelligence' about a potential enemy, whether political, economic or military, is now one of the most sophisticated branches of *government. Governments anxious about the security of their rule also gather intelligence about those subject to it, to the point where every citizen may regard every other as a potential policeman. (*See* *police state.)

The organization of the various internationally operative intelligence agencies – such as the CIA and the KGB – lies outside the scope of this dictionary; but it must be remembered, in any attempt to describe the nature of the modern state, that these agencies form an ever more powerful, and ever more autonomous, influence in the exercise of power. Fear of this autonomy in the CIA led to the formation in the US of a Senate committee (under Senator Church), which in 1976 called for stricter control of the intelligence service, and provisions for compelling it to be answerable to Congress. The accountability of the KGB remains as inscrutable as the KGB itself, but it, and its predecessor the NKVD, together with the many subsidiary organizations through which they have exerted themselves, have probably had a far greater influence in shaping modern history than the communist ideology which they purport to serve.

intelligentsia. Russian term, current since the mid nineteenth century, used to describe collectively all those *intellectuals who not only identify themselves as such, but do so in the course of attributing to themselves a particular social position independent of *class, and perhaps accessible from any class, together with a political outlook that reflects that position. Feebly defined as 'critically thinking personalities' by the Russian materialist and proto-Marxian philosopher D. I. Pisarev (1840–68), they were promptly portrayed (and condemned) as *nihilists by Ivan Turgenev, in his famous novel *Fathers and Sons*. Some find Turgenev's vision confirmed in the role of the intelligentsia before, during and after the Russian Revolution.

interest. Return from the deployment of *capital over time; consequently the sum of money due after financial capital has been loaned for a given length of time. The 'classical theory' of interest given by *Smith and *Ricardo represents interest as an income which attaches to capital, rather as *rent attaches to *land, a view which explains interest only given a satisfactory theory of rent. (*Marx argued that there *is* no true theory of rent in classical economics, and that the order of explanation ought really to be reversed.) The classical theory was developed further: the rate of interest was seen as being determined by the supply and demand for loanable funds. The former depended upon the expected profitability of investment, which according to the theory depended upon the marginal productivity of capital; the latter depended upon consumers' rate of *time preference: goods available today have more value than goods available tomorrow.

The classical theories, and related theories, were criticized by Keynes, who tried to explain the rate of interest in monetary terms, developing a more complex analysis in terms of expectations, in which interest is regarded as the reward for sacrificing the liquidity of other assets. However, the marginal productivity theory of interest still retains some support.

The receipt of interest has always been the subject of moral condemnation – for example, by *Aristotle in the *Oeconomica*, and by traditional *Christian and *Islamic doctrines of *usury. However, in times of *inflation, there can be little inducement to save without positive *nominal* interest, and, without private saving, new capital cannot be accumulated by the *private sector. So a condemnation of interest is sometimes thought to be tantamount to a conditional affirmation of socialism. For a brief survey of the arguments, *see* *just price, *usury.

interest group. A *group, united by common interest, which has sufficient *identity to act on its own behalf (e.g. by electing officers, and representatives, establishing common funds, associations, and reports, engaging in active *propaganda) and which therefore has some *influence either on public opinion or on government. An interest group may have sufficient political *access to become a *pressure group; alternatively its political influence may be only indirect, e.g. through the mobilization of popular support. The theory of the interest group is an important part of modern political science, and vital to the explanation of *collective choice.

interests. When it is said that some action or state is 'in John's interest', or 'one of John's interests', any one of four things may be meant: John desires it; he intends it; he values it; or he needs it either intrinsically, or in order to satisfy one of his desires, intentions or values. Not everything desired is intended, not everything intended is valued, not everything valued is needed, and vice versa for the whole sequence. The distinctions here – familiar to a philosopher – may be overlooked in political discussion, even though the concept of a 'real interest' (sometimes used with sinister implications) has evolved in order to distinguish those things which are really in a man's interest from those things which he merely thinks to be so.

Real interests are best seen as *needs, and these are indisputably objective – i.e. whether or not John needs something is determined independently of John's thinking that he does; John may or may not be right about this. The same is not obviously true of John's desires, intentions, and values, which, like his beliefs, are or seem to be subjective; there is no distinction between what they are and what John thinks they are – although Freudian psychology might lead one to doubt this, at least over a certain range of cases.

In sociology interests tend to be identified with *revealed preferences: that is with all aims that are actually pursued, whatever their source and justification. A distinction is then made between individual and 'common' interests, the latter being definitive of *groups, and invoked in the explanation of *collective choice.

In all political thinking, however, the distinction between needs, values, intentions and desires should be observed, so that it may be necessary to penetrate below the sociologist's analysis. For one thing, since a person may neither desire nor value what he needs, his real interests may diverge from his pursuits: is it then justified to restrain him? Some forms of liberalism regard any obstruction to desires as an interference with freedom. Others – perhaps influenced by *Kantian doctrines of *autonomy – argue that an interference in desires which permits the realization of intentions does not reduce, but on the contrary enhances, freedom. Still others – again perhaps under Kantian influence – may argue that an interference in intentions that permits the greater realization of *values is not only not a violation, but a liberation, of human autonomy. The last view seems to permit considerable invasion of ordinary human projects, but, says the Kantian, no *rational choice would ever be impeded by it, and this is the true justification of all those strictures that are contained in law.

In all discussions of this issue much will depend upon the philosophical question of the objectivity of values, and also on a conception of *human nature in terms of which the needs of the human being are to be specified. It is a frequent criticism of the application of preference theories to political decisions that the concept of a preference is indifferent between desires, intentions and values, while the aim of politics may be unintelligible if these are given equal weight, or even assumed to be commensurate.

interference. Left undefined in international law, but a term vital to the understanding of international relations. Interference is a form of *agency, which may involve *force or the threat of force, or the establishment of a system of *control or *coercion. It involves action designed to ensure compliance with certain requirements, in a sphere where another agent is morally, politically or legally *sovereign. It involves disrespect for sovereignty, and a refusal to recognize that things which affect one's interest may not be one's concern.

The precise nature of the agency involved is difficult to define. It seems to be a definite interference in the affairs of another state to make a show of arms and to threaten, or represent onself as threatening, force, should that state change its form of government. On the other hand, to refuse to ratify a treaty or a trade agreement after a change of government, in order to register disapproval, seems not to be an interference, but merely an attempt to influence.

international capitalism. Term used to denote not a theory but a force (cf. *international socialism). The idea is that, although there may be no political movement expressly devoted to the advance of capitalism throughout the world, there is a natural tendency in capitalism to do just that, whether behind the cover of *imperialism, or through its inherent tendency to expand and capture markets, and so induce economic dependence upon a market economy.

International Court of Justice. The judicial organ of the United Nations, established in 1946 at The Hague. All fifteen judges must be from different countries, and have *judicial independence, not being representatives in any legal or political sense of the countries from which they are appointed. Jurisdiction is limited to civil cases brought by and against *sovereign states, although the statute which constitutes the court contains an 'optional clause', whereby member states can choose to be bound by the court's decisions in any matter of international law, the interpretation of treaties, and so on.

The judgement is that of a majority, and the court is not bound by its own previous decisions: nevertheless it has written reports, and these have played a major part in the development of *international law.

International Labour Organization. Set up in 1919 by the Treaty of Versailles with the object of advancing the cause of *social justice, by working towards an international code of labour law and practice, in the form of conventions (legal instruments to serve as models for national legislations) and recommendations. It attempts to provide an international forum for labour demands, and to recommend to governments what are in effect constitutional means of answering them, through law and *conciliation. The ILO now has 135 member nations (including all major states within the Western and Soviet blocs) and, since 1946, has been a specialized agency of the United Nations.

international law. International law has two branches: public (applying between states), which is referred to in this entry, and private (applying to individuals), which is also known as *conflict of laws and described under that heading. In theory the first is a single body of law applying universally, while the second (which settles such questions as *jurisdiction) inevitably varies from place to place, being simply a branch of the law of the particular *sovereign state that applies it.

The possibility of an international law has been one of the great issues of Western political thought, not only since the collapse of *ecclesiastical jurisdiction, but also prior to that jurisdiction, when jurists and philosophers faced the question of adapting and justifying *Roman law in local conditions that differed markedly from those which had entered into its development, while trying to retain the universal character of the *jus gentium* and of the *natural law that had been used to support it.

The term 'international law' was coined in 1780 by *Bentham, but modern discussions have their roots much earlier, in the thought of *Aquinas, *Grotius, Pufendorf, Vattel and *Kant, all of whom attempted to give theoretical foundations for international *jurisdiction. Grotius advocated a mixture of natural law and *positive law, as providing the basis for the law obtaining between states, so that it is now normal to divide theorists of the subject into positivists, naturalists and Grotians, the leading naturalist being Pufendorf (*De Jure Naturae et Gentium*, 1672), and the leading positivist Vattel (*Le droit des gens*, 1758). According to the positivists international law is a summary of treaties, customs and agreements between states, with no authority beyond that provided by the voluntary submission of the parties; while according to the naturalists there is a universal source of this authority in *human nature, which can be neither disobeyed in good conscience nor overriden by contract. On either view the question of the intellectual basis of the law must be distinguished from that of its effectiveness, and it is clear that, in the lack of any single sovereign power to enforce international law, the agreement of nations to abide by it (for whatever reason) is the only material force that can ensure its enactment.

Complex problems of jurisprudence arise over the relation between international law and state (in this context usually called *municipal) law. Which takes precedence, and why? According to the 'monist' doctrine both systems of law are binding on those subject to them, so that international law automatically enters into the legal system of any state subscribing to it; according to the 'dualist' doctrine, the origins of the two kinds of law are so different as to define completely different spheres of action. Neither theoretical position alters the need to bring the two into harmony, since clearly any conflict will lead to municipal courts overriding decisions in international law, and hence to a *de facto* withdrawal of the state from the agreement to be bound by it.

International Monetary Fund. *See* *world organizations.

international organizations. Bodies set up by multilateral agreement between states, to be distinguished from transnational organizations, which simply *operate* between states. (Thus legally speaking, *international socialism, like *international capitalism, is a transnational and not an international movement.) Since the Congress of Vienna, international organizations have been of enormous importance in determining relations between states. The question of the *international personality of such organizations is often extremely important – without it, they cannot be party to disputes under *international law. (Thus it seems that the British Commonwealth lacks international personality, while the United Nations possesses it.) The most important of all international organizations, the United Nations, has a constitution that was embodied in a charter, ratified in 1945, following negotiations between the UK, US, USSR and China beginning in 1942. The membership consists of the original fifty states which adopted the charter, and states later admitted, which are peace-loving, accept the obligations of the charter and are deemed able and willing to carry out those obligations. States are recommended by the Security Council and admitted by a two-thirds vote of the General Assembly. The General Assembly comprises representatives of all members, and it inititates studies and makes recommendations concerning all matters, but without legislative power. The Security Council is composed of five permanent members (the UK, US, France, China, USSR), and six others elected for two years by the General Assembly. The functions of the Security Council are primarily executive and members agree to accept and carry out its decisions: the power of *veto possessed by each of its members ensures that these are few. In addition to those two principal bodies there are the Economic and Social Council, concerned with the promotion of better living conditions and the support of human rights throughout the member states; the Trusteeship Council, concerned with the administration of *trusteeship territories, and the *International Court of Justice. The partial effectiveness of the United Nations in adjudicating at least some disputes which might otherwise be settled violently has given some credence to these institutions, the working of which is as yet ill-understood by those who belong to them.

international personality. Status of a legal *person in *international law – accorded to every *sovereign state, and denoting the external aspect of *sovereignty in so far as this is a legally recognizable attribute. A state can remain the same international person despite changes of name, *territory, *dynasty, form of government, *constitution etc. The problem of the true identity of states is reflected in the difficulties posed by the international recognition of a new *regime. Recognition as an international person is, however, not the same as recognition as *legitimate: an *insurgent government and a legitimate government may equally acquire the status of legal persons. If that were not so, then there could be no international *adjudication of their dispute.

Individuals may also have international personality, for the purpose of laws dealing expressly with their interests, such as the laws concerning human rights, but how that helps them to enforce international law against a resistant municipal power is hard to say. It seems that the problem of enforcing human rights in those states where citizens are apt to express their grievances in terms of the definition of that concept embodied in the UN Charter, and thereby in international law, has remained unchanged by the existence of that law. This may be partly because individuals' rights are also determined by *municipal law, whereas the rights of a sovereign state are determined *only* by international law.

international socialism. The form of socialism advocated in the **Communist Manifesto*, which regards its aims as universal, and recognizes no national boundaries, seeking the emancipation of the *proletariat everywhere, from bondage imposed upon it by private property in the form of capitalism. The proletariat is sometimes held to be the only class that is truly international, having been stripped, according to the theory, of every asset that would attach its interests to a particular nation, territory, sovereign, or other object of localized political allegiance. Cf. *national socialism.

international trade. The exchange of goods and services between one state and another, which takes place because of differing costs of production, and because of the pursuit of a wider range of goods and services, and a greater quantity of both. The 'law of comparative average', due to Torrens and *Ricardo, holds that even when the costs of production are uniformly higher in one country than in another, mutual trade may be to the advantage of both. According to neo-classical theory, states will tend to export the commodities in the production of which their most abundant resources are most intensively employed. Hence trade will involve the exchange of 'labour intensive' goods, from states with a large labour force, against raw materials and technology, from states in which those may be found and produced in abundance. *Mercantilism and *protectionism are doctrines which hold that too much unrestricted trade between states can sometimes be bad for at least one of the parties, and which therefore advocate restrictions of *free trade, say through tariffs. The controversy here, which is ancient, seems to continue unresolved. Extensive international trade has, however, often been seen as a vital adjunct to *international law, creating the mutual dependence between states that provides the ultimate sanction in any dispute. It is sometimes argued, however, that trade has a tendency to create its own kind of political subservience: *see* *imperialism, *international capitalism.

internationalism. The doctrine that political activity should define its objectives not in terms of the constitution, history or geographical boundaries of any particular *nation, but in terms of a universal human condition.

Examples of internationalist doctrines include *Marxism (in its classical form), which thought of all political activity in terms of an international *class struggle (*see* *international socialism); the political theory of *Kant, who saw the aim of politics as the abolition of national *jurisdictions and the adoption of a single body of objectively determined and universally applicable law; and the medieval conception of *natural law, which associated an internationalist theory of the human condition with a defence of the international jurisdiction of the *church. The last example is, however, deviant, in that it preceded the widespread *nationalism against which internationalism is in part a reaction.

Internationals. Term usually applied to a succession of international federations formed from parties dedicated to *international socialism, the first (the international 'Working Men's Association') being founded in London in 1864, with the support of Marx, the second in Paris in 1889, both being split by faction, decay and hostility between the participants, divided over matters equally of doctrine and of policy. The third, the *Comintern, founded in Moscow in 1919, survived, due to ruthless leadership exercised first by Lenin and subsequently by Stalin, who dissolved it in 1943. Meanwhile the so-called Fourth International had been formed in 1938 by followers of *Trotsky, while an independent 'Labour and Socialist International' had been created in 1923 by a few powerless *social democrats. (There was also a 'fascist international' founded at the same time, although it had no influence.) Finally a Socialist International was founded in 1951 in Frankfurt, with members from forty countries. The history of the internationals evolved around various disputes, principal being that concerning anarchism, which split the first, that between *bolsheviks and *mensheviks, which split the second, that between *Stalinists and *Trotskyists, which split the third. Since the end of the Second World War and particularly since the Sino-Soviet dispute in the late 1950s, the international socialist movement has been bitterly divided, and the conditions for a unified international organization no longer exist.

intervention. In *international law intervention means dictatorial *interference in the domestic or foreign affairs of a state by another, in such a way as to impair the first state's *independence. The law of intervention has in the past suffered from the defect that the legality of any act of intervention can always be put beyond question by declaring it to be war. However, under contemporary law, war is illegal unless undertaken in self-defence. There is, however, an equivalent escape from legal sanctions, provided by the ease with which an aggressive power may secure an 'invitation' to give aid to a party or faction within the state. This expedient is easy to use when a fiction of friendship has been maintained, as between the USSR and its satellites, but it does not depend upon such a fiction, as is shown by the intervention of Vietnam in Cambodia.

interventionism. The belief in the right and necessity of government to interfere in the operation of the market in order to achieve economic or social ends. The means advocated might involve any or all of the following: *price control, *exchange control, *incomes policy, support for ailing industries, *nationalization. The outcome of such policies may be a *market economy with close state supervision, or it may be a *mixed economy.

investment. In economics, the expenditure on *capital goods rather than *commodities that are immediately consumed. In more common parlance, the purchase of any asset or the undertaking of any commitment which involves forgoing present for the sake of future benefits.

Part of the justification sometimes offered for capitalism on grounds of justice is that, in foregoing present for future benefits (and therefore in preferring capital to consumption expenditure), a person makes a sacrifice of a kind necessary to continuing *production (cf. *Austrian school theories of capital). Hence the *interest on investment, if it represents the price at which an individual is prepared to forgo present enjoyment for future enjoyment (together with the risk of no enjoyment at all should the project fail), is simply the *just price of investment (*see* *time preference, *usury). The description of this reward as just is not refuted by *Marxist claims that profit involves the extraction of *surplus-value through the extortion of hours of unpaid labour. But it does not follow that capital must be privately owned, and hence it does not follow that the investor was justly in the position to obtain this profit in the first place.

invisible hand. *Adam Smith argued in *The Wealth of Nations*, 1776, that, under the mechanism of a *free market, the pursuit of profit leads each participant to act to the material advantage of society as a whole, as though 'led by an invisible hand to promote an end which was no part of his intention'. This is a more optimistic formulation of the slogan 'private vices, public benefits', given prominence by *Mandeville, and some form of it may still be offered as part of the justification of the market economy – namely that it also embodies a mechanism which achieves common economic objectives to the greater satisfaction of its participants than any viable alternative.

Smith's idea was the precursor of *Hegel's 'cunning of reason' and also, in a very different way, of *Marx's idea that the functions of economic activity might, by their very nature, remain concealed to the participants. Recently *Nozick has generalized Adam Smith's dictum, so as to describe as 'invisible hand explanations' all those explanations which 'explain what looks to be the product of someone's intentional design as not being brought about by anyone's intentions'. Not surprisingly, he finds that such explanations are common throughout the *social sciences (*Anarchy, State and Utopia*, 1971). 'Invisible hand' mechanisms do not necessarily work to the benefit of the participants. Not only are there cases of 'private virtues, public evils', as Mandeville recognized; there are also many examples of *counter-finality, e.g. the *prisoners' dilemma.

iron law of oligarchy. The law postulated by the German sociologist Roberto Michels that in all organizations power tends to fall into the hands of a small number of leaders, regardless of the formal constitution of the organization. Applying this 'law' to the German Socialist Party he argued that, in spite of its democratic constitution and revolutionary goals, it was doomed to acquire bureaucratic and also conservative leaders. As Michels put it, 'who says organization, says oligarchy' (*Political Parties*, 1920).

iron law of wages. Expression coined by *Lassalle, to denote the process whereby wages are supposedly kept down to the minimum required for the subsistence of the wage-labourer. The arguments for such a 'law' had been given by *Malthus and *Ricardo, who argued that if wages rise above subsistence level, the population will increase, and with it the supply of labour, so that, by the 'law of supply and demand', wages will fall back to the subsistence level. *Marx accepted the 'iron law', but not for those reasons: rather, he argued, there will always be a 'reserve army of labour' under capitalism, and hence a substitute for any labourer not prepared to work for the subsistence wage. Only with the destruction of capitalism can the 'iron law' be broken, but it will be broken then, and therefore is not a law of nature, as Ricardo and Lassalle had wrongly represented it to be. The subsequent history of capitalism has refuted all versions of the law as thoroughly as the history of communism has confirmed the *iron law of oligarchy.

irredentism. Originally, the policy and programme of the 'irredentists', i.e. those activists who, in 1878 and thereafter, strove to unify all Italian-speaking regions into a single Italian state. Now used more generally to name any attempt to unify into one state regions some of which are regarded as subject to a power with no title to rule them, and all of which are thought to belong, by tradition, law, custom, and language, or by nature, together; cf. *nationalism.

isegoria. Greek; the equal right to be heard in the sovereign assembly of the state before any public decision is taken. An ideal and partial achievement of *Athenian democracy which is completely absent from all systems of *representation.

Islam. Arabic: submission. Like any religion Islam has had a profound influence on the political institutions of those peoples who have adopted it, and has produced its own legacy of political thought. Initially theorists concentrated on the problem of the *caliphate: the divinely sanctioned rule through the successor (*kalīf*, or *imām*) of the prophet. Actual powers in the Muslim world rapidly diversified, and the caliphate became an office with little or no temporal power; the question of the legitimacy of actual powers then became acute. The supreme source of authority was the *Islamic law, or *shari'a* (= divine legislation), and the *sunna* (= custom, generally used to refer to the precepts and examples that can be extracted from the exemplary life of the prophet). The source of the law is revelation, through the Qur'ān, and through such subsequent texts and commentaries as can be supposed to have been guided by right apprehension of God's purpose. The authority of the law is therefore absolute, and all legitimacy must be derived from it. Originally it was thought that any officer, including the Caliph, could be legitimately deposed for an action contrary to the law; later it was realized that this would be impracticable, and that it was necessary to derive a system of *legal fictions (*hiyal*), in order to reconcile the law with actual human necessities. The jurists became increasingly concerned with the problem of obedience to a power which is, from the point of view of the law, in the wrong hands. Their reflections were various, but in practice of little influence: the prince (**sultān*) continued to administer affairs according to his own law, which existed alongside the divine law, and which was regarded as justified in so far as the divine law left much human conduct undetermined.

Medieval Islam produced important political thinkers, many of them (the *falāsifa*) directly inspired by the Greek philosophers. The *falāsifa* influenced all medieval thought, by transmitting the works of Plato, Aristotle and the neo-Platonists, along with their own detailed interpretations, to the Muslim and Christian worlds. The various attempts to reconcile the Greek vision of the state with the divine law caused renewed attention to the nature of law, as the fundamental principle of government. The prophetic revealed law becomes the constitution of an ideal Platonic state. Man is recognized as a political being, who is part of a state and who can exist in this world only through a state. Unlike the Greeks, the Muslim philosophers were committed to the view that the law applies not only in this world but also in the next, so that whatever political order is ideal in this world must also describe a possible order in the kingdom of God; hence the ideal states described by the *falāsifa* did not correspond very closely to any recognizable kind of human government. One interesting exception is the theory of the Machiavellian sceptic Ibn Khaldūn (1332–1406), who saw the state as a system of temporal power, through which government is acquired by a *dynasty. His theory of the dynasty, as having a natural term of life (three generations of forty years each), contains a premonition of many later theories of history, and an interesting diagnosis of the causes of the ascendancy and decline of institutions. He distinguishes three kinds of state: that based on the divine law (the ideal *theocracy of Islam), that based on a law established by human reason (which only approximates to the first), and that based on the ideal state of the philosophers. Each possibility represents an *ideal type; nevertheless actual institutions will differ according to which type is seen as their ultimate aim and fulfilment. Khaldūn is interesting for his attempts to give a theory of *positive law, and to integrate his account of the state with an analysis of production and taxation.

More recent Islamic thinkers have been preoccupied with the problem of reconciling Muslim teaching with the structure of the *nation state. The emergence of *Kemalism has changed radically the attitude of Muslim theorists towards the exercise of secular powers, and the founding of the Islamic state of Pakistan, with a constitution devised expressly to be compatible with the divine law, has provided an example for Muslims everywhere. It seems that the truth of Islam has been thought by believers to be buttressed (if not actually proved) by its political and military success, and this is perhaps one cause of the crisis of Islam in the modern world. Many also argue that Islam is distinguished not only by the fact that its law leaves much of human life undetermined, but also by the fact that it seems to have permitted the foundation and evolution of no institutions of government that might survive the collapse of faith. In this, it is sometimes said, it is sharply to be distinguished from *Christianity, which has formed bodies of law, institutions of government and education, and political procedures, all of which have survived the declining influence of the religion which founded them. Whether or not this is so, the constitution of Pakistan remains an extremely important study for those interested in the possibility alike of an Islamic, and of a post-Islamic, state. *See also* *theocratic guardianship.

Islamic law. *Shari'a*: divine law. An important example of a system of law which is religious in meaning, and which applies not by virtue of *citizenship or *allegiance to a state, but by virtue of religious affiliation, and on condition that there is an Islamic ruler to enforce it. It is applicable primarily between Muslims (although it contains provision for non-Muslims within the jurisdiction), and takes the concept of *obligation, rather than that of *right, as central. The law originated in the Qur'ān and the traditions attributed to Muhammad and is regarded as immutable, since it consists in what Muhammad knew, by revelation, of the divine will. It makes room for property and contractual rights, and economic developments, partly by the extensive use of stratagems and legal fictions (*hiyal*) – particularly important being those invoked in reconciling the need for *interest in capitalist economies with the law forbidding *usury.

Although states sometimes declare adherence to Islamic law, no state is governed exclusively by it.

isolationism. The doctrine that a state may best promote its own interests by refraining from interfering in those of others, and by keeping clear of the large issues of international politics. It was practised by Imperial China, and often advocated in the UK in the nineteenth century (sometimes under the banner of 'splendid isolation'), but it is most widely known as a permanently recurring feature of US foreign policy, already advocated in Washington's farewell address of 1796, and confirmed in the *Monroe doctrine of 1823, which is sometimes said to have introduced a policy of 'hemispheric isolationism'. US isolationism has taken other forms – 'continentalism' (made somewhat inapplicable by the revolution in Cuba and by the USSR's interest in Latin America), and 'westward expansion into the Pacific', precipitated by Pearl Harbor and extending at least until the end of the Vietnam war. But despite repeated calls for isolationist policies, such as the Republican Party's advocacy of 'Fortress America' in the 1960s, it seems now to be a thing of the past.

isonomy. Greek: equality before the law. The ideal of isonomy is an ancient one, and its achievement is often regarded (especially by theorists of liberalism) as one measure of the legitimacy of the resulting government. For, in a condition of isonomy, the individual's dealings with the state (i.e. all dealings that are mediated by law) are not affected by who he is, by what power he has, or by what title, property or office distinguishes him.

The conditions of isonomy are difficult to determine. In one sense it could be said to be achieved so long as anybody who appears before a judge is given treatment according to the merits of his case. But in another sense that is not enough, since it could be that only the rich, powerful or politically influential are able to appear before a judge in the first place or able, at any rate, to ensure that they have the best advice when they do so. Thus some have argued that, without some effective system of legal aid, ensuring that any person, however lacking in privilege, may have access to the best legal advice, there can be no genuine isonomy. Even so, there will be many ways in which the influence of the influential may be felt, but perhaps it is vain to define isonomy so strictly that only the refutation of a tautology could bring it into being.

isoquant. In economics, a curve showing the various possible combinations of inputs required to produce a given output of a given product, e.g. the various combinations of quantities of capital and of labour that could produce a sack of coal. Perhaps 100 units of capital and 50 of labour produce the same as 75 units of each – in which case these two quantities define points on a single isoquant.

Isoquants are often supposed to exhibit a similar structure to *indifference curves, except that outputs are measurable and *utilities are not, so that quantities may be attached to isoquants but not to indifference curves. Isoquants feature in the theory of the *firm, and in summarizing the contributions made by the various *factors of production.

J

Jacobinism. Named after the Jacobin club in the French Revolution, a society of deputies, led by Robespierre, which acted so as to concentrate power in its own hands, believing that the truth of its vision was sufficient guarantee of its authority to act. Subsequently there were many such clubs, and the term Jacobinism has been used to denote any revolutionary movement which is determined to impose its aims at whatever cost, in the conviction that the end justifies the means, and that the people, being ignorant, must be compelled towards the aims of revolution and cannot be expected willingly to adopt them. The philosophy of the Jacobin club has often been thought to derive from *Rousseau, although the relation between Rousseau and Robespierre is certainly not closer than that between *Lenin, who described himself and his followers as 'Jacobins tied to the proletariat', and *Marx.

Jacquerie (sometimes: Jacquery). From the French 'Jacques', nickname for a peasant, and originally describing the revolt of the peasantry against the nobles in northern France in 1357–8; subsequently used to denote the mass of people taking part in an uprising based in peasant support.

Jefferson, Thomas (1743–1826). American essayist and statesman, drafter of the *Declaration of Independence*, 1776, President of the US (1801–9), and founder of the University of Virginia. Jefferson was a theorist of *constitution and *democracy, who left, in his *Manual*, 1796, a summary of the law and practice of *Congress which remains a standard work, and which is bound up and published with all the successive editions of the Rules of the

House of Representatives and of the Senate. In his *Notes on the State of Virginia*, 1784, he had expounded his own version of the theoretical basis of the ideal American constitution, which, while democratic in form, contains a strong residue of respect for the agrarian mode of life, and for the stable structures of government that would support it. He defended *bicameral government, the office of a *supreme court, and a *bill of rights. He also conveyed respect for the English *common law, and for the rights that had been enshrined in it, so that the *Virginia Declaration of Rights*, 1776, which he prompted, contained a résumé of rights extracted from or continuous with those implied in the common law. His observation of the French Revolution convinced him that, although there are universally valid principles of human rights, the form of government must be tailored to the conditions of a given society, and not dictated by the logic of abstract ideas. He also believed that generations as well as individuals have rights, and that a constitution and laws should not be immovably imposed on succeeding generations. The eventual adoption of the Bill of Rights owes much to Jefferson, as does the US constitution as a whole. *See also* *Jeffersonian democracy.

Jeffersonian democracy. The kind of *democracy advocated by *Jefferson, involving universal *suffrage, *bicameral government, stable *institutions, declared *freedoms and *rights (it was Jefferson who criticized the constitution of 1789 for its failure to include a *bill of rights), *division of powers, and effective *checks and balances to the exercise of power. In particular, Jeffersonian democracy is distinguished by its emphasis on *federalism, and on the need for individual states to retain powers against the federal government, so as to be able to nullify the latter's unconstitutional acts. It thus sees the principal constitutional guarantee as lying in the decentralization of power.

Jesuit movement. The Society of Jesus was founded by St Ignatius Loyola in 1534 and approved by Pope Paul III in 1540. It aimed to revitalize the *Roman Catholic Church in face of the threat posed by the *Reformation, and to undertake missionary work designed to convert people to the faith. Members of the order wear no distinctive habit, and their obligations are entirely contained within this aim of conversion, so that they have become types of single-minded devotion to *doctrine. Their influence was widespread, in educational institutions, in the administering of 'spiritual exercises', in the conduct of missions, and in the subtle use of *casuistry with which to adapt their doctrine to every prior disposition to believe it. Their rapid advance accordingly invoked considerable hostility, and the order was expelled from France in 1764, and then suppressed by Pope Clement XIV in 1773. Nevertheless they continued to function in a reduced way, were restored by Pope Pius VII in 1814, and still maintain missions and centres of learning throughout the world. Their methods, involving infiltration, and personal persuasion of those most able to exert public influence, have served as a model for many subsequent subversive movements.

Jevons, William Stanley (1835–82). English political economist, logician and philosopher of science, and one of the inventors of the *marginal utility theory of *price. Jevons extended this theory to generate the marginal productivity theory of *interest, and thus prepared the ground for modern economic analyses of *capital, as a separate *factor of production. He was extremely influential on many members of the *Austrian school and on neo-classical theorists, and thereby many of his theories have entered into the modern defences of capitalism.

Jewish law. The law contained in the Torah of Moses, as glossed and supplemented by subsequent scribes, commentators and priests, which was partly committed to writing in the Mishnah (AD 200), and ultimately collected in the Babylonian Talmud of AD 600. Among systematic treatises, those of

Moses Maimonides (1135–1205) – the Mishnah Torah – and Joseph Qaro (1488–1575) – Shulchan 'Arukh – are the most respected. Jewish law is construed as having its basis in divine revelation, but accommodates elaborate customary rules and procedures. Its effect on Christianity has caused it to exert an influence upon Western law generally, particularly in matters relating to marriage, to relations between *church and state, and to commercial contracts (where its international character has been influential in forming the laws of contract which permit and support international trade).

jingoism. From the refrain 'By Jingo!', attached to a music-hall song of 1878, which became the marching song of those citizens of the UK who in that year were spoiling for war with Russia. Hence: blustering, bragging *chauvinism, with aggressive inclinations of an *imperialist kind. Described by Julien Benda as 'the form of patriotism specially invented by democracies'.

joint stock company. A business association in which common stock, or *capital, is contributed by a group of persons. As a result, there may be effective *separation of ownership from control. The rise of the joint stock company in the seventeenth century proceeded without effective legal discipline until the South Sea Bubble of 1720. After that, company law, controlling the behaviour, and eventually limiting the liability, of members of a joint stock company, was introduced, thus ratifying the institutions through which modern capitalism finds expression. The phrase 'joint stock company' is now virtually obsolete.

journalism. The production of news and comment for widespread publication. The issue of the freedom of the press (and by implication of the *media generally) is one that journalism, the express purpose of which is one of *communication, irrespective of literary, scientific or any other merit, raises in its acutest form. The liberty to publish news and information is in most places subsequent to control, either through the operation of independent statutes, or through the exercise of *de facto* powers of *censorship. Like all such liberties it must be thought of as a matter of degree, curtailed by laws of libel, decency, *privacy and *sedition. Nevertheless the 'freedom of information', guaranteed under the Helsinki final agreement, is one that is often defended as a basic *human right, and which is opposed by many modern states (including half those that signed the Helsinki agreement) with a fervour that is sometimes thought to be a sign of political, if not mental, instability. (The accusation of mental instability is derived from the claim that only someone suffering from paranoid delusions, or whose life was in some similarly deranged way founded on a lie, would oppose the truth as though it were in itself a crime; this accusation against press censorship and the suppression of free information within the USSR has been made with great force by Solzhenitsyn.) A reply that is often made is that journalism in the West only *appears* to be objective, and that it is in fact so structured as constantly to reinforce a bias in favour of established interests. Hence 'freedom of information' never means more than freedom to disseminate established lies.

In the West discussion of this issue has involved the resurgence of a kind of *cultural conservatism, which represents journalism as too deeply degenerate for its freedom to be valuable, together with liberal attempts to define the ideal extent of the freedom of the press, and the true grounds for its restriction. To summarize these arguments is almost impossible, but some main points may be given here:

The cultural conservative argues that, whatever freedom exists, it can never have greater value than the value of the activity that is permitted by it. The forces which direct a 'free press' are inevitably given to the promotion of lies, distortions and vulgarities. That view might equally be upheld by a *Marxist as part of a theory of the ideological workings of the 'capitalist media'. But the conservative reason for it will tend to mention, not ideology, but style and manner: in particular the commercial necessity to appeal as widely and forcefully as possible. The existence of a large reading public makes high-toned journalism anachronistic and financially unrewarding. Moreover, the transference of journalism to media of mass communication such as television removes all qualifications (such as literacy, or education) which had previously been necessary for the reception of information about the public world. Content is determined by style, and the content of most journalistic utterance will accordingly be confined to those matters that have the widest appeal, irrespective of any intrinsic worth as subjects of communication. (Hence 'journalese' and 'journalistic' as terms of abuse.)

The liberal argument tends to begin from the idea that the widespread dissemination of information about the public world is not only a duty of those who possess it, but also a right of the recipient. This is particularly so in a democracy, where every citizen has to cast a vote at an election, and where every citizen therefore has a right to be informed of the likely consequences. Moreover, the dissemination of information has been seen as a fundamental factor in the breaking down of barriers, between individuals, classes, races, and societies, and it is – on one liberal view – only barriers that threaten civil and international peace. Vulgarity or paucity of literary merit are small prices to pay for such freedom of information, and even if it be true that journalism is too preoccupied with the immediate and the sensational to deliberate on its true significance, deliberation is in any case not its responsibility, but rather the responsibility of the citizen.

The liberal argument is, on the whole, accepted in the US and the UK, and what control there is is exercised through councils and professional bodies (such as the UK Press Council). These do not have any legal jurisdiction over journalism, but simply exert pressure to maintain certain standards of conduct among their members. However, many think that the individual has rights which are inherently threatened by journalism. The aim of journalism is to secure an audience, and the more sensational, violent and tragic an episode, the more likely that an audience will be secured for it. Hence the press constantly intrudes into the privacy of individuals, precisely at those points where privacy is most evidently necessary.

journeyman. A term that has an air of obsolescence, because the condition that it describes – that of the day labourer – is largely obsolescent. From *journée* (French: day), a journeyman is one qualified at a craft, trade or skill, who is able to work at it as a wage-labourer with frequent changes of employer, and who demands payment by the day. In the sixteenth and seventeenth centuries, journeymen formed a large and active rising class, and in their struggle for independence from their masters combined with security of employment, precipitated many important changes in production.

Judaism. Judaism, unlike *Zionism, does not stress the doctrine that the Jewish people constitute or should constitute a separate state or nation, but only that they are bound individually and collectively by a single law (*see* *Jewish law) which is of international application. Being founded in *natural justice, divine revelation, tradition, and domestic custom, this law enters into conflict with surrounding *positive law, if at all, only through no fault of its own. Because of this, modern Judaism (in contrast to the Judaism of the Old Testament) has generated no political doctrine or vision that is common to those who subscribe to it. However, profession of the Jewish faith, which has often been persecuted (*see* *anti-semitism), may still awaken political suspicions, and while persecution of the Jews in communist countries tends to represent itself as 'anti-Zionist', it exhibits a disconcerting continuity with the anti-semitism of the past.

judicial legislation *See* *judiciary, *legislation

judicial review. The challenging of acts performed by the *legislative branch of government before a judicial body. To the extent that this exists it grants a dominant role to the *judiciary in the exercise of political power. It is not recognized in UK law (although there is some dispute about this) nor is it explicitly sanctioned in the US constitution. Nevertheless, judicial review is practised by the *Supreme Court, and state constitutions are generally interpreted as granting the power of judicial review to their own courts. It is arguable that, unless the judiciary has this power, the effect of a written constitution in limiting the acts of a legislature is nugatory, since no body would exist to ensure that the constitution is applied. On the other hand, who is to supervise the Supreme Court? The old problem of 'quis custodiet ipsos custoder?' arises here in a particularly vivid form.

Sometimes the expression 'judicial review' is used more widely, to mean the judicial review of the exercise of any power of government, including the executive power, as expressed, for example, through administrative decisions. This is clearly both possible, and also necessary, if there are to be constitutional guarantees of individual *rights: *see* *administrative law, *judiciary.

judiciary. The judiciary comprises the whole body of judges within a legal system, and its nature, function, composition and procedure provide one of the focal points of modern political debate. Three main areas need to be reviewed; judicial independence, judicial legislation, and the class interests of the judiciary.

(i) Independence. According to the doctrine of the *separation of powers, the judiciary exercises a power within the state that is separable (whether or not separated) from the other powers of government – in particular from those of the *legislature and the *executive. To what extent is this idea a fiction? If it is not, to what extent ought it to be put into practice? If it is put into practice then how should it be done?

The idea of judicial independence seems not to be a fiction. However it refers to a condition that may be extremely difficult to achieve, since it requires that the power that appoints a judge must also be prepared to yield to him. The problem of how to achieve this through a *constitution has exercised some of the most influential political thinkers in modern times, notably *Montesquieu, and the *Founding Fathers of the US. It is not necessary that there should be a written constitution; in both the US and the UK it seems that there are definite procedures whereby a citizen may obtain redress before a court for abuses of executive power (*see* *administrative law). It is perhaps easier to imagine judicial independence from the executive than from the legislative power; for obviously a judiciary ceases to be a power of the state altogether once it ceases to apply the law, as enacted by the legislative assembly. Nevertheless it may be independent to the extent that judicial decisions cannot be overturned by the legislature, i.e. if there is no *retroactive legislation, and also no appeal from the courts to the legislature. (By an accident of the UK constitution the House of Lords is both a legislating body and also the highest court of appeal, but, by convention, its two functions are kept separate.) Judicial independence might exist *de jure* – it may for example be specified in a written document which purports to describe the constitution – but not exist *de facto,* say, because a judge is removed from office whenever his decision displeases the executive. However, it may be that judicial independence is a necessary condition for the *rule of law, and for a genuine constitution, in which case it could be said that, without it, the distinction between the *de jure* and the *de facto* is dissolved.

Ought judicial independence to exist? Some argue (as just noted) that without it there is no rule of law: law does not determine the outcome of any issue but only the will of those in power. Moreover, no constitution can guarantee rights if the citizen cannot contend for these rights in open court, and no citizen can contend for his rights against the executive power if the judge of his case is always identical with the executive power. (*See* *natural justice, *show trials.)

How is independence to be secured? This is in many ways the hardest question, since it really means, how is it to be secured without also dissolving the organic relations between the various powers of government? Components of judicial independence that are standardly accepted (although not necessarily by any one theorist) are: (a) promotion of judges on advice from the existing judiciary; (b) no retroactive legislation; (c) acceptance of the doctrine of *precedent, and **stare decisis;* (d) established judicial procedure that is not subject to constant executive and administrative review; (e) the possibility of *judicial review.

(ii) Judicial legislation. It seems that the separation of powers ought to vest the making of law outside the judiciary. However, the existence of *common law, of *equity, and the doctrine of precedent, together with the inescapable fact of *hard cases, all entail that, at least sometimes, a judge must come to a decision that is not uniquely determined by the existing pronouncements of the legislature. It might seem, therefore, that in such a case, the judge *makes* the law (since nobody else does). Others reply that this does not follow: he discovers the law, or else draws out its implications. That philosophical question is extremely hard to resolve. In any case, there is much independent discussion of the extent to which this 'judicial legislation' is, or should be, permitted. Some esteem it, on the conservative ground that judges tend to be freer from impetuous reformism than politicians, and usually have a better grasp of the effects of legislation in the lives of ordinary citizens. Others oppose it as an obstacle to reform, and perhaps also as an instrument of class *hegemony, hence:

(iii) The class interests of the judiciary, which are now a frequent object of political comment. The judges in Western democracies belong inevitably to the professional classes, and stand in relations that, viewed from the point of view of production, are sometimes described as bourgeois. Opposition to their independence often comes from those who see this independence as simply an indefinite permission given to a particular class to advance itself behind the shield of law. Moreover (on some views) law itself is only the rewriting in terms of positive rights of those relations of power which determine the ascendancy of the bourgeoisie. (*See* *rights and powers.)

junta. From the Spanish, and originally referring to the local councils established in 1808 to conduct the war against Napoleon, a junta is a deliberative council or committee. Now generally refers to any form of government involving a committee which holds power as a body, and especially to forms of military government in which a ruling council of officers takes responsibility for all executive and legislative acts.

jural relations. Relations such as *right, *obligation, *privilege and inability which define the application of the law. The study of jural relations has a large philosophical component, and such analytical jurists as Austin and Hohfeld have attempted to describe the logical relationship among them. The following table is now widely accepted:

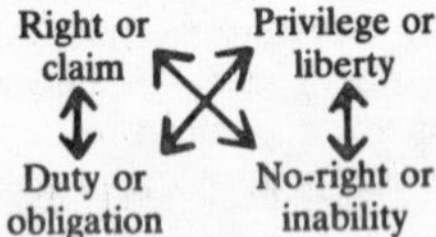

Vertical arrows indicate 'jural correlatives', in which application of either term to one party indicates the application of the other term to the other; diagonal arrows indicate 'jural opposites', in which application of one term to one party indicates the non-application of the other term to the other. Not all legal rights define a duty and some are correlated with a privilege; hence the above table enables one to work out the implications of any given doctrine of legal rights. One problematic case is that of the *right to work: for it seems that there can be no duty to provide work if there is no work to provide. (*Kant: 'ought implies can'.) Does this show that there can be no 'right to work' in a condition of unemployment, or that such a condition is always remediable, or that the above table of jural relations cannot be extended to *natural rights, or what?

jurisdiction. The sphere of authority exercised by a state. Hence, in *international law, the right of a *sovereign state to determine rights and duties of persons by legislation and to enforce those rights and duties. Jurisdiction extends over a certain *territory, and it seems that this territorial element in the concept is essential to settling questions as to its application. The idea therefore forms an essential part of the notion of a state as embodied in a territory – although whether there can be territoriless sovereign states is not settled only by the question of whether there can be a state without jurisdiction. Jurisdiction may be qualified by rights of asylum etc., and there may be disputes over jurisdiction, especially in the case of federations, in which the component states may possess local legislative systems in addition to the supreme legislature of the federation.

It is also common to speak of the 'jurisdiction' of a court, meaning the class of persons and issues which may be heard before it. Important problems of jurisdiction are raised by the powers of the *International Court of Justice, and by *ecclesiastical jurisdiction.

jurisdictional dispute. **1**. In US labour law, a dispute between unions concerning which workers should belong to which union. The thought here is that a union exerts a kind of *jurisdiction over its members by virtue of its representative and disciplinary functions, and that two such jurisdictions cannot be exercised over the same worker.

2. Sometimes also applied to a dispute over whether an administrative body has acted **ultra vires*, i.e. beyond the powers conferred on it by law. Such a dispute may be called 'jurisdictional' because administrative bodies often exercise powers which are quasi-judicial, and it is in respect of these (i.e. of the quality of their 'jurisdiction') that the action of *ultra vires* is usually brought.

jurisprudence. The study of *law, not the actual law of any particular *jurisdiction, but law as such – its origin, form and nature. It is to be distinguished (but can be distinguished only with difficulty) from the philosophy of law, which deals with the meaning and justification of the underlying concepts of law, such as *right, *obligation, *responsibility and *justice. Jurisprudence is both comparative and historical; it takes certain basic concepts for granted and deliberates on the problems generated by their application in this or that field of legislation. A question of jurisprudence such as, What is responsibility in law? is partly philosophical – dependent upon an analysis of the extra-legal concept of responsibility – and partly legal – dependent upon a collection of (and extrapolation from) the actual criteria used in assigning responsibility by the courts. But it is not exclusively either, and this explains the peculiar nature of jurisprudence: it tries to bring the order and system of philosophy into the reasoning of the law, by subsuming that reasoning under principles for which a philosophical explanation can be at least envisaged, if not produced.

jury. A body of laymen summoned to a court of law in order to decide questions of fact in a judicial (usually criminal) proceeding. Juries must not decide questions of law, and are always given legal guidance, either by the judge or by some officer of the court, in so far as this has a material bearing upon the matter that they must decide. The 'grand jury' in US criminal proceedings also has an accusatory function, but this does not give it authority in matters of law.

The institution of trial by jury was well established in medieval English law, but was increasingly confined to criminal cases; it is now exclusively an institution of Anglo-American law. It is often defended on the grounds that the participation of ordinary citizens in the administration of justice helps to enhance the reputation of the law, and also gives a criterion of the extent to which laws are in harmony with popular sentiment; moreover it provides some protection of the liberties of the accused. It is attacked on the ground of the frequent ignorance and prejudice of juries, who, while called upon to decide only questions of fact, nevertheless tend to see facts in terms of the legal consequences as they understand or misunderstand them.

just war. A conception frequently discussed by medieval philosophers and recently revived. *Canon law distinguished *jus in bello* (justice in the course of war) from the *jus ad bellum* (the just cause of war). A just cause may be pursued by unjust means – e.g. by the wholesale slaughter of non-combatants. *Aquinas summarized medieval thinking in his view that a war is just only if (1) there is sufficient *authority in the party who wages it; (b) there is just cause of offence, and (c) there is an intention to wage war solely for the sake of *peace, or for the suppression of the wicked and the sustenance of the good.

The major problems concern the idea of 'just cause' in (b), although many modern thinkers are unhappy, both about the concept of authority invoked in (a) (does the leader of an *insurgent army ever have authority? If so, in what sense?) and about the incorporation into (c) of some condition other than that of peace (who are the good? And who are the wicked? Is revolutionary subversion of a *democracy just, say, simply because it is the *bourgeoisie* who hold power? And so on). The best example of just cause, and the one almost universally accepted, is that of unprovoked *aggression from some other state. Indeed, *Grotius, and many thinkers who followed in his steps, found this to be almost the sole just cause of war.

The question of *jus in bello* is at least as complicated as that of the just war. It seems intuitively evident that a just cause can be pursued unjustly, and attempts have therefore been made (e.g. through the 'Geneva Conventions') to limit the procedures that may legitimately be employed by belligerents, whatever the justice of their cause. However modern forms of warfare are such as to involve non-combatants almost automatically and this has radically altered the character of the soldier's moral perceptions.

justice. *Plato's *Republic* begins with the question, 'What is justice?', and with the famous refutation of the view that justice is the *interest of those with *power: in other words, it argues for the non-identity of *rights and powers. (For the persistence of the doctrine refuted by Plato, *see* *rights and powers.) Since then, Plato's question has lain at the heart of all moral, political and legal philosophy, and is often considered to be the single most important question in political thought. *Aristotle, who thought of justice as the true subject-matter of political philosophy, and of its execution as a major purpose, perhaps *the* major purpose, of the **polis* (a view also expressed by Aeschylus in the *Oresteia),* made a famous distinction between 'distributive' and 'commutative' justice, the first being concerned with the distribution of goods among a class, the second with the treatment of the individual in particular transactions (e.g. when punishing him). In the second case justice involves giving to someone what he deserves, or else what he has a *right to receive. In the first case it is, according to Aristotle, a matter of 'treating equals equally'. These are not necessarily the same idea (although it could be said that, in the abstract, equals do have a right to be, and deserve to be, treated equally). If I have to distribute a cake among five starving people, then they may each deserve the whole cake, but it may be unjust not to divide it.

The Aristotelian distinction survives in various forms, although it would now be very unusual for a philosopher to think that there are really two concepts of justice, rather than two applications of a single idea. Contemporary use of the term *social justice makes extensive use of the distributive conception, while, in regulating actions between people, the commutative conception – justice as right or desert – seems to be prevalent. Many of the problems arise because the two may enter into conflict, as when Robin Hood acts unjustly (by taking what he has no right to take) in order to bring about social justice (through *redistribution). Is this conflict real, or would deeper reflection resolve it? Theories divide over their answer to that question. Those which take patterns of distribution as their model (among which the most influential recent theory is that of *Rawls) might find themselves resolving this issue only to admit that Robin Hood acts justly (provided perhaps that he dignifies himself with the title of *sovereign and redistributes in the name of the *state); those which regard the respect for individual rights as the central idea in justice (such as *Nozick's) might resolve the issue only to find themselves condoning distributions of goods so unequal as to be very oddly described as just. The important questions seem to be these:

(i) Is justice primarily the attribute of an act, of a person, or of a state of affairs? If of an act, then states of affairs (e.g. 'distributions' of goods) are just or unjust only to the extent that they are the outcome of just or unjust acts. If of a person, then rules of just action must be subordinate to a conception of human *virtue (e.g. an action is just if it would be recommended by the 'impartial judge' or the 'man of justice') – a conception which vastly complicates the discussion, and probably undercuts the desire of many modern philosophers to establish simple laws of justice. If of a state of affairs, then we might consider it unjust that one person is born more advantaged than another, even though human *agency has nothing to do with it. Aristotle seems to have favoured the second idea; much dispute between socialists and liberals in modern politics comes from socialists being attached to the third of those ideas, and liberals to the first.

(ii) Is justice a forward-looking or a backward-looking conception? In other words, does it look to the results of an action, or to its antecedents? The connection with desert and right suggests the latter, and this is at the root of the conflict – which many philosophers have thought to exist – between justice and *utility, itself cited as one of the principal failings of *utilitarianism. But some doctrines of social justice seem to construe justice as a forward-looking conception, nevertheless.

(iii) Is justice a constitutive or a procedural concept? That is, is the difference between the just and the unjust to be found in the nature of the action, or in the manner of its execution? Study of the law has sometimes led to the opinion that laws themselves are never either just or unjust, but that the process of their application may be one or the other, since it is only when legal rights have been determined that we can speak of 'treating equals equally'.

(iv) What *is* it, to treat equals equally? What is the relevant respect in which people are to be compared? If there is *no* respect, then the result of this maxim is *egalitarianism; if the respect is that of legal rights, and there is no natural limit on those (but only the limits embodied in *positive law), then rights may be unequally determined, and a slave may be justly treated as a slave.

(v) Is there, in other words, *natural justice? And are there *natural rights?

(vi) If so, does that solve the question, Why be just? *See* *value, *virtue.

In all those questions the problem of the objectivity of the concept of justice is paramount. There is a further problem suggested by them: the nature of the 'sentiment of justice' (cf. *Hume). Is there a real fact of human nature here, or could that sentiment be educated away? It always seems as though political systems that override the sense of justice thereby render themselves precarious. Is this because that sense is at the root of sentiments of *allegiance? Or is there a genuine conception of *political obligation that requires justice to be preserved? (Cf. *piety.)

K

Kaldor, Nicholas, Lord (b. 1908). See *Cambridge school, *compensation.

kangaroo court. A mock hearing in which all norms of justice and judicial procedure are ignored, and in which, as a rule, prosecutor, judge and executioner are one, and the verdict predetermined. The 'trial' by terrorists of their hostages is an example; most *show trials differ only in a fictional division between prosecutor and judge. (Originally US slang, already current in 1853.)

Kant, Immanuel (1724–1804). German philosopher, and the deepest and most systematic thinker of the *Enlightenment. Kant lived in relative isolation from the political upheavals of the eighteenth century, and wrote little of direct political import; nevertheless his direct and indirect influence on legal and political thinking has been enormous, and his philosophical exposition of the principles of *universalism is without compare. Kant believed that reason, which could lead to theoretical knowledge only when carefully circumscribed, has a natural tendency to transcend its limits, leading to empty and paradoxical beliefs which could never be rationally supported. However, this very same reason has a legitimate practical employment, in which it is *autonomous, a law-maker to itself, both postulating and obeying the 'categorical imperative' of pure practical reason. This stipulates that one must act only on that maxim which one can at the same time will as a law for all rational beings. Reason is the distinguishing feature of man and of human *agency, and the defining property of the *person, who is constrained by it to treat himself and all other persons as ends, and not as means only. However, the conditions for the harmonious exercise of practical reason are not present in nature, so that men must ascend towards reason with the aid of local and circumscribed political communities. These fail to instantiate the universalist *ideal of a 'kingdom of ends' in which reason alone is sovereign. However, as Kant argues in *Perpetual Peace*, 1795, the ultimate aim of reason is to realize that idea: this will require a universal 'league of nations', and a subsequent dwindling of the authority of the *nation state. Kant at first hailed the French Revolution as a sign of mankind's progress towards this condition of 'perpetual peace', but later withdrew his approval, and returned to a belief in mitigated monarchy as the best form of government for imperfect beings. Underlying Kant's famous and influential philosophy of *internationalism are the ruling ideas of his moral philosophy:

(i) The premise of all morality is autonomy. Autonomy is the kind of freedom that is unique to the will of a rational being, and which generates the ability to 'will an action as law' for oneself. I can will an action as law for myself only if I also will it as a universal law, since it is of the essence of reason to abstract from all 'empirical' conditions towards universal maxims. Hence from autonomy there stems:

(ii) The categorical imperative: I must act so as to will the maxim of my action as a universal law, and I can do this only if I respect the rationality of others (else my law is not addressed to universal reason); hence I must treat all rational beings as ends, and not as means. That in turn is possible only if I envisage myself and others as alike members of an ideal community, or 'kingdom of ends'.

(iii) The conflict between reason and the passions is one part of that between the rational will, which struggles always to realize the kingdom of ends, and the 'empirical conditions' which prevail in the realm of nature. Law will become truly universal only when it abstracts from those conditions and addresses itself to reason alone. Such a law can make no distinction among rational beings except in terms of the 'good' and the 'bad' will that motivates them. Moreover, as an expression of autonomy, it conflicts with the individual will only where that will is acting unfreely, in obedience to a force of nature, rather than to its own sovereign authority. Hence when this universal law is enforced it will not infringe the freedom of those who are governed by it, but only curb their unfree desires.

Those ideas provide a philosophical foundation for *liberalism in one of its most persuasive forms: they recommend a kind of law which aims at freedom, and which makes no arbitrary distinctions among those to whom it is applied. Freedom is the ability to realize oneself in autonomous choices. (*See* *self-realization.) But such choices will always contain an act of rational obedience towards the moral law. (The idea of freedom as obedience was later, in *Hegel and others, to be given interpretations that are far from liberal.)

On Kant's view the moral law, since it stems from reason alone, must be objectively binding on all rational beings, and there is no need to have recourse to theology in order to recommend it. Indeed, to invoke religion at this point is, Kant thought, to fall into the trap of 'heteronomy of the will'. (Making the rational will obedient to something other than itself.) Hence Kant is often held to have completed a task begun by *Grotius, giving a basis for natural law which does not invoke the will of God, but rather commands God himself to obedience. Moreover, the second formulation of the categorical imperative (the injunction to treat persons as ends and not as means only) has often been thought to capture the essence of the idea of justice, and has therefore been used as a basis for many philosophical doctrines of rights. (*See*, e.g., *Nozick.)

katascopic. Of a social theory: proceeding from a conception of society towards a description of the individual, as opposed to 'anascopic': extrapolating from the individual towards a conception of society. Since *Durkheim it has been common for *sociology to be katascopic.

Kautsky, Karl (1854–1939). The leading 'classical' exponent, after Marx and Engels, of *Marxism. Kautsky was influenced by *Darwinism, and found the *materialist theory of history irresistible, believing it to be an extension into the socio-political realm of the same persuasive thought that had motivated the theory of evolution. He accepted the Marxian distinction between base and superstructure, the thesis that capitalism would be destroyed by internal *crisis, and the theory that *socialization of the means of production was alone sufficient to end the contradictions of capitalism. The principal contradiction, for Kautsky, was that between the ability of capitalism to produce ever increasing wealth, and its inability to distribute it. Kautsky opposed the *revisionism of Bernstein, and at first rejected the 'parliamentary road to socialism'. However, at the Second *International, over which Kautsky was a dominant intellectual and political influence, he attempted to reconcile the revisionists and the left-wing group led by Liebknecht, Mehring and *Luxemburg. After the split in the Russian social democrat party, Kautsky favoured the *mensheviks against the *bolsheviks, began to oppose the 'revolutionary road to socialism', and attacked Lenin's theory of *imperialism. Subsequently he broke completely with Lenin, denounced Leninist practice, and became the object of fierce criticism from within the bolshevik camp. However, some of his economic theories, and in particular his work on agriculture (*The Agrarian Question*, 1899), entered into orthodox USSR thinking.

Kelsen, Hans (1881–1973). Austrian jurist and political theorist, who advanced a legalistic conception of the state as a system of *positive law, not founded in natural law or in any other conception of justice other than as a constraint upon procedure (*General Theory of Law and State*, 1945). Each system of positive law consists of norms imposed and enforced by the state, the validity of these norms consisting in their derivability from a basic norm (*Grundnorm*), such as the proposition that the constitution is supreme. The *Grundnorm*, which is the point beyond which justification cannot go, defines the essence of the state and the form of its (internal) *sovereignty. Hence states can be classified in terms of this *Grundnorm*, which might, e.g., enjoin subjects to obey a constitution, or a custom, or the will of a monarch.

While Kelsen's view of the state is legalistic, he refused to see law as anything but rationalized and systematized *convention, through which political power exerts itself. The value of this system is to be found, not in its conformity to any abstract ideal of justice, but in its ability to promote peace, order and well-being. Hence the ultimate justification offered for any system of law is *utilitarian.

Kemalism. Advocacy of the doctrines and policies of Kemal Atatürk (1880–1938), Turkish military leader and statesman, who abolished the *sultanate, and founded the modern Turkish republic in a spirit of Turkish *nationalism. Kemalism advocates the orientation of the state towards international relations, and the complete reorganization of all traditions and customs which hinder those relations, or retard the formation of modern political institutions. Hence, in order to create a modern state, a modern civil society must be simultaneously generated to be governed by it. All educational, administrative and legal bodies must be *secularized, and domestic life must be *modernized, even down to the details of dress and sexual conduct (Atatürk is famous for forbidding the wearing of the veil, and for his rejection of the Islamic laws of marriage and sexual relations). One of the most striking features of Kemalism was the attempt to give a serious practical politics of *language: it set out to reform the Turkish language both in alphabet and vocabulary, rejecting Arabic words in favour of native (i.e. Anatolian) words, and Arabic script in favour of the Roman alphabet. Hence it was able to break at the roots the bond with Islamic culture, and turn Turkey's face towards the West, fortified by a growing spirit of national *identity.

ketman. Persian term (from Arabic: *kitman*, concealment) used to denote a phenomenon recorded admiringly by *Gobineau: the elaborate concealment of one's deepest convictions, and the ironic and absolute pretence to adopt a rival system of beliefs. Ketman was practised by certain Muslim sects (Shi'ites and Druze) in the face of political, religious and philosophical persecution. The term has also been used by the Polish writer Czeslaw Miłosz (*The Captive Mind*, 1955), in order to denote the stance of the intellectual in the modern communist state, forced to simulate adherence to political doctrines which conflict with everything that he believes to be true, and learning to take elaborate, self-mocking pleasure in the techniques of concealment.

Keynes, John Maynard, Lord (1883–1946). English economist, who addressed himself to the problem of *unemployment, seeking both to explain and to remedy it, and who thereby invented the most influential twentieth-century theory of *macroeconomics. Traditional economics had attempted to explain unemployment by the inflexibility of wages in the downswing of the *trade cycle, arguing that the principal solution to unemployment was to cut wages, so that the prospect of greater profits would induce businessmen to invest. Keynes argued against this, suggesting that a cut in wages would probably lower *aggregate demand, which is in turn a factor involved in the stimulation of the economy, so that a lowering of wages might well, by reducing aggregate demand, cause a further decline in employment. Hence Keynes advocated the active stimulation of demand by the government, for example by spending on public works. He advanced a theory designed to justify this, and also to solve many of the outstanding problems left by older theories of *money, *interest, and *investment (*The General Theory of Employment, Interest and Money*, 1936). This suggested, as against the older theories, that the quantity of money in the economy determines, not just the level of prices, but also the real rate of interest. In order to increase output and to diminish unemployment it was not that wages should be cut but rather that aggregate demand for goods and services should be increased. The details of this theory are complex, and it has been both much criticized and much defended by subsequent economists. However, it has had considerable political influence. It suggested, first, that a capitalist economy may, at a certain point, require considerable government intervention if it is to survive; secondly that, given that intervention, it may very well survive indefinitely. Hence predictions of a *crisis of capitalism are unfounded, and the much discussed *falling rate of profit does not spell the doom of capitalist enterprise. Keynes thus gave theoretical foundations for a *mixed economy and for *interventionism; these have since become features of most Western European forms of government.

Keynes's theory implies that heavy unemployment is not necessarily a temporary aberration from the normal situation, but may represent an equilibrium, if there is no government intervention to remedy the problem. If aggregate demand is too high, on the other hand, it is argued that demand-pull *inflation will occur. Moreover sustained full employment may lead to problems of inflation, due to the strengthened position of workers and trade unions. (*See also* *over-full employment.)

Keynesianism. Advocacy of the kind of doctrine and policy recommended by *Keynes in the *General Theory*, and in particular of government intervention in the economy in order to stimulate demand. More recently, however, a distinction has often been drawn between (vulgarized) 'Keynesianism', and the (more subtle) ideas of Keynes himself.

kibbutz. Hebrew: *kibbus*, a gathering. A kind of *cooperative agricultural settlement, owned collectively by its members, in which the family is not abolished but replaced, as primary unit, by a form of *commune, forbidding all private property in the means of production. Children are educated collectively, and work is distributed without regard to class or influence. (Such is the theory, which advocates a kind of communal social life as an effective way of securing true community of interest in those concerned to operate an enterprise.)

The kibbutz system was introduced into Israel in 1909, in order to provide Jewish settlements which would operate within a *market economy, while being politically and socially independent. Kibbutzim were to be socialist and egalitarian in their internal organization (thus instantiating an ideal of *market socialism). Later they were favoured as a way to maintain an active military presence in the countryside.

kinship. The system of human relations derived from sexual reproduction, and including such relations as the *family. Anthropologists distinguish kinship (relation by blood) from affinity (relation by marriage). In practice, however, both relations are involved in a 'kinship system', which consists of a set of obligations, customs and social ties which unite people into a society of supposed blood relationship. Such systems are of great interest to anthropologists, and form what is perhaps the least institutionalized of political orders. Each member either is, or behaves as if he is, a relation, by blood or affinity, of every other, and owes his obligation to the leaders and to the tribe on that basis alone. Usually an aura of sanctity and religious prohibition surrounds and consolidates this vital bond of kinship, so making the obligations founded in it absolute and indefeasible. Such sentiments enable many tribes to dispense with developed systems of law, thus surviving as societies without the protective mantle of a state. This means that, legally speaking, they may be incorporated into a state without violation of sovereignty, since, from the legal point of view, they do not possess it. However, from the philosophical point of view, it is clear that statehood is a matter of degree, that many tribes do possess it to some degree, and that the prevalence of *custom and *tradition should not be thought of as a simple absence of institutions, but rather as the presence of institutions of a special kind.

The strain of adapting *allegiance so that it is directed towards a state and its attendant system of law has led to periodic attempts in civilized communities to reorganize the sentiments of *political obligation on the model of those deep bonds of kinship which seem to dispense with legalized conceptions of politics entirely. This attempt is characteristic of certain forms of conservative *organicism, of old-fashioned *nationalism and, in the limiting case, of *racism, where an attempt is made to underpin the entire structure of a modern state with a fiction of kinship.

Kropotkin, Peter Alekseievitch, Prince (1842–1921). Founder of anarcho-communism, who attempted to base an anarchist theory of society on a methodical science of social relations. Kropotkin opposed *Darwinism and argued, on the basis of observation both of men and of animals, that 'mutual aid' was the true principle of individual and social development, and not the 'survival of the fittest'. In *Law and Authority, an Anarchist Essay*, 1886, he argues that custom and voluntary agreement, rather than law and normative authority, represent the creative forces of history In *Mutual Aid, a Factor of Evolution*, 1890–6, he argues that sociability is, under all circumstances, the greatest advantage in the struggle for life, and therefore the natural condition of all evolutionary beings, who, were it not for the corruptions imposed by the state and law, would develop bonds of instinctive solidarity which would make government unnecessary. He advocated a form of 'anarchist communism', and opposed his view to that of Marx, which he regarded as 'statist'.

kulaks. Former peasants elevated into proprietors of medium-sized farms after the agrarian reforms of Stolypin in Russia in 1906. The kulaks became a kind of agrarian middle class, and they present perhaps the most striking example in modern politics of the deliberate creation of a class, the aim being political stability, the disintegration of the village commune, and the protection of the countryside against revolution. In 1929 Stalin ordered the 'liquidation of the kulaks'; ten million people are estimated to have died.

Kulturkampf. German: war of culture. Repressive political movement against the Roman Catholic Church, instigated in 1871 by Bismarck, with the intention of wresting all educational and cultural institutions from the church, and conferring them instead upon the state. Bismarck became convinced of the error of his policy, and concluded a concordat with Pope Leo XIII. The term has, however, remained, designating one aspect of a complex phenomenon, equally exemplified in *cultural revolution, where an attempt is made to transfer political power through gaining control over *education and *culture.

L

labour. The purposeful exercise of human capacity (whether physical or intellectual) in the transformation of nature into commodities. Labour is regarded by many economists as one among several *factors of production, and by *Marx as the primary *productive force.

Labour time is the time spent in productive activity, whereas labour *power* is the capacity to produce through labour. The distinction between the two is a cornerstone of the theory of *surplus-value, in the version defended by Marx. If it were the case that an employer gave to an employee the value of his labour time, then (it is held) there could be no explanation of the *accumulation of value in the employer's hands. Only when we see that the wage contract exchanges the value of labour *power* for the value of a certain labour *time* do we begin to understand how the second might be invariably greater than the first, resulting in a transfer to the employer of what Marx called (tendentiously) hours of 'unpaid labour'.

Nineteenth-century theories of labour as constitutive of the human personality, and the associated attempts to analyse the self-image of labour in its varied employments, have had considerable influence upon modern political thinking, notably through the theory of *alienated labour, which attempts to account for the distressed quality of the labour process under *factory production, sometimes in terms of the distinct mode of ownership that is associated with it. (*See* *work.)

labour law. The body of legal principles and rules governing the employment of *labour: more or less synonymous with *industrial law.

Legislation governing the terms of the *wage contract is of great antiquity, and a notorious medieval example (the Statute of Labourers 1349, which condemned labourers after the Black Death to work for wages current before it, despite the disparity between the demand for and the supply of labour) has been the subject of much political comment, partly because it is an early example of an *incomes policy. Most modern legislation has been aimed at improving the conditions of labour, and has arisen as a response to the *industrial revolution, and to the social changes consequent on large-scale *factory production and the employment of *detail labour. The first important statute in the UK was Pitt's Health and Morals of Apprentices Act 1802; but *see further* *factory legislation.

labour mobility. Labour mobility is of two kinds: (a) geographical, consisting in the power of the labour force to move from place to place, and (b) occupational, consisting in the power of workers to change occupations in response to changing needs and the availability of jobs. Art. 48 of the Treaty of Rome, 1957, attempts to guarantee mobility in sense (a) throughout the EEC, but it has been considerably qualified by local immigration laws. Within any economy both forms of mobility affect the rate at which economic *equilibrium can be achieved after radical changes in the place and character of production. The proliferation of factory production and detail labour increases mobility in sense (a), since it severs the social relations which attach people to particular places of work and leisure, while decreasing it in sense (b), since it encourages an increasing specialization and narrowness in the forms of work.

labour movement. The movement which seeks to further the interests of the working class, usually by gaining political power (either through *representation or through direct *control) for workers. The antecedents of the labour movement are found in the rebellions of slaves in antiquity, and in the 'peasants' revolt' of medieval Europe. The modern labour movement is, however, to a great extent an offshoot of *industrialization and of the consequent severance of the labourer from all traditional relations of obligation towards his employer. It began in France and England, among reforming radicals, during the eighteenth century, and took early shape in English *Chartism and French *Babouvism. Its history through the nineteenth century is intermingled with that of *Owenism, *Marxism, *ouvrièrisme* (the French movement pressing for working-class representation within a republican constitution), the *trade union movement, and the various responses from governments. In the UK these responses included *factory legislation, and the eventual extension of the franchise in 1867, as a result of which a considerable portion of the working class was able to vote in parliamentary elections. This permitted the emergence of new political movements, such as the Labour Representation League, formed in 1869, working for the representation of the labour movement in Parliament but 'without reference to opinion or party bias'. The movement culminated in the formation of the UK *Labour Party, which has provided the model for similar parties elsewhere. These have sought to give power to the working class through representation within a *constitutional democracy, and to use existing institutions in order to work for the betterment of the pay and conditions of labour, while maintaining a broadly *socialist political perspective. The labour movement has also had a developed international character, and has sought at every stage to create links between workers which transcend national boundaries.

labour organizations. Organized labour has taken many forms, both within and outside the *labour movement. Principal are: *trade unions, *labour parties, *international labour organizations and *cooperative movements. One of the motives behind such organizations is given by the following theory. The owners of property are automatically in collusion, and can force legislation and political action to protect their interests. The market unites them in the common aim of profit, and since law is the offshoot of market relations, it will always be bent in their direction. Labour, however, is in no such fortunate position, since it owns nothing but itself (which according to some is one stage better, according to others one stage worse, than *slavery or *serfdom), and so cannot enforce its interests. It has, therefore, an automatic tendency to economic and political disunity, arising from the wage contract, which puts labourers in competition with one another for jobs, exploits their need, and prevents spontaneous collusion in any action designed to ameliorate their common circumstances. The unequal balance between the labourer and the man who employs him can be restored only by the development of organized labour, either in the form of trade unions and other organizations within a capitalist economy, which restore some of the mutuality of the wage contract through *collective bargaining, or through anti-capitalist organizations which have social ownership as their aim.

labour parties. The political arm of the *labour movement. The UK Independent Labour Party emerged from an informal coalition with the Liberals in 1893, while the Labour Party as we know it was founded in 1900, as a combination of all *democratic socialist groups in the UK, including trade unions, the *Fabian Society, the Independent Labour Party and the left-oriented Social Democratic Federation. Other labour parties were formed in imitation of it, in various parts of the British Empire and (subsequently) Commonwealth, and Norway and Israel have both developed labour parties on the UK model. In so far as they have achieved an identifiable political character it is captured by the following features:

(a) explicit appeal to the working-class vote;

(b) affiliation with, and even partial direction by, the trade unions, with important constitutional provisions to preserve the relative autonomy of the parliamentary party;

(c) belief in representational government through democratic election, and in the constitution and institutions (such as parliament) that will be necessary for that end;

(d) belief in a planned economy, with the increasing use of government power to direct industry, to ensure *economic growth and full employment, and to bring about a more equitable distribution of property and opportunity. For the most part this has involved the advocacy of the nationalization of key private assets, and the furtherance of a mixed economy, permitting limited private ownership of the means of production;

(e) belief in the redistribution of wealth, usually through taxation, and the abolition of privilege (especially privilege which stems from class) in all fields, especially education and the professions;

(f) belief in the development of a *welfare state;

(g) the commitment to democracy, not only as a principle of government, but also as a necessary part of the just administration of all institutions, however subordinate. This last feature is part of the undercurrent of liberalism which motivates much labour party thinking.

On the whole labour parties have shown themselves to be constitutionalist in their activities, fairly conservative in their economic policy, and highly respectful towards popular symbols of government, such as the UK monarchy. Recent conflicts within the UK party have arisen partly because those on the left either reject that constitutionalist and parliamentarian stance, or else are believed to reject it by those on the right. The conflict resembles that between bolsheviks and mensheviks in the Second International, and has led to the formation of the first *social democrat party within the UK Parliament.

labour power. *See* *labour.

labour theory of value. A theory developed by *Ricardo, and adopted by *Marx, according to which the *exchange-value of a commodity is determined by labour and labour alone. The theory exists in at least three forms.

(i) Since exchange-value is an artefact, and cannot exist in nature, it must exist in virtue of some human activity. The only activity that could explain the rise of the institution of exchange is the activity which transforms nature into commodities. This activity is human labour. The theory exists in this form in Hegel and in the early Marx. It may explain the institution of exchange-value, but not the quantity of exchange-value that resides in any commodity.

(ii) (Ricardo.) The exchange-value of a commodity is uniquely determined (provided certain conditions are satisfied) by the quantity of labour that went into its production. Hence *price, or exchange-value in *equilibrium conditions, is directly proportional to labour hours.

(iii) (Marx.) The exchange-value of a commodity depends upon the labour time 'socially necessary' to produce the commodity. Marx sometimes speaks of value as 'congealed labour', a phrase that is ambiguous between (i) and (ii). It is important to note that Marx's labour theory of value was primarily intended not as a theory of price but as an analysis of the *exploitation of the worker. Marx differed from the previous classical economists in that he argued that the capitalist buys labour *power*, rather than labour, and that he pays the worker less value than he extracts from his labour, hence the *surplus value. So there is exploitation rather than a just price.

The differences between (ii) and (iii) are not always noticed. They are, however, enormous since by (ii) the value of a commodity is given by the labour used to produce it, while by (iii) it is given by the labour that is *necessary* to produce it at the time of exchange (when conditions of production might be vastly different). In all versions the labour theory attempts to dispense with demand as an independent variable in the creation of value. It also represents capital as economically subordinate, being itself no more than an accumulation of value, and hence to be explained as a by-product of labour. This formulates the fundamental Marxist intuition, that labour, not capital, is the prime *productive force. The view of capital as a productive force was stigmatized by Marx as 'capital fetishism'. (Cf. *commodity fetishism.) It is objected to the labour theory that it neglects scarcity rents, that it must reduce qualitative differences of labour to quantitative differences, that the special assumptions required for its conclusions are not fulfilled in modern economies, and that its most plausible version, (iii), requires a theoretical apparatus that has not been provided for it. Another objection is that the labour theory of value provides no theory of price levels unless one already knows the surplus value accruing to the supplier of each commodity.

laicism. The belief that civil functions performed erstwhile by a priesthood ought to be transferred to the laity, especially functions of a judicial and educational kind. Its extreme form might involve *anti-clericalism and the advocacy of a **Kulturkampf* against the church. It remains an important movement in Turkey and (to some extent) Tunisia. Laicism was regarded by *Kemalism as an essential part of the process whereby modern political institutions could be constructed, hence it remains one of the 'six arrows' of the Turkish Republican People's Party.

laicization. The transference of religious duties from a clergy to the laity. Not to be confused with *laicism, which advocates the authority of the laity in social and political matters, but usually concedes the exclusive competence of the priesthood in all matters of religion. However, a clergy which sees as 'matters of religion' what others see as 'simple politics' will often react to laicism as though it involved laicization, and so attempt to forbid it.

Laing, Ronald David (b. 1927). British psychiatrist. *See* *alternative society, *family, *psychotherapy.

laissez-faire. An expression which perhaps originated in a remark made to Colbert, finance minister to Louis XIV: 'Laissez faire, laissez passer.' The slogan was taken up by the *physiocrats, who believed that the state's role was simply that of protecting property rights and the natural order. *Classical economics shared this hostility to *interventionism, and the slogan *laissez-faire* is still used to characterize some of the doctrines of the *New Right, who believe with *Smith that a statesman who seeks to control the flow of capital within an economy 'would not only load himself with a most unnecessary attention, but assume an authority which could safely be trusted, not only to no single person, but to no council or senate whatever, and which would nowhere be so dangerous as in the hands of a man who had folly and presumption enough to fancy himself fit to exercise it' (*The Wealth of Nations*, IV, 2).

The theory of *laissez-faire* is part of a justification that is still offered for capitalism, although few now think that it indicates a feasible policy.

Lamarckism. The theory of evolution associated with the work of the French zoologist J. B. P. A. de Lamarck (1744–1829), according to which needs provide a motivating *force* behind evolutionary change, which does not therefore proceed in the random manner envisaged by some Darwinists. Lamarck believed in 'the inheritance of acquired characteristics': i.e. in the ability of an organism to pass on its achievements. Darwin himself was mildly attracted by Lamarckism, although it is not generally accepted by biologists. However, it has had its political followers, notable among them being Stalin, who adopted and, so to speak, enforced the version of Lamarckism known, after its propagator, as Lysenkoism. This view seemed to offer a biological basis for the reconciliation of *egalitarianism with human progress, since it suggested that an organism reared differently from its ancestors would tend to develop in a new way, and that distinctions between people might be eliminated by new conditions of development. A Lamarckian version of Marx's theory of history might also seem attractive, since it would account for the very small number of variations among *production relations that actually exist.

land. Land includes, for economic, political and legal purposes, all that is contained within the soil, all that grows on it, and also, in law, all that has been built on it (*see* *land law.) Early debates over the economics of agriculture often posed the question of whether land could be considered to be a *factor of production distinct from *capital. The free exchange of privately owned land is, legally speaking, a relatively new development, dating in the UK from the Settled Land Act 1856. But since land itself is productive often only when serviced by labour, it stands in a relation to labour that is comparable to that of any other means of production.

Some have argued that, while private property in such things as houses, commodities, and even factories may be permissible in the interests of security and production, private property in land violates a fundamental need or right of *common ownership. (Arguments along these lines were offered by Henry George, in *Progress and Poverty*, 1879.) Proposals for the social ownership of land have therefore been frequent in modern politics, even in the UK where, technically, no land is held except on tenure from the Crown. The problems for this new attempt to divide land from 'movable' goods are twofold: (i) all goods are produced from raw materials that were, originally, land; hence there has to be a transition from common ownership to private ownership if the latter is to be possible, and hence there must be a *right* of transfer. With whom does this right lie? If it lies with society as a whole (or with the state as society's trustee or guardian), then in effect there is common ownership of everything; (ii) in order to live on and produce from the land some security of tenure is necessary, and what is security of tenure if not a (defeasible) right of private property? (*See* *private property.) In which case social ownership becomes a legal fiction, like the ownership of land by the Crown.

Nevertheless the distinction between land and other forms of capital remains deeply entrenched in much political thinking, and not merely because the first is an ambiguous term which sometimes refers to agricultural as opposed to factory production. Many conservatives, for example, distinguish between the psychological stances involved in the ownership of land and the ownership of movable capital. The first stands as a symbol for permanent attachment to a place, and submission to the *jurisdiction there obtaining, while the second represents the desire to accumulate power in a manner that may avoid the responsibilities that attach to it, and to move from jurisdiction to jurisdiction in order to escape them. Although there is an exaggeration involved in that (for example, no man need live on land that he owns) it does suggest an argument for *exchange control which conservatives might be compelled to accept, on grounds summarized by Disraeli as the 'feudal principle': 'the tenure of property is also the holding of responsibility'.

land law. The branch of law which deals with the tenure of land provides one of the most interesting fields of political archaeology, since it contains strata from every era of social development, in which are fossilized the legal foliage of former social and economic orders.

As an example of a politically significant transition it is instructive to consider the case of settled land. Originally settled land passed intact to the legal heirs, so that the tenant for life was considered trustee for those who were to succeed him, with no right of use that would enable him to alter their right to the land and its fruits. The Settled Land Acts 1882 and 1890 established that the interests of the heirs could be 'over-reached', i.e. translated into a money interest, and would automatically be so translated whenever the tenant for life sold the land. Hence – whatever the form of the settlement – there would be no impediment to sale of the land by the present occupant, who would then hold money, rather than land, in trust for his successors. This legislation put land for the first time on an equal footing with all other property as an item of free exchange, so that land becomes simply a special case of capital. This might be thought to be a product of the transition from feudal to capitalist relations of production, and the abolition of the special status of land that was associated with the former. (It should be noted, however, that, while this interpretation is sometimes embraced by Marxists, the legal transition occurred some 500 years later than the supposed economic one: which suggests that the explanation cannot be so simple.)

Of equal interest is the feudal doctrine, still surviving in UK law, of 'estates in land'. Land, being definitive of *jurisdiction, is always held subject to *allegiance. However, according to the feudal doctrine, tenure and allegiance follow each other: the obligation owed by the 'tenant in chief' is direct to the sovereign, that by the one who holds from the tenant in chief is to him, and so on. One half of this idea survives in the fact that tenure is always a matter of degree, descending from freehold (which is subject only to forfeiture in favour of the sovereign), through leasehold, to sub-tenancies, down to the weakest form of security, known as 'squatter's rights'. This last arises sometimes from *prescription, and sometimes from the effect of the Statute of Forcible Entry 1381, which makes it a crime forcibly to evict someone without legal process, and which has thus protected most kinds of tenancy since those times which are regarded as feudal. Defenders and attackers of private property should attend to the idea, still enshrined in this kind of law, that property rights often exist in varying degrees, and always involve a third term. Besides the person possessing them and the thing in which they are possessed, there is also the sovereign power from which they are held. (*See* *eminent domain.)

No legal system is without some kind of security of exclusive tenure, and since legal security of exclusive tenure *is* private property, no legal system is without private property in land: see, for example, Art. 44 of the USSR constitution which insists that housing is socially owned while conceding that citizens have a right to it (and this right is clearly only a genuine right if it involves a right also to exclude at least some invaders from outside, otherwise it is not a right of tenure). It could be said that the onus lies on those who would think away all private property to describe how this variety of it might be eliminated without eliminating all the normal securities of domestic life. (*See* *production, distribution, exchange, consumption.)

The modern attempt to control relations between landlord and tenant by statute is an attempt to extend security of tenure and so rights in land to all citizens. It is sometimes held to violate the existing property rights of the landlord, although it is clear that every extension of ownership in land will violate the rights of *someone*, unless some land is unowned.

In the US the original settlements involved *common ownership of land; private property in land emerged only later, as a result of purchases from the common fund, and it is the economic success of private ownership in land in seventeenth-century Virginia that is partly responsible for the later universal approval and adoption of this transaction.

land reform. The breaking up of large estates, *redistribution of *land, and the facilitating of legal transfer of land, with the object of bringing about fundamental changes in the structure of power. Land, being identified with the state through the existence of *jurisdiction, and with life through its essential role in the production of necessary goods, seems to be fundamental to all relations of property. It is perhaps less true than it used to be that the *ruling class of a state is the class of landowners, but it is still the case that all radical changes in class structure proceed at least in part by land reform, and opposition to land reform may be a sign of the desire to conserve an existing social hierarchy. Since land is the object that most readily lends itself to doctrines of *common ownership it is less frequent to find such reform being opposed on grounds of *natural justice. *See* *hereditary principle.

landlocked state. A state with no coastal borders (e.g. Switzerland, Czechoslovakia), and which is therefore dependent upon the cooperation of its neighbours for all communications by sea. The importance of maritime communications for commerce and imperial expansion is sometimes offered as one explanation of the relative unimportance of landlocked states in international politics.

Lange, Oskar Ryszard (1904–65). Polish economist and politician. *See* *market socialism.

language. Language, as a symbol of social identity, came to have increasing political importance with the rise of *nationalism, so that the existence of a common language is now often thought to be an important precondition of political *identity. *Irredentism in the UK has been associated with moves to revive the Celtic languages, and the formation of the central European states after the dissolution of the Austro-Hungarian Empire took language as its starting-point. *Kemalism exerted towards the Turkish language much of its political energy, hoping to reform it in the direction of a desired political identity and away from cultural dependence upon the supposedly backward states of Islam. *Feminism also asserts a politics of language, sometimes arguing for the removal of distinctions of gender from English, or for the replacement of the masculine pronoun as the usual form of indefinite reference, on the ground that such grammatical habits merely perpetuate socially induced and 'irrelevant' distinctions between men and women, and also prevent the speaker from recognizing the arbitrariness of those distinctions. In opposition to such radical reformers the *cultural conservative is apt to defend the existing language as the embodiment of moral, spiritual and aesthetic values: the thought here has usually been vaguely expressed, and its implications are as obscure as those of the positions which it attacks.

Along with the many nationalist movements that take language as a political focus, there is also an international movement, which advocates an international language (Esperanto) that will be free from all the local and parochial affections that are contained in the older tongues. This movement seems to have flagged, perhaps because there were no native speakers to give it initial impetus. By contrast the use of Latin as a universal language by the Roman Catholic Church (now rejected by that institution, to the sorrow of many of its members) was enormously successful in helping it to found an international *jurisdiction, and to influence political and educational institutions everywhere.

Almost all discussions of the political significance of language engage in large and unfounded speculations, and, while there is no doubt that many of the above views are based in serious perceptions, it is extremely difficult to see how thought about this most difficult question should proceed. Some Marxists have attempted to present a 'labour theory' of language development (following the Marxian view of language as 'practical consciousness': *The German Ideology*, 1846), but despite Stalin's amateur linguistics, nobody has really succeeded in saying what this means. *See* *communication.

Lassalle, Ferdinand (1825–64). German *socialist, revolutionary of 1848, and for some time a friend both of *Proudhon and of *Marx. He advocated a form of socialism in which private property would be permitted if legitimately acquired, but in which the *iron law of wages would be broken by the abolition of *wage labour and the wage contract. He defended *co-operatives, which were to be established with assistance from the state, and which, when combined with universal suffrage, would lead not only to the economic but also to the political dominance of the working class, and the effective end of capitalist exploitation. Lassalle's socialism attempted to give concrete descriptions of future society, and to adapt itself to existing political institutions, so that changes in law within the existing constitition might be sufficient to bring it about. Hence it gave rise to many concrete programmes of reform, including the famous 'Gotha Programme', criticized as theoretically incoherent by Marx.

late capitalism. Term sometimes used by *socialist and especially *Marxist writers to denote the species of capitalism which has developed since the *industrial revolution and which survives in modified form in the US and Western Europe. It is called 'late' in obedience to the Marxist conviction that it is doomed soon to disappear, and in recognition of the fact that capitalist *production relations preceded the industrial revolution, although in a quite different form.

latitudinarianism. Term applied disapprovingly to those seventeenth-century Anglican divines who were without serious conviction in matters of liturgy and even of doctrine. Now often extended to denote any kind of doctrinal unconcern, especially in matters of religion and politics.

law. H. Kantorowicz (1877–1940) defined

law as 'a body of social rules prescribing external conduct and considered justiciable'. This definition, satisfactory so far as it goes, does not go far: what is meant by 'social'? 'rules'? 'prescribing'? 'external'? 'conduct'? 'justiciable'? And 'considered' by whom? The following observations seem pertinent:

(a) 'social' denotes the fact that law applies to more than one person, and that the subject of law is himself a social being (perhaps because he is a *rational being);

(b) 'rules' must embrace custom (since there is customary law), unformulated maxims (since there is *common law), as well as *statute. The common element here is that of repeatability: the same action can be performed on a variety of occasions, and in principle by any number of people. Thus laws, however qualified, must always have a universal form;

(c) 'prescribing' means that laws are not indicative but imperative in mood: they do not describe but command (although this is in one sense denied by legal realists: *see* below). Hence, if there is a motive to disobey the law, there must also be sanctions and *punishments to enforce it;

(d) 'external' is meant to exclude thought and belief and those emotions that are 'kept to oneself', and to apply only to behaviour that is recognized socially. The possibility of laws forbidding private thoughts and emotions is, however, a real one. It is sometimes thought that such laws would be deviant; however, many systems of law prescribe 'correct beliefs'. It is sometimes argued that such laws prescribe not beliefs but parades, rituals and customs which require at least an outward pretence of those beliefs;

(e) 'conduct' means conduct which issues from *agency of a *person, and for which it is intelligible to hold the agent *responsible;

(f) 'justiciable' means susceptible to evaluation before a *court of law, empowered to enforce a judgement;

(g) 'considered' is the most difficult term in this list. The simplest answer is 'considered by the state in its legislative capacity', which clarifies the matter only to someone who has a grasp of the idea of the *state and its *legislature. Many nineteenth-century theorists, notably *J. S. Mill, wrote as though law is the expression of a social requirement, so that 'considered' is to be interpreted as 'considered by society' – which seems to conflict with the observation that society, unlike the state, is not a decision-making body, and becomes one only by also becoming a state.

Law as roughly defined above has been theorized in three distinct ways:

(i) Natural law theory. This sees all laws as attempts by human reason to approximate to those rules of *natural law which enshrine an ideal of good conduct, and which are the universal property of rational beings. The doctrine has two forms, according to whether natural law is thought of as gaining its authority from God's command or from human reason. However, as *Kant pointed out, the first interpretation makes natural law into a species of *positive law, and so in effect abolishes it.

(ii) Legal positivism. First fully expounded in modern times by *Bentham and John Austin. This theory regards law not as an attempt to approximate to an objective law of nature, but simply as a human *convention or stipulation, whose authority derives from no other source than that of the legislating body which dictates it. On this view all law is by definition *positive law. But that does not mean that all law is *arbitrary: a law must still be validated by its pedigree, by the fact, for example, that it can be derived from a *Grundnorm (see* *Kelsen) or conforms to a 'rule of recognition' (a phrase used by H. L. A. Hart) which determines its constitutional validity. Nevertheless there is no extra-legal standard that a law must conform to in order to *be* a law. Such a view may yet be compatible with the doctrine of *natural law, as providing an independent criterion of the *merit* of any positive law. (Alternatively, a *utilitarian criterion may be invoked in the justification of any particular body of laws.) For the positivist, law is law by virtue of its form; for the naturalist, by virtue of its content.

(iii) Legal realism. A name sometimes given to the view which tries to discuss the basic *fact* of law, without reference to its prescriptive nature. Law is a form of social activity, with its attendant punishments and persuasions; since this is the only fact of the matter, then it is in these terms that law must be discussed. Law becomes 'the prophecies of what courts will do in fact and nothing more pretentious' (Holmes J.).

law and morality. What is forbidden by the law may be morally permissible and even morally obligatory; likewise what is morally forbidden may be permitted or even compelled by the law. To what extent should the two systems of *sanction correspond, and to what extent can they correspond? Those questions have been a major problem for modern political thinkers. Liberals in the Anglo-Saxon tradition have tended to follow *J. S. Mill in thinking that law is essentially *public, whereas morality has large *private areas into which the law can intrude only by violating individual rights or freedoms, and so undermining its own legitimacy. For example, sexual morality has recently been regarded as a private affair, or as public only in so far as it involves *harm to one of the participants. If that is so, it is often argued, the harmless varieties of sexual conduct, however morally obnoxious they may be or be thought to be, ought not to be forbidden by law. The only criteria should be those of harm and *consent. By contrast, thinkers who do not feel the liberal confidence in the absolute independence of *society and *state, may think of the state and its law as the guardian of an entire social order, and of all the values, whether moral, religious, or political, which that social order requires. For example, it may be argued that social order can endure despite the violation of many moral sanctions, but that moral sanctions must be recognized by the law if they are to be commonly accepted, and must be commonly accepted if social cohesion is to be maintained. That thought (which rests on a utilitarian premise) may correspond in its conclusions to more authoritarian pronouncements, such as those made on behalf of a divine law. Thus in the modern *Islamic state, the distinction between morality and law is apt to seem artificial, as is the corresponding distinction between the public and the private, precisely because all human affairs are regulated by a law which has been laid down by God. (*See further* *freedom, *liberalism, *liberty.)

law and order. The rallying cry of a certain kind of *populist conservatism, although plausibly held to be a main concern of *politics everywhere. To the extent that order exists without law there is no state (and perhaps no need for one); to the extent that law exists without order then the state exists only as an ideal and not in reality. Theoretically speaking the two terms correspond to the division between *rights and powers, and the slogan indicates the belief that political *constitution consists in their convergence: all powers should be sanctioned by right, and all rights enacted through an order that exactly corresponds to them.

Order without law may be spontaneous (the ideal of *anarchism), or forced (the actuality of *despotism). *Constitutionalists tend to argue that it is no accident that the preaching of anarchism leads to despotism.

law of uneven development. A supposed law, often alluded to by *Marx, and invoked, e.g, by *Trotsky, in order to explain and predict the course of *revolution in underdeveloped countries (especially Russia) and to reconcile the observed facts with the major claims of *Marxist theory. The idea is that, instead of developing uniformly from feudal to post-capitalist production relations, such societies develop in a way that, while beginning in feudalism, and ending in socialism, is in its intermediary stages 'planless, complex and combined' – 'combined' meaning that various stages in the process, such as *primitive accumulation and *industrialization, which should in theory be separated, occur in combination. The law is therefore sometimes called the 'law of uneven and combined development', and 'without this law. . .it is impossible to understand the history of Russia, and indeed of any country of the second, third or tenth cultural class' (Leon Trotsky: *History of the Russian Revolution,* 1930).

leadership. The capacity to inspire confidence in the rightness of one's purposes, courage in their collective execution, and *obedience in the threat of resistance. (*Contrast* *demagogue.) Leadership has sometimes been propounded as a supreme political virtue (*see *Führerprinzip*, *vanguard), although it is also one of the characteristics that make *politics impossible. Leadership is a matter of degree, and consists in the extent to which a single person can build *control on a foundation of *influence. Changes effected through leadership may be vaster and, despite the hardship of those affected by them, more easily accepted than those which derive from the deliberation of a party or a bureaucracy. At the same time, they are often considered, in retrospect, to be the inevitable outcome of irresistible and impersonal forces. Many recent sociological studies of leadership have attempted to explain these and related facts. Some argue that leadership results from *charisma – although this seems not so much to explain the phenomenon as to redescribe it. Others now reject attempts to explain leadership in terms of the personal characteristics of the leader, and prefer to see leadership as a relation dependent upon social context, so that those who are leaders in one situation may not be leaders in another. (See R. M. Stogdill: *Personal Factors Associated with Leadership,* 1948). Elias Canetti (*Crowds and Power,* 1960) has described the function of the leader as an integral part of a *crowd, and has argued that the principal quality that he requires, apart from those which make him prominent in the first place is survival. By showing himself able to survive while others succumb to the greatest dangers he perpetuates the myth of a more than human virtue; to do this he may even deliberately set out to kill his closest supporters.

left. The polar opposite of *right. The term originated in the habit of the democratic and liberal side of the French assembly, and of other European legislatures in the nineteenth century, of sitting to the left of the president's chair (a habit presaged in the French Estates General of 1789, in which the nobility sat on the King's right, and the 'third estate' on his left).

Terms like 'left', 'left of centre', and 'left wing' now denote a variety of things, and most of all a certain flavour of politics. Their use in Western democracies must be sharply distinguished from their use in most communist states (as in 'left-deviationism', for which see *leftism, *deviationism). The flavour signified in the West is produced by some combination of the following views (no one of which is necessary and each of which admits of degree):

(1) a hostility to *private property, and belief in *social ownership as the ideal alternative, with control by the state as a necessary means to that;

(ii) a hostility towards all *classes other than the *proletariat, and particularly towards the *bourgeoisie;

(iii) a hostility towards *establishment in all its forms, and towards *offices, *honours, and other symbolic expressions of the dignity of government;

(iv) desire for a classless society, without *privilege, *patronage or a *hereditary principle;

(v) belief in *democracy, or at least in popular participation in government; or government by consent;

(vi) belief in certain *natural rights (or *human rights), particularly those associated with the aspirations of the working class; together with a desire for *social justice;

(vii) a belief in *progress, to be furthered by *revolution or *reform;

(viii) *egalitarian leanings perhaps as

a result of a particular view of social justice;

(ix) anti-*nationalist (although not necessarily *internationalist) tendencies (although it should be noted that nationalists now constitute one of the largest classes on the left);

(x) belief in a *welfare state, and in state control over education, medicine, and important resources.

All of (i) to (x) show a tendency in a *socialist direction, and express a vision of politics which attempts to dispense with a theory of *institutions and with a theory of *political obligation. Not all of (i) to (x) are compatible in practice, although it is possible to believe that they are. (Thus some think that the state control advocated in (i) will tend to conflict with the natural rights supported in (vi), that the ideal of the classless society espoused in (iv) conflicts with the class loyalty expressed in (ii), that the belief in democracy expressed in (vi) conflicts with the contempt for establishment and office conveyed in (iii) (democracy being possible only within a framework of enduring institutions), and so on.) Most people on the left would describe themselves as socialists; the 'revolutionary left' is composed of those who wish to bring socialism into being by revolution, the rest being content with reform conducted through existing institutions. Left-wing theory is the attempt to synthesize all or some of (i) to (x), eliminate inconsistencies, and provide an underlying justification in terms either of a theory of history or a theory of *justice, or both.

Because there is a clear spectrum of opinion identified by the two poles of 'left' and 'right' it is now normal to refer, e.g., to the left wing of right-wing parties, and the right wing of left-wing parties. Very roughly the shift to the left is the shift in the direction of *Rousseau's 'compassionating zeal' for the poor and underprivileged, and away from respect for existing institutions, in particular those that confer power, property, privilege and social distinction.

left-liberal. Vague term denoting the spectrum of attitudes common among Western *intellectuals, and exemplified in the later expressions of English *Fabianism, and in the 'Lib-Lab' mentality. The main characteristic is an adherence to those items of *left-wing belief which are, or seem to be, compatible with certain basic *liberal convictions, notably the belief in *natural rights, in *freedoms (especially of thought, expression and association), and in legal *reform in the direction of increased *toleration. The attempt to reconcile those values with *social justice, and even with *egalitarian principles of distribution, has been responsible for many of the most important shifts in political opinion among Western intellectuals since the last war. Although left-liberal attitudes are often unsystematic there have been attempts to give them full theoretical foundation – e.g. in the theory of *justice espoused by *Rawls. These attempts are usually inspired by the sense that the two sets of values – those associated with the liberal doctrine of rights and freedoms, and those associated with socialist ideals of equitable distribution and social justice – are ultimately derived from a single *universalist intuition, concerning the equal value of every individual. It ought therefore to be possible to reconcile them within a single political doctrine. It is often objected that such a reconciliation is impossible, since the powers required to ensure socialist distribution can be exercised only by violating liberal rights and freedoms.

leftism. **1**. The adherence to the opinions of the *left.

2. In Communist Party official language, 'leftism' names a heresy, associated with *Bukharin, the main characteristics of which were originally a disposition to take socialist policies too far, and to insist for example on the *democratization of all social activities, rather than on the important tactical and supervisory role of the *Communist Party and its institutions. *Lenin's attacks on Bukharin and the 'left' in 1918 provide the main texts for this usage, in particular

Left Wing Communism: An Infantile Disorder, which defined the arguments and set the tone for subsequent discussions. Lenin there contrasts the 'principled' stance of his opponents with the 'tactical' stance of the Communist Party, especially in its operations outside the USSR.

legal fiction. A pretence that an instance of A is really an instance of B so that the law relating to Bs, but not to As, can be applied to it. The invention of a 'legal fiction' is a much favoured mode of legal development, enabling new cases to be accommodated and distinguished, without changing the structure of the law. Examples include many of the procedures for *manumission in *Roman law and for loans at interest in *Islamic law. Among examples in modern UK and US law are the doctrines that a girl under a certain age never 'consents' to sexual intercourse, and that a wife living with her husband always does. (The second of those is now, however, criticized, and probably soon to be discarded.)

legal privilege. A privilege in law is an authority to do something without fear of legal sanction. In UK law, members of *Parliament, barristers, *trade unions, and many others have privileges, protecting them against certain kinds of action which, could they be brought against them, would effectively prevent them from performing their functions. A privilege is sometimes described as a kind of *right; however the withdrawal of a privilege is not the violation of a right, so this usage is misleading. (It is sometimes said that it is a right, but not a 'claim right'. *See* *jural relations.) There is, for example, no 'right to strike' in UK law (although it is often spoken of); there is, rather, a privilege granting immunity to strikers from certain kinds of legal proceeding that might otherwise have been brought against them. (For the distinction here *see* *privilege.)

legalism. Excessive veneration for the law, and its procedures, and a reluctance to depart from the letter of the law, or to bend it in some new direction. Often used in a derogatory sense to mean excessive preoccupation with the *legality of an action and an associated reluctance to assess it on its independent merits.

Legalism is an important feature of many European forms of government. This has had important effects on the practice of *democratic centralism in Eastern Europe, where the Leninist commitment to a 'withering away of law' has been rejected, and all crimes are adjudicated under a traditional *adversary system, requiring complicated stratagems in political trials if the outcome is to be properly secured in advance.

legality. Conformity to *law. The principal ground on which a *subject may legally challenge the validity of an act of his *sovereign (i.e. an *act of state). The law, being an expression of the will of the sovereign, can be invoked against the sovereign without derogating from the sovereign's authority: a challenge based on illegality is simply a reminder to the sovereign of the internal necessity to be consistent. To the extent that such a challenge is not possible (e.g. by *judicial review, or by action on a charge of **ultra vires*) there is no true legal determination of the relations between subject and sovereign, and the system is one of *despotism.

legislation. The 'making' of law (inverted commas necessary since some believe that law is not made but discovered: *see* *judiciary, *law). This can involve any one of the following procedures:

(i) Express decree by the *legislature, which decree may be oral or written, and will always stand in need of subsequent interpretation by the judiciary. *See* *statute.

(ii) The establishment of a legal custom, with no express enactment of the legislature, but with an entrenched obedience to *precedent: *see* *common law.

(iii) A decision of the highest *court of the *jurisdiction concerning a case not covered by the existing legislation. The most famous case of this in English law is the decision of the House of Lords in *Rylands* v. *Fletcher,* 1868, from which most of the modern law of occupier's liability ultimately stems.

The third case is sometimes called 'judicial legislation', and is a special case of (ii); it is an instance of common law without precedent. What is the basis of such legislation? Is this merely an undetermined decision by the judges? Or are they working out implications in the existing law? Is their attitude one of invention or discovery? (*See* *hard cases.) Some thinkers dispute over the value of this third kind of legislation, and whether or not a *constitution should permit it (assuming that it could absolutely forbid it and still be a constitution). The US constitution, for example (Art. I, ss 1 and 7, and Art. VI), expressly confines the word 'legislation' to Acts of *Congress. But perhaps the only thing that is thereby confined is a word. The thing denoted by that word, say some, takes place in the law courts just as soon as there is a doctrine of *precedent.

legislator. The giver of law. That law should be given to a people, by a single legislator, sometimes seems strange to modern ways of thinking, but the idea of the wise legislator is an important conception in ancient and medieval theories of the state and also in the thought of *Rousseau, who wrote of the legislator as 'shaping the people like a god'. The most famous legislators were Lycurgus of Sparta, and Solon, who, at about 594 BC, was called upon to terminate the civil strife in Athens and give laws to the city, replacing those of Draco: some of these laws survive in fragments of verse (it being part of the authority of the legislator that he should express himself in memorable idiom). To think of the law as given is to think of it as directed to the purpose of order and good government. Thus *Machiavelli was able to say: 'that republic, indeed, may be called happy whose lot has been to have a founder so prudent as to provide for it laws under which it can continue to live securely, without need to amend them; as we find Sparta preserving hers for 800 years, without deterioration, and without any dangerous disturbances' (*Discourses,* I, II); and again: 'with very few exceptions, no commonwealth or kingdom ever has salutary institutions given to it from the first, or has its institutions recast in an entirely new mould, unless by a single person' (ibid. I, IX). The advocacy of legislation by a single man was not confined to Machiavelli: even *Harrington advanced this doctrine, on the grounds that a government should be made 'altogether and at once'. It is often remarked, however, that modern *revolutions, while they may end by giving power to a single person, seldom produce the 'immortal legislator' whom Robespierre sought. It is remarkable, for example, that, while Lenin achieved enormous concentration of power in the hands of a single party and its chiefs, he founded no institution or body of law that is independent of the power of the party or able to outlast it.

legislature. The part of government which exerts a *legislative power, i.e which is concerned with making and changing the law. Usually contrasted with the *executive, which applies the law, and engages in foreign and domestic *policy, and the *judiciary, which interprets the law and settles disputes. (For the theory of the relation between these, *see* *separation of powers.) There cannot be a *constitution without rules for determining who shall belong to the legislature. In the UK it is composed of the monarch, the House of Commons, and the House of Lords – i.e. 'The Queen in Parliament'. In the US it is composed of the President, the Senate and the House of Representatives. In both cases, however, *delegated legislation is (in certain conditions) permitted, so that other institutions are from time to time granted legislative powers, and ministers have powers to act by decree and directive which are also legislative. Moreover, the possibility of judicial legislation makes it difficult to draw the boundary between the legislature and the judiciary with any confidence in its absolute character.

legitimacy. A power is exercised illegitimately if there is no right to its exercise; otherwise it is exercised legitimately. Thus the crucial concepts in understanding legitimacy are those of *power and *right.

The main question that has occupied political thinkers is that of the legitimacy or otherwise of powers exercised in the name of the state, or of government. What gives a state the right to exercise such powers over the citizen, and which of the powers so exercised are rightly exercised? These questions are related to that of *political obligation: what obliges the citizen to obey the state? (Right and *obligation being 'jural correlatives': *see* *jural relations.) Expressing the question in terms of legitimacy emphasizes the *agency of the state, and questions that agency directly.

It is necessary to distinguish four questions:

(i) What makes a government, or the powers exercised by a government, legitimate? This is a question of political philosophy – identical in content, if not in emphasis, to that of political obligation.

(ii) What makes people believe a government to be, or accept it as being, legitimate? This is a question to which a politician, however sceptical or indifferent he may be towards the first question, will always give his attention. If a people have the rooted belief that only democratic election, say, or only hereditary succession, confers legitimacy, they can be governed in some other way only by force.

(iii) What is the legal determination of legitimate power? This is a question of law, perhaps of *positive law, the answer to which may vary from state to state. Thus a directive from the Crown *empowers* (i.e. confers legitimate power) upon its recipient in UK law. An exercise of power, if **ultra vires*, is by this criterion illegitimate. By extension, in *international law, the legitimate government may be distinguished from the illegitimate, by legal rules. These rules may in fact fly in the face both of the true grounds (if there be any) for legitimacy (question (i)), and of the true sentiments of those destined to accept the result (question (ii)).

(iv) What is the legal determination of legitimate succession to power? This 'hereditary' idea of legitimacy is the one most frequently discussed in practical politics. Thus democratic election is recognized by the US constitution as the legitimate means of transferring the executive power to a new President (in normal circumstances). But clearly the powers conferred by the constitution are not themselves made legitimate just because they are, in this sense, legitimately transferred. It might still be argued that the exercise of power over such and such a territory in accordance with this constitution is a violation of right (for example, the right of the original inhabitants of the American continent). Likewise, worries about 'legitimate succession' to the ruling house of the UK are not likely to impress someone who believes that monarchical government constitutes an illegitimate exercise of power.

It seems that illegitimacy, like injustice, is more easily recognized than its opposite, and that the resentment towards a government thought to be illegitimate is far stronger than the contentment with a government thought to have the sanction of right. This fact of human nature has been all-important in European politics, especially in determining allegiances during wars of succession.

legitimation. The process whereby power gains acceptance for itself in the eyes of those who are governed by it, by generating a belief in its *legitimacy. According to some Marxists it is a major function of *ideology to effect this legitimation, by representing the existing political institutions and offices in such a way that political obligation seems natural and right. (*See also* *naturalization.) In communist states legitimation tends to persist (despite the official view that, after the revolution, it will no longer be necessary), but has the novel character of issuing directly from the state, in the form of *doctrine. It is a fundamental conservative idea that legitimation, while it is necessary, cannot proceed from the state, but only from the institutions of *civil society, whether social, domestic or religious; the state draws upon the fund of legitimacy that is thereby generated, establishing ceremonies and activities with which to generate in the subject's mind the thought of an independent duty to be governed (as when, for example, the *sovereign has himself crowned by the Pope). The social phenomenon here is highly complex, but the political views divide between the following:

(i) legitimation is necessary only in some political conditions, dispensable in others;

(ii) legitimation is always necessary, and should proceed through *indoctrination or 'political education';

(iii) (the conservative view just referred to) legitimation is necessary, but should proceed independently of political doctrine, and by drawing upon civil institutions of a different order from the political. There is a natural disagreement over whether or not it would be *better* to dispense with legitimation or to create the conditions in which legitimation can be dispensed with – for example by establishing government by *consent (supposing this to be possible, and also distinct from government by legitimation). Some also argue that there is a *crisis of legitimation (e.g. Habermas and other members of the *Frankfurt school) which now imperils our civilization.

legitimist. Someone who believes in, and guides his political action by, an idea of the legitimate transfer of power. (*See* *legitimacy, question (iv).) Usually used to denote someone attached to a *monarchical government, governed by rules of succession, and to a particular person or family supposed entitled under those rules, the violation of which he deplores and resists. Such a person opposes not only *republican revolution, but also the ascent of a new ruling house, of a usurper or 'protector' or of any person other than the one prescribed by the (usually hereditary) rules for the transfer of government. The depth of legitimist feeling is great, and has often been compared to family feeling, perhaps because both are species of *piety.

Leibniz, Gottfried Wilhelm (1646–1716). German philosopher, mathematician, jurist, politician and scientist. *See* *rationalism, *theodicy.

leisure. Leisure is the freedom from the immediate need to *work; idleness is the lack of an occupation. The first is a value only to someone who thinks that he can be better occupied by not working. It is characteristic of a *profession that it may so invade the desires and ambitions of someone who pursues it as to eliminate the thought that he could be better employed in some other way; so that the professional may often not regard leisure as a value. The same does not seem to be true of the *wage labourer, who is occupied by work, but whose work does not usually generate a sense that he is well occupied. Does it follow that the wage labourer will desire leisure, or that he will know what to do with it when he has it? This question has become of increasing concern to political thinkers, since it seems that enforced idleness (or *unemployment) is now a normal condition; it generates social problems to the extent that there is no satisfactory form of leisure available to the unemployed.

Marx looked forward to the state of universal leisure that would supposedly follow upon the mastery of nature, and argued that in this state there will no longer be the fragmentation of human nature and activity that is characteristic of capitalist modes of production, since there will be no further dependence upon *detail labour and specialized employment. In this situation men would no longer be identified through *roles or occupations, but only as individuals – and all activities would be open to every man (even, it seems, hunting, fishing and literary criticism). That vision of leisure, as a 'restoration of man to himself', the condition in which all the faculties are developed in harmony with each other, and no one is stunted by too narrow an occupation in the productive process, is appealing, partly because it seems to reconcile the vision of a communist society with an individualistic ideal of *self-realization. However, it has often been objected that the condition is radically under-described by Marx. Do not human beings have a natural tendency to specialize, and is there not an inequality of abilities, skills and enthusiasms that makes this specialization necessary? And what satisfaction is there in doing everything by half? In what way would people existing in such a condition make their leisure into something that they could value?

Traditionally leisure was an attribute of *aristocracy, the privilege of a *ruling class. As such it was the subject of meticulous planning, and by no means thought of as the neutral condition from which self-realization took its departure. Leisure was rather an end in itself, developed into social life, manners, *ceremony, display, and high *culture, the whole of life given over to an elaborate play of aesthetic values. Some often attempt to envisage more democratic versions of that same laboured inactivity, perhaps out of a respect for the culture that is enshrined in it, perhaps out of a sense that it constitutes a valuable achievement in itself. Others regard that course as politically impossible, perhaps even as morally undesirable, and consider that, in so far as there can be a politics of leisure, it should be confined to those activities – such as *sport – which engage the attention of all classes. The older style of leisure, many say, is inextricably bound up with class domination, and gains its character from the elaborate ceremonies whereby ruling classes assert their determination to exclude those regarded as unsuitable for membership, while flattering their own ascendancy with activities which represent it as legitimate. Others, more pragmatic, regard the principal feature of a *leisure class as residing, not in culture, but in *conspicuous consumption, whereby those in whose hands wealth accumulates play a functional role in social organization, by spending as much and as fast as possible.

Pessimists, who argue that work is necessary in order to keep people fixed in social relations, tend to think of leisure as an evil, and to find the cure for *alienation, not in the provision of leisure, but in the transformation of work from something fragmented into something all-engrossing or at least fulfilling, in the manner of *craft (according to certain romantic visions of that mode of production).

leisure class. Expression coined by *Veblen (*Theory of the Leisure Class*, 1899), to denote the peculiarly inelegant class which, he thought, had appropriated the means of leisure in industrial countries and which had prevented full development of the potential that industrial production makes available. Despite its wasteful and stunted nature, having no style other than that of conspicuous consumption, this class performs the important economic function of returning the surplus product of production to the producers, by squandering it in a massive way, so stimulating again the process of production, and providing the employment through which producers subsist. It therefore maintains production at a level sufficient to reproduce itself, while preventing production from developing as it might.

Lenin. (V. I. Ulyanov) (1870–1924). Russian revolutionary, leader of the *bolsheviks during and after the Russian Revolution, and architect of modern communism. Lenin made some emendations to Marxist doctrine; these emendations did not, he thought, depart from the spirit of Marxism, but only made it possible to envisage its practice in twentieth-century conditions. In so far as Lenin's theory differs from the *dialectical materialism of *Engels, it is in such particulars as the following:

(i) The emphasis on revolutionary morality. 'Our morality is completely subservient to the interests of the one class of the proletariat.' What matters is always the end; and the means, however objectionable to the *bourgeois conscience, may still be justified by it. Action requires total commitment to the revolutionary purpose: 'everything that is done in the proletarian cause is honest'.

(ii) The theory of the *vanguard. The proletariat, left to itself, develops only 'proletarian consciousness'; hence a revolution of the proletariat is ineffective unless conducted by a vanguard of 'professional revolutionists', drawn primarily from the bourgeois *intelligentsia. They act and speak in the name of the working class, and subsequently hold power in trust for it. Together with the proletariat they must form themselves into a *party, and that party must be entirely united over all questions that really matter to the advance of revolution.

(iii) The doctrine of *democratic centralism: that the concentration of power in a centrally organized party is necessary both before and after a revolution, if the interests of the proletariat are to be served.

(iv) The attack on *revisionism, and on the view that there is a peaceful path to socialism, together with a reaffirmation of the doctrine of the *class struggle delivered by the **Communist Manifesto*. (These issues were at the root of the break from the *mensheviks.)

(v) The theory of *imperialism, as the last stage of capitalism, and of Russia as the 'weakest link in the chain of imperialism'. This was expounded in such a way as to explain (in the face of Marxist theory to the contrary) why revolution might take place in Russia, where *productive forces had not developed to the point recognized as the point of *crisis; why the revolution, when it did come, would be anti-bourgeois and anti-capitalist, despite the fact that Russian society was to some extent pre-capitalist in form; and why it would lead to the victory of the proletariat, and to an affirmation of its international character.

(vi) The theory of the *withering away of the state. While this is mentioned by Marx and Engels, the theory has a vital role in Lenin's prognostications. After socialism has been achieved, 'full communism' gradually comes into being as the state and all its machinery, including law, wither away, having been necessary only so long as antagonistic *production relations endured, in order to compel people to act against nature. But before this withering is possible, the central machinery must be strengthened and subjected to the rule of the party.

(vii) The theories of *cultural revolution, and of the double causality of revolution. Classical Marxism describes the 'objective conditions' of revolution. Before revolution is possible certain 'subjective conditions' must be fulfilled: including the changed consciousness of the intelligentsia, and the emergence therefrom of the revolutionary vanguard.

The force of Lenin's personality, his conviction of his own rightness, and his remarkable qualities of *leadership, were responsible for the success of the Russian Revolution and the eventual victory of the bolsheviks. This practical success has led to the acceptance of theories which, had they been uttered by someone else, might have been found less persuasive. (*See* *Leninism.)

Leninism. Adherence to the doctrines and in particular to the revolutionary methods of *Lenin. The main features are: furtherance of communist revolution as part of a worldwide struggle against capitalist imperialism; attachment to the organizational principles of 'the party of the new type' (i.e. the party which incorporates all functions of the state, and which systematically eliminates opposition); *democratic centralism; emphasis on the role of the revolutionary *vanguard, whose constitution naturally tends to be differently described depending upon who is in charge of it.

Leninism became a worldwide movement in 1920, when Lenin himself imposed on the *Comintern his 'twenty-one conditions', which in effect stipulated that communist parties everywhere should organize themselves according to the principles that he had laid down for the Russian party. However it is not solely because of this, but rather because of the extraordinary practical success of Lenin's party organization, that Leninism has become a feature of so many communist movements.

levellers. A radical political *faction among artisans and apprentices in mid-seventeenth-century England, who played some part in the formation of Cromwell's army, and who attempted, during the Putney debates of October 1647, to elicit democratic, *egalitarian policies in the Parliamentarians. They advocated universal suffrage for 'freeborn Englishmen', as a guarantee of government by consent; though it seems that the class of freeborn Englishmen did not include servants or the unemployed. Levellers were as much concerned by the vast disproportions of wealth between the lower and upper middle class, as by the rights of Englishmen and the undemocratic nature of existing political representation. Nevertheless they began a continuing movement in British politics, which was to flow into the labour movement in the nineteenth century, and lead to the distinctive modern forms of socialism in the UK, respecting both liberty and property, but wishing for a constitution which would combine democratic representation with equalized redistribution.

Lévi-Strauss, Claude (b. 1908). French social anthropologist. *See* *structuralism.

liberal education. A label, now going out of fashion, for the kind of *education which arose out of the Roman 'liberal arts' (aimed to train the 'orator' or man with the *virtues necessary for public life), and which was regarded as the appropriate education for a *gentleman. The form of liberal education has always been more precisely defined than its content: it consists in attendance at a reputable school and a reputable university, and the dilution of study with recreation of an improving kind, such as music, debating, wide reading, and competitive sport. The content of liberal education has usually been thought to derive from the humanities, on the understanding that the gentleman is a more useful member of his class the more useless his education. However in the US the phrase 'liberal education' is still widely used to describe any form of academic education as distinct from professional training: education designed for the citizen rather than the expert.

The idea has traditionally been that uselessness is an essential precondition of *culture, which is essential both to *rhetoric and to social grace, which are in turn essential to good government. Hence uselessness in education is the greatest utility in public life. None of those conceptions is now very fashionable.

liberal individualism. A term used in the history of ideas in order to denote the combination of *liberal doctrine with a metaphysical grounding in *individualism, on the assumption that the two qualify each other in ways that are both intellectually and historically significant. The outlook of liberal individualism is often ascribed to *Locke and his successors, although some (e.g. C. B. Macpherson: *Possessive Individualism*, 1962) also ascribe it to *Hobbes. It tends to be associated, by those who espouse some form of *historical materialism, with the rise of capitalism, and the market economy, it being supposed that an emphasis on individual rights and freedoms is the functional correlative of the relations embodied in the wage contract.

liberalism. A loose term used to mean a body of modern political doctrine, some parts of which have been given systematic exposition, and other parts of which have been left inchoate or tacit by its adherents. The history of liberalism is contemporaneous with the history of *limited government, i.e. with the successful attempts of those subject to government to curtail its powers, and to secure for themselves *charters, *statutes, *institutions, and forms of *representation, that will guarantee the individual's *rights against the invasions of the *sovereign power. There are recognizably liberal thoughts expressed in Magna Carta, 1215, although the modern doctrine is usually thought of as a seventeenth- and eighteenth-century creation, partly because of the political theory then produced in support of it, partly because of the rapid changes in political institutions which hastened its advance, and partly because the underlying *individualism received confirmation in so many aspects of economic, social and political life. Principal exponents of aspects of liberalism are *Spinoza, *Locke, *Montesquieu, *Kant, *Bentham, *J. S. Mill, *Jefferson and *Madison, together with many other significant figures of the *Enlightenment and subsequently. It is almost impossible to reduce liberalism to a single theoretical position, although the following ideas are fundamental to most forms of it:

(i) Belief in the supreme value of the individual, his freedom and his rights.

(ii) Individualism, in its metaphysical variant (*see also* *liberal individualism).

(iii) Belief that the individual has *natural rights, which exist independently of government, and which ought to be protected by and against government.

(iv) Recognition of the supreme value of freedom, usually glossed as the ability to secure that to which one has a right, together with the view that government must be so limited as to grant freedom to every citizen; perhaps even that government is justifiable only to the extent that it maximizes freedom, or to the extent that it protects the free individual from invasions of his rights.

All the above doctrines go together, and form a moral and metaphysical unity. In addition, the following propositions may sometimes be advanced in the name of liberalism (because of the supposed theoretical connection with the above four):

(v) An anthropocentric, rather than theological, view of human affairs, regarding human potential and achievement as the principal locus of *value (*see* *humanism).

(vi) *Universalism: i.e. a belief that rights and duties are universal, and stem from a human condition that transcends place and time. People should learn to renounce their particular local attachments so as to view things from the standpoint of an impartial *legislator.

(vii) Advocacy of *toleration in matters of *morality and *religion.

Liberalism expresses the political theory of limited government, and conveys the political sentiments of the *modern man, who sees himself as detached from *tradition, *custom, *religion and *prejudice, and deposited in the world with no guidance beyond that which his own reason can provide. Hence, if there is a reasoned account to be offered of fundamental human liberties and rights, the individual can judge the *legitimacy of political institutions by the extent of their respect for them, and extend his allegiance accordingly. The fundamental feature of all liberal theories of political obligation is that of overt or tacit consent, and the doctrine of the social contract is the prime example of a liberal theory of government. To make the underlying philosophy coherent it is necessary to say much about both the nature of the human individual, and the nature of freedom. One philosophy which brings these two subjects together is that of Kant, whose theory of the autonomy of the rational agent provides a grounding for all of the propositions given above, with the possible exception of the last. But this last – the advocacy of tolerance – is perhaps the least tenable, liberalism being itself a moral view, and often expressed with a bigoted aversion towards its opponents that is nothing if not intolerant.

One of the important modern problems for liberalism is that of the *free market. It was standardly assumed (or argued) by early liberals that the right of private property, and the freedom of exchange, are ineliminable postulates of individual freedom. If so, a free market seems to be the inevitable result of liberal ideals. (Thus liberalism has often been denounced as 'bourgeois ideology', precisely because it justifies the existence of capitalist production relations.) However, growing acceptance among liberals of the socialist arguments against accumulation, and of the argument that private property, if left to its normal course, provides freedom for those who possess it only at the cost of unfreedom for those who do not, has led some liberals to renounce their allegiance to the free market doctrines and to attempt to reconcile their beliefs with redistribution and egalitarian *social justice. This has led to the now fairly orthodox *left-liberal position, in which the major theoretical conflicts generated by this transformation are fought out.

The major effort of liberal political theory, apart from that new effort of conciliation between ostensibly conflicting positions, is devoted to the problem of what the English jurist Henry de Bracton (d. 1268) called the 'constitution of liberty': i.e. the framework of political institutions which make limited government possible, and which effectively preserve the individual and his rights from any invasion from above. (The antiquity of liberal ideas in English law is well illustrated by the quotation.)

liberal parties. The political heirs of the *Whigs in England came to refer to themselves in the 1830s as 'liberals', following an established continental usage, and in recognition of a similarity of outlook with those called liberal in France. Throughout the nineteenth century liberal parties were formed in Europe, and the UK 'National Liberal Federation' was formed in 1877, providing the main centre of opposition to the *Conservative Party. The party went into a decline, partly as a result of the ascendancy of the *Labour Party, and despite periodic revivals has not in recent years been a dominant political force, except on those occasions when an electorate wishes to express an attachment to *centre policies, having identified the two major parties as too far to the *left or to the *right of some convenient point of safety.

The US has no major party that calls itself liberal, but its constitution provides a kind of background of liberal principles (in particular the declared protection of *human and *civil rights), which has imposed a uniformity of outlook on the two major parties, compelling them to accept or to seem to accept many of the fundamental tenets of liberalism.

The politics of modern liberal parties tend to be open and corrigible. In so far as anything general can be said about them, it is that they have stood mostly for *free trade, *capitalist development, pacific attitudes in international relations, political *reform within the framework of enduring *institutions, extension of the *franchise, the support for *civil rights, *human rights, and *minority rights, and, in recent years, a qualified support for the *mixed economy. They have also shown support for *decentralization, and *community politics, and, at times, *democratization of industry and commerce.

liberation. The act of freeing, e.g. a *slave from his bondage, an individual from his *conscience, a nation from its conquerors, an oppressed class from its rulers. Modern usages concentrate on two contrasting kinds of movement: those designed to liberate the human individual from supposedly irrational and oppressive taboos and conventions; and those designed to overthrow supposedly oppressive regimes. (Roughly these may be contrasted as movements against *repression and movements against *oppression.) To the first kind belong women's liberation (although radical *feminists diagnose the condition of women in such a way that their movement is more naturally seen as of the second kind), 'gay liberation' and so on; to the second kind belong the 'wars of national liberation' undertaken in the name of a nation, or a people (although sometimes in the name of an oppressed working class or peasantry). It is an important doctrine of *Marxism-Leninism that such wars are justified, even when conducted by an outside party, provided that they have the liberation of the proletariat as their aim. This can be seen as a new addition to the doctrines of *just war; alternatively it might be seen as an extension of those doctrines (endorsed in existing international law) which permit intervention in the affairs of one state so as to liberate another that is in its thrall. The aim in the war of liberation is to intervene in the affairs of a state so as to liberate the *civil society that lies in its bondage. Since a society, unlike a state, is not a legal *person, and has no rights in international law, the doctrine by implication throws aside the question of legality, and applies the idea of justice independently. This provides one of the many illustrations of the way in which *international socialism is, ultimately, committed to an idea of *natural justice.

libertarianism. **1**. The form of liberalism which believes in freeing people not merely from the constraints of traditional political institutions, but also from the inner constraints imposed by their mistaken attribution of power to ineffectual things. The active libertarian is engaged in a process of *liberation, and wages war on all institutions through which man's vision of the world is narrowed (some would say focused) – among them the institutions of *religion, and the *family, and the customs of social, especially sexual conformity. Libertarianism is not so much a doctrine as an attitude, condemned by some as mistaking licence for *liberty, praised by others as the new temper of *humanism.

2. In economics, a radical form of the theory of **laissez-faire*, which believes that economic activity must be actively liberated from the bondage of needless political constraints in order to achieve true prosperity.

3. Often used as a name for the metaphysical theory that *determinism must be false, on account of the fact of human *freedom.

liberty. While 'liberty' (Latin root) is synonymous with 'freedom' (Saxon root), it has legal and historical associations that have caused it to be discussed in different contexts, and to accrue to itself different connotations. A theory of liberty is a theory of *political* *freedom; but it helps to clarify matters if the following historical applications of the idea are first attended to:

(i) Liberty and liberties. The 'liberties of the subject' under UK law are not guaranteed by any particular statute, but are implied in a general principle (itself an immemorial *custom) that anyone may do what he likes, so long as no law prevents him, and that the attempt to prevent him, in the absence of a law, is either a civil or a criminal wrong, itself a valid cause of legal action. Periodic attempts to embody the 'liberties of the subject' in a statute (from Magna Carta, 1215, to the Act of Settlement 1701) have provided a repertoire of *rights, some of which entered the *Bill of Rights attached to the US constitution; they have also helped to give legal cogency to the view that *natural rights are respected in UK law. (*See also* *freedoms.)

(ii) Liberty and licence. An *ad hoc* distinction is often made (borrowing terms put to contentious use by *Locke) between liberty and licence, the first being a necessary condition of human fulfilment, the second a sufficient condition of human degeneracy. Intuitively the distinction is easy to grasp: it is an infringement of my liberty to prevent me from walking out of my house, but only the removal of licence to prevent me from then abusing, assaulting or murdering my neighbour. But the theory of this distinction remains one of the deepest intellectual preoccupations of liberalism. Both liberty and licence consist in extension of permission (or removal of constraint), but the intuition is that sometimes this extension is right, sometimes wrong: if, however, that is *all* that can be said, the invocation of liberty becomes vacuous, either as the justification of a particular legal code, or as the assertion of an enduring human *value. The most plausible step in a theory of the distinction is to say that liberty is the permission to do what you have a *right to do, while licence is the permission to do what someone (usually someone else) has a right that you do not do. This shifts the discussion to the theory of rights, and is one ground for thinking that the idea of freedom cannot be discussed without also discussing that of *justice.

(iii) Liberty and value. If liberty is to deserve the place habitually given to it in political doctrine it must be shown to be a value, either as a necessary means to moral action, or as an end of moral action. Some philosophers (notably *Kant) have argued that liberty becomes a value through a connection with *autonomy, which is a necessary (and according to Kant sufficient) condition for moral agency. It is one of the deep questions of political philosophy to connect liberty, as identified through the liberties mentioned in (i), with autonomy, as specified through a theory of the nature of *rational agency.

(iv) Liberty and constraint. Some have argued that liberties make no sense without constraints, since constraints are necessary in order to nurture the being who can value liberties. This issue, which identifies another deep problem in political philosophy, is discussed under *freedom and also under *Hegel.

Liebknecht, Karl (1871–1919). German lawyer and left-wing activist. *See* *communist parties, *Kautsky, *Luxemburg, *Spartacists.

limitation. The doctrine in law that after a certain period an action cannot be brought. In English law the period is generally twelve years, but may for some types of action be less. The doctrine of limitation has been of great importance in establishing the right to the use of land. It implies that if someone has occupied land for twelve years, with the knowledge of the legal owner, and with no attempt on the part of the owner to remove him, then the owner's title to the land is effectively extinguished, since no action can be brought to enforce it. (In this connection *see also* *prescription.) A law without limitation must inevitably lead to social upheavals, as the burden of extinct agreements becomes intolerable.

limited government. Usually contrasted with absolute government (*see* *absolutism), and meaning any form of government in which the sovereign power (in particular the *executive power) is limited by *law, *constitution, or *institutions, presenting *checks and balances to its exercise. The forms of limited government are as varied as the ways of limiting power: sometimes power is limited through a constitution, sometimes through a balance against other powers. The two cases are importantly different, so much so that often only the first is called limited government. In the case of constitutional limitation the sovereign power possesses an *internal* constraint on its exercise: it is, in other words, limited by itself. It is the very same sovereign who exerts supreme political power who also upholds the constitution through which that power is restrained and channelled. Some think, however, that that is possible only if the constitution enacts a *separation of powers, so as in effect to decompose the sovereign power into separate elements, and balance the one against the other. In particular they tend to argue for *judicial independence, as giving a guarantee to the subject that he may enforce against the sovereign those rights and privileges which are granted in the constitution.

In the second case, of *de facto* limitation, there need be no constitutional balance, but simply a balance of powers. But some balance of power seems to exist universally; no government has been so despotic that the sovereign power has not had to limit its activities in the light of opposition from within society or the state (although some argue that both Hitler and Stalin came near to complete *autocracy, by generating effective machinery for eliminating opposition before it could gather momentum). Those monarchies which are called 'absolute', on the ground that there are no legal constraints upon the sovereign, have usually been severely limited in fact, by the need to reconcile the aristocracy, the common people and (sometimes) the church, to all policies of the sovereign. In a similar way modern governments may be limited by the aims and activities of a trade union, or a cartel, even though no legal powers of limitation have been granted to those bodies.

There is an interesting conceptual difference between limited government that arises as a result of the limitation of a power once deemed absolute (such as, on one interpretation, the *constitutional monarchy of the UK), and a limited government which arises from a constitution that grants no absolute power (such as the constitutional democracy of the US). Some argue that the second is a recent invention, made possible by building upon the experience and institutions of the first. Whether or not that is so, it is often said that the search for the conditions of limited government is the major task of political theory, for only in conditions of limited government is *politics (as opposed to *force) the condition of public life.

limited sovereignty doctrine. The view that certain states within the immediate *sphere of influence and protection of a larger power can retain their independence only by limiting their *sovereignty, so as to conform to the foreign policy of the larger power. Originally put forward in 1947 as a corollary of the *Truman doctrine, now rejected as legally incoherent by most Western powers, the view remains influential in the Soviet bloc, where it is known as the Brezhnev doctrine, following President Brezhnev's invocation of it to justify the invasion of Czechoslovakia in 1968.

limited war. War that is limited, usually by agreement between the parties, to certain objectives, or in which the *territory attacked and (most importantly) the weapons used are limited either unilaterally or by agreement. The practice of limiting armaments is not exclusively modern. There are anthropological examples of tribes who limit war by agreement with their customary opponents, say to certain seasons of the year, or to certain weapons. Nevertheless limitation is made particularly important by the invention of modern weapons. Suggestions concerning *arms control have therefore been in existence at least since the invention of gunpowder. *See* *war.

linkage politics. In the theory of systems analysis, or *cybernetics, a recurrent sequence of behaviour which originates in one system, and causes effects in another, is known as a linkage. The term has been extended to political thought, not with any precise theoretical intention other than to indicate that political bodies are also systems, and that actions between them may accordingly be recurrent and systematic in ways determined by their internal organization. Linkages are described as reactive (e.g. when increased armament in one *state causes increased armament in another); emulative (e.g. when industrial expansion in one state causes a desire for similar expansion among its neighbours); and 'penetrative', as in the penetration of the economies of southern African states by South Africa, or the penetration of the politics of the Caribbean states by Cuba and the US. Penetrative linkages are the most difficult to understand; and the adoption of this jargon seems to do little to explain them.

Lippmann, Walter (1880–1974). American journalist. *See* *cold war, *public opinion.

liquidity. The ease with which an asset can be exchanged for money: determined by the structure of the market, and by the ease with which goods of the requisite kind exchange. 'Liquidity preference' is another name for the desire to hold money as opposed to, say, land (which has low liquidity), while 'liquidity ratio' is the proportion of a bank's assets that are held in liquid form (i.e. as cash, or money on short-term loan). The liquidity ratio is a measure of a bank's ability to meet immediate public demand for money.

liturgy. In its primary meaning, the 'liturgy' denotes the prescribed form of worship within a *Christian *church (although it can also be used, especially in the Eastern churches, as a name for the eucharist). It has been a frequent object of political controversy, and, somewhat surprisingly, continues to be so, within both the *Roman Catholic and the *Protestant communities. It has always been accepted that liturgy must evolve in response to changing modes of expression, but in every religion its language tends to lag behind the spoken language; the sacredness of the message begins to attach to the words used to convey it, and this in turn makes people hesitate to change them. (The phenomenon can be witnessed equally in ancient Egypt and modern England, in Islam and Christianity, in established and nonconformist churches.) Hence rapid changes have a disorientating effect which may lead to considerable resistance.

In UK the peculiar constitutional position of the *Anglican Church grants parliamentary control over liturgy. This was exercised in enforcing the language and doctrine of the Book of Common Prayer in the Acts of Uniformity 1549, 1552, and 1662, and more recently in the Worship and Doctrine Measure 1974. The subsequent controversy over the Book of Common Prayer became a cause for *cultural conservatism, and led to a private member's bill in the Commons and Lords. At the same time the 'liturgical movement' in the Roman Catholic Church, originating in nineteenth-century France, has sought to make the Roman liturgies both more true to their meaning and more useful to public worship than they had been thought to be, by transcribing them into the vernacular, using words of common speech, and music of common enjoyment, and encouraging participation as opposed to *ceremony. Large questions concerning the politics of *language have been raised both by those opposed to, and those in favour of, these changes, and the only uncontroversial position is that ascribed to itself by the Church of England in the preface to the Old Prayer Book: 'It hath been the wisdom of the Church of England, ever since the first compiling of her Publick Liturgy, to keep the mean between the two extremes, of too much stiffness in refusing, and of too much ease in admitting, any variation from it.'

local government. A public organization authorized to decide and administer a limited range of public policies pertaining to a circumscribed *territory within a larger and sovereign *jurisdiction. In the UK, boroughs were originally granted independent status by royal charter, which recognized the limited autonomy that they had formerly practised; in time such charters became regularized and often allowed considerable discretion to those who received them. The modern history of local government dates, however, from the 1830s, and in particular from the Poor Law Act 1834, which assigned welfare administration to local 'Boards of Guardians', and the Municipal Corporations Act 1835, which defined a municipal corporation as a 'legal personification of the local community, represented by an elected council, and acting for, and responsible to, the inhabitants of the district'. The US system is largely modelled on the UK counterpart, but the relationship is with the government of a particular state, rather than with the federal government. In the USSR, local government is purely administrative, and there is no *decentralization of power involved in its exercise, only a certain 'deconcentration': the local soviet is an agent of the government and of the Communist Party and has no power to legislate on particular issues. This legislative power exists in the UK and the US, although it is controlled by statute (e.g. the UK Local Government Act 1972). The local organizations are also dependent upon central funds for many of their activities, and therefore constrained to obey orders from above. However, such financial dependence exists to a lesser extent in the US; in addition, certain states grant 'home rule' to municipalities by statute or by constitutional provisions, thus permitting autonomy in all matters that are not constrained by the general law of the state. In France the Napoleonic system of delegating responsibilities to the mayor of local communities has led to extensive powers of local legislation.

In the UK local councils are now elected along party lines, and even respond to party whips, where the parties are defined in terms of national politics rather than local issues. Thus local government may become a testing ground for politicians attempting to enter the national parliament. Local governments may attempt to defy the central government and its law, and now exert considerable powers over the ordinary citizen. Prior to the nineteenth century these powers were confined to those specified in the poor laws and the statutes relating to the upkeep of highways, but as the first were extended through welfare legislation and the second through the distinctly modern law of planning, and as the organization of the police and the provision for general education and also housing were entrusted to local administration, it became inevitable that a concentration of political power would result. But while the power of local government has increased, its local character has, in a sense, dwindled. Two changes have helped to bring this about: the creation of artificial boundaries, designed for administrative convenience rather than in obedience to any historically recognized local affiliation; and the generation of a large and unionized bureaucracy. It is, furthermore, a crime to withhold rates, so that the citizen's main powers of redress lie in *administrative law, or in the ability to vote at a council election.

In Europe, and the UK in particular, all this has generated a *de facto* delegation of power, together with an extensive limitation of *sovereignty, since the delegated powers are more or less impossible to recall once they are entrenched in the local machinery. Some defend this transfer of power as necessary to the creation of more local and particularized allegiances; others condemn it for the very same reason – namely that it destroys local allegiances by bringing local government into the hands of powers that are not truly local, and at the same time not truly bound to the sovereign power.

The argument is a vexed and bitter one. It is not possible to govern a modern state without extensive local government, but it is also impossible to govern it if local government is not responsive to the demands of a central power, nor answerable directly to the citizen. Some have argued that the citizen should have more power to withhold rates – although clearly such a power would render all local administration highly precarious. Others argue that the politics of national parties ought to be forbidden at local elections, or that the scope of the activities designated as 'local' ought to be substantially reduced (for example, by making education and the police a national affair). All policies seem to present insuperable difficulties, and the issue remains one of pure speculation.

Locke, John (1632–1704). English philosopher whose political writings contain one of the finest modern justifications of *limited government, and one of the first statements of the principles of modern *liberalism. Locke argued against the theory of *divine right, and defended a form of constitutional government within the framework of *natural rights; his theory was taken as an intellectual foundation by many of the *Founding Fathers of the US, and also by several of the French revolutionaries. His two *Treatises of Civil Government*, 1690, remain standard works of political theory, while his *Letter on Toleration*, 1689, contains a vigorous defence of the liberal principle of *toleration.

(i) There are natural rights which derive from a 'law of nature' implanted by God in all reasoning beings. It is given to reason to perceive these rights and they exist independently of any social order. Principal among them are the rights to life, limb and freedom of action: no one can deprive me of these without doing me wrong, unless I myself have done something to give him just cause (perhaps not even then, since Locke sometimes describes these rights as 'inalienable'). There is also a natural right to *private property: any object which is appropriated or produced by 'mixing my labour' with it is, given certain conditions, e.g. that it was not the subject of some prior right, mine, as much as the limbs that worked on it are mine. (This is a kind of 'labour theory of right' which indirectly inspired the *labour theory of value.)

(ii) Natural rights exist in a *state of nature, and do not require the absolute protection and control of *Hobbes's *sovereign for their recognition. They are specific individual rights and cannot be removed or limited except by the consent of those possessing them, a process which probably extends only to freedom of action and property, and not to life and limb (see above). All government, since it involves the limitation of the freedom of the subject and his subjection to a higher power, must, therefore, be the result of consent if it is to be legitimate, and no government is made legitimate in any other way. Locke brings powerful arguments against the idea of an independent *hereditary principle of government, and against other doctrines of legitimacy that try to bypass the need for consent on the part of the governed.

(iii) The model for legitimate government is therefore to be found in contract. The transition from the state of nature to the state of civil society would involve a legitimate transfer, renunciation and creation of rights were it to result from a *social contract (or 'compact'), by which free beings contract among each other to accept the curtailment of their several rights in exchange for the benefits and security of society. This compact is not a historical event, but, as it were, a structure concealed within society, which is revealed, whenever there is genuine *political obligation, by a species of *tacit consent.

(iv) Tacit consent is demonstrated in a variety of ways, but one extremely important criterion is that a citizen, given the opportunity to remove himself to some 'vacant place' outside the sphere of political obligation, chooses not to do so. This shows that he remains bound by the duties of the subject by his own choice, so that those duties are genuine obligations that he has incurred. Even travelling on the highway through some foreign place obligates the individual to accept the law there obtaining. (This aspect of the theory was much criticized, notably by *Hume.)

(v) Civil society forms itself into particular institutions of government which enshrine and protect the contractual relation among its members. Locke did not develop a complete theory of political institutions, but he advocated *limited government, *constitution, and some kind of (preferably *democratic) *representation. He also suggested that liberties could be better protected and the social compact better upheld by an effective *separation of powers – he thereby introduced a notion that was to have radical influence, partly through the more careful and systematic theory of it given by *Montesquieu.

Locke's political philosophy can be seen as a defence of the 'Glorious Revolution' of 1688, as an imaginative exposition of perennial ideas of liberty and justice, and as an apologetic for the legal system associated with a market economy, and with the contractual relation between worker and capitalist.

logistics. US term, introduced during the Second World War, to denote the activity and principles of supply for the armed forces, including transport and distribution; now extended also to non-military contexts.

long run. In *price theory, the time period sufficient for a *firm to be able to vary all its *factors of production: labour, raw materials, capital. Some industries can change their complete structure and composition only over a period of many years; for others it may be possible to do this in a period of weeks. It is only when the long run is considered that fully comprehensive economic planning can be undertaken, and this fact has influenced economic thinking throughout the world, in the smallest manufacture as much as in the 'five year plans' of the major communist states. It may be that five years is still too short.

lord. **1**. A title, bestowed in UK law on *peers and also by courtesy on some of the sons of some of the peers, and on judges of the Scottish Court of Session. A courtesy title brings no legal or political *privileges, whereas a peerage (which may also be held by a woman) normally denotes the right to sit in the House of Lords, and the loss of the right to vote for or sit in the House of Commons.

2. A social and economic position, formerly associated with 1. but no longer so associated, titles being created as *honours, and economic position determined by *market forces which ignore or override the feudal position associated with lordship. The lord was distinguished, under *feudalism, in three ways:

(i) economically, as the holder of manorial land, who takes a return or *corvée* on the product of all the land from his serfs;

(ii) legally, as the president of the manorial court, with jurisdiction over the serfs on his land, subject usually to rights of appeal to the sovereign;

(iii) politically, in so far as he could claim the privilege of a peer, which was granted by the crown in exchange for certain military duties.

(i), (ii) and (iii) did not always go together, and they converge probably only in the *ideal type of feudalism defined in this work. They define collectively a highly organized idea of established property, in which some conservatives have occasionally seen relations of mutual *responsibility miraculously conjoined with distinctions of class, and in which others have seen carefully concealed habits of *slavery and *exploitation.

The legality of the title of lord (sense 1.) is defined by the constitution, and upheld in the idea of constitutional monarchy; outside monarchy the use of such titles is either illegal (as in the US), or somewhat arbitrary; they have therefore largely fallen into disuse.

loyalists. Those who remain loyal, during some crisis, revolution or civil war, to an established, and usually monarchical, *regime. In Northern Ireland the term denotes those who profess loyalty to the Union, i.e. who believe that the sovereign of the UK is the legitimate sovereign over Northern Ireland. The term is sometimes put in inverted commas, to denote the paradox that someone, professing loyalty, might yet commit crimes (acts forbidden by the sovereign) in its name.

loyalty. The disposition to act and speak in the interests and defence of another, regardless of benefit or cost. Loyalty can be the expression of *friendship (i.e. a result of spontaneous liking or love), of *justice (i.e. a result of the judgement that loyalty is *deserved*), or of *piety (i.e. a result of some unchosen bond that transcends considerations of justice alone). Political creeds differ according to which (if any) of those models is taken as a basis for loyalty towards the state. Liberalism emphasizes *political obligation, and justice; some conservatives emphasize friendship (*see*, e.g., *Oakeshott), while others (not necessarily conservative) emphasize piety (*see*, e.g., *Hegel).

The difficulties posed by the idea were illustrated in the elaborate procedures adopted by Presidents Truman and Eisenhower for determining the 'loyalty' of the servants of the US government.

Lukás, Georg, or György (1885–1971). Hungarian philosopher and literary critic, an important influence on *neo-Marxism, and one of the first *Marxist thinkers to displace the theory of *historical materialism from the central place that it had occupied in revolutionary thinking, and to elevate in its place a Marxist theory of consciousness. The idea of *reification is important to his theory, as describing the consciousness of man under capitalist *production relations. Lukács's great respect for *Hegel's analysis of the human spirit led him to anticipate the theories which later became familiar with the publication of *Marx's manuscripts of 1844. Lukács to some extent shared those parts of Marx's philosophy which stem from Marx's *Young Hegelian origins, especially the theory of *alienation. He argued that the Marxist theory of history is correct but incomplete, needing to be supplemented by a theory of how the world is seen by the various classes at the various points of historical development. The structure of consciousness must be different for each class, and alters as production relations change; but all classes in capitalist society possess their own kind of *false consciousness. What philosophers had seen as the problem of knowledge (is the world as it appears to me?) is better understood as the problem of *praxis: do I act on the world so as to see it without false consciousness? The problem for all criticism of consciousness is to show how a vision that is fundamentally class-determined may yet be demystified, so as to give knowledge of the real world of social relations.

Lukács went on to give an ambitious account of the nature of philosophy and of art, and he can be regarded as the most widely influential of Marxist literary critics. His particular insights (e.g. into the realism of Balzac) are often esteemed more than the ambitious theories from which he supposed them to derive. As an articulate apologist for *Stalinism, and a thinker with a large fund of dark hatred for what others regard as normal features of the human condition, Lukács has inspired as much distaste as intellectual admiration, and is said to have provided the model for Naphta in Thomas Mann's *The Magic Mountain*.

Lutheranism. Martin Luther (1483–1546), founder of the German Reformation, famous advocate of the doctrine of 'justification by faith alone', and passionate preacher of the sovereignty of *conscience, could hardly have had more political influence than he had, despite the fact that he and his immediate followers produced few developed political doctrines. Unlike *Calvinism, Lutheranism involves no account of real or ideal *institutions, no clear theory of the *state, or of the relation between *church and state, and no very obvious economic analysis (although Luther accepted the doctrine of the just price, together with a primitive version of the labour theory of value). Lutheranism has often been thought to be just as significant a force as Calvinism in facilitating, or (on some views) generating, the rise of modern capitalism, partly because of its effects on later *puritanism, partly because its emphasis on the individual, his 'vocation', and his conscience gave credence to the new species of commercial transaction, of which the wage contract was one of the most important expressions. The individual is held to commune directly with God, and not through the mediation of any merely human institution; hence, no human institution can have an authority that enables it to override the call of conscience. The grace that is freely bestowed upon the soul may be expressed in social relations, but social relations are only ancillary to the life and duty of the spiritual being. Luther's famous polemic *Of the Bondage of the Will*, 1525, contains what many of his contemporaries saw as a denial of free will, asserting that God is always sovereign over the will and can direct it to his ends, faith being one result of God's power. This and related doctrines were uttered in the course of controversy with the more temperate *Erasmus, and most of Luther's voluminous writings are devoted to the expression and refinement of the themes rehearsed during that controversy. The religious movement which followed lent itself to the *universalist doctrines of the *Enlightenment, and the Lutheran paradox (that the will is most free when most constrained by the grace of God) is reiterated, with resounding metaphysical and political effect, in *Kant's theory of *autonomy: that the will is only free when reason compels its obedience. The influence of Lutheranism over capitalism has been often discussed, e.g. by *Weber and by R. H. Tawney: *see* *Protestant ethic.

Luxemburg, Rosa (1870–1919). Polish-born socialist and exponent of revolutionary *Marxism, who was one of the first to recognize the rise of despotism in the *bolshevik faction, and to warn against its influence. Luxemburg attempted to reconcile theoretical Marxism with respect for the 'will of the people'. She criticized Lenin for his dictatorial ways, his unscrupulousness and the innate tendency of his theory of the *vanguard to lend itself to the advance of tyranny.

Luxemburg's most important theoretical work is *The Accumulation of Capital*, 1913, in which she argues that pure capitalism cannot create the conditions necessary to maintain its own development. Capital accumulates faster than demand within capitalist countries can increase: hence capitalism attempts to absorb underdeveloped areas and spheres of non-capitalist production, initiating a period of capitalist imperialism. This thesis was badly received by other communist theoreticians, and only with the Keynesian revolution was her theory that lack of purchasing power causes a breakdown in the capitalist system rehabilitated. However, she correctly predicted the subsequent course of Russian communism and, together with her fellow *Spartacist Karl Liebknecht, had considerable momentary influence over the communist intelligentsia. She did not achieve political power, and was murdered by the Freikorps in Berlin in 1919.

Lycurgus. *See* *Sparta.

Lysenkoism. *See* *Lamarckism.

M

McCarthyism. Attitudes and policies named after the Republican Senator Joseph McCarthy (1908–56), Chairman of the 'Un-American Activities Committee', who in February 1950 alleged that he had the names of 57 'card carrying communists' in the State Department, and that 205 people employed by the department were well-known communist sympathizers. This, combined with the previous scandal caused by the trial of Alger Hiss for espionage, and Senator McCarthy's subsequent attacks on universities and intellectuals, led to a kind of hysteria which saw all liberal and socialist opinion as both communist and 'un-American'. Some recent writers have doubted that McCarthy deserved either the support that he initially achieved or the condemnation which his activities finally brought on him. Socialist opinion in the US still sometimes accuses those who connect socialist ideas with USSR foreign policy of McCarthyism. *See also* *anti-communism.

Machiavelli, Niccolò (1459–1517). Italian political theorist and historian, who, in two controversial and superficially contradictory works – *The Prince*, and the *Discourses on the First Ten Books of Titus Livy*, both begun in 1513 – expounded a political vision which attempted to bring the observed facts of contemporary despotism into relation with general ideas about law, liberty and the state. Machiavelli has often been thought of as the first theorist of the modern state – the first, that is, to isolate for study this particular political arrangement, rather than the **polis*, the *church, or some body of universal, or potentially universal, law.

The Prince speaks entirely of *power, how it is obtained and how preserved. Its **Realpolitik* and close observation of men as they are, rather than as we might wish them to be, have caused the adjective 'Machiavellian' to be bestowed on anyone who, indifferent to questions of morality, devotes himself to the pursuit of power. It is now more normal to interpret *The Prince* in the light of the *Discourses*: it deals with the necessary conditions of government, rather than the sufficient conditions of good government, arguing that the *rule of law is natural to *rational beings, but that it must be established by power, and power may have to use unnatural means in order to impose itself.

In the *Discourses*, Machiavelli reflects on the character of Roman constitutional government as described by Livy, and tries to ascertain what the rule of law ideally should be:

(i) He rejects *Aristotle's division of governments into three good and three bad

forms, and proposes as an ideal a form of mixed government, which is monarchical, aristocratic, and democratic at once. While he attributes this mixed government to *Sparta as formed by the laws of Lycurgus, it approximates in fact more nearly to the English constitutional monarchy that emerged from the Glorious Revolution of 1688. Machiavelli argues that, in mixed government, the separate classes will, through institutions of *representation, limit each other's power and so contribute to the *liberty of all. This defence of *limited government as a necessary condition of liberty began a tradition that continues to the present day.
(ii) Thus Machiavelli finds that dissent and *opposition are far from being the evils that they had been thought to be; on the contrary they might be necessary to the whole idea of a state in which liberty can be preserved. Such, at any rate, was the character of the opposition between Senate and Commons in Rome: without it, neither would have had the freedom which both enjoyed.
(iii) Machiavelli emphasizes the importance of the rule of law as superseding *faction and private vengeance; he therefore explores the constitution that might be necessary to uphold it. A constitution with established institutions, together with procedures whereby they may be renewed by 'being brought back to their beginnings', is defended, partly as a guarantee against *usurpation. Machiavelli also defends a distribution of power, sufficient to make possible the *impeachment of any officer of state, however highly placed. (His example is the impeachment of Coriolanus.)

This defence of *constitutionalism accompanies a detailed description of the political nature of man, as revealed in civil, military and religious usages. Machiavelli's view, voiced in both *The Prince* and the *Discourses*, that government is an artefact, made possible by force, and justifying all force that is used in its defence, has had many opponents and defenders. So too has his idea (influenced by Aristotle) that each constitution has its own peculiar *virtue, and that the value of a political arrangement cannot be discussed without reference to the human character that is engendered by it. The brilliant scepticism of Machiavelli's vision disguises from the sentimental mind the accuracy of many of his observations. His ultimate doctrine is less systematic than empirical, and its philosophical shortcomings are compensated for by its insight into human motivation.

Machtpolitik. German for *power politics.

McLuhan, Herbert Marshall (b. 1911). Canadian communications theorist. *See* *communication, *media.

macroeconomics. The economics of large aggregates, dealing with state finances, *fiscal policy, unemployment, aggregate supply and demand, and so on. Macroeconomics tries to treat of the total influence of all relevant economic factors on each other, and to provide the means of understanding and predicting *national income (hence it is sometimes called income theory). Modern macroeconomics takes much inspiration from the work of *Keynes, and has been largely concerned with *equilibrium, and with the consequences of the possibility – elaborately described by Keynes – that equilibrium may occur at less than full employment.

Madison, James (1751–1836). *Founding Father, friend of *Jefferson, and one of the principal architects of the US constitution, Madison gave voice to many of the underlying ideas of *federalism, arguing that a federal constitution is always a greater guarantee of stability and freedom than any attempted imposition of a unifying power. His writings in *The Federalist* are of exemplary clarity and power, and their translation of *Locke's and *Montesquieu's theories of natural right and limited government into real political terms was partly responsible for the philosophical consistency of the final constitution. In particular Madison was one of the main forces behind the adoption of the principle of a *separation of powers, and of a special process for amendment, which would 'guard equally against that extreme facility, which would render the constitution too mutable; and that extreme difficulty, which might perpetuate its discovered faults'.

magistrate. Traditionally any person, including the *sovereign, empowered to sit in judgement and to exercise judicial authority. Because of the important political role of magistrates in ancient Rome, the term was given wide application in the Renaissance, for example by *Machiavelli, to denote any political *office whereby the affairs of state are regulated in accordance with law.

Maistre, Joseph Marie, Comte de (1754–1821). French essayist and political thinker, a *reactionary, *legitimist and *ultramontanist, who defended a modified, belated and high-toned version of the doctrine of the *divine right of kings. His scepticism towards received liberal and democratic ideas was trenchant and influential, although what he tried to put in place of them has seldom been found wholly satisfactory. He argued that constitutions are not created but found, and that the rage of constitution-making which characterized the governments of his day was in part founded on a misconception of the American constitution, which was no more than a document making explicit a spirit already present in the *common law from which it grew. All constitutions and all states are inseparable from the spirit of the society that is governed by them; the attempt to separate them means social and political death. This idea is associated with an attack on the liberal analysis of *political obligation. No obligation to the sovereign can have a basis in contract or consent, but only in *piety towards established things. The true object of that emotion is not the state, but God, and it is in religious duty that the obligation towards all human institutions must ultimately be founded. Moreover it is God, and not man, who is the maker of constitutions, and the ultimate *legislator, all French revolutionary thought on this subject being nothing but unseemly blasphemy designed to fortify human incompetence.

De Maistre's thought is often criticized for its inexplicit character and its dismissiveness towards rival positions; however he is still admired for his insights into human nature, particularly by those of conservative political sentiment.

Maitland, F. W. (1850–1906). English constitutional historian, who, in his posthumously published lectures, *The Constitutional History of England*, 1908, gave the classic statement of the theory that the constitution of the UK is a definite entity, even though tacit and procedural, to be deduced from *custom rather than from any written document. Maitland also attempted to establish that *limited government had been the rule rather than the exception in England, that the *rights claimed by seventeenth- and eighteenth-century theorists had always been implied in the *common law, and that the process of political *conciliation had been the principal organ of constitutional change. These ideas have played a large part in supporting both conservative doctrines of law and constitution, and the opposition to the thesis of *historical materialism, which sees these things as developing in response to external (specifically economic) forces, rather than in response to innate principles of their own. Maitland also divided constitutional from *administrative law, in a manner that is now largely accepted.

majesty. The ability to command respect through solemn and ceremonious (but not necessarily ceremonial) display. The majesty of the *state was emphasized by Roman writers, and is often defended as a condition of political *stability. This majesty may attach to the subordinate institutions of government (especially to the *judiciary, where it is often regarded as a necessary means to impose a sense of the objective authority of the law upon those who violate it). What creates majesty or gives it cogency is hard to say; however, from the very definition, it is clear that it must, when it exists, enter into the reality (if not into the justifying thought) of political *allegiance. Robespierre, having as he thought discredited the old symbols which conveyed it, found cause to invent new ones (in particular the cult of Reason) in their stead; Napoleon, more perceptively, surrounded himself with all the old dignities, and all the new, consciously seeking to transfer monarchical ideas of majesty to himself. The modern *government through symbols is perhaps remarkable for its failure to create a similar effect of majesty, a fact which some say explains its frequent reliance on terror. The old crime of *lèse majesté* indicates the extent to which majesty was central to the political order; the nearest equivalent of this crime under the government through symbols is 'slandering the state'.

Malinowski, Bronislaw (1884–1942). Polish-American anthropologist; *see* *anthropology, *myth.

Malthus, Thomas Robert (1766–1834). English clergyman and *classical economist, who, in his *Essay on Population*, 1798–1803, argued that the natural rate of population growth is geometrical, while that of food production is arithmetical, thus posing a threat of ultimate starvation. Malthus also argued against *Ricardo's defence of *Say's law, and is now recognized as an original, perhaps eccentric, economist, and an important theorist of *economic growth.

managerial revolution. Phrase gaining currency from the book of that title by James Burnham, 1941, which depicts the rise of 'managers' as a new social *class, common to *capitalist, *communist and *mixed economies, and argues that the 1939 war is the 'first great war of managerial society', just as *Lenin had argued that the war of 1914 was the last great war of *imperialism. Burnham's particular theories are largely discredited, but the phrase is still used to denote the shift of power from the legal owner of the means of production to the effective manager (*see* *separation of ownership from control).

Manchester school (also: Manchesterism). Term applied to the defenders of *free trade, and **laissez-faire*, headed by Cobden and Bright and the Anti-Corn Law League, and relying for their intellectual credentials on the economic theories of *Ricardo.

mandate. Latin: something commanded. The doctrine of the mandate is highly influential in *democratic politics, although it is extremely difficult to see quite what it means, the problem here being inextricably bound up with the general problems of *collective choice. It is sometimes said that when a political *party stands for *election, it makes certain promises, and by virtue of this secures the vote of the electorate. In return for the voluntary act of the electorate, it therefore stands under a *contractual or quasi-contractual obligation to fulfil its promises, and has a 'mandate from the electorate' so to do. In other words, the relation between a party in office and the electorate is one of mandation. The mandate is held to be a sufficient (some say also necessary) condition for the legitimacy of acts performed in fulfilment of it. The whole structure of obligation stems therefore from the fundamental act of consent whereby democracies establish their claims to legitimacy. The problems for this view are several:

(i) The party programme may contain a variety of independent policies, and each voter might have been in a minority of party supporters on the issue which secured his vote; in which case, to whom has the ruling party promised what? (This case is in all probability the normal one.)

(ii) A large number of votes cast in favour of any party are cast independently of its programme, out of habit, allegiance or a liking for a certain 'style' of government. In which case, why is the obligation to keep promises the overriding one?

(iii) Political necessity, social policy, etc. may make it desirable or expedient to change a policy after election: does the party then no longer have a mandate? If parties were to promise only what they knew to be politically possible, then probably they would promise nothing.

The electorate presumably knows this, and presumably this tacit understanding between the two changes the structure of the obligation created by the party programme.

At the same time, a party programme seems to express some kind of commitment. It may be that the correct response is to say that there *is* a mandate after election, but that its basis is not to be found in contract, or promise-keeping; alternatively, that there is no such thing as a mandate, in which case, with what authority does the ruling party act? Some answer the question by distinguishing mandation from *representation and from *delegation.

mandates system. A system which transferred the government of certain territories and colonies of Germany and Turkey to a special commission of the League of Nations after the First World War. A related system of *trusteeship under the United Nations Organization was introduced after the Second World War to deal with the provisional government of certain territories of Italy and Japan.

Mandeville, Bernard de (1670–1733). Dutch-born English doctor and satirist, who, in his *Fable of the Bees*, 1705, set out to illustrate the political message contained in its subtitle: 'private vices, public benefits'. He tried to show, for example, how the accumulation of wealth through the egoistic pursuit of power and luxury leads to the public welfare, since vanity requires that wealth be redistributed after death in order to achieve posthumous fame for liberality. (Mandeville's arguments about luxury and leisure, and their contribution to aggregate demand, are to be found also in *Veblen's theory of conspicuous consumption.) Mandeville's caustic style disguised a serious economic doctrine, and he is often regarded as one of the founders of the *invisible hand justification of the market economy.

manichaeism (or: manichaeanism). A form of *gnosticism founded by Mani, and originating in Persia in the early days of Christianity. Manichaeans founded their religion on a metaphysical doctrine: the division of the world between light and darkness, the first representing the forces of good, the second those of evil. The world itself, suspended between these two principles which are in eternal conflict, offers to the individual soul a path to salvation. The soul must throw off its attachment to matter (i.e. to the body, which issues from the principle of darkness), and ascend towards the light, which is the substance of the spirit and of God. The sect spread rapidly and caused numerous heresies within the Christian church, the most striking being that of the Albigensians in thirteenth-century Provence.

The term 'manichaeism' has been appropriated to name any all-embracing doctrine which sees the world in terms of a fundamental division and opposition between two irreconcilable forces, one good, the other evil; e.g. certain naïve forms of *progressivism and *utopian socialism. The actual religion of Mani was, however, apolitical and ascetic in tendency.

manifesto. Italian: I manifest. The *OED* defines a manifesto as 'a public declaration, usually issued by or with the sanction of a sovereign prince or state, or by an individual or body of individuals whose proceedings are of public importance, for the purpose of making known past actions, and explaining the reasons or motives for actions announced as forthcoming'. In fact many important manifestos – such as the **Communist Manifesto* – have been issued by bodies of little consequence at the time of their utterance, and have neither summarized past actions nor given any very concrete explanation of future ones. Indeed, 'manifestos of accusation' are now the rule rather than the exception (typical being Zola's famous *J'accuse*, issued apropos the Dreyfus case). Such manifestos serve not so much to inform people as to give political *identity to the groups that issue them, by focusing their antipathies.

Mannheim, Karl (1893–1947). German

sociologist, and one of the founders of the *sociology of knowledge, which he argued must come to replace traditional philosophical theories of knowledge. In *Ideology and Utopia*, 1929, he argued that all knowledge is situation-bound; each age develops its own style of thought, and comparison between the styles is impossible. Within each age there is a conflict between the tendency to conserve a style of thought, and the tendency to renounce it in favour of some other; conservation produces 'ideologies' (modes of *false consciousness which make the world seem more stable than it is), while the impetus towards change produces 'utopias' (over-valuations of the future and celebrations of the dynamic forces of history). Mannheim admits the possibility of a realistic vision between ideology and utopia, but prefers the theory that society is polarized into hostile camps, from whose conflict a 'dynamic synthesis' may be forged by the impartial intellectual observer. The Marxian influences are everywhere apparent; in later life, however, Mannheim advocated 'planning for freedom', which he thought would overcome both the anarchy of liberal thought and the totalitarian implications of communism. He remains influential in sociology, although the discipline that he founded – the sociology of knowledge – and the theory of 'relationism', whereby he attempted to escape the charge that his vision left no room for the idea of truth, have since been widely regarded as intellectually disreputable.

manumission. The freeing of a *slave. In Roman law this was effected in a variety of ways, often by using *legal fictions of gift or purchase. The church later introduced simpler procedures, and conferred a right of manumission *in ecclesia*, thus effectively abolishing slavery.

Mao Tse Tung (Tse Toung, Zedong, or plain Mao) (1893–1975). Chinese communist leader, who attempted to adapt the theory and practice of Marxist revolution to China, where the peasantry, rather than the proletariat, was the main focus of social discontent. Mao was a populist, who attempted to make his thought accessible to the people; at the same time he is often supposed to have made substantial theoretical contributions to modern Marxism, not only in practice, but also in theory. The main features are these:

(i) 'Political epistemology'. Socialism requires us to 'revolutionize self and things'. People must realize that they are capable both of securing changes in things, and of changing themselves, before genuine revolution is possible. At the same time, material transformation is necessary in order to achieve the required transformation in consciousness. The circle here is not vicious, but 'dialectical'.

(ii) The priority of practice. Practice is the supreme test of truth, and all theory must be tested through its application, and rejected where required.

(iii) 'The necessity for error'. Mao was hostile to the dogmatism of the *bolsheviks, and argued that 'to say that mistakes can be avoided . . . is an anti-Marxist proposition . . . it amounts to denying the law of the unity of opposites'. Moreover, if the people do not respond positively to the party's plans for them, it is the party and its cadres, rather than the people, who are at fault.

(iv) The law of the *dialectic. For Mao 'the correct line is formed in the struggle with the incorrect line': i.e. opposition and conflict are necessary to all historical change, and to deny them is to deny the law of contradiction. This law pervades all social formations, classes, individuals and the Communist Party itself, and is not abolished by the achievement of socialism or communism. Revolution is not a final 'resolution', but simply a move forward in the desired direction; contradictions continue unabated, and it is folly to attempt to extinguish them by dictating a solution from above. 'Marxist philosophy holds that the law of the unity of opposites is the fundamental law of the universe. This law operates universally, whether in the natural world, in human society, or in man's thinking. Between the opposites of a contradiction there is

at once unity and struggle, and it is this that impels things to move and change.'
(v) The priority of politics. Ideological and political transformation are integral to the accomplishment of all economic objectives. There is no priority of the economic over the political; rather, they advance in concert, no revolution can succeed merely by devoting itself to increasing production, and when politics and economics conflict, politics must prevail. *Cultural revolution may often be more important than *industrial revolution, since it creates the new modes of knowledge which enable the people to perceive the value of industrialization.
(vi) The emphasis on the community. The aim of revolution is the achievement of a particular kind of community, based in cooperative principles, without specialization, and without distinctions of right, class or privilege among the members. Manual labour is ideologically superior to intellectual labour, and the latter must gradually be eliminated. The existence of a fundamentally peasant society must be taken as a premise in political planning, and while heavy industry is desirable, forced industrialization is neither wise nor dialectically possible. (But *see* *Great Leap Forward.)
(vii) Criticisms of Soviet domestic policy, particularly agricultural policy, which 'drains the pond to catch the fish'. Mao retains a kind of *democratic centralism, but seeks to reconcile it with a faith in the wisdom of the masses. Democracy and centralism are not only compatible but positively complementary: perhaps because they illustrate the 'unity of opposites'. Mao constantly emphasized the need to open the party to influence from below. (But *see* *control, *influence.) Criticism and self-criticism provide the only methods of resolving contradictions among the people.

Mao was a brilliant military strategist and tactician, and wrote extensively on the role of the army, specifically the *guerrilla army, in revolutionizing the peasantry (the theory of 'people's war'). Much of his social doctrine can be seen as instructions to an army, concerning the treatment of a society in which the army is the focal point of power. Mao himself rose to power through military means, and defeated the Chinese Nationalist forces after the Second World War, thereafter retaining the Chinese Red Army as a main instrument of policy.

Maoism. Political theory and practice along lines suggested or inspired by *Mao. Maoism involves the attempt to combine the aspirations of communist revolution with respect for the people, and openness to *influence from the people. It is also puritanical, and wishes to abolish the profit motive in favour of 'moral incentives'. Theoretically Maoism probably pays more attention to the idea of the *dialectic, and to the necessity for some kind of *opposition, than does *Leninism, although in practice 'opposition' does not include opposition to the Communist Party. It also involves emphasis on the community and the commune, as the true locus of revolutionary transformation, together with a respect for the peasantry, and a belief that a whole people is capable of transforming itself in a revolutionary direction without recourse to massive development of productive capacity.

Many adherents of the *New Left professed themselves to be Maoists during the 1960s and 70s, believing Maoism to be free from the oppressive bureaucracy and dictatorship of Soviet communism, and more in keeping with the ideal of *permanent revolution, as this had been described by Trotsky. Maoism has been an important force in international affairs, first because it effectively brought *international socialism to an end, by splitting the world communist parties into a Russian and a Chinese camp, secondly because it seemed to provide a model for communism in the Third World, in which predominantly agricultural production remains. It is currently criticized in China itself, and the claim that it has really been open to opposition or to influence from below has been doubted.

Marcuse, Herbert (1898–1979). German-American political philosopher, former member of the *Frankfurt school, and interesting apart for the intellectual *fashion which he inspired through his later libertarian and utopian writings on the subjects of sexual *repression and social *liberation. In *Reason and Revolution*, 1941, Marcuse presents a re-examination of *Hegel's political philosophy, and tries to show its centrality to understanding the theories that had been expressed in the early 1844 manuscripts of *Marx. He explored the Hegelian distinction between *state and *civil society in order to analyse *totalitarianism (in which civil society rules the state), modern communism (in which the state rules civil society), the withering away of the state, and civil liberty, which he regarded as the freeing of society from the bonds of the state. He emphasized the dialectical elements in both Hegel and Marx, and attempted to elaborate Marx's theory of *alienation in order to provide a thorough-going critique of modern industrial society.

marginal analysis. The analysis of relations between marginal (i.e. small) increments or decrements of variable quantities. Principally used in economics, but with applications elsewhere in the social and political sciences, it involves the application of differential calculus to the analysis of *cost and benefit. The 'marginal principle' (held by some to denote an essential feature of *rational conduct) holds that it is rational to proceed with a course of action to the point where marginal benefits are balanced by marginal costs; use of this principle underlies much *welfare economics.

In political theory marginal analysis is always important in situations where behaviour is affected not by the actual quantity of, say, armaments, goods, productive forces, but by the effect of increments and decrements. It seems plausible to suggest that in many areas (e.g. wages and food consumption), once above the level of subsistence, people are more affected by changes in the level of their expectations than by the level itself, so that predictions and decisions will respond to marginal rather than to actual costs and benefits.

marginal utility. Marginal utility is the change in *utility resulting from an incremental unit of a good. The 'marginal utility theory of price' holds that the price of a good in *equilibrium conditions is the price that the consumer is just prepared to pay for the last unit consumed. A good may have a very high utility and a very low marginal utility, for example water, and the marginal utility theory is held to explain why the price of such a good may yet remain so low, even when it is (as in this case) necessary to life. It thus explains what *classical economists called the 'paradox of value' – that the *use-value of a commodity might be very high, even when its *exchange-value is very low, and vice versa. It also replaces the classical idea that use-value and exchange-value are separate properties, by identifying the second in terms of the first.

The 'law of diminishing marginal utility' holds that, after some point, successive equal increments in the amount of a good yield successively smaller increases in utility, so that marginal utility always diminishes after a certain point. All such conceptions assume that utility may be measured in definite units, which is perhaps more plausible in the theory of price than in other areas. This much criticized assumption has led to the replacement of marginal utility theory by analysis based in the *indifference curve, which makes no such assumption.

marginalism. Economic, political and strategic thinking which gives special importance to *marginal analysis. The term can also mean the emphasis on small increases and decreases, for example in political conciliation, or in arms control and strategic planning, whether or not marginal analysis is also invoked. (Cf. *incrementalism.)

maritime law. The law of the sea and of shipping, governing salvage and related matters. It is part of the *municipal law of the individual state, and not a branch of *international law, although it has everywhere been formed in obedience to international *conventions agreed between sovereign states.

market. A system of exchange where the demands of buyers interact with the supply made available by sellers, thus, in *free markets, determining the resulting *price. More often, in practice, law, government intervention and the activities of *cartels and *monopolies exert some kind of control over its operation. Analysis of the market under various conditions is a major preoccupation of economists. It is also a preoccupation of political theorists, particularly those who believe that the existence of the market is a necessary condition of capitalism, or who wish to identify a particular kind of *production relation as characteristic of it. Some use their analysis to justify *capitalism, arguing on a variety of grounds, first that the market is unique to capitalism (but *see* *market socialism), secondly that it is to be preferred to every rival form of distribution, e.g., because it permits the emergence of *equilibrium despite the fact that buyers and sellers remain largely ignorant of each other's desires (whereas – a point often made by economists of the *Austrian school – equilibrium under a socialist *planned economy requires an immense amount of, probably unavailable, information about the consumer); or because it produces *collective choices which are also rational and perhaps even *optimal *social choices; or because it contains what *Hayek has called a 'harsh discipline' with which to regulate supply and demand, and to reduce profits and prices. Others have attributed to the market opposite effects, together with deleterious consequences of a more intangible order, such as *commodity fetishism, and the emergence of a 'market ideology', according to which even the human being and his *labour power are thought of as 'alienable' – i.e. as bought and sold like commodities. (This play on the word *alienation is partly responsible for its modern use in political rhetoric.) Some have praised the market as an ideal form of social union, involving the peaceful and occasionally festive expression of social projects, in an atmosphere of conciliation, agreement and tacit understanding.

market forces. In a capitalist economy, market forces are identified as the forces of *supply and *demand which together are held to determine prices and quantities bought and sold. The idea that these are forces, in the sense of having a power in themselves to generate economic activity, is sometimes criticized as a form of *fetishism by *Marxists (corresponding to Marx's 'capital fetishism'). The only *force* here, says the Marxist, is the productive force of labour; there is therefore a real ideological difference between those who explain price in terms of supply and demand, and those who explain it in terms of the *labour theory of value.

It is hard to know how to assess those claims, since if *x* really does *explain y,* it can be assumed that *x* is also a *cause of y*, and if a cause is not a force generating its effect, then what precisely *is* meant by 'force', and why should forces matter? Nevertheless, this controversy is often taken very seriously, since it connects directly with the Marxist critique of *bourgeois economics, as building assumptions about production relations into the explanation of production relations, and also with the more general criticism that ideology finds all its explanations in appearances, and not in the essence that they conceal. (*See* *essence/appearance.)

market socialism. Term sometimes used to denote a theory which attempts to reconcile the belief in the *market, as a system of exchange, with belief in *social ownership of the means of production. The argument is roughly this: a market is (at least to some extent) a self-regulating mechanism, and allocates resources without recourse to tyrannical measures designed to force an unwanted pattern of distribution on a reluctant society, and without all the manifold incompetences and inhumanities witnessed in the state-controlled systems of modern communism. At the same time, private ownership of the means of production leads to exploitation and injustice, together with unacceptable *accumulations of capital in the hands of the few. The ideal would therefore be to combine the benefits of the market mechanism with a social ownership that would remove its injustices. One suggestion has been that there should be cooperative ownership of every productive enterprise, but that each cooperative should be in free and open competition with others, thus stimulating production, and leading to the economical and useful exchange and distribution of the product. Supply and demand would determine prices, and the state would intervene where necessary only by adjusting supply or demand. Marx criticized all such theories on the grounds that *production, distribution and exchange are organically connected, and it is not possible for there to be private ownership only of one part of the chain. The controversy over this is still active; there was a certain measure of interest aroused by market socialist schemes in the 1930s (notably by the theories of the Polish economist O. R. Lange) and more recently, following the introduction of a kind of market socialism into Yugoslavia in 1950.

marriage. According to Christian theological doctrines which were, until recently, widely accepted, the marriage bond is unbreakable and eternal, and generates a peculiar 'affinity' between the partners (it is the impossibility of creating this affinity between blood relations that is supposed to explain the interdiction on incest). This doctrine can be seen as in part a rationalization of the more widespread view, enshrined in law, that marriage is an autonomous institution, with peculiar internal aims and constraints, arising out of and generating *obligations which are not contractual, and not to be explained merely in terms of promises given or benefits received. These obligations cannot be specified in advance, and although marriage begins with a kind of contract, it is a contract to be united precisely by a non-contractual obligation (this is part of the difference in connotation between a promise, which is the index of a specific intention, and a vow, which dedicates one's being and not just one's acts).

The philosophical idea of the non-contractual obligation has been explored in this connection by *Hegel (who used it partly to counteract the *social contract theory of the *state), and reflects intuitions embodied in the law. Laws relating to marriage are nowhere reducible to laws of contract, and have incorporated striking elements not to be found in any other sphere of law (but cf. *industrial law). Such laws always attempt to prevent rather than to facilitate divorce, to guarantee the duration of marital obligations even beyond divorce, and to make the grounds of divorce correspond to a socially accepted idea of the permanence of marriage. Many liberals find this feature puzzling, and often seek to reformulate the law in contractual terms – not 'till death us do part' but 'till death or mutual consent us do part'. The older conception is given its most extreme legal expression in the English common law doctrine that husband and wife are one *person (namely, the husband), a conception that nowadays causes considerable offence to the other person. The rival 'contractual' view strives to make divorce as easy as marriage (provided there is agreement), and to make all legally enforceable obligations transmutable into monetary terms; it also sees no reason for the announcement of a marriage through the adoption of the husband's name by the wife, or for any other symbolic or ceremonial display. The upshot of this contractarian view is, in effect, the abolition of marriage as a separate institution: it ceases to be intelligible that people should make *vows* of marriage, rather than promises of an enforceable kind. Between the two extremes there is room for the conception of the 'limited vow': i.e. of non-contractual obligations that are regarded as extinguished by the fulfilment of certain conditions, and this is in effect what the modern law of marriage upholds.

Those inspired by certain *feminist and also Marxist arguments concerning the relation between the family and private property might similarly seek to abolish marriage. Marriage may exist while it has its economic rationale in a particular system of *production relations, but it can only impede the free development of the individual when those relations disintegrate.

martial law. Law applied through the *courts martial or military tribunals established under the directorship of military institutions. Only exceptionally can martial law be imposed within the state *jurisdiction rather than in foreign territory temporarily occupied. In the UK it cannot be declared in time of peace. Its principal characteristics are procedural: justice is administered according to provisions laid down by military councils, standards of evidence are changed, and the right of appeal constrained or abolished.

It is commonly said that 'martial law' was declared in Poland in December 1981. This seems to imply (i) that after the declaration the law was administered by different tribunals, or by differently constituted tribunals, from those that had administered it before; (ii) that legal procedure became that of a military tribunal rather than a civil court; (iii) that the military institutions were separate from those of the *state; or else (iv) that there was genuine judicial independence under the former law that was removed by the imposition of martial law. In fact it is doubtful that any of (i) to (iv) is true, and it would therefore be better to refer to a sudden imposition of severe laws under a system that in any case never fully recognized judicial independence or the *rule of law.

The expression 'martial law' is also used (although legally this is not approved) to denote military law, i.e. the special bodies of law applicable to members of the armed forces during the course of their duties as such. In this sense it *could* be said that martial law in Poland was extended to the whole population.

Marx, Karl (1818–83). A *Young Hegelian turned social scientist, who lived for much of his life in exile, having lent support to the revolutionary activity of 1848. Together with *Engels he wrote the **Communist Manifesto,* and developed a philosophy of man, history and politics that would give hitherto unprecedented authority to the communist cause. This philosophy has undergone many changes (*see* *dialectical materialism, *Marxism-Leninism, *neo-Marxism). We give it here in the form in which it is found in Marx, where the doctrine has three distinct, but interdependent, parts.

(i) Human nature. This theory shows the influence of *Hegel and finds fullest expression in Marx's early writings (e.g. *The 1844 Manuscripts*). The nature of man is not immutable but historical, changing in accordance with social and economic conditions. But the prime mover of history is man himself who, through labour, remakes the world in his own image and changes his image in accordance with his powers. The nature of man therefore depends upon the conditions in which he labours. *Private property creates the division between the classes, and also the condition of *alienation which is overcome only by overthrowing the institution which creates it. With the abolition of private property man ceases to be a mere object or means; he is restored to his dignity as subject, or end in himself. He then becomes free, and his social relations become classless.

(ii) History. The philosophical idea of the 'historical essence of man' is recast in the later writings (notably *Capital,* vol. I, 1867) as a scientific claim concerning the evolution of human societies. All social forms have a function, and this function explains their existence, their survival and their destruction. Marx's theory is a form of *materialism: history is propelled by material forces – the *productive forces – whereby nature is transformed into *use-values and *exchange-values.

These productive forces compel the creation and destruction of successive systems of *production relations between men. These systems, or economic structures, form the material *base of society upon which the many-tiered superstructure of institutions is erected. Among the possible production relations are those of *feudalism, *capitalism, *socialism and *communism. The superstructure consists of the legal and other institutions which consolidate these arrangements, together with the *ideology that pertains to them. Productive forces have an intrinsic tendency to develop, as man's knowledge of and mastery over nature increase. As they develop successive economic structures arise and give way, and the social superstructure changes along with them. At a particular point of development the productive forces and the production relations enter into conflict: the latter being unable to contain the former. Society then enters a period of *revolution. Men become conscious of this by recognizing the existence of *class struggle, between those whose activity fits them for the new economic structure, and those who are guardians of the old. This consciousness is not the cause, but the effect, of the material conflict which generates revolution.

(iii) Economics. Marx put forward a version of the *labour theory of value. Since exchange-value enters the world only through labour, attribution to it of autonomous power is a form of fetishism (*see* *commodity fetishism). Exchange-value is in reality 'congealed human labour'. The accumulation of *surplus value is explained as the extortion of hours of unpaid labour; exchange-value therefore accumulates in the hands of the capitalist, and never in the hands of the worker. This is the only explanation of regular capital accumulation that is compatible with the truth of the labour theory (but cf. *primitive accumulation); it follows that capitalism is of necessity a form of exploitation.

The combination of these views leads to a prediction. At a certain point of development the economic structure of capitalism will no longer be able to contain and facilitate the ever-developing productive forces. Hence there will be a *crisis of capitalism to be resolved by revolution. This revolution will transfer power to the proletariat, and there will follow a development towards an economic arrangement that will be communist (since that is the only arrangement suited to the final mastery of nature), and also classless.

Marxian/Marxist. Two terms which are not now generally synonymous. 'Marxian' means pertaining to one or other of the theories expounded by *Marx: for example, to the theory of exploitation and surplus value, or the theory of historical materialism. 'Marxist' means pertaining to the theory or (more usually) practice of *Marxism: i.e. forming some part of the complex revolutionary movement that derived its initial inspiration from the writings of Marx. Thus a Marxian economist might well not be a Marxist economist – he might even be opposed to all revolutionary activity. It seems that there are even Marxian conservatives, just as there are Marxists who believe very few of the theories of Marx.

Marxism. Marxism has two distinct parts: theoretical, and practical. Theoretically it involves adherence to the ideas of *Marx, together with a political commitment to proletarian *revolution of the kind described and foretold by Marx. Practically, it involves Marxist *praxis, within the context of a 'bourgeois' state, which in turn involves, not necessarily revolutionary activity, but a preparation of the ground for revolution in social and institutional life.

Marxism is a vast movement and its theoretical and practical aspects do not necessarily correspond. Moreover, there are currents, strains, heresies and rival interpretations in the theoretical sphere which make it additionally difficult to pin down any particular doctrine as giving the essence of Marxism. It is normal to distinguish the 'scientific' strain of Marxism, with its emphasis upon the supposedly rigorous analysis of the economic structure and 'law of development' of capitalist society, from the 'Marxist humanism' which, because it seems committed to less bold predictions and less monumental claims about the nature of society, has recommended itself to many who cannot quite believe either the economics of Marx or the many available versions of *historical materialism. Marxist humanism involves the application of the concepts found in Marxian theory to the description of human consciousness, to social and cultural phenomena, and to all aspects of life in which classes and their ideologies gain ascendancy. It is humanistic not only in its emphasis on consciousness, but also in its concern for values which may seem to have no place in the 'scientific' claims of historical materialism. Within these two broad movements one must distinguish, as versions of the 'scientific': *dialectical materialism, *technological determinism, and some of the theories concerned with *exploitation and the *labour theory of value; as versions of the 'humanistic': *critical theory, the *Frankfurt school, and the work of *Lukács and (possibly) *Gramsci. Within those intellectual currents many more influences are felt – some pay more or less attention to the work of *Engels, to the *Leninist theories of *imperialism and *revolution and to attempts made by *Luxemburg and others to prevent the theoretical justification of *tyranny. Some have tried to synthesize Marxism with other doctrines, for example with *structuralism (*see* *Althusser), with *cybernetics (*see* *crisis theory), with *liberalism (*see* *left-liberalism) and so on.

Marxist practice seems to be more uniform than the theory. Revolutionary movements which call themselves Marxist will tend to see the world in terms of a *class struggle, and attempt to align themselves with the oppressed party in that struggle. They may be very little influenced by either of the two main theoretical movements mentioned, but nourish themselves instead upon a variety of *left, *socialist and *egalitarian doctrines, associating themselves with the name of Marx on account of the successful revolutions carried out in his name.

In USSR parlance many heresies within Marxism are singled out for condemnation (*see*, e.g., *deviationism). This practice was begun by the *bolsheviks, and continued by *Lenin, Stalin and their successors, with a fervour that is rarely encountered outside *religion – a fact that has been instrumental in persuading many to see the actual Marxist movement in communist states more as a quasi-religious than as a political phenomenon. Thus contemporary Marxism has been called by Raymond Aron 'the opium of the intellectuals', parodying Marx's own description of religion as 'the opium of the people'.

Marxism-Leninism. Term coined in the USSR after *Lenin's death, in order to denote the philosophy which Stalin held up as the true philosophy of the Russian Revolution. It purported to combine Marx's analysis of capitalism, in *Engels's slightly popularized version, with Lenin's doctrines of revolutionary action – notably *democratic centralism and the theory of the *Communist Party as *vanguard. The question whether the two strands of thought are consistent with each other is not usually raised, although it is arguable that they are contradictory. Some think that the doctrine, as put forward by Stalin, is so fraught with weaknesses and inconsistencies as to be unserious in everything except its consequences; others think that there is a real theoretical position which emerges when Lenin's emendations are incorporated into the Marxian theories, and that the result is a distinct doctrine, and not just an exercise in propaganda. Most modern communist parties, including the Communist Party of Great Britain, claim to be Marxist-Leninist.

marxizing (sometimes French: *marxisant*). Scattering references and allusions to *Marxian thoughts and technicalities through one's speech or writing, often in order to establish one's credentials as a serious member of the intellectual *left. Marxizing literary criticism had a vogue in France and Italy in the 1960s and 70s (e.g. in the early work of Roland Barthes), and some dismiss the work of the *Frankfurt school as marxizing, meaning to imply that it presents no new theory, and does not involve a serious application but only an affectation of Marxist language. The use of the term is, however, not necessarily pejorative. It may be thought that some degree of marxizing is necessary, e.g. in the composition of a dictionary of political thought, in order to give a modern perspective on the subject.

mass culture. Term of American sociology, now widely used, but perhaps without theoretical basis, to denote that part of popular *culture which is produced consciously for the *masses, rather than the traditional 'high culture' that had been the property of a ruling élite. (See, e.g., D. Macdonald: *A Theory of Mass Culture,* 1957.) Mass culture is sometimes thought to be a product of the *industrial revolution, which destroyed the previous 'folk culture'. The mass culture is also said to be 'consumed' by those who enjoy it, to be 'manufactured', usually under conditions of intense stimulation of demand, and without any suggestion that the value of any cultural product is to be measured in terms other than its price. That a cultural commodity is wanted by someone is said to be the sole criterion of its worth; that the want is artificial, say, produced by the stimulus of advertising or by the peculiarly riveting form of the product, that the want is depraved, and can exist only in a nature that has been in some way morally or spiritually degraded – all such factors supposedly play no part in determining the calculations either of the producer or of the consumer.

In such accounts terms from the theory of *commodities are used, and it is indeed normal to associate this kind of culture with *consumerism – i.e. with the reduction of all values to those of the market. Debate over the value of mass culture is therefore at least as old as the *cultural conservatism that arose in response to the massive stimulation of production during the nineteenth century. The cultural conservative is apt to argue that a critical stance, with an eye to moral and aesthetic values, is an essential part of the understanding of cultural products. Without it 'culture' forms a great tide of stimulation in which true human attachments are dissolved. The opponent of that line of thought may sometimes rest his case in the trivial and disputable ground that *de gustibus non est disputandum* (there is no argument about taste); alternatively he may adopt the more serious argument that the complaints of the cultural conservative are concealed justifications of *élitism, and have the effect, whether or not intended, of confining all serious recreation to a *ruling class.

mass hysteria. The phenomenon of infectious reaction in *crowds, where each member, with no understanding of the cause or object of his emotion, may respond sympathetically to the joy, pride, anger, fear or anxiety of his neighbours. Without this 'cohesive' principle crowds would have no character of their own, *demagogues would be without power, and revolutions hardly conceivable. Since the favoured candidates for explanation of historical transformation are the *leadership theory, and the theory of *revolution, this may be held to support the belief that all such transformations are really promoted by unconscious agency, of which mass hysteria is the immediate expression.

masses. 'There are no masses, only ways of seeing people as masses', writes Raymond Williams (*Culture and Society, 1780–1950,* 1958), who further argues that the term 'masses' has arisen in modern English to replace the once familiar 'mob' as an expression of indiscriminate abuse. In representing a class in its undifferentiated totality the term represents it also as random, irrational and without human qualities. (Cf. the French *canaille.*) In *The Revolt of the Masses,* 1930, José Ortega y Gasset expresses some of the disdain of an old ruling class for the uncontrolled and destructive activities of men no longer obedient to traditional moral and social order, and argues, not that the 'masses' exist only because they are perceived as such, but that they exist because a new form of political organization has made them possible. He identifies this as the modern kind of democracy, in which individuals are regarded as having equal rights regardless of power, and all privilege is treated with hostility and, where possible, undermined, so as to restore the uniformity of the whole.

The idea of the masses as the vehicle of progressive and irresistible historical forces is the Marxist equivalent of the French Revolution's idea of the *people, as the sole source of *authority. Among the practitioners of Marxism many have allowed little leeway to the masses, although *Mao assigned to them an enormous role in every political transformation, and therefore attempted to involve them actively in policy.

massive retaliation. In January 1954, J. F. Dulles declared that 'the way to deter aggression is for the free communities to be willing and able to respond vigorously at places and with means of our own choosing'. This was interpreted as advocating a *strategy of massive retaliation, i.e. immediate complete response to all identifiable attacks using all available means. Subsequently in 1966 NATO affirmed a policy of 'flexible response', i.e. the maintenance of forces designed to conduct any conflict at the lowest possible level until negotiation can be begun, and with the hope of avoiding 'escalation' towards nuclear war. The original NATO policy was in fact one of 'aggressive defence', Dulles intending to signal not a commitment to massive retaliation but rather a preparedness to overreach in counter-aggression the scope and consequences of any attack.

master and servant. The terms used in English law for the legal relation of employment, based in the *wage contract, but now overlaid and qualified by statutes that belie any simple contractual interpretation. (*See* *industrial law.) The master is vicariously liable in tort or delict to any third party injured by fault of the servant when acting in the course of employment – an old *common law doctrine that survives in UK and US law. This doctrine had always acted, even in the absence of statutory provision, to constrain conditions of employment so as to prevent acts dangerous to the public.

The survival of the old terms is one indication of the way in which the wage relation has been conceived in law, as a web of mutual duties, one party being dominant and the other subservient. The 'wage relation of the new type' prefers the terms 'employer' and 'employee', in order to deny the implication of dominance and subservience.

master and slave. A famous passage in *Hegel's *Phenomenology of Spirit,* 1807, describes a transition, represented as both historical and also essential to the individual self-consciousness, from the 'life and death struggle' in the *state of nature, to the acceptance of universal moral law. The transition is described as the 'moment' of lordship and bondage, or master and slave. One party to the original struggle overcomes and enslaves the other, so as to use the other as a means to his ends. The result is that the victor (the master) retires into a life of leisure and consumption which distances him from reality, while the loser, the slave, continues, even in his bondage, to imprint on the world the mark of his individual will. As producer, the slave is enabled to acquire a consciousness of himself as agent, and a sense of the world as containing not only means but also ends; as consumer, the master loses that consciousness, and with it the sense of the ends of his existence. The 'inner freedom' of the slave grows with the 'inner bondage' of the master, until the slave is in a position to rise up and bind his oppressor, so beginning the process again with a reversal of roles. The toing and froing between command and obedience is supposed to exemplify the structure of the *dialectic, and it is resolved only by the transition from this 'moment' of consciousness to that higher 'moment', in which each party sees the other as end and not as means, and thereby accepts the governance of a universal moral law (*see* *Kant).

The parable has many complex details and has had great influence on nineteenth- and twentieth-century political thought, inspiring philosophies of true (as opposed to 'artificial') *freedom, of *revolution and 'revolutionary consciousness', of *alienation, and so on. The influence was immediate on *Young Hegelians, and survived in *Marxist humanism.

materialism. 1. Metaphysics. A somewhat outmoded label for the philosophy that denies that the mind and its contents have a peculiar nature separate from physical reality and subject to autonomous laws of constitution and development. The 'materialism' of the *Enlightenment held that nothing exists except matter, and that the processes which we interpret as mental are really material processes seen in a peculiar and erroneous light.

The *dialectical materialism of *Engels, and *historical materialism generally, have held, not that mental processes *are* material, but rather that their development is in essentials dependent upon transformations in material circumstances, so that what is perceived as a change in consciousness is only the effect, and never the cause, of a transformation in material states of affairs (for example a transformation in *production relations). Milder forms might say only that *some* mental processes (e.g. those constitutive of a social and political vision) are dependent upon material circumstances, and powerless to influence them.

Philosophically speaking, historical materialism should be seen as an answer to a certain kind of *idealism. The term 'materialism' is often now avoided by philosophers, since it seems to imply adherence to the view that 'matter' is the fundamental stuff of the universe, a view long ago disproved by physical science. The modern preferred term is 'physicalism', which holds merely that whatever exists is subject to the laws of constitution and transformation which govern physical reality, and is, in that sense, part of physical reality. But what is physical reality? The best answer is: whatever is governed by the laws of physics.

As that paragraph intimates, there is a philosophical problem in identifying precisely what is being affirmed, and what denied, by those who say that the mind is, or is not, a physical entity. It is fair to say that the current philosophical debate over this issue surpasses in minuteness and sophistication anything that was envisaged by eighteenth-century materialists, or anything that occurred to the defenders of historical materialism.

2. Morals. The attachment to material *values, i.e. to those pleasures and profits which are intrinsically connected with the body, and might equally be attributed to beings without reason or self-consciousness (such as the pleasures of food, drink, sex), together with an attachment to *money, as material means to pleasure. Usually contrasted with attachment to the 'true' realm of human values, in which reason and self-consciousness are implicated, involving such intangibles as loyalty, love, courage, justice and *virtue generally.

materialist theory of history. *See* *dialectical materialism, *historical materialism, *historicism, *materialism.

matriarchy. The system of *kinship relations whereby authority tends to be vested in mothers rather than in fathers (*see* *patriarchy), and in which some or all of those rights and powers traditionally associated with the 'head' of the family belong to the mother (including the right to inherit and bequeath property). The study of matriarchy has done much to support *relativism concerning domestic values and institutions, and to illustrate part of the *feminist argument that many of the apparent distinctions between men and women (and in particular those associated with the granting of power and authority to men rather than to women) are not innate but 'culturally determined' (i.e. acquired).

Maurras, Charles (1868–1952). French writer, right-wing activist, and polemicist, *see* **intégrisme*, *royalism, **trahison des clercs*.

maximin. 1. A technical term of *decision theory and *game theory, denoting a strategy in which the player acts so as to achieve the best outcome that he can, given the worst possible pay-off that could result from the actions of the other players. Thus, the player maximizes the minimum pay-off.

2. A principle of social *justice according to which the best distribution of goods among a class of recipients is that in which the amount obtained by the worst off is the highest (in other words, which maximizes the minimum received). This criterion has recently been advanced by *Rawls as essential to the concept of distributive justice – it seems to capture the idea that justice must concern itself first and foremost with the situation of the worst off.

Rawls's appropriation of the term 'maximin' from game theory reflects his view that the theory of justice, like game theory, involves an application of principles of rational choice in a situation of conflict and coordination. It should not be thought to imply, however, that the reasoning underlying judgements of justice on this view is simply a special case of the reasoning behind the maximin strategies discussed by game theorists.

media. 'The media of communication': i.e. all those means whereby the public receives *communication, whether or not they also lie within public control. Much recent thought has been devoted to the issue of the *control of the media, and the difference made to the content of communication by that control. Social theorists such as Vance Packard (*The Hidden Persuaders*, 1957) have done much to display the power of *advertising in stimulating demand and in creating artificial appetites, often by means that bypass completely the reasoning powers of the subject. To the extent that this is regarded as deleterious, it has been normal to advocate some legal control over advertising. So far no one has been able to describe what form that control should take without advocating the introduction of extensive powers of *censorship.

Advertising apart, many social theorists have also tried to ascertain the extent to which the media in any *class society automatically fall into the hands of the class that owns the means of production, and so become directed to supporting the interests of that class. This aspect of the theory of class *hegemony has been extremely influential, partly because it counters what are often seen as *bourgeois celebrations of the 'freedom' of the media in capitalist countries, as opposed to their complete unfreedom in communist countries. Much of the dispute here is about words. It is a trivial consequence of certain theories of hegemony that the *ruling class controls all major sources of social and political power. Hence that class must also control the media. But the ruling class may be defined so vaguely as to mean nothing more than 'the class which controls the sources of political power', so making the accusation vacuous. In the absence of a better theory, the only serious distinction that could be drawn is that between control by forces within *civil society, which may be exerted against the state, and control by the *state. On all these issues *see* *communication.

The slogan of Marshall McLuhan, that 'the medium is the message', captures the idea, familiar to literary critics, that form and content are never completely separable, so that *how* something is said partly determines *what* is said. On this view it becomes impossible for a medium that is modelled stylistically on the advertisement (*see* *admass) to convey the same thing as a medium modelled stylistically on *propaganda, so that the capitalist and communist media will never be in full agreement about anything, and all appearance of agreement will be an illusion which lasts just so long as the stylistic contexts of the two are ignored. There must, naturally, be some exaggeration in a theory that has that consequence but, as literary critics have discovered, it is extremely difficult to see quite where the exaggeration lies.

mediation. The intervention of a third party in an attempt to resolve a conflict, especially an international conflict, where mediation is a recognized and sometimes mandatory procedure under the Charter of the United Nations. Mediation differs from *arbitration, since there is no agreement to accept the suggestions of the third party, and from *good offices, in that it involves active involvement in the negotiation. In US labour law mediation is recognized as a procedure for resolving industrial disputes.

Mencius (Meng Tzu) (371–289 BC). Chinese philosopher and politician; *see* *Confucianism.

mendésien. Follower of the policies of the French socialist statesman Pierre Mendès-France (b. 1907), sometime prime minister of a coalition government. The label signifies a kind of *constitutionalist socialism, within the framework of French republican institutions, reformist, ready for compromise, and mildly egalitarian. It therefore corresponds to the socialism of the UK *Labour Party, as this existed immediately after the war.

mensheviks. The *moderate faction within the Russian Social Democrat Party. At the party congress in London in 1903, directed by Plekhanov (1856–1918) and Martov (1873–1923), a division arose between those favouring revolution and those favouring reform. The first were the bolsheviks, the second the mensheviks (from the Russian *menshinstvo*, a minority, due to the minority vote which they received as a result of *Lenin's manipulation). The mensheviks formed a separate political party in 1917, despite a nominal reunion with the bolseheviks in 1906, and were a majority in most soviets after the February revolution. They were ousted by the bolshevik *coup d'état* in October, and then gradually liquidated or sent into exile.

The mensheviks were *Marxists, who believed that Russia must pass through a phase of capitalist development before proletarian revolution would be possible; they also rejected Lenin's theory of the role of the party in establishing a socialist administration.

mental illness. *See* *psychotherapy.

mercantile law. Old term for business and commercial law. Not a distinct branch of the legal system in *common law countries, but often so in those countries with a legal system founded in *Roman law.

mercantilism. Economic doctrine much favoured between the mid sixteenth and late seventeenth centuries, which explored the relation between national prosperity and *international trade, and which recommended intervention by the state to encourage exports and limit imports, and so increase both wealth and power. A leading exponent was Gerald Malynes (1586–1641), who advocated such measures as *exchange control, and made various important additions to the concepts of political economy. Later advocates of doctrines of *free trade criticized the mercantilists, partly on the ground that their equation of prosperity simply with the difference between export and import showed an insufficient grasp of the structure of the economy and of the potential gains from trade.

mercenary. A professional soldier who fights for pay, and regardless of political allegiance. Common from the thirteenth century in Europe, the widespread use of mercenaries was deplored by *Machiavelli, on the ground that it transferred power to untrustworthy bands without interest in the political stability or integrity of the state for which they fought. Mercenary armies declined, and virtually disappeared, after the Revolutionary and Napoleonic practices of *conscription had become universal. Moral indignation against mercenaries reflects acceptance by many of the idea that *war can be legitimately carried out only by *states and that individuals can legitimately involve themselves in it only to the extent that the state commands them. Otherwise their responsibility for what they do is personal, and they are no better than murderers. The paradoxical consequences of this doctrine are, however, evident. It implies that the command of a state can exonerate the individual from moral blame (which seems to imply that the state has some near-divine dispensation). For a *utilitarian, it may also imply that the result – including *total war, in which every citizen is bound by terrifying oaths and penalties to wage war absolutely and mercilessly and for whatever time his rulers should choose to commit him – is morally preferable to the activities of the self-seeking *condottieri*. The thought here is that there is something morally dubious about someone who fights and kills for money, and for whoever pays best, and something praiseworthy about someone who fights only when his country is in danger, and for the good of that country.

Standards of behaviour among mercenary soldiers have varied enormously, from the rapine and plunder of the *condottieri* to the disciplined fighting of the Gurkhas, circumscribed by a precise *ethic and with great emphasis on honour.

meritocracy. Term coined in 1958 by Michael Young (*The Rise of the Meritocracy*), to denote government by those thought to possess merit (cf. *aristocracy). 'Merit' means, roughly, intelligence plus effort, both of which capacities are early identified and selectively nurtured through an education system designed to advance 'merit' as rapidly as possible, so that it will emerge in the form of an *élite prepared to take charge of government. In addition all jobs and positions will be obtained on the basis of merit alone, with the implication that, wherever you are, whether at the top or the bottom of the pile, it's where you deserve to be.

Meritocracy has been characterized as promoting rule by *status group rather than by *class; it indicates a large measure of *social mobility selectively obtained. Many regard meritocracy as a distinguishing feature of modern government, and deplore, praise or ignore it accordingly.

messianism. Belief in and adherence to the Messiah, i.e. to one who comes as a messenger from God. More broadly messianic movements are those which are led by someone who claims to be, or to be licensed by, the Messiah. 'Messianism' is used to denote any social or political movement which importantly resembles the religious pattern, with emphasis on *leadership, inspiration, enthusiasm, or a vision of the promised land. Such movements frequently contain elements of *millenarianism, and even *mass hysteria, and tend to involve the deployment of *crowds rather than the building of *institutions. They are important in modern Asian and African politics, where they often build on existing religious sentiments, and upon an existing tendency to experience the world in terms of a 'mission'.

methodology. A word that should mean the study of methods, but is often used simply to mean 'method', as in 'the methodology of the social sciences'. If there is a subject then there is a method of investigation determined by it. There may be more than one method used to discover some matter, and in this case (which is probably more rare than commonly imagined) it is possible to speak of methodology, as the discipline which attempts to describe the method which best achieves the required result. Thus there is a 'methodology' of medical diagnosis, partly because diagnosis does not give the *theory* of what it discovers. In general the existence of a genuine methodology implies the absence of a conclusively established theory, since a theory of something will automatically deliver an account of the correct way of making and validating discoveries about it. When people speak of 'methodological individualism' this implication is precisely what they wish to convey: that they do not know whether or not individualism is true, but they are going to act as though it were. (Cf. also methodological *holism.) When people speak of 'Marxist methodology' or 'structuralist methodology' they might again mean that: more often, however, they wish to banish the implication that the premises from which they begin have less theoretical guarantee than the observations against which they propose to test them.

metropolitan power. The controlling power within an empire or colonial state: that part of the empire which is the privileged recipient of the benefits of expansion, from which the expansion originally occurred, and towards which all relations of accountability ultimately flow.

microeconomics. Branch of economics which treats of small 'decision units' – the *consumer, the *household, the *firm – in order to show how their decisions jointly determine relative *prices and quantities, and the allocation of resources to production. Microeconomics is distinct from macroeconomics, which is the study of the aggregate national income and those features of the economy that are associated with it. In a completely *planned economy, in which all economic activity occurs at the behest of and in response to central decision, it is not clear that the two studies could be truly separate.

middle classes. In the eighteenth century the term 'middle ranks' was used increasingly to denote the expanding section of society that was composed neither of 'nobility' nor of 'common people', and by the nineteenth century the term 'middle classes' was widely used to commend themselves by those to whom it applied. In current sociological usage the expression does not seem to denote a *class, but rather a large and fluid *status group, characterized most of all by its extent and flexibility, and by the ease with which someone can join, and the difficulty with which he can leave it. Cf. *bourgeois.

military-industrial complex. Phrase coined by President Eisenhower in 1960, to denote a pattern of relations sometimes thought to exist between high-ranking industrialists concerned in the manufacture of military technology, and military advisers, concerned in making themselves useful (perhaps even indispensable) to a government. The thought is that the two groups act in concert, perhaps even in collusion, so as to maintain high levels of spending on defence, and a military approach in international politics.

Mill, James (1773–1836) Scottish philosopher, historian and economist, influential in propagating the *utilitarianism of *Bentham, and forming on the basis of it a radical reforming political movement, dedicated to the extension of the franchise, and the representation of working-class interests in Parliament. His *Philosophical Radicals included *Ricardo. Mill himself was a keen student of the new political economy, and attempted to combine a respect for private property, dogmatic utilitarianism, sympathy for the underprivileged, and a libertarian attitude that extended to all aspects of production and trade. He devoted much attention to the problems of education, and was influential partly through his advocacy of the view that intelligence is as much acquired as inherited; the education that he gave to his son, *J. S. Mill, is vividly described in the latter's autobiography.

Mill, John Stuart (1806–73). English philosopher and political economist who made contributions to almost all aspects of political thought:
(i) Political economy. Mill wrote an updated version of *Smith's *Wealth of Nations* (*Principles of Political Economy*, 1848), in which *classical political economy is summarized and given what is perhaps its most accessible expression. Mill offers a qualified defence of **laissez-faire*, but argues that it can lead to just and orderly economic development only if trade unions exist, in order to restore parity of bargaining power between the owners of industry and those employed by them. (*See* *bargaining theory of

wages.) Price is regarded as determined by the equality of demand and supply – i.e. prices rise until demand has fallen to the level of supply, (Mill thus saw no cause to adopt *Ricardo's version of the *labour theory of value). Mill makes various proposals for redistribution in the interests of social justice, mostly through taxation, especially on death, and presents a classic statement of the argument against the *hereditary principle.

(ii) Utilitarianism. One of the more famous of Mill's writings is the pamphlet of this name (1863), in which he amends and restates the Benthamite view of morality that had been bequeathed to him by his father *James Mill. While criticizing many of the assumptions of that view, Mill endorses the 'greatest happiness' principle as the criterion of what is right. He argues that the principle is defensible only if one distinguishes happiness from pleasure (or at any rate recognizes that there are qualitatively different pleasures). He sometimes sees, sometimes does not see, that this vitiates the quantitative approach that had been a principal motive behind Bentham's *hedonism. Mill also offers various thoughts about human nature in order to justify his amendments. *Utilitarianism* has fascinated many subsequent philosophers, partly for its passionate conviction, partly for its failure wholly to reveal why it is so convinced about what.

(iii) Liberalism. Mill's essays *On Liberty*, 1859, and *The Subjection of Women*, 1869, written 1861, contain classic statements of liberal thought about law, liberty and rights. The first defends the view that 'the sole end for which mankind are warranted, individually or collectively, in interfering with the liberty of action of any of their number, is self-protection', from which premise Mill argues at length in favour of basic freedoms, guaranteed by law, and of a radical distinction between the public sphere of law and the private sphere of morality. In the course of this Mill adumbrates another view of law and liberty, the first as a system which maximizes, or ought to maximize, the second. In this sense liberty is seen not in terms of permission, but in terms of the opportunity for *self-realization, for example, through conducting 'experiments in living' in an environment that permits all faculties to be developed in harmony. *The Subjection of Women* is a classic argument in the *feminist cause, defending the proposition that there is no known difference between men and women that would justify attributing to them different *rights.

(iv) The theory of government. In *Considerations on Representative Government*, 1861, Mill outlines and defends an ideal system of government, based on *proportional representation, in which minorities will find spokesmen in the institutions of government, and in which the rights of all citizens will be effectively guaranteed, while allowing to them maximum occasion for self-development.

While Mill devoted most of his social and political writings to questions concerning law, constitution and economics, it seems clear that an *individualistic view of human nature underlies much of his sense of the value of the liberty that he defends. For this he has been criticized, by those opposed to individualism. He has also been accused of a certain naïvety about human nature. He himself recognized the possibility of such an accusation and sometimes thought that he had cured himself through studying the *cultural conservatism of *Coleridge and *Carlyle, and absorbing, if not their political doctrines, at least the German romantic view of the significance of culture which had inspired them. In any case, Mill's thinking about law, liberty and emancipation has been widely accepted in Anglo-Saxon jurisprudence, as giving the basic principles upon which legal reform should proceed. Much of the inner conflict in Mill's moral and political thought has been seen by later philosophers as the result of an intrinsic tension between the standards of liberty and utility, and this tension is expressed equally in the legal reforms (e.g. those concerning sexual conduct) which Mill's thinking has partly inspired.

millenarianism. Belief in the 'millennium'

– i.e. a future thousand-year period of blessedness. Based in the prophecy contained in Revelations 20, it has been spasmodically popular among Christians throughout the centuries. The term is now extended to denote any doctrine which is based in the promise of an eventual release from earthly miseries by an enduring security, preferably without political institutions: e.g. *Marx's belief that communism will bring the *prehistory of humanity to a close, as interpreted by certain of his early disciples. Such 'eschatological fantasy' (Norman Cohn: *The Pursuit of the Millennium*, 1957), is common to many political doctrines, ancient, medieval and modern.

The religious idea is sometimes thought to be particularly predominant in countries which have formed their social and political identity in response to *colonialism (see, e.g., G. Balandier: *The Sociology of Black Africa*, 1970). An interesting example is the New Guinea 'cargo cult' in which the Western 'cargo' is thought to be about to arrive, bringing the spirits of the dead and ushering in the millennium.

Milosz, Czeslaw, (b. 1911). Polish writer and diplomat. *See* *Asiatic despotism, *ketman, *New Right.

minimax. Technical term of *game theory. A minimax strategy is one in which a player attempts to maximize his minimum gain. If there is such a strategy open to either party in a two-person *zero-sum game, then the game has a 'solution', i.e. a strategy with an acceptable guaranteed result. In the case of such games, the minimax strategy is also called a *maximin strategy; the two terms are normally synonymous. However, there are games in which maximizing one's minimum gain is not also minimizing another's maxium gain; in these cases it may be important to distinguish the two kinds of strategy by employing two distinct terms to refer to them.

minorities. Exactly what constitutes a minority is an extremely difficult question. Numerically speaking, the English upper class is a minority, so, probably, is the lower middle class. But neither would be referred to as a 'minority' in a political discussion, largely because a grouping in terms of *class suggests a socio-economic theory, whereas a grouping in terms of 'minority' suggests that the important facts are *ethnic or *cultural. A minority might, however, form a class – either a ruling class (the Turks in Cyprus before 1974) or a subordinate class (the Tamils in Sri Lanka) – but this does not seem to be essential. There is a minority whenever there are (a) habits of association among members which involve an idea of separateness – perhaps imposed by the majority, perhaps accepted by the minority, perhaps both; (b) a sense of separate social *identity which expresses itself in different behaviour. Clearly (a) and (b) reinforce each other: a majority may single out a particular group as *not* belonging to it and, by denying to it privileges and rights, reinforce the group's own sense that it constitutes a separate social identity, perhaps causing it to seek a corresponding political identity. The basis for this pattern of social division may be religion, language, race or any other factor that is socially perceivable, though in fact the division of a people into 'majority' and 'minority' tends to become prominent as a result of nationalistic sentiment.

The existence of minorities has generated the problem of *integration and minority rights. On one view the state is a set of legal and legally determined institutions, not to be identified with the civil society that is governed by them. The first legislates, the second obeys, but there is no other reason besides that of law for the state to take an interest in the composition and habits of association of the society destined to be governed by it. On this view, unless there is legal provision to the contrary, the rights guaranteed by law and constitution must be extended to all, so that there can be no legal recognition of discriminatory practices against minorities, the category of 'minority' belonging exclusively to civil society, and not to the state. At the same time it may be necessary to provide additional stipulations guaranteeing to minorities those special practices which constitute them, asserting a constitutional right for civil society to fragment as its members should decide. Up to a point all constitutions now attempt these provisions, notably the US constitution, with varying degrees of success in their enforcement and varying degrees of seriousness in their intention. Clearly a constitution may purport to guarantee to Jews, e.g., freedom to worship, dress, and congregate as their traditions demand, while the executive arm of government always regards such practices as *prima facie* evidence of being, say, a *Zionist and an enemy of the state. Such situations are common, and that is one reason why the mere extending of rights by a constitution is never sufficient to guarantee *minority* rights. There must be additional procedures whereby a member of a minority can enforce his rights, by obtaining redress for all actions which discriminate against him on the basis of his membership of a minority, thus ensuring that he has the genuine right to practise his religion etc. without forfeiting *other* rights or benefits.

Views which see the state and civil society as more closely identified (say, because the authority of the first is thought to be only a legal translation of the real or potential unity of the second, as in *nationalism) might be more concerned to eliminate than to protect minorities. A state might attempt to force all minorities to relinquish their habits of association and join the majority, or it might provide different rights in law, so upholding the exclusion of the minority from benefits claimed by the majority.

The practice of making treaty stipulations guaranteeing minority rights has been known since the Reformation. As part of the peace settlement of 1919–20 most Central and Eastern European countries were required to make treaties or sign declarations protecting the rights of minorities. Such treaties proved unenforceable, in particular when faced with the persistent human tendency to seek vengeance for unexplained ills by attributing them to creatures regarded as *alien.

mission civilatrice. The 'civilizing mission' through which French colonial expansion in the nineteenth century justified itself, it being held that the the introduction of legal, political and cultural institutions was so much to the advantage of the developing countries as to justify their subordination to a *metropolitan power. Because of the deliberately *meritocratic nature of Napoleonic institutions, French law and especially French systems of education took root more effectively than those of many other colonial powers, and led, for example, to a uniform system of examinations throughout the French colonies and a comparatively flourishing colonial literature.

mixed economy. An economy in which private enterprise and state-controlled (or *socially owned) enterprises exist side by side, interacting and perhaps even competing with each other. All economies are to some extent mixed, even if illegally (say, through the existence of an extensive black market, as in most communist states). The UK economy is one of the most important examples, in that it contains extensive private and extensive public ownership which have come, over a period of many years, to depend upon each other. The arrangement has been praised for its supposed flexibility, continuity and responsiveness to social change, together with its ability to permit government action in times of crisis, and private enterprise in times of stability. It has been criticized recently by *monetarists and thinkers of the *New Right, for supposedly allowing too much public ownership, and so undermining the conditions for economic prosperity, equilibrium and the free market.

mixed government. Government which is neither monarchical, nor aristocratic, nor oligarchic, nor democratic, but some mixture of two or more of those categories. No government entirely corresponds to the traditional categories, which must be considered to be *ideal types; but some show a definite tendency towards stable synthesis of rival modes. A good example of such a mixed government is provided by the UK, which has recently tended towards a constitutional *monarchy, with an established *aristocracy represented separately in the upper house of Parliament, whose power is mitigated and for most political purposes overriden by that of an assembly elected on more or less *democratic principles. Mixed government was recommended by *Machiavelli as the appropriate form of government for a class society, and it provides an example of *limited government in which the limitation comes as much from the balance of forces within the government as from any specific constitutional provisions.

moderate. Used in two related senses, first to describe political opinions, secondly to describe a mode of government.

Opinions merit the label 'moderate' in popular usage when no one is particularly offended by them other than those who demonstrate, by their offence, that they are not moderate. The definition is not circular, so long as the form and content of inoffensive opinion can be described. The first three of the following conditions attempt to display its form, the last two its content:

(i) Primarily, a desire for *conciliation rather than *confrontation.

(ii) A preference for reform over revolution – which at one level is simply an expansion of the requirements implicit in (i).

(iii) A belief that political transformation should be gradual and involve no great violence to institutions.

(iv) Belief that there exists a *consensus among right-minded people, and that the process of politics consists in part in the discovery of this consensus and its translation into law. The consensus will shift with changing circumstances, which is why politics is necessary, but the coincidence between government and public opinion is or should be the ultimate aim of politics, and the premise from which conciliation begins.

(v) Tolerance towards views which do not match the consensus, provided that they are expressed in accordance with the formal principles (i) to (iii), all other views being disliked as instances of *extremism.

Features (iv) and (v) lead to some confusion between moderate and *centrist positions, the latter being defined in polar terms (as a mean between extremes) the former being defined, as here, quite independently of any contrasting position.

A government is called 'moderate' not necessarily on account of the opinions which motivate it, but rather because it attempts to balance and conciliate, rather than to confront or eliminate, rival powers within civil society. A characteristic of moderate government is that it should permit the existence of an *opposition. Some argue that only a *limited government can do that, and that the combination of limited government and permitted opposition requires a *rule of law. These plausible ideas depend, however, on intricate connections among institutions which can be laid bare only with the greatest intellectual labour.

modernity. The contrast between 'ancient' and 'modern' was introduced at the *Renaissance, but it seems that the distinctively modern sense of the term 'modern', as signifying the transformed consciousness of the world and the self that comes from living 'now', rather than 'then', is a later invention. Etymologically the term is connected with 'mode', and hence *fashion; it occurs with its modern sense – signifying that which is important and inescapable to the person who would live in the present – in *Rousseau, and thereafter in many writings of the late *Enlightenment and *Romantic periods. It was perhaps Hegel who gave the most solemn and far-reaching analysis of the condition of the modern man: the character who holds history before himself and himself before history and reflects upon whether the two are in harmony. Modernity, as the self-conscious placing of oneself in history, can take optimistic and pessimistic forms. In either version it has demanded changes not only in the rhetoric, but also in the substance of political thinking. The modern man exists in *conscious* relation to history; if he acts out of custom and tradition it is in a certain measure from a sense of irony: if he commits himself to a future it is either recklessly, or with a battery of predictions designed to tell him how history *must* proceed. Some argue that conservatism is a peculiar product of this modern consciousness; emerging perhaps for the first time clearly in the works of *Burke and Hegel, and consisting in celebrations of custom and prejudice by men who were detached from both, and whose very self-consciousness distanced them from the object of their veneration. Revolution is also said to be an idea which owes its currency to the modern spirit, perhaps because revolution destroys the history with which this spirit is constantly comparing itself. (The contrast between conservatism and revolution, as just described, is captured in *Mannheim's polar division of thought between 'ideology' and 'utopia'.) Some have argued that the essence of modernity is *nihilism, combined with the recognition of the impossibility of nihilism (thus Turgenev, *Nietzsche, Dostoevsky). Only a modern person could dream up, in answer to this predicament, the doctrine of *commitment, to programmes and policies which can be justified only by ceasing to be committed to them. (*See* *existentialism.)

Despite the self-obsessiveness of the spirit which identifies itself as modern, an ideal of modernity continues to appeal. Calls to 'modernize' laws, institutions, artifacts, lifestyles, religions, have become standard items of political rhetoric. This has led to the term 'modern' becoming synonymous, for some, with the habit, supposedly pernicious, of elevating ends over means, of preferring machinery in motion to persons at rest. But there seems to be no simple issue that is contended in debates over 'modernization', and the above must be taken only as a sketch of a vast and largely uncharted area of conflict.

monarchy. Literally, rule by one. As now understood, however, the form of government in which the *head of state holds office, usually with the title of King or Queen, either for life or until voluntary renunciation (by 'abdication'). Monarchies are of two fundamental kinds: absolute monarchy, and limited monarchy (of which the modern *constitutional monarchy is a variant). In the latter, the person who reigns does not necessarily rule, in the strict sense of *controlling the outcome of *executive decisions, but may perhaps exert no more than a merely ceremonial, or perhaps partly regulative, function. The absolute monarchy is obsolete, in one sense: that is, those who hold absolute *power* for life nowadays rarely do so as a matter of *law*, and tend to dignify themselves not with the title of King or Queen, but with that of Chairman (when government is through the machinery of a *party) or President. The distinction is a nice one. It is not that the title King is hereditary, while that of Chairman is not. There have been elected kings (as in Poland), and hereditary 'lord protectors' (Richard Cromwell): there might easily be hereditary party chairmen. It seems rather that a monarch is identified by a law of succession to office, and by a ceremonial and perhaps slightly mystical unity with the nation which he rules, whereby he takes its name, and becomes the personal embodiment of all its dignities and rights. (This has been called 'existential *representation' by Eric Voegelin.) A chairman derives his dignities more abstractly, and speaks for a doctrine and for the party that embodies it, as much as for a territory over which that party exercises its authority. Clearly, there need be no great difference in the kinds of power that are exercised in the various kinds of case: the distinction is one of law, history and *ethos.

Hereditary monarchy is often praised, on the ground that it enables the head of state to achieve office without having to scramble for it, and on the ground that it implants an idea of continuity and legitimacy at the heart of popular sentiments towards the state. It is criticized, like all applications of the *hereditary principle, on the ground that it is arbitrary – i.e. there is no relation between the office filled and the qualifications of the person destined to fill it. Some accept this argument, and reply either that in this area arbitrariness is a virtue (it is part of the mystical quality of the 'head of state' and therefore of the allegiance towards the state that he symbolizes), or that every other mode of filling so high an office must be equally arbitrary, and usually more dangerous. Whatever the truth of these arguments, it seems that the popularity of monarchy remains great, perhaps because the monarch now has so little actual power. By contrast the party chairman attracts popularity not usually as holder of an office but rather because, like Stalin, he embodies qualities of personal *leadership.

monetarism. Name now frequently given to an economic policy which sees the control of the *money supply as crucial to the control of *inflation and which, by implication, condemns government attempts to *reflate the economy through public spending (which must in normal circumstances increase the money supply).

The theoretical basis of modern monetarism is the so-called 'quantity theory of money': a long-established but disputed theory based in acceptance of the 'Fisher equation' (after the economist Irving Fisher (1867–1947)): $MV = Py$, where M is the stock of money, V is the velocity at which money circulates through the economy, P is the average price level of goods and services, and y is a volume measure of the flow of those goods and services (i.e the flow of *real income). Since the total money value of goods bought (= stock of money × velocity of circulation) is necessarily the same as the money value of goods sold (price level × goods and services sold), the equation is valid *a priori*. Thus V is sometimes defined as $Py \div M$. The theory receives its empirical application by assuming that y is constant (or growing at a given rate), that the economy is at *full employment and will remain there, and that V is constant, determined by independent and unchanging facts concerning the institution of money, such as the time intervals between wage payments. In which case M determines P, so that price level rises and falls with money supply. To keep down inflation (rising prices) it is therefore necessary, and sufficient, to keep down the money supply.

It is easy to find difficulties with the assumptions (a) of full employment (which here need only mean maximum possible employment), and (b) of constancy in the velocity of money circulation (which has certainly changed drastically with computerization and universal credit). Milton Friedman, one of the most recent defenders of monetarism, has argued that, nevertheless, although V varies, it is an 'endogenous variable' – one whose value is determined by institutional facts of the economy and not in a random way, so that, for the purposes of policy, V can be regarded as stable. Friedman has therefore argued that control of the money supply is still the one thing that governments can do which will exert a predictable effect on inflation, and cites in support of his theory the supposed empirical facts that only where such control exists has inflation been forced down, and only in the absence of it has it escalated to the point of *hyperflation. None of this shows, however, that it is or is not easy to control the money supply.

Critics sometimes confuse the doctrine that control of the money supply is necessary and sufficient to control inflation with the doctrine that control of the money supply is necessary and sufficient to produce a healthy economy. Clearly control of inflation is only one objective: *economic growth may be another, as may full employment, even when artificially created by the stimulation of demand, through an increase of the money supply (*see* *Keynes).

money. Anything acceptable in payment of a debt can be called money, provided its acceptance is sufficiently widespread, but the principal application of the term is to any sufficiently universal medium of exchange, such as 'coin of the realm' (i.e. liabilities of the government) and bank credit notes. In less sophisticated economies the coin itself has a value – i.e. an intrinsic capacity to exchange against other goods, independently of the government's promise to sustain or enforce that exchange – as when the coin is made of gold. The reliance on 'valueless' tokens as embodiments of official promises indicates a confidence in the stability of the economy: where this confidence disappears, *barter may come to replace the monetary system. (*See* *hyperflation.)

Money has the following functions: it is a medium of exchange which replaces barter, and so facilitates transactions; it is a store of value, which facilitates saving; it is a unit for the measurement of value, which facilitates accounting. In all of these its value lies in no use apart from its potentiality to exchange against what is useful independently. The 'money illusion' is the propensity to respond to changes in money magnitudes as though they were changes in *real terms, and not simply a revision in terms of measurement. Thus when offered double income and double prices, someone may suffer from the illusion that he is being offered something real, rather than a change in his habits of accounting. (*See* *real terms.)

The 'money illusion' is to be distinguished from certain illusions associated with money by *Marx, but more metaphysically characterized. Marx argued that there is a mystery contained in the very fact of exchange-value, and in particular in money as its principal embodiment. The possession of value in exchange is an appearance only, and does not correspond to the essence of money. (*See* *essence/appearance.) This essence consists in the socio-economic relations (the *production relations) which generate exchange-value from the only thing (*labour) that *can* generate value. The institution of money creates the permanent illusion of value as embodied in the things, including money, which are exchanged, rather than in the labour which produces them. (*See* *commodity fetishism.) This particular application of the essence/appearance distinction is highly controversial, and while it seems to be saying something extremely important, it is hotly disputed what that something is.

money supply. Many definitions of this are offered by economists. However, the most generally accepted is: the amount of *money (i.e. items conventionally accepted in payment of debt) which circulates in an economy at any given time. This generally includes current accounts at banks as well as coin of the realm. Difficulties arise in trying to ascertain which, if any, is the most appropriate way of conceiving of the money supply for the purposes of government policy. Instruments used by governments in the control of the money supply include interest rate policy (changing the lending rate at a central bank), and operations of the 'money market', as when a central bank buys or sells government bonds. Governments may also try to control bank lending and the rate of interest more directly (*see* *credit control). All these instruments are used in the instigation of monetary policy.

monism. 1. The belief that there is only one thing, or one kind of thing, that constitutes or explains events; or else that there is only one basic law or form of law which governs all transformations within a certain field.

In one version *historical materialism is a kind of monism, since it asserts that all historical development is to be explained in terms of transformations in production relations, which are in turn to be explained in terms of the development of one thing: productive forces. This version might be held to be implausible, for example, because there are other 'material' forces active in the shaping of human history – such as sexuality. But this objection might be accepted by someone who argued for historical monism at another level, saying, for example, that all these forces contribute to historical development in accordance with a single law, or a single kind of law, say a law of *functional explanation. Thus a monist is anyone who says 'one' to his opponents' 'many'.

2. Hence, the opposite of *pluralism, in particular the advocacy of a unitary state, in which one people obedient to one system of laws, and with one set of values and social relations, enjoys a single continuous territory. (*See* *nationalism.)

monopoly. A monopoly exists when a firm or individual is the sole seller of a given commodity. Lesser degrees of monopoly can be recognized, and in UK law an enterprise can be referred to the Monopolies and Mergers Commission if it possesses one third or more of the market sales of a commodity. The commission makes reports upon which a minister may act in order to control or destroy the monopoly. Monopolies have been a common grievance throughout history, and were made illegal, with certain exceptions, by the English Statute of Monopolies 1624. Exclusive control of a market naturally enables a firm to fix prices in its own favour and, it is argued, a just price could never result from this. Some also argue that the existing strictures against monopoly still permit the same effects, through permitting or encouraging *oligopoly in its place. Marxists sometimes add that the emergence of a monopoly is an inherent tendency of *late capitalism; and is merely the becoming explicit, in the (illusory) world of market relations, of the (real) constraint that all owners of the means of production exert over those who have property only in their own labour power. That there can be laws which *effectively* control monopoly is sometimes offered as an argument in support of the view that capitalism has the inherent means (through law) to overcome its own crises.

Others argue that these laws have not been truly effective, and that the monopolization of industry presents one of the most significant crises of modern capitalism. Thus Paul A. Baran and Paul M. Sweezy (*Monopoly Capital,* 1966) have argued that competition in a market economy leads to the concentration and centralization of capital, and this, in turn, leads to the formation of monopolies. This transition from competitive to monopoly capital is held to have profound and far-reaching effects, on accumulation, on the structure of profits and prices and on economic growth, the principal sign of which is the increasing stagnation of the economy, as monopolies attempt to protect their markets. This argument is not accepted generally, and even among those who accept it it is not always held to imply that capitalism is therefore in a state of crisis. But the question is far from closed, and is regarded by many as being immensely important in considering the future of capitalist economies.

Certain deviations from a competitive market towards monopoly may lead to a situation in which many firms are in competition with each other, say because their products are close to each other and can be substituted one for the other, and yet each possesses a downward-sloping demand curve. This situation is described by economists as monopolistic or *imperfect competition.

Monroe doctrine. The doctrine enunciated by President Monroe in 1823, and still important in rationalizing US foreign policy, that the US can countenance no intervention in the American continent by a foreign power and would not itself intervene in disputes in Europe.

Montesquieu, Charles-Louis de Secondat, Baron de (1689–1755). French philosopher and political theorist who attempted, in *The Spirit of the Laws*, 1734, to study human society 'scientifically', and to arrive at the principles of government which would explain the nature and extent of law, and the constitution best suited to guarantee the liberties of the subject, while maintaining order over all. Montesquieu admired *Locke, and the English constitution (or what he took to be the English constitution), praising it as 'the mirror of liberty'. He advocated a *separation of powers, and was the first to give the modern formulation of that idea, as part of a theory of *limited government. Montesquieu argued that only an aristocratic government on the English model could create an effective balance of powers within the state, avoiding the despotic tendencies inherent both in absolute monarchy and in government by the common people. He defended liberty; but his desire was to restore old liberties which the *absolutism of Louis XIV had eroded, rather than to advocate the new and, what he saw as, dangerous liberties of the Enlightenment.

According to Montesquieu, law and constitution are ultimately founded in the 'spirit' of a people. While there is a universal *natural law, it is not to be supposed that the conditions for its enforcement exist everywhere and at every time: on the contrary, only within the ideal constitution can the natural law be used effectively to guarantee the rights of the citizen, and this constitution is in turn dependent for its power upon a spirit that is in part determined by geographical, climatic and historical conditions. (It is no accident, therefore, that the liberties of the English subject are guaranteed by jurisdiction over an *island*.)

Montesquieu gave interesting, and sometimes penetrating, accounts of the spirit of a people under monarchy, and under the various forms of republican government, arguing that to each form of government there corresponds a fundamental moral sentiment that binds the citizen to the political order: in monarchy the sentiment is honour, in a republic it is 'political virtue' (*see* *virtue), manifest in a sense of public responsibility. These separate spirits are exhibited even in the smallest transactions inculcated by the various modes of rule. Montesquieu modified his constitutionalism by such sociological observations, tending to the conclusion that a constitution expresses a social condition that is not, in the end, detachable from it. (*Durkheim praised these observations as the first manifestation of modern sociology.) Thus, while Montesquieu influenced the liberal constitutionalists who attempted to divide state and civil society as far as possible, he himself did not countenance that division but, on the contrary, regarded the customs and *ethos of civil society as giving content to the laws which exist as its form. In this he influenced *Burke, who admired him, also, for what he took to be a thorough-going attempt to articulate the idea of liberty in terms of a conservative vision of *privilege.

moral rearmament. The slogan of a political campaign, founded in Oxford (as the 'Oxford Group') by F. Buchman (1878–1961), an American Lutheran minister, with the aim of reinvigorating the Christian countries through a regeneration of moral values, an opposition to corruption, and a strengthening of international ties. The movement has at times had an *anti-communist tendency, but its fervour has been largely expended in the attempt to resist the liberalization of the law.

moralism. The disposition to moralize – i.e. to cast judgement of a moral kind upon actions which are not appropriately so judged. Moralism in art and literature is a familar phenomenon, and some dismiss all moral judgement *of* art and literature as mere moralism, since it applies moral values in a sphere where they supposedly have no application. That view is no doubt already implausible; it is even less plausible to dismiss the relevance of moral judgement to actions done in the name of politics, although the Leninist theory of 'revolutionary morality' in effect dismisses as moralism most criticism of Leninist policies that anyone could ever be in a position to make. Here, as elsewhere, there is a dividing line between moral sense, which recognizes a moral issue when it sees one, and moralism, which curtails the possibilities of action by seeing everything in a moral light. But what that dividing line is depends upon a theory of *responsibility, which will settle the all-important questions of when the consequences of a politician's action are morally significant and when they are properly to be attributed to *him*.

Some *Marxists argue that all moral judgement of political action is *ideology, and call it 'moralism' for that reason, thinking that to give this kind of *explanation* of a judgement is also to expose it as a fraud. This somewhat technical usage of the term is very much dependent upon a theory of ideology: some would argue that it is a self-defeating usage, since it deprives the Marxist himself of the power to make moral recommendations.

morality and politics. What are the distinctions between moral and political judgement, and between morally and politically motivated action? Should moral values enter into political decision-making? If so, when and how? Those large questions have their parallel in all spheres where the actions of one person have consequences in the lives of others, but where the relation between the two is mediated by an *office or a *role. Thus a judge who condemns someone to punishment in accordance with the law is not normally thought to be acting *in propria persona,* but rather as the holder of an office; we do not normally criticize him in moral terms unless he exceeds that office – i.e. acts **ultra vires,* say by condemning someone of proven innocence in order to settle a private account. Intuitively, some such distinction might also apply in politics. How could war be conducted, unemployment created, or people left homeless or property-less, if there were not some way of exonerating the politician whose actions initiate these things from the *responsibility that might otherwise attach to them? If we could never carry out this exoneration, then most normal politics would have to be condemned as immoral. The issue is complex, and requires clarity in the following areas:
(i) The nature of roles and offices, in particular those through which political power is channelled. Is it really possible for a role or an office to change the moral nature of the act performed by its occupant? Or, if not, to change his responsibilities?
(ii) The concept of responsibility. Can responsibility for the known consequences of an act depend upon roles and offices?
(iii) The concept of political *virtue. Can one think of political actions as justifiable in terms of the virtuous character that is expressed through them? *Aristotle, *Cicero, *Machiavelli and many others have argued that moral virtues express themselves in the political sphere, but in a manner that shows a flexibility to the needs of politics. The politician is like a soldier: although the activity in which he is engaged may require him to harm people, there are only some things which a virtuous character will tolerate. Moreover, there are forms of virtue which find their highest expression in the political (as others in the military) sphere. It may also be part of virtue to accept the problems of political expediency and to adapt one's conduct to them, for what the just, wise and courageous man will do depends partly upon the circumstances in which he is required to do it.
(iv) To what extent can the sphere of politics be seen (as e.g. Machiavelli saw it) as a sphere of necessity, in which the freedom of choice which permits moral thought and action is constrained or abolished?
(v) Most importantly, the nature of moral judgement. Moral judgement is an expression of *value, where the object is a human act or character. According to one popular view, given system by *Kant, moral judgement takes the form of commitment to universal and exceptionless laws, governing the behaviour of all rational beings as such, irrespective of circumstances, consequences and roles. This view would not countenance the distinction between spheres of personal responsibility and political expediency, but at best allow that expediency may sometimes place the agent in a dilemma. According to a rival view – that of Aristotle – moral judgement concerns itself not with universal rules of conduct but with the specification of the dispositions of character that we all have reason to admire (the virtues).

Whatever the answer to those problems, it is intuitively clear that political *ideals are not independent of moral values, and that even a moderate, who thought of all politics on the model of conciliation, must recognize that some courses of action are ruled out as morally impossible, and that some forces ought to be, not conciliated, but confronted. (This might be one underlying intuition governing the idea of a *crime – as an act expressing a state of mind that will not admit of conciliation within well-ordered government.) Thus the imposition of any form of government also implies the preparedness to use *force; it could even be, as *Machiavelli suggested, that a *rule of law can be achieved only through violence.

Even if that were to prompt us to take a lenient view of politicians, it would not permit us to abolish the distinction between moral and immoral *procedure* in politics. Lenin's 'revolutionary morality' – which concerns itself only with ends, never with means – abolishes that distinction. Hence it is not surprising if arguments from *natural justice and *human rights leave it unmoved, since these concern essentially the way things are done. The more or less universal horror at *terrorism suggests that the sense of moral and immoral procedure is deeply seated in the ordinary conscience, and whether there can be a morality without it is open to doubt.

More, Sir Thomas (1478–1535). English humanist and Lord Chancellor; *see* *property, *utopia.

Morris, William (1834–96). English painter, poet and social critic, inspired by the writings of Ruskin, who founded, in 1861, the organization which was later to be known as the arts and crafts movement, and, in 1884, the Socialist League. The arts and crafts movement opposed what it saw as the degradation of labour by the industrial process, and sought for ways to restore to labour the dignity and wholeness which it felt to have been characteristic of *craft. This would not be possible, Morris thought, without radical social transformation, and he advocated a policy of socialist reform, with *common ownership, and workers' cooperatives dedicated to manufacture that would be conducted as nearly as possible in the spirit of craft, with a concern for aesthetic values, and a leisurely involvement of the whole person of the labourer in his task. This ideal of labour was associated by Morris with medieval morality, society and religion, on the assumption that the ideal form of labour, in which all participants had been on equal footing and equally fulfilled, was the construction of the medieval cathedral, through common industry, unmediated by property, and performed for the greater glory of God. Morris's utopian vision, expressed in *News from Nowhere,* 1891, involved rejection of industrial production; this caused some of his critics to condemn his views as romantic and even *reactionary, but his peculiar synthesis of socialism and *cultural conservatism has been highly influential in the English-speaking world, and finds echoes in contemporary thought.

multilateralism. *See* *bilateralism.

multinational corporations. The multinational corporations or enterprises are usually defined as those producing at least a quarter of their output outside their country of origin (which may or may not be the country where they are legally based). Because of the internal organization of such corporations they may form powerful international influences outside the direct control of particular governments, and so are now much discussed, both by those who see in *international capitalism the covert prolongation of that *imperialism which Lenin had designated as capitalism's last stage, and by those who seek to uphold the sovereign rights which such corporations may be tempted to violate. The facts here are much disputed: for example the extent of the involvement of such corporations in political **coups d'état* in order to secure governments favourable to their operations; the extent of the unseen network of influence or control which gives them power in governments generally. What seems to be generally agreed is that all such power is deplorable, either because counter-revolutionary and part of capitalist hegemony, or because effectively outside the control of law. Those who argue the second objection usually point out how easy it is for a company subject to several *jurisdictions to escape the effective control of each of them. In answer to this argument several organizations (notably the Organization for Economic Cooperation and Development) have attempted to devise codes of conduct with which to regulate the behaviour of multinationals, so as to sever their economic power from all political influence.

multiplier. A term introduced into economics by *Keynes, to denote a measure of the effect on the *national income or employment of a change in some autonomous component of aggregate demand For example, suppose that firms increase their rate of investment expenditure on plant, machinery etc.; this initial stimulus to the economy will generate new income and expenditure, so generating further investment, which in turn generates further income and expenditure and so on. The result will be that the increase in national income will be several times larger than the increase in investment. The multiplier is the ratio between the overall increase in national income and the increase in investment expenditure that stimulates it. The overall effect of the initial investment increase is called the multiplier effect.

The multiplier plays an important role in Keynesian macroeconomics, being applied not only to investment, but also to export demand, and in particular to government spending, and taxation. Because of the multiplier, government *fiscal policy may be a highly efficacious way of stimulating aggregate demand.

multipolar. A system is multipolar if it contains many poles (i.e. points of concentrated force) upon which the equilibrium of the system depends. In international politics 'multipolar equilibrium' is now widely thought to be the only available kind. It is contrasted with the 'bipolar' equilibrium which might exist between two powers who are either sufficiently dominant, or sufficiently isolated in their dealings with each other, to be able to determine the conditions of equilibrium between them, independently of any other power. With the concentration of economic and political potential in several different areas the problem of the conditions of multipolar equilibrium has become extremely important, but it is clear that nothing simple could be said concerning it.

municipal law. Since, in *Roman law, a *municipium* was any self-governing body within the Roman Empire, the term 'municipal law' has come to have two meanings:

1. The law of a state or nation, as opposed to *international law.

2. Laws made by a municipality, such as byelaws, through *delegated powers of legislation.

Muslim Brotherhood. *Islamic *fundamentalist movement founded in Egypt in 1929 by Hasan al-Banna. It aimed to reimpose the law of Islam which is 'creed and worship, fatherland and nationality, law and culture, tolerance and strength . . . religion and state; and Qur'an and sword'. The movement is anti-Western and founded in an ideal of Islamic self-sufficiency. Hasan al-Banna advocated dual allegiance, to the 'particular nationality', and to Islam as the overriding principle, and although he was concerned that there should be peaceful relations with the non-Islamic powers, the Brotherhood became increasingly militant, advocating the use of violence in the name of Islam even within the Islamic nation states. Variants and offshoots still constitute important movements within Islamic politics.

Muslim League. Movement founded in Dacca in 1906, which became the largest Islamic party in India, and which is largely responsible for the *separatist politics of Indian Muslims, and for the subsequent foundation of Pakistan, as a constitutional Islamic republic.

Mussolini, Benito (1883–1945). Italian statesman; *see* *concordat, **coup d'état*, *fascism, *Gramsci, *Pareto, *Sorel, *violence.

mutualism. A system of voluntary association for the exchange of services, in which credit is offered at cost (i.e. without profit), and services likewise; advocated by *Proudhon, and often suggested as an integral part of any developed system of *market socialism.

mutuality. The requirement in an agreement that each party do something to or for the other. Absence of mutuality makes an agreement unenforceable at law, so that a contract 'without consideration' is nugatory. Common moral thought, however, also upholds the obligation contained in a unilateral promise. Law and morality seem to agree in the thought that someone who claims rights over another, who has not bound himself by a promise, and to whom he concedes no rights in return, is asserting a claim which, in normal cases, has no force. Hence those who claim unearned rights are regarded as making unjust demands. Conservatives often reject *reformist claims of right on account of this absence of mutuality, although whether or not this is correct is never simple: never more simple, in fact, than the problem of *political obligation.

myth. Any false belief that is (a) of symbolic importance in the emotional life of the believer, (b) based in a need to believe rather than in rational conviction, (c) associated with stories that are accepted not as history (or not on historical evidence), but as illustrations or parables, (d) endowed with a 'sacred' quality, which it can confer on the social relations, institutions or political arrangements associated with it, so granting them an air of legitimacy. It is a familiar thesis of anthropology that myths are natural to man, and that they do not exist in isolation, but interconnect, so that to accept one myth is to accept a system of which it forms a part. *Structuralists, for example, believe that the true meaning of any myth is revealed only in the context of such a system. A rival view (that of Malinowski) sees myth in terms of *functional explanation: myths exist *because* of their capacity to justify institutions, rights and laws. (Although it is fair to say that such explanations are not the prerogative of modern anthropologists: Strauss, Feuerbach and other *Young Hegelians also advanced them.)

Whether or not Malinowski is right, it is not uncommon to find philosophers who think that he ought to be. Plato, for example, famously argued both that the myths associated with the religion of his contemporaries ought to be rejected because of their harmful nature, and also that no one could hope to govern without the 'noble lie' whose untruth could be perceived only from the height of philosophy, but whose symbolic and sacred force was necessary in order to motivate the citizen to obedience.

Plato's view is the ancestor of certain Marxian ideas concerning *ideology, although it is used to justify myth as a means to political stability, rather than to condemn a particular form of stability because of its foundation in myth. It is to be compared with *Sorel's view of myth (specifically the myth of the 'general strike') as the means to construct a new reality. Like many modern conservatives, and like Sorel, Plato sought to defend myths, without giving any reasons for believing them – an enterprise as precarious as politics itself. But if he was right, so that myth not only does, as Malinowski argues, underpin ideas of legitimacy, but is necessary for that end, then the precariousness of this exercise cannot be conclusive ground for not engaging in it.

Hence the modern art of 'mythopoeia', which is the deliberate creation of myth for others' consumption. This is sometimes known as 'remythologizing' and it has occupied many of the political practitioners of our century, notably those, such as Stalin and Hitler, who tried to dignify the forms of *totalitarian government. Some argue that much of the re-writing of history that occurs in totalitarian states should be attributed to mythopoeia, rather than to the desire simply to hide the record of crimes. A quieter form of mythopoeia has been practised by certain intellectual conservatives – e.g. W. B. Yeats, T. S. Eliot, Ezra Pound – and through them has had a certain influence on modern conservative thought.

N

Napoleonic law. The 'Napoleonic code' *(code napoléon)* is the unofficial name given to the codes of law adopted in France at Napoleon's instance between 1804–11, and exported in whole or in part to territories in Europe that came under Napoleon's sway, and also to other places (including some states of South America). The Napoleonic code still forms the basis of French law, and while its composition is rooted in conceptions inherited from the pre-revolutionary period, in *Roman law, and in doctrines of *natural law, it remains one of the most complete and masterly systems of *statute law in existence. The primary source of the law is *legislation, and reliance on *common law, *custom and the doctrine of *precedent is kept to a minimum. Decisions are not binding precedents, but rather examples of judicial interpretation of the provisions in the requisite statute. (However there is intellectual pressure to attempt to achieve consistency between successive interpretations, and this leads to an enhanced role of *jurisprudence and academic commentary in determining the interpretation of the codes.) There are a few overriding principles, corresponding to ideas of *equity and public order, which may be consulted in case of gaps in the law, but their invocation is exceptional, and equity, for example, does not play the constitutive law-making role that it has played in Anglo-American law (*see* *trust).

The supreme court in France is the Cour de Cassation, to which appeal lies in law only, and it is composed of a first president, four presidents, sixty judges, a procurer-general and advocates-general: this type of supreme court is the model for Napoleonic systems of adjudication, and sits as a kind of permanent intellectual commentator on the nature and meaning of the statutes.

narodnik. Russian: *narod,* common people. A follower of Narodnism, a socialist movement which arose in the 1870s in Russia. According to the narodniks capitalism arises here and there by chance, is not a necessary stage of development, and might never develop in Russia. If revolution is possible, then it is equally possible in the form of a peasants' revolt, although this could succeed only if organized by leaders with charismatic force. However, revolution is not necessary, since constitutional reform, *decentralization and *redistribution might suffice to remove existing evils. Criticized by Engels and by *Lenin, Narodnism is regarded in the USSR as heretical, being 'unscientific' socialism, and insufficiently respectful towards the *masses.

nation. A term often used rather vaguely, to mean any *sovereign state with political *autonomy and settled *territory. That usage represents a confusion between *country and *nation state. The definition given here is not political but social:

A nation consists of a people, sharing a common language (or dialects of a common language), inhabiting a fixed territory, with common customs and traditions, which may have become sufficiently conscious to take on the aspect of *law, and who recognize common interests and a common need for a single *sovereign. (The idea is that there is an *explanatory* unity among all the things mentioned.)

In this sense Czechoslovakia, for example, consists of two nations within the *jurisdiction of a single state, a fact recognized in Czechoslovak law, while the Germans are a single nation formed into two states. (The UK is a single state, but probably at least two, possibly four, nations, although here the decline of Celtic languages makes the matter difficult to decide.) Some argue that a further ingredient in nationhood is national *identity, in the form of a sentiment of unity – for which *see* *nationalism.

Although the definition given is social, it should be recognized that it describes a *civil society: i.e. one that is formed in the image of potential government: the legislation, and institution-building for a nation are matters already partly determined by its social structure, and this is one reason for thinking that, if it is necessary to create a new state, the recognition of a 'national' boundary will be a useful beginning.

nation state. A state organized for the government of a *nation (or perhaps of two or more closely related nations), whose territory is determined by national boundaries, and whose law is determined, at least in part, by national customs and expectations. The nation-state is often compared and contrasted with the Greek **polis*, or city state, and its emergence from the various international jurisdictions of Europe has been regarded as one of the major facts of modern political history. For the theory of the nation state, *see* *nationalism.

national bolshevism. An attempt, begun in Germany by Karl Radek in 1919, to found a doctrine which would reconcile the seemingly incompatible outlooks of *bolshevism and *nationalism, in order to create a truly German revolution, and resist both the Western alliance and bolshevik Russia. The movement did not survive the rise of *national socialism, despite a certain similarity of rhetoric.

national bourgeoisie. A term of Marxist politics, denoting the section of property owners in Third World countries who operate purely within national boundaries, as distinct from the sections of the bourgeoisie involved with foreign-based enterprises, *multinational corporations and so on. Because foreign enterprises compete with and often threaten to destroy smaller and weaker indigenous enterprises, the national bourgeoisie tends to support nationalistic and even anti-imperialist policies, and may enter into alliance with movements of *national liberation, as in the *united front of the Chinese Communist Party and the Kuomintang, 1936–46. (The matter is discussed by *Mao, in *The Role of the Chinese Communist Party in the National War*, 1938.)

national debt. The total outstanding debts of the central government. How one calculates the national debt depends upon which public bodies are regarded as liabilities of central government. For example, should one include or not include nationalized industries? Local authorities? And so on. The largest item of all in the UK national debt is government securities, for loans received from private individuals. These provide a maximum security investment, since no enterprise within a state is less likely to default than the state itself. Thus, by holding government securities individuals can obtain a safe return in money, if not in real terms, and banks can improve their own security, while, through buying and selling securities, the government can meet its financial requirements and exercise a convenient form of influence over the *money supply.

national health. The English Poor Relief Act 1601 was the first of a long series of statutory provisions governing the *health and social *welfare of the poorer subjects of the Crown, which led to the creation of a ministry of health in 1914. The process culminated in the founding, in 1948, of the National Health Service, by the then Labour government, thus providing the name by which this kind of welfare legislation is generally known, and also reinforcing, in the public consciousness, the connection between welfare provision and the *labour movement. The National Health Service aims to provide free medical treatment of an acceptable standard to every citizen, financed through taxation. Although the subsequent disputes over 'national health' focused tempestuous feelings, among those who regarded this as the most important achievement of modern socialism, and among those who attacked it as a gross interference with personal liberties, the debate has simmered down, and the health service is accepted as a legitimate and immovable part of government. The argument persists, to some extent, in the US, where certain thinkers of the *New Right remain opposed to such measures (and so distanced from the characteristic stance of English conservatism), and where the argument is often given that health is largely an individual and not a state concern, and that the poor should be relieved through *charity rather than through compulsory *taxation of the fortunate. (For the arguments here, *see* *health.)

national income. The money measure of the total flow of goods and services produced in the economy of a state over a given period. (*See* *gross domestic product, *gross national product.) The national income can be calculated through the total of incomes received in the state, through the total expenditure of all individuals and institutions, (including investment), or through the total price of all goods and services sold, net of tax, subsidies, etc. In principle the three measurements should give the same result, but technicalities of estimation and measurement mean that they do not do so exactly in practice.

National income is a measure of the flourishing of an economy, but not necessarily of the economic well-being of those contained within it, since that also depends upon how the income is distributed. A high *per capita* national income may in fact exist alongside a very low real income in the hands of the majority.

national interest. Something is in the national interest if it helps the nation to survive, or to flourish in the way that nations flourish. Thus national *interests are really national *needs. But what is a nation, and how do nations flourish? The question is not a quibble, since the term 'nation' is used ambiguously, denoting *either* the *state, *or* the *civil society under its governance, *or* both (on the assumption that they have the kind of unity canvassed by advocates of the *nation state). A state that is *despotic is one that flourishes at the *expense* of civil society, so that if the national interest means the interest of such a state, there may be every reason for the members of society to act against it. If, however, it means the interest of the society, then in this case the state itself is not in the national interest. This ambiguity is clear enough in times of peace, where the machinery of a state may be opposed by those subject to it without any consciousness of *treason; it is far less clear in times of war, when the state itself provides the necessary means to the society's survival, and where the interests of the two, however briefly, coincide. (This fact was of immense use to Stalin, and is also one of the explanations sometimes offered for the fact that *tyrants have a tendency to wage *war, although it may be contended that Stalin himself was more interested in waging war within his own dominions.) Despite the above problems of defining what is at issue in the concept of the national interest, it is clear that the idea is to be distinguished from that of national security, the latter denoting and allowing for its fulfilment a more limited range of state and social actions. For what, at least on one reading of the term, may be in the national interest may not also be in the interests of national security; consider, for example, the questions surrounding the 'freedom of information'. (*See also* *security.)

It is characteristic of traditional monarchy to attempt to personify the national interest in the monarch, by making him head of the armed forces, negotiator of all treaties, and symbolic substitute for the people in every act where their collective well-being is at stake. This idea of the king as 'father to his subjects' is one that was also borrowed by Stalin to considerable effect. (*See* **raison d'état*.)

national liberation. Literally, the freeing of a nation from a foreign power, but now also used to denote the *creation* of a nation by force from within, perhaps in defiance of some ruling élite which thrives on regional divisions. The liberation movements in Africa do not always aim to free nations from subjection, but often to break down institutions thought to be *neo-colonial, so as to remake the state as a nation, obedient to local customs and identity.

national socialism. Political movement founded in Germany in 1919, and subsequently led to power by Hitler. Theoretically national socialism was a mixture. As its name implies, it presented itself at first as a *nationalistic answer to *international socialism, and appealed to those who could not envisage any resurgence of government after the débâcle of the First World War except along socialist and nationalist lines. However, it was from the beginning combined with *racist doctrines and military ambitions, which reflected both the outlook of the peculiar leaders of the party and also the underlying doctrine. Thus, part of the nationalistic idea consisted in a belief in *Lebensraum* or 'living space' (*see* *geopolitics), and in a *Herrenvolk,* or ruling people with a right to expand into that space, expelling those peoples who had occupied it, and eliminating those races whose degeneracy justified their extinction. There thus resurged the idea of the **Volksstaat:* a state in which there would be no distinction between political institutions and natural relations, so that all political activity would bear immediately on society, and all social activity immediately on the state. In practice this meant the emergence of the one-party state (*see* *party), as a necessary part of the transfer to the state of the powers thought necessary to ensuring the maximum social unity; this in turn led to *totalitarian government. The socialist element survived largely in the form of commitment to extensive *welfare programmes and a *mixed economy, together with hostility towards the historical *ruling class, whose rule was to be replaced by that of the *leader (*see* **Führerprinzip*). The survival of private ownership in the means of production, the adoption of virulent *anti-semitism, and hostility to the *labour movement and to the left generally, serve to distinguish Hitler's transformation of national socialism from Stalin's, in other ways comparable, transformation of its international counterpart.

The name 'Nazi' is formed from the abbreviation for 'National Socialist German Workers Party'. *See also* *fascism.

nationalism. 1. The sentiment and ideology of attachment to a *nation and to its interests.

2. The theory that a state (perhaps every state) should be founded in a nation, and that a nation should be constituted as a state. Hence, the attempt to uphold national *identity through political action. National identity is something more than nationhood: it involves, not only the territorial integrity, common language, custom and culture noted above as essential to the idea of a *nation, but also *consciousness* of these, as determining separate rights and allegiances. This consciousness is held to render intelligible and to justify the habits of association among neighbours. (In its extreme form nationalism might involve the emergence of an *ethnocentric or even *racist ideology.)

Nationalism has often been thought to be a political reaction to the Napoleonic conquest of Europe, and to the break-up over the centuries of the Empire in Central Europe. However, that is misleading, if it is meant to imply, e.g., that the ideology of national self-determination neither preceded Napoleon in Europe, nor occurred independently elsewhere. It is more plausible to say that there emerged from the Napoleonic attempts at European government an association of nationalism and legal and political ideals of the *nation state. These ideals attempt to find the ingredients of *political obligation and political *identity in *allegiances which are in some sense less than wholly political - matters of geographical, cultural and ethnic association. The motive is to find some binding force between people that is stronger than any revocable agreement to be governed, wider than any merely personal affection, and sufficiently public to lend itself to the foundation of political *institutions and laws.

Some oppose nationalism to *patriotism. Any number of contrasts might be intended; for example, that between a sentiment of attachment (patriotism), and an ideology of national superiority (nationalism); or that between a respect for political institutions and laws (patriotism), and an attachment to race, language and custom (nationalism). Modern nationalism is often decried, on account, e.g., of its attempt to found political obligation in purely *social* allegiances, or its alleged irrationalism, or its opposition to *universalist doctrines, or its nascent belligerence or *imperialism. Patriotism might then be proposed as a beneficent alternative, a sentiment which fills the gap between obligations incurred and obedience required, without having recourse to a bellicose fiction of national integrity. However, both 'nationalism' and 'patriotism' are used loosely, and, as defined in this dictionary, they are clearly compatible.

nationalization. The acquisition by the state of property previously held by private persons or companies. This is one of the many uses in which 'nation' means 'state', and has no connotations of language, territory or custom. The acquisition by the state is itself often thought of as a temporary phase in the transfer of property from private into *social ownership (i.e. ownership by society, and not by any political institution). Nationalization may involve *expropriation, or compulsory purchase. The purpose may be overtly political – in order to abolish or reduce private ownership in the means of production, say – or simply one of economic or social expediency – for example, in order to uphold and keep in existence a network of railways vital to the economy as a whole, but which could not be run at a profit. Alternatively, nationalization may be deemed advantageous in order that the state should occupy a dominant position within the economy; or in order to prevent individuals from exploiting those industries whose nature requires that they be organized on a monopoly basis (e.g. electricity).

Defenders of the *mixed economy see nationalization in this second light, *socialists often see it in the first.

natural justice. The substantial idea of natural justice has to be distinguished from the procedural idea often referred to in systems of *administrative law.

1. Substantial. 'Natural justice' denotes justice that does not depend on *convention but only on *nature, so as to contain within itself a criterion of validity that is independent of *positive law. This criterion is human nature itself, which supposedly leads us towards natural justice just as reasoning and observation lead us towards scientific truth. Thus it is given to all men to see the injustice of rape, murder and (perhaps) theft, without having to consult a body of law that expressly forbids them. In this sense 'natural justice' simply means 'justice', in its philosophical sense of a set of principles of right that exists independently of human prescriptions, embodied in a system either of *natural law, or of *natural rights, or of both.

2. Formal. Those procedures which ensure the minimum standards of justice in *adjudication, whether or not the matter adjudicated involves natural justice in sense 1. The two standard principles accepted are that no man shall be judge in his own cause *(nemo judex in parte sua),* and that each side be heard and no one condemned unheard *(audi alteram partem).* The first requires a judge to be disinterested (e.g. not to have a financial interest in the result, or a motive for seeking a criminal conviction); the second requires that the person judged be given adequate opportunity to prepare and deliver his case. Neither *show trials nor revolutionary tribunals adhere, or can adhere, to those principles. The violation of natural justice is a fundamental ground of appeal, especially in administrative law.

natural law. Natural law and natural rights are those which are recognized by *natural justice, and the attempt to uphold them is the fundamental aim of any theory of *justice that is not merely sceptical of the whole idea.

Natural law, if it exists, is a system of law binding on men by virtue of their nature alone, and independently of all convention or *positive law. (*See* *nature and convention.) The usual attribute of human nature that is chosen as the basis for this law is reason, or *rationality. It is because we are rational beings that we recognize natural law, and it is because we recognize it that it binds us. (Thus animals without reason are not bound by natural law, and the lion who eats his prey does no injustice.)

*Roman law sought for a body of principles – the *jus gentium* – that would apply to all peoples over which the Roman law was required to exert jurisdiction, and which would therefore be independent of all customary law, and of the specific rights reserved for citizens of Rome. As the *jus gentium* developed theorists sought for an intellectual basis, and therefore turned their attention to *jus naturale*, natural law, relying on doctrines of justice expounded by Greek (and especially *Stoic) philosophers. The *jus naturale* came to function as a standard against which all civil law could be judged, and was elevated by *Cicero into the repository of reflective criticism and justification of positive law. It is, in intention, a résumé of all those truths about justice that have universal application.

There are many theories of natural law mentioned throughout this dictionary, but it is important to distinguish two fundamental kinds of theory. The medievals often attempted to derive natural law from a higher law (the divine law), which would be expressive of the will of God (*see* *Aquinas), while it is a characteristic of post-Renaissance thought (beginning with *Grotius and culminating in *Kant) to think that this reference to divine law is unsatisfactory, since it reduces natural law to positive law (i.e. natural law becomes the special case of a positive law laid down not by men but by God). Kant went further, and said that the reference to God's will is pernicious, since it absolves us from the responsibilities contained in the idea of an objective justice to which God himself must by his nature conform. The two kinds of theory are therefore quite different, not only in their theological claims, but also in the basis that they offer for natural law.

Theories of natural law have often been used to prescribe *natural rights, i.e principles which tell us, without reference to custom or institution, how human beings ought to be treated.

natural light. A name given by Descartes to the faculty of reason, whereby we perceive the immediate and certain truth of ideas. The phrase 'it is manifest to the natural light' is another way of expressing the view that a truth or maxim is *a priori*, or shown valid by reasoning alone. Many seventeenth- and eighteenth-century theorists of *natural law appealed to this 'natural light' as the ultimate source of their doctrines.

natural rights. Rights which belong to all human beings by nature, and independently of *positive law. The theory of natural rights, recast in the rhetoric of *human rights, is an important tenet of modern liberalism, even though described by one liberal theorist, *Bentham, as 'nonsense on stilts'. It is necessary to distinguish four questions: Are there natural rights? *Which* rights are natural? Under what conditions will people recognize or believe in them? Under what conditions will people uphold them?

In response to the third question, some legal *realists argue that natural rights are recognized only where there is legal procedure which conforms to *natural justice, and are, as it were, the psychological after-image of this procedure. The procedure seems to enshrine rights which transcend those merely legal rights that it adjudicates. Conversely, the attempt to secure recognition of natural rights in those states which have no *rule of law conforming to natural justice is a vain one. That argument is sometimes given in explanation of the failure of human rights treaties with certain communist states.

Many philosophers have tried to give positive answers to the first question based in a theory of *natural law (notable examples being *Hobbes, *Locke, and *Kant). Recently the emphasis on procedural ideas of justice has been significant. If there are to be *any* rights, it is sometimes said, there must be a legal procedure whereby to uphold them; so that there cannot be any positive rights at all, unless there is *adjudication. Hence, in this sense, there are either no rights at all, or else a universal right to adjudication in order to determine rights; hence a natural right to adjudication. This is one case of a popular modern form of argument, which has as its conclusion 'if there are any rights, then there is *this* one . . .', views which bear the mark of a procedural idea of justice. (*See* *justice.)

By contrast most traditional views have given detailed systems of natural rights, such as were offered by Locke in defence of life, limb, liberty, and property. Locke went on to suggest that at least some of these rights are *inalienable* – notably the right to life. Otherwise it would seem possible for someone to argue that, under the *social contract constitutive of some particular state, all citizens had forsworn that right, thus permitting their wholesale slaughter. If this possibility were allowed, then the doctrine of natural rights would no longer perform its desired function of providing a court of appeal in which the justice of every constitution and every law might be tried. Some have seen here a deficiency in the language of rights, and preferred to return to ideas of natural *law*. A right, they argue, is always alienable by agreement, but a law may still persist, imposing an independent obligation on the other party. Thus, whether or not I forswear my right to life. there will always be an obligation that binds you not to remove it.

Among sceptics it is necessary to distinguish those who dismiss the doctrine of natural rights in its entirety from those who, while thinking it to have no objective basis, yet find that it is part of human nature to believe in it, so that the idea that there are natural rights remains as an irremovable illusion, which must therefore condition all political decision-making designed to govern people suffering from that illusion. This sophisticated idea may go on to incorporate 'natural' rights into a system of law, even though motivated in doing so purely by **Realpolitik*.

naturalization. 1. The acquisition of citizenship on the part of someone who had previously been an *alien.
2. In *Marxian theory, the concept of *ideology is sometimes glossed in terms of, or supplemented by a theory of, naturalization, meaning the process whereby historical and changeable social conditions are represented to those subject to them as part of a natural condition, perhaps stemming from human nature. Thus it is an essential feature of *bourgeois economics, according to Marx, that it represents the condition of man in a market society as his natural condition, thus consolidating a particular and transient system of *production relations by making it impossible to think of human beings (beings with *this* nature) as related in any other way and still producing. (*See also* *reification.)

nature and convention. The ancient contrast between nature and convention was elevated into a principle in the discussion of moral, political and social problems by the *sophists, and through them influenced Greek and Roman philosophy and law. As defined in this work, conventions include all regular practices which issue in intentional action, and which may vary from place to place and time to time. Conventions indicate laws that men happen to obey, rather than those laws which they *must* obey by nature. Unfortunately that 'must' is ambiguous: it may indicate the necessity to act according to the laws which explain our actions, or according to the laws which justify them. What we *must* do in the second sense, we need not do in the first. For the second 'must' indicates moral obligation, the first scientific necessity – and the distinction is enshrined in the double sense of '*natural law', as denoting either the laws which explain things, or the laws which must be invoked in order to tell us what is right. If the two sets of law coincided, then there would be no need for the second: man would be naturally good.

Nazism. *See* *national socialism.

Nechayev, Sergei Gennadevitch (1847–82). Russian anarchist and terrorist; *see* *nihilism.

need. Needs form a special class of *interests. I have an interest in anything that I would, on rational consideration, desire, but not every such thing is necessary to me. I need only that without which I would cease to exist or cease to flourish in accordance with the norms of my nature (*see* *normality). This definition needs to be extended slightly, in order to cope with artificial needs, i.e. needs which arise because human nature is artificially changed, and with 'relative' needs, i.e. needs which a normal human being may have in a certain context (e.g. the need of a wounded man for treatment), as opposed to the absolute needs which stem directly from common human nature.

The distinction between desire and need is vital, since it is plausible to hold that I always have greater reason to pursue what I need rather than what I merely desire, even though the desire in the second case is far stronger than the desire in the first. (*See* *rational, for some of the difficulties caused by this fact for mathematical models of decision-making.) Thus many argue that, although all men desire private property, no man needs it, while the needs of all can be satisfied only when property is no longer private. That argument against private property justifies doing what is not generally desired, by referring to what is, nevertheless, needed.

negotiation. A means for settling disputes, whereby each party declares what he desires, and attempts to obtain as much of it as possible, by making concessions to the other side, or by displaying his purposes. Negotiation is characteristically the first step in international disputes, and made obligatory by the UN Charter, prior to any invocation of the jurisdiction of the Security Council. Likewise, in industrial disputes, negotiation is customarily regarded as the first step, and other measures are uncalled for until negotiation has broken down.

négritude. A term adopted by French-educated Negro intellectuals in Africa and the Caribbean, and current since the 1930s, used to denote a sense of common Negro *identity. The Negro is a distinct social and political being, with needs and emotions that are not necessarily catered for by the constitutional governments invented by the white man; he stands in need of a self-consciousness of his own devising, that will dignify his separateness, and generate institutions adapted to his needs. *Négritude* denotes a common inheritance, and perhaps a common destiny, among blacks, which would be sufficient, if respected, to unite them all against *colonialism and similar forms of exploitation. Its principal elements are nostalgia for traditional African society, and elevation of emotion, intuition and spontaneous social interaction over the rationalistic *hellenism of the white man's forms of government. Its principal exponents have been L.-S. Senghor and Aimé Cesaire.

neo-apartheid. Recent coinage to denote policies followed in South Africa, which involve permitting blacks and coloureds to mix freely with whites, and treating them in such a way as to defuse their resentment at the real difference in political rights accorded to the various races. In other words, it denotes a policy designed to uphold the main aims of *apartheid by partly concealing them.

neo-classical economics. Two schools of economic thought have been described as 'neo-classical', and there seems to be no agreement among economists as to which is correctly so-called:
1. The school which emerged after 1870 and which became dominant by the end of the nineteenth century, its main original theorists being *Jevons, Menger (*see* *Austrian school), Marshall, and particularly Leon Walras. Such economists were marked by their strong leaning towards *microeconomics, and the study of independent decisions made by many households and firms, in competitive market conditions. They analysed the *equilibrium conditions of markets, and attempted to explain *prices, quantities and income distribution; one of the major instruments used in this explanation was the theory of *marginal utility, the principle of diminishing utility being supposed to apply to the satisfaction of each particular desire. Members of this school tended to exaggerate their differences from their predecessors, although Alfred Marshall developed classical ideas in a manner that was to prove particularly influential. They emphasized the scientific claims of economics, although some have suggested that this emphasis too is exaggerated, and that the neo-classical economists were significantly less concerned with empirical evidence than were *Smith or *Ricardo. The theory was concerned with the elaborating of *ideal types, such as *perfect competition, and with giving mathematical models appropriate to the behaviour of ideally rational beings.
2. The school of economists which emerged after the Second World War in opposition to *Keynesianism and the *Cambridge school, which, while sharing many of the preoccupations of 1., has dispensed with the theory of marginal utility, and *marginalism generally, emphasizing consumer *preference as the fundamental factor in the explanation of economic activity, and the main determinant of value.

Both 1. and 2. have been variously criticized by *institutionalists, *Marxians, *Keynesians and others; in either case the term 'neo-classical' seems to indicate the similarity of their overall perspective to that of the classical economists, and an emphasis on competitive markets and equilibrium conditions, and on the general principles and operations of a liberal economy.

neo-Marxism. A term denoting various currents in twentieth-century *Marxism – perhaps starting with the work of *Lukács, and continuing in the *Frankfurt school. These currents diverge from traditional Marxism in emphasizing, not *historical materialism, but the description of consciousness, as the central component in Marx's social analysis. Some neo-Marxists find inspiration in the elements in Marx that derive directly from *Hegel, emphasizing, for example, the analysis of *alienation, the concept of the *dialectic, the supposed movement of history towards a *utopian ideal. Others, in reaction, try to detach Marx from Hegel, uniting his thought, perhaps, with *existentialism (*see* *Sartre), or with some kind of *structuralism (*see* *Althusser), often giving voice (as in the last case) to a kind of fundamentalist fervour and injunctions to return to the true interpretation of the doctrine.

neo-mercantilism. Term put about by the economist Harry Johnson, which denotes modern theories designed to justify the protection of home markets, by controlling imports or subsidizing exports. The term relates to the *mercantilism criticized in the name of *free trade by *Smith, and is used to describe theories which gained vogue in the 1930s, during the Depression, and which have been again revived by some *Keynesian economists of the *Cambridge school. *See* *protectionism.

neutralism. Not the declaration of neutrality, but rather the practice of showing an intention to remain neutral in any eventual conflict, and to treat the parties to that conflict with total impartiality. It was practised before 1939 by the Belgian and Nordic states, and subsequently, especially by Third World countries who fear domination by either the Western or the Soviet bloc, and who are determined not to be drawn into the conflict between them. Now, although the concept of 'neutralism' is still used to describe this attitude, it has been increasingly replaced by that of *non-alignment, which is held to be a kind of 'positive neutrality', reminiscent of the 'armed neutrality' of eighteenth-century Russia.

neutrality. The position of a state that is not party to a war, which stands apart from it, and which treats each side impartially. It was fully recognized in international law only in the eighteenth century, but since then certain states have used the idea assertively in times of war, to show their determination not to be involved in it, as in the 'armed neutrality' of Russia, Sweden and Denmark in 1780. Under the UN Charter no member of the UN can remain neutral in a war in which the Security Council has called upon it to take action against a state guilty of aggression; otherwise a state is presumed to be neutral unless it declares by some act or word that it supports one side or another. A state may make a declaration of neutrality which binds it to help either side in ways specified in international law. The UN Charter illustrates a general point of significance, namely, that there is a tension between the idea of neutrality and that of *just war.

new class. Term coined by M. Djilas to denote the ruling élite formed through the Communist Party in those states in which it asserts supreme control in accordance with the principles of *democratic centralism. Djilas argues that, through the total permeation of all institutions by the Communist Party, the restrictions on membership and the advantages that accrue to membership, a kind of self-perpetuating power structure asserts itself that has all the characteristics associated with a *ruling class (*The New Class*, 1957). Whether it is right to speak of a class in this context could be doubted: for the qualification for membership is radically different from anything historically encountered as definitive of class membership. (*See* *class, *élite, *status.) Djilas argues, however, that the new class has all the characteristics of earlier ruling classes, together with novel features of its own, in particular it comes to power not 'to complete a new economic order, but to establish its own and, in so doing, to establish its power over society'. The class is not identical with the Communist Party, but established through it; eventually, however, it becomes stronger than the party, whose unity of belief and iron discipline it has exploited, and the party cannot control it. At the same time it is the upsurge of this new class that explains the unity and discipline of the party, and the party's rise to power.

New Deal. Expression introduced in President Roosevelt's nomination speech of 1932, and now used to describe the policies initiated during Roosevelt's first administration, during 1933–7, when, in order to counteract the effects of the Depression, far-reaching measures of government intervention in the economy were introduced, including encouragement of private industry, together with state-financed industries and welfare legislation. The New Deal involved a radical departure from the previous US fiscal policy, of trying to secure a balanced budget, and had wide-ranging effects which have often been thought to be beneficial. It introduced the first substantial element of a *mixed economy into the US, together with expectations associated with welfare legislation.

new diplomacy. The methods of 'open' as opposed to 'secret' diplomacy advocated and followed during the aftermath of the First World War, and presaged in President Wilson's 'Fourteen Points', in which he advocated 'open covenants, openly arrived at'.

New Economic Policy (NEP). Introduced into the USSR in 1921 and ending the policy of 'war communism', the NEP sought to restore the economy, by making concessions to private trade and industry and abandoning the pressure towards *collectivization. The state was to maintain control of the 'commanding heights' of the economy, while leaving private enterprise to flourish in a small way. The economy recovered, but the NEP was abandoned by Stalin in 1929, by a process of 'revolution from above'; however, some of its provisions have probably crept back into practice, whether or not officially recognized.

New Left. Political tendency emerging among *Marxists during the 1950s, associated with an increasing disenchantment with *bolshevism and its offshoots. It led to the foundation, in the UK, of the *New Left Review,* which became one of the most important expressions of intellectual opinion on the *left. The New Left existed in a milder version in the US, and flourished in France, being grafted on to the native left-wing philosophies of *Sartre and other members of the wartime resistance, to become a nationwide political movement of the 1960s, culminating in the events of May 1968. In so far as there is any single consistent position that can be ascribed to the New Left, it consists in a belief in the *democratization of all institutions, so as to eliminate every focus of established power. This belief naturally generated in support of itself many critical analyses of existing institutions and power structures, together with a proliferation of theories with which to describe and condemn them: it is partly due to the New Left that this dictionary is, if not necessary, at least possible. From this critical analysis – which, while always left-wing in inspiration, did not necessarily involve the adoption of any specific Marxist theory (such as *historical materialism) – there arose an important school of English cultural critics and historians, among whom perhaps the most significant are Raymond Williams, Perry Anderson and E. P. Thompson. This school has done much to develop a Marxist analysis of modern history, emphasizing the component of *class struggle, and attempting to interpret events in a way favourable to left-wing politics.

Critics of the New Left have sometimes objected to a supposed negativity, arguing that its diagnoses of existing power structures – because they accompany only schematic representations of alternatives – serve more as vehicles for resentment than as serious proposals for a socialist future. Others even try to connect this resentment with the *sentimental anger of the German and Italian urban terrorists who arose from the movements of the sixties. However, it is not at all clear that there is sufficient system in the opinions of the New Left to warrant those judgements.

new man. The phrase 'new man', 'new communist man', or 'new socialist man', has been used since the 1920s, by both supporters and critics of USSR communism, in order to describe the transformation not only of the economic order but also of the individual personality, that has taken place, or should take place, either under socialism, or under the 'full communism' to which socialism supposedly leads. Since man has a 'historical essence' he is, in one sense, not the same creature under the new economic order, and values and aspirations which previously motivated him may no longer be understood or recognized.

New Right. Expression used to denote the recent resurgence of conservative and anti-socialist thought in the UK, the US, and France. There seem to be three distinct currents of thought that are comprised in this movement, at least as exemplified in the UK and the US, and it is not clear that they are compatible with one another:

(i) Revulsion against socialism as practised, together with an attempt to see the practice already implicit in the theories. A main stimulus for this attempt has come from Central European and Russian refugees from communism (Milosz, Kolakowski, Solzhenitzyn and others) who have attempted to show that Marxian theories already contain the seeds of

*Stalinism, because of their inability to envisage institutions that will be tolerant of *opposition, because of their *messianic fervour and *antinomian assurance that history must vindicate them, and because of their emphasis on historical necessity at the expense of individual choice.
(ii) Renewed attachment (especially in the US) to liberal values, and to libertarian justifications of capitalism and private property, sometimes tempered by an old-fashioned respect for institutions and customs (as in *Hayek), sometimes associated with a respect for the decencies of a 'moral majority', sometimes based in a thoroughgoing individualism that comes close to anarchism (as in *Nozick).
(iii) Reaction to the excesses of *left-liberal *enlightenment opinion, in matters of law, morality and social consciousness, perhaps combined with the advocacy of more authoritarian forms of government, or at least forms of government more sensitive to traditional values, customs and forms of association. The third current is likely to stand in partial opposition to the second, advocating acceptance of the *mixed economy, and of the actual historical conditions of modern politics, and attempting to replace dogmatic policies with traditional conservative hesitations and reluctances. It favours respect for institutions, pragmatic politics, conciliation and manoeuvre, all against a background of respect for the actual condition of civil society.

Examples of this third kind of thinking are to be found in Ian Gilmour, and other theorists of the UK Conservative Party, who acknowledge *Burke as their master. It should be pointed out, however, that the tension between the three positions is already manifest in Burke himself, who converted his reasoned hatred of the French Revolution (condemned on grounds resembling (i)), and his respect for the *free market and its ideology ((ii)), into a rhetoric which emphasized tradition and pragmatic politics as its fundamental ground (as in (iii)). The potential contradiction here provides one of the major objections raised against the New Right – that it seeks to be both conservative and liberal at once. Moreover, it is sometimes criticized for not tackling directly the problems of class and privilege as they are currently presented, and for a certain sentimental picture of tradition that seems to inspire it.

In France the New Right seems to be less concerned with tradition and more interested in liberal values, largely because of their role in permitting and encouraging human development. Some representatives of the movement (notably Alain de Benoist) have emphasized the biological need of the human being to assert, aggrandize, and expend himself, and have argued against socialism as a form of mass domestication, destined to bring about the degeneracy of the species.

Newman, John Henry, Cardinal (1801–90). English divine and writer; *see* *cultural conservatism, *tractarianism, *universities.

Nietzsche, Friedrich Wilhelm (1844–1900) German philosopher, critic and iconoclast, who gave an impassioned defence of *egoism, and who influenced some of the defenders of fascism, through his celebration of ancient values of strength, courage, pride and resolution. Nietzsche attacked first Christianity and all other forms of belief in a transcendent being, and secondly the modern 'secular religions' which had arisen in the place of it, and which had tried to perpetuate religious feeling through worship of a universal human nature. He identified socialism, humanism, and above all egalitarianism, as principal manifestations of this bowdlerized religion, arguing that all of them display the deep corruption of the modern consciousness, which seeks to hide from the responsibility of existence by taking refuge in a *sentimental vision of universal brotherhood. In *Thus Spake Zarathustra,* 1883–92, Nietzsche presented his rival morality, arguing that man has only one duty, which is to realize in himself the *Übermensch* (superman, or 'transcended man') who has overcome in himself mere 'human' nature, rejected the 'herd instinct' of common morality, and asserted himself as master of his own experience, justified not in what he shares with others, but in what distinguishes him. Such a being will be disdainful of all attempts to ascribe to him some universal body of rights, and will act so as to rise above the herd which seeks only to bring everything down to its own level. His aim is not to obey a moral law, but to 'will his own desire as a law for himself'. He will elevate passion above reason, and regard the world with a scepticism that undermines all claims to right and truth that do not stem from himself and from his will to life, joy, and power. The principal disease of the will is not morality as such, but pity, which is the foundation of the 'slave morality' that Nietzsche attributed to Christ. Pity remorselessly seeks out objects over which to rejoice, taking pleasure only in weakness, and cutting off sympathy for the strong, the dominant and the successful – those, in short, who are good, not in the sense of common morality (which contrasts good with evil), but 'good specimens', who exhibit strength, power, and vitality (*Beyond Good and Evil,* 1886).

Nietzsche advocated in those terms a species of 'joyful wisdom' which he thought to be uniquely suitable to men without religious belief. From this standpoint he constructed many brilliant satires of the intellectual and political fashions of his age. His own political vision was almost entirely confined to the critique of *universalism; he left it to others to draw from his philosophical egoism what political conclusions they could.

nihilism. The belief in nothing, as opposed to the absence of belief. The word has been used in English since at least 1817, but gained currency later on account of the Russian nihilists, modelled upon the character Bazarov, in Turgenev's *Fathers and Sons* (1862). Bazarov, detested by his creator, nevertheless inspired a generation of Russian radicals, who contrived to be politically active in the cause of nothing. Principal among them was S. G. Nechayev, who collaborated with *Bakunin in writing *The Revolutionary Catechism,* 1869, in which the nihilist hero, a terrorist, without property, identity, morality or attachments, is described. The basic idea was that, since society is founded on lies, and all moral, religious and humanitarian beliefs are just instruments of concealment, all beliefs and values must be torn down and the disposition to hope and worship be eliminated, so that the world could be seen as it really is. For some reason it was thought that things would then be better for the people.

Nihilism, as a state of mind, rather than a doctrine, has often been thought to underlie many modern political philosophies, including *existentialism, some forms of *historical materialism, and even the various kinds of *conservatism which advocate the acceptance of what is, rather than the vain pursuit of what might have been.

nobility. 1. A *class, identifiable in various ways, but usually thought to have arisen out of the social and economic position of *lord in *feudalism: i.e the position of the owner of land, bound by duties towards the sovereign, and with feudal rights over the occupants of his land. In UK law the membership of this class is still marked out by certain legal privileges, such as a title, and an associated *peerage, which confers the political power consequent on membership of the upper chamber of Parliament. Since the office of peer has usually been hereditary (at least since the thirteenth century and until the nineteenth) this legal privilege has reinforced the socio-economic determination of the nobility as a hereditary class. Outside the UK that class is more widely defined, it having been common to recognize grades of nobility short of peerage – such as the *petite noblesse* of France, the little nobility of Russia, and the *szlachta* of Poland. The idea of a nobility does not extend to the description of classes in societies that have not known feudal modes of tenure, and while the nobility might still be referred to in modern Europe, it is always with the implication of feudal or semi-feudal relations, either still existing or recently extinguished.

2. A virtue, associated with 1. for a variety of good or bad reasons, one being that the feudal position of lord was traditionally granted by the sovereign in exchange or reward for military service, so that the nobility became responsible for the levying and maintaining of armies, so forming an 'officer class'. Hence its distinct social position tended to become associated with the virtues proper to that class – e.g. courage and honour. In addition, because of the *leisure consequent on its economic position, the nobility was able to cultivate refinements of culture, social interaction and display which have become mingled with the military virtues to form an elaborate and ritualized conception of what a nobleman might correctly do.

The connection of sense between 1. and 2. is obvious, as is the fact that they may not go together. Rousseau attributed the virtue of nobility to savages (and perhaps only to savages), communists sometimes attribute it to the proletariat. The one class that usually escapes being called noble is the bourgeoisie.

noble savage. *See* *Rousseau.

nomads. People who maintain social and even political organization among themselves, while remaining attached to no particular *territory, and owning only movable property, together with rights of pasture, often of a purely customary kind. Certain modern systems of law (notably *Islamic law and *Jewish law) are adapted for nomadic use, since they involve a flexible idea of *jurisdiction (based partly in racial and religious affiliation), and of *municipality.

Theories of the state do not always apply to the case of nomads, since the absence of territorial jurisdiction leaves questions of legal *sovereignty undetermined. Nevertheless some nomadic peoples have developed political institutions, involving, for example, kingship, an aristocracy of tribal chieftains, a common law, and even parliaments and representative government. Modern legal conceptions of sovereignty attach, however, to territory, and such peoples will often find themselves subject to a jurisdiction which is not of their own law, and to *conflicts of law that can be resolved by no court. Nomad societies pose a problem for Marxist analysis similar to that posed by the *Asiatic modes of production.

non-alignment. The active refusal of a state to align itself with either party to a dispute between superpowers, in particular the continuing dispute between the Western powers and the Soviet bloc. Non-alignment developed in place of *neutralism, attempting to be both less *isolationist, and more positive in creating the conditions for ultimate peace. A conference of non-aligned powers took place (attended by thirty-five Mediterranean and Afro-Asian powers) in Belgrade in 1961, and the policies there advocated had considerable effect on world politics through the United Nations in the 1960s and 1970s. Heightened tension between the two major blocs has, however, led to a decline in the influence of the non-aligned states.

non-intervention. Until the mid nineteenth-century it was widely held that a state has the right to intervene in the affairs of another in order to protect its own citizens, property and rights that may be affected by the second state's inability or incompetence to protect them through the exercise of sovereign powers. Two Argentinians, Carlos Calvo in 1868 and Louis Drago in 1907, maintained that no sovereign state could have this right while still respecting the sovereignty of the other, and Drago's formulation of the idea of non-intervention was incorporated as Article 1 of the second Hague Convention in 1907.

The endorsement of non-intervention has been integral to the treaties negotiated by the USSR with its neighbours since the Revolution and still occasionally features in Soviet pronouncements on foreign policy. (But *see* *limited sovereignty.)

non-negotiable demands. Demands made during the course of negotiations which, it is implied, must be met if the negotiations are to be accepted, and their outcome *ratified, by the party who makes them. Non-negotiable demands have always been an important part of diplomacy, especially that of the USSR, it being assumed that the best way to advance your interests is to make sure that you negotiate only over those issues that do not really concern you.

The theory of the non-negotiable game has become an important part of *game theory, and points to important differences between the *strategies which are rational where negotiation is possible, and those which should be adopted where negotiation is ruled out.

non-proliferation. In order to prevent the spread of nuclear weapons to states not subject to the familiar military and political constraints against their use, treaties of non-proliferation have been proposed, and in 1968 a Nuclear Nonproliferation Treaty was signed by three of the major powers (the US, UK and USSR) who undertook not to transfer the appropriate technology, and by 100 or so minor powers, who undertook not to develop it. Several powers refused to sign (notably China, France, India, Israel and South Africa), on the ground that the treaty discriminates too heavily in favour of existing nuclear powers. The treaty remains open for signature, but its effect is unclear; it is not certain whether, e.g., Israel and South Africa have the potential to produce nuclear weapons. The thought behind the treaty is that the spread of nuclear weapons to a power whose traditional enemy does not yet have them offers a new temptation to use them – a temptation to which the US yielded during the Pacific war – and that, in any case, further proliferation of nuclear weapons to those states not already so endowed is to be avoided.

non-violent resistance. Resistance, especially to the occupation of one's country, without the use of *violence. (*See also* *passive resistance.) The policy was advocated by Gandhi under the name of *civil disobedience, and can be successful when conducted from below against an unpopular government. However, its success in India is probably not independent of the fact that the British were no longer convinced that the occupation of India was to their advantage. Non-violent resistance has been more or less completely ineffective when conducted against an occupying power that is determined to remain – as in Norway during the Second World War, and in Czechoslovakia since 1968.

norm. An ambiguous term, which can mean either that which is normal, or that which is normative, i.e. required, say, by an ideal, a standard, or a moral code. Biologists would tend to use the term in its first sense, sociologists in its second, although in sociological usage the distinction is extremely difficult to draw, for reasons given below:

1. The idea of the normal. The normal is not the same as the statistical average. All surviving lions may be abnormal (say, because they all suffer from some hereditary disease). Thus the properties of the average lion may not be identical with those of the normal lion. The normal lion is the lion who possesses the properties which determine the existence, continuance, reproduction and flourishing of his kind: i.e. he is the lion who obeys the laws of leonine nature. The idea of the normal is therefore no more clear than that of a law of nature – the subject of much debate in the philosophy of science, and beyond the scope of this dictionary. It is clear that this already raises special problems for the idea of human normality, since the concept of *human nature (and therefore that of the laws of human nature) remains essentially contested. According to *Kant, for example, we have two natures, one empirical, governed by the 'laws of nature' as these are applied to all inanimate and organic things, the other 'transcendental', governed by 'laws of reason' which turn out to be norms only in the second sense, of ideals of conduct.

Much debate over the normal response of the normal person is uncertain partly because of deep uncertainties about the 'laws of human nature', which recur throughout political discourse. It could be that, while the average man enjoys pornography, the normal man is revolted by it. Until we know the nature and role of moral sentiment in the normal man we cannot determine whether this is true. It could be that the average man desires private property, while the normal man (the man 'restored to himself') does not. And so on. Likewise we speak of normal and abnormal societies, which presents parallel problems concerning the 'laws of social nature'.

2. The idea of the normative. Conduct is normative if imposed by *sanctions. While this covers moral codes and ideals, sociologists also tend to consider other sanctions besides the moral. Thus there are legal norms, customary norms, norms of good behaviour and manners, norms of dress, speech and deportment, all of which may be held to fall outside the domain of morality, at least as commonly understood. A new ambiguity enters the discussion, for the following reason: when a philosopher discusses normative judgements, he is concerned with those that are actually put forward as valid, and the reasoning used to support them. But the judgements that are so defended may not be the judgements that are obeyed. The sociologist is concerned not only with how people represent their codes of conduct, but with the *sanctions* which they apply. The two may not correspond, not because of hypocrisy or self-deception, but because of the intricate way in which social influences are spread. Thus it is quite possible for a sociologist to argue that there is a norm of male dominance in a given society, in which most people sincerely believe that sexual domination is morally wrong. This is because the sociologist recognizes the existence of sanctions beyond those laid down by morality: sanctions of custom, manners, and so on, which may be exerted through many channels, but may never issue in a moral condemnation. Such an observation would be possible only if there is some measure of conformity to the norm, otherwise the existence of *social* sanctions would be in doubt. Hence norms as observed by the sociologist are *also* records of what is normal (sense 1.) within society. Nevertheless, the sociologist's concern is not with what is normal, but with what is normative.

normal. *See* *norm.

normal profit. To be distinguished from *profit, normal profit is that profit which is just sufficient to induce an *entrepreneur to remain in his present enterprise. Thus it is the amount necessary to cover the cost of the services supplied, disregarding *opportunity costs.

normalization. Used after the Second World War to refer to the re-establishment of friendly relations between states, rulers and peoples. Also a euphemism for the forced resumption of unwanted ties, as in the normalization of Czechoslovakia after 1968, following the intervention of the Soviet army.

normative. *See* *norm.

nostalgia. Greek: homesickness. Originally a yearning for home, but now used to mean any longing after an absent (and by implication past) state of affairs, accompanied by an idealization of that state, involving intemperate attention to its supposed virtues, together with a merely schematic representation of its vices. Nostalgia is a form of *sentimentality, and should be understood accordingly. It is normally thought to have the past as its object, and the accusation is often made against conservatives that their respect for what they take to be tradition is no more than nostalgia, i.e. sentimental attachment to something which can be loved with impunity partly because it has vanished, leaving only the memory of its virtues. When this objection comes from Marxists it is sometimes countered by a *tu quoque* – on the assumption that there is an equivalent of nostalgia which has not the past but the future as its object, and which dwells on a similarly schematized state of being. (The communist future, like heaven, is usually only negatively described, and hence may readily be deprived of its vices.) If this extension of the idea is allowed, then it could be that nostalgia is an ingredient in all political thinking that is based on foregone conclusions.

Nozick, Robert (b. 1938). US philosopher who, in *Anarchy, State and Utopia*, 1974, sets forth a complex restatement of what many have seen as a *Lockean theory of the state, justice, and private property. Beginning from the individualistic assumption that there is no true political entity other than individuals, and that only individuals have *rights, and relying on a *Kantian view of rights, he presents an influential defence of private property, of *accumulation, and of social and political inequalities, not as things good in themselves, but as things which can be removed only by denying the rights of individuals. He believes that conditions can be laid down for determining when property is justly acquired, and also justly transferred: crudely, the first when it is acquired without denying to anyone else any right or perpetuating any injustice, the second when property passes by voluntary and open transaction between fully knowing, and responsible beings. He then attempts to formulate 'justice-preserving' rules of transfer: if property passes justly from *a* to *b* and justly from *b* to *c*, then *c* holds it justly if *a* held it justly. It can then be shown that there may be just holdings of large accumulations, just distributions which are vastly unequal, and so on. Any theory of 'distributive justice', which concentrates not on just transfer, but on the *end state of a distribution, is, Nozick thinks, bound to do violence to our far surer and more philosophically defensible ideas of the just transaction, and so should be rejected as a covert justification of injustice. In this way he argues against many (e.g. socialist) ideas of *redistribution, and in favour of certain kinds of private property.

Nozick's argument is essentially liberal: it proceeds by arguing that everyone should be free to do what he has a right to do, but not to interfere with another's rights. From the same idea Nozick derives a defence of private medicine (*see* *health) arguing that no doctor can be justly compelled to offer his services in accordance with an ideal distribution of medical benefits, and independently of his voluntary agreements. And likewise, for many other received ideas of *social justice. However, Nozick finds cause to uphold, not a traditional conservatism, but rather what he calls the *minimal state, i.e. the least powerful political arrangement compatible with the protection of rights. All political order is a *prima facie* interference with a natural right to pursue one's ends, and – having considered seriously the arguments for *anarchism – Nozick concludes that political order can therefore be justified only if it can also be shown to contribute to the upholding of individual rights.

Nozick's arguments reformulate a debate that has long existed between those who think of justice in terms of patterns of distribution, and those who think of it in terms of transaction. His views have been criticized (a) because they do not take into account the difficulties posed by the idea of a 'just original acquisition'; (b) because they are based on an unargued individualism concerning human nature and human rights, which attempts to detach the individual from the history and social arrangement which has formed him; and (c) because Nozick seems not to attend to the many functions that a *state may fulfil besides that of policing the rights of its members.

nuclear family. *See* *family.

O

Oakeshott, Michael (b. 1901). English philosopher, who has attempted to give a theory of human conduct and human experience that will be free from the *empiricist presuppositions of much modern political philosophy. He has thereby tried in *Rationalism and Politics*, 1948, 1962, and *Human Conduct*, 1976, to uphold a vision of 'civil association' that reconciles the conservative respect for custom, prejudice and tradition with certain liberal values. Oakeshott's thought has *idealist antecedents, but it eschews system and attempts to present a vision of political society and allegiance that will be respectful of the historical complexities contained in them, and of the actual nature of the beings that are subject to them. The main elements seem to be:

(i) An attack on *rationalism, by which is meant the attempt to subsume all political activity within an overriding aim or formula, to which social life must be made to approximate.

(ii) An attack on ideology, in the specific sense of principles and *doctrines detached from the historical circumstances of their utterance, political principles being acceptable only if they are, as it were, saturated with the conditions from which they spring. Oakeshott's use of the term 'ideology' does not coincide exactly with either of the senses given in this dictionary, although 'doctrine' is perhaps an equivalent. According to Oakeshott, the aims of political association are not made, but discovered, and doctrine can never be a substitute for the 'intimations' which arise from active engagement in the political order.

(iii) An acceptance of certain forms of political life, and certain institutions, as 'given', i.e. as creating the framework within which political thought and activity is conducted, and therefore not to be construed as in any sense its product. Thus Anglo-American representative government is not to be thought of as a means to an end, or a solution to a given political problem, but as a form of political association, dictating both the end and the means, the solution and the problem.

(iv) A theory of political activity as the offshoot of, and dependent on, 'civil association'. This is the product neither of *contract, nor of any mutuality of purpose, but is to be construed rather on the model of a conversation, whose meaning and principle of development is to be seen at least partly in terms internal to itself. Hence the model for *political obligation is the diffuse obligation of *friendship rather than the precise and revocable obligation of contract.

Oakeshott develops a subtle, but somewhat elusive, view of human nature and human conduct with which to support those, and similar, views, and thereby to present a conservative defence of institutions, together with a critique of *dirigisme, of *egalitarianism, and of the socialist ideal of a society without property or class.

obedience. The acquiescence to a *command, whether express or tacit; by extension, the acceptance in action of the *authority of a person or office. Emphasis on obedience as the master concept in political order is characteristic of *absolutism and *paternalism, and it is often thought that this emphasis gave way during the late seventeenth and eighteenth centuries to a similar emphasis on *consent, the distinguishing feature being that, in the second case, the subject, in obeying only what he has consented to, obeys himself, and so is not only subject but also sovereign of his political existence. Without consent, obedience is to some person or office other than oneself, and it is often thought that, until the grounds for such obedience can be discovered, the basis of political obligation and sovereignty will not have been given. Some thinkers do not believe that there is any basis other than habit, or tradition, but that these are sufficient in themselves, and any attempt to replace them with an idea of *consent will be based in a fiction, and moreover a dangerous fiction. (*See* *legitimacy, *piety.) This is one aspect of the complex question of *political obligation.

objectification. Term of *Hegel's metaphysics (German: *Entaüsserung*), meaning the process of *self-realization through the 'positing' or creating of an objective world. For Hegel, *alienation is a specific 'moment' of objectification;

this idea was taken over and amended by the young *Marx, who associated alienation with private property, and objectification with its abolition.

obligation. 1. Legal. A bond between two legal *persons, which confers enforceable *rights and *duties. E.g. if *x* negligently injures *y*, then this confers on *x* the obligation in law to make due compensation to *y*, and *y* has a right to that compensation. (*See also* *jural relations.) In Roman law the law of obligations is extremely important, subsuming all of contract, quasi-contract and tort, and also any other civil relation in which one person imposes a legal liability on another.

2. Moral. The concept from which the legal notion derives is that of personal or moral obligation – the idea of being *bound* to do something. Some argue that this concept is primitive, in that it can be explained in no other terms; it is certainly one of the most difficult of all concepts to analyse, and creates major problems for moral philosophy. (*See* *duty.) The concept of moral obligation seems to be narrower than that of the morally right: thus it is arguable that I have no obligation to save the life of a man who, unknown to me, is at this moment starving in Lesotho; nevertheless to do so would be morally right. The use of the language of obligation seems to imply an additional bond of *responsibility between the parties.

Philosophical theories of obligation are of two kinds: those which take the concept as fundamental, and those which think it to be derivative from some other idea, such as that of *value. It is also important to distinguish subjectivist views, which see no ultimate justification for statements of obligation other than personal choice or *convention, from objectivist views, such as that of *Kant, who argues that there are obligations which are binding on all rational agents: to understand them is to be motivated to obey them.

obscenity. The attempt to define and suppress obscenity is an ancient one, and it has been recognized in English common law at least since 1727 that it is criminal to publish indecent matter. The Obscene Publications Act 1957 prohibited the publication of obscene matter but did not define 'obscene', although it provided a *test* of obscenity, namely, the tendency to corrupt and deprave those likely to come in contact with the material in question. It has been of considerable concern to attempt a definition, this being one of the areas where public law and private morality seem to enter into contact, and to generate conflicting intuitions. Without a definition of obscenity and a theory which accounts for its alleged evil, it becomes impossible to see how a law could forbid obscenity without also exercising an effective power of arbitrary *censorship. (Note that obscenity is not forbidden, but forbidden in *public*.)

Roughly speaking, obscenity is a property of representations and displays. The human body is not obscene, but it can be represented or displayed obscenely, in a photograph, picture, dance or gesture. The fault in the test given in the law is that it identifies obscenity through its effects, and these are largely unknowable. The common, and plausible, intuition is that the offence has already been committed in the very act of public display, whatever the consequences. Obscenity 'depersonalizes': it shows the human body, and the sexual act, as void of any personal responsibility or affection, a mechanical performance, indicative of an animal pleasure detached from any expression of commitment between the partners; and moreover, obscenity *negates* that commitment or shows it as irrelevant to the pleasures displayed. This need not be *true* of those engaging in the act, but the essence of obscenity is that that is how the act is *shown*. Thus the universal sexual attributes are divorced from the individual agents, and represented as interesting in themselves. On the wider issue of legal control, *see* *pornography.

obsolescence. There are two kinds of thing which might suffer obsolescence, those with and those without a function. A machine with a function becomes obsolescent when it can no longer perform that function as efficiently as some available alternative. A village community – which exists for its own sake, and not as a means to an end – may become obsolescent, for example, because conditions essential to its survival have been changed. (Communications with the town may have improved, agricultural work may have become difficult or unattractive, local customs and ceremonies may have lost their appeal or authority.) In such a case it is normal to speak of obsolescence, even though the community is not being judged as inefficient. The lack of independent function is compatible with the existence of internal functions: for example, ceremonies within the village may have a function relative to the village's survival (such is the basic tenet of much *functionalist anthropology). However, the village itself is not made obsolescent by the appearance of an 'alternative'; there can be no alternative. Such thoughts underlie *organicist doctrines of society, and also certain conservative theories concerning the nature of political institutions, e.g. those voiced by *Oakeshott. The obsolescence of a political institution is often said not to be like the obsolescence of a machine, since an institution, while it may perform functions, also partly (perhaps sometimes wholly) creates the functions that it performs. It then becomes difficult or even impossible to compare institutions with alternatives so as to see which 'does the job best'. The dispute here is vital to the philosophy of *reform (i.e. does one 'reform in order to conserve', as *Burke put it, or in order to improve?), and also to understanding the implications of organicism.

'Planned obsolescence' is a much-criticized feature of large-scale manufacturing: objects are said to be made to perform a certain function, but with built-in faults, so that in the course of time they will perform it only imperfectly, by which time, however, the function will have become indispensable. Hence other objects will be needed to replace them, and demand need never fall to the point where the manufacturing process must come to an end. Some defend this practice, on the ground that it maintains employment and stimulates aggregate demand. Others criticize it for its inherent irrationality, and its wastefulness of natural resources, not the least of which is human labour.

odium theologicum. 'Theological hatred': a medieval expression denoting the extraordinary acerbity of abstruse discussions between theologians over matters which seem quite insignificant to the uninitiated. The venom of the intellectual in defence of a theory is thereby explained in terms of a real feeling that underlies it – in this case a religious feeling – while at the same time recognizing it to be slightly comic and perhaps misplaced. *Odium theologicum* recurs in the discussion of secular beliefs, particularly in the writings of the *New Left, and in Marxist intellectual propaganda, where it sometimes has a sinister side to it; an intellectual heresy might also show you to be an 'objective class enemy'.

office. Offices are specified by determining three things:
(i) rights and duties of the holder of the office;
(ii) conditions of entry;
(iii) conditions of exit.
(ii) and (iii) are collectively known as the rules of succession, and they cover almost every way in which political power may be transferred: for example, office may be hereditary for life, or by election from a *college for a period of years, or by election from a *politbureau, but with no rules of exit; and so on. The rights and duties specified under (i) may be embodied in a law, a custom or a convention, or simply evident from the moral background against which the office is set. Offices must be distinguished into public and private, the former being characterized partly by the fact that the holder is entitled to influence the lives of others without their knowledge.

There is a tradition at least as old as

*Aristotle which describes a *constitution as a set of public offices, united under law. There can be government without office, but such government automatically raises the question of how it might be limited. The only constraints on those who exercise power will be custom (ineffective in itself), and the criminal and civil law. But either the law will be too strong to allow political action (since every action will be grounds for at least civil, if not criminal, redress), or else too weak to prevent *despotism, since it will be simply inapplicable to the rulers. Anything in between those extremes will be tantamount to a constitution of offices, since it will involve rules that circumscribe the responsibilities and define the obligations of someone when and in so far as he is acting in a certain capacity. Without such rules it is difficult to imagine such procedures as *impeachment, or redress for actions performed **ultra vires* – procedures which, on one plausible view, are integral to the whole idea of *limited government. (*See* *Machiavelli.) (One frequent criticism of *democratic centralism – at least as practised – is that it has created no effective political offices independent of the *party that occupies them; it is inevitable that government exercised according to this principle will be without a true constitution.)

Offices may outlast their holders, and are often treated as symbols of political continuity, attracting to themselves the ceremonies and symbols of *majesty. Some welcome this process, thinking it part of wise government to assail the citizen with representations of a political order greater and more enduring than himself. Such thinkers may welcome too the association of offices with *honours, so symbolizing the unity of responsibility and power: power attached to an office is power limited by responsibility, and hence perceived in terms of a conception of legitimacy. Others dislike the ceremonial aspect of office, and wish for more 'informal' government, thinking that offices – when too much dignified with the majesties of state – place a veil between the rulers and the ruled, thus preventing the powerless from having access to or audience with power.

official secrets. 'Official' means pertaining to *office and in political contexts this means public office. However, this is not the meaning of an 'official' secret as defined, for example, in the UK Official Secrets Acts 1911 and 1920. Here an official secret is taken to be (roughly) any confidential matter relating to the state which may be disclosed so as to be 'prejudicial to the safety or interests of the state'. Whether purposes are prejudicial to the safety or interests of the state is a question for the court on hearing evidence from the Crown as to the interests of the state, and not a question for the jury on which the accused could give evidence concerning his ultimate intention.

The problem of reconciling a law of official secrets with freedom of information is so great as to remain unresolved. Every such law seems to be either too narrow to be effective or else so wide as to enable the suppression of matters which – it is argued – ought to be publicly known.

oligarchy. Greek: rule by a few. Quite what this means in practice is as difficult to determine as the meaning of *democracy. *Aristotle contrasted oligarchy (where the few rule in their own interest) with *aristocracy, or rule by the best, in which rule by the few is nevertheless in the interest of the many. However, 'aristocracy' now has a specialized meaning, implying a particular kind of *class organization, and it is not at all clear that this kind of government is in the interests of anyone. Oligarchy has been held to include the concentration of power under one-party government, that exhibited by the UK cabinet, and so on. Clearly, some of these arrangements might be in the interests of the people, some might not.

In general, since power is held in different degrees by different people, it is very likely that it will concentrate in the hands of a few, who, whatever the institutions and laws which limit their power, will nevertheless be able to recognize each other and to act instinctively in concert. It is therefore arguable that oligarchy is the natural condition of government, even in states which are legally *monarchies, or *democracies. (*See* *iron law of oligarchy.) Judgement of oligarchy must depend, therefore, on the principles whereby the élite is held together, and whereby its power is limited. In particular, can the people exert any *control over the oligarchy (e.g. by ejecting it from office at an election)? Or are they able to exert nothing more than *influence? Some argue that true oligarchy should be confined to the second case, whereas the first has a genuine democratic component.

oligopoly. Oligopoly relates to *monopoly as *oligarchy to *monarchy. It denotes the condition of a market in which a small number of firms control a large portion of production. The various firms involved tend to recognize their mutual interdependence and potential power, and so try to come to whatever arrangements among themselves might be necessary to realize and retain that power. In practice such attempts may often be in vain, as mutual distrust and an underlying desire for individual power tend to prevail. However, agreements restricting price competition and similar attempts to control the market may emerge in a condition of oligopoly. Often governments attempt to prevent these and similar practices and this is one of the main purposes of *anti-trust legislation.

The crucial feature of oligopoly is that what is a rational act for each firm depends upon what the other firms will do. Hence *game theory has a very important role in the study of oligopoly.

Olympic Games. *See* *sport.

ontology. Literally, the study of being; but usually used in political theory in a sense which ultimately stems from modern *phenomenology, to mean the underlying assumptions about reality, especially social reality, that are made in some given outlook. What is held to exist in itself, what only as a mode or determination of something else? Sometimes an institution is thought to exist independently of its members; sometimes a political outlook is nonsense without the assumption of the existence of God; sometimes the law is regarded as existing objectively and independently of men's conventional recognition of its imperatives. All these are 'ontologies', reflecting, in the last case, a belief in natural law.

The word 'ontology' is used in a similar sense by some analytical philosophers (e.g. Quine) to mean, not the study of being, but rather the class of things supposed to exist by a theory. Such a usage is also familar among social scientists. It is often important to distinguish the ontology of a belief or practice from the ontology of the theory which explains it. Thus a *functional explanation of witchcraft, unlike the practice of witchcraft, will not normally imply the existence of disembodied spirits.

open door policy. Originally applied to a system for the economic development of China, proposed in 1899 by the US Secretary of State John Hay, according to which no nation was to have exclusive rights for the commercial exploitation of China. To put it cynically, China was to be made economically independent of each trading nation, by being made dependent upon all of them. The policy was rejected by the Chinese in the subsequent upsurge of *nationalist sentiment. The expression is now used to denote the policy of trading with all states on equal terms, without giving monopolies or preferences to any.

open society. Expression used by *Popper, to denote a society whose members may openly criticize the institutions and the structures of power without fear of reprisal; where education is distinct from indoctrination; where society is able to flourish freely in all the ways that are natural to it, without the impediment of supervision from the state; where freedom of thought, action and belief are allowed to the greatest possible extent;

and where there is neither the overbearing discipline of *totalitarian government, nor the rigid political structure of *absolutism. In short, it is a society which is as free from the state as is possible while maintaining good order, cohesion, and constitutional politics.

The positive description of the open society is less definite in the works of Popper than the trenchant attack on those taken to be its enemies – who include *Plato, *Hegel and *Marx (*The Open Society and its Enemies*, 1945). The rhetorical impact of the attack on Marx, in which Popper attempts to show that it is, to borrow a Marxist phrase, no accident that regimes based in Marxian doctrine end up as *totalitarian, has been great, although its intellectual content and value are disputed.

operations research. An interdisciplinary study which looks for the *optimal solution to problems in the management of a *firm, or any other complex organization dedicated to specifiable purposes. The normal method involves the construction of models which are tested and then modified in order to approximate as nearly as possible to the actual situation which needs to be understood.

opinion. A 'matter of opinion' is a matter over which there may be reasonable disagreement, either because the subject forbids objective determination, or because the evidence and arguments available to either side are, in normal circumstances, insufficient to establish either view. In normal parlance, therefore, an opinion is either a judgement of *value, concerned with the ends of conduct, or a judgement of technique (concerned with the means) where matters are so complex as to remain unsettled by existing expertise, or a judgement of fact about the past, present or future, which cannot be established by available evidence. It is a respectable philosophical doctrine that in matters of value, the opinion of the majority converges on what is correct; the same cannot be said about matters of technique, and the opinion of the majority in economics, law, and government, where these do not involve a reiteration of the *ends* of conduct, may be worthless, even when unanimous. 'Opinion polls' nevertheless range over both types of issue, so that it may often be rational (for this and other reasons) to ignore them.

Some have wanted to see a 'forum of opinion' in government: as was advocated once in *The Federalist* (vol. 49). This was part of the philosophy behind the upper chamber of Congress: it was supposed to generate an atmosphere of leisure and free discussion in order to represent, not *interests, but opinions, a process upon which 'all governments rest'. In so far as such an idea seems plausible it is because the instititional conditions are created under which opinions will be based on the maximum available understanding of their subject-matter. Other forms of consultation of opinion – say through a poll of the majority – tend to be less credible as an instrument of government. Some see *representation as separating out the two kinds of opinion, allowing the majority to determine the ends of political life, without imposing their opinion about the means. Others regard representation as a system whereby interests, rather than opinions, find expression in government.

Certain thinkers in the style of *Burke and *Tocqueville have fought against the 'tyranny of opinion' in all matters, believing that an opinion, as a conscious reflection, in words that the utterer may be unpractised to use, will probably reflect the attitude of the one who asks for it, rather than of the one who answers. This distrust of opinion was thought by Burke to be compatible with, and indeed one of the main reasons for, representative government. Others – notably *Lenin – have argued rather that since only the left intelligentsia is able to form opinions that approximate to the truth, only it should govern. That view, which smacks of *Plato's defence of the philosopher king, conveys a particular and much disputed conception of the relations between theory and practice, and between opinion and knowledge.

opportunism. Term applied in 1876 to the French republican leader L. Gambetta, and since then adopted as an important item of communist vituperation. In normal parlance, an opportunist is one who seizes every opportunity to advance himself and his cause, by compromise, pretended belief, and treachery; in communist parlance, it is someone who renounces the 'revolutionary road to socialism', repudiates various dogmas of Marxism-Leninism, and shows a willingness to compromise with the *bourgeoisie.

opportunity cost. The opportunity cost of some chosen course of action is whatever benefit is offered by the best available alternative forgone. Opportunity cost is an important concept in modern economics, and in *cost-benefit analysis. It is generally assumed that it is rational to choose x if the benefit of x is greater than the opportunity cost of x. Further, on the assumption of *perfect competition in a market, the opportunity cost of every commodity is equal to its market price, which is a simple measure of the benefits forgone in purchasing it. As in other cases of cost and benefit the concept has wider application than to financial costs alone.

opposition. Some forms of rule cannot tolerate opposition, and root it out wherever it arises. Other forms not only tolerate it, but make room for it *within* the institutions of government. This feature of 'internalized opposition' has sometimes been taken as a mark of *limited, as opposed to absolute, government, and also as the mark of *politics, as opposed to *coercion. It is hard to imagine the feature without extremely complex institutions and constitutional devices: it is one of the principal problems of political thought, to discover what makes such opposition possible.

The use of the term 'opposition', to denote forces within political institutions that resist the ruling officers or party, is comparatively recent. J. Cam Hobhouse, speaking in the House of Commons in 1826, remarked that 'it was said to be very hard on his majesty's ministers to raise objections to this proposition. For his own part, he thought it was more hard on his majesty's opposition to compel them to take this course.' Hansard records laughter at the phrase 'his majesty's opposition'. Although there are uses of 'opposition', to refer to a party or a caucus within an assembly, going back to the early eighteenth century, it seems that this suggestion of an *established opposition was relatively new. It is now, however, quite normal to refer to a 'loyal opposition', and to imply that the interests of the state are as well served by the opposition as by the government itself.

The 'opposition' in the modern UK Parliament consists not merely of opposition *parties or *factions, but principally of a 'shadow formation'. The offices of government are imitated within the opposition, which thereby forms itself into a body prepared to substitute for all the occupants of those offices at any time. The opposition has its leader, its base organization and committees, and usually responds to every move of the government with counter-proposals, representing, in theory, what it *would* do if it were in office.

The existence of such a structured opposition within the institutions of government contributes to the modern understanding of the idea of *party. It presupposes a form of government in which maximum unity within a party is combined with maximum separation between the offices of government and the party that occupies them. It is not surprising to find that this double feat of maximization is a rare achievement. (*See* *office, *representation.)

Because of the immense importance of oppositions in forming the character of modern governments they have become serious subjects of study among political scientists.

oppression. The use of *coercion, *force, or *violence by some holder of *power, in order to constrain another's freedom or deny his *rights. Defining oppression in that way explains the common thought that oppressed peoples have a right to rise up and throw off their yoke. Sometimes *persuasive definition generates easy inference from the existence of force to the justice of oppression, by passing through the term 'oppression', thus avoiding the major political question, as to whose rights and freedoms are being violated by whom.

Oppression may be overt (as in the occupation of a country by an invader not acting in a just cause), or covert, as in the oppression exerted by organized criminals through a system of 'protection'. A particularly important example of covert oppression is that in which the oppression is also unintentional, while the force stems from economic power working upon economic need. The best known example of this is 'class oppression', as represented in Marxist thought. This consists typically in the forcible denial of rights and liberties to a proletarian class by a bourgeoisie acting, not in collusion, but in concert, so as to maintain its economic power. (It is not clear that Marx thought that the *rights* of the proletariat are denied under capitalism, since he often wanted to remove all ideas of right and justice from his critique; it is clear, however, that he thought of the freedom of the proletariat as constrained.)

Oppression must be distinguished from *repression, although some (e.g. *Marcuse, *Reich) have regarded the latter as an effect of the former.

optimal. A solution to a maximizing problem (e.g. a problem posed by the desire to achieve as much utility as possible from expenditure on goods, subject to remaining within one's income or budget) is optimal if it is as good as any other. There need not be a unique optimal solution: a problem may have several optimal solutions which are equally good. Optimal solutions must be distinguished from satisficing solutions, which merely meet certain requirements whether or not there is some superior alternative. The search for an optimal solution in social and political problems is now a large preoccupation of political science, and the concept has an important role in *operations research, *welfare economics, and even the theory of *justice. Problems of optimization arise when there are several objectives involved, and when the maximization of one objective is incompatible with the maximization of another. A typical example is that presented by inflation and employment. A government may seek to promote both employment and the reduction of inflation; it may be that these are so related that the maximization of one is incompatible with the maximization of the other. (*See* *Phillips curve.) Moreover there may also be an unacceptable minimum below which one of the variables cannot be allowed to fall.

Criteria of optimality are contentious, especially in questions of distribution. The classical *utilitarian criterion, which seeks for the highest level of overall utility, is clearly compatible with vastly unequal distributions; the far weaker criterion of *Pareto optimality leaves many matters undetermined, while the *maximin criterion has often seemed to be applicable only in special cases.

Opus Dei ('the work of God'). A Roman Catholic organization, founded in Madrid in 1928, with the intention of fostering Christian principles of morality and religion in everyday life. It maintains educational institutions, and has played an important, but covert, political role, both in Spain (originally in opposition to the Republican government, subsequently securing the restoration of Roman Catholic institutions under Franco), and elsewhere.

organic. Now used to mean: exhibiting the kind of organization that pertains to living organisms. The definition has an air of circularity, because of the etymologically identical term 'organization' that is used in formulating it. Attempts to clarify the idea have not proved very successful, and often run up against intractable philosophical problems. The usual contrast is between the organic and the mechanical, but that only helps if we have a clear idea of the mechanical: some things popularly described as 'machines' may obey principles of organization which also characterize organisms – such, at any rate, is one of the plausible assumptions of *cybernetics. An important idea seems to be that of function: it is plausible to suggest that all the parts of an organism bear a functional relation to one another. Each part is a means to the functioning of every other. That is of course no clearer than the idea of 'function'. A related suggestion is that the *overall* function of an organism is internal – the maintenance of its own existence. That contrasts with the typical machine, which is constructed for an independent purpose, and which is not to be explained in terms of any principle of self-preservation. The two ideas are vague, but very important in political thinking. They underlie both the frequently made claim that societies are organic, and therefore not to be subjected lightheartedly to surgery, and also the opposing position that societies may occasionally be in need of a revolutionary 'purge'.

organicism. The view that certain composite entities – in particular social entities – are *organic, or sufficiently like organic things to be understood by the laws of organic life. The theory is usually put forward as a version of *holism, in order to argue that social entities, like organisms, cannot be understood merely as the aggregates of their parts, but only by invoking principles of organization that explain the functioning of the parts in terms of their relation to the whole. Organicist views are sometimes thought to be inherently conservative, since they suggest that social entities are delicate, not easily understood, and more likely to survive and flourish if not too much meddled with. However, some who accept that also advocate *revolution, out of a belief, for example, that the death of one society might involve the birth of another. (*See* *death.)

organization man. Expression introduced in a book of that title by William H. Whyte, in 1956, to describe the new human type supposedly generated by bureaucracy and large-scale management. Whyte's analysis dwells on the conformity, mediocrity and mechanical responses of the organization man, together with the ideology which arises therefrom, and which replaces the imperatives of morality and personal affection by new cold imperatives of impersonal order.

organization theory. The sociological theory of the function, mechanism and effect of organizations, especially of large-scale industrial organizations engaged in production. The foundations of the theory were laid by *Weber, but it is not clear that it is really a distinct branch rather than the whole of sociology.

oriental despotism. Term already used by travellers in the seventeenth century, and taken over by *Montesquieu. Traditional Chinese bureaucracy, the Mogul Empire, certain phases of the Russian Tsarist Empire, and even (although the intention here is no doubt ironical) the modern USSR, have been described as oriental despotisms. The principal characteristics are: concentration of power in the hands of a despot and his entourage; control of all social and political activity from above; absence of a rule of law, and immediate oppressive reaction to any challenge to the central power; emphasis on military power; rapid mobilization of the whole populace in order to override and eliminate *opposition, usually without regard to moral niceties. It is not clear whether 'oriental despotism' and '*asiatic despotism' are synonymous: it is possible that the second is described in relation to a mode of production, the first in relation to habits of violence, and that the two do not necessarily coincide. Various theories have been advanced to explain oriental despotism, including the now largely discredited hypothesis (K. Wittfogel, *Oriental Despotism,* 1954) that it is a system made necessary by centralized schemes of irrigation.

original sin. In *Christian theology, the sin which has belonged to all people since the fall of Adam. The doctrine is derived from St Paul's teaching that 'through one man sin entered the world' so that 'by the trespass of the one the many died'. According to *Aquinas, original sin consists in the loss of those supernatural privileges which had focused man's will upon his true eternal end; as a result of this loss man's reason is submitted to his senses. Original sin is transmitted, not because of Adam's personal failing, but because it is the condition of that human nature first exemplified in Adam, and growing organically from him. Original sin is redeemed in the sacrifice of Christ.

The doctrine represents in mystical terms, and by way of a thesis concerning the structure of man's relation to God, a sentiment that also has many secular and political equivalents: the sentiment of man's 'fallen' condition, which has been rationalized in this and various other ways. The same sentiment emerges in the (typically conservative) theory of the inevitable imperfection of all human beings and their works, according to which too much hope and too much trust in human capacities constitute one of the most dangerous manifestations of that imperfection. Original sin is thus an important concept for such thinkers as *de Maistre, who refers to it as 'explaining everything, and without which nothing can be explained'. It is also referred to ironically by Marx, who suggests that *primitive accumulation is the true original sin of capitalism, and who relies on the analogy for several details of the ensuing theory.

Ortega y Gasset, Jośe (1883–1955). Spanish writer and philosopher; *see* *masses.

orthodoxy. The 'straight' opinion – i.e. the opinion which adheres as closely as possible to a given set of beliefs. Not every political doctrine or theory defines an orthodoxy. When writers refer, e.g., to 'liberal orthodoxy', it is extremely unclear what is meant, and even 'Marxist orthodoxy' is a dubious phrase, given the potential conflict between the scientific theory of *historical materialism and the *neo-Marxist critique of consciousness. Some conservatives argue that their view is characterized by the impossibility of orthodoxy, being founded in respect for the actual, and for all the variations, flexibilities and impredictabilities that characterize the actual. But perhaps that rhetorical disclaimer has itself become a form of orthodoxy.

Orwell, George (E. A. Blair) (1903–50). English writer and satirist, who deserves a place in this dictionary partly because his novel *Nineteen Eighty Four,* well known for its description of an *ideal type of *totalitarianism, added certain words to political language which have proved irreplaceable. These words satirize the acronyms of bolshevism ('*Cominform'. '*Comintern', 'Proletcult', etc.) and include *Newspeak* (designed to meet the ideological needs of *Ingsoc,* or English socialism, and to make heretical thought – *thoughtcrime* – impossible), *prolefeed* (rubbishy entertainment and fictitious news for the masses, or *proles*), *unperson* (one who has been carefully removed from history) and *doublethink*: 'the power of holding two contradictory propositions in one's mind simultaneously, and accepting both of them'. Orwell also invented the 'thought police', as the last word in despotic efficiency, and wrote, in *Animal Farm,* the most famous of all satires of *Stalinism, which he epitomized in the phrase 'all animals are equal, but some are more equal than others'.

Orwell was himself an important influence on English liberal socialism.

Ostpolitik. German: East policy. The West German policy, initiated by Chancellor Kurt Kiesinger in 1966, and emphasized afresh by Chancellor Willy Brandt in 1970, of attempting to end hostile relations with the Soviet bloc by agreements to renounce the use of force, to recognize *de facto* borders, and to encourage trade and cooperation. The policy was a forerunner of **détente*.

over-full employment. Empirical investigation and certain macroeconomic theories suggest that it is impossible to have completely full employment without inflation. If unemployment falls below a certain minimum, i.e. when there is excess demand for goods and labour, then demand becomes high relative to productive capacity, and prices and wages will tend to rise. When unemployment has sunk below this minimum, therefore, the economy might be said to be in a state of 'over-full employment'.

over-population. A state is sometimes called over-populated when no increase in population will generate an increase in production, so that all increases strain resources. Whether or not a state is over-populated does not, on this definition, depend upon crowding, or density of population, but only on the actual ability to meet increased demand.

A state might also be called over-populated if increases in population fail to increase output per head, so that standards of living either remain stationary or fall with each addition to the population. Certain economists have attempted to provide theories of 'optimum population' along these lines, and have offered criteria in order to ascertain when population is at the optimum level. Such criteria are many and varied but oft-quoted versions include: that population at which average, or alternatively total, utility is maximized; that population at which income per head is maximized, and so on.

ouvrièrisme. *See* *labour movement.

Owen, Robert (1771–1858). British industrialist and philanthropist, early socialist, and pioneer of the cooperative movement. At his model cotton mills at New Lanark, Owen attempted to show that good wages and conditions for the workers are consistent with business success. Owen believed that social life is or should be continuous with work, and that the two are mutually dependent. He therefore built a model village for his workers, with communal facilities, education and welfare provisions. The great evil of competition is, he thought, the effect, and not the cause of social and economic institutions. Owen believed in private property in the means of production (specifically a nation of 'small independent producers') together with socialized distribution (through common ownership of markets and redistribution in favour of the needy). *Marx claimed to see a paradox here – *see* *production, distribution, exchange, consumption.

Owenism. The theory and practice of co-operative socialism on the model proposed by *Owen. Owenism is related to *market socialism, although less theoretical.

ownership. *See* *property.

P

pacific blockade. Coercion short of *war from a more powerful state towards a less powerful one. It consists in the blockade of ports with minimum ancillary violence: its object is to avoid war, hence rights of warfare cannot be exercised against ships of other states involved in the blockade. It has been recognized as a distinct form of coercion at least since the Anglo-Swedish blockade of Norwegian ports in 1814. The Declaration of Paris 1856 required that blockades be effective; since then blockades have been used by the major powers in preserving peace. The practice has been to some extent superseded by the provisions of the Hague Convention 1907, no. 2, which forbids the use of armed force in the recovery of contract debts, unless arbitration is unsuccessful.

pacifism. The belief that all *war is unjustified, and that all international politics should proceed by arbitration and treaties under international law. Pacifism may arise out of moral convictions so strong as to give grounds for *conscientious objection to military service, although the right to such objection is rarely recognized.

Attempts to build pacifism into a political doctrine have usually involved an element of *universalism – for example, a belief in universal *natural law, which is superior to, and ought eventually to replace, the municipal laws of states. This would abolish the nation state and subsume all human beings under a single universal jurisdiction. The thought here is that the main cause of belligerence is the sentiment of *territory associated with political division, and war will no longer be either necessary or possible when such division is removed. However, all that can really be inferred from the evidence is that war will then be called 'civil war'; experience also suggests that civil war is as bad as, if not worse than, war of other kinds.

Pacifism has been an important force in modern politics, partly because of its successful use as a strategy by Gandhi (*see* *passive resistance), partly because of the unacceptable destructiveness of modern warfare.

Paine, Thomas (1737–1809). English-born outlaw, and leader of the American Revolution, whose *Common Sense,* 1776, crystallized the sentiment that led to the Declaration of Independence, arguing that 'government even in its best state, is a necessary evil; in its worst state, an intolerable one'. Paine also wrote one of the major documents of radical reform, *The Rights of Man*, 1791, 1792. This, a response to *Burke's critical analysis of the French Revolution, contained a *universalist defence of the doctrine of *natural rights, and of revolution in the cause of such rights. Paine also defended democracy, redistribution on grounds of social justice, progressive taxation, and egalitarianism in all areas – such as education – where privilege is normally operative. His doctrine of natural rights is in the spirit of *Locke (although he claimed never to have read Locke), while his attempt to reconcile liberal principles of justice with egalitarian doctrines of property and opportunity anticipates later arguments in the *left-liberal tradition. Paine was seen by many contemporaries as a passionate exponent of *Enlightenment opinions, an enemy of *establishment in all its forms, a proponent of *deism, and champion of the oppressed.

palace revolution. A revolution against a *monarch or similar figure, or against the institution of monarchy, instigated by those close to the monarch, such as the higher nobility and officers of the court, and conducted within the precincts of the court, rather than in the towns or the country. Sometimes used to denote any relatively quiet but unconstitutional change of government which occurs at the instigation of forces within a ruling faction or party, such as occurred within the *Politburo in the USSR in 1964 when Brezhnev ousted Kruschev.

pan-Africanism. A movement attempting to unite black Africans behind a consciousness of their distinct political *identity and common political destiny. Pan-Africanism began among US blacks in the 1850s, and achieved its first conference on African soil in 1958. Its doctrines have been various, and seldom systematic; for a while the ideals of **né-gritude* were influential, particularly in French-speaking states.

pan-Germanism, pan-Slavism. Two movements which date from the late nineteenth century and which were strongly influenced by the intellectual currents of nineteenth-century *nationalism. They each aimed to unite under common political institutions people with a common language or related languages and, according to the theory, belonging to a common *race. Hitler's special brand of pan-Germanism tried to separate the ideas of language and race, in order to exclude those German speakers whom he found objectionable, while recent pan-Slavism in Eastern Europe has tended to emphasize common language, and to make no claims of a specifically racial character. Both movements have been largely discredited, the first because of its apotheosis in *national socialism, the second because of its role in legitimating the Soviet conquest of Slavonic nations.

pan-Islam. Movement for uniting the Islamic nations, both socially and politically, which originated in the Ottoman Empire in the 1880s, and which has undergone a chequered history of anti-

Zionism, anti-communism and (most recently) anti-Americanism

pantisocracy. A form of social organization without government, all being of equal rank and social position, and none having any right of ascendancy over any other. (The term was introduced in the course of defending the idea by Southey, and promptly satirized by Byron.) Pantisocratists in the early nineteenth century were mostly comfortable English intellectuals, whose egalitarianism consisted in a desire to raise everyone to their own level (which they believed to be such that it rendered government unnecessary) rather than to reduce themselves to the level of anyone else.

paradox of democracy. A paradox, emphasized by *Rousseau, which has been stated in many versions; the essence of the paradox is this:
(i) If I believe in the legitimacy of democratic choice, then I believe that the policy chosen as a result of democratic procedure ought to be enacted.
(ii) There are two incompatible policies, A and B.
(iii) Believing that A ought to be enacted, I vote for A.
(iv) The majority vote for B.

By (i) and (iv), I believe that B ought to be enacted; by (iii) I believe that A ought to be enacted; I also know the truth of (ii), i.e. that A and B are incompatible. Hence I seem compelled by my belief in democracy to embrace conflicting – perhaps even contradictory – opinions. The paradox is not to be confused with the *voting paradoxes that arise in the theory of *social choice. The main attempts to resolve the paradox involve analysis of the particular belief contained in (i): what exactly *does* a democrat believe about the majority decision in this case? That it ought to be enacted? Or that it ought not to be opposed in any way other than that made available by democratic procedure? And so on.

paramilitary. An organization is paramilitary if it affects the style and method of military institutions – with military discipline, a hierarchy of command, directed towards violent ends, and self-licensed to kill – while existing within civilian institutions. Many revolutionary parties have passed through a paramilitary stage. The function seems to be at least partly that of making murder easier, not just physically, but also morally, by suggesting that killing is performed under orders, and so is no more murder than the killing of an enemy combatant in time of war. This further reinforces the command structure of the paramilitary organization, through the thought that something which may legitimately dispense so dreadful a licence must itself have the authority of government.

parasitism. The charge of 'parasitism' is often levelled in the USSR and its satellites against citizens who do not work, and 'anti-parasite laws' were considerably strengthened in the late 1950s. The constitution guarantees, in theory, a *right to work, and the citizen is in normal circumstances under an obligation to seek (and, when certain conditions are fulfilled, accept) work. The 'parasite' may in fact have been ejected for political reasons from his former employment, so that the charge is sometimes used to enforce a political judgement; however, it can normally be avoided, by working a certain minimum number of hours or earning a certain minimum wage. Thus arises a special kind of *unemployment, in which what is in effect unemployment benefit is paid out as a fictional wage, in exchange for a few hours of attendance at a place designated by the state.

Paretian liberal, impossibility of. A result in the theory of *social choice, due to Amartya Sen, which shows the inconsistency of three requirements: unrestricted domain (no individual preference orderings are ruled out *ab initio*); the 'weak Pareto principle' (if everyone prefers state x to state y, then x is socially preferred to y); and 'minimal liberty' (at least two persons have their own minimal 'personal sphere', such that, if one of them prefers x to y in his personal sphere, then x is socially preferred to y). The theorem is an example of an 'impossibility theorem', similar in spirit to *Arrow's theorem. Intuitively it seems to establish that there is a conflict between liberal values (which imply that at least some individuals are sovereign in at least some minimal private sphere), and a plausible criterion of social welfare (the weak Pareto principle).

Pareto, Vilfredo, Marchese (1848–1923). Italian economist, sociologist and philosopher, one of the founders of modern sociology, and a vigorous political pamphleteer, who argued vehemently in the cause of *free trade on the one hand, and *authoritarian politics on the other, and against *socialism as enemy of the first, *liberalism as enemy of the second. Pareto was, however, no romantic conservative, but (at least in his own eyes) a hard-headed realist. His vision of politics and economics was founded in an ideal of rational conduct, which represented rationality as a perfect matching of end and means: his admiration for Machiavellian manoeuvres in politics came from this somewhat *scientistic vision of the rational man. Recognizing that most people do not behave according to his paradigms of rationality, he put forward ambitious (and often satirical) sociological theories of irrational conduct, the most influential being that many socially significant beliefs are *residues of socio-economic forces not themselves to be expressed in cognitive form.

Pareto is esteemed as a sociologist, partly because of his pioneering attempt to give an account of society as a 'system', with points of equilibrium, and mechanisms of adjustment, which may proceed independently of human attempts at voluntary control. He emphasized the importance of problems of social integration, and the functional interdependence of seemingly disparate social phenomena. His theories of social integrity and interdependence profoundly influenced his economics, and Pareto is often considered to be one of the founders of modern *welfare economics. He argued that economics is a science, but must always be seen as part of a larger framework provided by the social sciences as a whole, social and economic phenomena being interdependent. He gave a theory of economic efficiency which took account, not only of the level of income, but also of its distribution within an economy, and this led him to introduce certain important concepts, including the distinction between cardinal and ordinal utility (*see* *preference), many of the basic ideas of *marginalism, and the criterion of *optimality (or 'ophelimity') which has since become known as *'Pareto optimality'. Pareto optimality is the condition in which no one can be made better off without someone else becoming worse off – i.e. the position in which no change in *income will make *everyone* better off. This criterion contrasts, for example, with that proposed by classical *utilitarianism (the maximum welfare over all), and incorporates an intuition concerning *social justice, namely, that it is unacceptable to allow the welfare of anyone simply to be *sacrificed* in the interests of anyone else. Its utility in welfare theory has been doubted, partly because it does not determine a unique solution to welfare problems, and partly because it is compatible with every degree of social inequality between members of a society. However various versions of the criterion have proved useful in giving the structure of *social choices. (*See* *Paretian liberal.)

Pareto's mind was far-ranging, and on almost every issue in economics and politics he had something (though not necessarily something lasting) to say. There is, for example, a 'Pareto's law', which holds, largely on the basis of empirical observation, that whatever the political conditions or mode of *taxation, income will tend to be distributed in the same way, with the lowest paid being the largest group. The law is, at best, only approximately confirmed.

Pareto was praised by the *fascist government of Mussolini, but since he lived to see only one year of its rule, it is impossible to know what he would have thought of it. Many of his political intuitions align him with some of Mussolini's policies; on the other hand his keen sense of the ridiculous might have caused him to withhold commitment.

Pareto optimality. A criterion of social welfare (named from *Pareto's 'criterion of ophelimity'), according to which a situation is optimal if nobody in it could be made better off without someone being made worse off. Unlike the classic principle of *utilitarianism the criterion does not involve interpersonal comparisons of utility. Hence it can be applied to a social situation while making no assumptions concerning the relative force of individuals' preferences within that situation. For this reason the criterion has been extremely important in welfare economics, since it permits the theorist to drop one of the most contentious assumptions that have been made in that study. However, it suffers from the defect that there may be as many as infinitely many Pareto optimal solutions to a single problem. For a weak 'Pareto' criterion of social welfare which similarly avoids interpersonal comparisons of utility, *see* *Paretian liberal.

parity. Comparability. When philosophers say that there is 'no parity' between say, the values of morality and the pleasures of the senses, they mean that the two cannot be set against each other in a rational equation, so that reasons of sensual pleasure cannot count for or against reasons of morality. The claim that there is no parity between two classes of benefit is often used to rebut the view that a single quantitative method can be applied to both of them – as in *J. S. Mill's attack on *Bentham's *hedonism.

Among specialized uses of the term, the following should be noted:
(i) to denote the exchange rate of a currency against some internationally accepted standard (such as gold), which the government declares to be the norm;
(ii) in 'parity index', which denotes an *index of the normal outgoings of US farmers, and is used to compute the 'parity prices' for agricultural products – i.e. the prices which must be set in order to support the farmer according to those expectations that cause him to continue with his employment;
(iii) in 'purchasing power parity theory', which states that exchange rates are determined by the price levels in the separate states compared (in other words, changes in exchange rate offset changes in price levels). This is a widely accepted theory which is sometimes held to undermine the assumptions behind *exchange control.

Parliament. A term often used for institutions of consultative government, but here discussed as the name of the institution of government by *bicameral *representation in the UK, which has evolved continuously since the eleventh century and which has been taken as a model by many other states (*see* *Westminster model). Many of Parliament's procedures, rights and duties are derived from convention and custom, and much of what is important concerning its role and power must be phrased as discovery rather than as legal rule – e.g. 'It seems that there is no legal limitation on Parliament's power', and not 'There shall be no limitation on Parliament's power.' The institutional structure with two houses (Lords and Commons) was established very early and its fundamental constitutional principles – that all taxation without the consent of Parliament is illegal, that both houses must concur in legislation, and that the Commons have power to inquire into administration and accounts, and to impeach the King's ministers for maladministration – were asserted definitively in the reign of Edward III (b. 1312, r. 1327–77), thus establishing *limited monarchy in medieval England. Since then changes have occurred in the nature and quality of its membership, in procedures for election (the extension of the franchise beginning in 1832, and now reaching to almost every citizen over the age of eighteen), and by the emergence of *parties, a process which began in the late seventeenth century, but which took on its modern aspect after 1832.

Parliament is a system of representation, whose main present function is to legitimate and to limit in the name of the *Crown the power exercised by a political party, rather than that exercised by the monarch. Although legislation is still enacted by 'The Queen in Parliament', the thesis of the 'sovereignty of Parliament' – i.e. that Parliament is the true locus of sovereign power – has gained increasing acceptance since the seventeenth century, but, with the successive limitations of the powers of the House of Lords by the Parliament Acts 1911 and 1949, it would be more reasonable now to speak of the sovereignty of the Commons. That could not have been said before 1945, when the House of Lords played a major part in determining policy, providing ministers and amending legislation, and when the King himself was once (1931) required to intervene (under the 'royal *prerogative') in order to form a government.

Legislation must be passed first by the Commons, and then by the Lords, before gaining the 'royal assent'; the *Prime Minister is chosen, by convention, from the ranks of the majority party in the Commons, and is usually leader of that party. Most candidates for election to the Commons stand in the name of a party, and are subject to the discipline of a party, both before and after election. This has led to a radical change in the character of representation, which seems to be an inevitable result of the need to appeal to the electorate as a whole with a coherent legislative programme. (*See* *mandate.)

Parliament has 'privilege' – that is, things spoken in the course of parliamentary proceedings are immune from proceedings in the courts; however, the Speaker of the House of Commons has power to discipline members for speaking out of order, or for using insulting or abusive language. Officially all legislation from the Commons is preceded by, and emerges from, debate. What debate there is, however, is at a fairly low level, and most legislation is passed unamended in the form that the dominant party has chosen. The House of Lords may introduce bills and these will tend to be debated, but the Commons is jealous of its power, and will tolerate bills in the House of Lords, or amendments to its own bills from the Lords, only if they relate to matters over which neither government nor opposition has strong feelings. If any dispute arises, the Commons may (by the Parliament Acts), override the decision of the Lords, after specified procedures have been complied with.

parliamentarianism. The UK form of *constitutionalism, which upholds the *sovereignty of *Parliament, and which argues that the constitution, procedure and structure of Parliament must not be overruled or damaged in the interests of a *party. It may argue for the wisdom of parliamentary institutions, or for the view that they are all we have got. Either way, it will assert that government without institutions is despotic, and that parliamentary institutions are vital to *limited government, serving as the form which unites the content of successive acts of legislation, and which disciplines every change in the law in accordance with a recognized idea of sovereignty. Every act of government is performed, not by an individual, nor by a party, but by an officer, acting in the exercise of his office, who derives his authority in the last analysis from Parliament.

parochialism. Attachment to the parish; hence, any attitude which derives its sense and content from conditions too localized to permit generalization, and which evinces an unreasoning (and, by implication, unreasonable) attachment to those conditions. Just how circumscribed an attitude must be to be called parochial is not clear. Is Welsh Nationalism or Ulster Unionism parochial? Presumably not, since both seek political institutions that will correspond to social forces that supposedly already require them. Likewise, many nationalistic and irredentist movements endeavour to produce a correspondence between forms of government and local *identity which could be seen to be reasonable even by those for whom that local identity provides no coherent motive.

participation. The ideal of participation is captured in the slogan: 'What touches all must be decided by all'; but who is included in the 'all?' How heavily must one be touched? The difficulty here explains a certain preference for the weaker slogan: 'Those affected by decisions must be involved in making them'. Again, however, it is not clear what 'involvement' amounts to. It could mean a right to vote, or a right to be heard, or a right to decide autonomous and circumscribed matters, or a right of veto, or a right of representation, delegation or mandation. It is disputable whether any of these is tantamount to involvement in any independent sense – the issue here being that of the nature and validity of *collective choice. One aim is to ensure that decisions made are acceptable to those affected by them. But if that were *all* that involvement amounted to, then the real criterion would be consent, rather than some procedure of decision making. In which case, to consent to a situation in which all decisions are made by an independent body of managers is *itself* to be involved in their decisions. Clearly, therefore, something more active is meant by 'involvement'.

The call for participation has been extended from the institutions of state to all those subject institutions which have power, however limited and local, over the lives of people, particularly those which govern work. Hence the German call for *Mitbestimmung,* or coordination between workers and management in the place of work. Again, what is intended by this seems to vary from case to case. Similar calls have been made concerning the government of schools and universities, even armies and prisons. *See* *democracy, *democratization, *influence, *representation.

particularism. *See* *universalism.

partisan. 1. Adjective: applies to someone who 'takes a party line' (which may or may not be the line of a *party) on any issue. To be partisan is to close one's mind to thoughts that present difficulties for an established outlook or opinion.
2. Noun: used to describe the Russians who attacked Napoleon's supply-line during the campaign of 1812, and now denoting any armed group offering resistance behind the lines of an enemy. Because of the Italian and especially Yugoslavian resistance to German forces during the war, it is particularly associated with guerrilla forces fighting within an occupied country.

partition. The political division of a territory into autonomous sections, with or without migration of the peoples resident there, in order to establish two governments. This may occur as a result of outside belligerency or influence (as in the partition of Germany), as part of a reorganization of government following the departure of a colonial regime (as in India), or as a result of internal unrest, perhaps also aided and fomented from outside (as in the partition of Cyprus). In the latter two cases it may involve *irredentism, or a desire for modes of government that recognize cultural, social or racial bonds which exist independently.

party. Exactly what constitutes a political party, and what distinguishes it from a *faction, is an extremely difficult question. In fact the term 'party' seems to denote two distinct kinds of institution:
1. Under conditions of representative government, in which parties may succeed one another in office, according to the decision of an electorate, a party is a voluntary association of individuals, united for common political purposes, some of whom pledge their support, others of whom run for election, and some of whom will take office in government if the party is successful. It usually has a constitution, rules of membership, and procedure for determining officers. It tends to have agreed policies, divergence from which may mean expulsion or discipline, but it does not necessarily align itself with any *doctrine, or with any *class. It seeks to increase its membership as much as possible, and holds

office under a constitution that is superior to it, and which determines how it may conduct the affairs of state. It cannot make law, but only initiate legislation, law being made, not by the party, but by the sovereign institutions over which it exerts an influence, perhaps a dominant influence. Its constitution will be determined by the need to coincide with government offices as and when required or invited; it will therefore bear the stamp of the constitution under which it aims for power.

2. In a so-called 'one-party state', there is an entity called a party, but which may have little in common with 1. It is not normally a voluntary association, but rather a corporate body of undetermined legal status, with powers to expel from and, by virtue of its monopoly over all office and advancement, to coerce to, membership. Its purposes are not only political (except under the assumption, which it accepts, that all purposes are political), but also social, and it seeks complete control over all institutions. It does not seek power through election, although it may rehearse a fiction of election every now and again, while forbidding any party other than itself to participate. It defines the offices of state, determines their membership, and permits no organized *opposition within them. It proceeds not by representation but by delegation from above, and generates permissions which extend from the hierarchy downwards, giving powers to local bodies and police to act with its authority. It controls the making of laws, supervises their application, and is often bound by no precedent or constitutional constraint. It has a recognized doctrine and punishes all deviations from it, not only among its members but also among those who are excluded from membership. It does not necessarily seek to extend membership but often to curtail it, so as to exert the maximum discipline compatible with completely extended power. It usually makes other parties illegal, or else compels them to affiliate with itself. It infiltrates and gains possession of all autonomous institutions and often declares itself to be the enlightened *vanguard of a class.

passive resistance. A policy of unarmed and *non-violent resistance to an occupying force, or a government imposed by such force. It involves deliberate neglect of official and administrative functions, refusal to attend interrogations, non-participation in government activities, and so on. The strategy was advocated and pursued by Gandhi, in opposition to British occupation of India. It was followed also in Czechoslovakia, following the Russian invasion of 1968, but with little success. It is hard to organize passive resistance if opposition to it is determined, and the strategy is vulnerable to the self-interested defection of the majority.

passive revolution. The bringing about of revolution by withdrawing cooperation from all activities and institutions in which the existing *hegemony exerts itself, and so leaving it without a basis of power. The policy was advocated by *Gramsci as a form of non-violent social transformation from below, as opposed to the violent transformation from above practised by *bolshevism.

paternalism. 'The principle and practice of paternal administration; government as by a father; the claim or attempt to supply the needs or to regulate the life of a nation or community in the same way as a father does those of his children': thus the *OED*, capturing what the first Duke of Buckingham meant when he said that 'a king is father to his subjects'.

The term can be used as one of praise or of abuse, depending upon whether the responsibilities or the advantages of a father are emphasized. The idea of 'paternal' government is, on the whole, one of a benign arrangement, such as the romantic admirers of *feudalism have sometimes imagined it to be. If a government is truly paternal, then it is bound by responsibilities which are the equivalent of the responsibilities of a parent. In this sense many sociologists describe relations which combine power and responsibility (e.g. that between employer and employee) as involving a paternal component (the inspiration here being *Weber).

The term is also used to denote the attitude which sees people as so helpless and childlike as to stand in the same need of authority and government as children. Kindness may be resented by its recipient if it stems from a paternalistic attitude, since it implies that he is weaker than self-respect admits.

patriarchy. Literally, the rule by fathers. Used to denote:
1. Forms of *kinship relations in which the father is the source of authority, respect, property, and hereditary privilege (cf. *matriarchy).
2. In political writings, especially those of a *feminist persuasion, the dominance of social and political institutions by men, and the consolidation of male *hegemony throughout public and private life by means of law, especially family law. Since not all men are fathers, the term 'phallocracy' has been coined to replace this usage, generating the added implication that the dominion of men is also a form of irrational worship of the phallus.
3. The doctrine that political authority is inherited in the male line (perhaps from Adam), used as a justification for a particular kind of monarchy. *See* *divine right.

patrician. In early Rome, the privileged class of citizens who filled all magistracies and priesthoods until about 400 BC, when their power began to be limited by the *plebeians, so that, by the end of the Republic, their privileges were insignificant. Under the Empire only the Empress could create patricians, and, although the honour was hereditary, it was of no great political significance. The term is sometimes used of the European aristocracies, partly in order to denote the extent to which their class, like that of the patricians, is one determined by style and honour as much as by economic ascendancy.

patrimony. The inheritance from ancestors (the Latin root implies male ancestors, but the implication seems no longer to hold). The questions of patrimonial privilege and property are referred to under *hereditary principle.

patriotism. Love of country (literally, of fatherland). A vague term that is used differently for different purposes, and is in any case no clearer than the 'love' and 'country' employed in its definition. Patriotism is sometimes assimilated to, and sometimes sharply distinguished from, *nationalism. Thus the preamble to the USSR constitution declares that Soviet citizens are 'patriots and internationalists'. This makes it seem as though patriotism is more enlightened than nationalism, or at least, without the exclusiveness which is supposedly generated by too fervent an attachment to the *nation. If so, then 'country' may mean something like the laws and institutions of the state, together with whatever customs and conditions may be supposed in their application. 'Love' means, not only the attachment to those things, but the determination to defend them, perhaps at cost to one's life, when necessary. According to many of the traditional defenders of patriotism, it is a higher feeling than that of obligation to the sovereign, and one that the sovereign himself may respond to. Thus Bolingbroke (*The Patriot King,* 1738–9) argued that the sovereign title is itself conditional upon patriotic acts, so that the country (both state and civil society) is the true object of all allegiance, for subject and sovereign alike.

Such ideas survive, and in normal parlance a patriot esteems not only the institutions of a state but also, more especially, the people governed by those institutions, and the language, history and culture that is theirs. Furthermore, patriotism involves sentiments of territory, and tends to feed itself on visions of landscape which, while they may have social order as their focus, are nevertheless saturated with *nostalgia towards a place and climate. In which case, the sentiments underlying patriotism could be distinguished only with considerable difficulty from those attaching to nationalism. If there is a serious distinction here, it is that between a natural feeling, and an artificial and perhaps belligerent *ideology.

Patriotism combined with *xenophobia is *chauvinism; when bellicose and contemptuous it may also be *jingoism. The term suggests that the sentiment is conceived on the model of love from child to parent, presumably because it is held to be a kind of *piety, not reducible to any rescindable agreement or acquired affection. That would not make patriotism irrational, any more than love of parents is irrational, but it would do something to explain why the patriot himself may be able to give no reasoned basis for his emotion.

pax. Latin: peace. The Roman 'peace' was imposed partly by conquest, partly by tribes petitioning to be included within it, for fear of more powerful neighbours, or from the recognition of political and economic necessity. Thus the 'pacification' of Europe and North Africa was simultaneously the creation of an empire and the imposition of a form of *international law, the *jus gentium* (*see* *Roman law). *Pagus* (French *pays*, Italian *paese*) meant a pacified, i.e. subdued, community, and hence a village or commune within the Empire. Thus the term *pax Romana* came to designate the peace that stems from common subjection to a higher power, in this case often taken to be a blessing, because of the *rule of law made possible by it.

Similar ideas are involved in the *pax Britannica,* brought about by Britain during the eighteenth and nineteenth centuries, and still persisting within the Commonwealth, although with dwindling ability to assert itself as the separate legal and political systems diverge. Likewise the *pax Russica* which exists in Central Europe (but without a true rule of law, and imposed by constant *coercion). In medieval Europe there was also a *pax Dei* (peace of God), which could be invoked or imposed from time to time. This was designed to bring quarrels to an end by the threat of spiritual punishments, and to protect certain categories of noncombatants in time of war. It was an antecedent of the modern law of *neutrality, and administered largely by the church. It must be distinguished from the analogous *truega Dei,* or 'truce of God', a more temporary measure, designed to permit diplomacy.

peace. In negative terms, the absence of *war. Peace is supposed in *international law to be the normal relation between states, and legislation for 'peacemaking' and 'peacekeeping' has proceeded on this assumption. Plans for peacekeeping have been frequently proposed, for example by theAbbé de Saint-Pierre in 1713 (a perpetual alliance of Christian states in Europe), by *Bentham in 1789 (international court of judicature and a common *legislature), and by *Kant, whose proposals are perhaps the most interesting. Kant envisaged 'perpetual peace' as requiring a reorganization and bringing into conformity of the constitutions of all potential belligerents. It is necessary, Kant thought, for all states to be republics, submitting to a public law based on a federation of free states. The basis of that law would be the universal imperative of reason – the 'categorical imperative' – acceptable to all rational beings, and the only true expression of freedom. The law would therefore provide an automatic guarantee of freedom to all who submit to it, and the cause of belligerency would cease to exist. (The inclusion of provisions designed to guarantee universal *human rights into modern agreements aimed at peace – such as the Helsinki agreement – can be seen as in part exemplifying Kant's underlying idea.) Until Trotsky's '*peaceful coexistence' it was also assumed by *international socialist movements that perpetual peace could be achieved only by complete social and political transformation of all potential belligerents and alignment behind a common principle.

A positive definition of peace is hard to produce. There are infinite shades, from the absolute peace of reciprocated love in domestic security, to the internecine hatreds of civil war. In international law it is established that lack of belligerency is not sufficient for peace but only necessary, thus reflecting an intuition of daily existence. The ideal of pure personal tranquillity brings with it the notion of a complete rest from all consuming purposes. Poets have given us intimations of this condition, but it is unlikely that political thought can do any more than trouble it. War, with its concentrated purpose, is only one of many attitudes hostile to peace, in which the idea of a ruling purpose brings order into fragmented consciousness and exchanges small frustrations for absolute choices between life and death. Thus *Augustine argued that true peace requires not merely the absence of active hostilities but 'tranquillity in order'. Some have seen the *existentialist's philosophy of *commitment as construing personal fulfilment on the model of a transition from restlessness, not to rest, but to war, and have tried to explain its appeal accordingly. For nothing seems more tedious or futile than this state which, like heaven, can be only negatively described.

peaceful coexistence. Phrase coined by *Trotsky in 1917 (originally 'peaceful cohabitation'), and used first to designate the USSR policy of coming to terms with neighbouring capitalist states at the end of the First World War, and subsequently by Khrushchev to describe USSR policy towards capitalist states generally, despite the official commitment to supporting revolutionary working-class movements wherever they occur. China proposed its own form of 'peaceful coexistence' with India in 1954. The phrase is interpreted very broadly in communist countries so as to permit the encouragement of wars of *national liberation, and the fomenting of unrest and civil disorder in capitalist states.

peer. Latin: *pares,* equals. **1.** In sociological usage peers are those who compare themselves with one another, so that a peer group consists of those who, through whatever relation of interest, age, or social proximity, respond selectively to the advantages and disadvantages of other members of the group.
2. In the UK political system a 'peer' also denotes all members of the House of Lords. Originally the term 'peer' meant anyone 'on a par' with the sovereign, and entitled to be 'judged by his peers'. The peers in question were those barons and ecclesiastics recognized by the sovereign as having certain distinctive titles to land and jurisdiction, and parliamentary privileges appropriate to their military, economic and spiritual station. The modern idea of a peer as someone entitled to sit in the House of Lords records the only significant privilege remaining to those who bear titles of *nobility in their own right (although it seems that a peer may still demand 'trial by his peers').

The issue of the legitimacy of a second chamber of peers is frequently raised in modern UK politics. The House of Lords was abolished during the interregnum, but restored with the return of the monarchy, its legislative and administrative necessity being at the time indisputable. Its present composition – including life peers, law lords and others appointed expressly for judicial, administrative or political reasons – reflects in part the convention that its function as a legislative body should be separated as far as possible from its function as a court of law, and that it must be so constituted as to reflect *opinions current within the nation as a whole.

The arguments for and against a *hereditary principle determining entry into a second chamber are familiar and perhaps rather trivial. Reform of the House of Lords remains an outstanding political issue, however, and seems to be contemplated by all major parties. *J. S. Mill and Bagehot recommended life peers, some 100 years before their introduction, but apart from that little has been done about changing the constitution of the house: effort has been concentrated rather on reducing its powers, so that these are now very slight. One of the problems for radical reform lies in the unformulated and largely conventional nature of the UK constitution, which makes it impossible to predict with certainty what the consequences of radical surgery will be.

people. **1.** Definite. The designation *le peuple* or 'the people', as the collective noun denoting those subject to government, came into prominence at the French Revolution: it first stood for *menu* or *petit peuple,* and denoted small businessmen, grocers, artisans, workers, employees, salesmen, servants, day labourers, the peasantry, the proletariat and the indeterminate poor. The term rapidly became of great rhetorical significance. Arendt, for example, has held that 'the words *le peuple* are the key words for the understanding of the French Revolution, and their connotations were determined by those who were exposed to the spectacle of the people's sufferings which they themselves did not share' (*On Revolution,* 1963). On this view the term is saturated by the downward directed compassion of the privileged, towards *le peuple toujours malheureux,* as Robespierre described them. Since then, however, the term has become wider in its significance. 'The people' now designates all those subject to government within a jurisdiction, irrespective of status, class, or actual wealth and power: even happy people are people in the modern sense. Hence the modern usage recaptures the idea of the Roman *populus,* those subject to government, as opposed to the senate, those who govern. Such an idea is conveyed in the aim of 'goverment of the people, by the people, for the people', and in the modern conception of the *sovereignty of the people, according to which those who are governed also exert ultimate *control (and not just *influence) over those who govern them. The 'will of the people' is, it is commonly supposed, what democratic election aims to discover, while the *interests of the people provide a favoured criterion for the legitimacy of certain kinds of popular government – specifically in the *people's democracies. Here the term 'people' is used as part of the theory of *Marxism-Leninism, to denote 'the proletariat and its allies'.
2. Indefinite. When writers refer to 'a people', and discuss, for example, the rights, customs, and laws of that people, they intend to pick out a collective identity which is at least partly independent of political structure. A people has a history, and a continuity, which are not those of a state and, according to some *nationalist doctrines, it has a 'right' to that state which will express and conserve its existing identity. (*See* **Volksstaat*.) The idea presents difficulties similar to those presented by the idea of *race. However, it is clear that much modern controversy requires it, e.g. the dispute over the rights attributed to or claimed by, the Jewish, or the Palestinian, 'peoples'.

people's democracy. Term first used by Soviet Russian theorists after the Second World War, to denote the political and social organization of the socialist states of Eastern Europe and Asia, implying that ideologically such states were at a lower stage than the 'socialist democracy' of the USSR. In practice now used to denote the particular kind of supposed democracy, associated with rule by a tightly organized communist party, in which all consultation, representation and popular opinion achieves political expression through the machinery of the party, or not at all. This is democracy, since only the interests of the *people are consulted, and it is the people's, because it is their interest that counts.

perfect competition. A hypothetical condition important as an *ideal type in economic analysis. It is supposed that there are many buyers and sellers in the market, so that none individually can influence price, that there is no collusion between suppliers, and that both buyers and sellers are fully informed about prices throughout the market. Most actual competition deviates appreciably from this ideal, but it defines a model which, it is hoped, may be used to explain the actual behaviour of the actual markets that deviate from it. Some argue that it is absurd to explain actual competition in terms of perfect competition, without further theory as to how the two are related. Others, notably Friedman, argue that such objections are confused, since all scientific laws describe ideal situations, while generating explanations of a world to which the ideal only approximates.

permanent revolution. Expression coined by *Proudhon, and taken over by *Trotsky from Marx's 'Address to the Communist League' (1850), to denote the kind of revolution supposed necessary to the backward conditions of pre-revolutionary Russia. In the absence of a developed middle class, there must be direct confrontation between the lower and the ruling class, the peasantry and the proletariat being combined into a single force, the *people. Moreover, the defeat of capitalism would be possible only by the spread of revolution to other countries, in particular to Europe where the conditions for revolution were more mature. Permanent revolution would ensue, in which the proletariat everywhere would be engaged in the task of social destruction and reconstruction, in order to pass through all necessary stages on the road to communism.

permissiveness. The attitude of extreme *toleration towards all behaviour deemed to be *private – especially behaviour related to sexuality, human relations, forms of association, ceremony and leisure. The issue of how far permissiveness should be extended or prevented is identical with that of tolerance. The journalistic phrase 'permissive society' records the sense that a different form of social order may emerge from its widespread adoption. Hence arguments about the permission of individual actions may have to extend to the evaluation of a whole society.

person. One of the problems posed by *human nature is that of relating the idea of person to that of human being. In Latin the use of the term *persona* to refer to human beings was late: previously it had denoted a dramatic role (as it still does in critical usage), and then a legal person (see below). Philosophies of the relation between the person and the human being are various: *Locke distinguished them on the grounds of their incommensurate continuity, and thought of consciousness and responsibility as the defining features of the person. *Kant distinguished them on the grounds of the wholly different laws that determine the behaviour of each, the human being belonging to the 'empirical' world of nature, the person to the 'transcendental' world where laws of reason alone prevail. Kant's view is, in effect, an attempt to recast the legal concept as the idea of a distinct category of being.

1. In law. A person is an entity with rights and duties recognized in law. There are natural persons (including most human beings, but perhaps not confined to them), and also artificial or 'juristic' persons, such as *corporations, which have a legal identity quite distinct from the natural persons who may at any moment constitute them, and which may survive as a set of unoccupied *offices their rights and duties intact.

2. By extension, we can introduce the idea of the moral person, as the bearer of *moral* rights and duties. Such rights and duties are not the product of (although they may be confirmed in) a system of law, but have their basis in a system of moral values. They presumably include such natural rights as there may be. The metaphysical idea of the person introduced by Kant is meant to coincide with this idea, while also showing that persons are a distinct metaphysical kind of thing.

3. In politics it is clear that we are presented with many entities which, while not necessarily legal or moral persons, are analogous to them. They include the state (which is also an *international person in international law), many of its subject institutions, and even such socially defined entities as the *nation. These are thought to have rights and duties, although it is not always clear whether such rights and duties are legal or moral. The thought depends in part on the fact that states, nations and institutions contain natural persons as members. However, the membership may change completely, while the rights and duties remain (as when a state and its jurisdiction are repopulated by immigrants after a plague). The personal nature of the state is held by some (e.g. *Hegel) to go further, approximating indeed to the personal nature of human beings.

The construct of the legal person (sense 1.) has been of great interest, partly because of the suggestiveness of the idea that 'it is not the natural Ego which enters a court of law. It is a right-and-duty-bearing person, created by the law, which appears before the law' (Sir Ernest Barker). The idea of a *right as essential to that of the person creates many philosophical puzzles under sense 2. In particular, what is it about *human beings* that makes them moral persons? Kant attempted to identify a 'transcendental freedom' at the heart of human nature, and to show that all beings with that freedom must be treated as ends and not as means only. This can be seen as an attempt to show *why* humans are persons, and also to show just what is meant by a right. We have a sense that some human beings are not fully persons: a foetus, for example, or an unconscious relict made vegetable by a car-crash. Do we therefore think that they have *no* rights? That question is vital in considering issues of the *right to life. Again, animals are protected by the law: that is, we have legal duties towards them. Does that give them rights in law, and if so, are they too legal persons? More importantly, are they moral persons? Do they have moral rights, or are they merely the subject of moral duties? One reason for saying that they are not moral persons is that, while we have duties to them, they have, and can have, no duties to us. Hence it is misleading to speak of them as the bearers of rights. Such views are much contested, and derive ultimately from a theory that the distinguishing mark of the person is *rationality, or perhaps, more accurately, rational *agency.

persuasive definition. Phrase coined by the American philosopher C. L. Stevenson (*Ethics and Language,* 1949), to denote the attempt to attach the value of one thing to the reality of another, by defining the second as the 'true' or 'real' example of the first. Thus: 'National socialism is true democracy' (Hitler). Here an important argument is 'won' by defining the desired conclusion as true. (Likewise the persuasive definition of 'democracy' in *democratic centralism.)

***petit bourgeois*.** The class of small property owners, including those, such as small shopkeepers, with only indirect control over the means of production. The *petit bourgeois* form an imprecise class since, if the qualification is by *amount* of property held, then it seems to include members of society with quite disparate functions, such as teachers, brass-band leaders, smallholders and fortune tellers, while if the qualification is functional (for example, control over exchange and distribution) then it includes every level of wealth, and possibly overlaps with the *haute bourgeoisie* and the proletariat. It is the *petit bourgeois*, according to Marx, which suffers *proletarianization as capitalism advances towards its crisis. The term is used to denote a *spirit* in common to the small property owners in urban capitalism: the problem is to find a structural or functional explanation of that spirit, if there is one.

Petty, Sir William (1623–87). English political economist and polymath. *See* *political arithmetic.

phallocracy. *See* *paternalism.

phenomenology. Philosophical method due largely to the German philosopher Edmund Husserl (1859–1938) (although the term had been introduced by Hegel in a very different context). Phenomenology began as the theory of 'consciousness as such', studied in isolation from the material circumstances that surround it; the hope was to determine the nature and content of the various 'mental acts', such as belief, emotion, thought and desire. The term was later used to name a somewhat diffuse method in *sociology, which stays with the description of the perceived surface of social phenomena, believing that social consciousness represents the world in a unique way, and that until we understand the mode of 'representation' that is intrinsic to it, it is pointless to look beyond it to the material facts which provide its explanation, since we will not know what we are trying to explain. The principal exponent has been Alfred Schutz, but the language of phenomenology is frequently borrowed in the formulation of social and political theories. *See*, for example, *ontology.

philistinism. David's battle with the Philistine (literally Palestinian) Goliath became, during the early nineteenth century, a symbol of the battle between the sensibility of the poet and the blunt calculation of the man of affairs. Following a German student usage popularized by Robert Schumann and *Carlyle, *Arnold developed a influential theory of the philistine consciousness, designed to provide an explanation and justification of *culture and *humane education, both of which the philistine is held to lack. The philistine is contrasted with the barbarian, the first being a type of the *middle class, the second a type of the *nobility. The philistine lives in a world entirely conditioned by material and commonplace values. His consciousness is so taken up with the pursuit of measurable profit and loss that he cannot perceive the world in other terms. For him, therefore, the world of culture and enlightened human understanding is not merely valueless – it is imperceivable. The philistine cannot be argued with, since he must always fail to see his opponent's point of view. Arnold originally criticized *utilitarianism as a form of philistinism, because of its desire to find a measurable quantity for every human value; others have criticized *vulgar Marxism in similar terms (because of its emphasis on the material explanations of human thoughts and feelings, and its lack of perception of their content); as well as the attitudes engendered by capitalism and private property.

Phillips curve. The relationship between *inflation and *unemployment estimated in 1958 by the British economist A. W. H. Phillips (1914–75). The curve is so shaped that as unemployment falls the rate of inflation rises, so, it is argued, it is never possible to reduce both together. The empirical evidence adduced by Phillips was fairly persuasive. However, the relationship measured by Phillips appeared to have 'broken down' in the 1970s, when inflation and unemployment rose together (*see* *stagflation). Some, in particular the *monetarists, argue that there is no long-term relationship between inflation and unemployment; the latter being determined independently by market forces, the former depending upon the *money supply policy of the government. Opponents of this view point to the fact that attempts to reduce inflation by controlling the money supply have resulted in a rise in unemployment.

philosopher king. *See* *Plato.

philosophical radicals. Followers of *Bentham who attempted to translate *liberalism from philosophical premises into practical conclusions of law, economics and politics, and who formed, in the early nineteenth century in Britain, a kind of intellectual establishment, with some of the authority of the *left-liberal establishment formed (partly through the *Fabian society) in the twentieth century. They included *James Mill, *John Stuart Mill, *Ricardo, the jurisprudent John Austin, and the historian George Grote.

philosophy. Greek: the love of wisdom. A term with three main current meanings:

1. Any very general (but not necessarily systematic) set of beliefs in which an outlook on the world is founded, and from which the motives of human action may be drawn.

2. Traditionally (as in 'natural philosophy'), any form of systematic science. This usage has largely disappeared, but marks an important intellectual tradition which saw science and philosophy, in sense 3. below, as continuous.

3. Specifically the essentially contested subject-matter of philosophical writings, which treats all questions as abstractly as possible, and looks not for what is, but for what must be or might be. Philosophy examines the grounds of knowledge and the presuppositions of science (epistemology and method), together with the ultimate constitution of reality (metaphysics) and the essence of *value (ethics and aesthetics). Sometimes said to be the science of questions, philosophy asks for the ultimate meaning and justification of everything, including itself.

physiocrats. Group of French eighteenth-century economists, led by F. Quesnay (1694–1774), who argued against political interference in the 'natural' economic order, and thought that agriculture is the only source of wealth, and that it alone should be subject to taxation. They argued that the state should play no part in directing economic activity, other than that of upholding the natural order and safeguarding property. Their defence of *free trade and **laissez-faire* influenced *Adam Smith, while Quesnay himself made important beginnings in the science of *macroeconomics.

piecemeal engineering. An expression used by *Popper to denote his preferred manner of social reform: the replacement of worn-out parts of the mechanism, and the gradual sophistication of the whole, while keeping the machine in motion. The image, offensive to those who are opposed to mechanical models of political life (*see* *organicism), is not necessary to the thought that is expressed through it. (*See* *reform.)

piety. Latin: *pietas*. An important conception in Roman political thought, in Christian theology, and in certain (mainly conservative) theories of *political obligation. Piety contrasts with, and is also related to, justice, and in its basic meaning refers to the disposition to recognize and act upon obligations that are not based in contract nor in any other voluntary choice of the agent. Thus my duty to my parents (whom I neither chose nor chose to be related to, nor chose to be obliged towards) is one of piety, as is, on some views, my duty towards the state. (*See*, e.g., *Burke, *Hegel.) Piety is related to justice in that it involves a disposition to accord and to recognize obligations and rights; it is distinct from justice in that it is not concerned with the regulation of contract, exchange or distribution, or with the derivation of rights from free transactions. Hence it has often been thought to provide the model for theories of political obligation which deny the possibility of a *social contract, or of *tacit consent; and thus provides an important idea to anti-individualistic doctrines of *legitimacy.

Since, if God exists, we owe him submission not by consent but by our natural position as created beings, the term 'piety' was early appropriated to describe the condition of sincere religious belief, although the Roman virtue, celebrated in the character of Virgil's *pius Aeneas*, already had a religious tone to it, and this tone survives, detached from any religious doctrine, in Wordsworth's evocation of 'natural piety'. Conservatives who are attached to that idea are often accused of 'pious cant' – i.e. fragrant venerating words which fail to give grounds for any true obligation. They are also accused – because a defence of piety towards existing institutions may involve a neglect of *social justice – of a lack of 'pity', to use a later Christian derivation from the same Latin root.

planned economy. 1. A fully planned economy is one in which resources are allocated by a centralized administration, and not by the mechanism of *price. Decisions on outputs are taken by the administration, and the use of capital, land and labour is brought entirely within its supervision.

In the USSR the emphasis has been on planned heavy industry, while in China it has been on planned agriculture; the first seems to present fewer administrative problems than the second, and it is significant that almost all planned economies have had to concede some element of *market economy in the agricultural sector.

The arguments for and against a planned economy include those for and against *private property in the means of distribution. More important, since independent of general conceptions concerning ownership and control, is the argument which asserts the necessity of planning, in order to deal with shortages, social upheaval, underdevelopment, *unemployment and collapse of confidence in the mode of production. To the extent that those problems can be identified independently of questions of ownership, it is an empirical matter whether a planned economy is better equipped to solve them than the market mechanism that it is supposed to replace. Intuitively it would seem that it is; however, comparison between fully planned and market economies in postwar Europe has suggested that almost all of those problems have become worse in fully planned economies, and remained at least stable elsewhere. Some suggest that this is inevitable, the result of the insensitivity of the planned economy to *consumer preference, its susceptibility to large and devastating mistakes, and to large-scale corruption, and its lack of any natural tendency to *equilibrium. It is difficult to assess such arguments. It could be that the failures are in part due to dogmas of *common ownership which have led to the elimination of adequate incentives to produce – a fact (if it is a fact) which is independent of the existence of large-scale planning. However, it is also true that, while there is a theory of market equilibrium which has rough application, and which does suggest how equilibrium may come about without any deliberate striving towards it, there is no such theory for the planned economy, and this may be because it has no natural, but only a planned, equilibrium.

2. Partly planned economy. There has been increasing awareness during the twentieth century that, while markets have equilibrium conditions, it is not necessary that equilibrium will be reached or that the particular equilibrium reached will be compatible with other social and economic objectives, such as full employment and economic growth. Hence the emergence almost everywhere of partly planned economies, in which the government attempts to manage the flow of resources, while preserving as much of the price mechanism as is compatible with that aim. The partly planned economy is now the rule rather than the exception; for particular examples, *see* *interventionism, *Keynesianism, *mixed economy, *prices and incomes policy.

Plato (*c.* 428–348 BC). Greek philosopher, whose two most famous political works – the *Republic* and *The Laws* – differ markedly in tone and emphasis, the first enunciating an ideal state organized according to a concept of *justice, the second describing varieties of constitutional government, illustrated from Greek city-states, and endorsing a constitution not wholly unlike that of *Sparta. The first is based in the highest metaphysical speculation, written with extraordinary literary imagination and philosophical skill, and moves towards conclusions that have always impressed for their cogency, if not for their practicality. The second is dry, discursive, and tempered by a cynical awareness of human imperfection.

The *Republic:* Plato's opening question is 'What is justice?' He dismisses, in a famous argument, the suggestion that justice is 'the interest of the strongest' (i.e. that *rights are really *powers). The interest of the strongest varies from time to time and from place to place, while justice is always one thing; moreover the exercise of any power, however great, can always be judged on its merits, and it is precisely the function of the idea of justice to provide the grounds for that judgement. Justice is a human attribute, and consists in a certain harmony in the human soul. In order to analyse this harmony, Plato compares the human soul with its highest earthly manifestation, an ideal state or **polis*. This is a kind of super-person, constituted from the resolution of conflicting interests and aims. (The image here was to recur again, notably in *Hobbes and *Hegel.) The just state contains a social *division of labour, and encourages the *virtues proper to each kind of labour. These virtues are all particularized forms of justice, and serve to fit those who possess them to the station which is theirs. Thus justice is the supreme virtue, which enables the citizen to accept his station, and the duties pertaining to it.

There are three social classes: the rulers or guardians, the soldiers, and those engaged in production. These classes correspond to fundamental faculties in the human soul – the rational, which commands, the spirited, which attacks, and the appetitive, which desires. Wisdom controls the first, courage the second, and temperance the third. Justice is the disposition of all to harmonize under the rule of wisdom. Hence the just state is the state in which wise guardians ensure mediation and reconciliation among the classes beneath them. Plato's conception leads to the ideal of the philosopher king, who holds power with complete entitlement, because he knows things as they are and has sought and found the truth in the realm of ideas. This conception is often satirized, or linked with suspicion to certain forms of *Leninism, according to which a *vanguard party, being in possession of the 'truth of history', has unlimited entitlement to the exercise of power. It is doubtful, however, that Plato meant to draw attention to anything except an ideal of just government, from which all actual government, and all tyranny, must diverge.

In the course of elaborating his picture of the just state, Plato recommends abolition of the family, communal modes of ownership, censorship of art and letters, and propagation of the 'noble lie' which permits the multitude to acquiesce towards established power. (*See* *myth.) His discussion of the nature and place of education within the *polis* has been highly influential, along with his diagnosis of the various shortcomings of the actual forms of government in comparison with the ideal. He identifies these forms as timocracy, whose principle is honour, oligarchy, based in wealth, and democracy, which is the rule of licence. In his description of democracy he satirizes the Athenian constitution, and provides one of the first and most trenchant critiques of *liberalism as a political doctrine.

The Laws: this contains detailed constitutional recommendations. Plato advocates a kind of *mixed government, or limited oligarchy, such as was later defended by *Machiavelli. Under Plato's system, power is concentrated in the old, whose main duties lie in the conservation of political institutions, and the holding of offices. Plato moves away from the communistic principles of the *Republic,* allowing to each citizen a wife, a family, and private property, at least in so far as this is necessary to form a *household. But each individual is subordinate to the state, of which he is an organic part, and law, which is the dispensation of reason, penetrates into every aspect of life, regulating and controlling even domestic functions. Once again Plato lays great emphasis on education, and its role in preparing the citizen for political life, but he adds to his discussion many additional provisions. Again, Plato defends the view that the state has an interest in the private life and development of the individual, and needs to make complex legal provisions for every aspect of social existence. Hence his philosophy, in both *The Laws* and the *Republic,* has been held to have *totalitarian leanings.

play. The disposition to enjoy doing something with reason, but for no independent purpose: the essential human activity from which on one view (that of Schiller, *Letters on Aesthetic Education,* 1801) all aesthetic experience derives, and which forms an important underlying structure in *leisure. Not all leisure involves play, since play is essentially active, a recovery from over-activity not through rest but through a rival activity that lacks the purposive character of *work. While there are games with purposes, such as winning, scoring a goal, etc., these are not detachable from the game itself. Thus play has no overall purpose besides itself, even if it has a function, e.g. the function, in a child, of preparing for adult life. Schiller had in mind the importance of such purposeless activities (among which art is the highest) in the formation of character and civic virtue: it is this which frees the human being from the instrumentality of work, and gives sense to his *labour.

plebeian. In Rome, the general body of citizens, other than *patricians. Originally the plebeians were excluded from office, but gradually were accorded democratic rights, until in 287 BC a *Lex Hortensia* made plebiscites (measures passed by the council of plebeians) binding on the whole people.

plebiscite. Nowadays, any means for securing an expression of popular *opinion (for example, by a *referendum) for the purpose of political decision making. Originally, a measure passed by the council of the Roman *plebeians.

Plekhanov, Georgi Valentinovich (1856–1918). Russian literary critic, philosopher and social reformer; *see* *dialectical materialism, *mensheviks.

plural society. A *civil society in which several *societies coexist in a single *territory, interacting in a peaceful way, perhaps so as to become socially, politically and economically interdependent. The normal assumption is that such a society is formed through a liberal constitution, which builds some principle of tolerance and *minority rights into its procedure, so as to break down isolationist and separatist tendencies among citizens belonging to various racial, religious and ethnic groups.

pluralism. 1. The belief in the distribution of political power through several institutions which can limit one another's action, or through institutions none of which is *sovereign. Pluralism is the advocacy of a particular kind of *limited government.

2. The belief that the constitution of a state ought to make room for varieties of social customs, religious and moral beliefs, and habits of association, and that all political rights should be traced back to the constitution, and not to any social entity other than the state itself. In such circumstances the social and the political are as separate as can be, and uniform political institutions coexist with a *plural society.

3. Any view which, in opposition to *monism (and perhaps also to dualism), argues for a multiplicity of basic things, processes, concepts or explanations.

plutocracy. Rule by wealth – i.e any form of government in which institutions are so formed (whether or not by express design) that only a person of considerable wealth can hold office, either because of the expenses necessary to achieve, or those necessary to maintain it. Plutocracy should be distinguished from government in which holding office is the occasion for acquiring wealth. US democracy has a tendency to be plutocratic, whereas the non-plutocratic system of *democratic centralism seems to lead to vast acquisitions of wealth by important office-holders.

police. A recent invention, the paid police force dates from 1829 in the UK, although it was familiar before then in France, Russia and elsewhere. It rapidly grew in power and complexity, and is now considered to be necessary almost everywhere and by almost everyone. Its powers vary from place to place, and in accordance with the political structure; being the instrument to enforce the law, its nature is partly determined by the character of the law that it enforces. The following variables should be noted:

(i) extent, i.e. the quantity of policemen per head of population;

(ii) powers, e.g. powers of search, with or without warrant, of arrest, detention, interrogation and restraint;

(iii) provisions for redress; to what extent may the citizen (**de jure*), and to what

extent can he (*de facto*) obtain redress (e.g. through a controlling body, or a court of law) against a police officer who has acted **ultra vires?*
(iv) openness; to what extent can the police operate secretly, and in such a way as to penetrate the private life of the citizen? (*See* *police state);
(v) armaments; what weapons may the police use in enforcing the law, and when?

It is necessary to distinguish those systems which provide for constant active invigilation of the police, and those which merely provide redress for violations. Given the power which, on one plausible view, the police must possess in order to fulfil their function, it may be that legal provisions for redress are insufficient, in that they do not override the powers of intimidation which the police can bring to bear on any potential complainant. For this reason there have evolved, in many Western countries, commissions of inquiry which attempt to invigilate independently, and also to prevent abuses before they have become widespread. In English *common law, unlawful arrest and imprisonment have from early on been crimes, and since 1967 a distinction is made between 'arrestable offences' and 'non-arrestable offences' (where arrest requires a warrant), in order to curb police powers while replacing the traditional distinction between 'felonies' and 'misdemeanours'.

police state. A state in which political stability has come to be, or to seem to be, dependent upon police supervision of the ordinary citizen, and in which the police are given powers suitable to that. The police force is extended, and operates secretly, with powers to detain for interrogation without charge, to search, to interrupt correspondence and to tap telephone calls, and in general to keep detailed records on citizens accused of no crime, in order to enforce measures designed to extinguish all *opposition to the government and its institutions. The powers here may not be legally granted, but that is not normally an obstacle, since there is a presumption that there is no *rule of law in these circumstances, and the acquisition of large *de facto* powers by the police will simply be one aspect of a widespread defiance of *natural justice.

policy. Greek *politeia,* government. The general principles which guide the making of laws, administration, and executive acts of government in domestic and international affairs. Policy has to be distinguished from *doctrine – the system of beliefs and values which generate policy, and which purport to describe the ends to which policy is the means – and from *philosophy, the underlying justification given for doctrine and policy together. Political outlooks differ radically over whether policy is or should be a reflection of some underlying philosophical position, but most agree that policy should be consistent, reasonable and acceptable to those with power to oppose it. Some argue that it cannot have those qualities unless it also has the support of a (perhaps unexpressed) doctrine, which identifies, even if it does not justify, the ends that are pursued.

***polis*.** The Greek city-state, i.e. a system of independent *jurisdiction over a city. Usually the population was small enough for most citizens to be acquainted with those in power, and usually the economic life of the city involved trade with neighbours, supported by more or less extensive territories in the surrounding countryside and elsewhere. Western political thought began with the study of the *polis*, and its transference to the study of modern states and nations involves an extension of theory and concept that some have criticized as unwarranted. The *polis* was surrounded by other states whose citizens spoke the same language; it competed openly with its neighbours for territorial and economic privileges; its institutions were the object of observation, criticism and emulation from only twenty miles away; often it seemed to have a tribal character in which relations of kinship were as important as relations of law. Such features distinguish it, in part, from the modern *nation state;

nevertheless it is not at all clear that they render the observations of *Plato and *Aristotle inapplicable to modern constitutions.

politburo (sometimes: politbureau). The 'political bureau', i.e. ruling committee of the USSR *Communist Party, and the effective bearer of executive power within the state. Established as a subcommittee of the Party Central Committee in 1919 (members, Lenin, Trotsky, Stalin, Kamenev, Krestinsky) it gradually grew, until abolished in 1952, when it was replaced by a 25-member presidium. This has since contracted to ten members and is often called the Politburo from a sense that its nature and function are indistinguishable from those of the previous committee of that name. (Likewise for other ruling communist parties on the Soviet model.)

political. A term that is used in at least two important ways, first in the distinction between the political and the social, in which 'political' means, roughly, pertaining to the *state and its institutions; secondly in the distinction between political and other models of *government, for which *see* *politics.

political arithmetic. Term of seventeenth-century economics, made current by Sir William Petty, who used it to denote the whole science of political economy. Petty put economics on a new footing through attempting to give a mathematical analysis of the balance of trade, and to expose fallacies in the currently accepted forms of *mercantilism.

political economy. In contrast to domestic economy, political economy studies the economic behaviour and interest of the entire state. The term was introduced in 1613 by A. de Monchréstien, and became established in English usage with James Steuart's *Inquiry into the Principles of Political Economy,* 1767. It survives from subsequent eighteenth- and nineteenth-century usage, but retains, in the word 'political', an implication that factors other than the economic may be relevant to questions of political economy. *Welfare economics is an example of a theory of political economy, which attempts to build into its conception of 'welfare' some idea of the 'politically acceptable' which is not just reducible to the 'economically efficient'.

The term is current among *Marxists and thinkers of the *New Left, in order to denote systems of economics which take seriously the political implications of the science, and which (in contrast to 'mainstream economics') attempt to describe arrangements which are radically different from the capitalist market. Such thinkers often complain that *neo-classical economics relies on being able to isolate the economic from the political, and that this cannot be done. It seems that defenders of the *free market are also now returning to the use of the term.

political obligation. Roughly, the obligation of the *citizen towards the *state, or of the *subject towards the *sovereign. The expression is sometimes used to denote the reverse obligation from sovereign to subject, or the reciprocal obligation between the two.

The definition is rough since some theories of political obligation deny that there can be obligation towards a state, but admit the possibility of obligation towards *society; others deny even that, and argue that political obligation is held neither towards the state, nor towards society, nor towards any other abstraction or office, but towards each member of society individually. (The basis of this last view might be some sort of *individualism or, at any rate, a denial that abstract entities can be *persons.) The problem of political obligation – what it is and how it is justified – has come to be one of the central problems of political philosophy. The major theories can be classified thus:

(i) *Social contract theories, according to which the obligation arises from a contract, either with all members of society individually (*Locke), with society itself (*Rousseau), or with the sovereign (*Bodin).

(ii) Theories of consent which fall short

of contract – e.g. *tacit consent, whereby the citizen shows his acceptance of an arrangement by so acting under its protection as to bind himself in an obligation towards it. This is often presented as a part of (i), as by *Locke.

(iii) Theories of non-consensual obligation, which describe political obligation as arising independently from any choice of the subject, say from *piety (as in *Burke and *Hegel), or from the sovereign's right to *obedience.

(iv) Theories (of which (iii) provides some examples) which are framed in terms of conditions for *legitimacy, arguing that there is an obligation from the subject towards every legitimate sovereign. The *divine right of kings is such a doctrine, as is the very different doctrine of the *mandate, and similar theories emerging from the idea of *election.

(v) Negative theories. For example, the theory that the citizen is always under an obligation towards the state unless and until the state acts unjustly, or so as to negate some necessary human good, such as freedom. Most such theories can be rephrased as special theories of legitimacy, which argue that the concept of legitimacy is 'defeasible' – i.e. every government is legitimate unless. . . – upon which might follow a possibly open-ended series of conditions. It is possible that Aristotle's theory of political obligation was of this type, and that his reference to justice as the binding principle of the state was meant to indicate one among several unspecified conditions, the absence of which would suffice to take legitimacy away.

All the above theories are discussed elsewhere in this work.

political offence. The right of *extradition usually suffers exception in the case of 'political offences', although what counts as a political offence has not been defined authoritatively in UK or US law. Two criteria have been suggested:

(i) Do the facts alleged amount to a known crime, discounting political motivation?

(ii) Was there political motivation?

If the second criterion is used, then you can get away with quite a lot, perhaps even murder and terrorism. If the first criterion is used, then a suspect can be extradited only for those things recognized as crimes in the court before which he is brought. This will suffice to grant *sanctuary to victims of many oppressive laws, which make it a crime, say, to publish criticisms of the state, but not to an assassin or a terrorist. The UK courts tend to view as political any offence committed 'in connection with' a 'political disturbance', but the two apostrophized phrases indicate that this criterion is as vague in practice as the notion which it is used to define.

Why should there be this exclusion under extradition agreements? One plausible answer is that, without it, rights of sanctuary are ineffective. Another is that a foreign power may be in the course of being overthrown, and may attempt to make itself secure by inventing 'political crimes'. To return people wanted for such crimes is in effect to take sides in a political struggle which may result in a new regime offended by the fate of its supporters, and therefore disposed to regard with hostility those who had surrendered them. But many other considerations are relevant; it is, for example, important for extradition agreements to avoid what might amount to a declaration of war through judicial action.

political realism. *See* *realism.

political thought. This may mean any one of four things:

1. Political thought, in the sense of the title of this dictionary: thoughts, theories and values which motivate *policy, and political behaviour. Political thought includes the theories through which people attempt to explain each other's political behaviour, the values by which they judge it, and the mechanisms (such as law) whereby they attempt to control it.

2. Political theory. The theory of political institutions. This includes the theories of the state, of law, of representation and election. It is a comparative and explanatory science, exemplified in works of constitutional history and analysis.

3. Political philosophy. This seeks the most general answers to the most general questions of method and justification raised by the concepts and theories employed in 1. and 2. Thus the concept of justice, which may form a part of ordinary political thought, may also be a subject of philosophical analysis, with a view to determining its grounds.

4. Political science. An academic discipline which includes 2. and 3. along with *political economy, and perhaps also *sociology. It involves a developing synthesis of many contrasting disciplines, and incorporates all studies which have politically significant thought and action as their subject-matter. It is probably too wide and too ambitious to be an independent subject with a method of its own, and remains influential only as a projected unity rather than as an actual one.

politicization. To 'politicize' is to transform an activity that seemed to have no political connotations into one that is consciously bent towards political ends. Thus Walter Benjamin recommended that, in the interests of revolution, it is necessary to 'politicize art', meaning that the façade of impassive contemplation presented by art must be broken down, and its real potential as an agent of political transformation revealed.

politics. Sometimes used as a plural noun, sometimes and now more usually as a singular, 'politics' began its career in English as a term of abuse for the activities of those engaged in *faction, and gradually became respectable as modern forms of *representation evolved. Definitions are many and varied, ranging from the conciliatory ('the art of the possible' – Lord Butler), through the cynical ('the art of governing mankind through deceiving them' – Isaac D'Israeli), to the wilfully assertive ('the art of carrying out the life struggle of a nation for its earthly existence' – Hitler). As now used 'politics' denotes a kind of activity associated with *government, but there are conflicting views as to what this activity amounts to. Some follow the English legal theorist Sir John Fortescue in his praise of the English constitution (*De Laudibus Legum Angliae,* c. 1470), and distinguish political from regal forms of government, both involving the imposition of law, but the former distinguished by the attempt to gain consent for that law through representation and *conciliation. Others, similarly motivated, frame their definition in terms offered by *Aristotle, and see politics as the art of controlling and reconciling the diverse *interests* within a state. This influence can be seen in the following definition: 'Politics . . .can be simply defined as the activity by which differing interests within a given unit of rule are conciliated by giving them a share in power in proportion to their importance to the welfare and survival of the whole community. And. . .a political system is that type of government where politics proves successful in ensuring reasonable stability and order' (Bernard Crick: *In Defence of Politics,* 1962).

Such definitions are appealing, since they emphasize the centrality of balance and conciliation to the art of politics; however, in the looser sense exemplified in this dictionary there are activities and doctrines called 'political' which have no ability to tolerate *opposition, and a rooted antagonism to all conciliatory gestures – e.g. *democratic centralism *Leninism, **Gleichschaltung*. Moreover the definition is far from clear, even if we can take for granted some understanding of the terms (such as 'interests', 'rule', 'welfare' and 'community') that are employed in it. What of a share in power that is *not* according to the welfare of the whole? What if conciliation is accomplished by some other means than power-sharing? What kind of power is in question? (If we say, 'political power' then we are beginning to run in a circle.) Nevertheless, the idea of politics as involving the recognition and conciliation of opposing interests is now widely accepted. Some draw the conclusion that politics is therefore opposed to *sovereignty, although this is clearly wrong, since no conciliation can be effected between diverse interests without there being an entity more authoritative than both, even if that entity is nothing other than the contract or agreement that they will live in harmony. Out of that contract sovereignty is automatically born. More plausibly, sovereignty is its necessary precondition, and the condition of its enforcement.

polycentrism. The splitting of a political organization into independent centres of power. Used to describe developments in world communism after the twentieth congress of the USSR Communist Party in 1956. The term was popularized by the Italian communist leader P. Togliatti, and now refers to the general emergence of independent communist parties, a process which began with the dispute between the USSR and Yugoslavia, continued in the breach between Soviet and Chinese political practice and interests, and is exemplified in the various attempts by Western European communist parties to find an identity independent of the USSR (*see* *Eurocommunism), and by Eastern European communist parties to assert forms of national communism more appropriate to local conditions than those imposed on them by Stalin.

poor laws. The 'old poor law', created by the Poor Relief Act 1601, charged the relief of the poor to every parish, which had to provide work and to tax all residents in order to provide both the work and the relief that was earned by it. Parishes began to combine into poor law unions so as to administer this charge, and to appoint elected boards of guardians. The 'new poor law' of 1834 set up a central board of Poor Law Commisioners, and from then on social welfare was considered in the UK to be a national and not just a local concern. This can be seen as in part a response towards the increased mobility of labour, and the rapidity with which towns were growing and declining. Legislation culminated in the creation of the *welfare state during the twentieth century, and the end of the requirement that poor relief would be given only to those who suffered what was increasingly regarded as the ignominy of the 'workhouse'. 'Unemployment benefit' is now regarded as a right.

Popper, Sir Karl Raimund (b. 1902). Viennese-born philosopher whose study of scientific method has been extremely influential, both in the philosophy of science, and (because of his own application of it to political theory) in political thought and practice. Popper argues that all serious science is 'hypothetico-deductive', that is, it involves, not induction from accumulated instances, but rather the postulation of a hypothesis from which deductions are made. Since the hypothesis is universal, it can be confirmed by no finite number of instances; but it can be disconfirmed by one, and that is the clue to scientific method, which proceeds by 'conjecture and refutation' – i.e. the postulation of a hypothesis and the attempt to refute it through finding a counter-example.

Pseudo-science is recognizable, therefore, by the fact that either it is unfalsifiable, or else it shuns falsification, by the constant adoption of qualifications so as to accommodate every conceivable fact. One example of such pseudo-science is the Ptolemaic system of 'epicycles', which have no other rationale than to avoid empirical disproof of the Ptolemaic cosmology. Another example is the Marxian theory of history, which makes only wrong predictions, and yet which constantly amends itself so as never to regard itself as refuted in its fundamental tenets. That is an example of *historicism – the attempt to subsume all of history under a single principle which 'explains' everything. In *The Poverty of Historicism,* 1957, Popper sets out to refute all forms of historicism on two grounds, the first being that the growth of knowledge itself exerts an influence on the course of history, hence neither the growth of knowledge nor its general effects can be predicted, since to predict knowledge is already to possess it. The second ground is that social science is of such a nature that it cannot generate laws of total social development, but only laws for fragmented and isolated social units. From this 'methodological individualism' Popper draws the conclusion that there is no rational approach to social problems which can give grounds for total change, since to attempt such change is necessarily to act on assumptions about the whole of things, i.e. to act blindly. The only kind of social reform that can be rationally contemplated is *piecemeal engineering. In the earlier *The Open Society and its Enemies*, 1945, Popper had attacked three historicist views – those of *Plato, *Hegel and *Marx – and tried to show that the search for total explanations of society was in each case combined with visions of government that were totalitarian in their aims and principles. He suggests that the only scientifically acceptable answer to the question, Who should rule? is to reject it, and to ask instead, How can institutions be devised that will minimize the risk of bad rulers?, a question to which Marxism, for example, has never addressed itself. (*See also* *holism, *open society, *individualism).

populism. The populist (in Russian, *narodnik, where it is associated with a specific political movement) is one who wishes to solve all political problems by appealing to the 'will of the people', believing the people to have instincts and reactions which, if properly tapped, will be alone sufficient to provide guidance and authority to the statesman. The narodniks believed the people to have some special role in the process of social evolution; the US 'Populist Party' (founded 1891) thought that the people required support from the government, in their attempt to maintain the American tradition of small private enterprise and self-sufficient farming. English conservatives often look for the 'roots' of their doctrine in the spirit of a people thought to be deeply and inarticulately loyal to its main provisions. (A view which was entertained and in part endorsed by *Coleridge and by *Carlyle.)

pornography. The definition of this term is much contested. A first shot might be pornography is the production of an *obscenity which provides a fantasy object for *sexual desire. That definition can be extended to any object which provides a gratification for fantasy and which shows the structural characteristic of obscenity (i.e. which represents the human body as voided of human personality). Thus there can be, in an extended sense, a pornography of eating, of violence, and so on.

The dispute over the value of pornography concerns two concepts which are instruments of confusion: that of obscenity, and that of fantasy. Given the definition offered of obscenity, it would seem that no one would think that a sexual impulse that sought to gratify itself through obscene representations could ever be a vehicle of personal feeling; and if it is true that sexual impulses ought to be vehicles of personal feeling, then pornography can reasonably be said to minister to debased desires. In addition it is sometimes said that fantasy is in itself a species of corruption, in that it permits the indulgence of impulses that would otherwise be inhibited, and so nurtures what we wish to suppress. One reply is that the fantasy gratification of a desire acts as a safety-valve for feelings which might otherwise be expressed in more damaging ways. Those two thoughts about fantasy are seldom attached to any theory of human nature which would enable us to determine which is true.

The problem of pornography and the law is in part independent. Those who see the law as a protective device, designed to safeguard the innocent from *harm, but to permit to the guilty whatever perversions constitute their delight, may think that the law should content itself merely to forbid the open sale of pornography. One of the problems, even for that view, lies in the peculiar nature of the 'offensiveness' of pornography: to discover such things by accident may have a devastating effect, and the mere knowledge that it is possible to obtain pornography proves to be an irritant to the morally susceptible. To some extent the confused debates over this issue reflect the confusions in the criterion of harm. However there is a real question, in the case of sexuality, as to where the boundary between the private and the public might lie. (*See* *law and morality, *sex.)

positive discrimination. Synonymous with *reverse discrimination.

positive economics. 1. Economics of the actual, rather than the ideal: economics which takes its scientific pretensions seriously, and attempts to establish hypotheses that might be refuted by empirical evidence. (*See* *Popper.)
2. Alternatively, economics which attempts to detach itself from all statements of a *normative kind, on the grounds that the factual and the normative are distinct, and that science concerns itself only with facts, and never with *values.

positive law. Law 'posited', or laid down, by a particular body of *conventions; for example, through the will of a *sovereign, through the enactments of a *legislature (*see* *statute), or through the accumulation of customary rights. Positive law is distinguished from *natural law, being entirely the product of human design. Whether it can be justified by referring to some independent standard is one of the fundamental questions of political thought – whether, for example, there is an independent standard of *justice (which is the doctrine of natural law), or whether the only standard is utility.

positivism. 1. The philosophical and political doctrine propagated by *Saint-Simon and extended by *Comte, who gave it reputation. 'Positive' here means that which really exists and can be observed, as opposed to the dubious fancies of theology and metaphysics. Comte advocated a scientific sociology, and attempted to show that the *progress which attaches to scientific thought can be, and perhaps has been, transferred to the human condition generally. By extending scientific knowledge, the problem of providing for human needs in this life can be solved without referring to another, hence the worship of humanity was to replace the worship of God.
2. Certain schools of sociology, notably those influenced by *Durkheim, which concern themselves with questions of method, and regard their subject-matter as the realm of *social facts.
3. 'Positive science', i.e. the exhortation to study facts rather than values, and to eliminate all statements of a *normative character from scientific explanations. (*See* *positive economics.)
4. Logical positivism. The philosophy associated with the 'Vienna circle' of the 1920s and 30s, and influenced in England and America by Bertrand Russell and the early Wittgenstein. Logical positivism was based on the 'verification principle', according to which the meaning of every sentence is completely determined by its method of verification and by nothing else. Unverifiable propositions – such as those of theology and metaphysics – are meaningless. Logical positivism has had little effect on political philosophy, except indirectly through the work of *Popper (who changed 'verification' to 'falsification' in his criterion for scientific method), and through the ethos of resolute scepticism and hard-headed anti-mysticism which it briefly inspired. Sometimes a particular interpretation of, e.g., *liberalism or *historical materialism, is denounced as 'positivist', the intention being to condemn a narrowness of outlook concerning what can, and what cannot, meaningfully be said.
5. Legal positivism. The view of law which advocates the study of actual legal systems, and eschews the search for independent justifications in terms of *natural law: i.e. the view which assumes that all law is *positive law. The leading positivists are John Austin (1790–1859), who defined law as a command of the sovereign, expressing his wish, and backed by sanctions, and *Kelsen, who saw all law as a system of directives to apply coercion in accordance with a basic constitutional principle, or *Grundnorm*. Such theories see law as a system of rules backed by coercion, which do not owe their status as law to any independent

criterion, such as that supposedly provided by natural law. Both Austin's and Kelsen's theories have difficulty, e.g. in accounting for the law of *contract or *trust (*see* *equity), but both have been highly influential, the first in particular on *Bentham and the *utilitarians. Modern positivists attempt to preserve the spirit of such theories, while giving more sophisticated accounts of the process whereby a decision is 'validated as law'.

possession. What is it to possess something? I possess many things: my mind and talents; my *labour power, and certain things that I have produced or acquired through exerting that power; a house, a garden, a set of books. Do I possess all these in the same sense? *Locke argued that there is a *natural right of property which emerges from 'mixing my labour' with an object. This doctrine seems to give an affirmative answer, to say that the 'property' that I have in any object is like the property that I have in my labour power, which is in turn like the property that I have in my own limbs and talents. This transition from a 'natural' relation to a relation of *right has proved fascinating, but also unsatisfactory, to later thinkers. Despite Locke's argument, the concept of possession, and its role in the notion of *private property, remains obscure.

In *land law attempts have been made to define possession more precisely, with interesting political consequences. Possession seems to mean either *de facto* *control over some object or territory, or such control backed also by the sanction of the law (= legal possession). It is normal to consider legal possession to require two things: physical control, and an intention to exert it (an *animus possidendi*). The first element may be absent, as when a legal owner of property temporarily turns his back on it, and the law protects his right. But if the second element disappears, so too does the possession. This is what establishes the squatter's right to land. If John has resided at a place for some time without recognizing Alfred's right to it, and if Alfred has not asserted that right in any way, then, after a certain time (*see* *limitation) the law will step in to protect (or rather, to create) John's right to remain, thus conferring on him 'possessory title'.

Poujadism. Attitudes associated with a political movement, the 'Union for the Defence of Small Shopkeepers and Artisans', founded in France in 1954, by Pierre Poujade (b. 1920), and sometimes thought to be the quintessence of **petit bourgeois* politics: hostility to *taxation, to state ownership of industry, and to most forms of large-scale development and modernization. There were also elements of anti-semitism, Gaullism, and even fascism, among the Poujadists at the 1955 election.

poverty. An idea that is intuitively clear, but which is difficult to define except as the polar opposite of *wealth. A polar definition is unsatisfactory since, below a certain point, the difference between wealth and poverty is not just one of degree, but one of kind. Hence various analysts since the late nineteenth century have attempted to draw the 'poverty line' – the point below which *true* (non-relative) poverty exists. Charles Booth, in *The Poverty of the People,* 1899, took the average expenditure of families on food, rent and clothes and defined the poor as those with an income just equal to providing this average (but no more), and the very poor as those with less. Such ways of drawing the poverty line have since been attacked, in particular because they are insensitive to the different requirements and budgets that emerge in the state of poverty. Nevertheless poverty lines are still drawn for official purposes and used to define the 'poverty gap', which is the amount by which the aggregate income of the poor falls below what the line requires.

Two ideas seem important: first, that, in the polar sense, poverty consists in a relative absence of choice; i.e. the poor man is always circumscribed in his activity in ways which are overcome by wealth. Secondly, that the 'transition from quantity to quality' seems to occur when the inability to obtain what is desired becomes an inability to obtain what is needed. (*See* *need.) Hence the poverty line corresponds to the point below which freedom of choice is so curtailed that a person cannot obtain what he needs. The difficulty in defining it is a result of the difficulty inherent in the concept of need: what a man needs for animal subsistence is not what he needs for effective survival as a social being; and what he needs as a social being may not suffice for his thriving as a rational animal. (E.g. does he *need* a family? Does he *need* education?) Needs are controversial, partly because of disagreements over *human nature, partly because of the social relativity of that nature.

Some distinguish poverty from pauperism, which is the state in which a person has less than he needs for survival, and so is unable to maintain himself at all without outside assistance. Pauperism (unlike poverty) has often been regarded not only as a misfortune, but as somehow intrinsically shameful – an idea variously rationalized in terms of *caste, *providence, idleness, but in all of its forms imposing on the pauper a sense of himself as falling not merely materially, but also morally, below a *norm. At the same time, traditional moralities have tended to argue that some (relative) poverty is not only compatible with virtue, but perhaps more naturally suited to it, and more naturally productive of happiness, than the extremes of wealth.

power. The ability to achieve whatever effect is desired, whether or not in the face of opposition. Power is a matter of degree; it can be conferred, delegated, shared and limited. It may be based in *consent or in *coercion. The power of a charismatic leader may be based in consent, while that of a tyrant usually is not; the power of the first may yet be very much greater than that of the second. Power may be exercised through *influence, or through *control (although it should be noted that, for no very good reason, political scientists often distinguish power from influence, thus restricting the term 'power' to relations that are exerted through control).

Because power (unlike *authority, *legitimacy and *right) is an indisputable fact, and easily understood as such, and because it seldom exists without also being exercised, there have arisen various *power theories of politics, which see power as the fundamental substance of which politics is the form. On these views, the important feature of every institution lies in its transformation, limitation and rationalization of power.

Power may be economic: ability to influence or control the means of production; it may be political: ability to influence or control the institutions through which law is made or applied; it may be personal: ability to exert influence and control over people for whatever reason. Some theories argue that all political power is to be explained in terms of economic power (e.g. the common forms of *Marxism). Others regard all forms of power as different forms of a single thing, none of which is more basic to the explanation of human society than any other.

One of the important questions in political thought concerns the relation of power to authority. We distinguish: power with authority; power with the common belief in its authority; and 'naked power', such as that exerted by a lawless gang. Politics can be seen as the attempt to translate the third into the second: to eliminate from public life all powers that do not have the sanction of a public acceptance of their authority. Thus, even when there is no 'political process' – no way in which new powers emerge into the public forum and seek the authority that is there bestowed – there may still be a process of *legitimation, whereby the naked power of the ruler attempts to represent itself as sanctioned by right. Naked power is weaker than the same power publicly accepted, and so this process can still be seen as a pursuit of power. Only if we believe that there really is an objective authority to be gained, can we see the pursuit of authority as something other than the pursuit of power.

The above sense of 'power' must be distinguished from the legal sense, where it denotes, not **de facto* ability, but **de jure* permission. The 'powers' conferred by law are permissions to do things without legal sanction. An agent who exercises such powers can be legally restrained only from exercising them **ultra vires* (i.e. beyond the powers granted), in which case he is not exercising them.

power élite. Phrase coined by the American sociologist C. Wright Mills, to denote those who wield *power within the ruling institutions of modern society, and who act, sometimes collusively, and in any case from common interests, to preserve and enhance that power. An *élite is not, or not necessarily, a *class, so that this idea of *hegemony must be distinguished from Marxian theories, such as that of *Gramsci. (*See* *class, *status.)

power politics. German: *Machtpolitik.* The conducting of politics (including domestic politics) entirely as though there were no factor involved besides power, so that groups without power are not considered, and those with power considered only to the extent that they possess it. This *value-free approach to politics is sometimes also called 'political realism', or **Realpolitik,* and purports to see the world of men as it is, and not as men think it to be. However, power politics actually changes the nature of politics, overriding what are often considered to be *rights; this suggests that realism is not the same as power politics, since the first may recognize rights (to the extent that it accords to them real existence), while the second recognizes only the powers that would enforce rights, and not the rights themselves. (*See* *rights and powers.)

power theories of politics. Theories of political practice and institutions which attempt to describe and to explain those things in terms of the existence, transfer, development and division of *power, as opposed to the *rights theories of politics, which see their subject matter in terms of *rights. (*See* *rights and powers.) Among power theories the theory of *sovereignty offered by *Machiavelli in *The Prince* is perhaps the most striking, in that it regards the central fact of politics as the concentration and maintenance of supreme *control over all people within a certain territory, and evaluates all institutions as means to this end. Justice and law are admitted into the theory only because men's disposition to believe in those things is itself one of the powers that have to be subsumed by the sovereign. A very different, but in some ways comparable, theory is the *historical materialism of *Marx and *Engels, which identifies two major powers: *productive forces (a dynamic power), and the various kinds of control that can be exerted over them through *production relations, this control being vested differently in different *classes. All social and political powers are explained in terms of their functional relation to those basic powers. *Hobbes's theory of sovereignty is a peculiar hybrid, but contains elements of a power theory.

pragmatism. 1. A philosophical theory associated with the names of the American philosophers C. S. Peirce (1839–1914), William James (1842–1910), and John *Dewey, which identifies the meaning and justification of beliefs through the practical results of holding them. Pragmatism can be seen as a form of *empiricism which tries to make due allowance for the fact that the subject of knowledge is not just a recipient of sensation, but also an active inquirer. Even 'truth' is subordinate to practice for James, since the only credentials of true belief are that, in holding it and acting from it, we find ourselves more successful than we otherwise might have been. Pragmatism has been enormously influential, both on American philosophy and on American political science. It seems to give a grounding to concepts not only of science, but also of law and social theory. By explaining political thought in terms of its survival value, it also justifies political thought as a beneficial feature of the human condition.

2. More generally used as a name for any approach that emphasizes what can be done in the actual world rather than what ought to be done in an ideal world.

praxis. Derived from the Greek for action, the term *praxis* is used by Aristotle to denote practical reasoning, as opposed to *theoria,* or theoretical reasoning. Through *Hegel's use of the term, and the occasional reference in *Marx, 'praxis' came to denote the general capacity to act so that one's projects and beliefs are in harmony with the world represented through them, together with a presumption that belief and action are not so sharply separable as *empiricist theories of knowledge would require them to be. The term is much used in *neo-Marxism, (which contains a 'praxis school'), and means something like this: praxis is activity that removes the necessity for *false consciousness. It sustains itself without *ideology, since it is directed to the essential nature of social reality. At a time of incipient revolution, the only true praxis is 'revolutionary praxis'. All other forms of activity falsify the world, and hide from the participant his true social nature. Through praxis we not only overcome false consciousness, but also manoeuvre ourselves into a position from which we can assess the claims of Marxism and perceive that they are true. (Cf. *faith.)

precedent. In law the 'doctrine of precedent' holds that in all judicial proceedings, previous decisions by superior courts are binding. More precisely, each such decision contains a principle (*ratio decidendi,* i.e. reason for deciding) which, if *applicable* to the present case, must be *applied* in the present case. The principle can be revoked, but not by any court inferior to the one that first applied it. In the US, where the doctrine of precedent is far less influential than it is in the UK, principles can be revoked by the courts that first applied them. In the UK they can be revoked only by the superior court, although the embarrassment that this causes in the highest court has led to the House of Lords on several occasions refusing to be bound by its own decisions.

The *ratio decidendi* of a precedent may not be easy to discover, and it is part of the judicial function in the lower court to interpret the judgement of the higher so as to bring the *ratio* to light. Alternatively, the judge of the lower court may leave the *ratio* unformulated, and decide either that the decision in the previous case does apply to the present case, or that it does not. In the latter judgement, known as 'distinguishing a case', the judge must point to material differences between the present case and the previous one and argue that the differences are relevant, so that the previous decision does not bind him. The judge can do this without formulating the *ratio decidendi* of the preceding case; it suffices to show that the differences are so great that the *ratio,* whatever it was, does not apply.

The doctrine of precedent raises in a vivid form the question of judicial *legislation. The older theory in English law was that, in following precedents, judges were simply declaring the law that had always existed in custom and in previous decisions; but, this custom being the custom of judges, it must surely be the case that judges were agents in creating it. So such a theory is not a theory at all – it gives us no answer to the question of where law comes from when cases are distinguished and precedents made. The reasoning involved in following a precedent is in fact extremely complex, and it is very hard to present clear answers to philosophical questions as to its nature. What happens, for example, when a superior court *overrules* a precedent? Does it change the law, or does it rather record the conviction that the law had been wrongly understood? If the higher court changes the law, then it seems that it violates the *sovereignty of Parliament and the *separation of powers. If it declares that the law had been misinterpreted, then it says in effect that all previous cases under the precedent were wrongly decided, which seems hardly consistent with the fact that these cases can (as a rule) no longer be retried.

predestination. The divine decree under which certain persons are inexorably guided to eternal salvation, and perhaps others to damnation. The doctrine of predestination is a cornerstone of *Calvinist theology, according to which salvation is offered to the elect alone. Some have accepted predestination and sought to reconcile it with the view that the others nevertheless have a chance. (Such seems to have been *Augustine's position.) Secular forms of the doctrine exist, as in the *Nazi idea that the Aryan race was predestined to world-domination, and as in certain *vulgar Marxist views to the effect that history is *on the side of* the proletariat. In all its forms the doctrine may lead to *antinomianism and, according to *Weber, a disorderliness of such a deep-seated kind that a new kind of self-discipline and public regimentation may come in the place of normal moral sanctions.

prediction/decision. A prediction is a statement about the future which expresses a belief, and which is founded (if at all) in evidence for its truth. A decision is also a statement about the future, but it expresses an intention, and is founded (if at all) not in evidence but in reasons for action. The distinction between the two is fundamental to the understanding of practical reason, and has exercised the ingenuity of several recent philosophers. On one account, *alienation is the state of mind which ensues from the renunciation of intention in favour of prediction, even in those spheres where the self and its *agency might be supposed to hold sway.

Decisions involve responsibility towards the future, whereas predictions do not. Hence some say that *historicist doctrines, which subsume all politics within a vision of the inevitable course of history, leave no room for responsible action. The view is dubious, but some milder version of it may nevertheless be correct.

preference. A concept of increasing importance in both economics and political theory, and now replacing, for many theoretical purposes, older ideas of *utility, both because preferences can be associated with direct empirical tests (*see* *revealed preference), and because preferences may be treated mathematically in ways which do not raise unanswerable problems of measurement. For the purposes of mathematical treatment, a preference is an ordering of alternatives: when *a* is not preferred to *b* and *b* not preferred to *a* the choice between them is said to be indifferent. The relation between preference and indifference has been important in the adoption of the *indifference curve, as a theoretical device in the explanation, e.g., of prices.

A 'preference ordering' may be of three or more alternatives (when *a* is preferred to *b*, and *b* to *c*, etc.). This has led to important questions concerning the consistency of preferences. If preference is a transitive relation (i.e. if it follows from the fact that John prefers *a* to *b* and *b* to *c* that he prefers *a* to *c*), then the following preference ordering is inconsistent: *a* preferred to *b*, *b* to *c* and *c* to *a*. *Social choice theories explore problems posed by the search for a 'social preference ordering' based on individual preference orderings (*see* *social welfare function). They often attempt to show that, under certain conditions, no such ordering can be guaranteed to be consistent. (*See* *voting paradox, and cf. *Arrow's theorem, *Paretian liberal.)

Other problems of preference ordering can present themselves, for example, in the matter of preferences that concern different times. Given limited jam, preference for jam today over jam tomorrow is inconsistent with preference for jam tomorrow. The synthesis of preference theory and statistical analysis of *risk and uncertainty is the basis of *decision theory.

preference ordering. *See* *preference, *social choice.

prejudice. Belief without reasoned support, which serves as a premise for practical reasoning, and which is a constituent part of some ***Weltanschauung* resistant to refutation. Prejudice is held to be a vice in those who are capable of thinking, but some conservatives (e.g. *Burke) hold it to be a virtue in those who are not. Prejudice is a fixity of unreasoned belief, while *bigotry is a fixity of unreasoned *values; both contrast with *dogmatism, which is the tendency to translate both belief and value into articulate form, and to regard them as thereby conclusively established. Dogmatic beliefs are beyond argument because they have been put beyond argument; prejudices are beyond argument because they do not recognize that argument is possible.

prerogative. The pre-eminence which the sovereign retains in the UK constitution, and which other *heads of state retain elsewhere, consisting in certain rights of action allowed to no one else in law. In the UK the royal prerogative is created and governed by *common law, in certain instances modified by statute; it includes not only immunities from prosecution but also powers to initiate actions, exercised usually with the advice of ministers or of the courts. Among these actions the conduct of foreign affairs is particularly important. The powers exercised through the courts include the prerogative writs, such as ***habeas corpus*; it has been this common law doctrine of royal prerogative that has enabled the courts to assert some of the basic *freedoms associated with the English constitution. The royal prerogative has been defined and limited several times, notably in Magna Carta 1215, the Petition of Right 1628, the Bill of Rights 1689, and the Act of Settlement 1700.

prescriptive right. A right created by lapse of time. In *Roman law, and in English and US law, such rights tend to be most prominent in the case of *land law, occupation of land continuously and peaceably from time immemorial being sufficient to warrant the presumption that such occupation is an indefeasible right. ('From time immemorial', in English law, means 'from time whereof the memory of man runneth not to the contrary' which, curiously, means from the beginning of the reign of Richard I; twenty years being sufficient to presume that such occupation has obtained.)

It is sometimes argued that the idea of a prescriptive right is necessary if a law of *private property in land is to be applicable (and perhaps the same goes for a law of private property as such). For defenders of the *hereditary principle this question is neither more nor less difficult than the question of *legitimacy; for liberal theories of property which find their paradigm in just acquisition followed by contractual exchange, such an idea presents special difficulties. (Cf. *primitive accumulation, for the equivalent in relation to *capital of this observation concerning *land.)

president. The name usually given to a *head of state in a *republic. The powers of the president vary from constitution to constitution: they may be minimal, as when the president is a figure of ceremonial significance only; or they may be absolute, as when he appoints himself president by virtue of his existing powers as leader of a party which has taken control of the state. The most interesting intellectual invention which bears this name is the US Presidency, constructed in part on principles laid down by *Montesquieu. The President is not only ceremonial and titular head of state, but also the chief *executive (i.e. fount of the executive power) and leader of the armed forces.

pressure group. An *interest group which has sufficient *influence on central government to be able to put pressure on behalf of its interests. Examples include the Confederation of British Industry, which tries to impress on the UK government the interests of the managerial class, and the Trades Union Congress, which does the same for workers. On one view the activity of *politics is facilitated by pressure groups; on another view it is hindered by them. The first view sees conciliation as the main aim of government, the second prefers to see government in terms of the exercise, and subsequent legitimation, of power. A pressure group that is consulted regularly, and which has enduring institutions and a body of legislation to protect its aims, has ceased to be a pressure group, and has become instead part of the *establishment. Such is possibly the case with the Trades Union Congress. Not all interest groups are pressure groups: the difference is one both of intention and of power.

price. The rate at which an item exchanges against *money. (*See also* *exchange-value.) More generally, the rate of exchange between any two goods. Price theory attempts to explain the prices at which goods exchange, and it usually confines itself to the study of price in *equilibrium conditions. Theories are of various kinds. The older, 'classical' theory tended to explain price in terms of the *cost of production, the most sophisticated version of this being the *labour theory of value. This proposes a 'law of value': in those simple conditions of production, where there is no *profit, but simply the exchange of products by the producers, price at equilibrium will be directly proportional to the quantity of 'embodied labour'. This theory was developed so as to account for profits under capitalist modes of production, and received a sophisticated formulation in the Marxian theory of *surplus value. It was severely criticized, partly because of difficulties over the idea of 'embodied labour', and alternatives were suggested, notably theories of the market, which find the determinants of price in the interaction between buyers and sellers, against certain background conditions. One such theory is the theory of *marginal utility, which gives an underpinning to the theory that price is determined by the equilibrium between *supply and *demand. Writing in the 1920s the economist Piero Sraffa revived the classical analysis in modified form, and gave new credence to some of the intuitions underlying the labour theory of value. As a result the whole area of price theory has become contested among economists, and the *value controversy among Marxists has received a new impetus.

The 'price system', or price mechanism, is the system whereby price serves to coordinate activities within an economy, regulating supply and demand, and (so it is claimed) directing economic energy to areas where it is most profitably employed. The price system can be regarded as a mechanism which establishes economic equilibrium more readily and more surely than any government action, although governments sometimes try to control prices in order to control inflation (*see* *prices and incomes policy). It seems however that public ownership of the means of production is compatible with the use of a price system to regulate distribution and exchange, although the theory of the resulting arrangement is unclear. (Such is the normal practice, for example, in communist countries; *see* *market socialism.)

The conditions under which the price system can operate to produce an *optimal distribution of resources and incomes form one of the major preoccupations of welfare economics.

price control. *See* *prices and incomes policy.

prices and incomes policy. A policy which aims to restrain prices and incomes, thus reducing the rate of *inflation (e.g. by fixing a legal limit to pay rises and price rises). A prices and incomes policy was introduced in autumn 1974 by the then Labour government in the UK, as a 'social compact' between government and the trade unions (the curious language being derived from *Locke, and invoking an old theory of *legitimacy in support of a new attempt at *legitimation). In its direct form the policy involves *interference in the *price system, and has been criticized on the grounds that this can lead to serious misallocation of resources and unpredictable imbalances in a dynamic economy.

primary elections. Elections carried out,

usually by a *party, but in theory by any group, in order to determine who shall stand as candidate in some other, wider election. The person chosen in a primary election is chosen as candidate for his group or party: the next, 'true', election, determines whether or not he will also be received as a 'representative' under the constitutional office for which he contends. Whom, then, does he 'represent': the party that chose him in the primary, the people who voted at the second election, or both? This is one of the difficult problems posed by the theory of *representation.

primary relations. Sociologists and anthropologists sometimes distinguish primary from secondary relations between people, the first having an inevitable and unchosen character, the second being formed through agreements and associations into which the agent enters, and from which he might also withdraw. Among primary relations the most important are those of *kinship, and in particular those kinship relations within the *family which are regarded as defining responsibility for the nurture of the child – e.g. relations with parents in the nuclear family. *Marriage involves the generation of new primary relations. This has sometimes been held to explain its peculiar status in most societies, as a bond that is not easily to be broken, and not to be construed in contractual terms. It is even said to be a 'sacrament', i.e. a relation in which a third party, the divinity, intervenes.

prime minister. The officer charged with leading and speaking for the government in the principal assembly of the legislature: in UK the 'first minister of the *Crown'. The role of a prime minister as leader and instigator of *executive acts is greater or less, depending upon the executive power of the *head of state In *constitutional monarchies, where the executive power of the head of state has declined almost to the point of extinction, the executive power of the prime minister is such as to confer effective political leadership In republics, the president may be elected precisely in order to exert executive power (it being one of the ruling conceptions of democracy that executive power must be transferred by election, which is the real reason why a constitutional monarch, with purely hereditary entitlement, could never bear it). In a republic, therefore, if the office of prime minister exists, the prime minister becomes accountable to the president; if the president exerts major executive powers then this accountability will restrict the executive powers of the prime minister. Whether or not a prime minister exerts full executive power depends therefore on the powers that are vested in the head of state. (Here 'powers' is used in a **de facto* sense, and not in the legal sense mentioned in the definition of *power. In the legal sense the prime minister in the UK has no executive powers, and merely 'advises' the monarch, in whom all executive powers remain. Clearly many gradations can be envisaged here between legal fiction and political truth.)

primitive. Behaviour, institutions, customs and laws are primitive when they are 'first', that is 'early', examples of their type, the supposition being that there is some natural course of evolution which they have not yet undergone. That supposition is often in fact rejected in the case of those societies that were most frequently (until the development of modern *anthropology) called primitive It is not at all clear that the societies of Africa which were contemporaneous with their nineteenth-century explorers were early examples of something else, nor is it at all clear how such an hypothesis could be proved. The archaeological division of human *prehistory into ages (stone age, bronze age, iron age, and so on) seemed at first to give some objective idea of development against which all societies could be measured. Modern archeology has, however, cast doubt on the division, and on the theory which it is used to support, so that the main basis for the use of the label 'primitive rests in doctrines of human progress which probably seemed more believable in the nineteenth century than now. Naturally there is scientific progress, and therefore the technological progress that accompanies it. But it does not follow that other aspects of human existence – the building of institutions, laws, customs and values – can be assimilated to the model of scientific development, although some (e.g. Lucy Mair: *African Societies*, 1974) recognize similar principles of development in the political sphere. In these crucial respects it may be seriously misleading, and at any rate highly theoretically loaded, to speak of primitive political systems. (But *see* *primitive communism, *primitive law, *progressivism.)

primitive accumulation. If there is to be wage labour, there must be an owner of the means of production, and the labourer who, owning only labour power, must work for someone else. Hence the structure of capitalistic economy can arise only if control over the means of production first accumulates in some hands, but not in others. This process, called 'previous accumulation' by *Adam Smith, is called 'primitive accumulation' by *Marx. The acts of accumulation which bring the division between capital and labour into existence (e.g. enclosures, expropriation of peasant landowners) are called 'primitive' in that they are antecedent to the genuine *process* of *accumulation of *surplus value which occurs through the transformation of labour. It involves detaching the feudal serf from the means of production of which he was 'part and parcel'. 'The so-called primitive accumulation. . .is nothing else than the historical process of divorcing the producer from the means of production. It appears as primitive, because it forms the prehistoric stage of capital and of the mode of production corresponding to it. . .This primitive accumulation plays in political economy about the same part as original sin in theology' (Marx). Despite Marx's view that the history of primitive accumulation is 'written in the annals of mankind in letters of blood and fire' *Trotsky and his followers advocated it, as the necessary means to establish communism in Russia, by abolishing rural and pre-capitalist modes of production and creating an 'accumulation' in the hands of the state. The necessary consequence – the simultaneous creation of the rootless, propertyless labourer – was regarded as a necessary means towards socialist modes of production and also (as in late medieval Europe) as a justified act of emancipation.

primitive communism. Expression coined by *Marx to refer to an *ideal type of *production relations, which he supposed to be exemplified, in part, by tribal communities, and which, according to the theory of *historical materialism (which justifies, if true, this use of the term 'primitive'), precedes the formation of *slavery. Primitive communism is like an economic *state of nature in the Marxian theory of history. It is a society without true political organization, without exchange and barter, and in which food is produced for common needs by the whole tribe working together without the sense of private property. It differs from 'true communism' in that it is a state of subjection to, rather than mastery over, nature; true communism can be achieved only by passing through the intermediate stages of feudalism, capitalism and socialism, in order to permit the full development of human potential.

primitive law. The *conventions whereby *primitive communities are governed, and under which disputes within those communities are resolved. It has been much disputed whether primitive law is really law, since it seems often to dispense with vital distinctions – e.g. between law and morality, law and etiquette – that are made in the legal systems of most modern societies. However, definite procedures of adjudication exist even in the most primitive communities, together with rights that can be defined independently of the particular person who claims them. Complex bodies of customary law have been identified, together with judicial offices whereby they are applied. The study of primitive law – 'legal anthropology' – has done much in recent years to clarify the nature of these systems. See Simon Roberts: *Order and Dispute*, 1979.

primitivism. An admiration for the primitive in man, which supposedly survives as a *residue even in the most civilized conduct, and which it may be necessary to recapture in order to be fully human. Primitivism played a large part in the political development of *national socialism, which allied its *racist doctrines to ideals of the tribal warrior. It has also been influential in modern literature, partly through the writings of D. H. Lawrence (although Lawrence's primitivism is sometimes described as callow), in modern art, partly through Picasso's admiration for African artefacts, and in modern music, through Stravinsky and the Ballets Russes. Primitivism is thus one of the major themes of modern culture, and *modernity is part of what makes primitivism possible.

prior restraint/subsequent punishment. A distinction sometimes made between two remedies for libellous or in other ways injurious publication, or for illegal or harmful meetings, demonstrations, or actions. Subsequent punishment is a threat which may be ignored by someone determined to act, whether for gain or from conviction. It does not protect the aggrieved party, if the one who seeks to embark on a course of injurious action has grounds for thinking that he can, by doing so, mobilize public opinion to protect him from sanction. Prior restraint is usually available in UK law in the form of an *injunction, which can be sought by the individual at any stage. The effect of this is to transform all injurious action from a civil to a criminal wrong, since the action will be tantamount to 'contempt of court'. This has had considerable significance in the development of US *labour law.

An injunction can also be sought by any citizen against any threatened crime. But the effects of disobedience are simply the effects of crime, and obedience to an injunction can itself be ensured only through the threat of punishment. The only kind of prior restraint that is independent of the threat of subsequent punishment is the actual imprisonment of someone *lest* he should commit a crime. This is illegal in the UK, in the US, and in most systems of law which guarantee elementary *freedoms. (*See *habeas corpus*.)

prison. *See* *punishment.

prisoner's dilemma. A situation in *game theory which has been thought to be particularly significant in revealing the complexities of political choice. Two partners-in-crime have been arrested and put in separate cells. They can be convicted of robbery, if prosecuted; and could be convicted of murder, if either were to confess. Each is promised by the police that both charges against him will be dropped if he alone confesses to murder, thus condemning the other. If both confess, both will get a somewhat reduced sentence for murder. If neither confesses, both will be convicted of robbery. Each reasons that he does better to confess, if the other confesses; and also better to confess, if the other does not. So each confesses regardless, and so helps to produce an outcome worse for both. The formal structure of this 'game' has been applied to the arms race, the failure of voluntary incomes policies, the over-fishing of the seas and many other aspects of social life, where norms which would benefit all fail to emerge. It captures a kind of insight about the contrary effects of individually rational decisions, found in *Hobbes, in *Hegel, in *Marx, and in many other earlier thinkers.

privacy. A condition imperfectly defined and imperfectly respected in many legal systems, despite the Universal Declaration of Human Rights (adopted but not enforceable by the United Nations Organization) which denounces interference with privacy, family, home and correspondence (implying, with intuitive plausibility, that these four are intimately connected). It was first argued in 1890 that there is a right of privacy, and that this right should be protected by law (Warren and Brandeis, in *Harvard Law Review*, 1890). Such ideas have continued to be important in US constitutional thinking, and definitions have been attempted. A report to the US President's Office of Science and Technology in 1967 asserted that 'the right to privacy is the right of the individual to decide for himself how much he will share with others his thoughts, feelings and the facts of his personal life.' That is vague, but it is difficult to replace it with anything more precise. Such definitions are in part attempts to define the *sphere* of the private (as opposed to the public), in part attempts to describe matters in which the individual can tolerate no right of control in anyone but himself. (*See further* *private and public.)

The 'right to privacy' is not recognized, at least under that description, in UK law, and those things which fall under 'privacy' must be protected through the laws of nuisance, libel, breach of confidence, breach of trust, etc. It is not clear, therefore, that a crime is committed by someone who spies on another, or that the tort involved is any more than a nuisance.

private and public. The distinction between private and public is drawn in one way in economics (*see* *private property, *private sector), in another way in law, and in another way for the purposes of political thought, where it denotes separate but overlapping spheres of activity: the private is the sphere of personal affection, personal antipathy, individual satisfaction, while the public is really two spheres (as *Hegel and others have pointed out): *civil society and *state. Civil society involves all those larger, more open relations between people that do not depend upon affection, but rather upon recognized purposes and upon an ability to cooperate through *contract and *consent. The state involves all those relations which are mediated by *law.

In law the distinction between private and public is equally unclear The distinction is familiar in *Roman law, and the accepted boundary is that between affairs among individuals, and affairs among states, or between individuals and the state. The two spheres overlap inextricably so that, e.g., many *torts are also *crimes, and many individual contracts must have the state as a third and controlling party.

Some liberal views of the relation between law and morality argue that the 'private' (in the political sense) is a sphere which is, or ought to be, free from the supervision of the law. It is often argued that such a view is either tautological (the 'private' being defined as the realm in which individual choice is sovereign), or else crucially imprecise (e.g. is murder between consenting adults 'in private' to be permitted?). *See* *law and morality.

private enterprise. The undertaking of any economic activity using privately owned *capital and with a view to private gain. Ownership of capital may be single, joint, or through an association, such as a company. In private enterprise risk is undertaken, and the possibility of profit is essential to induce anyone to undertake that risk. (*See* *enterprise.)

private property. *Property is a *right of use. Not all property is private property, and it is in fact not easy to state the distinguishing conditions of the private. The following features seem to be important:

(i) The right to exclude. That is, what I own privately I can exclude you from using. This right may be conditional, as in a tenancy that is forfeited upon immoral use, or upon breach of some condition in the lease. Indeed all such rights may be conditional – in that the state may retain *eminent domain in all property. Moreover, exclusiveness is a matter of degree. I cannot exclude a police officer with a search warrant from my flat, nor the town surveyor, and so on. Nevertheless if I can exclude *anybody* from my flat, to that small extent it is mine.

(ii) The right to use as I will. This too is only limited. Nobody has the unqualified

right in UK law to destroy his house, nor, if it is a Grade One listed building, to alter it in any material particular. And so on.
(iii) The right to transfer. Some forms of transfer may be forbidden, or penalized by taxation (e.g. by a gift tax, or capital transfer tax). But without some right of transfer the 'freedom to alienate', which classical liberal thought has often considered to be particularly important among property rights, would not exist.

It is vital to separate (i) and (iii), since it is (iii) that opens the possibility to *accumulation, and to the inequalities of wealth which, according to some (e.g. *Nozick), can be prevented only by injustice, and according to others (e.g. most socialists) are an injustice in themselves. Many arguments against private property are really arguments against (iii) and not against (i). Many defenders of private property and many attackers seem not to realize that all of (i) to (iii) are matters of degree, and therefore that their arguments may be directed for or against only some degree of private property and not for or against the institution as a whole. Furthermore it should be noted that private property is a legal right, and may or may not be a natural right, even if the existence of that legal right is justified. For a brief summary of the arguments on this issue, *see* *property.

private sector. In a *mixed economy, that part of the economy which is not under government *control. In other words, all *private enterprise, together with non-profit-making organizations, and exchanges between individuals.

privatization. The creation and upholding of a right of *private property in an object formerly owned socially or publicly, or perhaps not formerly owned at all. The term is intended to denote the converse of *socialization; the privatization of *nationalized industries has been several times contemplated and even implemented in the UK, by governments opposed to public ownership of the means of production.

privilege. 1. In law, an entitlement or authorization to do or not do something which may involve, for example, immunity from prosecution or civil liability. A privilege is a kind of legally recognized *liberty which, by implication, is not generally available, but attaches, for whatever reason, to a certain role, office or organization. Thus trade unions have wide privileges in UK law, and there is a special privilege associated with actions for defamation, which is granted to parliamentary and official communications (where it is absolute), and to medical communications (where it is qualified). One of the important privileges in UK law is parliamentary privilege, granting freedom to each house to conduct its proceedings without interference from the Crown, the courts, bodies outside Parliament, or the public. Such privilege exists either by common law or by statute, but neither house may by its own resolution create new privileges. It was established in *Stockdale v. Hansard*, 1839, that the extent of this privilege is determined by law and could be examined by the courts, though the House of Commons has not subsequently relinquished its claim to decide for itself whether any privilege exists. Abuse of privilege is now frequently complained of, but it seems that there is no serious redress available to the victim.
2. General. A privilege is a benefit conferred which cannot be claimed as a *right. (NB. In some philosophical sense it might *be* a right; but the point is that it cannot be claimed as such.) Many of the disputes about the nature of welfare legislation concern whether or not some benefit is a privilege or a right, the difference being that in the second case, but not in the first, it would be an injustice to withold it.

Privileges may attach to class, to membership of a party, to wealth, or to any other social position which enhances the power, status or well-being of the recipient. Hostility towards privilege may proceed from envy, and the consequent desire to destroy privilege come what may, or from the sense of justice, based in the thought that a privilege has been unfairly acquired by the other, or unfairly lost by oneself. In the extreme case it may be argued (perhaps on *universalist grounds) that, because there are no distinctions among human beings sufficient to justify the conferring of *any* privilege, all privilege is unjust. That view is tantamount to *egalitarianism, and may additionally involve the (probably mistaken) assumption that all privilege is *conferred*. (Depending upon whether or not judgements of justice require a presumption of *agency.)

The usual object of dispute is political privilege. Some argue that all political offices should be, in a real sense, open to all, so that all have a right to compete for office on an equal footing. One main problem for such a view is how to ensure that all people really *do* compete on an equal footing, since clearly an equal right does not imply an equal ability. *See* *access, *egalitarianism, *equal opportunity.

production, theory of. 1. The branch of economics concerned with determining the choice of inputs, given the *price of those inputs, the *production function relating them to outputs, and the level of output desired. It is based on the assumption that firms seeking to maximize their profits will seek to minimize the cost of inputs.
2. More widely, sometimes used to describe the attempt to explore the *factors of production in their full social relationship, and to compare the various modes of production from the social and political point of view.

production, distribution, exchange, consumption. Four distinct but inter-dependent parts of the economic process, which are sometimes separated for the sake of theory, and sometimes brought together, in order to argue that they are in some way organically interdependent. Goods are produced from nature either by cultivation or manufacture, they are distributed through mechanisms such as a *market, exchanged against other goods or money, and finally consumed. It is a fundamental tenet of *Marxist theory that the first three, at least, and probably all four, are interdependent, so that every system of *production relations also determines systems of exchange, distribution and consumption. (The four processes are sometimes described collectively as 'reproduction' by Marx.) Thus Marx believed that he had demonstrated the impossibility of *private property in the means of production without the existence of a market economy (i.e. private property in the means of distribution), and the existence of *exchange-value alongside *use-value in every commodity. He criticized those socialists such as *Lassalle, and the *Owenites, who thought that the inequitable distribution attaching to capitalist modes of production could be remedied by a publicly organized redistribution of the product: any mode of distribution is determined by the mode of production, of which it is a functional part. This position cannot, in its pure version, be right, as modern economies show. Nowadays there is large-scale private ownership of the means of production, existing side by side with massive redistribution through taxation, legally enforced minimum wages and maximum working hours, and even *price control.

Some socialists have argued that the important thing that they wish to prevent is private property in the means of production, other kinds of private property being permissible or even necessary. Thus many concede that it is hard to imagine life without private property in the 'means of consumption', by which is usually meant the household and all that pertains to it. But those very same arguments that urge an organic interdependence between production, exchange and distribution, extend to consumption too. Consider the case of a nomadic tribe whose main product is carpets. Carpets are produced at home, primarily for domestic use but, when necessary, they are exchanged against other goods. Where does private ownership in the means of consumption end and private ownership of the means of production begin? Should we take away the needle that has dared to make a carpet for *sale?* Or should we allow only small-scale production in the home, and permit factories only when they are *socially owned? Those questions are difficult, and it is important to be clear about them when discussing issues of private property. Either the organicist argument is correct, and private ownership in the means of consumption cannot be permitted without also permitting private ownership elsewhere; or it is not, in which case private ownership can coexist with equitable redistribution.

production function. The relation between the quantity of output of some commodity and the quantity of inputs required to make it. The production function varies from economy to economy and from firm to firm.

production relations (or: relations of production). *Marxian and Marxian-influenced term for the relations between people in production, and between people and *productive forces, which are enshrined in laws of *property, and which define the *base structure of society. Production relations permit and facilitate the operation of *productive forces, a fact which, on one Marxian view, explains both their existence and their transformation. Thus *capitalism is held to be a system of production relations, in which the capitalist controls the means of production and the worker controls his own labour power; by bringing the two into relation through the *wage-contract, production is made possible. Likewise *feudalism, *socialism and *communism are all, for Marx, systems of production relations, whose other features are explained in terms of this basic fact.

The relations between people which occur in and through production are not only relations between individuals. One of the important tenets of classical Marxism is that the relations hold also between *classes. This thought is difficult to interpret. Sometimes it seems as though the existence of a class is *explained* by the production relations between individuals, who, by virtue of similar positions in production, acquire similar interests and therefore act in concert. At other times it seems as though the classes are the fundamental *terms* of the relation: production relations are between classes, and between individuals only as members of classes. The latter view suggests the need for some independent criterion of class membership; however it is sometimes invoked in order to characterize *exploitation under capitalism. (Thus it might be said that I am free not to contract with you, the capitalist, but the class of proletarians as a whole is *forced* to contract with the class of capitalists, and in that sense does not really *contract* with it.)

productive forces (or: forces of production). This expression has a large significance in *Marxian theories of production, which attempt to separate the productive forces from the *production relations which channel them. The assumption is that all production involves both a dynamic and a fixed part, rather as a water turbine consists of a fixed piece of machinery which is set in motion by the force of water, but which, left to itself, does not move. The turbine channels the energy from the water to the electrical cable which runs from it.

The classical Marxian position is that, among the factors of production, labour, and labour alone, is a productive force. People often think that capital too is such a force. But, Marx argued, there is nothing in the status of an object as *capital* which causes it to produce (to think otherwise is to suffer from 'capital fetishism'). A piece of machinery may be owned as capital: but even if not owned at all it might still serve as an instrument of production. What makes it productive is that someone works with it and produces by means of it. That person, the producer, provides the productive force. The machine enhances his productivity, and is itself the product of force, including the force of intellectual labour. The mode of ownership or control does not contribute any power of production to the machine, but simply situates it in a system of production relations, by establishing that control over the machine, and therefore permission to produce by means of it, are vested in someone other than the producer.

Some regard such arguments as attempting to prove the primacy of labour by *persuasive definition of the term 'force'. (For is not the electricity that powers the machine *also* a productive force? Why is it so important that someone had to do something to *make* it produce?) Others hold that Marx's arguments formulate a profound truth about the nature of production, from which the basis of a theory of history may be taken. On this second view, productive forces can be identified and described independently of production relations (i.e. independently of ownership and control), and can also be used to explain the latter. It is the development of these forces that necessitates the constant evolution of production relations, which in turn generates all historical change.

productivity. A measure of the rate of output from the use of given quantities of *factors of production. Thus there is labour productivity, capital productivity, and land productivity. (Economists also talk of '*total* factor productivity'.) The productivity of a factor of production can be measured either in average, or in marginal terms, usually the former. Where labour is plentiful labour productivity will tend to be low, since it will be more economical to employ 'labour intensive' methods – i.e. methods in which large amounts of cheap labour are employed in preference to small amounts of expensive labour in conjunction with expensive machinery.

productivity bargaining. A kind of *collective bargaining in which employers agree to pay more for the more efficient use of labour time. In other words rewards are offered for more effort, or more effective effort, at the place of work. It has been common in the UK since the 1960s, and is perhaps the natural consequence of a conventional maximum to the length of the working day.

profession. The distinctions between employment, trade and profession are difficult to draw precisely, and might be drawn differently for different purposes, although the first two obviously have something to do with, respectively, production and exchange. It is widely held that membership of a profession is an important determinant of social and political attitudes, even though it is not at all clear that the professions form, as such, either a *class or a distinct *status group. Some step would be made towards the view that the professions form a class, or a significant sub-class within the *middle class, if it were shown that they stand in some common and constant relation to the means of production. But it is hard to discover any such relation: the best that can be said is that the professions are essential in the long run to production, since they provide and foster the skills necessary to improve its efficiency, but that they are less essential in the short run than many other groups.

The term 'profession' was originally applied to the three 'learned professions' of divinity, law and medicine, but now includes, for example, teaching and accounting. The surface features that seem relevant to the classification (and which may or may not identify a significant class) are:

(a) acquisition of learning as a requirement of entry;
(b) a presumption of learning in practice;
(c) self-direction, and control over the pace and scheduling of work;
(d) the possibility of advancement, from level to level, *within* the profession.

The four features clearly go together, since what gives credence to the idea of advancement *within* a profession (rather than by means of the profession) is the fact that learning is cumulative; given talent for its acquisition, a professional will steadily master what he has to know.

A 'professional' is someone who has acquired the skills necessary to some practice, whether or not that practice is a profession in the above sense. In this sense there are professional criminals, and professional politicians.

professional ethic. The *ethic of a *profession. Sociologists tend to give a *functional explanation of the professional ethic (cf. *business ethic), arguing that what explains the existence of certain beliefs and *values among members of the professions is the fact that those beliefs and values facilitate the successful performance of professional tasks. Thus the professional believes that he is bound by a duty towards his client, and not by a wage contract: such a belief facilitates the adoption of irregular working hours, and the undertaking of highly demanding tasks. Similar beliefs concerning professional responsibility and decorum enable the members of a profession both to learn from one another and to avoid entering into the overt competition that would destroy the *career structure, and so remove one of the incentives to acquire more professional skill. Thus members of the legal profession are in the UK forbidden to advertise their services; they also form into clubs and societies where they meet socially. There is nothing that *forbids* other professions from advertising, but it is regarded as very bad form in doctors, and for most teachers it suggests a position of relative failure. In the US, where even lawyers advertise their services, the professional ethic is nearer to the business ethic. This is often found repugnant by those used to the English habits; this might be snobbishness, or it might be a disguised perception of dysfunctionality.

profit. Profit is the aim of private *enterprise, but there is little agreement over what produces it. Accountants distinguish gross profit (total receipts from sales, less immediate costs of production) from net profit (gross profit less interest on loans, and depreciation). But the real economic distinction is that between normal profit and *excess profit. The former is the income (i.e. the residue left after subtracting all *opportunity costs of inputs), which is just sufficient to keep the firm in business. In other words, it is the opportunity cost of remaining in business rather than switching to some other activity. Excess profits are all profits above normal (sometimes called 'supernormal' profits), and sometimes regarded as the (risky) return to the entrepreneurial activity.

The theory of profit is an important part of classical economics. This tended to support the thesis of the *falling rate of profit, upheld by *Smith, *Ricardo and *Marx. It is not at all clear that the thesis is true, or what the consequences of its truth might be. The Marxian theory of profit relies on the notion of *surplus value. Marx argued that surplus value is not identical to profit, and therefore tried to give an account of how profit is determined by surplus value. The problem of deriving the one from the other is part of the 'transformation problem', and thus forms one part of the 'value controversy' in Marxian economics.

progress. Movement forwards. Condorcet is usually cited as the first major theorist of the modern version of the idea of progress. However, the rhetorical importance of the idea is sometimes dated from the seventeenth century, e.g. by J. B. Bury (*The Idea of Progress*, 1920), who argued that the entry of this concept into the realm of human values was part of the scientific revolution, and the consequent *secularization of thought, that occurred in the post-Reformation world. The 'belief in' progress is a form of optimism, with two aspects – first, the belief that things *do* progress; secondly the belief that there is a recognizably 'progressive' *outlook* on the world, which involves distinctive values as well as distinctive beliefs. The second is sometimes called 'progressivism', and tends to take its credentials from the tradition of liberal *humanism. It regards all reform and social movement as tending towards the complete emancipation of the individual from oppressive *superstition. The first aspect – the belief that progress is the natural order of things – is a form of *historicism, and has itself been condemned (by Dean Inge) as a 'pernicious superstition'. It involved three thoughts. (i) Some states of affairs are better than

others, and all reforms that advance towards the former and away from the latter are to be commended.
(ii) This advance occurs, in fact, through the passage of time.
(iii) Scientific knowledge leads to the ever-increasing control over human destiny and understanding of the human condition.

(i) is a near tautology; (ii) involves, as it stands, a fallacy (the fallacy, pointed out by *Kant, of believing that time alone can have causal properties); (iii) is almost certainly false. However, the use of (iii) in support of (ii) is still given as a ground for the belief in progress. If the accumulation of scientific knowledge enables us to master our fate, then, since this accumulation *is* progressive, the human condition must steadily improve under its influence. (A very sophisticated version of that idea is contained in *historical materialism, particularly in that variety of it that is sometimes called *technological determinism; a naïve version of the idea is to be found in the *positivism of Comte.)

It is often said that the belief in progress involves a confusion between ends and means. Science, which enables us to improve the second, always stands in need of the guidance of the first. But our knowledge of ends, unlike our knowledge of means, is, it is sometimes said, not progressive, but rather rests in those enduring values which define the invariable aspirations of human nature. In which case one might agree with the member of the *Frankfurt school who wrote that 'no universal history leads from savagery to humanitarianism, but there is one leading from the slingshot to the megaton bomb' (Theodor Adorno).

progressivism. *See* *progress.

proletarianization. The process which, according to Marx, occurs to the lower middle classes with the industrialization of capitalist production, whereby they are gradually ousted from business, and cast down into the mass seething beneath them, losing their distinctive expectations and style of life.

proletariat. Latin: *proletarius*, one who breeds, from *proles*, offspring. Under the Servian constitution of the sixth century BC those who could not pay taxes were required to lend their offspring in military service to the state. The term *proletarius* reappears in the fifteenth and sixteenth centuries, to name men similarly required to give services, only this time in the form of their own wage labour, being made landless by enclosures or eviction. Its modern use first occurs in the Swiss economist Sismondi, from whom it was borrowed by the French radicals, and passed to *Marx and his followers. The proletariat is the class of labourers under capitalist industrial production, who are, supposedly, property-less, having nothing to sell but their *labour power, and being cast loose from all bonds of obligation and all attachment to place and land. They form a rootless, mobile, needy mass, united only by their similar station in the *production relations of capitalism, and by whatever class *identity might emerge from that. Since labour is the major *productive force, and since all labour power lies with the proletariat, it is in the proletariat that the forces destined to burst asunder the fetters of capitalism are being nurtured.

propaganda. The sacred congregation Propaganda Fidei ('for the propagation of the faith') was established in Rome by Pope Gregory XV in 1622. Since then the term 'propaganda' has come to denote any attempt – however disrespectful of truth, reason and the human intellect – to win acceptance for a cause, system, or state, either by praise of the thing itself, or by vilification of its known and unknown alternatives.

The emergence of the 'propaganda machine' in the twentieth century is largely due to the attention paid by the *bolsheviks and the *national socialists to the task of *legitimation. Their techniques have been the subject of much comment, and the attempt at mind-control (called 're-education' in China and Vietnam) has been contemplated with alarm by outside observers. The similarity of Nazi and bolshevik propaganda – despite the supposed contrast in their ideals – has seemed to suggest that there are patterns to which all propaganda must adhere. What matters is not so much the content of the resulting beliefs, as the feelings of loyalty to friends and hostility to enemies which they inspire. Thus the concept of the 'enemy' has become very important in modern propaganda, alerting people to the ever-present dangers by which they are surrounded. The Jew and the 'anti-socialist' class enemy are distinguished by the fact that the first is what he is from birth, while the second may become what he is by corruption, and perhaps without realizing it himself. This means that you can never feel sure under bolshevik propaganda that you are *not* one of the enemy. The consequent failure (in comparison with Nazi propaganda) to generate a sense of security has been held responsible for some of the rejection of the propaganda message in the USSR. The subject is a mysterious one, and study is made additionally difficult by the fact that those who have had sufficient experience of the propaganda machine to know what it is like do not usually preserve the peace of mind necessary to examine it.

property. The fullest right that can exist over anything, which includes (in its maximum extent) the right to possess, use, lend, alienate, use up, consume and destroy. More simply, property can be described as a right of use, which can exist in various degrees, and subject to various conditions. There is no limit to the kinds of thing in which property rights may exist – copyright, for example, is a right of intellectual property, and there can be rights in land, in debts or other obligations, in movable goods, in human beings (in which case at least one of the parties is a *slave). Principal questions raised by the concept of property are: is there any basis for property rights other than convention? And: ought there to be rights of **private* property? In considering both questions it is necessary to remember that property rights are both composite and also a matter of degree. Thus my property right in this typewriter is a right to use, to destroy and to transfer; to lend, to give and to hire. It is clear that a philosophical justification of one of those rights may not be a justification of the others. Moreover a justification of any of those rights might only show it to be conditional, or defeasible. Thus the right of use of land is normally regarded as conditional upon loyalty to the sovereign; the right of transfer of food conditional upon truthful declaration of its nature; the right to destroy food as conditional upon a minimum level of abundance, and so on. All the rights, therefore, will be justified to a certain degree only, and it should not be thought that property is unjustified simply because no property right can ever be made absolute.

The arguments for and against private property invoke need, justice, freedom and utility. Arguments from all of those conceptions have been put forward to justify (a) universal *common ownership; (b) ownership by small *communes; (c) ownership by units small enough to be considered private, e.g. *companies, *families; (d) private ownership by individuals. It is generally hoped by socialists that an argument can be given for (a) or (b) which will not also permit (d). Thus if it can be shown that there is a right of common ownership in all land and in the means of production (say, because we have common needs and an equal right to satisfy them, or because we hold all land and its products in trust for ourselves and future generations), then the assertion of a private right of ownership is inherently unjust, since it is an attempt to exclude people from what is rightly theirs.

Arguments for private property should be distinguished into those which generate conclusions about particular property rights, and those which justify the existence of an institution of property rights without determining what should belong to whom. An argument of the first kind is *Locke's, to the effect that, given certain conditions, someone can create a *natural right to property in that with which he has mixed his labour. All just transfers will preserve this natural right, so that it is, in theory, possible to trace the lineage of all present property to its original acquisition, and determine which item is rightly and which wrongly held. An argument of the second kind is *Hegel's, to the effect that the institution of private property is necessary for men to assert their full individual freedom. This argues that there must *be* property rights, but says nothing about who should own what.

The major problem for defenders of a right of common ownership is to give an argument for it that will not also permit the right of detachment – i.e. the right of the individual to detach his share from the common fund, say through exerting himself with the consent of the others. The major problem for the defender of private property is to show why its existence is not a massive interference in the freedom and rights of the majority, who are excluded from the enjoyment of every item that is privately owned. Some defenders of common ownership recognize the force of arguments such as Hegel's, and conclude that each individual needs a sphere of private right where he can exert himself exclusively. They therefore advocate private ownership of the 'means of consumption', while arguing against private ownership in the means of production, distribution and exchange. Whether it is possible so to separate production from consumption is, however, a matter of doubt: *see* *production, distribution, exchange and consumption.

The battle over private property is not new: it occurs in the dispute between Plato and Aristotle over common ownership, and is rehearsed in much medieval natural law theory (*see* *Aquinas). Sir Thomas More criticizes private property in these terms: 'so long as private property remains, there is no hope at all that [social evils] may be healed and society restored to good health. While you try to cure a part, you aggravate the disease of other parts. In redressing one evil another is committed, since you cannot give something to one man without taking the same from another' (*Utopia*). Thus More argues against *redistribution and *sumptuary laws as remedies for the evils of private property, and advocate its abolition, just as the **Communist Manifesto* was to do later.

proportional representation. The form of *representation in which the strength of the representation of a *party in the assembly is directly proportional to the strength of its support among the electorate. It does not exist in the UK or the US, but does exist in certain European assemblies. Thus in the UK candidates stand for election in a constituency, and they represent the people of that constituency once elected. On this system a party with minority support may procure *no* seats in Parliament; in the general election of 1974, for example, over a third of those elected to the House of Commons were elected on a minority vote, and the Liberal Party, with nearly 20% of the vote, secured only 2% of the seats. Some argue that such a result is inherently absurd, and that the House of Commons cannot really claim to represent the people if its institutional structure is so impervious to minority voting. It is replied either that *adversary politics requires a two-party system if political stability is to be achieved, and hence requires a form of representation which filters out minority parties, or else that representation ought to be by constituency if the interests of the people (rather than the interests of the parties with which they may wrongly identify themselves) are to be consulted. Various suggestions for reform are made, sometimes accepting both sides of that argument.

prosecution. Legally sanctioned action by the state against a citizen in charging with, and preparing the proof of, a crime. Often a public officer is appointed to take charge of prosecutions (as in the US and France), but in England anyone may undertake prosecution in the name of the *Crown, and then ask for an authorized officer to take over. When a police officer prosecutes for a summary offence he is in theory acting as a private individual.

protectionism. The theory and practice of protecting home markets by curtailing or prohibiting competition from abroad, traditionally by the imposition of *tariffs or quotas to restrict the flow of imports (*see* *mercantilism, *neo-mercantilism). Some *Keynesian protectionists argue that import controls will raise national income, and in the long run lead to a higher total level of imports than existed before. Hence the control of imports may be to the benefit, not only of home markets, but also of international trade, so that other states, perceiving this, will not necessarily resort to retaliatory measures.

protectorate. In international relations and UK constitutional law, a protectorate is not a colony, but a form of guardianship, with the emphasis on the duty of the protecting state to foster the social, economic and political development of the protectorate to the point where political independence is feasible. Many of the British colonies enjoyed protectorate status (e.g. Rhodesia), although it is disputed how far they were treated as the term implies. Czechoslovakia was made a 'protectorate' of Germany in 1939, but here the term simply denoted *annexation.

Protestant ethic. *See* *Protestantism.

Protestantism. The systems of Christian faith and liturgical practice based on the principles of the *Reformation. (In 1529, the reforming members of the Diet of Spyer had issued a *protestatio* against the decision of the Roman Catholic majority, hence the name.) The three original branches were *Lutheranism, *Calvinism and Zwinglianism, with *Anglicanism as a disputed case, sometimes regarded as a parochial synthesis of the principles of the Reformation and the practices of the Roman Catholic Church. The chief items of belief are acceptance of the Bible as the only source of revealed truth, the doctrine of justification by faith alone (*see* *Lutheranism), and that of the universal priesthood of all believers, which is tantamount to the rejection of the church as an independent source of authority, rather than a voluntary association of all believers. With the rejection of the church is associated also a rejection of papal indulgencies (which relieve the individual of his necessary *conscience), and of the rituals, liturgies and ceremonies through which the church has dignified its worldly offices, together with an *iconoclasm towards all practices and beliefs that are merely local in significance (such as the veneration shown towards local saints).

The rise of Protestantism is associated with complex social and political developments. The growth of trading towns and manufactures, the movement of the population from the land, the decline of serfdom and the swelling of the journeyman class – these and many related changes are regarded as important factors, to be taken into account in any assessment of the political impact of Protestanism. Hence in 1905 *Weber put forward the proposition that, while some measure of *capitalism is inevitable under normal conditions, the peculiar thriving of capitalism in Western Europe and its dependencies, its indomitable progress, accumulation, and economic despotism, were the effect of what he called the Protestant ethic: the spirit of self-dependence and individual autonomy which flowered at the Reformation, and took powerful political form in the writings and activities of Calvin (*see* *Calvinism). The phrase has stuck, although the theory is much criticized, both by those who think that it mixes cause and effect (e.g. *Marxists, who believe that Protestantism is part of the ideology of modern capitalist production relations rather than their cause), and by those who believe that it is not founded in fact, pointing, for example, to the spread of capitalism in pre-Reformation Italy, and to the effect of the Counter-Reformation.

There are significant differences between Calvinism and Lutheranism, the first involving a sustained attempt to develop new political institutions, the second being content to refer large areas of social and political life to the jurisdiction of the individual conscience. The interaction of conscience and commerce lent a peculiar tone to the ideology of modern capitalism in Protestant countries, and whether or not Weber's thesis is accepted, it is normal to recognize that Protestant capitalism has had, as a result, a distinctive character – see e.g. R. H. Tawney: *Religion and the Rise of Capitalism,* 1926, in which the connections with *individualism and the *universalism of the *Enlightenment are emphasized.

Proudhon, Pierre-Joseph (1809–65). The first writer deliberately to accept the title 'anarchist', and since sometimes regarded as the father of modern *anarchism. In *What is Property?*, 1840, Proudhon attacked many of the rights of property prevalent in nineteenth-century France, and in particular all those rights of property which conferred effective *control of another human being. At the same time he rejected communism, and upheld the individual's right to independence, and to the measure of private property necessary for that. Communism, he argued, was dependent upon authority and control for its enforcement, and was therefore not, in the end, preferable to the system of private property relations which it sought to replace. Thus property and communism, while antithetically related, must both be transcended in their synthesis, which is anarchism.

Proudhon envisaged a worldwide working-class organization, founded not in political but in economic principles, specifically in the practice of *mutualism, whereby everything needed for production would be made available on mutually beneficial, but non-profit-making, terms. Proudhon's views aroused considerable interest, and for a while he was friendly with Marx. However, Proudhon reacted against what he saw as the authoritarian and dictatorial implications of Marxian theory, and was himself attacked by Marx in *The Poverty of Philosophy*, 1847. Proudhon founded a newspaper, was elected to the Constituent Assembly, and later imprisoned for his attacks on Louis Napoleon and his regime. His posthumous *On the Political Capability of the Working Class,* 1865, summarized his lifelong dedication to the labour movement, although he is perhaps best remembered for the maxim 'property is theft'.

providence. That which is provided, specifically by God, through his foreknowledge and beneficent care of human things. Providence is a theological conception akin to that of *destiny, which rationalizes and makes acceptable the widely disputed and also widely confirmed hypothesis that human affairs are largely outside human control.

provocation. A term difficult to apply since, in its common usage, it refers to an idea of *normality. An act constitutes provocation if the normal person would be provoked by it, but precisely what features such a person might have is hard to determine. In law the test is that of the *reasonable man, which is designed to capture the idea of normality, and to give to it legal cogency. Thus an act or series of acts done by one person to another constitutes a provocation in law if it could cause in a reasonable man, and actually does cause in the victim, a sudden and temporary loss of self-control. (This is not a defence, but rather a fact which changes the nature of the crime – e.g. which changes murder to manslaughter.)

In international relations provocation seems to mean any warlike or declamatory gesture which promises a threat to the interests of one state by another. It has no precise meaning in international law.

prudence. 1. One of the cardinal *virtues, prudence consists in the disposition to take account of the consequence of action, to fit the means to the end and the end to the means, and to behave in all things so that fulfilment is, in the circumstances, as likely as it is possible. That sentence contains a summary of *Aristotle's account of the virtue of *sophrosune* (practical wisdom), which ne regarded as the root of all other virtues. Without prudence, ancient philosophers argued, courage becomes rashness, wisdom becomes obstinacy, and justice becomes sentimental pity or rage. Prudence is thus integral to the other virtues which, without it, are merely the vicious simulacra of virtue in a spirit that does not possess it.

2. In moral philosophy, however, prudence is often used in a technical sense, in order to draw a contrast between the prudential and the moral. Prudence is the virtue of the rational egoist, or *economic man, who weighs every consideration in the balance of his own reasoned preferences, and does not show that 'irrational' attachment to absolute *values which is the distinguishing mark of the moral being.

psychotherapy. This has become an issue in political thinking on several accounts, among which the following are noteworthy:

(i) *Freud's theory that civilization rests upon the *repression of fundamental instincts, and contains, therefore, an internal conflict and discontent. The actual political consequences that Freud drew from this theory were marginal. He seemed to accept the process of repression, and the sublimation associated with it, as essential to family and social life, and to the transformation of the infantile libido, activated by its 'pleasure principle', into the mature *universalism of adult moral sentiment.

(ii) The general effect of Freudian and post-Freudian analysis on received ideas about the human condition. The most important has been the theory of unconscious motivation, and the associated idea that the reasons given for an action may be *rationalizations, unconnected with the motive, despite the agent's own sincere conviction to the contrary. This view echoes in the sphere of individual psychology the fundamental tenet of *historical materialism. There has been, indeed, a movement to combine the two approaches, so as to argue that the repression which drives the libido underground, and so provides the reservoir of unconscious motives, is an instance of that *oppression which drives labour underground, to become the great motivating force of history, developing unseen from the illusory world of *bourgeois ideology. (See, for example, *Herbert Marcuse: *Eros and Civilization,* 1962.)

(iii) The emergence of schools which attempt to *politicize the theory and practice of psychotherapy, e.g. that of *Reich, and the school associated with the name of Laing in the UK. The second relies to some extent on theses of *phenomenology, on theories propounded by *Sartre concerning the 'existential' significance of mental illness, and on theories given by the French sociologist and historian of ideas Michel Foucault, concerning the nature of clinical treatment. From Sartre is derived the thesis that the patient diagnosed as psychotic suffers from an 'ontological insecurity' – i.e. a sense that either he does not exist as a *person, or else has no right to exist. From Foucault comes the thesis that it is the function of the therapist in bourgeois society to induce the patient to renounce his attachment to ways of being hostile to the social order, and to come to accept his allotted role as an undifferentiated part of it. The Laingian school sees ontological insecurity not as the cause but as the effect of institutionalized treatment. It is also an effect of the strenuous conflicts of family life, which requires conformity to social norms and a submission to authority. In the light of these alleged facts the Laingians propose a 'politics of experience', whereby the cure of the psychotic lies in upholding, rather than denying, the validity of his fundamental experiences. (*See also* *authenticity.)

(iv) Political questions are raised in addition by certain psychotherapeutic practices, such as the USSR practice of subjecting *dissidents to forced psychotherapy, often of a brutal and damaging kind (thus acting as though the Laingian thesis in (iii) were indeed true).

(v) Finally, the epidemic of psychoanalysis among the US middle classes, in which

American *individualism has taken a new and surprising form, with a priesthood of psychoanalysts who, through the confessional, reassure the individual of his irreplaceable value as an end in himself, while exploiting, according to some, his evident value as a means.

public goods. Goods which can be withheld from one person only by being withheld from all, and which must therefore be provided communally, e.g. street lighting, police protection, defence. It is sometimes argued that no economy, however weighted towards the *private sector, can rely on private enterprise to supply these goods, since no entrepreneur would have the power to compel payment for them. The evolution of modern economies might be seen as involving a progressive recognition of the extent to which this is true of the goods that are ordinarily needed by the citizen. The argument is not, however, universally accepted, and there are, particularly in the US, those who think that public goods can be and ought to be provided by private contract, suitably reinforced by the law.

public interest. Politicians and lawyers often refer to the 'public interest', arguing that such and such a policy is or is not in the public interest, or that publication of a document is or is not a public benefit. However, it is not clear what these and similar phrases mean. The public cannot be identified with the state, since a state can exist that is not in the public interest (e.g. a *tyranny). Nor can it be identified simply with the majority, since it might be in the majority interest to dissolve all social union and emigrate to the ends of the earth (say when the state is threatened with extinction by powerful neighbours), but it is doubtful that such a course could ever be in the '*public* interest'. It may be suggested that the public interest is the interest of a *civil society, and has, as one necessary component, the cohesion of that society and its continuance as an entity with interests of its own. It is then possible to define *interest as herein recommended: but what would be a *measure* of the public interest will always be hard to determine. Some argue that there is no 'essence' captured by the term 'public interest', which functions, rather, as a term of contrast, used differently for different purposes. For related problems *see* *collective choice, *common good, *social choice.

public morals. It has been held in England to be a crime to conspire to corrupt public morals. However the most important recent case (*Shaw v. DPP*, 1962), although a decision of the House of Lords, is now doubted, on account of the vagueness of the charge. It has also been held to exhibit unwarranted judicial *legislation, in that there is no law forbidding the corruption of public morals, so that the acts alleged (publishing a directory of prostitutes) were rendered criminal through a legislative application of the law of *conspiracy. However, it seems that the concept of conspiracy can, and arguably should, permit just such judicial legislation. The more problematic issue is that of 'public morals': what are they, and to what extent should the law attempt to protect them? *See* *law and morality.

public opinion. Not the *opinion of the majority but the opinion that is active in the public realm. Public opinion can thus be liberal at a time when the majority opinion is illiberal (as perhaps now in the UK, at least over matters of crime and punishment), revolutionary at a time when the majority are reactionary (as happens from time to time in France), and even reactionary when the majority opinion is mildly liberal (as perhaps has happened in Japan). The consulting of public opinion is an important part of politics, and presumably a necessary prelude to the conciliation which, on some views, is the essence of the political process.

Public opinion must always be distinguished from the criteria whereby it is estimated – such as opinion polls, pronouncements through the *media and so on. Nevertheless, there must be some relation between these and public opinion, and in the absence of any of them it is doubtful that public opinion exists as an independent force in politics. Thus it is doubtful that there is such a thing as public opinion in states where all means of expression are used for propaganda on behalf of the existing rulers; and, if there is, it is neither possible nor necessary to consult it. Others have doubted the utility of consulting public opinion even in ostensibly democratic states. Thus Walter Lippmann, in *Public Opinion,* 1922, argued that modern *communications have the effect of condensing all information into brief slogans. These slogans, he thought, create a wall of stereotypes between the citizen and the issues to which he is expected to respond.

public ownership. Ambiguous term which may mean:
1. *social ownership and control;
2. ownership and control by the *state;
3. ownership and control in part by the state;
4. any of 1. to 3. without ownership, or any of 1. to 3. without control. (*See* *separation of ownership and control.)

Defenders of 1. sometimes denounce 2. as *state capitalism, and feel that it is particularly pernicious to identify the public with the state, rather than with society. Defenders of *private enterprise feel that 'public ownership' is often in practice a euphemism for state control, and argue against it on a variety of grounds, such as the inefficiency, corruption, and tyranny that stems from state control. *See* *social ownership, for some of the counter-arguments.

public sector. That part of economic activity which is not privately owned, either because vested in the state, or because subject to *common ownership. It includes central government and local authorities, in addition to *nationalized industries and public corporations. It presently accounts for over one fifth of the *gross national product in the UK, as well as in most European countries, and often has a shortfall of receipts over expenditure which creates a semi-permanent 'public sector borrowing requirement'.

public spirit. *See* *consensus, *Montesquieu, *virtue.

Pufendorf, Samuel von (1632–94). German jurist; *see* *eminent domain, *international law.

punishment. Punishment may be defined as (i) the infliction of pain, privation or disadvantage, (ii) on the grounds of some wrong committed by the sufferer, (iii) by someone authorized so to do. Condition (iii) is sometimes disputed, partly because it involves the difficult concept of *authority. Perhaps it should be said only that the person who punishes must *think* himself authorized to inflict pain; however, he may derive this authorization merely from the belief that his victim deserves pain, i.e. from condition (ii).

The question of the justification of punishment, and of particular forms of punishment, is a major issue in legal and political philosophy, and one where conflicting intuitions abound. Theories of justification may be divided into the forward-looking and the backward-looking, the former finding the reason for punishment in its effects, the latter in its antecedents. It it also necessary to distinguish theories which attempt to give a justification for each punishment case by case, and theories which seek to justify only the practice of punishment, but which give no answer to questions concerning who should be punished when.

Forward-looking views may refer to the 'reforming' effect of punishment, to its effect as a 'deterrent', and to its effect as a 'restraint', it being clear that when maimed, dead or in prison a person is less likely to commit crime. In addition there is the 'expressive' theory, which justifies punishment in terms of its ability to express and relieve the feelings of public outrage at crime and to reaffirm the common moral sentiments of the community. The thought here is that, if not expressed through punishment, outrage will turn to private revenge, thereby endangering social order. All four forward-looking reasons might be offered together, and all may be used to justify the practice of punishment, and also the particular punishments which stem from it.

Among backward-looking views the most important is the 'retributive' theory. which says that the reason for punishing someone is simply that he deserves it because of what he has done. Punishment is, or tries to be, 'just retribution'. One defender of that view (*Hegel) even goes so far as to say that the criminal has a *right* to punishment and that not to inflict it is to treat him, not as a person, but as a thing. Hegel's idea, or something resembling it, is often offered in opposition to those who advocate forms of 'therapy', designed to 'cure' the criminal of his 'disease', in the place of the vivid sanction that picks him out as responsible for a wrong, and so acknowledges his freedom and the dignity that stems from it.

Against the retributive view it is sometimes said that it does not *justify* punishment, but only describes it: for this backward-looking reason is simply the element of the idea of punishment contained in condition (ii) above. Something more needs to be said if the practice is actually to be *justified,* and for those of a *utilitarian cast this something more must always be sought in the future and not in the past.

On the question of what form punishment should take the main dispute has concerned capital, and, to a lesser extent, corporal punishment. Some argue that these forms of punishment are never justified, since both violate a *human right of the victim, the first his right to life. the second (perhaps) his right to be treated so as to respect his dignity as a person. The US constitution forbids 'cruel and unusual' punishments, as do certain internationally applied treaties and charters of human rights, but the interpretation of this phrase seems to vary from place to place and from time to time. Some argue in favour of capital punishment on the grounds of its awe-inspiring effect, and perhaps of its power to 'concentrate the mind', as Dr Johnson put it. It is also sometimes said that, without this extreme punishment, there will be no way effectively to distinguish crimes like theft from crimes like cold-blooded murder which inspire a peculiar horror in the normal conscience. In this area it is clear that arguments of very different force and character are offered on both sides.

puppet regime. A *regime controlled by officials who act in the interests of, and under instructions from, the government of another state, usually sustained by threats of violence and economic coercion.

puritanism. **1.** The extreme forms of *Protestantism, in which the idea of the sovereignty of conscience is taken to require constant and scrupulous vigilance over one's every sentiment and action (and usually over everyone else's) in order to track down and extirpate all impure and irreligious thoughts and motives.
2. The secular survival of that doctrine, especially in Northern European and Anglo-Saxon countries, without its theological commitment, but with its same restless vigilance and self-examination, especially in matters of sexual morality, but also in any other area of personal life in which the self is of sufficient interest to provide the major subject of its own researches.

The influence of puritanism on English and American politics in the seventeenth, eighteenth and, to some extent, nineteenth century, has been so great that nothing brief can be said about it.

Q

quantity theory of money. *See* *monetarism.

quietism. Originally the name of a seventeenth-century mystical sect founded *c.* 1675 by a Spanish priest, M. de Molinor, which condemned all human effort, believing that perfection and salvation come only from God, and that man's task is to abandon himself passively to God's will, even to the extent of not caring about his own salvation. The term is now used to refer to any state of mind, or policy, that recommends prostrate acceptance of the principal fact – be it a conquering power, an economic order, an 'historical necessity', or whatever. Thus R. H. Hutton, in 1871: 'He was, in political and social conviction, a democratic quietist; one might almost say a fatalist.'

Quine, Willard van Orman (b. 1908). American philosopher. *See* *ontology, *relativism.

R

race. A term of varying significance, originally used to denote any class of people related by common descent in a manner significantly connected with their location, language and customs. Its use was extended to express what might be called a 'moral idea' of affinity. According to this usage, a race is defined by a significant common history, which causes people to react selectively towards one another, identifying with the triumphs and sufferings of the race to which they 'belong', and regarding the history, customs and outlook of that race as in some way closer to their own personal existence than those of any other race.

The moral idea is not to be confused with the later scientific and pseudo-scientific attempts to divide humanity into separate 'races' or subspecies, supposedly exhibiting separate genetic characteristics. This extension of the idea of kinship beyond all connection of place, language and custom was common in the nineteenth century. Thus *Gobineau thought it necessary to distinguish between races in order to explain the diverse physical characteristics and diverse states of development of mankind. Later it was even thought that human customs should be explained in racial terms, and not, for example, in terms of climate (as *Montesquieu had attempted). Some see the *nationalist theory of the **Volksgeist* as inherently racialist (i.e. as exhibiting a belief in the disparity of races); and certainly its late manifestation in *national socialism involved a deep commitment to that belief.

In the light of modern genetics the issue of whether there are separate human races in some scientifically acceptable sense has come to seem both obscure and – in all probability – of little consequence. It seems that characteristics such as skin colour and physiognomy, which are popularly taken as indicators of race, are genetically very superficial. The question whether there is something deeper and more significant in behaviour, of which these differences are a sign, is extremely hard to answer. Interbreeding among humans has taken place continuously throughout history, leaving only contested grounds for thinking that some important attribute might be possessed by one 'race' and not by another: at the most there might be a continuum of intelligence, say, or physical strength. The issue has become too emotive to be treated with scientific objectivity, and hence the term 'race' is still used in the popular sense of common descent, construed independently of any relation of custom, language or territory, of which the supposed signs are skin colour and physiognomy. It is in this sense that the term is involved in the consideration of *racism.

racism. The terms 'racialism' and 'racism' are sometimes used interchangeably. It is probably best to use the first to mean the belief that there are significant distinctions (whether moral, intellectual or cultural) between *races, and the second to denote the belief not only that there are such differences, but that they provide adequate grounds for different treatment, in particular for granting rights and privileges to members of one race, and withholding them from members of another. Such a belief may or may not be accompanied by some *theory* of the differences between races. The emotional root of racism lies in a sense that some people are *alien, not necessarily on account of those physical characteristics that are used to identify them (although the appeal to such characteristics is a very important part of racism). Some have tried to explain this sense of the 'alien' in sexual terms – thus *Sartre, in his attempted diagnosis of *anti-semitism. Others have looked for economic causes, such as the need to recruit and also to confine a class of slave labourers, and the associated need for ready signs whereby to identify members of that class. Neither explanation can really account for the variety and extent of modern racism. 'Racial discrimination', i.e. *discrimination on grounds of race, is now the subject of legislation in many states, which often expressly reaffirm as illegal practices which were illegal already.

radical. From Latin *radix,* a root, the radical is one who wishes to take his political ideas to their roots, and to affirm in a thoroughgoing way the doctrines that are delivered by that exercise. It is a mistake to think that a radical must be on the *left, although the popular association between the radical and the *extremist is not so far-fetched as it might appear. The radical will tend to be hostile to the **status quo,* and anxious for sweeping changes, since the *status quo* generally expresses a balance between conflicting opinions and temperaments, and presents a loose imperfect order that lacks the ready intelligibility of systematic ideas. For this reason, while there may be 'radical right' views, 'radical conservatism' is apt to seem oxymoronic.

radical chic. Phrase coined by the American journalist Tom Wolfe, to denote the affectation of radical left-wing views among middle-class intellectuals in order to achieve *status. *See also* *snobbery.

raison d'état. French: reason of state. A reason for state action which is of such importance as to involve the welfare and interests of the entire society, and to override all countervailing considerations, in particular those of an international character. The idea of the 'reason of state' entered political thinking during the sixteenth century, following the collapse of *ecclesiastical jurisdiction in international disputes. The principle that there are and must be such reasons was expounded by Giovanni Botero (1544-1617) (*Della Ragione di Stato,* 1590), and is implicit in *Grotius; it has been acknowledged in *international law since the Peace of Westphalia, 1648.

rastafarianism. *See* *ethiopianism.

rate of exploitation. *See* *exploitation.

rate of interest. The rate of interest is the difference between what is lent and what must be repaid after a specified time, expressed as a proposition of the amount lent; it is the price paid for borrowing a unit of money over that time. At any one time there tend to be different rates of interest prevailing for different types of loan. There are various explanations offered for the existence of a positive rate of interest:
(a) *time preference: money lent represents a sacrifice of present consumption for future income;
(b) sacrifice of *liquidity: the lender may not be able quickly to convert the asset back to money, except perhaps by selling it, which may be risky;
(c) risk and uncertainty: e.g. the borrower might not repay;
(d) inflation: without interest the sum repaid will be less in real terms than the sum lent.

ratification. 1. In *international law, the confirmation of a treaty or agreement. In UK ratification is by the *Crown, in US by the Senate. Since treaties are not binding unless ratified, this gives to the Senate large powers in international relations which might otherwise – had the English model been followed – have vested in the President.
2. The endowing of a **de facto* power with *authority, whether legal, moral or political, either by express act, as when a parliament legalizes the activities of an autonomous organization (for example, the initial legalization of the free trade union movement in Poland), or im-

plicitly, by the progressive *establishment of a power within the constitutional structures of a state. An example of the latter has been the gradual incorporation of trade unions into the mechanism of government in the UK, whereby legal *privilege has grown into quasi-constitutional right.

Ratification is a process whereby *power transforms itself into *authority, by gaining its title from offices and institutions which already possess it.

ratio decidendi. *See* *precedent.

rational. Human beings are rational beings, in that they are able to present and be guided by reasons for belief, reasons for action, and reasons for feeling and desiring. Moreover their choices and beliefs may or may not comply with the demands of reason. Hence 'rational' has two related senses in political discourse: it denotes the rational (as opposed to the non-rational) being, and the rational (as opposed to the irrational) act.

1. The rational being: a being who thinks and acts for reasons. Some philosophers argue that such a being must possess language, and that the possession of symbolism and reasoning powers is not an isolated capacity that can be thought of simply as an addition to the mental repertoire of a living being. On the contrary, reason permeates and transforms every element of the life of the being that possesses it. A rational being acquires intentions (in addition to desires), self-consciousness (in addition to consciousness), remorse and regret (in addition to disappointment), hope and determination (in addition to expectation), *values and ends (in addition to preferences and means). In short, it is argued that a rational being is a being of a different kind from a non-rational being, and this is often presented as a ground for the views that only rational beings are natural *persons, and that only rational beings have *rights.

None of the above thoughts is uncontroversial, but it is accepted on every hand that rationality is no simple matter, and makes the greatest possible difference to the life of the being who possesses it. *Aristotle argued that all and only rational animals are political animals: if this is so, then it would be right to be suspicious of political theories that apply equally to rational beings and to the biological affinities of herds and shoals. It seems implicit in the Aristotelian thesis that the rational being is essentially social. Some argue further and construe rationality as a social artefact, something that we possess, as we possess language, *by virtue of* our social relations. That is sometimes offered as a criticism of *individualism, which supposes that the individual can exist outside society, in a *state of nature, and still possess the rational capacities from which choices and values spring.

2. Rational choice. What makes a choice rational? This question has been subjected to extended quasi-mathematical treatment, e.g. in *decision theory, *game theory and the theories of *social choice. All such theories begin from premises concerning the ends of action (i.e. what is preferred), and try to examine the conditions under which ends may be rationally combined, and conditions for the rational choice of means. One obvious way of being irrational is to have inconsistent ends – and the exploration of inconsistency of choices plays a large part in all these theories. Another kind of irrationality is that involved in choosing means with a higher probability of failure than some equally feasible and equally desirable alternative. Furthermore, we have intuitions concerning time and rational choice: to choose a good now, rather than later, all other things being equal, may be more rational than to choose it later rather than now (*see* *time preference). All such intuitions can be built into the structure of a theory of rational choice, and the consequences delivered, and this is the main aim of decision theory.

Note that the intuitions mentioned concern either the choice of means to ends, or the reconciliation of ends. They do not settle the outstanding question of moral philosophy, whether there can be reasons given for an end of action which do not reduce it to a means. Aristotle thought that a rational being is fulfilled only through *virtue, and that virtue circumscribes the ends of conduct. Hence the ends of the vicious man, however consistent, ordered and susceptible to *optimal solution, are against reason. *Kant argued, from a quite different standpoint, that a rational being is constrained by reason to accept only some ends of conduct, and to reject others as inconsistent with reason's demands. This whole subject, while of the greatest importance, remains shrouded in darkness.

rational economic man. *See* *economic man.

rationalism. 1. The philosophical doctrine that the world is knowable to reason, and only to reason, and that the deliverances of the senses stand to be corrected in the light of reason. Rationalism has its origins in ancient metaphysics, especially in *Plato, but it is particularly associated with the modern 'rationalists', i.e. with the philosophers belonging to the movement which began with Descartes and which reached its culmination in the German academic philosophy of the *Enlightenment, to be rebutted by Kant in his *Critique of Pure Reason.* The principal exponents of rationalism were *Spinoza and (the main object of Kant's critique) Leibniz. Rationalism survived Kant's attacks, and indeed incorporated them, to re-emerge in the metaphysical idealism of *Hegel and his immediate followers. The debate between rationalism and *empiricism over the nature and object of knowledge still continues.

2. In *Weber, rationalism denotes the preference for 'legal-rational' over traditional and customary modes of *legitimation. Weber's thesis, that modern society has suffered a progressive *rationalization of all institutions, is often accepted as casting light on the peculiar difficulties that the ideas of *allegiance and *obedience present to members of those societies, since there will always be some point at which the appeal to rules of legitimation gives out, and what then?

3. Sometimes used as a general designation of the search for rational solutions in the place of prejudices, and for scientific explanations in the place of what are regarded as mysteries. *J. S. Mill called himself a rationalist in this sense, although he was far from being a rationalist in sense 1.

4. More widely, 'rationalism' is used to denote the disposition to favour clear and explicit solutions, based on principles, whatever the problems, and to attempt to force reality into the mould of an ideal of reason-governed behaviour. According to some (e.g. *Oakeshott), rationalism is a political vice, involved in every attempt to force political realities into the convenient contours of pre-established theory. Rationalist doctrines are held to conceive human nature as better fitted to the solutions proposed for it than to those that it would discover through its own innate capacity to adapt itself to reality and reality to itself, e.g. through *custom and *tradition. (*See also* *tacit communication.)

5. Sometimes, in sociology, 'rationalism' is used to denote the thesis, due to *Dilthey, that the action of a rational being is *sui generis,* to be understood through *hermeneutics, and by reference to assumptions of rationality, rather than through scientific prediction and explanation of a kind that might equally be applied to the rest of nature.

rationalization. 1. In *Weber, the appeal to *authority based on 'legal-rational' principles, i.e. principles that can be formulated as laws, and given the structure of a rational justification, however lacking in ultimate foundation. To rationalize the institution of monarchy, for example, is to give a theory of the nature and function of the monarch that justifies his authority in terms of legal precepts and constitutional rules, rather than in terms of his inherent right to *obedience.

2. In normal parlance, and also in *Freudian theory, the justification of a course of action by proposing a reason that is not its motive. Rationalization is a way of justifying action in terms that do not explain it. The *Marxian theory of *ideology involves the thought that rationalization might be both *systematic,* and determined by class.

raw materials. Those *factors of production that are not artefacts, excluding *labour. Raw materials include land, and the contents of land, e.g. iron ore.

Rawls, John (b. 1921). American philosopher who, in his *Theory of Justice,* 1971, attempts to reconcile a liberal ideal of political obligation with a redistributive conception of *social justice. The elements are:
(i) *Social contract. The contract is neither explicit nor tacit, but hypothetical: to determine the justice of an arrangement involves asking whether it *would* be the outcome of a social contract made under certain conditions.
(ii) The original position. The idea of the just arrangement is formed by abstraction from all actual social conditions so as to appeal to rationality alone. We suppose a 'veil of ignorance' to be drawn over social reality, and we choose from behind this veil the social arrangement that would then be acceptable to all. (The idea here has its roots in *Kant's categorical imperative.)
(iii) The original position is fair, and what is chosen in it is just, since it makes no ungrounded discrimination among members of society. Hence the resulting theory is one of 'justice as fairness'.
(iv) Two principles supposedly emerge from the thought experiment involved in the postulation of an original position. An arrangement is just if and only if (a) each person has an equal right to the most extensive basic liberty compatible with a similar liberty for all; (b) social and economic inequalities may exist only if they are reasonably expected to better the position of the least advantaged, and are attached to offices and positions open to all. Condition (b) is not supposed to apply until (a) is satisfied, and is itself an application of the *difference principle, which will be chosen in the original position because, by virtue of the element of abstraction (ii), rational choice must concern itself with the position of the worst off, whoever he might be. (*See* *maximin.)

The two principles define the just original position; all other arrangements are just to the extent that they can be traced back, via just transactions, to such a position. The resulting theory is worked out in considerable detail, and is interesting partly for its attempt to incorporate results from theories of *rational choice, while being expressly anti-*utilitarian (although some commentators have argued that the theory is in fact very utilitarian, differing largely in the constraints that it imposes on rational choice). It is often criticized (e.g. by *Nozick) for its supposed emphasis on the *end state of a transaction at the expense of the rights that are upheld and abused in the *course* of a transaction. Moreover, the status of the theory is unclear. It is not certain that it provides an account of justice that is binding on all rational beings, rather than a rationalization of moral intuitions which may themselves be rationally rejected. Nevertheless, the theory has been highly influential, partly because of its attempt to reconcile intuitions taken respectively from liberal and from socialist doctrine.

reactionary. The idea of 'forces of reaction' which seek to arrest or reverse the achievements of revolution or reform was introduced into political thought by the philosophical radicals of the nineteenth century. At the time it was normal to identify these forces as the church, the aristocracy, and the institutions of the *ancien régime*. The term is still the property of the *left, although it has been used by *national socialists and *fascists. A reactionary is anyone who opposes changes that the left desires, or who seeks to re-establish a political order that has been overthrown in the name of left-wing ideals. The implication is usually that such a one merely 'reacts' to change, and does not initiate change, so that he has no claim to be heard, being without serious recommendations.

real terms. The value of some variable, such as price or wages, when adjusted for changes in the purchasing power of money. Thus, if my income in money remains unchanged over a year during which inflation runs at 10%, my income in real terms decreases to 100/110 of its initial rate – i.e. by 9%. The 'real wage' is given by the money wage divided by an *index of the overall price level. Aggregate values, such as total investment or national income, are often expressed in real terms.

realism. 1. Political. The disposition to see things as they are, rather than as they ought to be, and to recognize that the principal aim of all agents in the political sphere is power and self-aggrandisement. Certain critics of US postwar foreign policy have commented on its lack of realism, meaning, whether fairly or not, that it has taken a 'legal-moralistic' view of international conflict, rather than perceiving it in terms of the real struggles for power and influence which the profession of legal and moral values tends to conceal. Such critics (including H. J. Morgenthau, *American Foreign Policy*, 1952) argue, not that ideals, values and law are irrelevant to international relations, but that they must be tempered by a vision of the real underlying tendency in terms of power, and that the *national interest must be rendered secure enough to make action in the name of values effective. Most defenders of *power theories of politics are identified as realists by those who now identify themselves by that label.
2. Legal. *See* *law.
3. Metaphysical. A realist is someone who believes some object, class of objects, or property to be real and independent of our perceptions. Thus 'social realism' denotes a belief in the reality of social entities, such as society, the state and institutions, over and above the individuals who compose them (to be contrasted with *reductionism); 'moral realism' denotes the view that moral values are part of the fabric of reality and not merely a projection of human attitudes; and so on.

Realpolitik. German: politics of the real. A term introduced by the German publicist Ludwig von Rochau in his *Grundsätze der Realpolitik,* 1853, in which he criticized the lack of *realism in the policies followed by German liberals during the revolutionary years of 1848–9. The term was popularized later, since it seemed to capture the essence of Bismarck's policy during and after the years of German unification: a scrupulous attention to what is possible, a shrewd estimation of what one's opponent really wants, rather than what he says he wants, and a preparedness to assert *force when necessary. This particular brand of political realism should be distinguished from *power politics, or from the politics of the *non-negotiable demand, neither of which need be realistic.

reasonable man. A creature known at *common law (which has yet to recognize the reasonable woman), as the standard against which human conduct is to be judged, and who remains undefined except through the social judgements of courts and juries. The 'reasonable man' test (for example, for negligence) suggests that the fundamental characteristics are prudence, stability and foresight, but not so much of any of these as would prove offensive or unnatural to others. The use of the attribute of 'reasonableness' to define what is in effect *normal human conduct has the interesting implication that human nature is to be defined at least partly through study of rationality. The invocation of the reasonable man in a proposed test for *obscenity (*The Williams Report,* 1979) suggests that reasonableness can also be understood as qualifying susceptibilities.

rebellion. Violent opposition by a substantial body of persons against the lawfully constituted authority of a state, in the attempt to overthrow it. A rebellion can succeed in installing in power members of the same *class as those whom they replace; this is sometimes supposed not to be the case in a *revolution.

recession. A temporary period of underuse of labour and capital resources, producing unemployment and decline in production. Cf. *depression. The term may also be used to denote the decline of an economy, i.e. the falling of the level of activity.

recognition. In *international law, any political and executive act which expresses or implies a legal significance in the acts of another state. An extremely complex idea, which has led to the need to distinguish **de facto* from *de jure* recognition, the first being extended, in the absence of any legal constitution, to powers with which it is necessary to deal while they last.

redistribution. **1.** A reorganization of the boundaries between electoral districts in order to change the relation of *representation. This has often taken place in the UK, in response to the growth of towns and the depopulation of the countryside, although time-lags have led to notorious anomalies. Thus during the early nineteenth century, a country district of a few hundred might return two members to Parliament, and a swelling industrial town only one. (The problem of the 'rotten boroughs'.) On the larger issue of justice, *see* *representation.
2. The redistribution of *land, in accordance with conceptions of efficiency, justice or jurisdiction. *See* *land reform.
3. The redistribution of income and rewards in order to achieve some economic or social objective, usually that of *social justice in the distribution of goods. Modern moves in this direction have tended to advocate either direct state control over salaries and wages, usually combined with public ownership of the means of production, or else progressive *taxation, designed to ensure that the differential between the highest and the lowest paid is offset by a heavier burden of taxation on the former. Some argue that these measures do not work and that income distribution will always remain unaffected by them (*see* *Pareto). Others argue that questions of distribution cannot be separated from questions of ownership, so that effective state redistribution must accompany state control of production. Others reject progressive taxation, as involving an injustice towards the rich, in asking them to surrender not just a higher amount, but a higher proportion of what they earn. It is sometimes added that a person has a high earning capacity because of his social function, and progressive taxation will therefore discourage the most useful from taking on the work that is required from them. On these issues, *see* *sumptuary laws, *taxation.

reductionism. The attempt, in philosophy, the social sciences, and elsewhere, to avoid reference to entities regarded as non-existent, usually by systematic replacement of the language which seems to refer to them. Thus a philosopher might attempt to replace all reference to social entities by references to individuals, and suggest some systematic replacement for all sentences in which terms like 'state', 'society', and 'institution' occur. In political thought reductionism is often not carried through in that way, although in the debate concerning methodological *individualism, as opposed to *holism, the discussion is very much influenced by analytical philosophy, and therefore directs itself at least to the *possibility* of such systematic reduction. Recent philosophy has suggested that there may be fundamental errors involved in the assumption that reduction could be carried through (e.g. it seems that any replacement for the offending sentences will either fail to capture the original meaning, or else be unintelligible because infinitely complex). In the face of difficulties, reductionists tend to take refuge in an appeal to common sense, characteristically making use of the locution 'nothing but. . .', as in: 'authority is nothing but established power'; 'values are nothing but ideology'; or 'law is nothing but the will of the ruling class'.

re-education. The process whereby political opinions and attitudes are deliberately changed or suppressed, through education and *propaganda, sometimes accompanied by threats and *coercion. The process is sometimes called 'rectification' (term introduced by *Mao in 1929), and may have a relatively benign significance. In the West, however, it is normally thought to be a euphemism for a process designed to change the outlook of the victim regardless of reason, involving forced attendance at institutions of a disciplinary nature.

Threats are irrelevent to the inculcation of belief, but they may certainly cause their victim to simulate belief. When the re-educated individual emerges, therefore, he may be an adept at **ketman* and, as such, regarded with yet greater suspicion by those in power. Hence the process of re-education may be never-ending. It is much practised in China and Vietnam, and is there thought to reflect traditional habits both of education and of *indoctrination.

referendum. The referring of a political question to the *electorate for a direct decision by popular vote. In some constitutions (e.g. that of Australia) the constitution can be amended only with the consent of the electorate at a referendum, and the device is frequently used (although not required) in France, in order to validate constitutional change. It has recently been used in the UK, but is unknown in the US.

A referendum involves a decision by the electorate without the intermediary of *representation, and therefore exhibits a form of *direct democracy. However, to say that is to assume that the question asked of the electorate is intelligible to the majority, and also that it is one that is sensibly submitted to its vote. Some have doubted that either of those conditions was fulfilled in the case of the UK referendum on the Common Market; but it seems that in any case a referendum has no legal or constitutional authority in the UK. (This is part of the doctrine of the *sovereignty of *Parliament.)

reflation. The deliberate policy of expanding aggregate demand in the economy, e.g. by expanding the *money supply. According to *monetarists reflation automatically causes *inflation, and indeed *Hayek has referred to 'reflation' as 'a fraudulent term meaning inflation'.

reform. A process of political change within the framework of a *constitution, and without questioning the *legitimacy of the *sovereign power. The net result of continuous reform may be a change of constitution (whether in fact or in law), but the essential feature is the absence of challenge to the received political process. 'Reform' in the UK has meant, from the nineteenth century at least, electoral reform, particularly the extension of the *franchise through the Reform Act 1832 and the Representation of the People Acts 1867, 1884 and 1918.

Reformation. The religious movement that swept through Europe in the sixteenth century challenging the authority, doctrine and liturgy of the *Roman Catholic Church, and leading to the rise of *Lutheranism, *Calvinism and the *Protestant churches. The Reformation must not be confused with the changes introduced into the Church of England during the 'Reformation Parliament' of 1529–36, which were of a political rather than a religious nature, designed to unite the secular and religious sources of authority within a single sovereign power: the *Anglican Church did not until later make any substantial change in doctrine.

reformism. The advocacy of improvement by *reform, rather than by *revolution, either out of the conservative respect for constitution, as embodying unspoken wisdom condensed and applied in customary usage (cf. *Burke: 'one must reform in order to conserve'), or out of a sense that, without a frame of constitution and legitimacy, no political change is sufficiently predictable to be cogently intended. Many also regard the absence of any provision for reform as dangerous, arguing that a rigid constitution will not adapt to changing social circumstances, will therefore enter into ruinous conflict with social forces that it cannot control, and will so precipitate revolution, anarchy and, in the wake of anarchy, tyranny. Reformism is often identified as the principal enemy of revolutionaries who wish to exacerbate existing conflicts, and not to conciliate or soften them.

regime. French: a regimen, i.e. a form of rule. Now generally used to denote the actual holders of office within a government, considered independently of the offices which they hold. On this definition there can be a change of regime without a change of *constitution or *office, and vice versa, as when a ruling party recasts the constitution in order to preserve its power. (An example of the former: the change of ruling party after a UK election; an example of the latter, the proposals of the Zanu Party in Zimbabwe to perpetuate its own power through the creation of a one-party state.) Since the nature of a regime is determined in part by the offices which it occupies, 'regime' and 'government' may be used synonymously, but on the definition given they are no more synonymous than are 'the Queen' and 'the Crown'.

regionalism. The advocacy of forms of government which permit and encourage the development of indigenous culture and institutions within separate regions of the *jurisdiction, and which involve the *delegation of substantial political and legal powers to regional authorities with less than full *sovereignty but more than merely administrative functions.

rehabilitation. Term of political science used, for example, of the posthumous restoration to favour and acquittal of a victim of a purge, under a *Stalinist regime. Often the victim will have been already executed, and the process of rehabilitation will involve careful planning in order to avoid bringing law and government into total disrepute. Thus only six of those convicted in the notorious Moscow Trials have been rehabilitated, although statements have been made implying that all were innocent. Some observers also refer to 'de-rehabilitation', when some rehabilitated politician is again denounced as a traitor.

Reich, Wilhelm (1897–1957). Psychoanalyst, and student of *Freud, who attempted to *politicize Freud's theory of sexual *repression. In modern society (both communist and capitalist) the libido is repressed in ways which profoundly affect the individual character, and the nature of political institutions. Reich disagreed with Freud's view that repression performs a functionally necessary role in society, and argued (in *The Invasion of Compulsory Sex-Morality*, 1932) that the patriarchal family suppresses individual expression and fulfilment, and causes those subject to its influence to experience all social relations in terms of sanctions and fear. It is misguided to attempt to overcome this stultification of the individual by transforming the economic *base of social relations, as Marxists seek to do. Class distinctions too are largely irrelevant, since the oppression which Marx rightly discerned at the heart of the social order occurs at a deeper level; it is there, on the plane of individual sexuality, that it must be overcome.

Reich criticized both fascism and communism ('red fascism') for their coercive nature, and saw them both as expressions of the same warped instincts, and as inherently exploitative of the masses' propensity to submit to external control (*The Mass Psychology of Fascism*, 1933–4). His naïve and sentimental view of human sexuality was shared by *Marcuse, and he had, at one point, considerable influence over *libertarian thinking.

reification. German: *Versachlichung* or *Verdinglichung*. Term introduced by Marx and popularized by *Lukács (see *History and Class Consciousness*, 1971), and by *Marcuse and others of the *Frankfurt school, in order to describe the process whereby, in a society organized according to the principles of capitalism, the labourer endows commodities, *exchange-values, the economic laws which seem to govern them, and the institutions which protect them, with a real existence independent of himself. By virtue of this process, Lukács argues, the labourer is unable to perceive that he alone is responsible for the existence and nature of these things, their reality being derived entirely from his own labour. Reification is a form of *false consciousness. It also causes the labourer to see himself as diminished, unreal, inert, to the extent that he transfers through his actions the real powers that belong to him to the illusory world which commands his attention. The concept thus brings together the two Marxian ideas of *alienation and *commodity fetishism.

relativism. **1.** Moral. The view that *ideals and *values do not have universal validity, but are valid only in relation to particular social and historical conditions. ('What is truth on one side of the Pyrenees, is error on the other' – Pascal.) Moral relativism is to be distinguished from moral subjectivism, which says that no moral judgements have any validity whatsoever, beyond the fact of recording someone's subjective conviction. The relativist might think that moral judgements are objective while denying that they are universal.
2. Cultural. 'Cultural relativism' is the view that particular beliefs and practices make sense in one cultural context but not in another, and cannot be transplanted into another culture. Such views tend to be *organicist, and to argue that cultural transplants are a surgical impossibility.
3. Epistemological or cognitive. The view, associated with such philosophers as W. V. Quine and T. S. Kuhn, that observation and theory are inseparable, so that 'data' are intrinsically interpreted in terms of a theory, and cannot be regarded as 'given' independently. Epistemological relativism also implies (according to Quine) a relativism of *ontology. It has been extremely influential both directly, in philosophy, and also indirectly in the social sciences, and the *sociology of knowledge.

religion. The belief in, worship of, and attempt to obey, transcendent beings, usually on the assumption that they possess the power to regulate affairs in this world, and to distribute rewards and punishments in another. For some the single most powerful motive in human history, for others a mere device whereby the injustice of the existing social order is made tolerable to those destined to suffer it, and due to decline with the eventual mastery over nature and the tearing away of the veil of *ideology.

Religion and politics can never be separated in the minds either of believers or of those who seek to govern them, and religious conceptions have influenced almost all of the concepts and institutions of modern Western government: the law, through *canon law and *natural law; *sovereignty, through the doctrine of international *jurisdiction; property, through the doctrines of the *just price and *usury; social welfare and education, through the command of *charity; political obligation, through the commands of *piety and obedience; and political stability, through the belief that perfection belongs not to this world but to another.

rent. **1.** In economics, a technical term, defined as the factor price received *minus* the lowest factor price which would have induced the factor unit in question to remain in its current employment. (Thus a philosophy lecturer earning £11,000 who would stay in his job even at £7,000 (though not less) has a 'rent' of £4,000.)
2. In normal parlance, the price paid per unit of time for the use of something durable, especially land and the buildings upon it. The problem of the nature of rent, and the factors which determine it, exercised the *classical economists – *Malthus, *Ricardo, and others – who produced, in effect, a *marginal productivity theory of the rent accruing to agricultural land.

The moral and legal problems of rent (particularly of residential accommodation) and of rent control have been important in European politics during the present century. Some argue that rent control is intrinsically unacceptable, in that it involves massive interference in contractual relations in favour of one party, and sometimes after the bargain has been struck. This, it is sometimes said, infringes a requirement of *natural justice, so that rent control and, in particular, legislation providing security of tenure, are unjust. Others argue that the payment of rent for land and buildings should not be considered under the ordinary philosophy of contract, but rather under the philosophy of *land law, in which *prescriptive right and security of tenure are of the essence. The arguments here are various, but one important consideration is obviously that security of tenure of property is at the root of every other security that a person may enjoy. In which case statutory controls over rent and tenure serve merely to ratify what ought already to be judged as a tenure of land.

reparations. A form of war indemnity, whereby the loser pays large sums to some party of the winner's choice, usually the winner itself. Reparations were demanded of Germany by the peace treaties of 1919–20; the demand was heavily criticized by economists, especially *Keynes, and is thought to have furthered the economic collapse of Germany, to have absorbed money in unpaid loans from the victors, and to have contributed to the turmoil from which Germany was to emerge with another burden of reparations, this time to Israel.

representation. **1**. The process whereby the interests of the governed are 'represented' to those who govern them, for example through parliamentary institutions. The practice of representation in the UK is as old as the English Parliament, although its form has changed radically over the centuries. It is still not wholly clear what representation consists in, or what conditions determine its just and efficient functioning. *Burke made a celebrated distinction between representation and *delegation thus: 'a delegate merely mirrors and records the views of his constituents, whereas a representative is elected to judge according to his own conscience'. However, it is clear that if the representative's conscience told him to disobey all petitions from those who elected him, it would be odd to describe him as continuing to represent them. A further complication is introduced by the idea of mandation, and the doctrine of the *mandate, which suggests obedience to promises as a criterion for the legitimacy of a representational office. It is probably most useful to distinguish representation, delegation and mandation as three separate relations between an officer and those to whom he is answerable. These relations may or may not occur together:

(i) mandation: the relation between an office-holder and an electorate, by virtue of the promises of the former to the latter, under which he is obliged to fulfil those promises;

(ii) delegation: the relation between an officer and an electorate, when the electorate has instructed him to convey certain requests and commands to another body;

(iii) representation: the relation between an officer and an electorate who have no power over the officer other than that provided by an election, and in which the officer is bound (a) to obey the principles and constitution of the assembly in which he sits, and (b) within that framework, to urge consideration of the interests of his constituents.

The essential feature here is that a representative is bound by a double duty, that towards the institution in which he sits, and that towards the electorate. Neither duty is the result of a promise, but each must be upheld in obedience to the constitution under which the representative holds office. Thus representation is a conventional relation, mediated by conventions and rules, while delegation and mandation are both natural relations, founded in obligations undertaken by the appointee.

On this view, what makes someone a representative of a constituency or a group is not to be found in the existence or extent of the franchise. For example, representation may be by command from the sovereign; it seems that this was the case in the early days of the English Parliament, when representation of a borough was often undertaken with great reluctance by those commanded. However, many argue that it is impossible that someone should really represent the interests of a group if that group has no power either to elect or to eject him from the assembly, and hence that representation without franchise is not really the same thing as representation with it. The point here is that the representative must be not just *influenced but, in some crucial sense, *controlled, by those whose interest he represents – otherwise he will represent the state to its subjects, but not the subjects to the state. (Cf. *democratic centralism.)

This raises, however, the problem of the nature of the franchise. Some argue that a representative is more likely to respond to the interests of those who appoint him if they are identified with a specific place, where he himself is resident, and with the social and economic conditions with which he is familiar. In which case, the idea of the 'constituency', as enshrined in UK electoral law, emerges as denoting the second term of the relation. Others argue, perhaps in the interests of *proportional representation, that the UK system does not lead to an assembly which fairly represents the differences of opinion within the state, and that representation by interest ought therefore to be made explicit. For example each candidate ought to state, say through his allegiance to a party, where his interest lies, the votes of the electorate for the various parties then determining how many seats in the chamber are allotted to each. Roughly speaking, the first conception reflects a view of representation as involving an obligation towards a group of people identified in terms of an existing social and territorial relation, the second involves a view of representation as involving obligations towards a group identified in terms of their opinion. In fact, under the second view, parties and not people take the leading role as the principal channel through which public opinion influences government, and some argue that this makes representation of the **people* less likely, and not more.

2. Existential representation. Term coined by Eric Voegelin, in order to designate the traditional relation between a prince and his subjects, whereby the prince took the name of a territory, and was identified by the people of that territory as a personal embodiment of their political unity.

representative government. *See* *representation.

repression. A term introduced into the theory of psychoanalysis by *Freud, to refer to two supposed processes whereby impulses are buried in the unconscious: primal repression, whereby the young child defends itself from mental tension by endowing objects with the power to overcome that tension, and repression proper, which is the defence mechanism against those unconscious wishes and impulses that might, were they to rise into consciousness, cause unbearable tensions in the 'ego'. Repression involves mechanisms and subterfuges whereby such wishes and impulses are kept blocked in the unconscious.

The Freudian language is dense with dubious metaphors of the mind; nevertheless it has had a wide influence on political thought, proving persuasive in its redefinition of the process of moral education, and also useful to certain *neo-Marxist theories of *structural violence, which construe the allegedly oppressive character of bourgeois society in terms of the repression of instincts vital to *self-realization.

reprisals. When a state has failed to secure redress against another for a legal wrong by diplomatic means it may, in certain circumstances, commit injurious acts short of war, of a kind which would otherwise be illegal. Frequently what one state calls reprisals the other state will call acts of *aggression, and in modern times reprisals have usually come from greater powers towards smaller ones, so ensuring that war will not be the outcome. Reprisals are not permitted in the case where the delinquent state discharges whatever vicarious responsibility it might have for the injurious acts of its officials or armies.

Reprisals may be performed only by the state or its officials or forces, and against everything belonging to the delinquent state and its citizens. Negative reprisals consist in refusals to perform obligations, such as the repayment of a debt. Reprisals should be proportionate to the wrong done and limited to the compulsion necessary to obtain redress. In times of war reprisals may also exist, in this case to compel the other side to obey the laws of war.

reproduction. Important term in communist economic theory, taken from Marx's analysis of the reproduction of the means of production (*Capital*, vol. II). Reproduction includes *economic growth, but it is said to exist whether or not there is positive *accumulation, or rising *national income. A decline in production still involves reproduction.

republic. Latin: the public thing, in other words the state and its institutions. The term is now normally used to denote any state that is not a monarchy, or any non-monarchical federated part of a state which retains sufficient autonomy to exercise its own *jurisdiction.

Debates concerning the utility or otherwise of republics as opposed to monarchies now have a slightly antiquated air, and, although the Irish Republican Army is 'fighting' in a cause said to be republican, it is clear that the abolition of the UK monarchy would not suffice to remove its grievance. In comparison with a modern *constitutional monarchy, a republic tends to be distinguished by the enormous concentration of power in the head of state. This fact, which accords with the eminently progressive character of republics, was not foreseen by Ambrose Bierce when, in *The Devil's Dictionary*, he defined 'republic' thus: 'a nation in which, the thing governing and the thing governed being the same, there is only a permitted authority to enforce an optional obedience. In a republic the foundation of public order is the ever lessening habit of submission inherited from ancestors who, being truly governed, submitted because they had to. There are as many kinds of republics as there are gradations between the despotisms whence they came and the anarchy whither they lead.'

Bierce's definition usefully suggests that the distinction between republic and monarchy has, historically, corresponded to two rival theories of political obligation, one based in an idea of *consent, the other in an idea of *obedience.

Republican Party. The US Republican Party was founded in 1792 by *Jefferson, in order to defend agrarian interests and *states' rights, although the lineal heirs of Jefferson's Republicans are probably to be counted among today's Democrats. The Republican Party was re-formed as an anti-slavery coalition in 1854, and since then has gradually fitted itself into the common mould which the US constitution imposes on the main parties contending for office. It has gradually incorporated sections of public opinion that could be said to be *right of centre, but has shifted from the rural federalism of Jefferson to the free enterprise urban capitalism defended by the economists of the *New Right. The successes of the party since 1932 have been spasmodic, but it is now able to call upon considerable popular support through its image of tough-minded patriotism and international **Realpolitik*.

The name of the party originally signified Jefferson's theory that truly republican government required a federal constitution, and that only by the constant affirmation of states' rights could the office of President be kept from becoming monarchical. (For Jefferson the idea of monarchy was the idea of executive power of an overbearing, whether or not absolute, kind, vested in a single person.) The name persisted, as did the emphasis on states' rights, but it is now of no more than vestigial significance. Parties calling themselves republican exist elsewhere, even in one-party states, but they are united by no common principles, not even that contained (under Jefferson's interpretation) in their name.

resale price maintenance. The practice whereby a producer requires distributors to resell a product at a certain minimum price. There have been major inquiries by governments in the UK with the object of determining whether or not this practice is in the public interest. In 1964 it was decided (the Resale Prices Act) that all resale price agreements are to be deemed against the public interest, and therefore unenforceable at law, unless proved otherwise in court.

reserve army of labour. *See* *industrial army.

residue. A term used by *Pareto to denote fundamental impulses which motivate human conduct and which, while they appear to the agent as 'ideas', 'values' and 'convictions', exist independently, as enduring features of the human condition, unaffected by any rational argument or intellectual change. The theory of the relation between an idea and its residue bears some similarity to the *Marxian theory of the relation between an *ideology and its material conditions. The difference is that, for Pareto, a residue is not itself historically variable, but rather a more or less permanent datum of human nature, whereas for Marx the material conditions which determine ideology are themselves subject to, and also the principal locus of, historical change.

resistance. *Opposition which is denied legal recognition, either because all opposition is denied legal recognition, or because it is of such a character as to fall outside those categories of opposition recognized in law. Resistance must therefore be either clandestine (as in the underground resistance in the Second World War) or *passive.

resources. Another name for the *factors of production, and conventionally classified into land, labour and capital, the first being given a wide sense to include *raw materials, the second covering every known employment, including book-keeping, accounting, etc., the last covering all produced means of production (goods made to produce other goods).

Resources are always scarce relative to the desired level of production, and hence there is major political dispute over their allocation, and over the role of government in determining their allocation. It is a familiar anti-capitalist thesis that capitalism is wasteful of resources. It is a familiar anti-communist thesis that communism is even more wasteful. It is possible that both are right, or that the order should be reversed.

responsibility. 1. The feature of *agency without which there can be neither praise nor blame for what is done. If you and I are forcibly confined in a sealed container, then every breath of mine deprives you of air; but I am not responsible for your death by asphyxiation, as I would be were I to confine you and then deliberately to extract the air. The difference is intuitively obvious, but not easy to define. Old ideas of metaphysical *freedom, according to which the uncaused spontaneous act of will intercedes in the processes of nature, tend now to be rejected, not the least because they cannot account for responsibility. (Responsibility is often said to involve a *kind* of causation, not freedom from causation). Lawyers are used to laying down negative conditions for responsibility, i.e. conditions in which someone is *not* responsible for the consequences of his acts, as when he is *coerced into doing them, and likewise conditions of 'diminished responsibility'. But the attempt to specify positive conditions meets with nearly insuperable obstacles, deriving in part from obscurities in the idea of agency. We hold people responsible for the consequences of negligence, even though negligence is not something 'done'. And among things done and done deliberately we still distinguish cases where responsibility is lifted. Self-defence is an obvious example; less clear is the case of the soldier acting under orders. (The concept of a *war crime is that of an action that cannot be excused, even by orders from a superior officer.) Some argue that responsibility is affected by *office, and that this must be borne in mind when assessing the responsibility of President Truman for the deaths that resulted from the bombing of Hiroshima. Others go further and argue that responsibility may even be affected by belief, so that, for example, Lenin's belief that the powers assumed in the name of the party would be temporary, exonerates him from the terrible consequences that have ensued from that. All those cases are disputed (*see* *morality and politics), and it is fair to say that nothing is very clear about the concept of responsibility, not even its purpose. (Some say that the purpose is to channel praise and blame towards those actions which they might actually influence; others say that it is simply to describe the character of the person who is held responsible.)

2. Sometimes 'responsibility' is used to denote an action or sphere of action which is part of someone's duty, either as holder of an office, or as moral or political agent. In this sense responsibility is the converse of *accountability, and a person's responsibilities may indeed determine that sphere in which he is also responsible, in sense 1., for the outcome of whatever he does or neglects to do.

restrictive practices. All practices which, while they may be valid in *common law, have the deliberate effect of restraining open *competition in a market. In the UK the Restrictive Practices Act 1956 created a new judicial tribunal to investigate such practices, for example *resale price maintenance agreements. Some restrictive practices have always been considered invalid under common law rules of restraint of trade and conspiracy.

retaliation. Response to an act of *aggression; see especially *massive retaliation. It is sometimes regarded as proof that international relations remain in a *state of nature that the threat of retaliation is still the main factor to be considered in aggressive foreign policy, and the main force behind a policy of *deterrence. However, if it is possible to *recognize* aggression, and to distinguish it from retaliation, to that extent the state of nature has been superseded by something else, even if not by a *rule of law.

retribution. *See* *punishment.

retroactive legislation. Sometimes called 'retrospective legislation'. A law which expressly or by implication renders illegal, or otherwise affects, actions performed before it was passed. There is a presumption against such legislation in both UK and US law, but it is not unknown, especially where the consequences of not rectifying a legislative oversight might be politically or socially disastrous (see, for example, *Burmah Oil Co. Ltd.* v. *Lord Advocate*, 1965) or in the levying of taxes, where deliberation might have to come later than enforcement. Whereas retroactive legislation in civil law may sometimes be tolerated, it seems that it is almost never explicitly tolerated in criminal law, and may even be unconstitutional in the US. The grounds upon which it is criticized are two: (a) it is an offence to *natural justice, since it implies that a person cannot know the legal consequences of an action for which he is subsequently judged; (b) it violates *judicial independence, since it enables the legislature to reverse judicial decisions. The two criticisms are independent: Frederick the Great reversed judicial decisions in the *interests* of natural justice in the famous case of Miller Arnold, 1779, in which judges were prosecuted for applying the law as it was. It is sometimes said that (b) is not in itself an objection, since *judicial independence is tantamount to judicial legislation, which is in turn tantamount to retroactive legislation (on which, *see*, e.g., *hard cases).

***revanchisme*.** The policy and procedure of revenge as a coordinated political activity. Revanchists are those with a grievance which they seek to rectify at all costs, the world being out of joint for them until retribution is exacted. Examples among modern political movements include certain movements within the Palestine Liberation Organization, and others within Armenian separatist groups in Turkey.

revealed preference. A preference that is revealed in an actual choice of one bundle of goods over another. Revealed preferences are said to provide an empirical test of economic theories. The resulting theory is associated with the name of P. A. Samuelson, who uses the concept of revealed preference rather than the classical and, it is supposed, less empirically based ideas of utility.

reverse discrimination. *Discrimination in favour of members of a certain group, in order to rectify an inherent inequality of opportunity experienced by that group. Reverse discrimination has been advocated in the cause of the rights both of women and of blacks, and in the US it is occasionally practised. It has been criticized on the ground that it exhibits precisely the kind of injustice (favouring someone on grounds irrelevant to the purpose) that it is supposed to overcome. The reply is sometimes made that the aim is to rectify a 'structural' injustice, and therefore that there are competing claims for justice – that of the present contenders for advantage, and that of social groups as a whole – which must be balanced against each other. It is only by practising reverse discrimination, for a period, that such 'structural' injustice will be overcome.

revisionism. **1.** Defined by *Lenin as 'opposition to Marxism from within Marxism itself' (*Marxism and Revisionism*, 1908). The charge of 'revisionism' was first levelled by *Kautsky, in a polemical attack on the *social democrat Eduard Bernstein (1850–1932), and denoted a critical reinterpretation and partial rejection of Marxist theories, so as to make room for the social democrat vision of institutional change. Bernstein believed that *revolution is not essential to the transformation from *bourgeois democracy to 'true communism' and to *socialization of the means of production. He held that existing institutions should be used in order to instigate radical reforms, modifying production relations and modes of ownership by degrees, until the ideal of communism is achieved by legal and peaceful means. Bernstein did not rule out radical *confrontation, as in a general strike, but he thought that the proletariat would always be the loser in a contest of arms. This last idea brought down on him the fury of Lenin, so that 'revisionism' has since been used in the USSR as a label for some of the most serious heresies within communist ideology. Hence:

2. As described in the *Political Dictionary*, edited by party ideologist Boris Ponomaryov, revisionism is 'a trend in the working class movement that, to the benefit of the bourgeoisie, seeks to debase, to emasculate, to destroy Marxism by means of revision, that is by way of re-examination, distortion and negation of its basic tenets'. The heresies denoted by this term include those of the social democrats, and all other philosophies which suggest that classes ought to be reconciled. In addition, it seems, the following crimes are to be included: denying the aggressive essence of capitalist *imperialism; denying the directing and guiding role of the Communist Party; denying the universal importance of Lenin's theory of the dictatorship of the proletariat; rejecting *democratic centralism and demanding 'liberty of factions and factional struggles' (i.e. legalized *opposition); rejecting proletarian internationalism and sliding into 'national communism'. Many ideologists also include rejection of the *labour theory of value (e.g. through emphasis on the role of capital in generating value) as one of the facets of revisionism.

All those crimes can be seen to be parts of a single thought: that the Communist Party might not be entitled to the absolute power that it exercises. Hence the extreme seriousness of the charge.

3. The label 'revisionism' is sometimes

used to denote those American historians who reinterpret the history of the *cold war, so as to transfer blame on to the US.

revolution. Political scientists are deeply divided concerning both the meaning of the term 'revolution' and the true explanation of the phenomena denoted by it. To some extent the chosen explanation will determine the chosen meaning, so that theoretical discussions over whether the American Revolution, say, was a 'true revolution' will not be resolved merely by a dictionary definition. It is clear that the meaning of the term has changed, since it was first used of the 'Glorious Revolution' in England of 1688. What was then meant was the 'revolution' to some previous and lamented state of affairs, the term denoting the turning of the wheel of fortune. Now it seems to mean any major transformation that occurs simultaneously on the social and the political level, upsetting expectations and conformities that were sufficiently well established to define all important forms of association under the preceding order. The element of violence is sometimes considered necessary – although this is partly because those who advance this idea are influenced by a theory of 'revolutionary transformation' which requires it. An exception to such a thesis is the American Revolution, which was relatively pacific, and culminated in the calm and reasonable adoption of a constitution that has sometimes been thought to be the most imaginative piece of applied political science in human history. One theorist (Hannah Arendt: *On Revolution*, 1963) chooses to regard this example, not as exceptional, but as the prime example of a successful revolution. She argues that all political transformations called revolutions are united by the straining of subject peoples towards liberty, and the search for a constitution that will guarantee liberty. The Glorious Revolution, and the American Revolution, thus seem to be examples of revolutions which have achieved their ends, partly because they avoided the violence and social upheaval of later revolutions, and partly because transformation occurred at the political level, while retaining sufficient social continuity to guarantee stability.

Modern theorists are for the most part unpersuaded by Arendt's account, which, in the light of such phenomena as the recent 'Islamic Revolution' in Iran, can only seem stipulative. They tend to argue that violent transformations are of a different kind from non-violent ones. The ancestor of such a view is the theory of *Marx, which regarded the French Revolution as the paradigm, and which was, if not obsessed, at least fascinated by the enormous and hitherto undiscovered *forces* which that revolution unleashed. Thus there emerged the Marxian theory of revolution, which exists in two possibly compatible versions. The first version holds that revolutions occur when *productive forces develop to the point where *production relations begin to fetter them and, those enormous forces having been contained only briefly, the fetters burst asunder, toppling all institutions along with them. The second version says that revolution is the product of *class struggle within production relations, which grows until all existing institutions are invaded by it, when open conflict breaks out, leading to the replacement of the *ruling class by those that had been ruled by it. This second version of the theory originates in French revolutionary thinking, and gains some inspiration from *Hegel's diagnosis of the relation between *master and slave. The two theories are usually held together, partly because both are thought to explain revolution in terms of the existence of a *contradiction within the foundations of the social order. It is thus a fundamental thesis of Marxism that revolutions involve the defeat of one class by another; hence there are two revolutions involved in the transition from feudalism to socialism: that in which the bourgeoisie overthrows the aristocracy ('the bourgeois revolution'), and that in which the proletariat overthrows the bourgeoisie ('the proletarian revolution'). USSR propaganda calls the *bolshevik *coup d'état* in October 1917 the Great October Proletarian Revolution, on the assumption that it was the natural sequel to the 'bourgeois' revolution that had occurred in February.

*Leninist theories of revolution emphasize the role of the revolutionary *agent*, believing that revolutions occur at least in part because their 'subjective' conditions (and not only the 'objective', or what Marx had called 'material' conditions) are fulfilled. A simpler way of saying that is to say that revolutions are also *rebellions by active and organized groups within the state. The important difference between Leninist and Marxian views is that the former regard the accumulation of political power as an essential element in revolution, whereas the latter think of revolution primarily in social terms – for it is at the social level that the vast uncontrollable forces that swept the French Revolution to its conclusion seemed to originate. Modern theorists tend to recognize that the important modern events called revolutions have always involved the seizure of political power, usually by soldiers or intellectuals – hence the element of *coup d'état* has, since the Russian Revolution, come to seem indispensable (thus John Dunn, e.g.: *Modern Revolutions*, 1972). However, this does not settle the question of how the violent transformation of political power comes about, nor whether there is any single end towards which all revolutions are directed. The manifest lack of agreement among observers has a strong ideological cause: it seems to validate a *coup d'état* to say that it was part of an inevitable, and socially based, revolution; to confess candidly that it was motivated by the desire for power is to suggest that its credentials are no better (and probably worse) than the regime that it sought to replace.

rhetoric. The presentation of thought in accessible language, esteemed as a fundamental component in political *virtue by *Cicero, and considered to be an important part of all *education in the medieval systems of schooling. The conflict between rhetoric – the art of persuasion – and philosophy – the pursuit of truth – is responsible for much of the brilliant synthesis of the two which *Plato called 'dialectic'. To understand this conflict remains crucial to social criticism and to political theory. A belief has political appeal only to the extent that is is persuasive and it may be persuasive without being true, and even because it is not true. For example, a belief which hides an unpleasant reality appeals on account of its falsehood, and the art of rhetoric may be to dress that belief up to the point of *doctrine, with associated theories, policies, and ideals, all expressed in a language accessible to the common political animal. Much of the success of *Nazi ideology and of *Maoism has been attributed to rhetoric, as has the appeal of the belief that *revolution will bring *emancipation, despite the weight of historical evidence to the contrary.

Ricardo, David (1771–1823). English economist and, after *Smith, perhaps the greatest of the *classical economists, and a founder of nineteenth-century *political economy. Ricardo's *Principles of Political Economy and Taxation*, first edition 1817, set out 'to determine the laws which regulate the distribution [between the different classes of landowners, capitalists and labour] of the produce of industry'. The emphasis was on land and the use of land: demand grows as a result of increasing population, and therefore more and more land of a less and less fertile nature is brought into cultivation, until the *diminishing returns to land make the process unprofitable. However, if profits were higher at one place than another, this would encourage capital to be invested there until, by the law of diminishing returns, profit falls to the profit in the previous least profitable area. Since labour costs are the same everywhere a surplus will be earned on non-marginal land, and this surplus is *rent.

Ricardo's *labour theory of value, adapted from *Smith, was also to prove profoundly influential in purporting to explain natural *price and distribution without reference to demand.

right, the. Defined by contrast to (or perhaps more accurately, conflict with) the *left, the term 'right' does not even have the respectability of a history. As now used it denotes several connected and also conflicting ideas. To be 'on the right' is to believe (or for the political realist, to affect to believe) some bundle of the following:

(i) *conservative and perhaps *authoritarian doctrines concerning the nature of *civil society, with emphasis on *custom, *tradition and *allegiance as social bonds;

(ii) doctrines of *political obligation framed in terms of *obedience, *legitimacy and *piety rather than *contract, *consent and *justice;

(iii) reluctance to countenance too great a divorce between *law and morality – i.e. between the enactments of the state, and the sentiments of society, hence a resistance to *liberalizing reforms in the law;

(iv) *cultural conservatism;

(v) respect for the *hereditary principle and *prescriptive rights;

(vi) belief in *private property, not as a *natural right, but as an indispensable part of the condition of society;

(vii) belief in elementary *freedoms, and in the irreplaceable value of the individual as against the collective;

(viii) belief in *free enterprise and a capitalist economy, as the only mode of production compatible with human freedom, and suited to the temporary nature of human aspirations;

(ix) varying degrees of belief in human imperfectibility and *original sin.

Other items might be added to the list, and the above is suggested only as a cross-section of current significances. It should already be clear that not everything attributed to the 'right' is compatible with everything else, a fault that may lie either with the right itself or with those who so describe it. Thus the emphasis on freedom and capitalist production relations is probably not compatible with the belief in tradition and obedience, free capitalist production relations being the great solvent of social allegiance based in custom and authority, rather than in the 'legal-rational' principles that *Weber attributes to the world structured by contract. Nor is the belief in *human rights underlying (vii), with its individualistic emphasis, obviously compatible with respect for prescriptive right and the hereditary principle. These ideological conflicts are to some extent internal to the conservative position, which, if founded in 'intimations' of social order (as *Oakeshott suggests), is bound to suffer conflicts in an age of social flux. To some extent they stem from the fact that the right is defined by opposition to the left, which, while it discerns contradictions in history, is adamant that it contains none within itself. Since the left sometimes opposes economic liberalism, sometimes individualism, and sometimes social conservatism, the term 'right' is applied indifferently to all of those outlooks.

right to life. This is often given as a basic *right in systems of rights, and is sometimes said (e.g. by *Locke) to be inalienable, meaning that I can never confer on someone else the permission to take my life away. Problems arise, however, concerning the basis of this right, and its extent. It would seem that, if it exists at all, it exists universally, i.e. in every possessor of rights. For without it, no other right would seem to be possible, the holder having no right to endure long enough to exercise it. Nevertheless there are many who think that the right does not extend to the unborn human being, and others who believe that it may be relinquished by the aged and incurable. (*See* *abortion, *euthanasia.) In the first case it is sometimes argued that the foetus, while indisputably a living human being, is not a *person, and therefore cannot bear rights. It is often replied, first that the question of its personhood is undecided at best, secondly that rights may perhaps be possessed by things other than persons, thirdly that in any case we have duties of *piety (i.e. not founded merely in *justice, or the respect for rights) which extend to all human life. That is what explains, for some, the duty to respect human *life*, as a mysterious quality which inspires our awe and dread, in itself, and without reference to any idea of 'just transaction'.

right to work. A right sometimes claimed, ostensibly guaranteed by the USSR constitution, and inserted into the basic rights stipulated under the Helsinki Accord 1975, at the insistence of the countries of the Eastern bloc. It is often objected that there cannot be such a right, or at least that it cannot be a universal, *human right, since rights define obligations, and the corresponding obligation in this case either does not exist, or cannot be made universal. It seems reasonable to say that I have a right to life, since it is reasonable to suppose that everybody is under an obligation to respect my life. But it is contentious to say that everybody is under an obligation to provide work for the jobless, partly because this involves positive action on the part of those obliged, and partly because such action is not generally possible. It may be said that the obligation to provide lies with the state; but this does not overcome the complaint. While the state may be more powerful than any individual, it is still not *all*-powerful, and therefore may not be able to provide work for all of its citizens.

The reference to a 'right' to work is probably no more than a rhetorical emphasis on a supposed obligation of the state to endeavour to the best of its abilities to provide work. In which case, I do not have a right to work; the best that I have is a right that the state endeavour to provide work, whether or not for me. On the other hand, on some Hegelian and Marxian views of the person, *self-realization requires labour, so that without labour, life is not truly human. Thus the right to life and the right to labour are on a par: both must be respected if there are to be rights at all. But this only supports the belief in a right to work if 'labour' and 'work' are synonymous. *See* *labour, *work.

rights. In law rights form one of the sub-classes of legal advantage, the others being liberties and powers, the three advantages corresponding to the three legal burdens of duty, disability, and liability – *see* *jural relations. Some think that there are also *natural rights, in which case rights do not exist only in law, but also independently, through binding precepts of morality that do not depend upon a legal code for theii validity. However not every moral code is formulated in terms of rights: the ten commandments, for example, impose obligations, but do not specify rights, unless it is thought that every obligation creates a right in some other party. It is unclear whether that is the case. For example, it may be my moral duty not to be gluttonous, but whose rights are violated by my gluttony? Or, more contentiously, it may be my moral duty not to treat animals cruelly, but does that fact alone confer rights on animals? (There may be independent arguments for saying that animals are not *persons, and therefore can have no rights.)

Nevertheless, it seems to be the case that every right defines an obligation. To deny someone his rights is to do what ought not to be done (the 'ought' being legal or moral depending upon whether the right is considered to be a positive or a natural right). Rights are also advantages which may legitimately be claimed: which would illuminate the concept of a right only if the idea of *legitimacy was clear, whereas in fact it is commoner to explain the idea of legitimacy through its relation to the concept of right than vice versa. The idea of a right seems, indeed, to be as basic as any other. We might even define *justice in terms of it, as the disposition to accord to every person his rights.

Many philosophers and jurists have tried to detach the concept of right from the bewildering complexities that surround such ideas as legitimacy and justice, and have affirmed, instead, that the only true rights are created by *positive law. In other words, a right is simply the creation of some convention or rule (whether or not a legal rule), and the only fact of the matter here is that people are given to make and to respect such rules, not that there are independent rights that correspond to them.

Whatever the plausibility of that view, it is certainly not what is commonly believed. Most rights that are asserted with immediate confidence are asserted independently of any law or convention – such as the right to life and the right to limb. It is the sense that these *are* rights which causes men to rebel against laws which violate them.

The language of rights has the function in moral and legal discourse of laying limits to what can be done: a right is 'to be respected', and can be disrespected only by doing wrong. That idea was taken up by *Kant in his ambitious philosophy of practical reason. Kant argued that all persons must be treated as ends in themselves, that this is the fundamental right, and that reason alone compels us to comply with it.

Declarations of Rights have occasionally been made, as conditions to be complied with by every power that wishes to rule legitimately; e.g. by *Jefferson following the American Revolution, and also in the aftermath of the French Revolution under the influence of *Paine. The surprising degree of agreement as to which rights to declare has suggested to many that, even if we cannot presently find an objective basis to the idea of right, there certainly must be such a basis, else it would be impossible to understand how it is that people so readily and immediately reach agreement over so complex a matter. But there are contentious cases, and two articles above discuss two of them.

Lawyers distinguish positive and negative rights (e.g. my right that you fulfil your contract, and my right that you do not injure me); also rights *in personam*, availing against a definite person, and rights *in rem* (in a thing) availing against persons generally in respect of that thing (of which the most important is the right to exclude that lies at the heart of *private property). These distinctions are technicalities that do not bear on the central questions.

rights theories of politics. Political theories which use such concepts as right, obligation, law and justice in describing and explaining political arrangements; to be compared and contrasted with *power theories of politics. Rights theories include the major varieties of Western constitutionalism, in particular the systems of *Aristotle, *Locke and *Hegel. For Hegel, for example, the political world is identical with the sphere of right, and is constituted, and evolves, in accordance with the principles contained in that notion. Hegel's view contrasts radically with the power theory of *Marx, who saw all rights as institutional reflections of underlying relations of power. Thus for Hegel my power to exclude you from my home is to be explained in terms of a right of property; while for Marx all property rights are to be explained in terms of powers rooted in *production relations.

risk and uncertainty. 'Risk' denotes the situation where precise numerical probabilities can be assigned to the various possible outcomes of a choice; 'uncertainty' the situation where they cannot. In the former case the odds can be calculated, and a decision made on the basis of them; in the latter case this is not so.

The economic theory of risk and uncertainty, based on the calculus of probability first formulated by D. Bernouilli (1700–82), provides a theoretical explanation of one of the most important ideological notions of modern capitalism – the notion that an *entrepreneur's *profit is offset by his risk.

rites of passage. Expression coined by the French anthropologist Arnold van Gennep, in a book of that title (1909), to denote the *ceremonies which accompany the transition of an individual or group from one socially important condition to another – e.g. ceremonies of birth, puberty, maturity, marriage and death. The ceremonies tend to involve three components: *separation* of the individuals or groups from their previous condition; *transition* (French: *marge*), when the subjects remain suspended in limbo; and *incorporation* (*agrégation*) as participants in their new condition. Such ceremonies survive in a variety of forms in modern communities, and are sometimes thought to have an important function in securing transformations of *identity that would otherwise be hard to bear, and in reinforcing a sense of the objective validity of social *norms.

ritual. An action which follows a repeatable pattern, which has the sanction of *custom, and whose meaning is symbolic, even though it cannot usually be captured by what the agent may say in explanation of it. Ritual tends to be inflexible, or resistant to change, and to be understood as compelled by a moral or spiritual command that it would be sacrilegious, or at least outrageous, to disobey. Ritual is often thought to be an essential instrument of social cohesion, since it unites people behind a common form of action saturated by social significance. Hence the importance of ritual in military and civil institutions, in trade union gatherings, coronations, and trials.

Although psychologists sometimes misleadingly call the routine activities of animals 'rituals', it is arguable that only a rational being could feel the intimation of transcendent significance that provides the motive of ritual behaviour.

Robespierre, Maximilien de (1758–94). French revolutionary statesman. *See* *Jacobinism, *legislator, *majesty, *people, *social question, *terrorism.

role. A term with at least two meanings, and which has won an important place for itself in contemporary sociology.

1. Dramatic role, or 'persona': the character or state of mind which the actor simulates. From this idea have grown many modern usages of the term 'role', as a form of 'representation'.

2. In sociology. Sometimes defined as the 'dynamic aspect of a social position', i.e. the form of *agency connected with a social position. The social position is usually defined in terms of *norms of behaviour. Roles are like *offices, in that they are distinct from the person who occupies them, and bear their normative character independently. However, they are less well defined than offices, and arise more naturally out of social conditions, so that it is hard to see them as matters only of convention. Hence the 'norms' in question are not usually seen as matters only of responsibility and right.

There is a close connection between 1. and 2., and some sociologists (e.g. E. Goffman: *The Presentation of Self in Everyday Life*, 1956) regard the occupation of a role in sense 2. as very close to the kind of representational activity described in 1. The individual uses the roles that he occupies to control the impression that others may have of him: what is represented is not a dramatic character, but the self, in a particular, quasi-dramatic aspect.

Natural relations, such as 'father' or 'uncle', may be as much associated with roles, as artificial relations ('doctor', 'judge' etc.). Both may be matters of responsibility and competence, and both serve a like function of mediating between the individual and society, and providing circumscribed fields of intelligible action. Roles are sometimes important in *casuistry: since they define responsibilities, they may also limit them, so that, for example, the doctor who obeys the ethic intrinsic to his role may be released from blame for at least some unfortunate consequences. (Cf. *morality and politics.)

Roman Catholicism. The *church centred on the Bishop of Rome, which has represented itself as the mysterious body of Christ incarnate, has throughout the development of modern forms of government exerted a continuous influence upon law, upon ideas of sovereignty, and upon the institutional structure of societies developing under its tutelage. It is called 'catholic' because it claims universal validity, 'Roman' because this claim has, since the *Reformation, been disputed by other equally 'catholic' churches of *Protestant believers. It is through its claim to universality that the Roman Catholic Church has exerted a powerful political influence, and it is through the Roman Catholic Church that many of the distinctive institutions of *Christian countries took their form. The ideas of international jurisdiction and of a combined rule of *natural law and *sacrament were put forward from the earliest times, and built into a Christian political theory by *Augustine. It is sometimes held to be a significant achievement of Christianity (in contrast, say, to *Islam) that the institutions thereby founded and authorized were able to survive with their full political effectiveness even after the collapse of the Christian faith among those governed by them. Thus the doctrine of natural law, and the specific application of it through *canon law, have entered most of the legal systems of Europe. The idea of *limited government, and of the inviolable rights of the individual, repeatedly upheld in the name of the papacy by medieval jurists and theologians, achieved early acceptance, and endured to form the basic premise of most forms of liberal constitutionalism; the claims to international jurisdiction have persisted in modern international law, to a great extent founded on speculations already active in the ecclesiastical jurisdiction of the Middle Ages; the recurrent attempts to forbid or control usury and speculation, which have been a striking characteristic of Western governments, also have their origin in Roman Catholic teaching, as have the ideas of the just war, and the just practice of war, which have been important in shaping the forms of treaties and alliances among the European nations.

The Catholic Church retains its significance as a major force of international politics, and papal encyclicals continue to project moral and spiritual doctrine from Rome to the corners of the earth. It is almost impossible to summarize the political tenor of this doctrine. On issues such as *abortion and contraception, for example, its doctrines have seemed to many to be illiberal, while its defence of an international code of *human rights reiterates a piece of liberal orthodoxy. Its internal structure is authoritarian, and it supports an important hierarchy of offices which has, through its penetration of secular institutions, tended to uphold hierarchical organization everywhere (notably in Spain, where the church entered into open conflict with forces of radical reform during the present century). At the same time it seems bent on discarding hierarchical principles of government, and has recently begun to encourage the *laicization of its functions, and the revision of its *liturgies.

Roman-Dutch law. A legal system produced by the fusion of medieval Dutch law with the *Roman law as recorded in Justinian's *Digests* and *Institutes*. It was accepted at the Reception, and applied in Holland during the sixteenth, seventeenth and eighteenth centuries, after which it was replaced by the *Napoleonic law. It was exported to the Dutch colonies, including South Africa, and has there remained as the main basis of the legal system. Since it upholds ideas of judicial independence and natural justice it has proved an obstacle to the application of some of the oppressive legislation of *apartheid; this has led to several judicial qualifications of executive acts in recent years, notably over the right of residence in the black townships.

Roman law. A system of law developed over 2,000 years, and largely identified through the *Digests* and *Institutes* commanded in AD 530 by order of the Emperor Justinian, in which the whole body of existing law was condensed and *codified, providing a unique system of rationalized legality, which purports to describe the nature of jurisdiction throughout the Empire.

Roman law as applied to citizens consisted in the *jus civile* – the civil law of contract, tort, property etc. – together with the criminal law in so far as it dealt with the private affairs of individuals (all those branches constituting the *jus privatum*), and also the criminal law governing the relations between the individual and the state (the *jus publicum*). The civil law introduced many of the conceptual achievements upon which later codes have rested. Thus Roman law introduced the ideas of the juristic *person, of the corporate person, of *legal fiction, of the distinctions between kinds of *right, and kinds of *association, of 'quasi-contract' (actions which must be adjudicated as though they formed part of a contract), of implied and explicit contracts – in short, the ideas required for a complete description of civil obligation in legal terms. It was therefore inevitable that many later political theorists should phrase their conceptions of the state and *political obligation in terms borrowed from Roman law (*Hegel being a noteworthy example).

In addition to the *jus civile* Roman law acknowledged also a *jus gentium* and a *jus naturale*, the first being a system of international law designed to adjudicate disputes among those subjects of the Empire who were not citizens, whatever their local and customary legal practice, the second being largely a philosophical rationalization of the first by jurists influenced by the writings of Greek philosophers.

The *jus gentium* was free from the technicalities of the civil law, and involved principles of *natural justice and procedures of appeal from local tribunals to the jurisdiction of Rome. The *jus naturale*, or *natural law, seems to have been more or less identical with it, except in one particular, that *slavery was recognized as legitimate in the *jus gentium* but not in the *jus naturale* (although this may be due to a philosophical gloss). The two systems are interesting in showing the extent to which the search for a universal jurisdiction involves the invocation of rights thought to be natural rather than conventional. Thus the relation between the *jus gentium* and the *jus naturale* has come to symbolize the relation, both in power and in authority between *positive and natural law.

romanticism. Primarily used to denote the artistic and cultural movement which began in eighteenth-century Europe, and of which the following are regarded as early manifestations: in France, the writings of *Rousseau; in Germany, the *Sturm und Drang* movement; in Britain, the poems of 'Ossian' and the literary movement which culminated in the publication of *Lyrical Ballads* in 1798. However, the various phenomena attributed to the romantic movement are so many and various – from Gothic novels to the French Revolution – that it is impossible to describe the phenomenon without invoking contentious critical and philosophical theories.

The romantic movement is usually thought to have marked the transformation of the intellectual's self-image from objective to subjective; the intellectual ceased to be an acknowledged part of the world and became a suffering observer of the world, passing from social being to outcast. (Hence the fascination of Goethe, who seemed to be social being and outcast together.) The romantics sought to show how the suffering and aspiration of the solitary individual was nevertheless a route to salvation; and so produced visions of peace and renewal which were dependent upon no society for their realization. An example of the latter is Wordsworth's idyll of a unity between the self and nature unmediated by social artifice; that idea has since become a familiar datum of the *modern consciousness.

Through Rousseau romanticism was to recast the eighteenth-century vision of the social contract as a eulogy of the *state of nature; through *Herder it translated itself into a philosophy of *nationalism; through *Hegel it attempted to reconcile its idea of the ultimate validity of the self and *self-realization with a philosophy of institutions; through *Coleridge it provided the foundations of later *cultural conservatism, and through Shelley it produced the greatest existing poetic invocation of *utopian socialism. It must therefore be considered to be a fundamental ingredient of modern thought, which cannot be summarized in a single political doctrine.

By extension, the term 'romanticism' is often applied to any philosophy or state of mind that is more than normally redolent of the sentiments of the original romantics: for example, it has been applied to the writings of the *Frankfurt school, to the early *Marx, and to the irrationalist philosophy of *Sartre.

Roosevelt, Franklin Delano (1882–1945). American statesman and US President. *See* *democratic parties, *four freedoms, *freedom, *good neighbour policy, *New Deal.

Rousseau, Jean-Jacques (1712–78). Swiss-born writer and philosopher, whose *Social Contract*, 1762, and *Émile*, 1762, contain one of the first attempts to translate the spirit of *romanticism into political doctrine. *Émile* describes the education of the free being, and the process whereby the liberty and nobility which man possesses by nature can be preserved and enhanced through self-expression, and through an education that encourages at every point development rather than inhibition of the moral sentiments.

The *Social Contract* begins with the famous words 'Men are born free, yet everywhere they are in chains.' It can be read either as a celebration of liberty and the rights of man, which condemns all forms of absolute or arbitrary government, or as a recipe for the abolition of human liberties and the absorption of the individual into a sovereign collective. The work is unsystematic, rhetorical and fraught with paradoxes. Nevertheless its fundamental conceptions have been highly influential, and its very contradictory nature has often been esteemed, as the mark of a vision that recognizes the contradictions implicit in all social order.

Man is good by nature, just as he is free by nature. He is made bad, as he is made unfree, only by institutions which negate his powers. (The doctrine of the 'noble savage' to some extent summarizes these intuitions, although Rousseau argued that the savage requires society if he is to be *truly* free.) *Direct democracy is the only form of decision-making that can preserve man's natural liberty, since it is the only form in which his consent is the sole ground of legitimacy. But this extreme form of (non-representative) democracy has its paradoxes. In particular, in surrendering to it, the citizen chooses to be overriden by the rest of the community whenever his choice conflicts with theirs (*see* *paradox of democracy); in this way he surrenders part of his freedom to the community. This act of surrender has the form of a *social contract, between each member of society and every other, for the *common good. This contract creates an association which has corporate identity and personality. The association is called, when passive, 'the state', when active, 'the sovereign'. Like any legal person it has will. Rousseau calls this will the *general will, which is to be distinguished from the 'will of all' (the aggregate will of individual members of society). The resulting doctrine of sovereignty, which influenced *Hegel among others, shows in turn the influence of *Roman law conceptions of corporate identity.

It seemed to Rousseau to follow that he whose will conflicts with the general will is in conflict with himself. Such a man attempts to live a *contradiction; if he is not made to bend to the general will his own freedom will therefore be negated; so he must be 'forced to be free'. This paradox of freedom was very influential, as was the idea of the 'lived contradiction'. Rousseau himself saw that it admitted of *tyrannical interpretation, but did not avoid that consequence, since he believed that the problem of political freedom is genuine and serious, and certainly more mysterious than the empiricists had represented it to be. Such paradoxes were to be expected in any serious attempt to cast light on law and freedom. Thus Rousseau compared the problem of the *rule of law with that of squaring the circle, and argued that every freedom which the law provides, it must also curtail. Rousseau rejected Locke's version of the social contract theory, and also the idea of a *natural right. The condition of society is one in which *all* rights are alienated to the sovereign power.

routinization. Term used by *Weber, to denote the transformation of *charismatic *leadership into institutionalized leadership, where an office takes the place of a personality as the focus of authority.

royalism. The belief in the *legitimacy of monarchical government, and of a particular person's or *dynasty's title under that government. Royalism has been influential in modern French politics, particularly through the anti-parliamentarian movement, Action Française, founded in 1899 by Leon Daudet and Henri Vaugeois, and given direction by Jacques Bainville and by Charles Maurras, who was its major theorist. According to Maurras the true France (*pays réel*) must be distinguished from the republican system (*pays légal*) that had been imposed on it. All political practice requires certainty, which comes only through knowledge of the immediate environment; no abstract idea of legitimacy can be a motive to action until made part of a 'subjective synthesis' which relates to the actual historical conditions in which it must be applied. The embodiment of this synthesis in the person of a monarch gives to the legal idea of legitimacy its true 'particularized objectivity' – the sovereign has objective authority through law, and also subjective power, through his immediately intelligible identity with the traditions and social condition of the nation.

rule of law. The form of government in which no power can be exercised except according to procedures, principles and constraints contained in the law, and in which any citizen can find redress against any other, however powerfully placed, and against the officers of the state itself, for any act which involves a breach of the law.

The rule of law is an artefact, and the fundamental search involved in modern theories of *constitution is for the conditions which make it possible. It is obviously not enough for a constitution to *declare* that the law is supreme; it must also be possible for any citizen, however placed, to enforce that law. This suggests *judicial independence as a minimum requirement, at least if the law is to be enforced against the state. But that notion involves paradoxes, as does the idea of a *separation of powers upon which it is founded. In the end it is the state which controls the appointment and dismissal of judges, as it is the state which makes and revises the law.

In conditions of social collapse, or widespread terror and intimidation, a rule of law will no longer be possible; hence a rule of law also requires laws of *sedition and public order through which it may be upheld against the busy subversion of the lawless. This leads to a further paradox, noted by *Machiavelli, namely that a law of sedition must be as determined and as violent as the forces which it may need to overcome, and, since these include the extremes of military violence, it must itself be prepared to resort to extremes (although not to the same extremes, since that would be tantamount to permanent civil war). This means, in effect, that the rule of law must be prepared to disregard *natural justice and judicial procedure while combating some types of offender. At the same time, it must in other cases give untrammelled freedom to judicial procedure, and to the natural justice which, on one plausible view, is repeatedly invoked in it. So that the rule of law is itself indebted to the violence that it seeks to condemn.

ruling class. A *class which, by whatever mechanism, is able to fill all important *offices within the state, or every important position through which power over the people is exercised. Whether or not such a class will exercise power in its own interest is a question which *Aristotle, for one, regarded as open, thinking that it all depends upon the nature and education of the ruling class. That it *will* exercise power in its own interest (whatever it in fact *intends*) is a familiar doctrine of *historical materialism.

For the notion to be a useful one, there must be some way of determining membership of the ruling class other than through the occupancy of positions of power, else the 'ruling class' simply means 'those in power'. Many criteria proposed have proved unsatisfactory, and many discussions of the nature and value of a ruling class seem to peter out in the helpless tautology that 'power belongs with the powerful', often with some kind of protest against that elementary and indeed necessary truth.

The idea of a ruling class ceases to be empty if, for example, class membership is determined by economic control, and 'rule' by political control. Then the idea that there is a ruling class is in effect the idea that those who control the means of production will, for that reason, control all government offices. That is, in effect, the *Marxian position with regard to the *bourgeois state (whether or not true). The inverse of that is the view that control of political power leads to the control of economic power: in which case it would be better to speak of a class of rulers, rather than a ruling class. Such is, in effect, the position in modern communist societies, at least as described by Djilas (*see* *new class).

Ruskin, John (1819–1900). English writer, painter and social critic. *See* *aesthetics and politics, *architecture, *craft, *cultural conservatism, *Morris.

Russell, Bertrand Arthur William, third Earl Russell (1872–1970). English mathematician and philosopher. *See* *empiricism, *gentleman, *positivism.

S

sacrament. According to the Book of Common Prayer: 'an outward and visible sign of an inward and spiritual grace given unto us, ordained by Christ himself, as a means whereby we receive the same, and a pledge to assure us thereof'. A sacrament is an act whose significance, while it may sometimes be understood in earthly terms, is so great that it must eventually direct us towards the transcendental. It is through the idea of a sacrament (as exemplified in the communion) that Christian thinkers have tried to make sense of the non-contractual and peculiarly binding nature of *marriage, and of like human relations in which *piety seems to be the ruling principle. Similar views can be found in other religions, which tend to call God to witness to those transactions which are of enduring and formative importance, including sometimes the appointment of a ruler (*see* *caliphate).

Saint-Simon, Claude-Henri de Rouvroy, Comte de (1760–1825). Founder of French socialism, and initiator of the critical analysis of social conditions that was to prevail in nineteenth-century political thought. Saint-Simon was associated with *Comte in the founding of *positivism; however, he was less systematic, more analytical and, although without Comte's rhetorical gifts, indisputably less naïve and more circumspect. He developed a theory of *class conflict, identifying the principal classes as the producers (*industriels*) and the parasites (bureaucrats), and further argued that revolutionary and reforming activity is always useless if not accompanied by a proper theory of the conditions that determine and mould political change. He dismissed *utopian socialism for its indifference to the real facts of history, and advocated what he took to be a realistic theory of historical transformation, together with an ideal constitution of the socialist society which he wished to bring about. He thought that the time had come when the *industriels* could take control of society and organize it according to the actual needs of its members. The resulting constitution would consist of three chambers, that of invention, that of examination and that of deputies. The first would consist of artists and inventors, the second of critical scientists, the third of the 'captains of industry' who would initiate change and control education. It was so clear to Saint-Simon that this arrangement would be perceived to be in the public interest that he neglected to propose any laws that would enforce it. However, he thought that this kind of constitutional organization, combined with common ownership of the means of production and redistribution in the cause of social justice, would, taken together, ensure that the future society would embody as much of socialism as is compatible with the historical conditions from which it must arise.

salami tactics. The 'slicing off' of successive parts of opposing factions until no effective opposition remains, in the manner practised by the communist parties in Eastern Europe after 1945, especially by the Hungarian communist leader Mátyás Rákosi (1892–1971), who coined the term.

samizdat. Russian: self-publishing. The name for the increasingly important literature in the USSR and Eastern Europe which, while being denied official publication, circulates in legally permitted (but nevertheless illegally persecuted) ways, as duplicated typescript. It includes all significant literature expressing political views opposed to the thought and practice of the ruling Communist Party.

Samuelson, Paul Anthony (b. 1915). American economist. *See* *compensation criterion, *revealed preference.

sanction. 1. In law. Any provision for the enforcement of a law, by rewarding its obedience or punishing its transgression. Legal *positivism tends to regard sanctions as essential to law, thinking that this *power is the material reality which exists in appearance as the law's *authority. (*See* *command.)
2. In *international law, punitive action by one state against another, usually of an economic kind, designed to force a change of policy without resorting to overt aggression. Opinions differ as to the relation between sanction and *pacific blockade, and as to the precise extent to which either is inevitably the prelude to belligerence.

sanctuary. The practice of fleeing to a sacred place for refuge, especially from criminal proceedings. Sanctuary has more or less ceased, although it was long protected in English law, and by 'sanctuary and abjuration' (i.e. forswearing all civil rights and leaving the jurisdiction) a criminal could often escape prosecution. Now the term is used in a wide and vague sense for the protection offered – e.g. by a criminal organization – to persons who enter into a certain place in order to escape the law that may prevail there *de jure*, but not in fact.

sansculottism. The sansculottes ('without breeches') formed the undisciplined and destructive mass which emerged at the French Revolution, endowing republican principles with a promptness and barbarity of execution that until then they had not possessed. Hence sanculottism came to be used to name any violent republican fervour thought to be based more in unthinking resentments than in a reasoned comparison of the virtues of monarchical and republican government.

Sartre, Jean-Paul (1905–80). French philosopher, novelist and playwright, a leading advocate of *existentialism and, since 1945, one of the most important and influential of French left-wing intellectuals. Sartre's political philosophy evolved from an attempt to synthesize existentialism and *Marxism, towards a complex philosophy of 'revolutionary *praxis', and a rejection of what Sartre took to be the central theses of *dialectical materialism (*Critique of Dialectical Reason*, 1960). It is difficult to synthesize the many and varied strands in Sartre's political thought, which was constantly in a state of flux, but the following picture is perhaps not wholly inaccurate:

The essence of man's stance towards the world is freedom, which condemns him either to exercise true 'existential' choice, or to lose himself in the 'bad faith' of otherness. In bad faith a man is for himself what he takes himself to be for others; in particular he loses his freedom by adopting *roles, and moral codes, which bind him to public expectations in a public world. This attempt at a spurious 'objectivity' constitutes the loss of the true 'subjectivity' of freedom. The only remedy for bad faith is *commitment, construed as the total identification with one's freedom and the casting in of one's lot with life. (Sartre gives a trenchant and poignant account of this subjective freedom in his great work of *phenomenology, *Being and Nothingness*, 1945.)

But towards what should I commit myself? By Sartre's own theory that question should have no answer, since the self and its freedom are strictly transcendental. However, he also accepts the idea of the intellectual as the agent of social transformation, and believes that there can be no *authenticity that does not involve, through its transcendence of all publicly available roles, moralities and classes, identification with the *proletariat of Marxist theory. However, the Marxist theory of history gives a partial and mechanistic account of man's situation in the world, and does not speak directly to the free agent. No historical materialism will ever provide a substitute for political action, and no theory of the *dialectic will ever make room for the agent's own perspective on the social world in which he is condemned to act. The role of praxis is to transcend all such partial theories, and to 'totalize' the experience available to the modern consciousness. This totalization occurs *in* action, and also shows the world as *open* to action, and transformed through action.

Such totalization can be achieved only by the person who rejects all bourgeois morality and custom, and for the modern intellectual the true saint or hero is not the man of 'good heart' but rather the demonic anti-hero, the traitor, the person who turns morality inside out to reveal its empty inside. Such a saint (the writer and criminal Jean Genet is Sartre's example) speaks directly to the modern spirit, by *showing* all values to be subjective, and by inciting the free being to disobey all laws that are not affirmed subjectively, from the totalizing viewpoint of revolutionary praxis.

By a deft stroke of rhetoric, Sartre tries to recommend his philosophy to others (although no such recommendation can be obeyed without bad faith). Many have found in it the ultimate expression of the ethic of *autonomy that Kant brought into the world, while others have condemned it as a tissue of rhetorical confusions. It can be seen both as an imaginative dramatization of the post-romantic soul, which rejects both the world and its own isolation from the world; and also as a fine flight of intellectual snobbishness, in which bourgeois values are mocked in the name of a criminal chic.

satellite state. A state that is bound by economic, political and ideological gravity to another and more powerful state, which dictates its policies while permitting a fiction of self-government. States within the USSR *sphere of influence are in fact more usually described as satellite states, since 'influence' is in this case a euphemism for *control.

Savigny, Friedrich Carl von (1779–1861). German jurist; *see* *historical jurisprudence, **Volksgeist*.

Say's law. The 'law of markets' (*loi des débouches*) proposed by J.–B. Say (1767–1832). The basis of the law is that resources are never under-used, or, in common language, 'supply creates its own demand'. *Keynes criticized the law as underlying many of the errors of what he called classical macroeconomics.

scarcity. In economics, any condition where there is less of something than would be demanded at zero price (i.e. if it cost nothing). Thus cars are scarce, air is not. It is usually assumed that, in a market economy, scarcity is a necessary condition of positive price, so that absolute *abundance of something means that it will cost nothing.

Schelling, Thomas Crombie (b. 1921).

American strategic theorist. *See* *brinkmanship, *strategy.

Schiller, Friedrich von (1759–1805). German poet and essayist. *See* *play.

Schumpeter, Joseph Alois (1883–1946). US economist and sociologist, whose *Capitalism, Socialism and Democracy*, 1942, did much to revise prevailing sentiments concerning each of the phenomena referred to in its title. Schumpeter argued that capitalism, as it had been known in the West, was gradually giving way to a new economic order which, if it was not called socialism, would differ from socialism only in name. He identified certain main processes which were contributing to this transformation: constant increases in scale which, if extrapolated to their natural limit, would eventually entail *socialization of the means of production; an increasing tendency to rationalization and bureaucratic management, and an erosion of the role of the innovative *entrepreneur; the decay of vital features of the social and institutional framework of capitalism, with the loosening of family ties and inheritance, which undermines the motive to *accumulation; the corrosive role of intellectuals, who will always tend to take an anti-capitalist stance in any dispute; and the sheer success of capitalism in raising the *absolute* standard of living, and improving the *relative* power of the lower classes. Schumpeter was a staunch critic of democracy detached from the traditional institutions which would serve to direct the democratic choice, and sometimes advocated, sometimes merely predicted, 'socialism', by which he meant massive central planning of all economic activity within the political framework that would make that possible.

scientism. The belief that scientific method is applicable to all human problems, and that it will generate the only possible solution to them.

'Scientific method' denotes a disputed idea, but usually involves the following four features: (i) the search for laws of cause and effect; (ii) the introduction of theory which may involve reference to entities not normally observed (e.g. the atomic theory); (iii) the derivation of predictions from theory; (iv) the division of reality into 'natural kinds' – i.e. fundamental classifications (such as those involved in (ii)) which reflect, not actual human interests, but rather independent laws of nature (e.g. the classifications introduced by the periodic table of the elements).

Many oppose scientism on the grounds that scientific method cannot be applied universally, say because of human metaphysical *freedom. Others oppose it on the slightly more sophisticated ground that, while it may apply universally, it is not the only way of understanding (or even of explaining) that to which it is applied, and in certain cases the more misleading of the available ways (*see* **Verstehen*). Others oppose it on the grounds that it gives a false sense of knowledge in a state of actual ignorance – as, for example, in certain nineteenth-century theories of history and society which, by generating confidence in their 'scientific' basis, have also justified appalling mistakes which human intuition would have instinctively avoided.

Others, of course, accept scientism, or some modified form of it, although not usually under that label; *see*, for example, *Comte, *progress.

Scots law. The system of law prevailing in Scotland. Although part of the UK, Scotland retains its own legal system and its own judiciary, and has never been fully integrated into English legislative practice, despite the Act of Union. The law is more fully codified than English law, being based in *Roman law rather than Anglo-Saxon *common law, and it is one of the strongest arguments given for *devolution that laws conceived and made in the English Parliament are now imposed on a legal system which is often structurally recalcitrant to their judicial application. Final appeal is now to the English House of Lords, and this has tended to impose uniformity and to force some of the structure of the common law on to the previously codified arrangement. Nevertheless the complexity of Scots law and its acknowledged adaptation to the customs of Scotland are such that it constantly reasserts itself, and causes uncertainty as to how UK statutes can be applied within its *jurisdiction.

secession. The voluntary removal of a state from some *federation of which it forms a part, most famously exemplified in the secession of the eleven southern states of the US in 1860–62, to form the 'Confederate States of America', thus precipitating the American Civil War.

secondary boycott. *See* *industrial action.

secrecy. Secret societies (e.g. the Fenians, the Carbonari, the Ku Klux Klan) are not easily tolerated within any political arrangement which permits freedom of assembly, since, unless purposes and membership are declared, it is unclear whether or not an assembly is also a *conspiracy. However, at least one secret society – the *freemasons – has established an international identity, with some political consequences. *Official secrets are, however, everywhere reserved as a right of government which no citizen can challenge in open court. At the same time, there must be some limits on secrecy if the *rule of law is to be maintained, and those limits must be public, so that, if we cannot know what the secrets are, we can, so to speak, know where they are. The existence of secret laws (as at times in the USSR) is a fundamental violation of the rule of law, since it makes it impossible for any citizen to know that he is obeying the law. There is a common-sense presumption that too much secrecy undermines trust, and that a state which relies on secret laws, and a secret police to survey its citizens, is at least partly dependent upon terror. (*See* *police state.)

sectarianism. The advocacy of *separatist policies by, or on behalf of, a sect, where 'sect' usually means a part of society which has broken away from the established church due to differences over doctrine and/or religious practices, while being neither sufficiently organized, nor sufficiently distinct in terms of belief, to found a new religion. The word is sometimes used more loosely, to denote any kind of separatist movement, where 'sect' may have connotations of national, linguistic, even political, rather than religious, identity.

'Sectarian violence' may occur in the absence of sectarianism; i.e. sects may express their antagonism towards each other violently while desiring to continue in the close proximity which renders their mutual hatred so inspiring.

secularization. The transfer of *authority from religious institutions to secular bodies. Secularization has both a subjective and an objective aspect. The first involves the gradual disappearance of religious thought, feeling and imagery from the understanding of worldly things, so that religion either ceases to exist as an independent force, or else is confined to an abstract worship of the transcendental. As a result people experience the obligations, transactions and institutions of everyday life in terms that make no reference to the divine. This may be evident, e.g., in relations between the sexes, which some religions view as *sacramental; it is also evident in the gradual decline in the felt significance of non-consensual grounds of *political obligation, such as *piety and *obedience. Some have even argued that the associated secularization of political theory has been the most momentous of the intellectual changes which brought about the modern consciousness (e.g. J. N. Figgis: *From Gerson to Grotius*, 1916).

The objective aspect of secularization consists in the process whereby religious offices, institutions and ceremonies are extruded from public life – in education, law-making, administration and government. Conservatives sometimes oppose this objective secularization, on the assumption that the subjective secularization that would warrant it has not occurred, or is undesirable, or is precipitated by objective secularization. In *Islamic states this sentiment is very strong, and desecularizing movements abound; some argue that this is because the complete secularization of Islamic institutions of government would leave no remainder.

security. The guarantee of safety: i.e. the political arrangements which make *war less likely, which provide for negotiations rather than belligerence, and which aim to preserve peace as the normal condition among states. 'National security' also denotes all purposes of defence: i.e. the preparation for belligerence in order to deter or deflect it; in certain conditions therefore policies of national security may precipitate insecurity (the problem of the arms race and *arms control). Sometimes the term 'national security' is used so widely as to refer to any 'vital' interest.

The United Nations Security Council is a body designed to mediate in all conflicts that threaten war, in order to avert it. Its core consists of those powers strong enough to make others feel insecure, acting by mutual threat, in order to avert what they principally are threatening.

sedition. A crime less serious than *treason, but provided for under various names and descriptions in all systems of law, and consisting in the *subversion of the state through words and preparatory acts rather than through deeds. In the UK it is a *common law offence, described thus in *R.* v. *Burns*, 1886: 'acts, words or writings published with the intention to bring into hatred or contempt, or to excite disaffection against, the person of Her Majesty, her heirs, or successors, or the government and constitution of the United Kingom . . . or either House of Parliament, or the administration of justice, or to excite the Queen's subjects to attempt, otherwise than by lawful means, the alteration of any matter in Church or State by law established, or to incite . . . crime . . . or to raise discontent or disaffection amongst Her Majesty's subjects, or to promote feelings of ill-will and hostility between different classes of subject' The definition is clumsy but the intent is clear: to make criminal all those acts which seek to undermine the conditions that make the *rule of law under a given constitution possible. It is plausible to suggest that every rule of law requires a law of sedition, but it is clear that the crime here described is committed every day by those who try to stir up racial or class hatred.

The Soviet-style crime of 'slandering the state' can be seen as a variant of sedition, the main difference being that, *de facto* if not *de jure*, no *mens rea* is required to prove it, and seditious publication is defined very widely, so as to include many common criticisms of the state, the party, and their institutions.

segregation. The establishment by law or by custom of separate institutions of education, separate facilities of leisure and recreation, and perhaps even separate kinds and places of work, for people belonging to different groups, usuallly defined in terms of *race or *caste. *Apartheid is an extreme case, and the 'Jim Crow' legislation of certain southern states of the US another. *Integration aims at reversing segregation.

self-defence. An act performed in self-defence may not be criminal in law, even if of a kind that normally would be considered such. Thus violence offered in self-defence is permitted, provided, roughly speaking, that it is such that a *reasonable man would have thought it to be necessary in order to avert or reduce the risk of serious harm to himself.

Under *international law every state has a right of self-defence against armed attack, but the right is vague, subject to abuse, and also subject, under the UN Charter, to review by the Security Council. 'Collective self-defence' denotes agreements between states for mutual assistance in the event of armed attack.

self-determination. The aspiration of some group – grounded in some existing sentiment of national or racial *identity associated with common territory, language or religion – to form its own sovereign state and to govern itself This aspiration was recognized and encouraged in President Wilson's 'Fourteen Points', upon the breaking up of the Austro-Hungarian Empire, and provides a powerful political motive in modern Africa, where tribal affinities provide the 'pre-political' background to its emergence. This background is always presupposed, otherwise there is, so to speak, no 'self' to 'determine'. Only if a single social entity can be identified before and after the change – first as a society, and then as a state – can there be any recognizable process of self-determination.

self-help. 1. The ethic popularized during the nineteenth century through the writings of Samuel Smiles, and sometimes thought to be characteristic of **petit bourgeois* *ideology, advocating as a virtue what is already contained in the possibilities of that class position and so encouraging *social mobility. Natural disabilities and low inherited social status are to be overcome by dedicated effort, by self-reliance and saving. This policy will invariably prove to be the best one, since it is the least dependent upon unpredictable social transformations for its success.

The ethic of self-help has elements of the *Protestant ethic; it is also a popularized form of *individualism, which makes minimum moral and religious demands upon the believer.

2. 'Self-help' groups: i.e. groups with common interests that they seek to promote through association amongst themselves, rather than through influence over government, or appeal to other bodies.

3. In international relations, activities, such as reprisals, aimed to compel a state to obey law or agreement, without recourse to adjudication.

self-realization. Literally, the making real of the self: i.e. the actualization of those potentialities for thought and action which are distinctive of self-knowledge and self-identity, and which provide the individual with a sense of who he is, that he is someone, and that he has an intrinsic value which justifies his existence. The concept of the 'self' is so puzzling that few philosophers would be happy with the implications of that, or of any other, definition. However, most people have an intuitive understanding of what is meant by 'I', and of the value to us of the unique perspective on the world of thought and action which that word encapsulates. And the idea that the self exists first as potential, and then as reality, seems to be fairly common. Few thinkers are agreed over the nature of this process, and the term 'self-realization' is perhaps best considered to be a technicality of idealist philosophy, occasionally put to polemical use by psychotherapists and popular moralists, but without fixed significance outside the context which gave it sense.

Thus, in *Hegel, the term is associated with a critique of *individualism. Freedom is the property of the self – i.e. of the self-identifying, self-conscious centre of thought and action. But the self is not 'given' in a state of nature, nor is its existence an all-or-nothing affair. The self exists to a certain degree, and its realization is brought about through a process of *dialectical interaction with its kind. The process has various stages, including that of *master and slave, and involves the eventual 'positing' of the world of ethical life (or **Sittlichkeit*) in which the individual achieves free agency, and the perspective of the 'I', by understanding the world in moral terms.

Outside idealist philosophy the term may be used more loosely, in order to emphasize the role of expression in the making of the individual. Thus, broadly, political philosophies may be divided into the 'expressive' and the 'instrumental', according to whether they see the fulfilment of an individual in terms of internal self-development (*Rousseau), or in terms of external utility and success (*Hobbes). For the first kind of philosopher, categories such as *alienation will replace ideas of disutility, and labour will be seen as an externalization of the self rather than as a 'cost' or investment. The idealist theory of self-realization is part of the metaphysical attempt to uphold the expressive view, by showing that the individual described in the instrumental view is the achievement, and not the initiator, of social order.

senate. 1. Under Roman government, the assembly of senior men, which succeeded the council of kings. Membership depended upon wealth and hereditary privilege, and the senate evolved into a body not unlike the UK House of Lords, with nominal sovereignty and vestigial legislative powers.
2. The upper house of the US *Congress, composed of two senators from each state elected for six-year terms by popular vote, and presided over by the US Vice-President. It operates largely through standing committees, and enjoys wide executive powers.
3. In general, any upper house in *bicameral government constructed on the US model, which is not a house of *peers, and which reflects political divisions exemplified equally in the lower house.

The problem of the nature and powers of a senate exercised the makers of the US constitution. Originally the US Senate was designed to be a forum of *opinion, in which issues of public concern could be discussed with the leisure necessary for their proper consideration. It was intended that the chamber should serve, not merely as a revising and endorsing chamber, but as an additional organ of government, able to take a wider perspective than that forced on the House of Representatives by its representational function. This contrasts with the UK House of Lords, at least as it now is, which has virtually no powers other than powers of revision and endorsement. The problem of the ideal composition of a senate continues to exercise political theorists. It is clear that a main factor leading to the reduction of the powers of the House of Lords is its hereditary constitution, which means that its claims to legislate are differently founded from the claims of the lower house, and so can plausibly be attacked and disqualified by that house. At the same time, it is widely felt that a senate must consist of experienced statesmen and people of public repute, who are not necessarily politicians, but who have wide knowledge and understanding of political matters.

sentimentality. The enjoyment of emotion for its own sake, without regard to the true character of its object. The fundamental feature of sentimental emotion is that it is founded, not in a belief about and desire to understand its object, but rather in a belief about and admiration for the subject, as the vehicle of heroic, dignified or tender responses. Hence it accompanies and necessitates a lack of real interest in its object, a preference for fantasy over reality, and a disposition not to observe but to falsify the world. It has even been described (by Oscar Wilde) as the other side of cynicism and, contrary to its own self-image, is apt to seem cold-hearted to those directly affected by it. The thought of the true lover is 'This deserves my love', that of the sentimental lover, 'I am admirable, loving this'; it is evident that the first has, while the second has not, an interest in, and a motive to understand, the object of his emotion.

In politics sentimentality is an important motive, since it is a public and recognition-seeking state of mind. Thus there is sentimental grief, such as the frequent conservative regret over the nation and its lost traditions, and also sentimental anger, which searches the world for supposed injustices in order to say 'I am admirable, being angry at this.'

separation of ownership from control. The development of the *joint-stock company, and corporations of limited liability, in which the managers and directors have no more than a limited financial interest, is part of the process whereby, in modern capitalism, ownership has become separated from *control. Thus a large industry may be owned by shareholders who have next to no control over what occurs in any particular factory.

A similar separation occurs in *socialist countries, where ownership vests in the *state, and control in executives. The result is that the division between labour and management has taken on an increasingly similar form in the two different types of economy, and that, in both cases, it is a division between two kinds of *employee*. Some have found this fact to be significant in the study of the politics of production, since it suggests that, in both cases, capital has begun to take an increasingly anonymous form, leaving conflicts to be fought out, not between labour and capital, but between two kinds of labour. Many of the nineteenth-century critiques of private property were really critiques of a certain kind of control over others which private property permitted. The attenuation of this 'control through property' has seemed to many to explain the parochial character which those critiques now have.

separation of powers (sometimes: division of powers). The theory of the separation of powers, implicit in *Aristotle, but first given independent expression by *Harrington and *Locke, is known in its modern form largely through the writings of *Montesquieu, who thought that this separation was already exhibited by the English constitution, providing one of the principal safeguards of the *liberty of the English subject. Following Montesquieu, the three powers normally considered to be separable in the exercise of government are the *legislature, the *executive, and the *judiciary, the first of which formulates policy and enacts it as law, the second of which carries policy into action and the third of which applies the law according to rules of procedural justice, and resolves disputes. (There is some confusion over what, in fact, the executive power comprises; foreign policy and the waging of war had been assigned to a separate power by Locke, but are incorporated within the executive by Montesquieu.) The sign of the despot, Montesquieu argued, is to subsume these powers under one, and to hold that one to himself. In particular, the despot will never permit an independent judiciary, who might impede him from having his way in every dispute. In this condition of despotism nothing in the structure of power acts as a brake upon power, and hence no freedom can be *guaranteed*. In order to limit power, Montesquieu thought, the three powers that he had identified must be separated as much as possible, and balanced against each other. Thus the executive power should not be exercised by members of the legislature but (Montesquieu thought) by a monarch, subject to *impeachment for actions performed **ultra vires*. (This notion was carried into reality with the creation of the office of *President under the US constitution.)

In the UK it is now clear that the executive power lies with the *cabinet, which is formed from members of *Parliament (i.e. of the legislature), and which effectively controls the operation of Parliament. Moreover, in the UK the highest court of the land – the House of Lords – is also part of the legislature, and judges in that court can, and do, influence legislation. A convention prevents peers without judicial office from sitting in judgement, so that in effect the complete collapse of the powers does not occur. Nevertheless, it is clear that the UK constitution is very far from being as Montesquieu imagined it; and whatever guarantees of liberty are contained in it cannot be attributed simply to a separation of powers. Even the US constitution does not separate the powers completely, nor indeed could it do so without destroying the necessary unity of government. If the three powers ceased to function in harmony, then clearly government would be impossible. Thus, laws enacted by the legislature must be applied by the executive, and upheld by the judiciary, and if a judge acts *ultra vires*, it must be possible for the legislature to hold him to account, and for the executive to remove him from office. In contemplating the relation between the three powers we therefore encounter a problem not unlike that of the Holy Trinity: these things said to be three must also be one. In practice it seems that the greatest guarantee of liberty under the UK constitution is the existence of an independent judiciary; but, as Montesquieu himself observed, the judiciary is less a power than a brake upon power. The other two powers are instigators of policy, and must therefore always act in concert.

*Democratic centralism is strictly incompatible with any separation of powers, and this is manifest most of all in judicial procedure when the executive (the party) has an interest in the outcome.

separatism. 1. The aim of some group within a state to renounce allegiance to that state, and to form a sovereign state of its own. (See also *irredentism, *nationalism, *self-determination.)

The ambitions of a separatist movement must inevitably raise two vital questions: is there sufficient pre-political cohesion to achieve a true political *identity? And: is it in the interests of either party that this identity should be brought into being? Clearly not every group which has a social identity can also have a political identity; economic, institutional and other dependencies may forbid it. (In that sense my street can have no political identity, although, thanks to the residents' association, it is a definite social entity.) Equally a group with the capacity for political identity may well not wish to achieve it: the Protestant community of Northern Ireland being perhaps one example, the Sardinians another.

2. The aim of some radical *feminists, who maintain that, in the company of men, women are bound to be oppressed and so must seek only each other's company for social and political purposes.

serf. *See* *feudalism.

service/manufacture. A service industry produces services rather than goods – for example, haircuts, banking, railways, communications, and so on. A manufacture produces physical commodities.

servitude. 1. The state where one person is controlled by another, without being owned by him (cf. *slavery). Servitude is not necessarily an evil, and mutual servitude by consent is often a good. Love is a familiar form of involuntary servitude, and one that has been generalized into highly abstract visions of the government of the universe by Aristotelians and neo-Platonists. However, in the absence of consent, love, or friendship, servitude is sometimes regarded as an outward form of *alienation; since the *wage contract seems to give control to one party and not to the other, it is sometimes thought to be a form of servitude. (*See* *master and servant.)

2. Technical term in Roman and Scots land law roughly equivalent to easements and profits in English law.

3. In *international law a servitude is an international agreement imposing a certain permanent status – e.g. that of a demilitarized zone – on a certain territory (a development from 2.). A servitude may exist, e.g., in order to provide to a *land-locked state a means of access to the sea: it is analogous to a burden, such as a covenant, in land law.

sex. The biological difference between men and women, which is identified in terms of reproductive function, provides the material basis of a distinction that is perceived and experienced in many ways. Human sexuality presents philosophical and psychological enigmas which have their repercussions in political thought and practice, and not only when it comes to deciding questions of the role of law in mediating relations of erotic love, but also in questions concerning *sexism, *marriage and its political significance, the relation of civilization to *repression, and *sexual conduct generally.

Roughly speaking, philosophers and psychologists may be distinguished into those who think that human sexuality is simply a special case of animal sexuality, overlaid perhaps with distinctive but artificial rituals, and those who think that it is an altogether distinct phenomenon, sharing with the sexuality of animals nothing significant besides the reproductive function. Thinkers of the first kind include *Freud, and those of the second kind *Hegel and *Sartre. The problem arises because, while human beings are animals, they are also persons, and their personality seems to be deeply compromised in all their sexual acts: hence they may feel embarrassment, shame, and many other vulnerabilities that it would be nonsense to attribute to a creature without the idea of self. Moreover, human sexual desire does not seem to have the same object as animal desire. The animal desires stimulation of its sexual organs; the human desires another person, the particular him or her who captures his attention. And this personalized object is also *individuated* by sexual desire: it is James who is wanted, not someone else, and no other will 'do just as well'. This is one of the group of peculiarities in human sexuality which have led some philosophers (including Hegel and Sartre) to think that sexual desire contains a contradiction. As Sartre puts it, I want to possess the individuality of the other, which is his freedom: I want to possess him in his freedom, and therefore I desire that he be both wholly free and also wholly enslaved. From this account Sartre attempts to describe the peculiar relation of the human to his sexual organs, and to the pleasures of these organs, which seem to compromise him in a way that no other pleasures do.

By contrast Freudian and related schools of psychoanalysis have tried to understand human sexuality, and its admitted peculiarities, in terms of the simultaneous repression and preservation of animal instincts. These may be 'sublimated' into the strange activities of erotic love, but retain their inherently 'general' character, and can be studied as impersonal drives in all human beings.

On either view, it cannot be denied that sexuality is affected by and affects many of the customs, manners and attitudes of social life, so that the distinction between the sexes has gathered to itself a kind of universal social significance, leading to the recognition of a masculine and a feminine in everything, from the tone of a voice to the movement of a finger. This penetration of the human world by a radical division of kind is regarded by some as beneficial, by others as unjust or even disastrous, and by all as a fact. What to do with this fact is a question the answer to which has inevitable political overtones. A society which builds upon the biological distinction between the sexes further distinctions of *role, obligation, activity, dress, custom, and style, in effect creates two societies, interlocking and influencing each other in ways that perhaps reinforce the distinctions further. A society which abolishes those distinctions is a different kind of entity. Whether it can retain the same institutions – such as marriage and the family – may be doubted.

sexism. 1. Mild: the view that distinctions of gender are morally or politically significant, in such a way as to justify assigning different rights and different standards of behaviour to the two sexes. **2.** Strong: the view that one of the sexes is in some respect inferior to the other, in such a way as to justify assigning inferior rights (or perhaps no rights at all) and devaluing those tasks and characteristics which traditionally pertain to the 'inferior' sex.

Either sex may be the object of sexist attitudes (in sense 2.); however, it is commonly held that, in developed societies, women have been the usual victims. Sexism in its mild form need not mark out either sex as the 'victim', and must therefore be sharply distinguished from the stronger version with which it tends to be confused. As currently discussed, the strong form of sexism is considered to be, not merely a view about the rights of the two sexes, but a systematic way of perceiving and evaluating their activities and relations. It is sometimes claimed by *feminists that many men, perhaps most men, tend to perceive women as sex objects, or as instruments for the gratification, consolation and reproduction of men, rather than as persons, and that this attitude may be expressed in as many ways as male dominance can secure. It is claimed, for example, that men dominate and control the employment of women, their domestic lives, their relations to each other and to their children, even the language which they speak. Some go so far as to argue that the persistence of gender distinctions in language and the use of the pronoun 'he' to refer indifferently to people (as in this dictionary) are vestiges of a sexism so intransigent as to have enshrined itself in grammar. It is sometimes replied that the fact that men are dominant in the public sphere is a fact of nature, to be offset by the dominance of women in the private sphere. (Metaphysical embellishments of this theory may – e.g. in the thought of *Hegel – add 'active' and 'objective' to 'public', 'passive' and 'subjective' to 'private'.) The accusation of sexism, it is said, fails to take account of the need, experienced by every social being, for a public and a private sphere, and for the cultivation of different talents, achievements and susceptibilities within the two spheres. This need, which explains the appearance of male dominance, could never be satisfied by the fact of it. It requires, rather, a social framework which effectively divides roles, employments, and attitudes, and which then facilitates the separate but complementary development of the two sexes within that division.

Needless to say the dispute between the two views just outlined is bitter and confused. In both forms, sexism must raise the question of when a difference is relevant to a determination of rights. If it is true that some men do not think that women are persons, then this may explain the claim that some men seek to deny *all* rights to women, on the assumption that all and only persons have rights. For the most part, however, argument over 1. and 2., in so far as it concerns rights, tends to focus on the practice of assigning *different* rights to the two sexes – as in the argument over *equal pay. If we think that all persons have or should have equal rights, since the only ground for the possession of any rights is the mere fact of being a person, then presumably we shall oppose both forms of sexism. However, it is possible to believe that personality can be of two kinds, and that the division of kinds is relevant to the assigning of rights. Thus it could be that female sexuality is so different from male sexuality as to determine in a significant way the nature of the female person (a view that we are likely to hold if we think that the personality of the agent is involved in and moulded by the sexual act – *see* *sex). Thus it seems that there are many crimes, notably sex crimes, which tend to be differently regarded according to whether the victim is male or female, and many rights in civil law, such as property rights, which are or have been differently specified for men and for women, usually greatly to the detriment of the woman who seeks to free herself from unwelcome bonds of marriage, or guardianship. Matrimonial law is replete with such unequal rights, and the inequalities follow an obvious pattern. Thus UK and US law recognize a superior right for a mother to be with her children than for a father to be with his, and a superior right to support upon the breakdown of a marriage. It is clear that such inequalities reflect the fact that the law upholds existing divisions of roles, the superior rights granted to women in the private sphere being offset by the inferior rights granted to them in the public sphere of contract and employment. The greatest inequalities of all, however, lie in the domain of obligations rather than in that of rights (e.g. the obligation of women to care for their children, that of men to fight in wars), and can be attributed to a similar cause.

sexual conduct. Political questions concerning sexual conduct include:

(i) The general question of *law and morality. To what extent is sexual conduct really a *private matter, of no *public concern? And should the law seek to free itself of the marks of a moral code that does not have universal assent?

(ii) The politics of the sexual act. To what extent does the sexual act express and reinforce a political vision? Some (e.g. *Reich) have argued that the nature of sexual conduct is the crucial factor in social well-being. Others have devised forms of sexual 'protest' which, whether because they shock others, or because

they liberate the agent, serve as a main vehicle for political sentiment.
(iii) The issue of rape. *Feminists claim that rape should be seen not just as a sex crime, but as a way in which men assert and maintain their dominion over women. The peculiarity of rape is that only men commit it, and, in normal circumstances, only against women. It is therefore seen as a 'political' act; the threat of it, and the fear of it, are active forces within a community, which cow women into submissive *roles.
(iv) The problem of the sexually normal. Is this a coherent idea, and if so, should the law take cognizance of it? For example, some argue that the reluctance of the law to reduce the 'age of consent' for male homosexual intercourse shows a lingering attachment to the view that homosexuality is abnormal. Is there a concept of 'normal sexual relations' which requires that the parties be of different sex?

shame culture and guilt culture. A distinction introduced into *anthropology by Ruth Benedict (*The Chrysanthemum and the Sword,* 1946), and for a while highly influential. The distinction is between those cultures which rely on 'external sanctions for good behaviour', and those which rely rather on 'an internalized conviction of sin'. In the first the offender is shamed publicly before his fellows; in the second he confines his guilt within his troubled heart. The superficial appeal of the distinction (which to some has seemed to capture some of the difference between Mediterranean Catholicism and Northern Protestantism) should not lead us to exaggerate its explanatory potential. Rather it refers to two distinct but intimately related ways in which remorse may express itself. The sufferer may regard himself as horrible in the eyes of others, and redeemed when others reaccept him; or he may regard himself as horrible in his own eyes, and therefore as alone responsible for the expiation of his sin. It has sometimes been thought that guilt must therefore engender a heightened consciousness of oneself as an individual, with unshiftable burdens of responsibility – hence its association with the *Protestant ethic and other codes which might be thought to be based in a philosophy approximating to individualism. Shame, on the other hand, has an intrinsically social quality, and represents the sufferer as an organic part of the community which condemns him.

show trials. Trials on the model of the Moscow trials of the 1930s. The essential features are: large publicity, and a carefully selected victim, who is chosen as an example of some characteristic which the state wishes to eradicate. The verdict is predetermined by the prosecution and the judge instructed accordingly, so that there is no separation between judge and prosecution, no application of *natural justice, and no genuine *adjudication. The purpose of such trials is to stage a large-scale threat, directed at the population as a whole; they are 'trials' only in the sense that someone appears in court. They still occur, especially in China and Czechoslovakia, although to a lesser extent in the USSR than previously.

Sidgwick, Henry (1838–1900). English philosopher; *see* *immigration, *utilitarianism.

Sismondi, Jean Charles Léonard Simon de, (1773–1842). Swiss author; *see* *proletariat.

Sittlichkeit. German: morality or ethical life. Often used in the specific sense given to it by *Hegel, where it includes customary behaviour, respect for *persons, and a comprehensive stance towards the social world, rather than obedience to any specific moral code (*Moralität*), the assumption being that *Sittlichkeit* is a phase of development of the soul or **Geist,* through which it must pass if true individuality and freedom are to be achieved. (*See also* *self-realization.)

Skinner, Burrhus Frederic (b. 1904). US psychologist; *see* *behaviourism, *social engineering.

slavery. A slave is someone who is controlled and also owned by another, and who has either no *rights against the other, or only diminished rights. (Cf. *servitude.) The crucial factor here is that of ownership. It is fairly normal for people to possess legal or moral rights in others: such as the right to redress possessed against the person who has injured you. But rights of *private property are not normal. These rights have been interpreted as involving the right to exclusive use of the *labour power of the slave (restricted, however, by law), and the right to transfer ownership in the slave to another. It is clear that the owner of a slave does not have to be an individual human being. The state may assert rights of exclusive use in the labour power of its citizens, commanding and controlling them in all activities in which labour is expended, and it may even exert a limited right of transfer. Such would be *despotism, and actually existing slavery is for the most part of that kind. But the slave himself is normally considered to be an individual human person, and the injustice of slavery is held to follow from the idea of ownership of such an individual. It is generally thought that an individual person cannot be owned without also denying to him at least one of his (presumably *natural) rights: his right to dispose of his labour power as he wills. At the back of many of the *Marxian arguments about *exploitation is the thought that the situation of the slave is not really changed if you give to *him* the right of ownership in his own labour power and then promptly force him, through need, to alienate that right by selling it to another. (Hence Marx refers at times to 'wage slavery'.) There are, perhaps, elements of *persuasive definition in that idea; but it also suggests that a deeper account must be given of the injustice of slavery, which will show, if it can be shown, that slavery is unjust while the wage contract is not.

When classical writers – e.g. *Aristotle – defended slavery it is not clear that they were defending any absolute form of it. Slaves had extensive rights in Roman law, the practice of *manumission was not only widespread but also normal, and the actual conditions of slave labour were often to be favourably compared with the conditions of much factory labour in the nineteenth century (although the state slaves of Athens were forced to work the silver mines). This makes it additionally clear that abolitionist arguments need to be carefully phrased if they are to show that this arrangement is unjust, but comparable arrangements not so. Some, for example, think that the abolitionist arguments can be made cogent only by also denouncing the rights that a husband may exert over his wife's body under some laws of marriage.

Smith, Adam (1723–90). Scottish philosopher and political economist, whose *Theory of the Moral Sentiments,* 1759, presented an influential account of the emotional life of the moral being, and whose *Inquiry into the Nature and Causes of the Wealth of Nations,* 1776, completely transformed the subject of *political economy, and introduced many of the thoughts, problems and conceptions which have since lain at its heart. In the *Theory of the Moral Sentiments* Smith gave an account of justice as a negative virtue, which consists in refraining from injuring another and from taking what is rightfully his. This virtue is the essential foundation of a well-ordered society, but it is a sentiment too feeble to exist without the firm support of law. Smith later developed this view and made concessions towards some kinds of egoism, which he came to think to be a social value. In *The Wealth of Nations* he opposed the *mercantilist beliefs that a state's power depends upon its wealth, and that the best policy for a state is to retain as much of it within its borders as possible; on the contrary, Smith argued that there are great potential gains from trade and exchange, and he praised the virtues of competition. Thus Smith also rejected the idea of the primacy of agriculture (*see* *physiocrats), and gave a systematic account of the importance of manufacture in production.

Smith also pointed to the benefits, in terms of increasing production, which stem from specialization and the *division of labour, the products of which could be exchanged in the marketplace. Productivity depends on the skills of the labour force and the proportion of productive to unproductive labour. The detail division of labour enhances the first, while the accumulation of capital enhances the second. Smith thus initiated the inquiries into the nature and function of *capital that were to dominate nineteenth-century political economy.

Smith emphasized the distinction between *use-value and *exchange-value, suggesting labour as a measure of the second: however, he did not subscribe to the *labour theory of value in its subsequent form, since he thought prices to be determined by supply and demand. He defended **laissez-faire,* and believed that a market economy left to itself, while not without its evils, nevertheless has a natural tendency to *equilibrium possessed by no rival economic system. In it: 'Every individual is continually exerting himself to find out the most advantageous employment for whatever capital he can command.' This will be in producing and selling the goods which satisfy as many needs as possible. So that, through intending his own gain, a capitalist contributes to the general welfare, 'led by an invisible hand to promote an end which was no part of his intention'. This justification of capitalism, which echoes various thoughts of *Mandeville's, was to prove extremely influential, and still has its adherents. In fact what it justifies is not capitalism as such, but rather the profit motive, attached to an equilibrating mechanism which produces benefits for all. Critics tend to point out that without attention to problems of distribution, the market system may produce vast inequalities, and that this may in itself destroy the possibility of equilibrium in the political sphere.

Smith produced important recommendations concerning public finance and *taxation. In particular, he argued that a tax ought to be proportionate to the ability to pay; this argument was influential in forming taxation policy after Pitt.

snobbery. The affectation of a *class or *status, by cultivating the manners and society of those thought to possess it. It is usually accompanied by contempt for the class or status to which the subject least wishes to belong. If the class or status aspired to is lower than the one denied, then snobbery is called inverted: a special case of that is *radical chic, in which political posturing is regarded as an index of class membership.

Snobbery is possible only given the belief that there is something to class or status *other* than the affectation of it; hence its widespread persistence suggests that, whether or not class and status are mere appearances, there is a common belief that they are something more than that.

social choice. A technical term meaning a choice for a society derived from the choices of its individual members. The aim of social choice theory is not, typically, that of the theory of *collective choice (although, as noted, the term 'collective choice' is also used to refer to what is here described as 'social choice'). The theory is concerned not so much to describe and explain the actual inputs to social choices or to determine how the various kinds of influence and control regulate the making of political decisions, but rather to investigate the relation between social choices and individual preferences, when the second are taken as the ground and justification of the first. The theory of social choice is a complex area of applied mathematics, and many definitions are in fact current in the literature, both of 'social choice' itself, and of the *social welfare function which is the theory's principal device (the device which generates a statement of social choice from the statement of individual preferences). Much current work studies the derivation of social choices from the choices and *preference orderings of *all* individuals, and pays great attention to 'impossibility theorems'. These are results such as *Arrow's theorem and the *Paretian liberal which imply that, given certain requirements (e.g. that no member of society should dictate the outcome, that a social choice satisfies some given principle of *optimality, etc.), it is impossible to derive a social welfare function for a society. In other words, those requirements turn out to be inconsistent with the desire that social choices be determined by individual choices. The impossibility theorems have sometimes been thought to capture intuitive difficulties in the concept of *voting, and of collective choice generally.

social contract. Expression introduced into political theory by *Plato, and taken over by *Locke (who also spoke in this connection of a 'social compact'), and now used as a general label for views which try to found all ideas of *legitimacy and *political obligation in a contract, whether express, implied, or hypothetical: e.g. the views of *Hobbes, *Locke, *Rousseau and *Rawls. The essence of the view is this: since to contract is to put oneself under an obligation, the grounds of political obligation could be objectively determined if all such obligation could be traced to a contractual promise. For Hobbes the contract is between *subjects, to set up and obey a *sovereign; in accepting the sovereign's protection, the subject implicitly contracts with all other members of society to obey him. Hobbes wavers between the view that this obedience is absolute and the view that it is circumscribed by *natural law (i.e. by a system of rights that cannot be alienated under the terms of the contract). Locke similarly argued that sovereign power is not a party to the contract but at best the result of it; the contract is between the members of society, who mutually forswear certain freedoms that they enjoy in a *state of nature for the benefit of the security provided by society. But the terms of the contract do not permit the alienation of certain inalienable *natural rights. (Locke wished to oppose *absolutism in the name of *limited government, and foresaw the objection that absolute government might be precisely what had been contracted for.) Rousseau developed more fully the idea that sovereignty is the *outcome* of the contract, and countenanced a partial return to the more absolutist stand of Hobbes. The *general will that emerges from the contract has indisputed sovereignty over the particular wills that might conflict with it.

There are four possible kinds of social contract theory, according to whether the contract is construed as explicit, as implied, as hypothetical or as quasi-contractual:

(a) Explicit. Political obligations actually stem from explicit contracts. For example, a contract may be held to have preceded the formation of society. Or a constitution may be thought to be a contractual document, which is held before the citizen as he reaches the age of consent, and to which he then may signify his assent. (Hence the importance of a *bill of rights, as in the US constitution, or Magna Carta, and the importance of an 'oath of allegiance'.)

(b) Implied. The contract is to be inferred from social behaviour, but is not explicit, for example because the faculty to make explicit contracts emerges in the individual only long after his behaviour has shown his *tacit consent to the arrangement that surrounds him.

(c) Hypothetical. A state is legitimate to the extent that a contract *could* be constructed that its subjects *would* accept, and which does confer on them an obligation towards the state. This is the basis of a view offered by *Rawls, and it is sometimes criticized on the ground that nobody could be *really* bound by a hypothetical contract, so that the problem of political obligation remains.

(d) Quasi-contractual. On the analogy of *Roman and *common law doctrines of quasi-contract, it could be held that contract provides the best *model* for the understanding of obligations which arise through the mutual encouragement of interacting parties, and that a quasi-contractual obligation is to be inferred wherever this interaction is voluntary and accompanied by manifest and intended advantages to the participants. This is perhaps the most plausible view, but it stands in need of theoretical elaboration.

Moreover it does little to solve the general problem of political obligation, and can therefore be thought not to have succeeded in its principal purpose, which is one of justification rather than explanation.

social credit parties. Based on the theory, advanced by C. H. Douglas (1879–1952), that the weakness of modern capitalism lies in a deficiency of purchasing power. Social credit parties arose during the Depression with the aim of instigating monetary reform designed to make 'social credit' available to consumers – e.g. by discounts paid to retailers. The success of such parties was greatest in Canada, but is now dwindling, along with the belief in the underlying doctrine.

social Darwinism. *See* *Darwinism.

social democrats. **1**. 'Social democracy' is sometimes used to mean the theory and practice of *democratization, applied to all social institutions and all social rewards, and not merely to the institutions of government.

2. In a more specialized sense, 'social democrats' are defined by political affiliation. Originally all parties affiliated to the *international socialist movement assumed the title 'social democrats', but the modern use of the term emerged in 1905 following the split between the *bolshevik and the *menshevik wings of the Russian Communist Party, the second adhering to the label 'social democrat' in order to emphasize its adherence to a policy of peaceful social change by popular consent.

Now 'social democrat' denotes, roughly, any view, with some elements of socialist belief, which seeks reform rather than revolution, that respects constitutional procedures (even when the reform of the constitution is part of its aim), and which adheres to the principles of democratic election. The underlying belief is that what makes a party democratic is that it seeks to rule, not merely in the name and the interests of the people, but also by consent from the people. This means that social democrats must seek to retain the means whereby consent is offered, and must accept the existence of *opposition parties, and of elections which might lead to their own removal from office. Social democrat parties were originally dominated by Marxists, whether orthodox or *revisionist, but in Germany, where the movement has dominated politics, the Social Democrat Party (SPD) definitively broke with Marxism in 1959.

The recent emergence of a social democrat party in the UK has been partly in reaction to a tendency in the *Labour Party to show sympathy for some Leninist views and procedures. While it retains socialist sympathies, its *centrist and *moderate proposals, together with its reserved attitude towards the *labour movement and the trade unions, make it very difficult to assimilate to the parties which have previously gone by this name.

social engineering. The planned reconstruction of society. The phrase was used, for example, by the American jurist Roscoe Pound to denote the rule of law in a democratic society, but has often been thought to have rather sinister overtones. Hence it is contrasted with *piecemeal (social) engineering (by *Popper), and with social architecture, the first expressing hostility to the *totalitarian, the second hostility to the *utilitarian, implications of the phrase. A variant is the 'behavioural engineering' advocated by B. F. Skinner (*see* *behaviourism).

social fact (also: societal fact). An expression used, especially by *Durkheim, to indicate acceptance of the fundamental tenet of *holism in sociology. There are statements about society which cannot be rephrased as statements about individual members of it, and therefore there are facts about society over and above facts about its membership (*see* *reductionism). An example of such a social fact is the existence of a state of war between two societies; or the existence of a rule of law, or of any other constitutional artifact. Not all social facts are intentional artifacts of that kind: e.g. unnoticed *norms are also social facts. Durkheim argued that sociology is the study of social facts; and that their existence provides the refutation of *individualism.

social imperialism. Term used in China since 1960 in order to denote the authoritarian and expansionist policies attributed to the USSR ('socialism in words, imperialism in deeds').

social-industrial complex. Term introduced by J. O'Connor (*The Corporations and the State*, 1974), to denote industrial organization under capitalism in which the state actively intervenes in the process of production and distribution (with or without *nationalization), in order to achieve social objectives.

social justice. An application of the concept of distributive *justice to the wealth, assets, privileges and advantages that accumulate within a society or state. The idea is vague, partly on account of the lack of precision indicated in that last disjunction: society or state? If the latter, then what about the just distribution among states? If the former, what principle guides us in drawing the line between those qualified, and those not qualified, to be considered under the distribution?

As currently applied the idea seems to be this. Consider a state or system of laws; this identifies a society and ultimately determines, through those laws, the distribution of distributable benefits within it. We can then ask, which system of laws would achieve an equitable distribution of benefits? And that seems like a reasonable application of the concept of distributive justice.

Some object, however, that until something is produced, there are no benefits to distribute, and the very fact of production might create *rights* in the thing produced which would be violated by any distribution that does not have the consent of the producer. (*See* *Locke and, for the inverse application, *exploitation.) If that is so, then the whole picture of social justice as a form of distribution might involve a covert affirmation of a kind of *agency in an area where there is no agency, and a right of *control where there is no such right. (Such is the view, for example, of thinkers like *Nozick.) It is certainly true that appeal to this idea involves, if it is to be consistent, a radical rethinking of all existing rights of acquisition and exchange which, while they may be allowed to survive that process, are also put in question by it. Some find this radical rethinking paradoxical or impossible, arguing that it involves an extrapolation of our common ideas of justice to a point outside the situations which make them applicable. Others (notably *Rawls) argue that, on the contrary, it is just such a rethinking that occurs in every application of the concept of *justice.

One source of confusion concerning this topic is that European discussions have tended to introduce, under the idea of 'social justice', questions of *need, *welfare, and *poverty, giving arguments designed to be as responsive as possible to relations of social interdependence. American discussions, on the other hand, have emphasized the concept of *justice*, and so seen the discussion largely in terms of individual rights. Tensions arise partly because 'social' and 'justice' pull in different directions, the first towards the whole condition of society, the other towards the self-affirmation of the individual.

social mobility. The movement of individuals, families and groups from one *class or *status group to another. For example, the ascent of a nineteenth-century shopkeeper to the upper middle class through the profits of trade, or to the aristocracy through the acquisition of a peerage. Or the ascent of a party member within the Communist Party system. Or the supposed descent of the lower middle classes who suffer *proletarianization. Social mobility is in both directions, although inertia and the manner in which upper echelons legitimate and dignify their position tend to make the downward descent less frequent – at least in so far as status is concerned, since the loss of a fortune or public disgrace are not sufficient for loss of status.

The description of the process is as difficult as the description of the classes and status groups between which people are alleged to move. Thus 'upward mobility' is often thought to be a feature of modern 'post-industrial' society, on account of the increasing importance of skilled, and the decline of unskilled, labour. But whether this is mobility from one class or status group to another, rather than the reformation and reconstitution of the lower class, is extremely difficult to determine. For it is not possible for *everyone* to move upwards, without *someone* moving downwards. (The entire Congolese army was once promoted by one rank, though it is doubtful that any member of it was gratified.)

Social mobility is one of the phenomena that have led sociologists to doubt the utility of nineteenth-century theories of class membership, which suggest easily recognized gradations of 'higher' and 'lower', but which rely on theories of control over the means of production that no longer clearly apply.

social ownership. A form of *common ownership which is sometimes put forward by some *socialists as their defining purpose, and in reference to which 'socialism' originally acquired its modern significance. Social ownership is to be contrasted with private ownership on the one hand and 'state ownership' on the other. The latter is still a form of exclusive ownership, but by a public rather than a private individual, whereas social ownership is supposed to be genuine ownership in common. It is exemplified in some forms of *cooperative, but the aim of many socialists is that it should extend more widely than that (since cooperatives still may thrive under systems of private property). How wide it can be while still being a form of ownership (i.e. a right of use) is debatable. The original *Marxist idea, that social ownership precedes the withering away of the state, is meant to indicate that the state exists just so long as it is necessary to uphold laws granting rights in things: that is, just so long as it is necessary for things to be socially *owned*, while people adjust to the new *production relations which will make *all* forms of ownership unnecessary.

The programme of the Russian Revolution involved, in Stalin's words, the 'socialization of the principal instruments and means of production, in the process of violent proletarian revolution'; it led in fact to a combination of state ownership and private control. (*See* *state capitalism.)

social question. Term used since the eighteenth century to denote that area of political concern which calls not merely for conciliation, adjudication and legislation in the interests of stable government, but for positive action in order to ameliorate social conditions. It was the 'social question' that was partly responsible for the changed role of European government since the French Revolution and its transformation into an active instigator and purveyor of social change. Thus the programme of the French revolutionists was drawn up in response to what Robespierre called 'the most sacred of all laws, the welfare of the people, the most irrefrangible of all titles, necessity'. Throughout the nineteenth century in UK politics the 'social question' was used to denote the condition of people who until then had not had a vote; it was therefore an important phrase in the rhetoric surrounding the introduction of the second Reform Bill. Now that the legitimacy of government action to alleviate want is acknowledged, except perhaps by a small hard core of thinkers from the *New Right, the phrase has tended not to be used; the question is no longer debated, only the answer.

social services. Those services which are provided by the state for the benefit of society. What they include varies from case to case, but it is common to count *education, *health, some *communications, and the maintenance of law and order as social services which a government can be expected to provide and maintain, under the conditions in which a modern government must inevitably find itself. To what extent social services benefit from, or are damaged by, the co-existence of private services catering for the same benefits – i.e. private schools, private medical facilities, private means of communication – is one of the major issues of European politics, discussed in this dictionary under the various separate headings.

social stratification. The development of systematic inequalities of wealth, power, influence, education and privilege within a society. Such inequalities are normally seen as discontinuous; that is, difficult of access from outside, so that each stratum is separated by a barrier from its neighbours. It might be part of a theory of the *systematic* nature of stratification to explain this phenomenon of the barrier.

Social stratification may not exhibit the neat divisions of ownership or control invoked in theories such as the classical theories of *class. As in the case of class, however, the problem of describing the true character of social stratification is not separate from that of explaining it. Those who favour *functional explanations in social matters may identify the strata of society in terms of certain functions performed in upholding and facilitating the continuance of a social order. Those who adhere to *power theories of politics might identify strata in terms of levels or types of power. *Marx took both of those approaches together in his theory of class. Without those explanatory aims 'social stratification' has the vague sense of 'discontinuous inequality'. *See* *status.

social welfare function. 1. A relationship which associates a number with each possible allocation of resources within an economy; the higher the number, the higher in the social *preference ordering is the associated allocation of resources, while two resource allocations with the same number are 'indifferent' from the social point of view.
2. In the theory of *social choice, the term 'social welfare function' is usually used in the sense given to it by K. J. Arrow, i.e. a set of procedures for devising an entire social preference ordering over alternative states of society, given the set of preference orderings over those states possessed by the individuals in society. Such a function is compared by Arrow to a 'constitution': it is a way of translating individual desires and choices between alternative states of affairs into a social choice between them. For an application of this device that has been thought to be of considerable importance in political thought, *see* *Arrow's theorem.

socialism. A wide term, with two principal related meanings:

1. In Marxian theory and official communist language, socialism denotes a system of *production relations that is supposed to characterize the transitional stage between *capitalism and (full) *communism. The means of production are taken into *social ownership, and the state persists as an administrative machine, upholding a new order of legality, and a new system of rights, in such a way as to permit the emergence of true *common ownership, and the eventual abolition of the state.

2. The theory and practice of 'socialism', construed as a broad and comprehensive outlook on the human condition. Socialism envisages a political system that will be, not transitional, in the manner of 1., but permanent, and fitted to the changed conditions of life since the industrial revolution. As a political theory, socialism is a relative newcomer, and probably lacks both the system of traditional *liberalism, and the pragmatic character of *conservatism. But it has emerged in the present century as an increasingly ambitious set of doctrines, with both philosophical and practical components, and a vision of human nature that will lead from the one to the other. The principal ideas seem to be these:

(i) The premise of *equality. This may be variously stated in terms of *equal opportunity, *egalitarianism, etc. The main

consideration is that human beings have equal *rights, since they are equal in every respect relevant to their rights.
(ii) The state as administrator. The state is seen, not as the legal and ceremonial manifestation of civil society, but rather as a complex administrative device, designed to guarantee individual rights, and to distribute benefits among the citizens in accordance with those rights. The state is, therefore, primarily concerned with *distribution, and must provide and maintain the institutions which ensure that human goods – food, medicine, education, recreation – are made available to everybody on terms that are as equal as possible. Law is necessary as a means to good order, and to effective administration. But neither it, nor any other aspect of the state machinery, is an end in itself. Moreover, the state should be *confined* to administrative functions, and not, for example, set up as the propagator of religious doctrine, or nationalist ideology.
(iii) The elimination of systems of *control. Men exert control over each other in various ways – e.g. through the *class system, through political institutions, and through hereditary privileges. All such systems violate the fundamental axiom of equal rights. Private property is permissible, but only in so far as it does not amount to a system of control. While most socialists in sense 2. deny the Marxian thesis that *all* private property in the means of production is a form of control over other men's lives, they accept that *some* is. Hence private property, while in itself right and permissible, and perhaps even a proper expectation of a citizen in a well-ordered society, should not be allowed to accumulate inordinately, lest vast systems of private control should emerge and prove damaging to the interests of society as a whole. Hence the state must always be prepared to *nationalize major assets, and should curtail or forbid the transactions that lead to large-scale private accumulation – such as gifts and inheritance.

Those three main principles explain most of the details of socialist policy: in particular the attempt to eliminate privilege in all its forms, the opposition to the *hereditary principle, and the defence of the *welfare state. Historically socialism has had strong affiliations with the *labour movement, for the obvious reason that, while it promises very little and threatens much to the class of property owners, it promises much and threatens little, or seems to threaten little, to the workers. It has been an important force in European politics, and has acquired some of the pragmatism and ability to compromise which is integral to parliamentary government, so that, under the actual conditions of Western government, none of the three principles is expressed or applied in its pure, theoretical form. Some would add that the attempt to combine (i) to (iii) with the commitment to representative democracy is what is distinctive of Western, as opposed to 'communist', socialism, and that this 'parliamentary road to socialism' is in fact a creature so different from the socialism of the communist states as to be only misleadingly called by the same name.

Critics of socialism have argued, for example, that there is a potential conflict between principles (ii) and (iii). The massive control that needs to be exerted by the state if it is to be seen as an administrator with full responsibility for everyone's welfare is incompatible with the attempt to free people from the control of others. All that will be achieved is the transfer of control from an old *ruling class of aristocrats to a new *élite of bureaucrats. Moreover, some add, a ruling class with a monopoly of government is a better guarantee of freedom and justice than a bureaucracy of self-made men. Others object to the idea of the state as a means, and argue instead that the true character of the state is as an end in itself: only as such can it command the obedience and allegiance of those whom it governs. As means it comes to seem arbitrary and dispensable, and therefore holds increasing power with increasing instability. Others reject the premise of equality, on a variety of grounds mentioned elsewhere in this dictionary, while others argue that the ideal of *social justice implied in (i) to (iii) is incompatible with the assertion of *natural rights and *freedoms.

socialism in one country. The modified aim of the Russian revolutionaries, proposed by Stalin after he had perceived that *international socialism was not feasible. The original theory of the bolsheviks was that, since the *proletariat is an international class, and owes allegiance to no bourgeois nation state, its revolution in one place must precipitate revolution everywhere. The obvious fact that this spread of revolution had not occurred (whether or not it had occurred in Russia) led to the official doctrine that it must be achieved in one country, in order to demonstrate its possibility, and to create a focus of international power upon which the proletariat elsewhere might draw. Socialism in one country was to be brought about by the adoption of five-year plans, and other measures, imposing a centrally controlled discipline on the population.

socialist law. General term for the systems of law developed in the USSR since the revolution, but especially since 1967, and adopted by East European regimes subject to Soviet control. Socialist law is the result of an attempt to use existing Romano-Germanic law as the vehicle through which communist conceptions of property relations and contract, and of the role of the party, can be expressed. The basis of civil and criminal law is retained, in so far as it is necessary for the regulation of common social relations, the prevention of crime, and the protection of the citizen from tortious injury. The technical terms of Roman and German law have also been retained, although the outlawing of many property transactions and private associations has made it uncertain how some of them apply. Moreover, although there are written codes of law in all the countries affected, the absence of *judicial independence makes the passage from the written statute to its meaning and application uncertain, and it is commonly assumed that all laws ostensibly guaranteeing rights, liberties or privileges to the citizen will not be applied against the state or its agents.

socialist legality. Term in use in the USSR since the 1930s, first as a justification of Stalin's acts of tyranny, then as a name for the *rule of law, as this is interpreted by the party: i.e. the rule of law *subject* to the recognition of the leading role of Marxist ideology and the Communist Party. Some doubt that any such thing can be called a rule of law.

socialist parties. Expression now normally used to denote parties which are not affiliated to the communist movement and which, while advocating *socialism, make efforts to separate themselves ideologically and politically from the *Communist Party. Roughly speaking the term means any party with socialist aims, which seeks power within, and also seeks to preserve, a constitution permitting organized opposition to those aims. (*See* *labour parties, *social democrats.) Most such parties are affiliated to the 'socialist international', established in Frankfurt in 1951 as a continuation of the Labour and Socialist International, 1923, and as successor to the second *International, 1889. This has fifty-six affiliated parties from fifty-two states, and it attempts to provide the necessary support to the expression of non-communist ideology among socialists outside the communist states.

socialist realism. First proclaimed by the writer Maxim Gorky and such politicians as *Bukharin, socialist realism summarizes the artist's duty to the party under communism. He must eschew all *formalism, and represent the world of the proletariat in a dignifying, optimistic and generally intelligible manner so as to achieve 'the reflection of reality in its revolutionary development'. He must also endeavour not just to interpret the world, but to change it, in the direction prescribed by 'party-mindedness'. Socialist realism is often condemned as a form of *philistinism, and is now more or less universally despised for its cliché-ridden sentimentality. However, there are occasional revivals of the idea in the USSR, and a version of it has been influential in China, where it is still affirmed under Article 12 of the 1975 constitution.

socialization. 1. In sociology, the process whereby the individual acquires the characteristics that fit him for membership of society, including, most importantly, the perception of himself as an immovably social being, guided by *norms, *roles, and relations with others.

2. In politics, the transfer of an object from private into *social ownership. *See* *nationalization.

societal fact. *See* *social fact.

society. Any aggregate of individual human beings who interact in a systematic way, so as to determine criteria of membership. There are as many ways of counting societies as there are forms of systematic social interaction, and the distinction – essential to political thought, although often ignored by it – between *state and society is by no means easy to draw. In one sense the UK includes countless societies; in another sense only one. Here the *Hegelian concept of *civil society, as a 'moment' of the very same entity which is also a state, is useful. We might then describe the UK society as a collection of societies united into a single civil society. A civil society is a social system which bears the marks of political organization, and is ordered according to the constitution and legislation of a state. Such a society might precede and survive the state, just as a mass of bronze might precede and survive the statue into which it is cast. At the same time, it is no more *separable* from the state than the bronze is separable from the statue (while it lasts). To construe the relation between state and society thus – on the model of form and matter – is not wholly satisfactory, partly because the relation between matter and form itself presents conceptual difficulties. But it enables us to know more or less what we are talking about. Consequently the expression 'civil society' is used in this dictionary to denote a society identified through its political order.

Society in the wider sense is the subject-matter of *sociology; it includes every group of people who selectively respond to other members of that group: all groups of people who form 'systems' in the sense of *cybernetics. The narrower term *association refers to those systems which are also socially recognized as such, and perhaps accorded, on that account, separate status in law. Thus the upper class may form a society, given to systematic interaction, but it does not form an association.

sociobiology. Any theory or would-be theory which studies *society and social behaviour as a feature of the 'biology' of the participants, and which thus hopes to cast light on the social nature of man by studying 'social' features of other animals and the biological determinants (if there be such) of that 'social' behaviour. Some doubt that such a science is possible, arguing that social behaviour is essentially connected with *rationality, i.e. the attribute of men that animals are often supposed not to possess. For such thinkers sociobiology involves an illegitimate *reductionism. Others defend the utility of such a science, thinking that it helps to resolve the perennial question of *human nature, and also to remove some of the mystery which human social arrangements possess.

sociology. The study of *society, in its widest sense. Rival schools of sociologists emerged during the nineteenth century, perhaps the most important being the *individualists, who thought that all true explanations of facts about society must show them to be the consequences of separately identifiable facts about individuals, and the *holists, who believed that individuals are unintelligible outside their social context. Some now remain neutral with regard to that debate, or take an intermediate position; and for the most part prevailing schools no longer present themselves as rivals so much as complementary 'models' of inquiry into facts so unsystematic that it is not to be expected that any premature system will cast light on them. The most important theoretical device that has found its home in sociology is that of *functional explanation; apart from that, the main attempt has been to find either illuminating classifications of social phenomena, or else underlying mechanisms of social change (as in *Marx and *Weber).

Sociology has had enormous influence on political thought, partly through Marx and Weber, who revolutionized the understanding of class relations and their role in social coordination as a whole, partly through theories, such as *Durkheim's trenchant critique of individualism, which have seemed to undermine the foundations of many political doctrines. Dispute still remains, however, concerning the pretensions of sociology. Some regard it not as a science, but as a *scientistic substitute for what should be, if it were to exist at all, a *humanity. Such critics tend to point to the mass of unexplained jargon (sometimes called 'sociologese') which the discipline has generated, together with its more or less complete failure to present a body of established results, or falsifiable predictions. (*See* *Popper.) Others defend the subject on the grounds that one should not criticize it simply on the basis of the products of its second-rate adherents, nor derogate from the real achievements of the great sociologists (such as Marx, Weber, and Durkheim) who have transformed not only our vision of society, but also our vision of all political institutions within it. Some of the disputes in this area concern the extent to which sociology can be, or ought to be, *value-free. Some concern the nature of scientific method and its relation to the 'human' world (*see* **Verstehen*). Some concern the extent to which societies are really intelligible to those who do not belong to them (*see* *relativism).

sociology of knowledge. The branch of *sociology which concerns itself with discovering the social causes (if there be such) of beliefs and ideals. 'Knowledge' is a misleading term, since it implies the truth of what is known. 'Belief' would be better, since the sociology of knowledge often concerns itself with explaining beliefs in ways that show that they are neither caused by, nor in any other way related to, the truth of what they describe: a good example being the *Marxian theory of *false consciousness, which presents in a striking form the epistemological problem to which all such explanations give rise.

The sociology of science is a burgeoning area of sociology, partly because of the growing influence of epistemological *relativism.

socio-technics. Term due to Polish sociologists (e.g. A. Podgorecki: *Principles of Socio-Technics*, 1966) and now the preferred term in the Soviet bloc for *social engineering. 'Socio-technics' have a practical and progressive air which has in part overcome the party's ideological suspicion of *sociology.

solidarity. Common attachment which is so strong as to create a 'solid' resistance to attack. Originally a term of sociology, e.g. in *Durkheim, who used it to denote the internal forces of social cohesion, it later became a left propaganda word, used to describe the political consciousness of an emerging class struggling against *oppression. The term was taken over by the Polish free trade union which emerged in 1980 in opposition to the dictatorship exerted in Poland by the Communist Party.

Sombart, Werner (1863–1941). German economist and social theorist, who, in *Der Moderne Kapitalismus*, 1902, 1916–27, tried to overthrow the analysis of *capitalism given by *Marx, by refuting the fundamental premise of *historical materialism. Sombart argued that the modern Western consciousness is not a consequence of the development of capitalist *production relations, but that those relations are the consequence of a particular spirit, the 'Faustian' spirit of expanding knowledge and opportunity (also described by *Spengler in his less rigorous account of the condition of modern man). Sombart attempted to show how social, cultural and economic values interpenetrate in such a way as to generate the *dialectical movement of history. He repudiated Marxism completely after the Russian Revolution, denouncing it as 'uninhibited Mammonism', i.e. as a congeries of utilitarian values and pure hatred. His work remains important because of its attempt to reverse the order of explanation given by Marx, and so to formulate an intuitive objection to historical materialism, based on the fact that capitalist development seems to have been a local phenomenon.

sophists. Itinerant and professional teachers of the art of *rhetoric (hence the word 'sophism' for a spurious but deceptive argument), who thrived in Greece around 400 BC. The most influential doctrine associated with this heterogeneous body was that of the distinction between *nature and convention. The sophists also gave some of the earliest formulations of the idea of *natural law.

The sophists were noteworthy for their belief in *progress, and for their attempt to persuade people that *virtue, and therefore the art of government, could be taught to all rational beings. This had a revolutionary impact on Athenian society, and also was partly responsible for Plato's attacks on them, by virtue of which so many of their doctrines have survived, albeit perceived only darkly through Plato's bias. The sophists have sometimes been taken as the archetypal 'liberators', those who induce in their hearer the confidence in human capacities, and the confidence to make the world anew.

Sorel, Georges (1847–1922). French philosopher and social theorist, a Marxist turned *revisionist, turned eccentric, who lent his weight to the *anarcho-syndicalist movement, and influenced the development of modern political thought through his *Reflections on Violence*, 1908. In this he argues that *violence is not the single phenomenon normally described by that name, but extends through all social order, so that there is a 'violence of principles' exerted in the name of morality and religion, and various forms of *structural violence contained within the law and institutions of every enduring society. All serious political opposition must develop its own form of violence if it is to be successful; *confrontation, rather than *conciliation, is the true political process. Sorel proceeded to advocate the general strike as the preferred way of precipitating radical social change. He gave a curious theory of *myth in support of this idea. Having opposed Marxism on account of its *deterministic attitude towards the future, he argued that men control the future not through scientific understanding but through myth. The role of a myth is to rehearse the imminence of some event, and so to concentrate human will towards it, as eventually to bring it about. There are only two attitudes to the future – that of myth, which eventually masters the future, and that of *utopia, which swoons away from it. Some have found this analysis useful in the sociology of modern *fascism and Marxism, the first of which Sorel influenced through Mussolini.

sovereign. 1. General: the person, body, or system of offices in which *sovereignty is vested.

2. Specific: the person who, under a *monarchy, exercises the functions associated with the *head of state. Who this person shall be is determined in the UK by the Act of Settlement 1700, which can probably be altered only with the consent of those states within the Commonwealth which are also monarchies presided over by the sovereign of the UK.

The divergence between 1. and 2. is illustrated by the theory that sovereignty in the UK vests not in the sovereign but in Parliament.

sovereignty. 'There is and must be in every state a supreme, irresistible, absolute, and uncontrolled authority, in which the . . . right of sovereignty resides.' Thus wrote Blackstone in the *Commentaries on the Laws of England*, 1765–70, arguing that this absolute authority lies not with the sovereign, but with 'the Queen in Parliament'. It is now unclear what is meant by sovereignty, and the concept seems to focus disputes in political science and philosophy which no dictionary article could possibly resolve. The concept derives its contemporary significance from *Bodin, *Hobbes, *Rousseau, *Hegel, and many more, and seems to have at least two distinct parts:

1. External sovereignty. This is an attribute which political bodies possess in relation to other such bodies. Thus 'sovereignty' in *international law implies the recognition of a *state as having rights of jurisdiction over a particular people and territory, and being solely answerable for that jurisdiction in international law. This legal idea is meant to correspond to an actual power to assert itself over the territory in question. However, legal sovereignty can diverge from actual power, as in the case of the major states in Eastern Europe, which are sovereign states in international law, but which have no real power to act independently of the Soviet Union in any matter which concerns the Soviet interest. Here, it might be said, employing a distinction elaborated below, that legal and coercive sovereignty diverge.

There are many theories of external sovereignty; perhaps the most important distinction among them is between those which regard sovereignty in instrumental terms (e.g. as an institution existing in order to protect a society from internal and external violence), and those which see it in expressive terms, as the 'realization' or embodiment of social and political order. Hobbes's theory is an example of the first, Rousseau's an example of the second.

2. Internal sovereignty. This is an attribute possessed by a political body in relation to a society that falls under its government. Sovereignty in this sense lies in supreme *command over a *civil society, and it has a *de jure* (legal) aspect, as well as a *de facto* (coercive) aspect. Legal sovereignty vests in that person, office or body whose decisions cannot legally be challenged in the court. Coercive sovereignty vests in that person, office or body which in fact *controls the powers exerted and enforced in the name of government. Thus in the UK legal sovereignty is vested in the Queen in Parliament, whereas all *executive decisions are made by the *cabinet, which some say controls the political process as best it can (although it may be that the cabinet's *influence falls short of control). It is arguable that, because of constitutional pressure, coercive sovereignty can only be exercised in accordance with the law, and that all exercises of political power are thus eventually subject to scrutiny by Parliament. This 'coming together' of the legal and the coercive seems to be the ideal of internal sovereignty. It can be described as a uniting of power and (legal) authority. Quite what it involves has remained disputed since Bodin. The USSR constitution, for example, which leaves the question of legal sovereignty undetermined, purports to vest all 'power' in the people (Art. 2), but at the same time affirms the leading role of the Communist Party (Art. 6) in such a way as to imply that both legal *and* coercive power vest in it. In point of fact it is impossible to give a clear answer to the question where sovereignty in such an arrangement lies, and it may be doubted that the concept is here a useful one.

The US constitution purports to vest internal sovereignty in itself, but that seems incompatible (a) with the fact that the constitution can be amended, (b) with the fact that, unless some body can *enforce* the constitution, it is without coercive power. In this case legal and coercive sovereignty seem to fall apart. This shows why the concept of sovereignty has served as a focus for the question how it is that power and legal right might be so conjoined that the second informs and controls the first, while the first gives substance to the second. (*See also* *separation of powers.)

Once a body – e.g. a *legislature – has legal sovereignty there is clearly no limit to its legislative competence; it can be challenged by no one and is not bound by its own decisions. The UK Parliament conforms to that rule (although the great extent of *judicial independence might lead one to doubt that Parliament really could enact legislation that is in flagrant breach of *natural justice). The US Congress does not conform to the rule, since its legislative powers are limited by the constitution, the interpretation of which, however, constantly changes as Congress presses up against its previously defined limits. Some legal *positivists try to argue that, in such a case, true legal sovereignty must lie with whomsoever has power to change the constitution, but this seems absurd, since the body empowered to do this has hardly ever met and does not exist continuously. It is interesting to note, therefore, that while the concept of sovereignty might still be thought to be useful in describing the workings of the UK constitution, its application to modern states such as the US (with true constitutional government) and the USSR (with a fiction of constitution) is in both cases problematic.

sovietization. The forming of 'soviets', i.e. the workers' councils, which emerged in Russia during the 1905 revolution. Sovietization is the process whereby all economic, political and administrative power is transferred to such councils, in theory in order to facilitate grass-roots *democracy, in practice permitting control by the central party, which acts in the name of the 'Supreme Soviet'. The Supreme Soviet is the highest organ of state in the USSR, consisting of two chambers filled through one-party elections. Originally the mensheviks had the strongest support among the soviets, but after the bolshevik seizure of power they were gradually eliminated. At the lower level it is still possible for people who are not members of the Communist Party to be elected to a soviet, provided that their candidature is approved by the party.

Sparta. Greek *polis*, whose remarkable constitution, attributed to the legendary *legislator Lycurgus, provided one of the two most important *ideal types for ancient discussions of government (the other being *Athens). The following features (which seem to have existed from the sixth century BC onwards) are noteworthy: the division between citizens and helots (the latter being a conquered race destined from birth to a condition of slavery); the forbidding of the alienation of land within the city: the hereditary transfer of land to the head of the household; the forbidding of all commerce or trade to those with full citizenship; the lack of a monetary system (the last four features amounting to a more or less complete absence of the phenomena of exchange and *price); collective education of a military rather than academic kind, until the age of thirty, and collective meals for all men until the age of sixty. The political system consisted of two hereditary kings, a senate of elders which also functioned as a supreme court, an assembly of all male citizens over thirty and fifteen elective *ephors*. The last gradually came to acquire legislative, judicial and executive power, and could even sentence the king to fine or imprisonment. The whole organization of the state was directed towards war, and towards the continuing suppression of the ever-rebellious helots. Nevertheless the communal organization of Spartan social life, together with its strict curtailment of all property dealings, were often admired, e.g. by *Plato.

Spartacists. Members of the movement founded as the Spartacus League in 1916 in Germany, by *Luxemburg and Karl Liebknecht, and named after the Roman slave Spartacus, who led an unsuccessful rebellion of slaves, and who died in 71 BC. The Spartacus League was a revolutionary Marxist organization, strongly opposed to the war, and later became the nucleus of the German Communist Party.

species being (or: species life). Normal English translation of the term *Gattungswesen*, introduced by *Hegel and used by Feuerbach to signify the social essence of man (i.e. the fact that human beings are not truly such in isolation but only when joined in social relations with their kind), and taken over by *Marx in his early writings, in the hope that it indicated a theory of society that would be materialist in its assumptions and anti-individualist in its results.

Spencer, Herbert (1820–1903). British philosopher and social theorist; *see* *evolutionism.

speculation. Buying and selling with a view to profit as a result of changes in price. From the earliest times this practice has been condemned, the idea being that the speculator makes no contribution to the economy, either as producer or distributor, and furthermore that he profits from instabilities and that his activities may even encourage them.

The most common defence of speculation lies in the argument that it is an integral part of the self-regulating price mechanism, and facilitates the return of the market to *equilibrium.

Spengler, Oswald (1880–1936). German philosopher of history whose *Decline of the West*, 1919–22, presents in Wagnerian imagery a compendious vision of world history, as the 'comparative morphology' of cultures. Each culture has a life cycle, of about 1,000 years, and Western culture is now at its end, entering the period of 'civilization' where administration and technology take over from the flowering of the spirit in its summer forms. The Western spirit is 'Faustian', consisting in a constant urge to reach out into infinite space and fill it with significances – it is this spirit which explains the soaring gothic cathedrals, the perspectival paintings, the ever expanding fugal forms of music. The ancient Greco-Roman spirit, by contrast, was 'Apollonian', confined in a local finite space, practising the severe circumscribed life of the **polis*. Spengler's vision was unscholarly and impetuous, but his very modern version of the cyclical theory of history proved influential, and his poetry was captivating to a generation that had seen the crimes committed in the name of progress. His later adulation of the 'beast of prey' and the nobility of the 'irrational' man lent some support, or at least hot air, to the Nazi ideology, although he himself disapproved of Nazism, arguing, in reference to Hitler, that Germany stood in need of a hero, not a heroic tenor. The conception of the 'Faustian' spirit was shared with *Sombart, who put it to comparable use.

sphere of influence. Territory over which some powerful state claims preferential rights of a political and economic kind, but which may be united with that state neither by direct alliance, nor by any imperial or quasi-imperial tie. Spheres of influence may be proclaimed unilaterally (as under the *Monroe doctrine), or by agreement, as between the UK and Russia in 1907 in the case of Persia.

The idea is said to be important in understanding USSR foreign policy. However, it is normal to distinguish *influence from *control, in a way that seems to be of little significance in Soviet thought. The 'sphere of influence' in Eastern Europe, for example, is also a sphere of control, even of *force, and is probably better understood in such terms. The US 'sphere of influence' in Latin America may be similar, although many doubt this. The boundary between influence and control is difficult to draw, and is always drawn differently by the two sides in an international dispute.

Spinoza, Baruch (Benedict de) (1632–77). Dutch Jewish philosopher, a thoroughgoing *rationalist, and a *determinist, who nevertheless believed that intellectual freedom was the condition without which all civil order must be opposed to reason. Spinoza's *Tractatus Theologico-Politicus*, 1670, written under the influence of *Hobbes, presented a systematic treatment of the nature of the republic, in which many modern liberal doctrines achieved expression. Like Hobbes, Spinoza believed that the essence of government is power, and he made no distinction between *rights and powers (partly because of a metaphysical doctrine which implied that rights *are* powers). Nevertheless he defended a doctrine of *natural rights, supported by *natural law, which in turn is revealed to the *natural light of reason. Like *Grotius, Spinoza argued that the natural law is not law because it is laid down by God, but because it is the expression of necessities perceivable to all reasonable beings. All *positive law should be seen as an attempt to maintain the discipline of government, while conceding and protecting natural rights. Political obligation arises from an implicit *social contract, and consent rather than fear must establish the true authority and power of government. Hence the aim of government is liberty, since without liberty there can be no consent.

Spinoza attempts to reconcile a near-absolutist view of *sovereignty (arguing that the natural rights of the subject are, with a few exceptions, transferred to the sovereign), with a defence of *limited government, for which he sees *judicial independence as a necessary condition. The conflict here is redolent of similar conflicts in Hobbes; and like Hobbes, Spinoza is not anxious to see men in a state of nature, believing that, even though there are natural rights, they can be perceived only in the state of society. Hence, without political power, the value of limiting that power could never be understood. The right of the sovereign must be as absolute as his power; however, although it may seem supreme to the senses, it must always be limited by reason, whose power in the end is higher than that of anything that would oppose it. Here Spinoza relies on the Socratic defence of the life of the intellect as the exercise of true freedom, which he develops further in his posthumously published *Ethics*. Hence the absurdity of all laws designed to control human thought, or the expression of human thought. Spinoza's metaphysical determinism implied that the only freedom available to us is that of understanding the necessities which govern us, and it is to this intellectual freedom that political freedom is the means.

Spinoza's impassioned defence of free speech and also of religious toleration was highly developed. He argued that the real disturbers of the peace within any commonwealth are not those who express their sincere opinions, but rather those who seek to curtail the liberty of judgement over which they cannot tyrannize. Such people force a contradiction into the structure of law, and so bring it into disrepute, remove its limiting function, and destroy the sovereignty which the law proclaims.

Although he upheld Hobbes's idea of sovereignty, Spinoza concluded that the ideal sovereign was not a monarch, but a democratic assembly filled by those who represent the owners of property: i.e. those who exercise the powers that must be ruled.

sport. A leisure activity recognized as the common property of every class, and the focus of much political interest in both domestic and international affairs on account of its inherently associative character, and also because it is the most available form of *play, and therefore the most common active relief from *work. Institutions of sport are institutions of society, and it is significant that ideologies, such as fascism, which attempt to close the gap between society and state, requiring a point-by-point correspondence between law and social life, have invaded the institutions of sport and attempted to politicize them. This is partly because sport provides, through the player, the team and the captain, ready objects of human allegiance symbolic of local, territorial and national virtues. The identification between a team and its home town and the idea of organized competition between towns are both of great interest in the study of nationalism, since they embody in embryo the feelings of locality, associated with prowess and a right to rule, which are tapped by that political movement.

Nationalism has, in fact, more or less completely dominated the major attempt to use the institutions of sport to further peaceful international relations – the Olympic movement, founded in 1894 by the Comtean optimist Baron Pierre de Coubertin (1863–1937). The ceremonial and ritualistic character of the Olympic contest was exhibited in the Olympic Games of Antwerp in 1920, and later put to dramatic use by Hitler at the Eleventh Olympiad, in Berlin, 1936. (However, to Hitler's disgust, an American black, Jesse Owens, failed to demonstrate the inferiority of his race.) The last Olympiad, in Moscow 1980, was equally an exercise in propaganda, although by this time the ceremonial had been reduced to Disneyland idiocy.

stabilization. **1**. Political. The securing of a *regime from the threat of internal overthrow by revolution or rebellion. Stabilization is a major preoccupation of US foreign policy in Latin America, where precarious regimes are stabilized through economic and military support. However, political stability does not depend only upon money and arms, but also (so it seems) upon ideology and felt social unity, both of which may be provided by a religion. Neglect of the vital role of religion has sometimes been held responsible for the failure of the policy of stabilization in Iran, although that is clearly only one element in a complex episode.

2. Economic. The attempt by governments to reduce the extent of fluctuations in both income and level of employment.

stagflation. The situation in which rapid *inflation accompanies stagnation of production and high and rising unemployment. It is one of the most difficult of all problems faced by a government, since there seems to be no remedy for the one evil that will not also exacerbate the other.

Stakhanovism. In 1935, Alexei Stakhanov, a miner in the Ukraine, increased output by organizing a group of subordinate workers, and thus became the hero of Soviet labour, a kind of ideologically purified version of the entrepreneur, motivated not by material but by 'moral' incentives, and paid accordingly. As a result, a system of 'norms' was introduced which determines the minimum amount which must be produced by every labourer at a certain wage. Stakhanov, hated ever since by Soviet workers, has given his name to the system of organized labour and pay differentials in the USSR.

Stalinism. The form of *despotism exemplified by Stalin's exercise of power in the USSR, the main characteristics of which are: complete control of all media for propaganda purposes; systematic elimination of opposition, without respect for morality or law (although suitably glossed by ideas of 'revolutionary morality' – *see* *Lenin – and *socialist legality); mobilization of popular support around the leader; 'five-year plans' designed to secure production by force; elaborate justifications of *socialism in one country designed to reconcile every aspect of policy with Marxist-Leninist principles; unswerving dogmatism in all matters, regardless of competence; fear of and pitiless retribution against all those thought to be traitors to the ruling party and its purposes.

Some argue that Stalinism is implicit in Leninism, and the necessary consequence of the attempt to use Marxist doctrine as a programme of action rather than a theory of history (cf. *myth, *Sorel). The infrequency of Marxist-Leninist governments without dictatorship might be held to confirm this. Others prefer to see Stalinism simply as the offshoot of the criminal characteristics of Stalin himself, although this thought continues to present difficulties to a certain kind of historical materialist, since it seems to imply that history is made by individuals, rather than by the 'material forces' which project them into eminence.

stare decisis. More precisely: *stare decisis et non quieta movere*: to stand by decisions and not to move what has been settled. *Stare decisis* is the fundamental axiom of the doctrine of *precedent, and the root of all *common law, according to which previous judicial decisions must be followed if applicable. A decision can in fact be questioned, but only by a higher court, and when deemed binding by the highest court is immune from appeal in law. However, a decision is binding only in respect of its *ratio deci-*

dendi – i.e. the principle of the original judgement – and not in respect of *obiter dicta*. The *ratio decidendi* may be implied rather than express, and hence there is still room for the judicial manoeuvre of 'distinguishing a case', whereby it is decided that a precedent, while binding, does not apply. Making sense of the doctrine of *stare decisis* is vital to understanding both law and judicial independence.

state. A term which derives its modern usage from *Machiavelli, but concerning which there is no commonly accepted definition. A fundamental divide separates those who adhere to the *rights theory of politics, from those who adhere to the *power theory, and this is often reflected in definitions of 'the state'. As an example of the first, consider *Hegel: 'the state is the actuality of the ethical idea'; as an example of the second, *Weber: the state is the organization which 'monopolizes legitimate violence over a given territory' (where a 'legitimate' power is simply one that has bestowed upon itself the artificial sanction, itself no more than a special kind of power, of law). Marxists, who tend to adopt this second view, also add that the state is a 'product of society at a certain stage of development', and perhaps even 'the admission that this society has become entangled in an insoluble contradiction with itself' (*Engels): the idea being that the state is part of the institutional consolidation of capitalist *production relations.

Both views begin from the same fundamental distinction, that between state and *society, and both recognize that law is essential to the first, but may not be essential to the second. This same intuition underlies the idea of the state in *international law: an *association of persons, living in a determinate part of the earth's surface, legally organized and personified, and associated for their own government. Two special cases recognized in the literature are the city state (**polis*), and the *nation state, both of which accord well with that definition. While somewhat perfunctory, the legal idea serves to identify the class of objects that have been discussed by such thinkers as Machiavelli, *Hobbes, *Bodin and Hegel. The many obscurities are revealed, however, once we break down the definition into its components:

(i) association among persons for the end of government;
(ii) legal organization: i.e. the power of the government is exercised partly through law, and hence may be determined and limited in certain cases by a *constitution;
(iii) attachment to a particular *territory over which *jurisdiction is exercised;
(iv) personification: i.e. the state is both a juristic *person in international law, and a kind of quasi-person in popular thinking, with rights, obligations, and also a personal identity over time distinct from the identity of its members. Furthermore the state has *agency and *responsibility, whether or not in law.

Each of the four components presents difficulties, some of which are explored elsewhere in this dictionary. It is worth noting that (ii) is not the same as a *rule of law, which exists only as a special case of it; there can also be states which are without *constitutions. (Despite those legal positivists, such as *Kelsen, who try to identify a state with a system of *positive law.) Moreover the idea of *sovereignty is not explicitly mentioned in any of (i) to (iv), although, on some views, it could be thought to be implied by (i) and perhaps also by (iv).

In the light of all the many sceptical disputes concerning the idea of the state, it is not to be thought that (i) to (iv) do any more than capture a core idea. Since (i) to (iv) are probably all independent, or at least separately discussable, it is open to theorists to deny any of them while attempting to keep the remainder. Thus some would deny (i), arguing that political association is not 'for an end' and, even if it were, it would not be for the end of *government*. (*See*, e.g., *Oakeshott.) Others might deny (ii), on the grounds that it is parochial, over-influenced by the procedures of Western politics, and does not take account, for example, of *oriental despotism, whether historical or 'actually existing'. (iv) too meets with opposition, largely on ideological grounds, from those *individualists who think that only human beings can have rights and obligations, and that to personify the state in any other than a legal sense is to begin to worship it (*see* *minimal state). Finally (iii) can be seen to be of a different character from the other conditions, on account of the extra-legal reference to territory. Again this might be thought to be a parochial condition, expressive of the localized sentiments of attachment to the *polis* and the nation state. Could there not be a state without territory (e.g. the Jewish state, at certain periods during its history: *see* *Jewish law)? On the other hand it is very difficult to detach the idea of *jurisdiction from that of territory, just as it is difficult to imagine the fully political being who has *no* local attachments.

That last idea, however, introduces a fairly common use of the concept of the state, in which the state and the citizen are collectively contrasted to the sovereign and the subject; it being supposed that the first two define a distinctively modern kind of relationship, and a corresponding virtue of citizenship, which abstracts from blind obedience and unthinking attachments towards a reasoned respect towards the law. Thus the state might be held to be a name for a special sub-class of associations conforming to (i) to (iv): that in which the 'legal-rational' system of authority has come to replace the traditional system of obedience. (Such a view takes inspiration from Weber.)

state capitalism. An economic arrangement in which there is state ownership of the means of production. Control may be with a managerial class, or with a ruling party, and many of the features of capitalist *production relations remain – including, for example, the relation between the controllers and the proletariat, and including the wage contract, exploitation, and many other features imputed to capitalism. Sometimes *actually existing socialism is said to be a form of state capitalism, by which is meant that there is no true *social ownership, and certainly no true communism, since in communism there should be neither state nor property, but only collective control. However, 'state capitalism' is also a term of communist usage, which, together with '*state socialism', belongs to a collection of idioms used to describe the period of economic history which has defied the Marxian laws of development.

state of nature. The state of man outside society which is invoked by political philosophers either as a deliberate fiction, in order to separate *nature from convention in human affairs, or as a hypothesis about the condition of man before the existence of society, or as a hypothesis about his condition should society be taken away. If there is a *natural law, then it is valid in a state of nature. However it may not be *upheld* there, and *Hobbes, who believed in natural law, thought that, without a coercive *sovereign, such a law would not and could not be upheld, so that the life of man in the state of nature is 'solitary, poor, nasty, brutish and short'. Others (e.g. *Locke) have taken a more sympathetic view of it, while yet others (especially *Hegel and *Marx) have rejected the whole conception as incoherent, for example because it supposes the existence of rational, autonomous *persons outside the condition of society which alone makes the existence of such beings possible (Hegel), or because it imagines men in a state of nature disposed to form just those relations which capitalism and the market economy fit them for (Marx, glossed by C. B. Macpherson).

state socialism. Term sometimes used to denote large-scale state interference in the economy, roughly along the lines of *state capitalism, but sweetened by a fiction of *social ownership. The term has some importance in *Fabian writings, and also among communists anxious to draw residual moral boundaries, between forms of capitalism in which the state is involved as a principal agent, and forms of socialism in which the state is supreme.

states' rights. The US constitutional doctrine that the states of the Union should enjoy exclusive exercise of any powers not expressly granted by the US constitution to the federal government. Advocates of states' rights have been active in US politics since the beginning of the Union, their initial inspiration coming partly from *Jefferson's insistence upon the principle of *federalism as essential to a certain kind of limited government. Movements for the advancement of states' rights continue to oppose the accumulation of legislative and political authority in the federal government, especially in matters of local concern. In this they may often enter into conflict with bodies such as the *civil rights movement, which attempt to force local communities to conform to strictures contained in the federal constitution.

statism. *See étatism.*

status. A term sometimes used by sociologists (notably *Weber) to denote a kind of *social stratification that is not a matter either of *class or of political position. The term is used vaguely and inconsistently, but the main idea is that of a stratification based in social recognition rather than in any kind of material power, although, because social recognition is itself a kind of power, it is hard to draw the line with precision. Thus a group that sets itself apart through social relations, style and manners, may be composed of members from a variety of economic divisions within society, and yet be regarded, both by itself and by others, as somehow 'at the top' of a social scale. Some think that this might still be true of certain traditional European aristocracies, despite their more or less total loss of control over economic and political life.

It is sometimes argued that 'status groups' have replaced classes as the recognizable social divisions in modern societies, e.g. those of the US and of the USSR. Such groups are characterized by rapid *social mobility within the *hierarchy, and the absence of any hereditary qualification for membership: hereditary power and influence may be a sufficient condition for membership of a high status group, but it is never a necessary condition.

Traditional ideas of class may be associated with *functional explanations: that is, the division between classes may be due to some social function which it performs. Such explanation might also underlie the analysis of status groups (especially when analysed as 'income brackets'), so that in this respect class and status group may be difficult to separate. Thus some sociologists estimate status in terms of the 'reward system' in a society, where reward includes every kind of advantage offered by social life. This leads to more status groups than traditional class theories cater for, but it is not clear whether the status group theory is supposed to replace those theories or merely to add to them. Others, influenced by Weber's original claims that the system of privilege and honour is independent of the system of economic control (the class system), try to analyse status groups in terms of the opinion of distinction that is attached to each of them. Some even argue that the *media are one of the most important influences in the creation of modern status groups, so that TV personalities lie at the highest point in the social scale, with subordinate positions identified in terms of their greater or lesser proximity to that position of eminence. Defenders of traditional class analysis are apt to say that opinions of distinction are themselves to be *explained* in terms of class, and do not constitute class. The area is one of confusion, exacerbated by the fact that social groupings have all been subjected to the solvents of *democratization and the media in the West, and to that of party organization in the Soviet bloc. These have radically altered the kind of hierarchical structure that was observed by Marx and Weber.

status quo. 'The existing state of affairs', or 'previous state of affairs' (*status quo ante*). The expression has been in use since the 1830s to refer to the maintenance of or return to an existing social or political order. There is always *a status quo* at the back of conservative thinking on society, which furnishes the idea of an imperfect but nevertheless achieved social order which it would be better to conserve than to destroy.

statutes. Those laws which are laid down in statutes and statutory instruments, as distinct from *common law, which is the sum of principles contained in and developed through the decisions of judges, but not otherwise sanctioned by a legislative body. Statutes may be written, or they may be preserved (as were certain parts of Anglo-Saxon law) in the form of an oral tradition of maxims. The verse form of some of the ancient systems of law (e.g. the fragments of Solon that remain to us) may be explained by the need to memorize the law for recital at the critical moment.

Under UK law statute is in theory of higher authority than common law, and always prevails when the two conflict. However, statutes can usually be applied only after judicial interpretation, so that, despite being supreme as the expression of the will of the Queen in Parliament, they may be made to conform to the common law. While it may sometimes be inexpressible, the common law is always by its nature intelligible; the same is not true of statutes.

Stirner, Max (1806–56). Political theorist and polemicist; *see* *egoism, *Young Hegelians.

stoicism. A system of teachings named after the *stoa poikile* (painted porch) in Athens, where Zeno of Citium began to lecture around 300 BC. Stoicism flourished over 500 years, and it is normal to distinguish the early, middle and late stoas, the last being exemplified by Epictetus and Marcus Aurelius (slave and emperor) in Rome. Stoicisim was a systematic attempt to describe nature, beginning from principles of reason or *logos*. The resulting view of the world was a form of *materialism. Human reason is of the same stuff as the cosmic reason, which we understand as fate, necessity or providence, and to which we must submit in consciousness of its governance over our lives. That consciousness is our highest freedom and aim, and the thing which secures our happiness. This stoic paradox of freedom – that freedom is the consciousness of necessity – recurs throughout the history of social and political thought, for example in doctrines that might be attributed to *Spinoza, to *Kant and to *Hegel. Actual stoic morality was varied, and although all stoics preached the need for virtue, and identified the happiness of man with a kind of spiritual calm (*apatheia*), not all of them accepted (what their name now implies) a strenuous resignation in the face of suffering and misfortune. The stoic political doctrines tended to be *universalist, founded in a conception of man as *rational agent, with universal rights as a citizen of the 'cosmopolis' (*see* *Cicero, *cosmopolitanism).

stop-go. A description applied to UK economic policy in the 1960s, when the government would first use fiscal and monetary controls to reduce aggregate demand in order to reduce a balance of payments deficit and/or to reduce inflation, and then cautiously reflate the economy, in order to remedy the unemployment caused. Frequently the consequence of the 'go' was that conditions worsened, thus demanding a further 'stop'.

strategic capability. The military capacity of a state with 'strategic' weapons (*see* *strategy). First-strike capability is possessed by a force which can itself be destroyed by an enemy strike, and so which must be deployed first, in a 'pre-emptive strike'. Second-strike capability is possessed by a force that can survive a strike sufficiently intact to inflict unacceptable damage. Counter-value capability is that of a force sufficient only to destroy the enemy's cities and installations; counterforce capability is that of a force that may cripple the adversary's strategic military powers and still leave room for the destruction of his cities and industries. These technical terms are of some use in formulating the various levels at which strategic thinking must be conducted in modern conditions.

strategy. Greek: *strategia*, the office of a general, from *stratos*, an army. The art of the commander-in-chief; i.e. the art of projecting and achieving the larger objectives of a campaign; as opposed to 'tactics': the art of local deployment and small-scale manoeuvre through which a strategic purpose is achieved. The division is not exact, but corresponds to a division among weapons between the strategic (those which intimate the final aim of battle), and the tactical (those that are employed during battle as a matter of course). Roughly speaking this distinction has come to mean, weapons which will bring the show to an end, and those that will ensure its continuance. (*See* *strategic capability.)

The term 'strategy' has been given a more precise meaning in *decision theory, where it means a set of plans to cover all contingencies, and the study of those conflicts which require such overall planning is now an important part of *game theory, recent thinkers having attempted to use that theory to cast light on the nature of strategic problems. (Although it should be noted that, in game theory, 'strategy' may sometimes mean simply 'option'). It is sometimes argued that certain modern strategies are based on illegitimate or ill-considered attempts to extend the solutions for two-person games to what are essentially *n*-person games, and that a proper attention to the theory of the latter will show such strategies as *deterrence, for example, to be far from *optimal. Game theory has thus influenced both the vocabulary in terms of which strategy is discussed, and the situations with which it is compared. One theorist writes: 'Strategy . . . is not concerned with the efficient *application* of force but with the *exploitation of potential force*. It is concerned not just with enemies who dislike each other but with partners who distrust or disagree with each other. It is concerned not just with the division of gains and losses between two claimants but with the possibility that particular outcomes are worse (better) for *both* claimants than certain other outcomes. In the terminology of game theory, most interesting international conflicts are not "constant-sum games" but "variable-sum games": the sum of the gains of the participants involved is not fixed so that more for one inexorably means less for the other. There is a common interest in reaching outcomes that are mutually advantageous' (Thomas C. Schelling: *The Strategy of Conflict*, 1960).

strict liability. In the law of *tort, the kind of liability that may often be created by statute, but which, until *Rylands* v. *Fletcher*, 1868, was not known in *common law; strict liability occurs when a person may be held liable for the consequences of some act or omission, whatever the state of mind from which it flows, and whether or not he has acted as a *reasonable man. It is an important feature of English and American common law that they do not tolerate strict liability in the criminal law, and judges will interpret statutes which create crimes in such a way as to suppose that an element of 'guilty mind' is required, unless the statute is very carefully worded.

Some criminal codes allow a distinction between 'felonies and misdemeanours' (now abolished in UK law), and allow only the latter to include offences of strict liability. It is also normal to provide that offences of strict liability cannot later be cited so as to damage the interests of the person who committed them.

strike. 1. A form of *industrial action.
2. A term used in the theory of *strategic capability, as in 'strike first', and 'strike second' strategies.

structural unemployment. Unemployment created by some basic change in the structure and conditions, especially technological conditions, in an economy. It may persist for a long time, because such change tends to make the skills of a whole class of workers redundant. To overcome structural unemployment governments have paid much attention to the problem of the location of industries and the re-training of the work force.

structural violence (also: structural oppression). An expression used by *neo-Marxist critiques of bourgeois society, probably under the influence of *Sorel. The supposition is that *violence can take many forms besides that of *confrontation, and is often concealed within the 'structures' of a society, so as to oppress particular classes or particular groups of opinion within it. Thus some argue that the economic structure of capitalism does repeated and systematic violence to the workers. This structural violence may be contained even within those institutions – such as parliamentary representation – that are most often put forward as proof of the peaceable and conciliatory character of the bourgeois state. This is because the 'freedoms' and 'rights' thereby protected are selectively defined, so as to coincide with the existing privileges of the bourgeoisie. Hence (supposedly) the institution is used (rather like a court of law in a *show trial) to legitimate the continuing violence which one class directs against another.

The idea has been very influential; a notable use of it was by the French *New Left philosopher Maurice Merleau-Ponty (1908–61), who in his *Humanism and Terror*, 1947, excused some of the crimes of *Stalinism by comparing them advantageously with the more concealed, insidious and ineradicable crimes contained within the bourgeois economic order.

structuralism. A much misused term for any science, pseudo-science or critical method which finds the significance of human things (especially social and cultural products) in their structure. Structuralist theories have been proposed for the interpretation of all of the following: actions, rituals, religions; texts, clothes, buildings; poetry, music, architecture; and, most important perhaps, since it is often thought to be the root product of any culture, language.

To have structure, an object must have parts united under ordered relations. To say that structure is *the* determinant (rather than *a* determinant) of meaning is to say that it is not the parts themselves but the relations among them that are significant. This does not mean that the meaning remains unchanged when parts are changed, but that it remains invariant with respect to any *systematic* change of parts. Thus a short tone followed by a long tone has a Morse Code meaning. If the short tone becomes long, the signal may retain its meaning, provided the long tone becomes proportionately longer.

Confusion has been caused by the fact that there are two kinds of theory which might be called 'structuralist':

(i) the structuralist *anthropology of Lévi-Strauss and his followers, which finds significances by discovering repeated patterns. It is supposed that relations (exemplified, e.g., by rituals) remain unchanged from culture to culture, while the parts related may be systematically different. It is then supposed that meaning attaches to the recurring pattern of relations (the 'structure') and not to the local variants that are fitted into it;

(ii) the linguist's theory of grammatical structure, according to which the meaning of a sentence is determined in part by its structure – i.e. not merely by the words employed, but by the rules governing their conjunction.

In case (i) what is interpreted is the pattern divorced from its component parts; in case (ii) what is interpreted is the *whole*, as structured from its parts. The two kinds of interpretation are entirely different, since only in the first is the structure thought to have an independent significance. (Hence the word 'meaning' does not mean the same in (i) and (ii).) The confounding of the two has led to the impression that everything that has significant structure (architecture, music and literature, for example) also has the structure of language, and is to be interpreted in terms that might be equally used in the interpretation of linguistic signs. (One of the thoughts behind 'structuralist' criticism.) The confusion has even been extended to political theory, e.g. by *Althusser.

subject. A being subject to the power of another, and compelled therefore to obey the other's commands. *Spinoza wrote that 'it is the fact of obedience, not the motive for obedience, which makes a man a subject', meaning to imply that the relation of subject to sovereign is not dependent upon consent but simply upon the ability of the second to command the first.

It is often pointed out that the relation sovereign/subject has been superseded in political thinking by that of state/citizen. The change is not merely a change in words, since it has been accompanied by changed ideas of *sovereignty and *political obligation. The relation between sovereign and subject is one of *command and *obedience, whereas (it is supposed) that between state and citizen is one of mutual *obligation. However the distinction is not as clear cut as that implies, since the two relations are not incompatible, and on some views occur together in all political arrangements.

subsidization. The payment of sums by a government in order to make the price of a good lower than free *market forces would otherwise cause it to be.

substitution. 1. Economics. In many areas one consumer good may provide a substitute for another should conditions prevail which prevent attainment of the good desired initially. Thus two goods are substitutes if a rise in the price of one causes an increase in demand for the other. Such substitute relationships depend on the goods in question having similar functions or administering to a similar taste. Burgundy and claret, for example, may be mutual substitutes.

Third World countries often adopt 'import substitution policies', i.e. policies encouraging the substitution of home-produced goods for imported ones, and it seems that the 'politics of substitution' is increasingly important, as governments attempt to persuade citizens to buy the goods made at home.

2. Politics. A *strategy advocated by *Trotsky, whereby a militant organization (in the particular case, the Red Army) takes over the functions of the professional classes – especially schools, hospitals, local councils – and substitutes for the holders of every office some individual allied to the central cause. At a certain moment the whole of the *bourgeoisie finds itself suddenly and unexpectedly without effective power.

subversion. Undermining of an institution or of the state, often by *infiltrating offices and turning them against themselves, but also by any clandestine activity designed to influence the victim and/or to leave him without the support of the institutions upon which he relies. (Cf. *substitution.) 'Subversion of the republic' is a familiar crime in systems of *socialist law, and corresponds only approximately to Western laws of *sedition and *treason. The possibility of subversion is often not recognized in Western law, except in relation to military institutions. However, the US Subversive Activities Control Act 1950, designed to root out communists from offices of state, recognized subversion as a danger to which the US was exposed, while leaving the question of what constitutes subversion more or less unanswered. In the USSR it may be subversive to utter private criticisms of the Communist Party; in the US subversion requires an intention to damage the interests of the Union.

A 'war of subversion' is one carried on by giving military means and moral and economic aid to subversive groups within another state.

succession. The passing on of a title, whether to property, to kingship, or to rights of government. Expectations about *legitimacy are active in determining legal rights of succession. The principle of the 'entail' in feudal and quasi-feudal law, whereby an estate is held under a right of use for life, and then passed to a legally determined successor or heir, is not accepted in modern systems as a normal property right. In English law, all entails become *trusts of property, and are construed so as to permit transfer of the property during the lifetime of any tenant. Some feudal laws operate as though all property reverts on death to the sovereign, to be redistributed by him in accordance with the law (which is also his will). The idea that someone might *appoint* his successors, by will, seems to imply the right to transfer property even after death, and so has the effect of making a person sovereign over his own property. The feudal principle of 'succession according to law' still applies to titles of nobility and kingship (the latter subject to the Act of Settlement 1700 in the UK). Moreover, the idea of the sovereign as party to all succession has re-entered political practice, in the form of 'death duties' and other taxes designed to return property to the state on the death of the tenant.

succession states. Those states which, on the break-up of the Austro-Hungarian and Ottoman empires in 1918, succeeded to the full sovereign rights previously possessed over their territories by the Emperor or the Sultan.

suffrage. Originally an intercessionary prayer, then a vote or opinion for or against something, finally the power to vote at an election. 'Universal suffrage' thus denotes the right of all to vote, and 'extension of the suffrage' an extension of that right to persons formerly deprived of it. Hence, since 1906, a 'suffragette' has meant any woman active (or perhaps militant) in the cause of the right of women to vote in an election.

suicide. The causes of suicide are as many as the ways in which the will to live may fail. *Durkheim argued, however, that suicide in modern society owes its extent to the upsurge of a single set of closely related causes which show this most private and individual of acts to be, he thought, a gesture whose meaning is inherently social. Suicide does not occur outside society, and has to be seen as a response to social conditions, rather than to individual misfortune. The normal condition responsible is that of **anomie* in the social order, which causes the individual to become obsessed with the arbitrariness of his own existence to the point of finding no answer to the question, Why not die? In effect, *anomie* causes the rejection of the individual from the social organism in which he has his being, so that his suicide can be seen as analogous to the death of an amputated limb.

Durkheim also identifies other kinds of suicide, e.g. that inspired by a spirit of *fatalism, and draws a broad division between 'altruistic' and 'egoistic' motives for suicide, all having a social explanation similar to the one given. His statistical methods have, however, been criticized, since they may serve to explain variations, but not the actual level of suicide at any particular moment.

sultanate. The dominion of a sultan (Arabic: sovereign or sovereign power). 'Sultan' was the title normally borne by an Islamic prince or ruler under monarchical government. A sultanate is to be distinguished from the *caliphate, which, while technically a form of rule, has its ultimate significance in religious conceptions of legitimacy. The difference between the title Caliph and the title Sultan roughly corresponds to the distinction between *authority and *power. The former title has often been held by men who were the subjects, even the near prisoners, of the 'sultans' whose rule they authorized.

summit diplomacy (from 'parley at the summit', a phrase from Winston Churchill's election speech of 1950). Personal negotiations between heads of state or ministers of government, usually of *superpowers. Summit diplomacy is a new kind of diplomacy, so little noted for its success that 'summiting' has become a term of abuse, like 'slumming'.

sumptuary law. A law restricting extravagance and display in food, drink, furnishings, dress, and so on. In other words, a law controlling *conspicuous consumption. Originally such laws had the function of confining ostentation to the sovereign and his immediate court, but they were also imposed for moral and religious reasons. Their effect was to separate economic power from the display of power, so that men could not, by the mere fact of *accumulation, create about themselves the magnificence and dignity which attracted sentiments of obedience.

Some argue that certain modern laws of *taxation – such as those imposing capital transfer tax – ought to be seen as sumptuary laws. The rationale of such taxation is to be found, not in the small revenue that it might produce, but in its punitive effect. If the extremely wealthy must part with a portion of their wealth at every major transaction, then this will confirm their subject position, and compel them to recognize that each transaction takes place only by grace of the sovereign power.

superpower. A term which seems to mean any state able to threaten and negotiate on behalf of uncountably many, and which in fact denotes the US and the USSR.

superstition. From Latin, *superstare*, 'to stand over or against something' (i.e. in awe). Superstition means any unreasoning awe and reverence towards non-existent things, or towards actual things on the supposition that they are signs of something which is non-existent. Superstition is to be distinguished from *myth, in that it is based in a sense of human fragility before the unknown, while myth may indicate human confidence, leading to a description of the world as already bent in the direction of *agency. Superstition is also to be distinguished from other kinds of unreasoning belief – such as *prejudice.

Traditionally superstitions were associated with *religion. However, some profess to find 'secular superstitions' in the beliefs of modern people, such as that in inevitable human *progress. This is regarded as a superstition on the ground of a structural similarity with traditional examples: it is an unreasoning belief caused by awe and by fear of the unknown.

superstructure. *See* *base.

supply. The quantity of a good or service which suppliers make available for purchase at a given price; it generally varies (often increasing) with the price; hence the 'supply function', or 'supply curve', which plots that variation.

supply and demand, law of. Supply and demand are often identified as the principal market forces, which make themselves felt through the *price system. The 'law of supply and demand' states that these forces have a *natural* tendency to equilibrium, since if supply exceeds demand, price will fall, causing supply to fall and demand to rise; and vice versa when demand exceeds supply.

supply of money. *See* *money supply.

supranational. Institutions and laws are supranational when not confined in their power and application to any one *state, and when not of such a kind as to have power and application internationally (i.e. to all sovereign states). For example, the European Economic Community is a legally organized supranational body.

supreme court. 1. In common parlance, a court from whose decision there is no appeal. The function of a supreme court is usually to settle, either by interpretation of statute, or by exercise of judicial reasoning under the principles of common law, questions of law that have been disputed in some lower court. It does not normally concern itself with questions of fact, but has a decisive political influence in settling the interpretation of law. The powers of the supreme court may indicate the nature and the extent of the rule of law in a jurisdiction. For example, the US Supreme Court is a third body, separate from either house of Congress, which has supreme powers of *judicial review, and which can question the legality of all executive decisions under the constitution. Its judges can be removed only by *impeachment, and its special relation to the constitution, of which it is guardian and interpreter, endows it with enormous political power, exercised for example during the controversies over the *New Deal.

In the UK, by contrast, there is no supreme court separate from the legislature. The House of Lords (which might otherwise deserve the name) sits sometimes as a court, sometimes as a legislative body. Judges may influence legislation, and usually have a great impact when criticizing the technicalities of the drafting of a statute. But apart from that their political influence is secured only by the normal provisions of judicial independence.

2. The phrase 'supreme court' is in fact a technical term in UK constitutional law and applies, under the Judicature Act 1873, not to the House of Lords but to the Court of Appeal and the High Court, which rank successively as inferior courts. Hence the term 'supreme court' is used highly ambiguously in discussing the UK judicial system: appeal to the highest court is *from* the supreme court. This quirk of usage in fact serves further to reveal the great difference between appeals to the House of Lords and invocation of the US Supreme Court. The second is an essential recourse in securing constitutional rights, whereas the first is simply a final measure in the judicial process, and provides no special guarantee of the rights of the appellant. Hence, political controversies concerning judicial powers have a completely different character under the two constitutions.

surplus value. A term from the *labour theory of value, specifically in its Marxian variants. The capitalist pays the labourer the *exchange-value of his day's labour, which is, it is supposed, the value required to reproduce his *labour-power. This value is in fact produced by hours of work less than the amount contracted for under the wage contract. During the remaining hours of work the labourer produces surplus value – i.e. value over and above that which the capitalist pays him. This surplus value, it is supposed, accumulates not in his hands but in the hands of the capitalist, though by right it belongs to him.

Marxian theory wishes to explain profit in terms of surplus value, but for a variety of reasons 'surplus value' cannot be a direct measure of profit. The problem of deriving profits from surplus value has become known as the 'transformation problem', and exercises many Marxian economists. In order to state the problem in its normal form a standard measure of value must be given: the usual one chosen is 'embodied labour hours'. Critics of the labour theory of value argue that this phrase contains a confusion, even an animistic confusion of the kind criticized by Marx in his theories of *fetishism. What the labour theory really says is that the value of a commodity is the labour time *socially necessary* to its production: which may be much more or much less than that actually 'embodied' in it, depending upon the efficiency and competence of the worker and his tools. On this view there is no such thing as 'value', construed as some real quantity lying behind and explaining such phenomena as profit and price. The Marxian theory had held, however, that profits and prices are 'appearances', behind which their essence – 'value' – lies concealed. Attempts to rescue the Marxian theory have become, in recent years, highly sophisticated, and the problem has come to be known as the 'value controversy'. The most influential work which revives some of the fundamental conceptions underlying the Marxian theory of profit and price has been that by Piero Sraffa (*Production of Commodities by Means of Commodities*, 1960), but it is argued that these very conceptions can be used to dismiss the labour theory of value (Ian Steedman: *Marx after Sraffa*, 1977). (*See also* *essence/appearance.)

surrender. In *international law, cessation of resistance by one belligerent. Traditionally, 'surrender' has been taken to mean 'surrender on terms', the terms including at least survival and often survival as a political unit, even a unit of a certain sort. The terms may or may not include *capitulations. The idea of surrender has, therefore, been that of an 'arrangement for ending war', a social practice in which reciprocal concessions are made. The demand for 'unconditional surrender' is a new departure, a refusal to abide by that practice. (Unconditional surrender is not a legal concept, but simply a reference to the absence of any informal agreement established through diplomacy, or any express or implied assurance on the part of the victor.) Roosevelt's insistence on unconditional surrender after the Second World War has been denounced, not only for its breach of traditional conventions, but also as a 'theoretical' mistake, and an 'incomprehension of the relations between strategy and policy' (Raymond Aron: *Peace and War*, 1962).

syndicalism. French: *syndicat*, a trade union. Syndicalism was a militant trade union movement begun in France in the 1890s, and which for a time had the support of *Sorel, who gradually attempted to synthesize the syndicalist ideas with anarchism (*see* *anarcho-syndicalism), and to import his ethic of violence into the practice of *industrial action. The syndicalists wished to transfer all control over the means of production not to the state but to the trade unions, conceived as free associations of workers. The syndicalists were influenced by *Proudhon's attacks on the state and property, and rejected politics in favour of industrial action, seeing the strike as the true vehicle of guaranteeing that when control of the means of production was lost by one class it would be gained by the other, rather than transferred to some new centre of privilege and power.

Syndicalism was influential at the turn of the century, leading to the Charter of Amiens, 1906, in which its fundamental claims were enunciated, and to the formation of the American Industrial Workers of the World (the 'Wobblies'). Its influence declined, partly through suspicion among workers of its anarchist tendencies, but a kind of syndicalist spirit has remained alive in French trade union activity, manifesting itself with some force in 1968. Something of the same spirit has also made itself felt inside the Soviet bloc, notably through the Polish free trade union movement, which, however, is essentially non-violent.

systems theory. *See* *cybernetics.

T

taboo. A Polynesian word, used to mean any activity which is prohibited, or object which is untouchable or unmentionable, as a result of some deep and inarticulate fear of a superstitious or religious kind. On account of *Freud's attempt to explain taboo, and to relate it to states of mind that he thought to be civilized survivals of taboos, it is normal for the word to be used of all kinds of activities which are morally forbidden, but which fall outside the range of our moral rationalizations, incest being the most important example. Freud thought that in this case what is forbidden is also unconsciously desired; because of the strength of the passion, the interdiction must be absolute and unquestionable, and therefore surrounded by superstitious fears.

tacit communication. *Communication which takes place without exchange of words, or explicit agreement – for example the communication between two car drivers at an unmarked intersection, resulting in one giving way to the other. Such communication may take the form of 'tacit bargaining', in which each participant acts from a sense of what the other may concede in return for a favour; or it may take the form of a 'team spirit', whereby collective *strategy emerges spontaneously among people with an immediate common purpose. Such phenomena are of great importance in social action, underlying foreign policy and military strategy, as well as most forms of *association. The fundamental element consists in the usually rapid and often mysterious exchange of information about reflexive states of mind – i.e. states of mind of the following kind: 'He intends that I intend that he intends that. . .' or 'She expects that I expect that she intends that I intend that. . .' Some thinkers estimate the importance of *tradition, *culture and *custom as lying, at least partly, in their ability to bring order and intelligibility to the tacit communication upon which social cohesion rests. Some conservative hostility towards *rationalism could be seen as an attempt to define the large area of tacit bargaining in which man's greatest efforts towards the rational solution of conflict are expended, and to defend it from the oversimplification which purely explicit bargaining inevitably requires.

tacit consent. Consent that is not expressed but is to be inferred from the intentional activities of the agent. In *Locke's version of the *social contract theory tacit consent to a political arrangement can be inferred when an individual knowingly stays subject to its laws, even when free to leave to some 'vacant place' where he will be subject to no laws at all. *Hume pointed out that even if this *is* a criterion of consent, it is one that can never be applied, since most places fall under *some* jurisdiction and those that do not are without the necessary comforts and conveniences of the present arrangement, whatever the grounds of its legitimacy. Some reply that, even if alternatives are unattractive, this does not mean that people are *compelled* to remain where they are, so that the existence of consent can be inferred from their remaining. A sovereign who expressly forbids emigration, however, cannot argue that his subjects consented, even tacitly, to his rule.

By analogy other theories of *political obligation can be given a 'tacit' form. Thus some speak of the relation between sovereign and subject as one of tacit *command, meaning that the two parties intentionally behave as though one were commanding the other, even though no commands are actually issued.

tariffs. Import tariffs are taxes imposed on imports which may have the purpose either of raising revenue or, more usually, of effecting some long-term economic policy, such as the diminution of a *balance of payments deficit. (*See also* *protectionism.) Tariffs may also be used to counter 'dumping', to protect an industry, or to retaliate against some other state's tariffs. Export tariffs are less frequent, although they may be used to protect or prevent the exportation of essential *raw materials or works of art.

Tawney, Richard Henry (1880–1962). British historian and social critic; *see* *gentry, *Lutheranism, *Protestantism.

taxation. A lawful levy by the state on the property of its citizens. Taxation can be of income or of capital. The first has been preferred in capitalist countries, in order not to damage accumulations of capital thought essential to continuing *private enterprise. Capital taxation is often the declared aim of those who seek to make large-scale private enterprise impossible. Capital transfers and capital gains may also be taxed: the first is a tax on capital (which occurs, however, only at the moment of transfer); the second is a tax on income from capital. However, as the example illustrates, the boundary between capital and income taxation is a fine one, and, viewed from one point of view, capital gains tax can also be seen as a tax on capital, especially if it applies to all profit, whether or not there is a profit in *real terms (i.e. whether or not there is a real income). Capital transfer tax is a penalty on the exchange of property, whether by sale, gift or will. It therefore restricts the right of transfer which many have thought to be fundamental to the right of property.

The questions of the justice of taxation and of its ideal form have exercised political theorists and philosophers repeatedly. Clearly taxation has a different significance in socialist and in capitalist economies: in the latter the disposition of private capital is essential to production under existing production relations, so that taxation – if it is not to be an instrument of radical social change – has to respect capital. Within that broad requirement, however, there are many possibilities. Roughly speaking, theorists divide according to whether they see taxation as a necessary burden which should be distributed as justly as possible upon those destined to bear it, or whether they see it rather as an *instrument* of justice (specifically *social justice) which should be used in part to secure a more equitable distribution of material goods than currently obtains. It is true that there are some eccentrics who reject taxation more or less entirely. Thus *Nozick seems to regard taxation as an intrinsic violation of justice, since it involves forcing the citizen to work for the state for a certain number of hours without reward. (This is like the Marxist view that the worker is compelled to work a certain number of hours in each day for the capitalist and is therefore exploited.) The obvious reply – namely that the state returns the benefit received in the form of public goods and services – is argued not to be sufficient, since the exchange, even if mutually profitable, is forced. Others take for granted that, since the *rule of law is itself based in force, and since there can be no rule of law without the government necessary to sustain it, taxation is a precondition of the arrangement in which voluntary transactions, of the kind esteemed by Nozick, may occur. Moreover, it is argued, it is the state which makes private accumulations possible, by guaranteeing the law under which they are held, whether or not they are also held justly. It is therefore entitled to address itself to the question whether they *are* held justly and to redistribute them accordingly.

Whether our view of taxation is of a relation conditioned by justice, or of an instrument of justice, two questions seem particularly important in determining its preferred nature: (i) should there be total taxation on death? (for which *see* *hereditary principle, *succession); (ii) should there be progressive taxation? The latter is assumed now to be normal, although it should be noted that there is a sense in which it requires different classes of citizens to be treated 'unequally', the rich being compelled to part with a greater portion of their wealth than the poor. This is not because the government seeks to protect the very poor from the burden of taxation: that is an independent provision, usually secured by allowing all income below a certain amount to go tax free. It would seem then that the advocacy of progressive taxation goes more naturally with the second view of taxation, as an instrument of justice, rather than as a necessity conditioned by justice. For progressive taxation certainly has an effect of redistribution, but it is uncertain that it makes any serious difference to government revenues, since it may depress economic activity. (The arguments here are topical, complex and seemingly inconclusive.) Another view of progressive taxation is as a kind of highly sophisticated *sumptuary law; but that is perhaps too anachronistic an idea to be of any great contemporary relevance.

Some have suggested the need for a *negative* income tax, as a means of supporting those whose income is too small to supply their needs, although clearly the problems of administration here would be enormous.

technocracy. The 'rule by technicians', proposed in 1919 by the Californian engineer W. H. Smyth, and celebrated in *Veblen's *Engineers and the Price System,* 1921. In fact the ideal of technocracy had already had its supporters in the nineteenth century, such as *Saint-Simon and *Comte. Under the universal *separation of ownership from control real power vests increasingly in those who are able to control the means of production, and chief among these are the technicians with the knowledge necessary to operate the complex machinery of modern production. Hence the actual economic power of technocrats is always increasing: that they should also rule, i.e. translate that power into political terms, is a suggestion that is sometimes greeted with horror, perhaps on the assumption that the technician's view of his fellow human beings is likely to be somewhat *utilitarian, perhaps even *philistine. The thesis of economic determinism, which argues that those who control the means of production will also, and for that reason, control the political process, seems to imply that technocracy is unavoidable.

technological determinism. The interpretation of *historical materialism which sees the steady growth of *technology as the principal factor in the development of *productive forces, and which therefore regards all major historical transformations as effects of technological change.

technology. Any practical application of scientific method and scientific conclusions whether in peace or war. Technology is the science of means, and as science advances so does technology. It seems that the increasing sophistication of means must also affect the ends of human conduct: some ends which were not previously possible may now be seriously intended. Hence technology, which solves many problems, also poses a problem for the moralist as much as for the politician. *Cultural conservatism set itself against the harsh purgative effect of technological transformation, believing that the multiplication of possibilities was in danger of destroying the seriousness of human attachment to all of them. The believers in *progress seemed, on the other hand, to take inspiration from technology, whether in the form of an economic theory of constantly developing productive capacity, or in a more *scientistic vision of moral improvement. Most modern thinkers take some intermediate position; it is impossible not to recognize the profound change in human aspirations that has been precipitated by the technology of *communications; or the irreversible changes that have occurred in the nature of social relations, partly as a result of that. But it is also difficult to contemplate the result with complete satisfaction. The major divide is between those who think of technology itself as the only cure to the ills that it generates, and those who seek to control and inhibit it directly, and by other means.

Among the economic and political effects of technology, the following have elicited considerable discussion: the change in patterns of supply (producing an abundance of manufactured goods but a comparatively small increase in food); the change in the character of labour; the change in the nature of culture (which itself becomes saturated with symbols of technology); the change in the techniques of war, and of medicine.

teleological explanation. Any explanation of some event or process in terms of its end rather than its origins. For example, an explanation in terms of purpose ('he did it in order to annoy her'), which must be contrasted (at least initially) with an explanation in terms of antecedent conditions ('he did it because of indigestion'). In both cases, a crucial factor is singled out as providing an explanation, but in the first case this factor lies (or seems to lie) in the future, in the second in the past. The distinction here was once known as that between 'final' and 'efficient' causation; now it is more normal to distinguish two kinds of explanation, the first teleological, the second causal. Among teleological explanations it is important to distinguish those which refer to a definite mental process, e.g. intention or desire, those which refer to a teleological motivation while remaining open as to whether that motivation should be described in mental terms ('the cat is stalking in order to catch the bird'), and those which apply in circumstances where mental processes are not in issue ('the plant turns in order to catch the sunlight'). Philosophers of science sometimes argue that the last are really *functional explanations – i.e. a special kind of causal explanation. *Functional explanation has sometimes been thought to be a kind of teleological explanation, but this seems wrong, since a function is not a condition which necessarily postdates the occurrence of what it explains.

Many philosophers of science have wondered *how* there can be teleological explanations, and whether all such explanations involve the invocation of purpose. Such explanations are certainly frequent in all the human sciences, but whether they can be introduced elsewhere is doubtful: a fact which might suggest that the reference to purpose is indeed necessary. Nevertheless social scientists still wonder whether the purpose invoked in teleological explanation has to be a human purpose, or whether there might be a 'social teleology' which proceeds independently. This may or may not reduce, in the end, to the question of the possibility of functional explanation in the social sciences.

teleology. The study of the end (Greek: *telos*), goal or purpose of something. The term is now often used to refer to the theory that all evaluation should be by reference to consequences: i.e. to *consequentialism.

terms of trade. The ratio of the *index of export prices to that of import prices. An improvement in the terms of trade is therefore a consequence of export prices rising more rapidly than import prices.

territory. Portion of the earth and its atmosphere which is such that it may fall under the *jurisdiction of a sovereign state. Modern international law recognizes territorial claims over part of the sea, and over air space, but how far these claims extend or should extend is a constant source of dispute. Modern territorial sovereignty has developed from the personal sovereignty exercised by feudal and absolute rulers, which was conceived in terms of an actual property right, albeit under a law more hypothetical than enforceable. The frequent redress of sovereigns to the Pope or to some individual said to be Caliph in order to establish this property right led to important attempts to develop an international law of territory. The rise of *nationalism can be seen as involving, at least in part, an attempt to replace a conferred property right by a *prescriptive right, by identifying a particular tract of land with the immemorial customs of people associated partly because of it, and also through their language, customs, race or kinship. Modern international jurisdiction begins from the premise that the world is divided up haphazardly into territories, by irreversible facts of history, and that *prima facie* rights to jurisdiction must be accorded to those governments which currently claim them. It then seeks to confine each state to that territory currently claimed by it, by the 'principle of territoriality', which holds that a sovereign state ought not to engage in jurisdictional acts outside the limits of its territory.

Certain *sociobiologists have identified the search for territory as a fundamental human instinct, the equivalent of which is to be found in many of the lower animals, who are presumably not motivated by any sense of the right of ownership or jurisdiction. Whether there is anything in common between animal and human territorial behaviour is open to doubt; nevertheless there is something about the manner in which men fight for territory which demands explanation in other than legal terms.

terrorism. Defined in the UK Prevention of Terrorism Act 1976, s. 14 (1) as: 'the use of violence for political ends [including] any use of violence for the purpose of putting the public or any section of the public in fear'. This definition seems to confuse two ideas: the use of *violence for political ends, and the use of violence in order to put the public in fear. Clearly it is the second idea that is important: the intentional creation of widespread fear and dismay by violence, in particular by violence of a random and arbitrary kind. It has frequently been defended, most famously by Robespierre: 'They say that terrorism is the resort of despotic government. Is our government then like despotism? Yes, as the sword that flashes in the hand of the hero of liberty is like that with which the satellites of tyranny are armed . . . The government of the Revolution is the despotism of liberty against tyranny.' Robespierre's defence is the one that is usually offered, and it is common now to recognize even some acts of state as 'terrorist' – e.g. the violence perpetrated by Stalin against the Russian people.

The question of the justification of terrorism is a special case of that posed by *consequentialism. If all acts could in principle be justified by their consequences, then so might terrorism. If some acts can never be justified by their consequences then some acts of terrorism must be among them. The argument given by Robespierre is usually generalized by making use of the idea of *structural violence. Terrorism merely opposes violence with violence in the name of freedom from violence. Whether this is so depends in part on the meaning of the term 'violence'.

theft. Dishonestly appropriating property with the intention permanently to deprive another. A statutory offence since 1968 in the UK, and defined more or less as above in a badly drafted act. Theft has always been recognized under a variety of names (larceny, embezzlement, fraudulent conversion) at *common law. It is still a common law offence in US and Scots law.

When *Proudhon declared that 'property is theft' he meant that all *private property involves the exclusion of others from what is, in effect, a *natural right of common possession. If that is so, then it may seem that no theft is greater than that involved in the maintenance of private property relations through a law of theft. Others argue that everything possessed lawfully either is, or has been made from, something which has been wrongfully appropriated, so that theft is merely a 'conventional' crime, a creation of arbitrary stipulations of positive law, designed to protect existing relations of *control.

However, the important point is not who has the right to own some object (whether or not this be a natural right or a right of some other kind), but rather who is being dishonest in taking and retaining something. The arguments about the thief's act focus not on the question whether his victim had a right to what he held, but rather on the question whether the thief acted dishonestly. Dishonesty is not an easy notion to define. It involves such things as deceit, covert dealing, breach of agreement – in short a whole range of human activities in which one person is abused by another. What is wrong with theft is what is wrong with that abuse. *Kant held that all such abuse involves the use of a rational being as a means only, and that that is the essence of interpersonal wrongdoing. In which case theft is morally the same kind of thing as (although no doubt less serious than) rape or murder. The problem here is immensely complex, but it is what is really at issue between Robin Hood and those whom he seeks to rob.

theocracy. Literally, 'government by God', but often, in common usage, 'government by priests'. The term was coined by the Jewish historian Josephus, to denote the Jewish conception of government as embodied in the Torah, where divine laws are treated as creating both religious and civil obligations (*see* *Jewish law). Theocracy as practised in the ancient world involved not direct government by priests, but the tenure of judicial and legislative offices by priests, and this idea has survived under *Islam into the modern world.

The ruling conception of a theocracy, according to *Spinoza (*Tractatus Theologico-Politicus,* XVII), is that all civil obligations are thought to stem from a covenant with God, and no other source of authority (such as a contract with the sovereign, or with other members of society) is recognized as binding. Even the 'general-in-chief or dictator' rules only because chosen by God to do so. Spinoza points out that in ancient Jewish custom the office of interpreter of the law was vested, not in the sovereign, but in the Levites who had no part in government. The sovereign, however, was not normally a priest. Hence there was an effective *separation of powers within the state, leading to the *limitation of the powers of the sovereign. Here, therefore, the idea of divine governance produced an effective *rule of law. The case should perhaps be contrasted with modern Iran, where both executive and judicial offices are held by divines.

theocratic guardianship. A political stance advocated by Ayatollah Khomeini, according to which there should be secular government and the institutions necessary to that end, superintended by religious institutions, which provide the means to resolve difficult moral, legal and social problems, and to redirect the 'political will' so as to align it with the will of God.

theodicy. Term coined by Leibniz, to denote any theory which shows the order of the world to be compatible with God's absolute goodness, and so justifies the ways of God to man. (Greek: *dike,* justice.) An example is Leibniz's own famously satirized view that the actual world is the best of all possible worlds: a view the subtlety of which is badly misrepresented when thus quoted out of context.

Third World. *See* *three worlds theory.

Thompson, Edward P. (b. 1924). British historian and social theorist; *see* *Althusser, *class consciousness, *New Left.

three worlds theory. The Third World (French: *tiers monde*) comprises those states and territories which exhibit neither developed capitalist nor developed socialist economies, many of which have recently 'emerged' from colonial or primitive rule, to adopt untried political institutions, sometimes bequeathed by or borrowed from states in another 'world'. 'Three worlds' theory consists in the comparative analysis of the economic (and to some extent political) conditions of the three 'worlds', and an attempt to understand the Third World, perhaps as an *ideal type (in comparison with the ideal types of capitalism and socialism). The description of Third World economy is extremely difficult; it is not possible to think of it either as 'pre-capitalist' or as 'pre-socialist', because all developments take on a character that is *sui generis,* there being little competence in economic management, only a very rudimentary *middle class, and little 'national consciousness' (as opposed to local or tribal consciousness) to which a government may appeal in its attempts to mobilize production. There is a dominance of subsistence production, very little unemployment (since much employment is of low productivity), a low accumulation rate, a small public sector, a low *per capita* income, and a markedly unequal income distribution. The Third World countries rarely have an interdependent market network, with prices tending towards uniformity and moving flexibly. The absence of this mechanism, which provides immediate signals for economic decisions, is often held to be a key feature in under-development.

The assumption of 'three worlds' is tendentious: within capitalism and socialism there are extensive variations; China declared herself a Third World country at the Bandung Conference in 1955; the capitalist countries provide *aid in a way in which the socialist countries cannot, thus drawing the Third World into relation with themselves; much of the socialist 'world' is more like the Third World than it is like capitalism, and so on. The real rationale behind the distinctions might be political rather than economic: i.e. it might consist in the reluctance or inability of the Third World to fit comfortably into either of the major political blocs, and its tendency to act as a self-dependent political system (although, in the case of international conflict, it is unlikely that the Third World could or would sustain itself as an independent unit). Some prefer a 'four worlds theory', believing that the Third World divides significantly into those states that have access to rich natural resources, and those which do not; but again the division is significant at least partly because of its effects at the political level, on account of the increased influence that a state rich in resources may exert over others.

thrift. Originally the fact of thriving or being prosperous, and hence, by transfer, the virtue traditionally thought necessary for that end. Thrift is a species of narrow *prudence – so narrow, some think, as not really to be prudence, and not a *virtue. Thrift involves the disposition to save rather than spend, to invest wisely, and accumulate diligently; above all to avoid debt. Thrift is sometimes described as a peculiarly capitalist virtue, part of the ideology which consolidates and legitimates the activity of capital accumulation. It should perhaps be pointed out that the parable of the prodigal son, from which much of the morality of thrift traditionally took its authority, was uttered in pre-capitalist Judaea, by someone who regarded prodigality as an eminently forgivable failing.

time preference. Preference for present as opposed to future consumption. Consider the question, Suppose there is no inflation, then how much money would I have to give you in one year's time to induce you to forgo £1 now? The existence of this (positive or negative) 'subjective rate of interest' is of crucial importance in all economic decisions concerning time, and must be taken into account, for example, when constructing a model of the *rational agent in terms of *decision theory.

The concept of time preference is important in certain theories of *interest and *profit. It is also a factor that seems to be overlooked in many traditional arguments concerning the justice or injustice of *usury. Pure time preference is to be distinguished from preferences arising from risk. Thus there are further grounds for preferring satisfaction now rather than at any later time, since I exist now, and it is always to some degree possible that I will not exist later.

timocracy. Term used by *Plato to denote the government of honour, which arises out of *aristocracy (government by the best), when the military character of the state comes to be the focus of all ambition. Culture, philosophy and the arts of peace decline, and are respected only in so far as they confer honour on those who achieve military prowess and public power. Such a description might perhaps be applied to Sparta, to certain orders of medieval knighthood (e.g. that of Malta), to the local rule by the Samurai in Japan, and perhaps to the (first) Napoleonic state.

Titoism. The socialism of Marshal Tito's Yugoslavia, characterized by a refusal to be absorbed into the Soviet bloc, a *neutralist foreign policy, and an economic policy which is sometimes described as *market socialism, but is perhaps more correctly considered to be a form of centralized socialism in which there is legitimate small-scale private property in the means of production, and in which autonomous cooperatives are encouraged. The party retains its central organizing role, and *opposition is not permitted, so that some of the characteristics of *democratic centralism are retained. However, considerable regional autonomy has been permitted, together with more freedoms of association, information and assembly than is normal in Eastern Europe. The relative popularity of Titoism in comparison with Leninism is perhaps shown by the fact that Yugoslavia has been able to reintroduce laws permitting emigration.

Tocqueville, Alexis, Comte de (1805–59). French politician and historian, whose shrewd observations of France and America have become classics of social and political analysis. In his first major work, *Democracy in America*, 1835, he argues that the 'principle of equality', whereby all distinctions of social status are gradually eroded, is the ruling principle of modern history. The tendency towards equality had, he thought, been dominant since the Middle Ages and, with the American and French Revolutions, had entered its final stage. The major problem facing modern society is that of reconciling equality with liberty, in the increasing absence of the diversity of power that had characterized traditional aristocratic regimes. The lower classes undermine the upper by increasing centralization, which erodes all social hierarchy, regionalism and local feeling, and results in an unprecedented concentration of power. Nevertheless, in a prescient and in many ways laudatory account of the US constitution, Tocqueville praised the American system for its ability to encourage decentralized government, even in a condition of complete democracy, and the constitution as an instrument able to shape society in accordance with democratic expectations, while still retaining the mechanisms by which the blunderings of democratic politics could be rendered revocable errors. He described the *jury as a political system, enacting the sovereignty of the people in the courtroom; at the same time he saw judicial independence in the US as endowing the judiciary with some of the stabilizing influence and inherent political privilege of the European aristocracy. Tocqueville's criticisms of American democracy and of the ethos of equality were many and various. He argued that liberty is threatened by public opinion ('the tyranny of the majority') which, with the egalitarian loss of individuality, self-assurance and social ease, must increasingly tend towards uniformity. Not only liberty, but also culture and intellectual distinction are threatened by equality; all class distinctions are destined to be replaced by increasingly arbitrary-seeming distinctions of status, without the dignifying attributes of culture and leisure that might render them permanent and authoritative. The 'imperfect phantom of equality' haunts the mind of all, destroying alike obedience, honour and the capacity to command, so that men, increasingly unable to find solace in the social order, will be confined within the solitude of their hearts.

In *The Old Regime and the French Revolution*, 1856, Tocqueville gave a highly influential account of the causes and effects of the French Revolution, arguing that revolutions occur when things begin to improve, or when things go wrong after a period of improvement – a view that many have seen confirmed in subsequent history. Although revolution speeds up the real change, that change – towards centralization, bureaucracy, and the increasing levelling of social hierarchy – is not caused by revolution but precedes it, being itself one of the major causes of revolution, since it undermines the old privileges which made preventive measures possible. Tocqueville blamed the old aristocracy for much of its loss of power; it had become a *caste* and, unlike the English gentry, had been willing to exchange political power for social exclusiveness and fiscal privilege, thus becoming both obnoxious to the majority, and unable to defend itself.

toleration. The policy of patient forbearance towards that which is not approved. There is toleration only where there are also things that are disapproved; if men were perfect, tolerance would be neither necessary nor possible.

The extent to which toleration can and should be extended has occupied many political theorists in modern times, most famously *Locke, whose *Letter on Toleration*, 1688, put forward arguments which are now widely accepted. Locke's concern was with religious toleration; he argued that no sovereign could found his right to rule on the truth of his religion, for it is not within the competence of a state to discern the truth of religious doctrines, nor is it the function of a state to save men's souls; rather the state exists to protect men's rights, and may use force to that end alone. Hence there ought to be tolerance in all matters of religion. Locke did not think that toleration should be extended to Roman Catholics, however, since he doubted that someone could be such and still owe first allegiance in political matters to the English sovereign. The principles behind Locke's view were soon widely accepted, and later extended from the religious to the moral sphere by *Mill, although Mill's arguments are widely disputed. (*See* *law and morality.)

Modern discussions tend to concern the further extension of toleration not just to that which is spiritually alien or morally disapproved, but also to that which is politically opposed. Toleration of *opposition to communism is rare in communist states but it is sometimes argued that toleration ought to be extended so far as is consistent with political stability (perhaps even further) in those political arrangements which recognize the legitimacy of opposition, and seek to permit freedom of *opinion. The position of the US in relation to communism illustrates to some extent the difficulties of the position. Some argue that in so far as communists can be supposed to be bent on destroying the existing form of government they can be compared to the Catholics whom Locke wished to exclude from toleration. (An argument influential at the time of *McCarthyism.) Others think that it is a right, that either is or ought to be protected under the US constitution, to work by peaceful means for whatever form of government is sincerely judged to be best for the American people. It is, however, reasonable to suppose that if the form of government projected is one that explicitly rejects the legitimacy of opposition, then there is no real right to political toleration, since anybody who claims that right must himself be prepared to grant it. Moreoever anybody who seeks to overthrow the US constitution and replace it with one that does not guarantee civil rights cannot claim to be protected by any right under the US constitution.

Tolstoy, Lev Nikolayevich (1828–1910). Russian novelist and social theorist; *see* *anarchism, *country, *leadership.

Tönnies, Ferdinand (1855–1936). German sociologist; *see* **Gemeinschaft* and *Gesellschaft*.

tort. The term in *common law for all wrongs that are actionable in civil law, in contrast to crime on the one hand, and breach of contract on the other. The law of tort is a branch of the law of obligations, where the legal obligation arises, not under an agreement, but under a general obligation to refrain from harming another, or to make good any harm done. The principle is to endeavour to shift the loss sustained to the person responsible for it. An important consequence is that a person who is injured through another's fault receives damages in law, while a person injured through no one's fault does not. Some argue that there is an injustice in this, since an injured person ought to be compensated simply because of his injury, and not because of any wrong done. However, it is clear that for the law to function as a law of obligation it must continue to enforce sanctions on grounds of responsibility; it is an instrument not of distributive but of commutative justice.

torture. Any form of violence that causes, and is intended to cause, acute mental or physical pain to the victim. Torture may be used as a form of *punishment, or as an act of vengeance upon defeated enemies. In its more institutionalized forms, however, torture is to be distinguished from punishment, being a means of coercion of the victim, intended to elicit evidence or confession. Thus torture has been part of the legal system of most of the European powers, and 'judicial torture' generated its own jurisprudence, rules, treatises and doctors of law.

In England torture as punishment and as coercion was, officially at least, virtually abolished in 1640, and most modern states explicitly rule out the use of torture either by statute or by constitutional provisions. Its persistence, however, is widespread, despite a declaration issued in 1975 by the United Nations Organization forbidding the use of torture by any member state. One major cause is that torture is often resorted to by the police forces of coercive regimes, which, while they have constitutions forbidding its use, do not have adequate provisions for the control of the police, being too much dependent upon the power of the police for their own stability.

Only rational beings are able to take pleasure in torturing each other, since only rational beings have the capacity to relish what another is feeling. Torture is sometimes said to proceed from a state of mind that not only overrides respect for persons, but which also desires to show persons as unfit for respect, by showing the ease with which the person can be overcome by the animal.

Toryism. Doctrines and policies associated with the English *Conservative Party, and its predecessor, the 'Tory' faction in English government since the Restoration. (The term comes from the Irish *tóraighe*, a pursuer, used in the seventeenth century to denote the dispossessed Irish who subsisted by plundering and killing English settlers, and extended later to those with Popish sympathies, and then to the loyalists who opposed the exclusion of James, Duke of York from the succession to the Crown.) Toryism has never been one thing, and is often divided into 'high' Toryism, which has a traditionalist and aristocratic flavour, and 'low' Toryism, more redolent of the *business ethic and the spirit of *free enterprise. The modern Conservative Party, with commitment to *monetarism, *free trade, the *market economy, widespread *democracy and *human rights, is partly a product of the recent import of ideas that were once exported to America as unfit for home consumption, there to take shape in a form that eventually antagonized one of the *Whig faction at home. This man was *Burke, whose denunciation of much that had been done in the name of liberty and rights has since become a received text of high Toryism. The following features seem important at the 'high' end of the thermometer:

(i) Belief in a *legitimacy founded in *custom, history and the **status quo*, rather than in *doctrine.

(ii) Belief that the devices of *legitimation should not be political - e.g. should not consist in published opinion or propaganda – but social, lying in popular morality, religion and ordinary patriotic sentiment.

(iii) Belief in the role and value of a *ruling class, and adherence to the view that politics is a natural activity of that class, but a dangerous device in the hands of any other.

(iv) Belief in the validity of private property, combined with a certain contempt for *mere* property, or for property that has been acquired too quickly or too recently.

(v) Belief in political restraint of economic activity in the interests of larger social questions, leading to a suspicion of unbridled capitalism, free trade, and perhaps even of *industrialization.

(vi) Belief in 'one nation', and the 'feudal principle' (both phrases bequeathed to Tory rhetoric by Disraeli), according to which class divisions may be legitimate and beneficial, but only so long as they are tempered by *conciliation and reciprocal obligations. (A view which sometimes leads to 'welfare Toryism' – the active fostering of a *welfare state in the interests of social continuity.)

(i) to (vi), overlaid and eroded by varying degrees of commitment to *democracy, to *liberalism, and to the *market economy, form the infinite grades of opinion that are now thought of as 'Tory'. All of (i) to (vi) could be thought of as survivals of a feudal aristocratic mentality, although they all have received the backing of serious political thought, both before and after Burke. 'Tory democracy' – initiated by Disraeli – to some extent marked the break with the old high Tory mentality.

total war. War involving the participation of all citizens, military and civilian, and in which all forces of production are directed towards the military effort.

totalitarianism. A state is totalitarian if it permits no *autonomous institutions, i.e. if the aims, activities and membership of all *associations are subject to the *control of the state. For this to be the case freedom of association cannot be permitted – and it is significant that the value of this freedom is doubted both by *Hobbes and by *Rousseau, two thinkers who offer arguments useful to totalitarian government, despite the fact that totalitarianism, as distinct from absolutism and autocracy, is a distinctly twentieth-century invention. Complete state control of the means of communication is also essential, together with an ideology (sense 1.); for the sole origin of all legitimation is the state itself, there being no autonomous institution, such as church, universities, clubs and societies, through which respect for the civil order can be independently inculcated. If such institutions exist it is only by permission of the state, and in accordance with strict instructions from the state.

Totalitarianism is not necessarily violent, but it is frequently argued to be unjust, since it involves encroachment by the state on many *natural rights, and an abolition of all forms of society that are not coerced from above. This 'withering away of society' often takes place under a rule that promises the *withering away of the state. It is, however, disputed that *collectivization, or *social ownership, or any other aim of communism, in itself requires totalitarian government.

Tractarianism. Name given to the early stages of the 'Oxford Movement', derived from *Tracts for the Times*, 1833–41, many written by J. H. (later Cardinal) Newman, defending the Apostolic and Catholic claims of *Anglicanism, and presaging the subsequent defection of many tractarians to the Roman Catholic Church. Tractarianism involved criticism of *liberalism in social and moral matters, and hostility to the Reformation, and to many of the effects of *industrialization. It had roots in a conservative and even reactionary view of English religion and society, and sought to articulate many doctrines of *cultural conservatism in the form of doctrine, at the same time claiming religious sanction for its views.

trade cycle. Regular oscillations in the level of economic activity, in which *depressions and *recessions follow upon periods of high employment and accelerating production. Theories of the trade cycle include most of the most important modern macroeconomic analyses, such as Keynes's theory (according to which depressions result from aggregate demand falling below the productive potential of the economy), and the theory of *monetarism, which sees the money supply as the key factor in the regulation of economic activity.

trade dispute. A concept introduced into UK law in order to designate the disputes in which trade unions claim a right of intercession, and in respect of which they may be granted legal privileges. It was defined in the Trades Disputes Act 1906, and again in the Trade Union and Labour Relations Act 1974, as a dispute between employers and workers or between workers and workers, relating to: terms and conditions of employment; allocation of work or duties; discipline; membership or non-membership of a union; facilities for union officials; negotiating machinery.

The sub-classes of dispute recognized, and the provision that dispute may be between workers and workers illustrate the extent to which *industrial law can no longer be considered as part of the law of contract, the relation of employment having achieved separate legal structure.

trade union (or: trades union). Originally an association for the self-protection of employees, particularly in response to the conditions of industrial production, and existing since the eighteenth century. Deemed a *conspiracy in restraint of trade at *common law, trade unions were finally fully legalized in the UK in 1871, by a Conservative government under Disraeli, after several decades of agitation. In 1875 the modern concept of a *trade dispute was adumbrated in a statute which, by implication, permitted peaceful picketing. Finally, after a case in which a union was held liable in damages for the loss caused by a strike, the Trades Disputes Act 1906 made most forms of trade union association and *industrial action legal. Since then the legislation concerning trade unions has been such as to confer on them privileges beyond those of any other associations (with the exception of the churches) which are not themselves branches of government. The objections to these privileges take two basic forms: first, that they seem to countenance the violation of essential freedoms and rights (*see*, e.g., *closed shop); secondly that they make certain actions initiated by trade unions injudiciable, despite their enormous social consequences, and therefore destroy the correspondence between grievance and legal remedy defended by some advocates of the conciliatory role of government. Many reject such arguments, usually on the ground that the privileges granted are nothing more than a necessary counterweight to the bargaining advantage of employers, and therefore the precondition of any relation of employment in which rights are respected, or in which adjudication of dispute is anything more than a perfunctory ratification of the employer's *coercion. Moreover, it is sometimes said, there is a quasi-constitutional role to be performed by the trade unions, which can reasonably be thought of as a separate *estate, demanding its own mode of representation before government.

The UK and US examples are of the 'free trade union' – i.e. unions formed under a law permitting freedom of association, and not disciplined from above by the state (although perhaps disciplined from within by a *party, it being important, in the UK, that the trade unions and the Labour Party, having emerged together from the *labour movement, remain closely affiliated). In modern communist countries trade unions are not usually free in that sense, nor is there a 'right to strike' such as has been recognized for 100 years in English law. Trade unions are conceived, rather, as representative devices within the framework of *democratic centralism, whereby the opinions of workers may be heard, and local disputes adjudicated, without disturbing the discipline of production.

The *de facto* power of unions in the UK, together with the legal recognition of that power, and the role given to trade union officials in negotiations over policy and economic planning, have changed the trade union movement from a movement of protest within the lower class to a slightly disputatious but more or less *accommodated part of the *establishment.

tradition. A highly charged and often commendatory term, which is used by certain forms of conservatism in order to assert the validity of its respect for the past, together with a belief that the present must be understood as a continuation, and never as an initiation, of social and political *identity. The term substitutes for a considerable lack of theory, and indeed is apt to embody the important conservative theory that theories (and especially theories of history) are dangerous – perhaps even, in the area of political practice, nonsensical. The following elements seem to be contained in the idea, as standardly invoked:

(i) A tradition denotes a class of intentional actions, together with the thoughts, beliefs, perceptions and associations which motivate them. Like *custom, tradition must be distinguished from *habit, and from mechanized response.

(ii) In virtue of (i), traditions contain a principle of development. Intentional actions are founded on reasons, thoughts and perceptions, and develop as understanding develops.

(iii) Nevertheless the reasons for traditional behaviour are 'immanent'; that is, they exist not as explicit doctrines, but as perceptions of the validity of an act while performing it, together with an intimation of further reasons which it may be impossible, and perhaps undesirable, to state.

(iv) Traditions are essentially shared, and understood as such. There are solitary habits, but no solitary traditions. And part of the motive of traditional behaviour is *that* it is shared; it involves the sense of a practice as possessing social and not just individual validity, so that, in conforming to it, the agent enjoys the sanction of a social norm.

(v) Traditions create a background of shared expectations, against which deviance and originality can be achieved. It is also partly by seeing people against this social background that their individual moral character is perceived. Hence, on one view, traditions are an essential ingredient in the production of the individual. The individual is an artefact, who becomes individual only because he has first absorbed into himself the common background of social behaviour against which to define himself.

The ruling thought of those who seek to uphold tradition is that it indicates a form of wholly peaceful attachment to a place, a time, a past, and the many social and institutional arrangements which make that past present. However, different traditions structure the understanding of tradition. Thus it is characteristic of British conservatism to emphasize (iii) (*see*, e.g., *Burke, *Oakeshott), and to underplay (v), which in turn is a preoccupation of German idealists and their progeny (*see* *Hegel). Moreover, it is more characteristic of the English than of the French or German defence to oppose tradition to *doctrine as a mode of *legitimation, although all seem to agree that tradition is required if other political values are to be enacted, since all such things as justice, liberty and community can be achieved only in a social order where the spirit of social continuity is dominant. (*See also* *tacit communication.)

Traditions can be both social and political. The emphasis is usually placed on the former, since the idea tends also to go with the theory that the state and its institutions are themselves offshoots of intimations contained in the experience of *civil society.

traditionalism. Any doctrine or policy founded in the defence of tradition, but specifically the philosophy of history and political programme developed by the *counter-revolutionary movement in eighteenth- and nineteenth-century France. Its main exponents were *de Maistre, Vicomte de Bonald (1754–1840) and F. R. de Lammenais (1782–1854). All were *ultramontanists, and defenders of a religious view of civil obligation, together with some sophisticated variant of the doctrine of *divine right. As a doctrine traditionalism was condemned by a papal decretal in 1855. Its spirit was revived in the twentieth century in **intégrisme* and the associated *royalism.

trahison des clercs. French: the treason of the clerks; in other words, betrayal by intellectuals. The title of a book by Julien Benda (1927), directed in the first instance against the political agitation of certain right-wing French intellectuals (notably Charles Maurras) but including a more general criticism of the role of the intellectual in modern politics, and of the increasing addiction of intellectuals to *Plato's myth of the 'philosopher king' – i.e. that knowledge bestows the right to rule.

transcendentalism. Romantic anti-rationalistic movement in nineteenth-century New England centred on R. W. Emerson (1803–82), who shared with *Coleridge and *Carlyle a view of human nature derived from German idealism, and who attempted to synthesize that view with native American individualism. Emerson criticized the civilization generated by industrial production, and all modes of mass existence, advocating self-knowledge, self-reverence and self-determination as universal ideals. Transcendentalist communities flourished for a while in New England but had little lasting influence.

treason. Breach of *allegiance to the *sovereign. Treason is defined in UK law by the Statute of Treasons 1351. It comprises, e.g., levying war against the sovereign in his realm, being an adherent to his enemies in his realm, or giving them aid and comfort elsewhere. The US constitution defines treason as levying war against the US or adhering to their enemies. There have been very few treason trials in the US and relatively few in the UK. Their relative abundance in the USSR is sometimes attributed to the fact that sovereignty rests, at least **de facto*, with the ruling party, which has had to impose its rule by force.

Treason remains one of the few crimes punishable by death in English law, and everywhere it is looked upon with the utmost seriousness. It has often seemed unjust that someone who feels no true allegiance to a sovereign power, and seeks to escape the jurisdiction of that power, should nevertheless render himself liable to the penalties meted out to a traitor when he is driven to oppose it, in obedience to his conscience, with the aid of outside help. The remedy, say those influenced by *Locke and *social contract doctrine, is to ensure that all citizens are free to leave the jurisdiction; they are then bound in conscience to defend the arrangement that they tacitly consent to enjoy. On that view, a state which forbids emigration commits an injustice when it accuses its uncooperative citizens of treason.

treaty. An agreement, normally written, concluded between two or more states or other subjects of *international law, intended to create rights and obligations between them that will be governed by that law. The word 'treaty' is normally reserved for the more formal kinds of agreement; *conventions and pacts are generally either less important or less formal. But to some extent the three terms, along with 'charter', 'act' 'declaration', 'protocol', can be used interchangeably, besides having various technical uses of their own.

In many respects the principles of private contract apply to treaties, but with one important exception: treaties are not made invalid by *duress, a party who enters a treaty by duress still being taken to have consented to it. Reasons for this rule are not hard to find: treaties must be dictated to the vanquished at the end of every war; moreover, there is no coercive sovereign in international law who can restrain the parties, so that both will threaten force (however covertly). Dictated treaties cannot, however, be contractual, and other treaties, to the extent that they share the nature of dictated accords, must be seen as exhibiting the peculiar synthesis of force and law which constitutes much of international adjudication. Moreover, it is sometimes argued that if the terms of a treaty are manifestly unjust, then they are not binding.

Treaties are not normally valid unless *ratified (the exceptions concern for the most part minor matters). Each constitution contains its own provision as to the agent in whom this power of ratification is vested. In the UK it is the monarch; in the US in theory it is the President, but he can ratify a treaty only with the consent of two thirds of the Senate, so that in fact the power of ratification vests in the Senate, with the President as solely empowered to *make* treaties.

Many problems of interpretation arise. Treaties are framed in order to deal with present exigencies, and later inherited by *regimes either unable or reluctant to fulfil, or even to understand, the original terms. Some international lawyers argue that in every treaty there is implied a clause which provides that the treaty is to be binding only so long as things stand as they are (*rebus sic stantibus*), so that a treaty is never more than conditional. But conditional on what? If the only answer is 'conditional on the present disposition of power' the function of a treaty as limiting the exercise of power is effectively denied, since as soon as a state emerges from the necessity that induced it to accept a treaty, it could repudiate it.

tribe. A form of social organization which is determined by *kinship rather than by *territory, but which nevertheless retains a distinct *chain of command. Legal anthropology has tended to the conclusion that no tribe is wholly without law, if only in the form of customary procedures for settling disputes. Law implies *jurisdiction, and jurisdiction *sovereignty. However, it seems that tribal jurisdiction is not like modern forms of territorial jurisdiction: those who come under the law are defined only by their kinship relation. This has meant that no tribe is in fact recognized as sovereign in international law, or as an *international person. The clash between modern territorial notions of sovereignty and older ideas of allegiance based in kinship is responsible for much political disorder in Africa and elsewhere.

trimmer. A term borrowed from nautical usage to mean someone who 'trims', i.e. who adjusts his position, between opposing parties or factions, inclining now to the one, now to the other, as interest requires.

The term was originally applied to Lord Halifax and his associates in 1680–90; the description was accepted by Halifax as a compliment, since it suggested to him that he always acted so as 'to keep even the ship of state'. It is now largely a term of abuse, on account of the prevalent idea that allegiance is owed, and perhaps primarily owed, to a doctrine or party. That idea is coherent in a one-party state, but Halifax's response would perhaps be more reasonable in a state that aims to have authority and sovereignty over and above the authority and influence of a party.

Trotsky, Leon (Lev Bronstein) (1879–1940). Russian revolutionary, writer and orator; *see* *Trotskyism.

Trotskyism. A collection of *Marxist doctrines and policies associated with Trotsky, who organized the first soviet in 1905, at first opposed and then supported Lenin, and was later Stalin's unsuccessful rival for leadership of the USSR Communist Party on the death of Lenin. Trotsky was expelled from the USSR in 1929, organized opposition to Stalin among exiles, and founded a fourth *International in 1938. He was murdered at Stalin's instigation in 1940.

Trotsky's opposition to Stalin ostensibly had a theoretical base, in that Trotsky remained wedded to the ideal of an international socialism, and opposed Stalin's policy of *socialism in one country: he continued to advocate 'world revolution' after his exile, making repeated use of a rhetorical phrase derived from Marx's *Address to the Communist League*, 1850, which has since become a principal identifying slogan of Trotskyism: *permanent revolution. Trotsky was also one of the first Marxists to proclaim that the initiative for anti-capitalist revolution in the twentieth century would come from underdeveloped countries, and advocated a theory of multiple systematic development which he thought would account for this, while remaining compatible with some form of *historical materialism. (*See* *law of uneven development.) He wrote widely and eclectically on many themes, and was an acute analyst of culture and institutions.

Apart from his doctrines Trotsky remains influential, first, because of the tactics with which he helped to lead the *bolsheviks to power: *entryism, *substitution, the use of *front organizations, and the organization of the 'Red Army', which was a crucial factor in the ultimate triumph of the bolshevik **coup d'état*; secondly because of his trenchant criticisms of the 'Bonapartist bureaucracy' that he saw emerging under Stalin's dictatorship.

In the USSR Trotskyism is often singled out as one of the main failings of the intellectual critics of *actually existing socialism, and is condemned as a *petit bourgeois* heresy. In the West, where it is sometimes argued that, had Trotsky been successful in gaining leadership of the USSR Communist Party, communism might subsequently have worn a more human face, Trotskyism has been influential, partly because it forms a focus for communist activity that is independent of, and over many issues opposed to, the Communist Party. Trotskyists usually claim to have more respect for democratic procedure and human rights than *Stalinists, which is plausible enough, since they could hardly have less. They also argue against centralization and bureaucracy, emphasize the role of politics in social transformation, and argue that revolution requires the transformation of *all* institutions, however small.

truce. Originally truth or fidelity to a promise, often given by one belligerent to another. The term now means the cessation of hostilities between belligerents, usually by declaration and common consent, and usually for a specified period. For 'truce of God', *see *pax*.

Truman doctrine. The doctrine contained in a message from President Truman to the US Congress in March 1947, which pledged US support for 'free peoples who are resisting attempted subjugation by armed minorities or outside pressures'. This marked the break with the *isolationism implied in the *Monroe doctrine, and laid the ideological foundation for subsequent US policy towards communist regimes.

trust. The legal arrangement whereby a trustee holds the legal title to property subject to the interest of a beneficiary, and bound by trust to safeguard that interest. In UK and US law, because of the doctrine of the primacy of *equity, the beneficiary's interest will be protected, and the beneficiary is, in equity, the true owner of the property. Thus the separation of legal from equitable ownership has become an important legal conception, by which judicial decision has created a network of property rights either unrecognized, or even denied, by the law. From medieval times the device has been used to avoid the effect of property statutes, and in particular to avoid taxation on property, by transferring the legal title to an untaxable trustee.

Trusts may be created expressly, by statute, declaration or will. Or they may arise through the operation of the law of equity, as in the 'constructive trust', where a judge, in the interests of justice, infers the existence of a trust that might have been known to neither party. (An important example is the constructive trust sometimes discerned when property is acquired with the help of another – e.g. a mistress – who is then dismissed without reward.) The law of trusts therefore has two important political applications: to override legal provisions in the interests of what might be argued to be *natural justice; and to uphold classes of extra-legal property rights through technicalities and fictions of ownership. The first use is often applauded, the second often denounced, in particular because it constantly acts so as to remove property dealings from the supervision of the legislature, and so permits the creation of *monopolies, *cartels, and other objectionable agreements, even when these are forbidden by statute. The purpose of *anti-trust legislation is in part to break down the influence of equity in this area (although here the term 'trust' has a slightly different sense, and such legislation may be directed against things which are not trusts in the precise legal sense).

Some charitable trusts show private property at an extreme point of attenuation, where the legal holders of the property (the trustees) may have no rights, but only obligations, and where the beneficiaries may be impossible to list, so that the funds of the trust cannot be divided among them. This case is sometimes cited as an example of the immense complexity of *private property rights, so that, if private property is objectionable, it is unlikely that it is in every case for exactly the same reason.

trusteeship. 1. The position of the legal owner of property under a *trust.

2. In *international law, the relation of the United Nations Organization, through its 'trusteeship council', to certain 'trust territories', about which the council concerns itself, formulating questionnaires, reporting on their political, social and economic conditions, and doing what it can to foster progress in those respects. The 'trust territory' stands to a *sovereign state roughly as equitable ownership stands to legal ownership in the doctrine of the *trust in law. The ownership of these territories vests in the people there resident, but they have yet to achieve the recognized sovereignty whereby their rights over the territory may be recognized in international law. A state which is appointed trustee of such a territory is held accountable to the UN for its government, and also to the people in the territory concerned.

The trusteeship system replaced the *mandates system, and now applies only to very few territories. It is, nevertheless, of considerable intellectual interest, in that it attempts to transfer a highly developed section of *municipal law into the international sphere.

tyranny. From Greek: *turannos*, an absolute ruler. Now normally used more or less synonymously with '*despotism', to denote any form of government which is oppressive, cruel, and without a rule of law, and in which there is considerable concentration of power, in the hands of a single individual or a single organization. The fascination of tyrants, for whom all spheres are seemingly spheres of will, so that the objective is absorbed into the subjective, has led to their frequent deification by poets. *Nietzsche's injunction to each man to will his own desire as a law for himself was accompanied by a respect for tyranny, as the highest example of that principle. The poet's refusal to recognize a world beyond the subjective is redeemed by a gift of imagination, whereby he may, in Hamlet's words, be bounded in a nutshell, and yet count himself king of infinite space. The tyrant, who lacks that gift, may yet have the grandeur of vision which substitutes for it, and this may be one reason why he is so frequently extolled.

The question of the justification of tyrannicide exercised ancient moralists and philosophers. One answer seems to be that it is justifiable in the circumstances where, were the tyrant an alien, war would be justified: so that the problem becomes one with that of *just war.

U

Übermensch. The 'overman' or 'superman', a concept introduced in *Nietzsche's philosophy of self-mastery and later vulgarized in the Nazi doctrine of the 'master race' (*Herrenvolk*). According to Nietzsche human nature defines the essence, not of an individual, but of a class, and the individual owes it to himself to transcend every class, and every principle, creed or custom that might confine him to one (including, incidentally, the class of the *Herrenvolk*). The individual is essentially *contrasted* with the universal. Hence human nature must be overcome, and true excellence belongs to the creature who emerges from this overcoming: the *Übermensch*. The doctrine relies on a rather dubious metaphysics, but has its parallel in certain *existentialist ideas concerning the priority of 'existence' over 'essence'. Nietzsche used it to revive ideas from *Aristotle's ethics. Aristotle argued that all men ought to cultivate *virtue, that virtue belongs to the entire character, and that its highest form is that of the *megalopsuchos*, or great-souled man, who surveys the human scene with a kind of lordly disdain that is unavailable to the mass of common mortals.

ultra vires. 'Beyond the powers': i.e. beyond those *powers conferred by law. Action *ultra vires* is an important ground for legal proceedings in all areas where powers are conferred on individuals who are tempted to exceed them: e.g. administration, delegated government, police action, company direction. The ability to bring such proceedings, and to enforce judgement against all officers of government should they exceed their *office, is often held forth as the principal mark of genuinely *limited government, since it is the sign that a citizen can effectively confine the powers of those who govern him, to those sanctioned in law. This is one part of that 'negative power' which John C. Calhoun celebrated in his *Discourse on the Constitution of the United States*, 1852, when he argued that 'it is . . . the negative power which makes the constitution, and the positive which makes the government'. However, Calhoun argued, the proceeding for actions *ultra vires* is not enough. He proposed the far stronger 'rule of concurrent majority', according to which 'every major interest in the country. . .is to possess a veto power on political decisions directly affecting it'. This power to prevent the very formation of policy is of a quite different order from the power to prevent the exceeding of office in its execution:

it is arguable that it must limit government to the point of non-existence.

ultramontanism. ('Beyond the mountains'; meaning, beyond the Alps.) The tendency in the *Roman Catholic Church to favour the centralization of authority in the papacy and its court (the *curia*) and to oppose national and diocesan independence in religious matters. After two centuries of vacillation ultramontanism triumphed in 1814, with the revival of its principal advocate, the *Jesuit order. It became a political force among French *traditionalists, who invoked the support of the papacy for their *legitimism, and who regarded the universal spiritual authority of the church as necessary to all civil order born out of Christian conceptions of sovereignty.

underground. A name applied to movements and associations opposed to some established order, who are compelled to conceal their opposition for fear of official reprisals. The name is sometimes appropriated by movements and associations who openly defy censure from an *establishment, and also by certain non-political associations which continue peacefully within a *police state, even when not forming a genuine *opposition, as in the underground universities, schools and religious associations that struggle for survival in the USSR and its dominions. Here opposition is not the *purpose* of association, although it is the normal result; hence there arises a real need for concealment.

unemployment. Used to denote involuntary, rather than voluntary, lack of paid employment, and divided into various kinds: e.g. cyclical, *frictional, seasonal, and *structural. It is a feature of much *neo-classical economics, and of the economic assumptions that are sometimes encapsulated in *Say's law, that structural unemployment, and any other enduring unemployment, becomes inexplicable; it is a virtue of *Keynesian economic theory that it attempts to explain such kinds of unemployment, in terms of *underconsumption. The Keynesian theory and its offshoots are not generally accepted as explaining every kind of unemployment, and the emphasis on technological factors has become increasingly important. If the means of production become so sophisticated that enormous productivity can be achieved while employing only a fraction of the work force, then, at some point of development, demand can be met in a condition of less than full employment. Some (including *Marx) have welcomed this possibility, thinking of *leisure, or some state analogous to leisure, as the natural condition of man; the problem becomes that of organizing the great machine of production so that the product is fairly distributed. Others have regarded the state of man so 'returned to himself' as either impossible, or undesirable. Leisure is often perceived as a *problem*. This effect, variously attributed to **anomie*, *alienation, and *human nature, is recognized in the so-called *right to work. If the 'right' were based in a need only for the product of labour, then it would be satisfied by providing an unearned stipend. This 'unemployment benefit' is not what is requested, nor is it what is given by those regimes that purport to uphold the right. What is usually given is work (paid at a rate lower than the proportionate equivalent of the unemployment benefit given in many states that do not concede a 'right to work'). If what is sought is not just the product of work, but work itself, then this is wholly intelligible. It is of course true that work is not uniformly pleasant or interesting; nevertheless it could be that it is functionally necessary to the human being that he *earn* his living and not just that he receive it.

In actual conditions it is socially necessary to work in order to enjoy any measure of material comfort. Most post-war governments have therefore taken it as a major policy objective to keep the level of unemployment to a minimum. Various more or less arbitrary figures have been suggested as the 'acceptable' maximum of unemployed: it was once 2%, then, throughout the 1950s and

1960s, 1.5% was considered normal. The 'acceptable' maximum has perforce risen as unemployment has risen; some even argue that unemployment below a certain level (Lord Beveridge argued 3%) marks a condition of *overfull employment, which cannot be sustained without damage to the economy.

Many economists believe that reduction of unemployment is incompatible with certain other basic economic objectives, such as control over the rate of *inflation (*see* *Phillips curve), or a stable *balance of payments. Alternatively it may be that the seeming difficulty of reconciling control of inflation with full employment is the result of deep structural factors within the economy, and that the two objectives could be reconciled only by overthrowing the economic order that makes each of them desirable. (There is, here, the seed of one of the many alleged *contradictions of capitalism, although it must be pointed out that inflation and unemployment are problems equally for communist regimes.)

unification of laws. The elimination of national peculiarities from law, so that states which frequently deal with each other commercially and politically should be able to do so without unnecessary legal impediment, and so that *international law should be able to connect as easily as possible with *municipal law. A movement for the unification of laws began in the nineteenth century, and has continued, despite serious obstacles and interruptions, up to the present. Important agencies of the movement have been the Universal Postal Union (established 1874), the *International Labour Organization (established 1919), and the Hague Conference (begun 1893).

unilateral act. An act which affects the relations of two or more parties, but in which only one party is involved as an *agent. The contrast is with bilateral, trilateral, etc. acts, in which there is always some element of agreement, collusion or common responsibility.

unilateral nuclear disarmament. Voluntary renunciation by one side to a potential conflict of at least some (including the most destructive) of the weapons of war. The usual argument given for unilateral nuclear disarmament is this: if nuclear armaments are kept by both sides then there is a probability of war by accident and war will in this case mean total destruction; if nuclear armaments are kept only by one side then there is a probability of deliberate war, which will involve conquest but not total destruction. However small the first probability and however large the second, the negative value of total destruction is incommensurably greater than that of conquest, so that it would always be irrational to choose the first alternative over the second.

The strength of such arguments depends upon the method for assigning probabilities, and also upon assumptions about accidental war, and about the destructive effects of nuclear weapons. It is always to be supposed, however, that, if men have not yet invented a weapon that will destroy the world, this is only through lack of time.

The argument for unilateral nuclear disarmament is often accepted, partly because it suggests a single clear course of action. Those who reject it tend to emphasize what they take to be the low probability of nuclear war and the near certainty of conquest if there were no weapons of mass destruction to prevent it. They may further argue that the potential enemy is such that no 'conventional' weapons could resist him, and that, in any case, he would not scruple to use nuclear weapons just because they could not be used against him. To know the truth about all these matters is hard. Some have felt that the enormous reservoirs of hatred that have been stored by the USSR propaganda machine are so dangerous that it is necessary to guard against them by all available means, any war being certain to involve the mass destruction of the vanquished. Others think that all these fears are based in fantasy, and perhaps in an equal hatred. The clearest view of the matter is that given by *Lenin: 'It would not matter one bit if three quarters of the human race perished. The important thing is that the remaining quarter should be communists.' But presumably, by that reasoning, one communist is enough, or perhaps two, an Adam and an Eve.

unincorporated association. *See* *incorporation.

USSR, constitution and laws. The constitution and laws of the Union of Soviet Socialist Republics present great difficulties to the student. Although a 'constitution' is contained in a written document, adopted by the Supreme Soviet (the legislative assembly) on 7 October 1977, this document is more descriptive than prescriptive, and does not explain how its provisions are to be enforced. It begins with a mythopoeic history of the revolution and its effects, describes the Communist Party as the 'leading and guiding force' of Soviet society, and declares certain rights and privileges of the Soviet citizen, and of the various nationalities within the Union. It describes in detail the federal structure, economic organization, and parliamentary institutions of the state, together with the functions of all the important offices within the state. Even as a description it is wildly inaccurate, and, in so far as it prescribes rights, either to citizens or to constituent nationalities, it seems to be largely ineffective. The procedure for claiming rights is left out of consideration, and *judicial independence is disposed of in a single line (Art. 155), which says merely that judges are independent and subject only to the law: how they become so, how they remain so, and what the citizen may do to compel them to be so, are not discussed. In fact the Communist Party controls the appointment of all judicial and administrative officers, and is thought by most observers to have large powers of coercion, even in the law courts.

Nevertheless, it is important to distinguish the structure of government from that of the party. There are in fact two partly independent but interlocking structures of power, the one nominally legal and embodied in representational offices of government, the other partly coercive, and embodied in the various committees and conferences of the party. The fact that only party members may fill state offices is important in assessing the actual extent of the party's power. However, the party remains distinct from the institutions of representation. In theory government proceeds on the principle of open discussion, whereby complaints and suggestions received at the village soviet are gradually passed upwards, through county soviet, provincial soviet, and republic soviet to the USSR 'Council of Ministers', which is, in theory, the centre of *executive power. The Council of Ministers is controlled by the Supreme Soviet and its Presidium. The Supreme Soviet (the *legislature) consists of two chambers, the 'Soviet of Union' and the 'Soviet of Nationalities', the first representing interests uniformly and without reference to place, the second representing specific nationalities within the Union.

Most observers consider that supreme executive power does not reside in the Council of Ministers, but in the *Politburo of the party. This is a small inner council of the central committee of the 'All Union Communist Party Congress', which stands in relation to the grass-roots party organizations roughly as the Supreme Soviet stands to the village soviets.

Soviet law is usually called *socialist law. The relative absence of a rule of law (*see* *socialist legality) means that it is not easy to know what is permissible and what is not; the complex inference from written statute to actual law must be conducted by a trained legal anthropologist. 'Sovietology' is the term coined for the new kind of anthropology which attempts to understand Soviet institutions, and 'kremlinology' for the study of the high command.

united front. Term used by communists to denote the various forms of cooperation in a particular state between the Communist Party and other left-wing parties, and also, in exceptional cases, non-left-wing parties. After seizure of power non-communist parties may survive in name, on condition that they accept the 'leadership' (i.e. dictatorship) of the Communist Party, so that many communist countries are now governed by party organizations with names such as the 'Fatherland Front' (Bulgaria), or the 'National Front' (Czechoslovakia).

UK constitution and laws. The United Kingdom comprises the kingdoms of Scotland and England, the principality of Wales, and Northern Ireland (which is that part of the former kingdom of Ireland which elected in 1920 to be bound by the Act of Union 1800, and which has in that sense remained loyal to the *Crown). The UK is not a federal state, since there are no sovereign legislative bodies outside Westminster. Nor is it a true unitary state, in that there has been and still is *delegation of power and regional autonomy on a scale more familiar in federations. In particular the legal systems of Scotland and, to some extent, Northern Ireland are substantially different from that of England and Wales and necessitate separate systems of courts and judicial offices (*see* *English law, *Scots law). It is usual, therefore, to acknowledge that, constitutionally, the UK is *sui generis*, and to be understood neither on the federal nor on the unitary model.

Furthermore the constitution remains unwritten and probably unwriteable, contains large elements that are the effect and residue of long-established custom and convention, rather than legal or executive recognition, and is completely open to amendment in every particular, containing (and probably able to contain) no equivalent of the *entrenched clause. *Sovereignty resides, according to many observers, in 'the Queen in Parliament', an expression which indicates the peculiar combination of hereditary monarchy and parliamentary representation that has led to present institutions. The actual locus of this sovereignty is in fact hard to determine: *executive power has been thought to reside not with the monarch but with the *Prime Minister or, to be more exact, the *cabinet, while legislative power resides only in both Houses of Parliament, as well as being exercised by judges through the operation of *common law and *equity. The *separation of powers is incomplete and dependent largely on convention, although *judicial independence seems to be as well guaranteed as anything else, by the nature of the law, and by rights and privileges enshrined in custom. Custom is in fact the most important part of the arrangement, and provides the background from which Parliament emerges as a definite shape, but without which parliamentary institutions are far from easy to understand.

United Nations Organization. *See* *international organizations, *world organizations.

US constitution and laws. Although the United States of America has the most famous of all written *constitutions, its actual constitution at any moment can be determined only by examining two centuries of judicial decision, and observing the extent to which the written words have been qualified, clarified and 'interpreted' in their application. The constitution of 1788 establishes a federal system of government, with considerable limits to its power, but with absolute sovereignty in all matters that concern the existence of the US as a single state. The federal government consists of legislative, executive and judicial branches, interrelated but distinct, and constructed expressly so as to accord with the theory of the *separation of powers, as this had been understood by the *Founding Fathers. The federal legislature is the *Congress, in which two main parties contend for power, while the federal executive is the *President, affiliated to one of the parties in Congress (although not necessarily to the majority party). The President has power to appoint a *cabinet, who are not members of Congress, in order to facilitate the exercise of executive power. The judicial power resides in, and depends on, the *Supreme Court which, because it can interpret and enforce the constitution, has considerable political influence.

The legal system is dualistic, with federal and state courts acting side by side to determine the rights and obligations of the citizen, the federal courts having jurisdiction in all matters arising under the constitution or in connection with the existence of the US as a sovereign state, the state courts adjudicating in most matters of civil and criminal law. The federal courts also exercise the supremely important function of *judicial review of administrative decisions.

Case law is as important as legislation, and the doctrine of *precedent is effective in practice, even if not fully recognized in law. Hence, although there is not a true *common law system in the US, the law of the separate states exists against a background of accepted decisions which are tantamount to common law, and which usually evolved out of an inheritance of European (e.g. English) common law. (Originally the settlers had tended to prefer written codes of law, and the Carolinas had a complete written code, compiled by *Locke, from 1668; this code gave way in 1712 to the English common law, as the only workable system, and this return to common law was universal by the time of the federal constitution.) The division between common law and *equity was originally recognized in the US, but has since been gradually diminished, and the enshrining of ideas of *natural justice in the *Bill of Rights has led to an automatic expectation of equitable remedies, which therefore have needed no procedural guarantee.

universalism. **1.** In Christian theology, another term for 'apocatastis', the doctrine that all moral agents, angels, men and devils, will ultimately be saved.
2. In political thought, the belief in universally valid principles of government and individual rights, usually founded in a doctrine of universal human nature. Typical universalist doctrines are those of *international socialism, *human rights, and the moral law of *Kant. Opposition to universalism is exemplified by *nationalism (sometimes called, in this context, 'national particularism', to emphasize that the universal is being contrasted with the particular), and by those varieties of conservatism which stress the view that man as a political animal is always the product of, and always incorporates into himself as part of his political nature, local conditions and attachments.

The opposite of universalism should be called particularism, and not individualism, which is a doctrine about human nature, and may well be compatible with universalism. Thus the universalist doctrines of *liberalism are also often individualistic. Only some individualists, notably *Nietzsche, have also advocated forms of individualism which have particularism as a consequence.

universities. Associations incorporated by charter or statute, for the purpose of the development and transmission of knowledge. The idea of a university is ecclesiastical in origin, and derives from the *Roman law concept of the *universitas*, a corporation created for a specified purpose. The distinctive structure, powers and educative role of the universities for a long time reflected their medieval origin, although the newer universities in the US and the UK are institutions of a kind that have very little outward resemblance to their medieval forebears.

The question of the ideal nature of university education, and of the role of the university in public life, are in fact older than the universities themselves. The medievals recognized their predecessors in the academy of *Plato, and in the school of Constantinople, founded AD 425, while the question of the nature and function of university education has its antecedents in the ancient dispute between *rhetoric and philosophy. Philosophy – the pursuit of wisdom – seems sublime but useless, while rhetoric – the art of persuasion – seems useful but degrading. Plato set out to show that philosophy is not only useful but indispensable both to the happiness of the individual and to the good government of the **polis*. The debate now centres on the relative merits of arts and sciences, but it has the same structure. On the one hand there are the graceful but useless accomplishments of the humanities; opposed to them stand the eminently useful sciences. Defenders of *humane education have tried to describe further, and more serious uses, which the arts satisfy through their very uselessness; while defenders of the sciences have emphasized the need for new recruits to management. The conflict between *utilitarians and *cultural conservatives in the nineteenth century led to several important attempts to examine the nature of universities as institutions and their role in the modern state, notably that of Cardinal Newman, in *The Idea of a University*, 1852.

In more recent years, discussions have centred upon the question, How widely distributed should university education be, and who should finance it? (*See* *education.) The extent to which universities have been funded and expanded under public initiative in the UK is some indication of the acceptance of their utility (and perhaps of the fact that those who gain high office are themselves university graduates). However, the old debates persist, and now concern the relative merits and comparative nature of the university and the polytechnic, the first supposedly focused on knowledge, the second on its application.

use-value. Classical economists' term for *utility, normally contrasted (following a usage introduced by *Smith) with *exchange-value which is explored by theories of *price. It is often held that 'use-value as such lies outside the sphere of investigation of political economy' (Marx), meaning that, from the economic point of view, the fact that someone has a desire which some object satisfies is the ultimate fact. The structure of the desire itself, and its merit, depth and moral or spiritual significance lie outside the economist's purview. Thus an apple has use-value, so does a work of art. But the desire for an apple is based in physical need, that for a work of art in a conception of aesthetic value. Many are unhappy with theories that treat these two things as on a par and have sought to take account in their economics of the multifarious nature of human desire. Is, for example, a desire for medical treatment to be considered as similar to a desire for cosmetics? And if not, what does this entail for the use-value of each? For reflections on this type of question see J. K. Galbraith's *The Affluent Society*, 1958.

usurpation. The illegitimate seizure of political power. Usurpation is to be distinguished from *revolution, in that the power seized in the first case precedes the seizure, and endures through it. Revolution consists not in the seizure of power but in its abolition and replacement by another power (sometimes represented as temporary). 'Illegitimate' means either illegal or (more widely) contrary to *natural justice.

usury. Originally, lending at a profit, and hence lending money for *interest. This is the narrow interpretation sometimes given to *usuria* (literally: putting to use) in *canon law, and to *ribā* (literally: increase) in *Islamic law. However, what has been intended by both terms has been a matter of considerable dispute, so that, while both *usuria* and *ribā* are forbidden, this has not always meant that people have been unable to lend at interest. It is now more normal to reserve the term 'usury' for interest judged to be unjust or excessive, which denotes the original idea only if *all* interest is such. Over this issue both Christians and Islamic jurists have given contradictory opinions and there seems to be no settled view in either religion. The transition from the original to the modern meaning has sometimes been thought to be explained by the rise of capitalism, but this is now doubted.

Clearly, lending money at a rate of interest equal to the rate of inflation is not lending money for profit in real terms. The blanket condemnation of usury also seems to neglect both the concept of *time preference, and the fact that individuals independently prefer goods now to the same goods later (there being, for example, a probability that I may not be here to enjoy them at a later time). Suppose I could be induced to forgo £1 now only if I could receive £1.10 in a year's time; does it not follow that someone who wishes to borrow £1 from me must offer 10% interest if he is to have my consent? One can imagine all kinds of sophisticated variants of that case and of the accompanying question. Moreover, according to the *Austrian school of economic thought, resources that are saved can be put to productive use in order to produce *more* goods in the future (*see also* *capital). Such considerations clearly influenced the Islamic jurists, who developed elaborate *legal fictions on this principle in order to avoid the charge of *ribā*: for example, I sell you my piano for £110, payable in a year's time; I then promptly buy it back from you for £100. The net result of the transaction is a loan of £100 at 10%; technically, however, it is a double contract, neatly capturing the idea of time preference in its terms.

Philosophical condemnations of usury have been of two kinds: the general and the particular. The first purports to find something wrong in any human relation in which someone enjoys a (legal) right to part of the product of another's labour, while not himself producing. Such arguments include criticisms of the feudal practice of *corvée*, and Marxist arguments concerning the *exploitation of the worker by the capitalist, who extorts hours of 'unpaid labour'. Such arguments are of a great generality, and clearly do not invoke any quality specific to usury. The more specific arguments tend to criticize, not usury in its original sense, but rather the modern idea of an unjust, oppressive, or exploitative loan. It may be, indeed, that this is what has always been intended by critics of usury. Typically critics concentrate on the case where one man grants a loan to another who is genuinely needy, in order to secure his dependence, making sure that the rate of interest is so high that the loan can never be repaid, so that the borrower in effect binds himself for life to provide an income to the lender. Some find elements of this kind of usury in modern credit systems – particularly the system of the bank card, which tempts people to spend to the limit of their capacity, and then binds them by interest rates that force them to try to raise their earnings. It is not clear that the cases are exactly parallel, although it is certain that no medieval moralist could have tolerated such modern forms of credit. A celebrated defence of usury on utilitarian grounds was offered by *Bentham (*Defence of Usury*, 1787), but here 'usury' means 'lending at interest, according to the market rate'.

'Usurocracy', the rule by usurers, is a coinage of Ezra Pound's, in which he mixes Latin and Greek etymology for expletive effect.

utilitarianism. The philosophy of morals, politics and legislation, associated with the names of *Bentham, *James Mill, *J. S. Mill, and Henry Sidgwick (1838–1900), which founds all practical reasoning in the concept of *utility, and argues that the right action, the good character, and the right law are those which maximize utility. Utilitarianism exists in many forms, but its most representative definition is that given by J. S. Mill, partly in order to endorse, and partly in order to criticize, the moral philosophy of Bentham: 'The creed which accepts as the foundation of morals Utility, or the Greatest Happiness Principle, holds that actions are right in proportion as they tend to promote happiness, wrong as they tend to produce the reverse of happiness. By happiness is intended pleasure and the absence of pain; by unhappiness, pain and the privation of pleasure'. The theory can be divided into three parts:

(i) the merits of an action lie in its consequences, and not in the motive or character from which it springs. Hence utilitarianism is often criticized as a form of *consequentialism and held, as such, to countenance injustice for the sake of however slight an increase in the overall good.

(ii) Consequences are to be assessed in

terms of something first called happiness, and then later identified in terms of pleasure and pain. The theory therefore provokes (as Mill realized) two powerful objections: that there is not one single end of human conduct, and that, even if happiness is an end, it is not to be described merely in terms of pleasure or pain. Happiness is the fulfilment of the *person or *rational agent, and is not reducible to the pleasures which an animal might equally feel. ('Better a Socrates dissatisfied than a pig satisfied'.) The emphasis on pleasure and pain stemmed from Bentham's *hedonism, itself an attempt to reduce ethics to measurable quantities, and so to solve the problems of morals and legislation through *cost/benefit analysis.

(iii) The *optimum to be achieved is overall maximization, untempered by any idea of distribution or desert. The theory has therefore prompted objections from those who, while perhaps accepting (i) and even (ii), wish to adopt a more just, intelligible, or politically feasible criterion of optimality: *see* *Pareto optimality, *maximin. (When *welfare economists refer to the 'utilitarian criterion of optimality' they have this idea of overall maximization in mind, whether or not conjoined to (i) and (ii).)

There are further difficulties – especially the practical difficulties of applying such a principle – and philosophers, attracted by what seems to be the eminent common sense of the doctrine, have sought to overcome some of them by distinguishing act utilitarianism (just discussed) from rule utilitarianism. According to the latter an action is judged right by its conformity to some rule, and the rule itself judged right by its conformity to the greatest happiness principle. It is sometimes argued that no such sophistications will escape a general difficulty for consequentialist doctrines, which is that they describe, not the moral reasoning of the agent, but the moral rationalizations of the observer, and hence provide no guide to action. It has also been argued, by *Hegelians and their progeny, that utilitarianism is founded in a mistaken and unduly *individualistic view of human nature.

utility. A term sometimes used by economists to denote what was classically called *use-value, and by philosophers to denote a variety of things, for example happiness (*see* *utilitarianism), pleasure (sometimes identified with happiness), and function. Modern economics, however, tends to dispense with the concept of utility, employing only the notion of *preference orderings. All these things are brought together in the thought that an object with utility is a means to an end, and is desired for that reason. If the ends of human conduct are given, then the utilities of all objects can be estimated in relation to them. *Bentham thought that, if I desire something, then I desire it as a means to pleasure. By adroit manipulation of that idea he came to believe that the utility of every object is a measurable quantity, to be estimated in terms of the intensity, duration, propinquity, fecundity and probability of the pleasure to which it is a means. Philosophers have objected that many less measurable dimensions have been left out of this account – e.g. those of depth, seriousness, and *value. Moreover we distinguish in our practical reasoning between desires, needs, whims, and values: yet all these distinctions seem to have no place in the Benthamite calculus. It may be replied that the objection is not to the actual terms of measurement that Bentham used, but to his claims as to what he was measuring. If 'utility' is thought of simply as another name for preference, and if preferences are construed in the terms of *decision theory, then comparative utilities can be seen as parts of a preference ordering. To say that one state of affairs has greater utility than another for John, is simply to say that John prefers the first to the second. This replacement of any real notion of utility with the notion of preference ordering is often thought to signal a great advance. It does not overcome the philosopher's worries about the incommensurability of the many things which might be weighed in the balance of preference, but it satisfies the economist's worries that the theory of utility might be associated with nothing empirically discernible whatsoever. (*See* *revealed preference.)

utility function. A mathematical device for representing a consumer's preference orderings.

utopia. Term coined by Sir Thomas More (*Utopia*, 1516), to mean (although the Greek derivation is incorrect) 'No place'. More portrays a social arrangement without violence, oppression, or property, and presents a comprehensive view of ideal institutions. The term has since been appropriated to name any such picture, usually with the implied criticism that a 'utopia' must idealize human nature, and gain its plausibility from neglecting recalcitrant facts. However, in the vast literature devoted to the construction of idealized societies one may distinguish the following quite different endeavours:
(i) to make political recommendations, in the form of an ideal, without examining the actual policies that might realize it. More's *Utopia* is an example of this.
(ii) To show what it would be like for an 'ideal' to be realized, thereby criticizing it. Huxley's *Brave New World* is an example of this. (On one theory of the literary imagination (ii) is always a greater imaginative task than (i) since it involves the labour of concrete description.)
(iii) The construction of an *ideal type of political arrangement, in order to explain actual forms of government. It is possible that Plato's *Republic* is at least partly of this kind, as are certain parts of Aristotle's *Politics*. Such a theory may attempt to give a full account of human nature, and to illustrate the ways in which actual arrangements fall short of the ideal.
(iv) The construction of an ideal in terms of which to *justify* actual approximations to it. Plato's theory is also of this type.

Early socialists such as *Fourier and *Owen were sometimes criticized for their 'utopian' character by the Marxists (in particular by Marx and Engels): their theories were of type (i), and involved the postulation of an ideal without the investigation of the actual conditions which must make it unrealizable. By contrast the socialism of Marx was held to be 'scientific', not just in the sense of being based in a scientific theory of social development, but also in the sense of taking account of actual social conditions, and of the transformations that will be necessary if a socialist community is to be brought into being. Some socialists try to justify utopias as *myths, which have the function of spurring men to action, so *hastening* the conditions which will make them actual. (*See* *Sorel.)

Objections to utopianism are made, not only in the name of scientific socialism, but also in the name of political *realism, and of the conservative attachment to existing social conditions. Some argue that much type (i) utopianism, in its reluctance to accept the proven realities of human nature, shows a diseased and egocentric consciousness. On this view, it is not surprising to find that those who are galvanized by utopian ideals are so often able to perpetrate cruelties, with consciences that are automatically washed clean by the never-ending absolution from that source. (*See* *antinomianism, *millenarianism.)

V

value. Worth, desirability, goodness: an idea which generates more questions than it answers. It is important to distinguish two uses:

1. In economics it is normal to follow *Smith in distinguishing *utility – or *use-value – from *price – or *exchange-value. Thus Smith wrote: 'The word value, it is to be observed, has two different meanings, and sometimes expresses the utility of some particular object, and sometimes the power of purchasing other goods which the possession of that object conveys. The one may be called "value in use", the other "value in exchange"' Smith adds that 'the things which have the greatest value in use have frequently little or no value in exchange; and, on the contrary, those which have the greatest value in exchange have frequently little or no value in use'; he gives water as an example of the first, a diamond as an example of the second. This observation is sometimes referred to as the 'paradox of value', and it is one of the things that theories of value have attempted to explain (success in explaining it being one argument sometimes offered for the *marginal utility theory).

2. Generally, the term 'value' is applied to all those objects thought to be worthy of human pursuit, say on moral, aesthetic, or religious grounds. Thus value attaches to goods in economics; but to ideals, motives, sentiments, actions and so on in the wider context. The principal question in the theory of value is that of the objectivity of moral value judgements; judgements of what is good, right or worthy. In normal philosophical usage, such judgements are of two kinds: (i) judgements of the worth, goodness or intrinsic desirability of a state of affairs, or of the *virtue of a character, or of the admirable quality of a motive; (ii) judgements of obligation, of the rightness or wrongness of an act, of duty, of what ought to be done, and so on. Sometimes the term value judgement is reserved for type (i), in order to separate what are thought to be the distinct logical structures of 'good' and 'ought'. Sometimes type (ii) is taken as primary, since it captures explicitly the normative element that is already implicit in (i).

The philosophical question may be expressed thus: are such value judgements mere expressions of preferences, dressed up in a language that claims the concurrence of others, or can they be objective, binding on all who understand them? Theories of the objectivity of value judgements can be divided into two: (a) 'realism', which holds that value judgements, like any other judgement in the indicative mood, describe reality and are therefore true or false according to whether or not they correspond to reality; (b) theories of practical reason which deny (a), e.g. because value judgements are not really indicatives but imperatives, but which go on to assert that, despite the fact that there is no 'moral reality', value judgements are still binding on all rational beings as the essential expression of the principles of practical reason. *Kant's view is an example of type (b), certain types of *utilitarianism may be of type (a), while *Aristotle's theory of *virtue contains a subtle mixture of both.

Theories of *justice are more or less useless if they accompany a sceptical or subjectivist theory about the value of justice. In general, any political ideal which seeks not only to exist but also to recommend itself must, in the end, uphold the objectivity of judgements of value. It is sometimes said that Marxism can never so recommend itself, since it dismisses value judgements as *ideology.

value controversy. *See* *price, *profit, *surplus value.

value-free. German: *wertfrei*. A judgement is sometimes held to be more 'scientific', and therefore more suited for incorporation into a scientific theory of society, if it is freed from all expressions of *value (in sense 2.). So at least thought *Weber, who introduced this usage, and who recommended a 'value-free' social science while also doubting its possibility. Some have argued that there can be no value-free social science, because there is no value-neutral language for the description, and therefore analysis and understanding, of social life. Others have argued that a value-free social science is necessary since value judgements are subjective, or unscientific, or possess some other defect that forbids them from serving as vehicles for an objective science of man.

vanguard. Those who are foremost in a battle. The term was appropriated by *Lenin, to denote the role of the Communist Party in the Russian Revolution and subsequently. Since the proletariat is disorganized, easily subverted, and without an understanding of its revolutionary mission, it stands in need of a disciplined organization that will organize and lead it, and which will articulate its needs and ideals: this is the vanguard, which represents the synthesis of the 'objective conditions' of revolution (i.e. the development of *productive forces and the beginnings of 'class warfare'), with the 'subjective conditions' – the understanding of past, present and future that will enable the cogent formulation of policy and tactics.

Vatican Councils. The two 'Vatican Councils,' 21st and 22nd 'Oecumenical Councils' respectively, were called, first, by Pope Pius IX in 1868, when *ultramontanism resurged and was victorious, with the affirmation of the doctrine of papal infallibility; second, by Pope John XXIII in 1962 (lasting until 1965), in which far-reaching liturgical reforms were instigated, together with measures of *secularization from within.

A Vatican Council is a convocation of bishops and others holding high office within the *Roman Catholic Church, in order to settle disputed questions of vital importance to the role of the church in society. The effect of the first was to redefine the role of the church as an international (but 'apolitical') organization; the effect of the second was to emphasize social transformation and secular morality, rather than faith, mystery, and eternal truth.

Veblen, Thorstein Bunde (1857–1929). American economist and sociologist, whose imaginative description of the transformation of social relations under the impact of technology and mass production has had a lasting influence on modern social and political science. Veblen was influenced by *Marx, and accepted the latter's dichotomous view of social development, replacing the dualism of *productive forces and *production relations with his own close equivalents, technology (which is the dynamic and constantly developing force) and institutions (the static and constraining structures which are functionally related to that force). However, Veblen was sceptical about the idea that there might be general 'laws of motion' of capitalist society, as of virtually everything else in Marxian social analysis. (See especially *The Theory of Business Enterprise*, 1904.) He argued that capitalist institutions would differ from place to place according to cultural factors, and that the class structure could not have a single universal form or function. His *Theory of the Leisure Class*, 1899, identified the function of the *leisure class at a certain stage of technological development in terms of a propensity towards conspicuous consumption. This tendency causes the class of parasites to act as a stimulus to production, and also an impediment to production beyond a certain level, while impressing on the labourer an image of the social distinction which consumption confers, thus prompting his emulation. Such a theory is characteristic of Veblen's irony: it is both a serious piece of social analysis, and also a satirical portrait of human futility. He was pessimistic, and although he sometimes allowed a socialist vision to break through his scathing portraits of modern capitalism, he was convinced of nothing so much as the inevitable 'triumph of imbecile institutions over life and culture'.

***Verstehen*.** German: understanding. A term appropriated by philosophical anthropologists during the nineteenth century (notably by *Dilthey and others influenced by *Kant's philosophy of human nature), in order to denote the peculiar mode of understanding necessary for the perception of human affairs. It is supposed that scientific explanation sees the human being as an organism motivated by physical causes; *Verstehen* sees him as a *person, acting from reasons, and in accordance with fundamental *values. The two visions represent the world in contrasting, perhaps even conflicting, ways. Some argue that without *Verstehen* no social reality is perceivable, since its lived essence lies outside the observer's grasp.

The idea of a duality of vision, the scientific (explanatory) and the human (justificatory), is often mooted, but not always in these terms. Fundamentally it involves an attempt to recast the old metaphysical idea of *freedom – that there are events outside the laws of nature – in a less paradoxical form, by saying that events can be seen under two aspects, that of nature, and that of 'freedom'.

The term was later imported into *sociology by *Weber, who accepted (but without much explanation) Dilthey's theory. (*See also* *hermeneutics, *humane education.)

veto. Latin: I forbid. A right to prevent an act or policy by a single negative vote. The veto is an important device, since, by granting it to every member of a body, you also ensure that no action can be undertaken unless they all consent to it. In international affairs this has seemed essential, if there is not to be recourse to force. Thus the veto granted to permanent members of the United Nations Security Council ensures that no issue will be decided by the United Nations Organization against the perceived interests of its more powerful members. This is sometimes thought to be necessary if those powerful members are to accept the rulings of its international jurisdiction.

Vico, Giambattista (1668–1744). Italian philosopher of history, who, in his *Scienza Nuova*, 1725, final version 1744, presented what was perhaps the first theory of history in the modern sense. He also anticipated the doctrine of **Verstehen*, and made a pioneering study of *myth and its social significance.

Vico rejected the idea of a fixed, static human nature, and believed that the essence of man changes with historical development. All *social contract theories ultimately assume that man can be abstracted from his social conditions and yet be seen as a freely choosing being, obeying laws of natural justice and able to engage in contracts and exchanges with his kind. On the contrary, such theories simply project into a hypothetical state of nature the image of man at one particular historical moment, and then suppose that the historical conditions which created him are also part of 'nature'. Such theories are examples of 'pseudo-myths', which misrepresent the early stages of man's development in accordance with a theoretical requirement. True myths, like poetry, art and language itself, should be seen as the embodiment in imaginative form of genuine perceptions of surrounding social conditions and preoccupations.

Vico thought that history exhibits a pattern, and that all events at a given moment bear some intrinsic relation to each other – although he presented no developed theory as to what this relation might be. The law of historical development is that of the recurring cycle, and the understanding of history ('the world of nations') is a special case of that human understanding which has people rather than physical processes as its object. Human nature must first be understood in terms of its expressions in language, culture and myth; then it will be seen that there is an underlying cyclical movement in all things. From bestial conditions men emerge, through an 'age of heroes', to an oligarchical society which gradually transforms itself into the law-governed communities of the 'age of men', established through class conflict. Upon the achievement of democracy and equal rights, society gradually disintegrates, lacking internal authority and cohesion, so giving way to a renewed bestiality.

That doctrine contains in embryo some of the most important of the thoughts that are characteristic of the *modern mind; hence the interest in Vico, who seemed to anticipate by 100 years the ideas that have lent tone to the confusions of post-romantic consciousness.

vigilante. Italian: a look-out. A volunteer police force, exercising rough justice in the absence of adequate enforcement of the law, on the model of those that were formed in the West of America during the 'gold rush', when groups of adventurers spread lawlessly into the wilderness.

It is usually thought that no state can recognize the legitimacy of a vigilante force, since this would be to grant to an autonomous force actual legislative and executive powers. In which case the state ceases to be *sovereign, and so ceases to have authority to grant those powers. It is sometimes replied that, if the state does not enforce the law, then it does not really make law, so that it has in any case renounced its jurisdiction and therefore its sovereignty, once a vigilante force becomes necessary. (At times these arguments have been relevant in describing the situation in Northern Ireland.)

violence. Violence is a property of *force. A force is violent if it 'violates', i.e. if it breaks and destroys that to which it is applied. It is an act of violence to strike my neighbour, an act only of force to steer him uninjured but against his will from the room. (*See* *coercion.)

Questions concerning violence repeatedly recur in political dispute, and while some of them are semantic, there is usually a serious issue of justification involved. Thus it is generally assumed that an act of violence needs to be justified; if no justification can be offered then violence is always a violation of right, unless it is of such a kind as to impute *responsibility to no *agent (e.g. the violence of the wind, or of some uncontrollable human passion). It is for this reason that certain radical thinkers have tried to find violence concealed within existing social structures, for if there really is such *structural violence contained in seemingly peaceful institutions, then violent opposition to them would be more easily justified.

One advocate of that position – *Sorel – did not much care whether violence was justified or not, so long as the proletariat could be brought to perceive its necessity. In his *Reflections on Violence*, 1908, he argued that all existing class conflicts must be exacerbated to the point of open violence, since attempts to render them peaceful served the interests of neither protagonist. Curiously, he argued that the bourgeoisie too would be vitalized by genuine conflict; through violent conflict energy would again enter social relations, changing them from uncreative apathy to dynamic instruments of change. Moreoever, open violence, construed in a spirit of war is free from hatred – in this it differs from the persecutions carried on through the law courts in the name of the state. Sorel's romanticized view of the essential decency of war enabled him to attack all the 'prejudices against violence', that he discerned in the parliamentary socialists of his day, and to advocate a politics of 'violence enlightened by the idea of the general strike'.

Sorel's encomium of violence (which contains no attempt to define what he praises) has been the object, from time to time, of veneration, by such romantics as Mussolini and the French *New Left of 1968. The question that he raises, and which has interested subsequent philosophers, is that of whether a particular class may be in such a position that, without violence, it could never achieve rights which it ought to enjoy.

virtue. Excellence of character, or 'dispositions which we praise' (*Aristotle); the subject-matter of much ancient morality, and of theories which have been profoundly influential, through Aristotle, *Plato and *Cicero, on Western political thought.

It was a commonly accepted view among ancient political thinkers that each kind of state generates and is generated by a character in its citizens, and that each particular virtue will correspond to its own political order. (This idea recurs in *Machiavelli and in *Montesquieu.) It is also an important thesis, advanced both by Plato and by Aristotle, that *true* virtue is one; to be truly courageous a man must also be wise, to be wise he must be just, to be just he must be prudent, and so on. Only the virtuous man can be happy, and hence there is, in the end, only one ideal state, that in which the true virtues flourish in the harmonious relation which defines their unity. In Plato the idea is taken further; the ideal state is itself conceived on the model of a human character, and Plato tries to find in *it* the harmonious disposition of human virtue. But in all versions, the implication of a deep correspondence between the character of the citizen and the order of the **polis* is defended. Some modern thinkers have regretted the fact that this idea has entered a decline, and that questions of constitution are discussed in terms of such abstractions as freedom, right, and distribution, rather than in terms of the quality of individual experience with which they are conjoined. Others have rejected the ancient enterprise as over-ambitious, perhaps even dangerous in its imputation of a political significance to every aspect of personal life.

The best account of virtue is Aristotle's. A virtue is a disposition; it is expressed in intentional action; it involves characteristic thoughts and motives; it consists in a readiness to obey reason, whatever the opposing temptations; it 'mediates' between emotions, by permitting the subject to make up his mind in defiance of them (the doctrine of the 'mean'); it is intrinsically connected to success in action; it defines the ends of action and not only the means (the distinction between virtue and technique); its application is more likely in the long run to lead to fulfilment than any of the emotions which it counters, and it defines the type of the fulfilled rational being. An example is courage, the disposition to face present danger in defiance of the two warring passions (fear and aggression) which tempt us, the one to cowardice, the other to rashness. Courage always makes a general contribution to success in action, by providing the motive to overcome obstacles and to do what is right despite the temptations of passion. Its motive is honour, and this provides the end of action, in circumstances however terrible.

Courage, when not conjoined to prudence, is merely the disposition to give way to that passion (aggression) which wars naturally with fear. Hence 'true' courage requires prudence. And so, it is hoped, through all the virtues, showing that the courageous man must also be just and wise. Justice presents a special problem, since it is an 'other-regarding' and not only a 'self-regarding' disposition. However, Aristotle thought that without justice no man could experience friendship, and that without friendship a rational being, who is also by nature a social being, could not be fulfilled. Without justice, moreover, courage is mere bullying, prudence small-mindedness, and wisdom no more than the cunning of the fox. To complete the picture Aristotle argued that virtue is a constituent part of happiness (which is the ultimate end of rational conduct). So all men have reason to acquire virtue. That was Aristotle's answer to the question of *value: there are objectively desirable states of character, and every rational being must see that he has reason to acquire them.

Voegelin, Eric (b. 1901). German political scientist; *see* *gnosticism, *monarchy. *representation.

Volksgeist. German: the spirit of a people; a term employed by writers of the late eighteenth century, especially by *Herder, and used to give theoretical foundation to the *nationalist position, by arguing that each people has its own 'spirit', from which language, customs and institutions emerge organically, and which constitutes the real bond of unity among them. (This is the nationalist basis for *political obligation.) Thus the jurist F. C. von Savigny (1779–1861) argued against *codification, in favour of customary law, on the grounds that the latter was the immediate expression of the *Volksgeist*, and that law inconsistent with the *Volksgeist* is law inconsistent with the people that it seeks to rule. This opposition to codified law was highly influential, and overcome only in 1900. The idea requires that it be possible to identify a 'people' independently of a state, and then in turn to identify the spirit which unites them, and with which the state must be brought into harmony.

Volksstaat. The people's state. The unified social and political arrangement which is supposed to emerge from aligning state institutions with the **Volksgeist* of the people who will be ruled by them. Based in *nationalist doctrines of the nature of a *people, it was an attempt to recast in terms intelligible to the people themselves the famous and flattering doctrine of their *sovereignty. In theory every institution is to be animated by the single spirit of the *Volksgeist*. The idea was popular with some Nazis.

voluntarism. In the context of the theory of historical development, 'voluntarism' denotes any view that emphasizes (or perhaps overemphasizes) the role of human design, and intention, as against the role of the 'material' factors emphasized by *historical materialism. The thesis that the human will is a determining factor in history seems uncontentious to the innocent, nor is it refuted by the manifestly true assertion that the will itself is determined by other (perhaps 'material') things. (*See* *determinism.) Nevertheless it might still be true that the overall *pattern* of history (the 'course of events') can best be explained by a theory that does not mention the will, not even the will of Napoleon or of Lenin. If that were the case then one fairly plausible form of voluntarism would have been refuted.

voluntary associations. *See* *associations.

voting. The expression of a preference as a contribution to a *collective choice. Voting by a show of hands is to be distinguished from voting by secret ballot. The second is no more than a contribution to a collective choice, while the first is a way both of making a choice and at the same time of declaring one's choice to others. It is determined, therefore, not only by one's preference, but also by one's attitude to others' opinions of one's preference. This is why the introduction of the secret ballot is often regarded as a necessary condition of 'free elections'. (*See* *elections.) 'Tactical voting' occurs when people vote for a candidate who is not their preferred candidate, but who may, e.g., be more likely to win than the better alternative, or likely to precipitate another election sooner, and so on. It is important in that it shows that voting cannot be taken as a direct index of *ultimate* preferences.

voting paradox. One of the paradoxes in the theory of *social choice, which suggests that there may be no *social welfare function which will deliver a consistent social preference ordering from individual preference orderings. Suppose a vote shows a majority preference for policy x over policy y, and also for y over z; it does not follow that there is a majority preference for x over z. (Suppose there are three citizens, A, B, and C; A prefers x to y and y to z; B prefers y to z and z to x; C prefers z to x and x to y.) The discovery of this paradox is sometimes attributed to Condorcet.

vox populi, vox dei. The voice of the people is the voice of God. The expression occurs in a letter to Charlemagne from the poet Alcuin in 800 and was also used by Archbishop Reynolds when crowning Edward III in 1327. This extreme version of the doctrine of the *sovereignty of the people, which suggests that the people is right whenever it believes anything at all, is compatible with any kind of government, on the assumption that for the most part the people have no beliefs. Their 'voice' is heard only at those moments of crisis in which God too enters the fray.

vulgar Marxism. Expression sometimes used to denote crude forms of *historical materialism, which attempt to explain all beliefs and values as the offshoots of economic factors and class position, and which then imagine that, in providing the explanation of a belief, one is relieved of the need to refute it.

W

wage. Remuneration under a contract of employment, usually extended on a weekly basis, and outside the special terms and expectations associated with a *profession. The distinction between wages and salaries (which are usually paid monthly) is at first sight a superficial one; however, it may be of considerable sociological interest, since it is often thought to correspond roughly to a distinction between kinds of employment (manual and administrative), and even (according to some) between classes, that of *wage labour, and that of the 'salariat'. (*See* *class, *social stratification, *status.) The contractual nature of the wage relation is nominally upheld in law, but the institution of *collective bargaining and the recent developments in *industrial law make the idea of a contract into a *legal fiction.

Explanations of the level of wages include the *classical 'wage fund theory' (the theory that in the short run there is a given amount of savings to pay the wages of the labour force); *Marx's theory that wages are the *exchange-value of *labour power (*see* *surplus value); and the marginal productivity theory of wages. One thing that needs to be explained by such theories is why the wages of manual labourers are so often lower than salaries.

wage labour. The condition of someone who, in order to exist, sells his labour power, and does so under the terms of a *wage contract. Practical reasoning for such a person is determined by a weekly cycle of labour and reward. Whether or not one accepts the view of the 'propertyless' condition of the proletariat (which has property only in the means of consumption necessary to reproduce itself), or whether one thinks that the *affluent worker is as much a propertied being as the bourgeois, it is clear that wage labour creates an important structural component in most modern societies. Wage labourers must associate with each other, since they are employed as a 'work force'; they share values, expectations, and institutions of *leisure, which may have a functional relation to the economic role that they play. Hence wage labour will always be a plausible candidate for a social *class, whatever the actual standard of living associated with it.

war. A forcible contention between states with the purpose of overpowering each other by armed force, in order to secure certain demands or claims. All wars involve a measure, however small, of *violence. War is to be distinguished from domestic upheavals and rebellions, however violent, in that it occurs between *states or powers seeking to constitute themselves as states; as such it is recognized and regulated by *international law, which incorporates legal rules originating in traditional discussions of the *just war.

The problem of enforcing laws of war is a perpetual one: if a party is already fighting, then it is not usually disposed to take legal advice. The threat of reprisals offers some coercion, but the *fact* of reprisals tends to lead only to escalation and ever more horrifying breaches of the law. The recent concept of the *war crime has arisen partly from the need for international judicial procedures (preferably conducted at a time of *peace) whereby to emphasize the binding quality of the law of war.

The study of war distinguishes various kinds of war, some of which are discussed elsewhere in this dictionary: *cold war, *insurgency, *limited war, and so on; also 'catalytic war' (conflict between two states deliberately catalysed by a third which has an interest in respect of one or the other or both). To some extent these classifications stem from the desire to relate the kinds of war to the causes of war. There seems to be, for example, a broad distinction between wars which result from the aggressive and expansionist policies of one of the belligerents, and wars which arise out of a mutual and perhaps long-standing hostility which may not, in itself, reflect any territorial claims. (Wars of religion are perhaps examples of this, as are some modern 'wars of ideology'.) The attempt to explain war *as such* involves going behind all such distinctions, in order to find that thing in human nature which requires violent resolution of *conflict. Some assert that there is an innate principle of belligerence which may be diverted into peaceful uses, but which is always ready to break out in violence when prompted. It was fashionable among post-romantic philosophers to sing the praises of this alleged instinct (thus *Nietzsche, *Sorel), although it has less following now that everyone has reason to fear it. Whether or not we accept the theory of innate belligerence, there is still a problem in explaining the outbreak of *war*. Those who attach belligerence to ideas of territory, purporting, say, to bring evidence from *sociobiology in order to demonstrate the primitive nature of the territorial instinct, may not in fact succeed in explaining war. For this is to explain how whole masses of people, who do not wish to fight, and who have no ambitions over the territory of their opponents, may yet find themselves acting under orders in ways from which their nature normally recoils. Further, modern anthropological studies of warfare between tribes, e.g. in Africa and North America, have emphasized the relative insignificance of territorial factors, in comparison with such motives as revenge (the blood-feud, which may become so institutionalized as to confer on war the character of a customary obligation), religious duty, e.g. towards a 'god of war', and personal prestige. The last motive is particularly important in tribes where the exhibition of personal prowess in war is the means by which a young man can increase his influence in the community and induce his fellows to bestow on him the political authority that normally vests in the elders. All the above motives are perceptively characterized by Homer, and underlie many of the systems of *honour that still prevail in modern societies.

war communism. Term used to describe the aims of the Red Army during the civil war which followed the Russian Revolution: i.e. the establishment of communism by the *substitution of communist military personnel for all civilian officers, and the total military organization of all production and distribution. The term gained currency as part of the need to emphasize that the harsh conditions initially prevailing were temporary, and in order to shift blame for them on to the 'imperialist war' that was taking place elsewhere.

war crime. Conduct during war which goes beyond legitimate hostilities under the laws of war. The allied powers set up a United Nations War Crimes Commission in 1943, which introduced the new category of the 'crime against humanity', partly in order to cover those atrocities that were being committed against people who were citizens of the very state whose agents were oppressing them. The problem with the jurisdiction over both kinds of crime is that, in the nature of the case, it is the victor who tries the vanquished, and similar crimes committed by the first may remain unmentioned or deliberately concealed behind the persecutory venom directed against the second (although there have been exceptions to this rule). Very rarely therefore has a state either tried, or been in a position to try, one of its own citizens for a 'war crime'. The US is an exception to this (the case of My Lai during the Vietnam War.) However, there have been trials of military personnel who have 'overstepped the mark of duty', although usually without reference to the concept of a war crime.

warfare state. A state whose main economic, social and political structure is created by or directed towards conditions of war, and which exists by virtue of perpetuating those conditions, or by engaging in ceaseless preparations for war, whether or not under the guise of self-defence (expression introduced by Archbishop Temple (1941)).

wealth. The total stock of possessions, tangible or intangible, which have *value. Wealth may be regarded as a stock of provisions, to be slowly expended in catering for present requirements, or as *capital, to be invested in the expectation of an *income. Moralists tend to favour the first use, economists the second (in so far as they regard *accumulation and *investment as necessary). It is sometimes said to be a peculiar feature of capitalism that wealth can generate an income for the holder of wealth; it could be that wealth might exist without that power. However most observers of *actually existing socialism seem to agree that it contains both private accumulation and private investment, although both are usually illegal.

Objections to wealth tend indeed to be objections to capitalist investment, either as a form of *usury, or as a form of *exploitation. Taxes on wealth are sometimes proposed, partly in order to give voice to those objections, partly because it is thought economically or socially justified to bring all large accumulations under the control of the state. Sometimes the intention is to formulate a kind of *sumptuary law, designed to diminish the prestige and potency of property and to make sure that no private citizen can dispose of an actual power greater than that of the state. Sometimes the intention is the redistribution of wealth, in accordance with an ideal of *social justice.

Webb, Beatrice (1857–1943), and Sidney (1858–1947). British socialists and social theorists; *see* *Fabianism, *gradualism.

Weber, Max (1864–1920). German sociologist and economic historian (not to be confused with his brother Alfred), who is often regarded, together with *Comte, *Durkheim and *Marx, as laying the foundations of modern sociology. Weber defended the idea of a *value-free social science. Social phenomena are identified in terms of a 'sense', which is attached by social beings to all their actions, and which is the true object of social knowledge. 'Sense' can be understood only by **Verstehen*, which therefore becomes the distinguishing mark of the social sciences. However *Verstehen* needs to be supplemented by causal explanation, and both require a theoretical model or *ideal type. (This last expression has probably acquired a significance other than the one that Weber gave to it. For Weber an ideal type describes what an agent *would* do, if he were acting entirely rationally in accordance with the 'sense' of his own behaviour.) The ideal type facilitates *Verstehen* by providing the language with which the far from ideal social reality can be described; it also suggests (but does not provide) causal explanations of reality. The concept of the ideal type was applied by Weber to the analysis of capitalism, and, in *The Protestant Ethic and the Spirit of Capitalism*, 1920–21, Weber tried to show that the Marxian theory of economic determination could not explain the actual history of capitalist development, which must be understood at least partly in terms of the ascetic and secular morality of *Calvinism.

Weber attempted to update the nineteenth-century theories of *class, distinguishing class from *status, and trying to show the importance of socially nurtured opinions in determining the second. In general, he felt that the neglect of the peculiar categories through which we observe and create our social behaviour had been responsible for many of the failings that he claimed to discover in the older theories of class.

Among the famous theories associated with the name of Weber is his treatment of the idea of *authority. He tried to define authority in terms of statistical laws; which express 'the probability that a command with a given specific content will be obeyed by a given group of persons'. He thought that command and obedience can be observed only by *Verstehen*. He then made his famous distinction between traditional authority (which rests on *custom and *prescription), *charismatic authority (which is a major source of social change), and 'legal-rational' authority of the kind exercised by the modern bureaucrat, where legitimacy rests on a belief in the legality of a pattern of normative rules, and the right of those elevated to power under those rules to issue commands. Weber's theory is not really an analysis of the concept of authority, but rather a sociological explanation of why it is that people come to believe in it (command and obedience already involving the ideas of authority). Nevertheless it is often taken as a starting point for discussions of the idea.

Weil, Simone (1909–43). French essayist and philosopher of Jewish extraction, and a modern proponent of *stoicism. Weil's mystical Christianity, and identification with the victims of modern European politics, compelled highly influential, if eccentric, reflections on the state of contemporary society, together with proposals for its political revitalization (*The Need for Roots*, 1949). She identified the chief evil of modern civilization as **déracinement*, and attempted to analyse the nature of the *enracinement* (putting down of roots) that had protected in the past, and might again protect in the future, humanity from social corrosion. A human being has roots by virtue of his active participation in a collectivity, which conserves in living form an inheritance of social existence, and which continues to offer presentiments of a future continuity. Weil attempted to reconcile that emphasis on particularized attachments with *universalist views of obligation, derived from *Kant, and also with a respect for hierarchy, diversity, private property and territory. This led her to support true *patriotism (a local intimation of world citizenship) against *nationalism (a form of *déracinement* comparable in its effects to the corrosiveness of industrial production). At the same time she claimed both Christian and Marxian inspiration for her rejection of the effects of industrialization, and proposed *utopian schemes for the amelioration of the condition of labour, by preventing the emergence of large-scale industry. She wished labour to be an exercise in willing obedience, founded in allegiance to others and to the social order. Her profoundly moral view of the relations of production influenced also her idea of law, which she thought (with Kant) could enforce morality without infringing freedom. She admired the UK constitution as a seeming expression of that ideal of law.

welfare. A disputed concept, meant to describe the flourishing or happiness of human beings, but defined by *welfare economics in terms of *preferences. Some philosophers have argued that the individual may not be better off simply for having what he prefers, and that, although *values, for example, are preferences, not all preferences are values. Some of our preferences (e.g. those concerning food) we regard as reflections of our own constitution – as *mere* preferences that we are under no obligation to justify when challenged. Values on the other hand have an authority greater than that, and indeed we learn to perceive and understand the world in terms of them. Thus a value seems to have not only strength, like a preference, but also 'depth', a quality whereby it brings order to experience by determining the interpretation of experience. It is said to be absurd to incorporate such a thing into a system of measurement, and some have for this reason looked with scepticism upon the aims of welfare economics. However it is better to see that theory as concerned with a limited set of questions concerning economic values (values in sense 1.) and the distribution of goods, rather than with the larger philosophical issue of the 'good for man'. At the same time, that larger issue cannot be neglected in any consideration of the social significance of 'welfare legislation'.

welfare economics. Branch of economics concerned with economic efficiency and resource allocation, as a means to the welfare of society. For the most part welfare economics tries to avoid assumptions regarding ethics, justice, and political desirability, and proposes instead measures of efficiency which are *value-free. Effieiency is usually taken to mean *optimality (often *Pareto optimality) in the satisfaction of *preferences. The theory inquires into the relative economic efficiency of the various economic systems, such as the price system. Welfare economics has generated the theory of *social choice, and the problem of the *social welfare function, and has thereby come to have far-reaching significance for political theory.

welfare state. Colloquial term (originally introduced by Archbishop William Temple (1881–1944), in *Citizen and Churchmen*, 1941) for a state which makes substantial provision through law and administration for those in need: e.g. the sick, poor, elderly, disabled and indigent. Even the US is now a welfare state in this sense, though clearly less so than many. Moves in the direction of the welfare state, through *poor laws and welfare legislation, accelerated appreciably during the nineteenth century, in particular with Bismarck's social welfare legislation of 1883–9, which was later taken as a model by other European states. In post-Second World War Europe, both capitalist and communist, *health services, *education, unemployment benefit and pensions are in almost every case provided out of government funds. This has met with opposition on the ground that it involves illegitimate government expenditure, and therefore illegitimate taxation, perhaps because it is held to encourage indigence and discourage *self-help. The favoured alternative, of private insurance schemes as practised in the US, is often attacked for the abuses and injustices to which it seems to give rise, while the welfare state is defended as involving not only social justice, but also a task for government which (unlike many of the tasks that it seems to arrogate to itself) is both necessary and could be effectively performed by no other *agent. The controversy is now more or less dead, but *see* *health.

***Weltanschauung*.** German: world outlook. A general conception of the world, in which beliefs, values and metaphysical presuppositions are all woven together so as to instil the world with significance, and facilitate the transition from thought to action.

westernization. The importation of customs and institutions thought to be characteristic of 'the West', i.e. of that *culture which *Spengler (among many) held to be in a state of irreversible decline. Westernization was advocated as a serious policy by influential figures in the Ottoman government in the nineteenth and twentieth centuries, and much more wholeheartedly by Atatürk, on the supposition that the Western way of doing things was necessary if Turkey was to adapt its social structure and political institutions to the conditions of twentieth-century life (*see* *Kemalism). Elsewhere, the aspects of the West that have been emulated with success have been those which confer *status (*consumerism, vulgarization of dress, speech and manners, the admiration for purposeless machinery) rather than those which have been thought to confer well-being, such as the institutions of law and government, and the modes of production and communication. Although these appealed to Atatürk and were advocated by him, they failed to win the sympathy of the people. This has led (especially in *Islamic states, and other places with moral outlooks hostile to conspicuous consumption) to a reaction against westernization, and against the capitalist system with which it is, rightly or wrongly, identified.

Westminster model. *Bicameral government on the model of the UK *Parliament, i.e with a lower house of representatives answerable to the electorate, with extensive legislative powers, and a *cabinet exercising major executive powers; together with an upper house structured in some other way, so as to embody the dignity and durability of the state and of the interests within it, but with limited legislative power, consonant with its non-representational character. Normally the upper house would be thought of as a revising chamber, while the lower house contains the principal powers and the principal initiators of policy.

Whig. The 'whigs' were rebels who held out in the Scottish lowlands in 1679, resisting the Act of Uniformity 1662, in the interests of their own religious eccentricities. The label was borrowed, from 1680 onwards, as a name for the English political faction which sought the transfer of power from the monarch to Parliament. Primarily the Whigs were a faction of Protestant noblemen, united in opposition to *Toryism, as it then was. However, because of their *parliamentarian leanings, they gradually became identified with the more liberal movements in

English politics and, during the course of the eighteenth century, brought about the realignment of parliamentary forces which permitted the emergence of the UK Liberal Party. By 1868 the term 'Whig' was no longer widely used, except as the name of the peculiar mixture of ardent eccentricity and rooted belief in the right of aristocrats to govern irrespective of their views, which some saw as a persisting principle in English politics. Later thinkers have continued to identify 'whiggism' with the liberal faction and have thought of it as a progressive, perhaps individualistic and even capitalistic, movement within the aristocracy, rather than as a form of *liberalism in the modern sense. *See* *Whig interpretation of history.

Whig interpretation of history. Expression coined by Sir Herbert Butterfield in a book of that title (1931), to denote the vision of history as generated by a conflict between *progress and *reaction, in which the first is always, in the end, victorious, bringing about the ever increasing prosperity, enlightenment and emancipation of mankind. The identification of this view as 'Whig' reflects the theory that the aristocratic faction which went by that name was given to an exaggerated estimate of its historical mission. However, it is clear that, in so far as anything so schematic can be believed as doctrine, there have been plenty of American, French and German Whigs in history.

withering away of the state. Phrase coined by Engels to denote the process whereby, according to Marx, and also to Lenin who made much of the idea, the state under socialism gradually becomes redundant, its existence as an instrument of *coercion being necessary only in order to sustain the oppressive production relations of capitalism, and only so long as people have the character and expectations induced by those relations. Gradually, under the practice of *collective choice, as the friendliness of the social order without private property in the means of production is recognized, law is no longer required, and men enter a condition ('full communism') in which society exists and flourishes without a controlling state. Then the 'government of people' gives way to the 'administration of things' (Marx).

Wollstonecraft, Mary (1759–97). English philosopher and novelist, wife of *Godwin, and champion of the libertarian and egalitarian ideals which she associated with the French Revolution. Wollstonecraft's *Vindication of the Rights of Men,* 1790, a reply to *Burke's *Reflections on the Recent Revolution in France,* defended the liberal position that 'The birthright of man. . . is such a degree of liberty, civil and religious, as is compatible with the liberty of every other individual with whom he is united in a social compact. . .'; the work argued rhetorically for Reason against prejudice, for impartiality and equality against privilege and hierarchy, for a political system dedicated to the satisfaction of human needs against one dedicated to the accumulation of power. Wollstonecraft's attack on the *hereditary principle and on the vested power of the family presaged her subsequent rejection of all self-perpetuating systems of control and, in *A Vindication of the Rights of Women,* 1792, she argued vigorously for the view that women, as rational creatures, should reject the vision of their nature, role and education that had been imposed on them by men, and cease to regard themselves as creatures subject to the control of another and stronger sex. The weakness and dependency of the female is, she argued, largely a consequence of the education chosen for her, while the sexual role and *mores* to which women conform are likewise the creation of men, designed for the advantage of the male, who confines the female within a sphere of submissive chastity while permitting himself the conduct which extends his influence and power.

Wollstonecraft's thoughts were disjointed and unsystematic: nevertheless they provoked widespread reaction, and have since been regarded as important early statements of the modern *feminist position.

women's movement. The movement to promote the *emancipation, *liberation, *rights and interests of women, as these are defined *by* women, which has existed as a political force in modern times since the early nineteenth century. While individual eighteenth-century writers (both men and women) made statements in support of *feminism (the most important being, perhaps, *Wollstonecraft's *Vindication of the Rights of Women,* 1792), there was no organized movement to which women, and particularly working-class women, substantially contributed, over which they had control, and through which their particular interests could be fostered. During the nineteenth century the demands for female suffrage came through the *labour movement and other agents of reform, but were not as a rule associated with any attempt to articulate the thoughts which are characteristic of modern feminism. An exception was the Nottingham Female Political Union (1838); it had few successors until 1889, when the Women's Franchise League began to campaign, not only for female suffrage, but also for complete equality of women in divorce, inheritance and the custody of children. Subsequently, many similar organizations emerged. Since the granting of female suffrage the main concerns of the movement have included *equal pay, *equal opportunity, equal *access, and the eradication of *sexism. Equal pay has been widely achieved in the *professions, but not in wage labour; statutes forbidding sexual discrimination have been adopted in the UK, US and USSR, and women have begun to ascend to high offices of government (although this is still rare in the USSR).

work. An activity which is of such a nature that it will not be voluntarily undertaken without reward. It is sometimes thought that the activity should be part of the economic process of *production, distribution, exchange and consumption, but that requirement is perhaps too stringent, except in the trivial sense that all paid employment is a part of the process of distribution, even that of the entertainer.

Some theorists (e.g. Arendt: *The Human Condition,* 1958) distinguish work from *labour, taking inspiration, e.g., from the earlier writings of Marx. Labour is seen as an essentially expressive activity, the activity in which *self-realization and the creation of human life have their locus. Labour becomes the social essence of man, and it is labour, rather than reason, which distinguishes man from the other animals. On this view 'work' might be usefully reserved as a name for that excrescence of the labouring process in which things are produced not for consumption but for exchange. Work is the instrumental, as opposed to the constitutive, aspect of human production. Too great an emphasis on work leads to the 'instrumentalization' of the world, the devaluation of everything to a means. Thus work becomes *alienated labour.

The 'work ethic' is the outlook which sees a major value of human existence in work, and which deprecates idleness as a deviation from a human norm. It involves a belief that people are, as it were, created through their employments, and a disposition to judge everyone in terms of his employment, so that the question 'What do you do?' stands in place of the question 'Who are you?' For this attitude someone without work is existentially disturbing, since he continues to appear like a ghost at social gatherings, despite the fact that he does not exist. The work ethic is sometimes held by sociologists to be associated with the emergence of *status distinctions in the place of distinctions of *class, but it is part of a large phenomenon of social transformation which probably cannot be explained so simply.

In popular parlance the name 'worker' is reserved for the person whose work is a form of *wage labour, thus reflecting some measure of conscious or unconscious acceptance of the view that only wage labourers really *produce* anything.

workers' control/workers' ownership. Expressions which denote the partial or complete ownership or control over an enterprise by those whose work is necessary if it is to function. Ownership involves the legal right to transfer, and to realize the *value of the enterprise as a capital asset. This may be vested in an individual, a company or the state, even though workers have effective control over the enterprise in every other respect. Workers' ownership in effect amounts to the creation of a *cooperative.

Workers' *control was an ambition of many radical and even anarchist elements within the nineteenth-century socialist movement, and was the express aim of *anarcho-syndicalism. It is often advocated on grounds of justice, since the workers are a major factor of production (and, on some views, the only force of production), and therefore ought to exert rights of control over the means of production; on grounds of utility, in that the increased interest that they might then take in the enterprise can only increase their disposition to work; on more philosophical grounds, such as that workers' control is the solution to *alienation, and the abolition of the treatment of the worker as a means.

working class. 1. In common parlance, the class (if it be such) of *wage labour, whether or not that class has substantial holdings of *private property, and whether or not it has ownership in or control over the means of production.
2. In Marxist theory, another name for the industrial *proletariat.

1. includes some peasants, 2. does not. 1. is based in intuitions and *class consciousness; 2. is based in a theory, which seeks to explain those intuitions and not merely to reiterate them.

world government. The *universalist ideal of a single unitary system of government, in which all disputes between people would be settled not by *force but by *adjudication, under a single *jurisdiction, and a *rule of law upheld through truly representative institutions of government. Under such a government there cannot be war, but only crime, and all disputes take on the air of justiciable grievances.

World government has been the dream of many exponents and theorists of international law. It was advocated by *Kant, as the logical corollary of the universal validity of the moral law, and has inspired many of those active in founding the League of Nations (a term taken from Kant), and the subsequent United Nations Organization. Sceptics argue that world government will mean simply that wars are no longer called wars, but insurrections, that nations are equal only because they are equally oppressed by the central power, that law is universal only because all local disputes are governed not by law but by force. Clearly vast issues of theory and practice are invoked by these contentions. To what extent, for example, could the differences between customs and languages be recognized under world government, and *how* would they be recognized? To what extent could the citizen from Cambodia make his grievance heard by a judge appointed from the Peruvian judiciary and expect equal treatment to a Peruvian? And so on.

world organizations. Organizations of an international character, with a status not necessarily recognized in *international law, which aim to promote cooperation between nations, and to achieve uniform institutions of a peaceable kind. They include the United Nations Organization, the World Health Organization, and the subsidiary institutions of the United Nations such as the *International Court of Justice. (*See* *international organizations.) Various specialized agencies of international administration, such as the Food and Agriculture Organization, the *International Labour Organization and UNESCO (UN Educational, Scientific and Cultural Organization), are brought into relationship with the UN by agreements between them and the Economic and Social Council.

Important forces in international economic policy have been the 'World Bank' (the International Bank for Reconstruction and Development), set up under the auspices of the United Nations in 1944, and the International Monetary Fund, which came into operation in 1947, with the aim of encouraging international cooperation in the monetary field, removing *exchange controls, and stabilizing exchange rates, so as to permit multilateralism among those who elected to belong to it. The fund is used to tide member states over temporary balance of payment difficulties, by borrowing money in exchange for their own currency, which they are then obliged to buy back in five years' time. The effect of this fund has been considerable, and its use of revenue from gold sales to provide aid for developing countries has caused it to have a wide influence, besides the real stabilization achieved in the currencies of its member states.

Both the World Bank and the International Monetary Fund are looked on with suspicion by *international socialists, because of their air of capitalist imperialism. There are organizations which ought, however, to be more readily acceptable to them, such as the International Labour Organization, and the World Federation of Trade Unions. However, due to the divisions within the international socialist movement, neither of these is particularly effective, the second largely because of Western suspicions that trade unions in the USSR and its satellites do not represent the interests of the workers within those states, and are instruments of state *coercion.

Other significant world organizations include the Organization for Economic Cooperation and Development (OECD), established in 1961 with the aim of encouraging *economic growth and stability among member states while contributing to the economic growth of the developing countries, whether or not members; and the World Health Organization, which is one of the agencies of the United Nations, and one of the most successful in persuading states to accept that there might be organizations with international purposes which are neither instruments of international law nor capitalist or communist conspiracies.

world wars. Wars which involve a substantial proportion of existing states. Such wars are precipitated by alliances and treaties which bind nations in a chain of belligerence. But their cause is often held to be deeper than that, for why were such alliances and treaties originally made, if not to contend with a 'common enemy'? Hence many seek to trace such wars to underlying class interests or economic interests, which need to be exerted over a larger area than that contained in any single jurisdiction. The classical exposition of such a theory is *Lenin's theory of the *imperialist war that was fought in Europe in 1914–18. However the theory is not widely accepted, and the Second World War is very implausibly described in terms of it.

X

xenophobia. Pathological hatred of strangers, usually accompanied by a conviction that they belong to a group that is *alien. Some forms of *racism are also forms of xenophobia, just as some anti-racism is motivated by 'xenophilia', the pathological love of strangers caused by contempt for one's traditional community. Xenophobia arises most readily where there is a conflict of interest between the two groups, for example when an immigrant group appears to an existing working class to be competing with it for scarce jobs and resources. Hence it is sometimes thought to be rarer among those classes for whom strangers are not competitors, such as the traditional European aristocracy in times of peace.

Y

Yeats, William Butler (1865–1939). Irish poet and dramatist; *see* *ceremony, *myth.

Young Hegelians. Philosophers, theologians, and political theorists in the 1830s and 1840s, with whom both Marx and Engels came into contact, and who attempted to adapt and transform Hegel's philosophy so as to give it a coherent critical and practical application. They included the theologians David Strauss (1808–74) and Bruno Bauer (1809–82), who were strongly influenced by Hegel's theory of universal history, the reactionary individualist Max Stirner (1806–56), a brilliant polemicist who foreshadowed Nietzsche's philosophy of self-enhancement, and the critic and philosopher Ludwig Feuerbach (1804–72), whose sophisticated iconoclasm had a profound effect on the younger generation of intellectuals. Feuerbach was interested in giving a *materialist version of the Hegelian philosophy of the self. He argued that man's essence is social, and resides in the *species-being that he shares with his kind. Only man has species-being, since only man has to *find* his own nature, by interacting with his kind. The alienated character of religion, as Hegel had described it, comes about because men carry that search beyond their social existence, into a transcendental realm which they do not understand. They then project out of themselves, and make into properties of the divinity, the perfections that might have been theirs. These perfections can have no reality outside man's social life, but there they have real existence. In removing his perfection from himself and bestowing it on a transcendent being, man makes his own perfection unobtainable, since it now lies outside the sphere of social action. This is the *fetishism which constitutes the essence of religious belief, and also the true divorce between man and his species-being (*The Essence of Christianity*, 1841).

All the Young Hegelians shared this interest in, and to some extent reaction against, religion, and all of them endeavoured to detach the Hegelian philosophy from its uncompromising metaphysical idealism. Feuerbach's theories recur in the early theories of Marx, particularly that concerning *alienation.

Z

Zeitgeist. The 'spirit of the times'. A term belonging to *Hegel's philosophy of history, denoting the successive stages of development of the universal **Geist* or spirit, as it generates history from itself in accordance with the logic of the *dialectic. The term is used more simply and vulgarly to imply that, when two events in the human world are contemporaneous, they must each be expressions of a single *Zeitgeist* which compels them. This is one of the simplest fallacies of *historicism, and consists in interpreting the retrospective order that we impose on history through our cultural and critical classifications, as a kind of *causal* order. The fallacy is often identified in historians and critics of art, where it is sometimes said to have done much harm.

zero-sum. Term from *game theory, denoting the situation in which one player's gain is another's loss, as in a duel, so that the several pay-offs of the players add up to zero for every possible choice of strategies. The idea of the zero-sum game has proved intriguing to political theorists, since it seems to provide a model for war, diplomacy, and some domestic politics. Some have even argued that political *freedom is a zero-sum game, on the ground that every freedom that is granted to one person involves restricting the freedom of others so as to make room for it.

Zionism. Jewish movement to establish, or re-establish, a Jewish *nation in Palestine, so as to resurrect the Zion of the Jewish kings and prophets. The movement is characterized by nationalist aspirations, based on a religion, law, custom and language which have survived without jurisdiction and without the territory over which it could be exercised. Zionism was founded in modern times by Theodor Herzel at the World Zionist Conference in Basle in 1897, and became a political reality with the Balfour Declaration of 1917.

Zionism stands for the aspiration of Jews everywhere to gain the territory with which to complete the legal and political identity of the Jewish state. Its claims to the particular territory of Israel are founded in an idea of the unbroken connection of the Jews with the 'Land of Israel' through which an image of national identity has persisted throughout the diaspora. In addition its claims to *a* territory are founded on the absolute need for the Jews to combine as a state, and no longer to seek to survive merely as a loosely joined international society. It is this absence of a state, Zionists often claim, that led to the *holocaust.